CONTENTS

THE MATURATIONAL
PROCESSES AND THE
FACILITATING
ENVIRONMENT

Studies in the Theory of
Emotional Development

BY

D.W. WINNICOTT

KARNAC

LONDON   NEW YORK

First published in 1965 by
The Hogarth Press Ltd

Reprinted 1990 with their permission
by H. Karnac (Books) Ltd.
6 Pembroke Buildings
London NW10 6RE

Reprinted 2002, 2003, 2004, 2005

British Library Cataloguing in Publication Data
A C.I.P. for this book is available from the British Library

ISBN: 0 946439 84 2

www.karnacbooks.com

EDITORIAL NOTE

This volume brings together Dr Winnicott's published and un-published papers on psycho-analysis and child development during the period 1957–1963. The series of papers presented here complements those published in *Collected Papers: Through Paediatrics to Psycho-Analysis* (London: Tavistock Publications, 1958).

There are two bibliographies at the end. The first includes all the books and papers referred to in the text. The second gives a list of Dr Winnicott's writings from 1926 to 1964.

In order that the text itself shall not be encumbered with too many cross-references and footnotes the inter-relationships of the themes and concepts discussed in Dr Winnicott's papers are provided in the index. The major themes are also broken down into sub-categories and indexed in such a way that the various implications and connotations of an idea become readily available to the reader. The basic concepts of Freud are indexed in relation to Dr Winnicott's discussions or elaborations of them. Quite often Dr Winnicott has taken a Freudian concept as his given frame of reference but has not discussed it as such, and it is intended that the index should in part remedy this by pointing out the links between Dr Winnicott's ideas and those of Freud.

M. MASUD R. KHAN

Associate Editor

INTRODUCTION

The main theme of these collected papers is the carrying back of the application of Freud's theories to infancy. Freud showed us that psycho-neurosis has its point of origin in the interpersonal relationships of the first maturity, belonging to the toddler age. I have played a part in the exploration of the idea that mental hospital disorders relate to failures of development in infancy. Schizophrenic illness in this way shows up as the *negative* of processes that can be traced in detail as the *positive* processes of maturation in the infancy and early childhood of the individual.

Dependence in early infancy is a fact, and in these papers I have tried to take dependence right into the theory of personality growth. Ego-psychology only makes sense if based firmly on the fact of dependence, and on the study of infancy as well as on the study of primitive mental mechanisms and psychic processes.

The beginning of ego emergence entails at first an almost absolute dependence on the supportive ego of the mother-figure and on her carefully graduated failure of adaptation. This is part of what I have called 'good-enough mothering'; in this way the environment takes its place among the other essential features of dependence, within which the infant is developing and is employing primitive mental mechanisms.

One aspect of the disturbance of ego emergence produced by environmental failure is the dissociation that is seen in the 'borderline case' in terms of the true and the false selves. I have developed this theme in my own way, seeing the representatives of this dissociation in healthy persons and in healthy living (private self reserved for intimacies, and public self adapted for socialization), and also examining the pathology of the same condition. At the extreme of illness I see the true self as a potentiality, hidden and preserved by the compliant false self, which latter is then a defence organization that is based on the various functions of the ego apparatus and on self-caretaking techniques. This relates to the concept of the observing ego.

Following up the idea of absolute dependence in earliest infancy I put forward a new way of looking at classification. My intention here is not so much to label personality types as to promote thinking and research into those aspects of the psycho-analytic technique which relate to meeting the patient's need in terms of dependence in the analytic relationship and situation.

9

The origin of the antisocial tendency is discussed. It is postulated that the antisocial tendency is a reaction to *deprivation*, not a result of *privation*; in this way the antisocial tendency belongs to the stage of relative (not absolute) dependence. This point of origin of the antisocial tendency in a child's development may even be in latency, when the child's ego has established autonomy and now therefore the child can be traumatized instead of distorted in regard to ego-functioning.

As a corollary to all this, the more psychotic disorders are seen to be closely related to environmental factors, whereas psychoneurosis is more essentially natural, a result of personal conflict, and not to be avoided by satisfactory nurture. It is further discussed how it is in the treatment of borderline cases that these new considerations find practical application, and indeed such treatments provide the most fruitful and accurate data for the understanding of infancy and of the dependent infant.

ACKNOWLEDGEMENTS

First I wish to acknowledge my debt to my psycho-analytic colleagues. I have grown up as a member of this group, and after so many years of inter-relating it is now impossible for me to know what I have learned and what I have contributed. The writings of any one of us must be to some extent plagiaristic. Nevertheless I think we do not copy; we work and observe and think and discover, even if it can be shown that what we discover has been discovered before.

I have found great value in travelling abroad and in discussing my ideas with those who work in analytic, psychiatric, paediatric and educational settings, and in society groupings that differ from those that obtain in London.

I wish to thank my secretary Mrs Joyce Coles whose accurate work has been an important part of each of these papers at its original coming to life. I am also grateful to Miss Ann Hutchinson who has prepared the papers for publication.

Lastly, I thank Mr Masud Khan, who has provided the drive which has resulted in the publication of this book. Mr Khan has given a great deal of his time to the work of editing. He has also made innumerable valuable minor suggestions, most of which I have accepted. He is responsible for my gradually coming to see the relationship of my work to that of other analysts, past and present. In particular I am grateful to him for his preparation of the index.

D. W. WINNICOTT

Part One
PAPERS ON DEVELOPMENT

1

PSYCHO-ANALYSIS AND THE SENSE OF GUILT[1]
(1958)

In this lecture I shall reach to no more profound statement than that of Burke, who wrote two hundred years ago that guilt resides in the intention. The intuitive flashes of the great, however, and even the elaborate constructs of poets and philosophers, are lacking in clinical applicability; psycho-analysis has already made available for sociology and for individual therapy much that was previously locked up in remarks like this one of Burke.

A psycho-analyst comes to the subject of guilt as one who is in the habit of thinking in terms of growth, in terms of the evolution of the human individual, the individual as a person, and in relation to the environment. The study of the sense of guilt implies for the analyst a study of individual emotional growth. Ordinarily, guilt-feeling is thought of as something that results from religious or moral teaching. Here I shall attempt to study guilt-feeling, not as a thing to be inculcated, but as an aspect of the development of the human individual. Cultural influences are of course important, vitally important; but these cultural influences can themselves be studied as an overlap of innumerable personal patterns. In other words, the clue to social and group psychology is the psychology of the individual. Those who hold the view that morality needs to be inculcated teach small children accordingly, and they forgo the pleasure of watching morality develop naturally in their children, who are thriving in a good setting that is provided in a personal and individual way.

I shall not need to examine variations in constitution. We have indeed no clear evidence that any individual who is not mentally defective is constitutionally incapable of developing a moral sense. On the other hand, we do find all degrees of success and failure in the development of a moral sense. I shall attempt to explain these variations. Undoubtedly there are children and adults with a defective guilt-sense, and such defect is not specifically linked with intellectual capacity or incapacity.

[1] Lecture given in a series as part of the celebrations of the centenary of Freud's birth: at Friends' House, April 1956, and first published in *Psycho-Analysis and Contemporary Thought*, ed. J. D. Sutherland. (London: Hogarth, 1958.)

It will simplify my task if I divide my examination of the problem into three main parts:

(1) The sense of guilt in those individuals who have developed and established a capacity for guilt-feeling.
(2) The sense of guilt at the point of its origin in individual emotional development.
(3) The sense of guilt as a feature conspicuous by its absence in certain individual persons.

At the end I shall refer to the loss and recovery of the capacity for guilt-sense.

1. *A Capacity for Sense of Guilt Assumed*

How does the concept of guilt appear in psycho-analytic theory? I think I am right in saying that the early work of Freud in this field had to do with the vicissitudes of guilt-sense in those individuals in whom a capacity for guilt-sense could be taken for granted. I will therefore say something about Freud's view of the meaning of guilt for the unconscious in health, and the psycho-pathology of guilt-sense.

The work of Freud shows how it is that true guilt resides in the intention, in unconscious intention. Actual crime is not the cause of guilt-feeling; rather is it the *result* of guilt—guilt that belongs to criminal intention. Only legal guilt refers to a crime; moral guilt refers to inner reality. Freud was able to make sense of this paradox. In his early theoretical formulations he was concerned with the id, by which he referred to the instinctual drives, and the ego, by which he referred to that part of the whole self that is related to the environment. The ego modifies the environment in order to bring about id-satisfactions, and it curbs id-impulses in order that what the environment can offer can be used to best advantage, again for id-satisfaction. Later (1923) Freud used the term superego to name that which is accepted by the ego for use in id-control.

Freud is here dealing with human nature in terms of *economics*, and deliberately simplifying the problem for the purpose of founding a theoretical formulation. There is an implied determinism in all this work, an assumption that human nature can be examined objectively and can have applied to it the laws that are known to apply in physics. In ego-id terms the sense of guilt is very little more than *anxiety with a special quality*, anxiety felt because of the conflict between love and hate. Guilt-sense implies tolerance of ambivalence. It is not difficult to accept the close relationship between guilt and the personal conflict that arises out of coincident loving and hating, but Freud was able to trace the conflict to its roots and to show that the feelings are those associated with the instinctual life. As is now well known, Freud found in analysis of adults (neurotic rather than psychotic) that he regularly came back to the early childhood of the patient, to intolerable anxiety, and to the clash of love and hate. In the simplest possible terms of the Oedipus complex, a boy in *health* achieved a relationship with his mother in which instinct was involved and in which the dream contained an in-love relationship with her. This led to the dream of the death of the father, which in turn led to the fear of the father and the fear that the father would destroy the child's instinctual potential. This is referred to as the castration-complex. At the same time there was the boy's love of the father and his respect for him. The boy's conflict between that side of his nature which made him hate and want to harm his father, and the other side by which he loved him, involved the boy in a sense of guilt. Guilt implied that the boy could tolerate and hold the conflict, which is in fact an inherent conflict, one that belongs to healthy life.

This is all quite simple, except that only through Freud has it been recognized that in health the climax of anxiety and guilt has a date; that is to say, has a first vitally important setting— the small child with biologically-determined instincts living in the family and experiencing the first triangular relationship. (This statement is purposely simplified, and I shall not make any reference here to the Oedipus complex in terms of sibling-relationships, nor any statement of the equivalent to the Oedipus complex in a child brought up away from the parents or in an institution.

In the early psycho-analytic statement there is but little reference to the destructive aims in the love impulse, or to the aggressive drives that only in health become fully fused with the erotic. All this needed eventually to be brought into the theory of the origin of guilt, and I shall examine such developments later. In the first statement guilt arises out of the clash of love and hate, a clash which is inevitable if loving is to include the instinctual element that belongs to it. The prototype has reality at the toddler age.

All psycho-analysts are familiar in their work with the replacement of symptoms by the more normal development, a sense of guilt, and an increased consciousness and acceptance of the content of the fantasy which makes the sense of guilt logical. How illogical the sense of guilt can seem! In Burton's *Anatomy of*

Melancholy there is a good collection of cases illustrating the absurdities of guilt-feeling. In long and deep analysis patients feel guilt about anything and everything, and even about early environmental adverse factors that we can easily discern as chance phenomena. Here is a simple illustration:

A boy of eight became increasingly anxious, and eventually ran away from school. He was found to be suffering from an unbearable sense of guilt because of the death of a sibling that took place some years *prior to his own birth*. He had recently heard about this, and the parents had no idea that he was disturbed by the news. In this case it was not necessary for the boy to have a long analysis. In a few therapeutic interviews he discovered that the crippling sense of guilt which he felt about this death was a displacement from the Oedipus complex. He was a fairly normal boy, and with this amount of help he was able to return to school, and his other symptoms cleared up.

The Superego

The introduction of the concept of the superego (1923) was a big step forward in the inevitably slow evolution of psychoanalytical metapsychology. Freud had done the pioneer work himself, bearing the brunt when the world was disturbed by his drawing attention to the instinctual life of children. Gradually other workers gained experience through the use of the technique, and Freud had many colleagues by the time he used the term superego. With his new term, Freud was indicating that the ego, in coping with the id, employed certain forces which were worthy of a name. The child gradually acquired controlling forces. In the over-simplification of the Oedipus complex, the boy introjected the respected and feared father, and therefore carried about with him controlling forces based on what the child perceived and felt about this father. This introjected father-figure was highly subjective, and coloured by the child's experiences with father-figures other than the actual father and by the cultural pattern of the family. (The word introjection simply meant a mental and emotional acceptance, and this term avoids the more functional implications of the word incorporation.) A sense of guilt therefore implies that the ego is coming to terms with the superego. Anxiety has matured into guilt.

Here in the concept of the superego can be seen the proposition that the genesis of guilt is a matter of inner reality, or that guilt resides in the intention. Here also lies the deepest reason for guilt-feeling related to masturbation and the autoerotic activities generally. Masturbation in itself is no crime, yet in the total fantasy of masturbation is gathered together all the conscious and unconscious intention.

From this very much simplified statement of the psychology of the boy, psycho-analysis could begin to study and examine the development of the superego in both boys and girls, and also the differences that undoubtedly exist in the male and female in regard to superego formation, in the pattern of conscience, and in the development of a capacity for guilt-feeling. Out of the concept of the superego a great deal has developed. The idea of the introjection of the father-figure has turned out to be too simple. There is an early history of the superego in each individual: the introject may become human and father-like, but in earlier stages the superego introjects, used for control of id-impulses and id-products, are subhuman, and indeed are primitive to any degree. Thus we find ourselves studying guilt-sense in each individual infant and child as it develops from crude fear to something akin to a relationship to a revered human being, one who can understand and forgive. (It has been pointed out that there is a parallel between the maturing of the superego in the individual child and the development of monotheism as depicted in early Jewish history.)

All the time while conceptualizing the processes which underlie the sense of guilt we are keeping in mind the fact that the sense of guilt, even when unconscious and even when apparently irrational, implies a certain degree of emotional growth, ego health, and hope.

The Psycho-pathology of Guilt-sense

It is common to find people who are burdened by a sense of guilt and indeed hampered by it. They carry it round like the load on the back of Christian in *Pilgrim's Progress*. We know that these people have a potentiality for constructive effort. Sometimes when they find a suitable opportunity for constructive work the sense of guilt no longer hampers them and they do exceptionally well; but a failure of opportunity may lead to a return of guilt-feeling, intolerable and inexplicable. We are dealing here with abnormalities of the superego. In a successful analysis of individuals who are oppressed by a sense of guilt, we find a gradual lessening of this burden. This lessening of the burden of guilt-feeling follows the lessening of repression, or the approach of the patient towards the Oedipus complex and an acceptance of responsibility for all the hate and love that this involves. This does not mean that the patients lose the capacity for a sense of guilt (except in so far as in some cases there may have been a false superego development based in an abnormal way on the intrusion of a very powerful authoritarian influence derived from the environment of early years).

We can study these excesses of guilt-feeling in individuals who pass for normal, and who indeed may be among the most valuable members of society. It is easier, however, to think in terms of illness, and the two illnesses that must be considered are melancholia and obsessional neurosis. There is an inter-relationship between these two illnesses, and we find patients who alternate between one and the other.

In obsessional neurosis, the patient is always trying to put something right; but it is quite clear to all observers, and perhaps to the patient, that there will be no success. We know that Lady Macbeth cannot undo the past and get away from her evil intentions by washing her hands. In obsessional neurosis we sometimes get a ritual which is like a caricature of a religion, as if the God of the religion were dead or temporarily unavailable. Obsessive thinking may be a feature whereby every attempt is made to annul one idea by another, but nothing succeeds. Behind the whole process is a confusion, and no amount of tidying that the patient can do alters this confusion, because it is maintained; it is unconsciously maintained in order to hide something very simple; namely, the fact that, in some specific setting of which the patient is unaware, hate is more powerful than love.

I will cite the case of a girl who could not go to the seaside because she saw in the waves someone crying out for help. Intolerable guilt made her go to absurd lengths in arranging for vigilance and rescue. The absurdity of the symptom could be shown by the fact that she could not tolerate even a picture postcard of the sea coast. If she saw one by chance in a shop-window she would have to find out who took the photograph, because she would see someone drowning, and she would have to organize relief, in spite of the fact that she knew perfectly well that the photograph was taken months and even years previously. This very ill girl was able eventually to come through to a fairly normal life, much less hampered by irrational guilt-feeling; but the treatment was necessarily of long duration.

Melancholia is an organized form of the depressed mood to which almost all people are liable. A melancholic patient may be paralysed by a sense of guilt, and may sit for years accusing himself or herself of causing the world war. No argument has any effect whatever. When it is possible to carry out an analysis of such a case, it is found that this gathering into the self of guilt for all the people in the world gives way in the treatment to the patient's fear that hate will be greater than love. The illness is an attempt to do the impossible. The patient absurdly claims responsibility for general disaster, but in so doing avoids reaching his or her personal destructiveness.

A little girl of five reacted with a deep depression to the death of her father which took place in unusual circumstances. The father had bought a car at a time when the little girl was going through a phase in which she was hating her father as well as loving him. She was, in fact, having dreams of his death, and when he proposed a car ride she implored him not to go. He insisted on going, as would be natural since children are liable to these nightmares. The family went for a ride, and it happened that they had an accident; the car was turned over and the little girl was the only one who was uninjured. She went up to her father who was lying in the road and kicked him to wake him up. But he was dead. I was able to watch this child through her serious depressive illness in which she had almost total apathy. For hours she stood in my room and nothing happened. One day she kicked the wall very gently with the same foot that she had used to kick her dead father to wake him up. I was able to put into words her wish to wake her father whom she loved, though in kicking him she was also expressing anger. From that moment of her kicking the wall she gradually came back into life, and after a year or so was able to return to school and to lead a normal life.

It was possible to have an intuitive understanding of unexplained guilt and of obsessional and melancholic illnesses apart from psycho-analysis. It is probably true, however, to say that it is only Freud's instrument of psycho-analysis and its derivatives that have made it possible for us to help the individual who is burdened by guilt-feeling to find the true origin of the sense of guilt in his or her own nature. The sense of guilt, seen this way, is a special form of anxiety associated with ambivalence, or co-existing love and hate. But ambivalence and the toleration of it by the individual implies a considerable degree of growth and health.

2. Guilt at its Point of Origin

I now come to a study of the point of origin of this capacity for guilt-sense, a point which exists in each individual. Melanie Klein (1935) drew the attention of psycho-analysts to a very important stage in emotional development to which she gave the name, 'the depressive position'. Her work on the origin of the capacity for guilt-sense in the human individual is an important result of the continued application of Freud's method. It is not possible to do justice to the complexities of the concept of the depressive position in a lecture of this length, but I will attempt a very brief statement.

It should be noted that whereas the earlier work of psychoanalysis dwelt on the conflict between love and hate, especially in the three-body or triangular situation, Melanie Klein more especially has developed the idea of conflict in the simple two-body relationship of the infant to the mother, conflict arising out of the destructive ideas that accompany the love impulse. Naturally, the date of the original version of this stage in an individual's development is earlier than the date of the Oedipus complex.

The accent changes. In previous work the accent was on the satisfaction that the infant obtained from instinctual experience. Now the accent shifts on to the aim, as it gradually appears. When Mrs Klein says that the infant aims at breaking ruthlessly through into the mother to take out of her everything that is felt there to be good, she is not of course denying the simple fact that instinctual experiences yield satisfaction. Nor was the aim altogether neglected in the earlier psycho-analytic formulations. Klein has developed the idea, however, that the primitive love impulse has an aggressive aim; being ruthless, it carries with it a variable quantity of destructive ideas unaffected by concern. These ideas may be very restricted at the beginning, but the infant we are watching and caring for need not be many months old before we can be fairly certain that we can perceive also the beginnings of concern—concern as to the results of the instinctual moments that belong to the developing love of the mother. If the mother behaves in that highly adaptive way which may come naturally to her, she is able to give plenty of time for the infant to come to terms with the fact that the object of the ruthless attack is the mother, the same person who is responsible for the total infant-care situation. It can be seen that the infant has two concerns; one as to the effect of the attack on the mother, and the other as to the results in the infant's own self according to whether there was a predominance of satisfaction or of frustration and anger. (I have used the expression primitive love impulse, but in Klein's writings the reference is to the aggression that is associated with the frustrations that inevitably disturb instinctual satisfactions as the child begins to be affected by the demands of reality.)

A great deal is being assumed here. For instance, we assume that the child is becoming a unit, and is becoming able to perceive the mother as a person. We also assume an ability to bring together the aggressive and erotic instinctual components into a sadistic experience, as well as an ability to find an object at the height of instinctual excitement. All of these developments may go wrong in their earlier stages, those stages which belong to the very beginning of life after birth and which depend on the mother and her natural handling of her infant. When we speak of the origins of guilt-sense, we assume healthy development at earlier stages. At what is called the depressive position the infant is not so much dependent on the mother's simple ability to hold a baby, which was her characteristic at the earlier stages, as on her ability to hold the infant-care situation over a period of time during which the infant may go through complex experiences. If time is given—a few hours maybe—the infant is able to work through the results of an instinctual experience. The mother, being still there, is able to be ready to receive and to understand if the infant has the natural impulse to give or to repair. At this stage in particular the infant is not able to deal with a succession of minders or prolonged absence of the mother. The infant's need for opportunity to make reparation and restitution, if oral sadism is to be accepted by the immature ego, is the second contribution of Klein tc this field.

Bowlby (1958) has been particularly interested in making the public aware of the need of every small child for a certain degree of reliability and continuity in external relationships. In the seventeenth century Richard Burton listed among the causes of melancholy: 'non-necessary, outward, adventitious, or accidental causes: as from the Nurse'. He was thinking partly in terms of the passage of noxious matters from the nurse via the milk, but not entirely so. For instance, he quotes from Aristotle who '. . . would not have a child put to nurse at all, but every mother to bring up her own, of what condition soever she be: . . . the mother will be more careful, loving and attendant, than any servile woman, or such hired creatures; this all the world acknowledgeth. . . .'

The observation of the origin of concern is better made in the analysis of a child or an adult than by direct observation of infants. In formulating these theories we do, of course, need to allow for distortions and sophistications that come from the reporting back that is inherent in the analytic situation. We are able, however, to get a view in our work of this most important development in human individuals, the origin of the capacity for a sense of guilt. Gradually as the infant finds out that the mother survives and accepts the restitutive gesture, so the infant becomes able to accept responsibility for the total fantasy of the full instinctual impulse that was previously ruthless. Ruthlessness gives way to ruth, unconcern to concern. (These terms refer to early development.)

In analysis one could say: 'couldn't care less' gives way to guilt-feeling. There is a gradual building up towards this point. No more fascinating experience awaits the analyst than the observation of the gradual build-up of the individual's capacity to tolerate the aggressive elements in the primitive love impulse. As I have said, this involves a gradual recognition of the difference between fact and fantasy, and of the mother's capacity to survive the instinctual moment, and so to be there to receive and understand the true reparative gesture.

As will be readily understood, this important phase of development is composed of innumerable repetitions spread over a period of time. There is a benign circle of (i) instinctual experience, (ii) acceptance of responsibility which is called guilt, (iii) a working through, and (iv) a true restitutive gesture. This can be reversed into a malign circle if something goes wrong at any point, in which case we see an undoing of the capacity for a sense of guilt and its replacement by inhibition of instinct or some other primitive form of defence, such as the splitting of objects into good and bad, etc. The question will certainly be asked: at what age in the normal child's development can the capacity for guilt-sense be said to become established? I suggest that we are talking about the first year of the infant's life, and in fact about the whole period in which the infant is having a clearly human two-body relationship with the mother. There is no need to claim that these things happen very early, although possibly they do. By the age of six months an infant can be seen to have a highly complex psychology, and it is possible that the *beginnings* of the depressive position are to be found by this age. There are immense difficulties in fixing the date of the origin of the guilt-feelings in the normal infant, and although it is a matter of great interest to seek an answer, the actual work of analysis is not affected by this issue.

There is a great deal in Melanie Klein's further work that I shall not be able to describe in this lecture, although it is relevant. In particular she has enriched our understanding of the complex relationship between fantasy and Freud's concept of inner reality, a concept that was clearly derived from philosophy. Klein has studied the interplay of what is felt by the infant to be benign or malevolent in terms of forces or objects within the self. This third contribution that she has made in this particular field reaches towards the problem of the eternal struggle in man's inner nature. Through the study of the growth of the infant's and the child's inner reality, we get a glimpse of the reason why there exists a relationship between the deepest conflicts that reveal themselves in religion and in art forms and the depressed mood or melancholic illness. At the centre is doubt, doubt as to the outcome of the struggle between the forces of good and evil, or in psychiatric terms, between the benign and persecutory elements within and without the personality. At the depressive position in the emotional development of an infant or a patient, we see the building up of the good and bad according to whether the instinctual experiences are satisfactory or frustrative. The good becomes protected from the bad, and a highly complex personal pattern is established as a system of defence against chaos within and without.

From my personal point of view, the work of Klein has enabled psycho-analytic theory to begin to include the idea of an individual's *value*, whereas in early psycho-analysis the statement was in terms of *health* and neurotic *ill-health*. Value is intimately bound up with the capacity for guilt-feeling.

3. Sense of Guilt Conspicuous by its Absence

I have now reached the third part of my lecture, in which I shall first briefly refer to the lack of a moral sense. Undoubtedly, in a proportion of people there is a lack of capacity for guilt-sense. The extreme of this incapacity for concern must be rare. But it is not rare to find individuals who have made a healthy development only in part, and who in part are unable to achieve concern or guilt-feeling, or even remorse. It is tempting here to fall back for an explanation on to the constitutional factor, which of course can never be ignored. However, psycho-analysis offers another explanation. This is that those who lack moral sense have lacked at the early stages of their development the emotional and physical setting which would have enabled a capacity for guilt-sense to have developed.

It should be understood that I am not denying that each infant carries a tendency towards the development of guilt. Given certain conditions of physical health and care, walking and talking appear because the time has come for these developments. In the case of the development of a capacity for guilt-feeling, the necessary environmental conditions are, however, of a much more complex order, comprising indeed all that is natural and reliable in infant and child care. In the earliest stages of the emotional development of the individual, we must not look for a guilt-sense. The ego is not sufficiently strong and organized to accept responsibility for id-impulses, and dependence is near absolute. If there is satisfactory development in the earliest stages, there comes about an ego integration which makes possible the beginning of a capacity for concern. Gradually, in favourable circumstances, a capacity for guilt-sense builds up in the individual in relation to the mother, and this is intimately related to the opportunity for reparation. When the capacity for concern is established, the individual begins to be in a position to experience the Oedipus complex, and to tolerate the ambivalence that is inherent at the later stage in which the child, if mature, is involved in triangular relationships as between whole human beings.

In this context I can do no more than acknowledge the fact that in some persons, or in a part of some persons, there is a stunting of emotional development in the earliest phases, and consequently an absence of moral sense. Where there is lack of personal moral sense the implanted moral code is necessary, but the resultant socialization is unstable.

The Creative Artist

It is interesting to note that the creative artist is able to reach to a kind of socialization which obviates the need for guilt-feeling and the associated reparative and restitutive activity that forms the basis for ordinary constructive work. The creative artist or thinker may, in fact, fail to understand, or even may despise, the feelings of concern that motivate a less creative person; and of artists it may be said that some have no capacity for guilt and yet achieve a socialization through their exceptional talent. Ordinary guilt-ridden people find this bewildering; yet they have a sneaking regard for ruthlessness that does in fact, in such circumstances, achieve more than guilt-driven labour.

Loss and Recovery of Guilt-sense

In our management of antisocial children and adults we can watch the loss or recovery of the capacity for guilt-sense, and often we are in a position to assess the variations in environmental reliability which produce these effects. It is at this point of loss and recovery of moral sense that we can study delinquency and recidivism. Freud wrote in 1915 (referring to adolescent and pre-adolescent acts, such as thefts, frauds, and arson, in people who have eventually become socially adjusted): 'Analytic work . . . brought the surprising discovery that such deeds were done principally *because* [my italics] they were forbidden, and because their execution was accompanied by mental relief for their doer. He was suffering from an oppressive feeling of guilt, of which he did not know the origin, and after he had committed a misdeed this oppression was mitigated. His sense of guilt was at least attached to something' (Freud, 1915, p. 332). Although Freud was referring to late stages in development, what he wrote applies also to children.

From our analytic work we can roughly divide antisocial behaviour into two kinds. The first is common and closely allied to the ordinary naughtiness of healthy children. In terms of behaviour the complaint is of stealing, lying, destructiveness, and bed-wetting. Repeatedly we find that these acts are done in an unconscious attempt to make sense of guilt-feeling. The child or adult cannot reach the source of a sense of guilt that is intolerable, and the fact that the guilt-feeling cannot be explained makes for a feeling of madness. The antisocial person gets relief by devising a limited crime which is only in a disguised way in the nature of the crime in the repressed fantasy that belongs to the original Oedipus complex. This is the closest that the antisocial person can get to the ambivalence belonging to the Oedipus complex. At first the substitute crime or delinquency is unsatisfactory to the delinquent, but when compulsively repeated it acquires the characteristics of secondary gain and thus becomes acceptable to the self. Our treatment is more likely to be effectual when we can apply it before secondary gain has become important. In this, the more common variety of antisocial behaviour, it is not so much the guilt that is repressed as the fantasy that explains the guilt.

By contrast, in the more serious and more rare antisocial episodes it is precisely the capacity for guilt-feeling that is lost. Here we find the most ugly crimes. We see the criminal engaged in a desperate attempt to feel guilty. It is unlikely that he ever succeeds. In order to develop a capacity for guilt-sense, such a person must find an environment of a specialized kind; in fact, we must supply for him an environment that corresponds to that which is normally needed by the immature infant. It is notoriously difficult to provide such an environment, which must be able to take up all the strains resulting from ruthlessness and impulsiveness. We find ourselves dealing with an infant, but one who has the strength and cunning of the older child or adult.

In the management of the more common type of case in which there is antisocial behaviour we are frequently able to produce a cure by rearrangement of the environment, basing what we do on the understanding that Freud has given us.

I shall give an example, that of a boy who was stealing at school. The headmaster, instead of punishing him, recognized that he was ill and recommended psychiatric consultation. This boy at the age of nine was dealing with a deprivation belonging to an earlier age, and what he needed was a period at home. His family had become reunited and this had given him a new hope. I found that the boy had been under a compulsion to steal, hearing a voice that ordered him about, the voice of a wizard. At home he became ill, infantile, dependent, enuretic, apathetic. His parents met his needs and allowed him to be ill. In the end they were rewarded by his making a spontaneous recovery. After a year he was able to return to boarding-school, and the recovery has proved to be a lasting one.

It would have been easy to have diverted this boy from the path that led to his recovery. He was of course unaware of the intolerable loneliness and emptiness that lay at the back of his illness, and which made him adopt the wizard in place of a more natural superego organization; this loneliness belonged to a time of separation from his family when he was five. If he had been thrashed or if the headmaster had told him that he ought to feel wicked, he would have hardened up and organized a fuller identification with the wizard; he would then have become domineering and defiant and eventually an antisocial person. This is a common type of case in child psychiatry, and I choose it simply because it is a published case and reference can be made to it for further details (Winnicott, 1953).

We cannot hope to cure many of those who have become delinquent, but we can hope to understand how to prevent the development of the antisocial tendency. We can at least avoid interrupting the developing relationship between mother and baby. Also, applying these principles to the ordinary upbringing of children, we can see the need for some strictness in management where the child's own guilt-sense is still primitive and crude; by limited prohibitions we give opportunity for that limited naughtiness which we call healthy, and which contains much of the child's spontaneity.

More than anyone else it was Freud who paved the way for the understanding of antisocial behaviour and of crime as a *sequel* to an unconscious criminal intention, and a symptom of a failure in child-care. I suggest that in putting forward these ideas and showing how we can test them and use them Freud has made a contribution to social psychology which can have far-reaching results.

2

THE CAPACITY TO BE ALONE[1]

(1958)

I wish to make an examination of the capacity of the individual to be alone, acting on the assumption that this capacity is one of the most important signs of maturity in emotional development.

In almost all our psycho-analytic treatments there come times when the ability to be alone is important to the patient. Clinically this may be represented by a silent phase or a silent session, and this silence, far from being evidence of resistance, turns out to be an achievement on the part of the patient. Perhaps it is here that the patient has been able to be alone for the first time. It is to this aspect of the transference in which the patient is alone in the analytic session that I wish to draw attention.

It is probably true to say that in psycho-analytical literature more has been written on the *fear* of being alone or the *wish* to be alone than on the *ability* to be alone; also a considerable amount of work has been done on the withdrawn state, a defensive organization implying an expectation of persecution. It would seem to me that a discussion on the *positive* aspects of the capacity to be alone is overdue. In the literature there may be specific attempts to state the capacity to be alone, but I am not aware of these. I wish to make reference to Freud's (1914) concept of the *anaclitic relationship* (cf. Winnicott, 1956a).

Three- and Two-Body Relationships

Rickman introduced us to the idea of thinking in terms of three-body and two-body relationships. We often refer to the Oedipus complex as a stage in which three-body relationships dominate the field of experience. Any attempt to describe the Oedipus complex in terms of two people must fail. Nevertheless two-body relationships do exist, and these belong to relatively earlier stages in the history of the individual. The original two-body relationship is that of the infant and the mother or mother-substitute, before any property of the mother has been sorted out

[1] Based on a paper read at an Extra Scientific Meeting of the British Psycho-Analytical Society, 24 July 1957, and first published in the *Int. J. Psycho-Anal.*, **39**, pp. 416–20.

and moulded into the idea of a father. The Klein concept of the depressive position can be described in terms of two-body relationships, and it is perhaps true to say that a two-body relationship is an essential feature of the concept.

After thinking in terms of three- and two-body relationships, how natural that one should go a stage further back and speak of a one-body relationship! At first it would seem that narcissism would be the one-body relationship, either an early form of secondary narcissism or primary narcissism itself. I am suggesting that this jump from two-body relationships to a one-body relationship cannot, in fact, be made without violation of a great deal that we know through our analytic work and through direct observation of mothers and infants.

Actually Being Alone

It will be appreciated that actually to be alone is not what I am discussing. A person may be in solitary confinement, and yet not be able to be alone. How greatly he must suffer is beyond imagination. However, many people do become able to enjoy solitude before they are out of childhood, and they may even value solitude as a most precious possession.

The capacity to be alone is either a highly sophisticated phenomenon, one that may arrive in a person's development *after* the establishment of three-body relationships, or else it is a phenomenon of early life which deserves special study because it is the foundation on which sophisticated aloneness is built.

Paradox

The main point of this contribution can now be stated. Although many types of experience go to the establishment of the capacity to be alone, there is one that is basic, and without a sufficiency of it the capacity to be alone does not come about; *this experience is that of being alone, as an infant and small child, in the presence of mother.* Thus the basis of the capacity to be alone is a paradox; it is the experience of being alone while someone else is present.

Here is implied a rather special type of relationship, that between the infant or small child who is alone, and the mother or mother-substitute who is in fact reliably present even if represented for the moment by a cot or a pram or the general atmosphere of the immediate environment. I would like to suggest a name for this special type of relationship.

Personally I like to use the term *ego-relatedness*, which is convenient in that it contrasts rather clearly with the word *id-relationship*, which is a recurring complication in what might be called ego life. Ego-relatedness refers to the relationship between two people, one of whom at any rate is alone; perhaps both are alone, yet the presence of each is important to the other. I consider that if one compares the meaning of the word 'like' with that of the word 'love', one can see that liking is a matter of ego-relatedness, whereas loving is more a matter of id-relationships, either crude or in sublimated form.

Before developing these two ideas in my own way I wish to remind you how it would be possible to refer to the capacity to be alone in well-worn psycho-analytic phraseology.

After Intercourse

It is perhaps fair to say that after satisfactory intercourse each partner is alone and is contented to be alone. Being able to enjoy being alone along with another person who is also alone is in itself an experience of health. Lack of id-tension may produce anxiety, but time-integration of the personality enables the individual to wait for the natural return of id-tension, and to enjoy sharing solitude, that is to say, solitude that is relatively free from the property that we call 'withdrawal'.

Primal Scene

It could be said that an individual's capacity to be alone depends on his ability to deal with the feelings aroused by the primal scene. In the primal scene an excited relationship between the parents is perceived or imagined, and this is accepted by the child who is healthy and who is able to master the hate and to gather it into the service of masturbation. In masturbation the whole responsibility for the conscious and unconscious fantasy is accepted by the individual child, who is the third person in a three-body or triangular relationship. To be able to be alone in these circumstances implies a maturity of erotic development, a genital potency or the corresponding female acceptance; it implies fusion of the aggressive and erotic impulses and ideas, and it implies a tolerance of ambivalence; along with all this there would naturally be a capacity on the part of the individual to identify with each of the parents.

A statement in these or any terms could become almost infinitely complex, because the capacity to be alone is so nearly synonymous with emotional maturity.

Good Internal Object

I will now attempt to use another language, one that derives from the work of Melanie Klein. The capacity to be alone depends on the existence of a good object in the psychic reality of the individual. The good internal breast or penis or the good internal relationships are well enough set up and defended for the individual (at any rate for the time being) to feel confident about the present and the future. The relationship of the individual to his or her internal objects, along with confidence in regard to internal relationships, provides of itself a sufficiency of living, so that temporarily he or she is able to rest contented even in the absence of external objects and stimuli. Maturity and the capacity to be alone implies that the individual has had the chance through good-enough mothering to build up a belief in a benign environment. This belief is built up through a repetition of satisfactory instinctual gratifications.

In this language one finds oneself referring to an earlier stage in the individual's development than that at which the classical Oedipus complex holds sway. Nevertheless a considerable degree of ego maturity is being assumed. The integration of the individual into a unit is assumed, otherwise there would be no sense in making reference to the inside and the outside, or in giving special significance to the fantasy of the inside. In negative terms: there must be a relative freedom from persecutory anxiety. In positive terms: the good internal objects are in the individual's personal inner world, and are available for projection at a suitable moment.

To be Alone in an Immature State

The question which will be asked at this point is this: Can a child or an infant be alone at a very early stage when ego immaturity makes it impossible for a description of being alone to be given in the phraseology that has just been employed? It is the main part of my thesis that we do need to be able to speak of an unsophisticated form of being alone, and that even if we agree that the capacity to be truly alone is a sophistication, the ability to be truly alone has as its basis the early experience of being alone in the presence of someone. Being alone in the presence of someone can take place at a very early stage, when the *ego immaturity is naturally balanced by ego-support* from the mother. In the course of time the individual introjects the ego-supportive mother and in this way becomes able to be alone without frequent reference to the mother or mother symbol.

'I am Alone'

I would like to take up this subject in a different way by studying the words 'I am alone'.

First there is the word 'I', implying much emotional growth. The individual is established as a unit. Integration is a fact. The external world is repudiated and an internal world has become possible. This is simply a topographical statement of the personality as a thing, as an organization of ego-nuclei. At this point no reference is being made to living.

Next come the words 'I am', representing a stage in individual growth. By these words the individual not only has shape but also life. In the beginnings of 'I am' the individual is (so to speak) raw, is undefended, vulnerable, potentially paranoid. The individual can only achieve the 'I am' stage because there exists an environment which is protective; the protective environment is in fact the mother preoccupied with her own infant and orientated to the infant's ego requirements through her identification with her own infant. There is no need to postulate an awareness of the mother on the part of the infant at this stage of 'I am'.

Next I come to the words 'I am alone'. According to the theory that I am putting forward this further stage does indeed involve an appreciation on the part of the infant of the mother's continued existence. By this I do not necessarily mean an awareness with the conscious mind. I consider, however, that 'I am alone' is a development from 'I am', dependent on the infant's awareness of the continued existence of a reliable mother whose reliability makes it possible for the infant to be alone and to enjoy being alone, for a limited period.

In this way I am trying to justify the paradox that the capacity to be alone is based on the experience of being alone in the presence of someone, and that without a sufficiency of this experience the capacity to be alone cannot develop.

'Ego-relatedness'

Now, if I am right in the matter of this paradox, it is interesting to examine the nature of the relationship of the infant to the mother, that which for the purposes of this paper I have called ego-relatedness. It will be seen that I attach a great importance to this relationship, as I consider that it is the stuff out of which friendship is made. It may turn out to be the *matrix of transference*.

There is a further reason why I put a special importance on this matter of ego-relatedness, but in order to make my meaning clear I must digress for a moment.

I think it will be generally agreed that id-impulse is significant only if it is contained in ego living. An id-impulse either disrupts a weak ego or else strengthens a strong one. It is possible to say that *id-relationships strengthen the ego when they occur in a framework of ego-relatedness*. If this be accepted, then an understanding of the importance of the capacity to be alone follows. It is only when alone (that is to say, in the presence of someone) that the infant can discover his own personal life. The pathological alternative is a false life built on reactions to external stimuli. When alone in the sense that I am using the term, and only when alone, the infant is able to do the equivalent of what in an adult would be called relaxing. The infant is able to become unintegrated, to flounder, to be in a state in which there is no orientation, to be able to exist for a time without being either a reactor to an external impingement or an active person with a direction of interest or movement. The stage is set for an id experience. In the course of time there arrives a sensation or an impulse. In this setting the sensation or impulse will feel real and be truly a personal experience.

It will now be seen why it is important that there is someone available, someone present, although present without making demands; the impulse having arrived, the id experience can be fruitful, and the object can be a part or the whole of the attendant person, namely the mother. It is only under these conditions that the infant can have an experience which feels real. A large number of such experiences form the basis for a life that has reality in it instead of futility. The individual who has developed the capacity to be alone is constantly able to rediscover the personal impulse, and the personal impulse is not wasted because the state of being alone is something which (though paradoxically) always implies that someone else is there.

In the course of time the individual becomes able to forgo the *actual* presence of a mother or mother-figure. This has been referred to in such terms as the establishment of an 'internal environment'. It is more primitive than the phenomenon which deserves the term 'introjected mother'.

Climax in Ego-relatedness

I would now like to go a little further in speculating in regard to the ego-relatedness and the possibilities of experience within this relationship, and to consider the concept of an *ego orgasm*. I am of course aware that if there is such a thing as an ego orgasm, those who are inhibited in instinctual experience will tend to specialize in such orgasms, so that there would be a pathology of the tendency to ego orgasm. At the moment I wish to leave out consideration of the pathological, not forgetting identification of the whole body with a part-object (phallus), and to ask only whether there can be a value in thinking of *ecstasy* as an ego orgasm. In the normal person a highly satisfactory experience such as may be obtained at a concert or at the theatre or in a friendship may deserve a term such as ego orgasm, which draws attention to the climax and the importance of the climax. It may be thought unwise that the word orgasm should be used in this context; I think that even so there is room for a discussion of the climax that may occur in satisfactory ego-relatedness. One may ask: when a child is playing, is the whole of the game a sublimation of id-impulse? Could there not be some value in thinking that there is a difference of *quality* as well as of *quantity of id* when one compares the game that is satisfactory with the instinct that crudely underlies the game? The concept of sublimation is fully accepted and has great value, but it is a pity to omit reference to the vast difference that exists between the happy playing of children and the play of children who get compulsively excited and who can be seen to be very near to an instinctual experience. It is true that even in the happy playing of the child everything can be *interpreted* in terms of id-impulse; this is possible because we talk in terms of symbols, and we are undoubtedly on safe ground in our use of symbolism and our understanding of all play in terms of id-relationships. Nevertheless, we leave out something vital if we do not remember that the play of a child is not happy when complicated by bodily excitements with their physical climaxes.

The so-called normal child is able to play, to get excited while playing, and to feel *satisfied with the game*, without feeling threatened by a physical orgasm of local excitement. By contrast, a deprived child with antisocial tendency, or any child with marked manic-defence restlessness, is unable to enjoy play because the body becomes physically involved. A physical climax is needed, and most parents know the moment when nothing brings an exciting game to an end except a smack—which provides a false climax, but a very useful one. In my opinion, if we compare the happy play of a child or the experience of an adult at a concert with a sexual experience, the difference is so great that we should do no harm in allowing a different term for the description of the two experiences. Whatever the unconscious symbolism, the quantity of actual physical excitement is minimal in the one type of experience and maximal in the other. We may pay tribute to the importance of ego-relatedness *per se* without giving up the ideas that underlie the concept of sublimation.

Summary

The capacity to be alone is a highly sophisticated phenomenon and has many contributory factors. It is closely related to emotional maturity.

The basis of the capacity to be alone is the experience of being alone in the presence of someone. In this way an infant with weak ego organization may be alone because of reliable ego-support.

The type of relationship that exists between an infant and the ego-supportive mother deserves special study. Although other terms have been used, I suggest that ego-relatedness might be a good term for temporary use.

In a frame of ego-relatedness, id-relationships occur and strengthen rather than disrupt the immature ego.

Gradually, the ego-supportive environment is introjected and built into the individual's personality, so that there comes about a capacity actually to be alone. Even so, theoretically, there is always someone present, someone who is equated ultimately and unconsciously with the mother, the person who, in the early days and weeks, was temporarily identified with her infant, and for the time being was interested in nothing else but the care of her own infant.

3

THE THEORY OF THE PARENT-INFANT RELATIONSHIP[1]

(1960)

The main point of this paper can perhaps best be brought out through a comparison of the study of infancy with the study of the psycho-analytic transference.[2] It cannot be too strongly emphasized that my statement is about infancy, and not primarily about psycho-analysis. The reason why this must be understood reaches to the root of the matter. If this paper does not contribute constructively, then it can only add to the existing confusion about the relative importance of personal and environmental influences in the development of the individual.

In psycho-analysis as we know it there is no trauma that is outside the individual's omnipotence. Everything eventually comes under ego-control, and thus becomes related to secondary processes. The patient is not helped if the analyst says: 'Your mother was not good enough' . . . 'your father really seduced you' . . . 'your aunt dropped you.' Changes come in an analysis when the traumatic factors enter the psycho-analytic material in the patient's own way, and within the patient's omnipotence. The interpretations that are alterative are those that can be made in terms of projection. The same applies to the benign factors, factors that led to satisfaction. Everything is interpreted in terms of the individual's love and ambivalence. The analyst is prepared to wait a long time to be in a position to do exactly this kind of work.

In infancy, however, good and bad things happen to the infant that are quite outside the infant's range. In fact infancy is the period in which the capacity for gathering external factors into the area of the infant's omnipotence is in process of formation. The ego-support of the maternal care enables the infant to live and develop in spite of his being not yet able to control, or to feel responsible for, what is good and bad in the environment.

[1] This paper, together with one by Dr Phyllis Greenacre on the same theme, was the subject of a discussion at the 22nd International Psycho-Analytical Congress at Edinburgh, 1961. It was first published in the *Int. J. Psycho-Anal.*, **41**, pp. 585–95.
[2] I have discussed this from a more detailed clinical angle in *Primitive Emotional Development* (1945).

The events of these earliest stages cannot be thought of as lost through what we know as the mechanisms of repression, and therefore analysts cannot expect to find them appearing as a result of work which lessens the forces of repression. It is possible that Freud was trying to allow for these phenomena when he used the term primary repression, but this is open to argument. What is fairly certain is that the matters under discussion here have had to be taken for granted in much of the psycho-analytic literature.[1]

Returning to psycho-analysis, I have said that the analyst is prepared to wait till the patient becomes able to present the environmental factors in terms that allow of their interpretation as projections. In the well-chosen case this result comes from the patient's capacity for confidence, which is rediscovered in the reliability of the analyst and the professional setting. Sometimes the analyst needs to wait a very long time; and in the case that is *badly* chosen for classical psycho-analysis it is likely that the reliability of the analyst is the most important factor (or more important than the interpretations) because the patient did not experience such reliability in the maternal care of infancy, and if the patient is to make use of such reliability he will need to find it for the first time in the analyst's behaviour. This would seem to be the basis for research into the problem of what a psycho-analyst can do in the treatment of schizophrenia and other psychoses.

In borderline cases the analyst does not always wait in vain; in the course of time the patient becomes able to make use of the psycho-analytic interpretations of the original traumata as projections. It may even happen that he is able to accept what is good in the environment as a projection of the simple and stable going-on-being elements that derive from his own inherited potential.

The paradox is that what is good and bad in the infant's environment is not in fact a projection, but in spite of this it is necessary, if the individual infant is to develop healthily, that everything shall seem to him to be a projection. Here we find omnipotence and the pleasure principle in operation, as they certainly are in earliest infancy; and to this observation we can add that the recognition of a true 'not-me' is a matter of the intellect; it belongs to extreme sophistication and to the maturity of the individual.

In the writings of Freud most of the formulations concerning

---

[1] I have reported (1954) some aspects of this problem, as met with in the case of a female patient while she was in deep regression.

infancy derive from a study of adults in analysis. There are some childhood observations ('Cotton reel' material (1920)), and there is the analysis of Little Hans (1909). At first sight it would seem that a great deal of psycho-analytic theory is about early childhood and infancy, but in one sense Freud can be said to have neglected infancy as a state. This is brought out by a footnote in *Formulations on the Two Principles of Mental Functioning* (1911, p. 220) in which he shows that he knows he is taking for granted the very things that are under discussion in this paper. In the text he traces the development from the pleasure-principle to the reality-principle, following his usual course of reconstructing the infancy of his adult patients. The note runs as follows:

> It will rightly be objected that an organization which was a slave to the pleasure-principle and neglected the reality of the external world could not maintain itself alive for the shortest time, so that it could not have come into existence at all. The employment of a fiction like this is, however, justified when one considers that the infant—provided one includes with it the care it receives from its mother—does almost realize a psychical system of this kind.

Here Freud paid full tribute to the function of maternal care, and it must be assumed that he left this subject alone only because he was not ready to discuss its implications. The note continues:

> It probably hallucinates the fulfilment of its internal needs; it betrays its unpleasure, when there is an increase of stimulus and an absence of satisfaction, by the motor discharge of screaming and beating about with its arms and legs, and it then experiences the satisfaction it has hallucinated. Later, as an older child, it learns to employ these manifestations of discharge intentionally as methods of expressing its feelings. Since the later care of children is modelled on the care of infants, the dominance of the pleasure-principle can really come to an end only when a child has achieved complete psychical detachment from its parents.

The words: 'provided one includes with it the care it receives from its mother' have great importance in the context of this study. The infant and the maternal care together form a unit.[1] Certainly if one is to study the theory of the parent-infant relationship one must come to a decision about these matters, which concern the real meaning of the word dependence. It is not enough that it is acknowledged that the environment is

---

[1] I once said: 'There is no such thing as an infant', meaning, of course, that whenever one finds an infant one finds maternal care, and without maternal care there would be no infant. (Discussion at a Scientific Meeting of the British Psycho-Analytical Society, *circa* 1940.) Was I influenced, without knowing it, by this footnote of Freud's?

important. If there is to be a discussion of the theory of the parent-infant relationship, then we are divided into two if there are some who do not allow that at the earliest stages the infant and the maternal care belong to each other and cannot be disentangled. These two things, the infant and the maternal care, disentangle and dissociate themselves in health; and health, which means so many things, to some extent means a disentanglement of maternal care from something which we then call the infant or the beginnings of a growing child. This idea is covered by Freud's words at the end of the footnote: 'the dominance of the pleasure-principle can really come to an end only when a child has achieved complete psychical detachment from its parents'. (The middle part of this footnote will be discussed in a later section, where it will be suggested that Freud's words here are inadequate and misleading in certain respects, if taken to refer to the earliest stage.)

The Word 'Infant'

In this paper the word infant will be taken to refer to the very young child. It is necessary to say this because in Freud's writings the word sometimes seems to include the child up to the age of the passing of the Oedipus complex. Actually the word infant implies 'not talking' (*infans*), and it is not un-useful to think of infancy as the phase prior to word presentation and the use of word symbols. The corollary is that it refers to a phase in which the infant depends on maternal care that is based on maternal empathy rather than on understanding of what is or could be verbally expressed.

This is essentially a period of ego development, and integration is the main feature of such development. The id-forces clamour for attention. At first they are external to the infant. In health the id becomes gathered into the service of the ego, and the ego masters the id, so that id-satisfactions become ego-strengtheners. This, however, is an achievement of healthy development and in infancy there are many variants dependent on relative failure of this achievement. In the ill-health of infancy achievements of this kind are minimally reached, or may be won and lost. In infantile psychosis (or schizophrenia) the id remains relatively or totally 'external' to the ego, and id-satisfactions remain physical, and have the effect of threatening the ego structure, that is, until defences of psychotic quality are organized.[1]

[1] I have tried to show the application of this hypothesis to an understanding of psychosis in my paper, 'Psychoses and Child Care' (Winnicott, 1952).

I am here supporting the view that the main reason why in infant development the infant usually becomes able to master, and the ego to include, the id, is the fact of the maternal care, the maternal ego implementing the infant ego and so making it powerful and stable. How this takes place will need to be examined, and also how the infant ego eventually becomes free of the mother's ego-support, so that the infant achieves mental detachment from the mother, that is, differentiation into a separate personal self.

In order to examine the parent-infant relationship it is necessary first to attempt a brief statement of the theory of infant emotional development.

Historical

In psycho-analytic theory as it grew up the early hypothesis concerned the id and the ego mechanisms of defence. It was understood that the id arrived on the scene very early indeed, and Freud's discovery and description of pregenital sexuality, based on his observations of the regressive elements found in genital fantasy and in play and in dreams, are main features of clinical psychology.

Ego mechanisms of defence were gradually formulated.[1] These mechanisms were assumed to be organized in relation to anxiety which derived either from instinct tension or from object loss. This part of psycho-analytic theory presupposes a separateness of the self and a structuring of the ego, perhaps a personal body scheme. At the level of the main part of this paper this state of affairs cannot yet be assumed. The discussion centres round the establishment of precisely this state of affairs, namely the structuring of the ego which makes anxiety from instinct tension or object loss possible. Anxiety at this early stage is not castration anxiety or separation anxiety; it relates to quite other things, and is, in fact, anxiety about annihilation (cf. the aphanisis of Jones).

In psycho-analytic theory ego mechanisms of defence largely belong to the idea of a child that has an independence, a truly

[1] Researches into defence mechanisms which followed Anna Freud's *The Ego and the Mechanisms of Defence* (1936) have from a different route arrived at a re-evaluation of the role of mothering in infant care and early infant development. Anna Freud (1953) has reassessed her views on the matter. Willi Hoffer (1955) also has made observations relating to this area of development. My emphasis in this paper, however, is on the importance of an understanding of the role of the early parental environment in infant development, and on the way this becomes of clinical significance for us in our handling of certain types of case with affective and character disorders.

personal defence organization. On this borderline the researches of Klein add to Freudian theory by clarifying the interplay of primitive anxieties and defence mechanisms. This work of Klein concerns earliest infancy, and draws attention to the importance of aggressive and destructive impulses that are more deeply rooted than those that are reactive to frustration and related to hate and anger; also in Klein's work there is a dissection of early defences against primitive anxieties, anxieties that belong to the first stages of the mental organization (splitting, projection, and introjection).

What is described in Melanie Klein's work clearly belongs to the life of the infant in its earliest phases, and to the period of dependence with which this paper is concerned. Melanie Klein made it clear that she recognized that the environment was important at this period, and in various ways at all stages.[1] I suggest, however, that her work and that of her co-workers leaves open for further consideration the development of the theme of full dependence, that which appears in Freud's phrase: '. . . the infant, provided one includes with it the care it receives from its mother . . .' There is nothing in Klein's work that contradicts the idea of absolute dependence, but there seems to me to be no specific reference to a stage at which the infant exists only because of the maternal care, together with which it forms a unit.

What I am bringing forward for consideration here is the difference between the analyst's acceptance of the reality of dependence, and his working with it in the transference.[2]

It would seem that the study of ego-defences takes the investigator back to pregenital id-manifestations, whereas the study of ego psychology takes him back to dependence, to the maternal-care–infant unit.

One half of the theory of the parent-infant relationship concerns the infant, and is the theory of the infant's journey from absolute dependence, through relative dependence, to independence, and, in parallel, the infant's journey from the pleasure principle to the reality principle, and from autoerotism to object relationships. The other half of the theory of the parent-infant relationship concerns maternal care, that is to say the qualities and changes in the mother that meet the specific and developing needs of the infant towards whom she orientates.

[1] I have given a detailed account of my understanding of Melanie Klein's work in this area in two papers (Winnicott, 1954b, and Chap. 1 of this volume). See Klein (1946, p. 297).

[2] For a clinical example see my paper, 'Withdrawal and Regression' (1954).

A. THE INFANT

The key word in this part of the study is *dependence*. Human infants cannot start to *be* except under certain conditions. These conditions are studied below, but they are part of the psychology of the infant. Infants come into *being* differently according to whether the conditions are favourable or unfavourable. At the same time conditions do not determine the infant's potential. This is inherited, and it is legitimate to study this inherited potential of the individual as a separate issue, *provided always that it is accepted that the inherited potential of an infant cannot become an infant unless linked to maternal care*.

The inherited potential includes a tendency towards growth and development. All stages of emotional growth can be roughly dated. Presumably all developmental stages have a date in each individual child. Nevertheless, not only do these dates vary from child to child, but also, *even if they were known in advance* in the case of a given child, they could not be used in predicting the child's actual development because of the other factor, maternal care. If such dates could be used in prediction at all, it would be on the basis of assuming a maternal care that is adequate in the important respects. (This obviously does not mean adequate only in the physical sense; the meaning of adequacy and inadequacy in this context is discussed below.)

The Inherited Potential and its Fate

It is necessary here to attempt to state briefly what happens to the inherited potential if this is to develop into an infant, and thereafter into a child, a child reaching towards independent existence. Because of the complexities of the subject such a statement must be made on the assumption of satisfactory maternal care, which means parental care. Satisfactory parental care can be classified roughly into three overlapping stages:

(*a*) Holding.
(*b*) Mother and infant living together. Here the father's function (of dealing with the environment for the mother) is not known to the infant.
(*c*) Father, mother, and infant, all three living together.

The term 'holding' is used here to denote not only the actual physical holding of the infant, but also the total environmental provision prior to the concept of *living with*. In other words, it refers to a three-dimensional or space relationship with time gradually added. This overlaps with, but is initiated prior to, instinctual experiences that in time would determine object relationships. It includes the management of experiences that are inherent in existence, such as the *completion* (and therefore the *non-completion*) of processes, processes which from the outside may seem to be purely physiological but which belong to infant psychology and take place in a complex psychological field, determined by the awareness and the empathy of the mother. (This concept of holding is further discussed below.)

The term 'living with' implies object relationships, and the emergence of the infant from the state of being merged with the mother, or his perception of objects as external to the self.

This study is especially concerned with the 'holding' stage of maternal care, and with the complex events in infants' psychological development that are related to this holding phase. It should be remembered, however, that a division of one phase from another is artificial, and merely a matter of convenience, adopted for the purpose of clearer definition.

Infant Development During the Holding Phase

In the light of this some characteristics of infant development during this phase can be enumerated. It is at this stage that

> primary process
> primary identification
> auto-erotism
> primary narcissism

are living realities.

In this phase the ego changes over from an unintegrated state to a structured integration, and so the infant becomes able to experience anxiety associated with disintegration. The word disintegration begins to have a meaning which it did not possess before ego integration became a fact. In healthy development at this stage the infant retains the capacity for re-experiencing un-integrated states, but this depends on the continuation of reliable maternal care or on the build-up in the infant of memories of maternal care beginning gradually to be perceived as such. The result of healthy progress in the infant's development during this stage is that he attains to what might be called 'unit status'. The infant becomes a person, an individual in his own right.

Associated with this attainment is the infant's psychosomatic existence, which begins to take on a personal pattern; I have referred to this as the psyche indwelling in the soma.[1] The basis for this indwelling is a linkage of motor and sensory and functional experiences with the infant's new state of being a person. As a further development there comes into existence what might be called a limiting membrane, which to some extent (in health) is equated with the surface of the skin, and has a position between the infant's 'me' and his 'not-me'. So the infant comes to have an inside and an outside, and a body-scheme. In this way meaning comes to the function of intake and output; moreover, it gradually becomes meaningful to postulate a personal or inner psychic reality for the infant.[2]

During the holding phase other processes are initiated; the most important is the dawn of intelligence and the beginning of a mind as something distinct from the psyche. From this follows the whole story of the secondary processes and of symbolic functioning, and of the organization of a personal psychic content, which forms a basis for dreaming and for living relationships.

At the same time there starts in the infant a joining up of two roots of impulsive behaviour. The term 'fusion' indicates the positive process whereby diffuse elements that belong to movement and to muscle erotism become (in health) fused with the orgiastic functioning of the erotogenic zones. This concept is more familiar as the reverse process of defusion, which is a complicated defence in which aggression becomes separated out from erotic experience after a period in which a degree of fusion has been achieved. All these developments belong to the environmental condition of *holding*, and without a good enough holding these stages cannot be attained, or once attained cannot become established.

A further development is in the capacity for object relationships. Here the infant changes from a relationship to a subjectively conceived object to a relationship to an object objectively perceived. This change is closely bound up with the infant's change from being merged with the mother to being separate from her, or to relating to her as separate and 'not-me'. This development is not specifically related to the holding, but is related to the phase of 'living with' . . .

[1] For an earlier statement by me on this issue see my paper, 'Mind and its Relation to the Psyche-Soma' (1949c).
[2] Here the work on primitive fantasy, with whose richness and complexity we are familiar through the teachings of Melanie Klein, becomes applicable and appropriate.

Dependence

In the holding phase the infant is maximally dependent. One can classify dependence thus:

(i) *Absolute Dependence*. In this state the infant has no means of knowing about the maternal care, which is largely a matter of prophylaxis. He cannot gain control over what is well and what is badly done, but is only in a position to gain profit or to suffer disturbance.

(ii) *Relative Dependence*. Here the infant can become aware of the need for the details of maternal care, and can to a growing extent relate them to personal impulse, and then later, in a psycho-analytic treatment, can reproduce them in the transference.

(iii) *Towards Independence*. The infant develops means for doing without actual care. This is accomplished through the accumulation of memories of care, the projection of personal needs and the introjection of care details, with the development of confidence in the environment. Here must be added the element of intellectual understanding with its tremendous implications.

Isolation of the Individual

Another phenomenon that needs consideration at this phase is the hiding of the core of the personality. Let us examine the concept of a central or true self. The central self could be said to be the inherited potential which is experiencing a continuity of being, and acquiring in its own way and at its own speed a personal psychic reality and a personal body-scheme.[1] It seems necessary to allow for the concept of the isolation of this central self as a characteristic of health. Any threat to this isolation of the true self constitutes a major anxiety at this early stage, and defences of earliest infancy appear in relation to failures on the part of the mother (or in maternal care) to ward off impingements which might disturb this isolation.

Impingements may be met and dealt with by the ego organization, gathered into the infant's omnipotence and sensed as projections.[2] On the other hand they may get through this defence in spite of the ego-support which maternal care provides. Then the central core of the ego is affected, and this is the very

---

[1] In Chapter 2 I have tried to discuss another aspect of this developmental phase as we see it in adult health. Cf. Greenacre (1958).

[2] I am using the term 'projections' here in its descriptive and dynamic and not in its full metapsychological sense. The function of primitive psychic mechanisms, such as introjection, projection, and splitting, falls beyond the scope of this paper.

nature of psychotic anxiety. In health the individual soon becomes invulnerable in this respect, and if external factors impinge there is merely a new degree and quality in the hiding of the central self. In this respect the best defence is the organization of a false self. Instinctual satisfactions and object relationships themselves constitute a threat to the individual's personal going-on-being. *Example:* a baby is feeding at the breast and obtains satisfaction. This fact by itself does not indicate whether he is having an ego-syntonic id experience or, on the contrary, is suffering the trauma of a seduction, a threat to personal ego continuity, a threat by an id experience which is not ego-syntonic, and with which the ego is not equipped to deal.

In health object relationships can be developed on the basis of a compromise, one which involves the individual in what later would be called cheating and dishonesty, whereas a direct relationship is possible only on the basis of regression to a state of being merged with the mother.

Annihilation[1]

Anxiety in these early stages of the parent-infant relationship relates to the threat of annihilation, and it is necessary to explain what is meant by this term.

In this place which is characterized by the essential existence of a holding environment, the 'inherited potential' is becoming itself a 'continuity of being'. The alternative to being is reacting, and reacting interrupts being and annihilates. Being and annihilation are the two alternatives. The holding environment therefore has as its main function the reduction to a minimum of impingements to which the infant must react with resultant annihilation of personal being. Under favourable conditions the infant establishes a continuity of existence and then begins to develop the sophistications which make it possible for impingements to be gathered into the area of omnipotence. At this stage the word death has no possible application, and this makes the term death instinct unacceptable in describing the root of destructiveness. Death has no meaning until the arrival of hate and of the concept of the whole human person. When a whole human person can be hated, death has meaning, and close on this follows that which can be called maiming; the whole hated and loved person is kept alive by being castrated or otherwise maimed instead of killed. These ideas belong to a phase later than that characterized by dependence on the holding environment.

[1] I have described clinical varieties of this type of anxiety from a slightly different aspect in a previous paper (1949b).

Freud's Footnote Re-examined

At this point it is necessary to look again at Freud's statement quoted earlier. He writes: 'Probably it (the baby) hallucinates the fulfilment of its inner needs; it betrays its pain due to in-crease of stimulation and delay of satisfaction by the motor dis-charge of crying and struggling, and then experiences the hal-lucinated satisfaction.' The theory indicated in this part of the statement fails to cover the requirements of the earliest phase. Already by these words reference is being made to object rela-tionships, and the validity of this part of Freud's statement depends on his taking for granted the earlier aspects of maternal care, those which are here described as belonging to the holding phase. On the other hand, this sentence of Freud fits exactly the requirements in the *next* phase, that which is characterized by a relationship between infant and mother in which object rela-tionships and instinctual or erotogenic-zone satisfactions hold sway; that is, when development proceeds well.

B. THE ROLE OF THE MATERNAL CARE

I shall now attempt to describe some aspects of maternal care, and especially holding. In this paper the concept of holding is important, and a further development of the idea is necessary. The word is here used to introduce a full development of the theme contained in Freud's phrase '. . . when one considers that the infant—provided one includes with it the care it receives from its mother—does almost realize a psychical system of this kind'. I refer to the actual state of the infant-mother relationship at the beginning when the infant has not separated out a self from the maternal care on which there exists absolute dependence in a psychological sense.[1]

At this stage the infant needs and in fact usually gets an environmental provision which has certain characteristics:

It meets physiological needs. Here physiology and psychology have not yet become distinct, or are only in the process of doing so; and

It is reliable. But the environmental provision is not mechanic-ally reliable. It is reliable in a way that implies the mother's empathy.

[1] Reminder: to be sure of separating this off from object relationships and instinct-gratification I must *artificially* confine my attention to the body needs of a general kind. A patient said to me: 'A good analytic hour in which the right interpretation is given at the right time *is* a good feed.'

Holding:

Protects from physiological insult.

Takes account of the infant's skin sensitivity—touch, temperature, auditory sensitivity, visual sensitivity, sensitivity to falling (action of gravity) and of the infant's lack of knowledge of the existence of anything other than the self.

It includes the whole routine of care throughout the day and night, and it is not the same with any two infants because it is part of the infant, and no two infants are alike.

Also it follows the minute day-to-day changes belonging to the infant's growth and development, both physical and psychological.

It should be noted that mothers who have it in them to provide good-enough care can be enabled to do better by being cared for themselves in a way that acknowledges the essential nature of their task. Mothers who do not have it in them to provide good-enough care cannot be made good enough by mere instruction.

Holding includes especially the physical holding of the infant, which is a form of loving. It is perhaps the only way in which a mother can show the infant her love. There are those who can hold an infant and those who cannot; the latter quickly produce in the infant a sense of insecurity, and distressed crying.

All this leads right up to, includes, and co-exists with the establishment of the infant's first object relationships and his first experiences of instinctual gratification.[1]

It would be wrong to put the instinctual gratification (feeding. etc.) or object relationships (relation to the breast) before the matter of ego organization (i.e. infant ego reinforced by maternal ego). The basis for instinctual satisfaction and for object relationships is the handling and the general management and the care of the infant, which is only too easily taken for granted when all goes well.

The mental health of the individual, in the sense of freedom from psychosis or liability to psychosis (schizophrenia), is laid down by this maternal care, which when it goes well is scarcely noticed, and is a continuation of the physiological provision that characterizes the prenatal state. This environmental provision is also a continuation of the tissue aliveness and the functional health which (for the infant) provides silent but vitally important ego-support. In this way schizophrenia or infantile psychosis or a

[1] For further discussion of this aspect of the developmental processes see my paper, 'Transitional Objects and Transitional Phenomena' (1951).

liability to psychosis at a later date is related to a failure of environmental provision. This is not to say, however, that the ill-effects of such failure cannot be described in terms of ego distortion and of the defences against primitive anxieties, that is to say in terms of the individual. It will be seen, therefore, that the work of Klein on the splitting defence mechanisms and on projections and introjections and so on, is an attempt to state the effects of failure of environmental provision in terms of the individual. This work on primitive mechanisms gives the clue to only one part of the story, and a reconstruction of the environment and of its failures provides the other part. This other part cannot appear in the transference because of the patient's lack of knowledge of the maternal care, either in its good or in its failing aspects, as it existed in the original infantile setting.

Examination of One Detail of Maternal Care

I will give an example to illustrate subtlety in infant care. An infant is merged with the mother, and while this remains true the nearer the mother can come to an exact understanding of the infant's needs the better. A change, however, comes with the end of merging, and this end is not necessarily gradual. As soon as mother and infant are separate, from the infant's point of view, then it will be noted that the mother tends to change in her attitude. It is as if she now realizes that the infant no longer expects the condition in which there is an almost magical understanding of need. The mother seems to know that the infant has a new capacity, that of giving a signal so that she can be guided towards meeting the infant's needs. It could be said that if now she knows too well what the infant needs, this is magic and forms no basis for an object relationship. Here we get to Freud's words: 'It (the infant) probably hallucinates the fulfilment of its internal needs; it betrays its unpleasure, when there is an increase of stimulus and an absence of satisfaction, by the motor discharge of screaming and beating about with its arms and legs, and it then experiences the satisfaction it has hallucinated.' In other words, at the end of merging, when the child has become separate from the environment, an important feature is that the infant has to give a signal.[1] We find this subtlety appearing clearly in the transference in our analytic work. It is very important, except when the patient is regressed to earliest infancy and to a state of merging, that the analyst shall *not* know the answers except in so far as the patient gives the clues. The analyst gathers the clues and makes the interpretations, and it often happens that patients

[1] Freud's later (1926) theory of anxiety as a signal to the ego.

fail to give the clues, making certain thereby that the analyst can do nothing. This limitation of the analyst's power is important to the patient, just as the analyst's power is important, represented by the interpretation that is right and that is made at the right moment, and that is based on the clues and the unconscious co-operation of the patient who is supplying the material which builds up and justifies the interpretation. In this way the student analyst sometimes does better analysis than he will do in a few years' time when he knows more. When he has had several patients he begins to find it irksome to go as slowly as the patient is going, and he begins to make interpretations based not on material supplied on that particular day by the patient but on his own accumulated knowledge or his adherence for the time being to a particular group of ideas. This is of no use to the patient. The analyst may appear to be very clever, and the patient may express admiration, but in the end the correct interpretation is a trauma, which the patient has to reject, because it is not his. He complains that the analyst attempts to hypnotize him, that is to say, that the analyst is inviting a severe regression to dependence, pulling the patient back to a merging in with the analyst.

The same thing can be observed with the mothers of infants; mothers who have had several children begin to be so good at the technique of mothering that they do all the right things at the right moments, and then the infant who has begun to become separate from the mother has no means of gaining control of all the good things that are going on. The creative gesture, the cry, the protest, all the little signs that are supposed to produce what the mother does, all these things are missing, because the mother has already met the need just as if the infant were still merged with her and she with the infant. In this way the mother, by being a seemingly good mother, does something worse than castrate the infant. The latter is left with two alternatives: either being in a permanent state of regression and of being merged with the mother, or else staging a total rejection of the mother, even of the seemingly good mother.

We see therefore that in infancy and in the management of infants there is a very subtle distinction between the mother's understanding of her infant's need based on empathy, and her change over to an understanding based on something in the infant or small child that indicates need. This is particularly difficult for mothers because of the fact that children vacillate between one state and the other; one minute they are merged with their mothers and require empathy, while the next they are separate from her, and then if she knows their needs in advance she is dangerous, a witch. It is a very strange thing that mothers who are quite uninstructed adapt to these changes in their developing infants satisfactorily and without any knowledge of the theory. This detail is reproduced in psycho-analytic work with borderline cases, and in all cases at certain moments of great importance when dependence in transference is maximal.

Unawareness of Satisfactory Maternal Care

It is axiomatic in these matters of maternal care of the holding variety that when things go well the infant has no means of knowing what is being properly provided and what is being prevented. On the other hand it is when things do not go well that the infant becomes aware, not of the failure of maternal care, but of the results, whatever they may be, of that failure; that is to say, the infant becomes aware of reacting to some impingement. As a result of success in maternal care there is built up in the infant a continuity of being which is the basis of ego-strength; whereas the result of each failure in maternal care is that the continuity of being is interrupted by reactions to the consequences of that failure, with resultant ego-weakening.[1] Such interruptions constitute annihilation, and are evidently associated with pain of psychotic quality and intensity. In the extreme case the infant exists only on the basis of a continuity of reactions to impingement and of recoveries from such reactions. This is in great contrast to the continuity of being which is my conception of ego-strength.

C. THE CHANGES IN THE MOTHER

It is important in this context to examine the changes that occur in women who are about to have a baby or who have just had one. These changes are at first almost physiological, and they start with the physical holding of the baby in the womb. Something would be missing, however, if a phrase such as 'maternal instinct' were used in description. The fact is that in health women change in their orientation to themselves and to the world, but however deeply rooted in physiology such changes may be, they can be distorted by mental ill-health in the

[1] In character cases it is this ego-weakening and the individual's various attempts to deal with it that presents itself for immediate attention, and yet only a true view of the etiology can make possible a sorting out of the defence aspect of this presenting symptom from its origin in environmental failure. I have referred to one specific aspect of this in the diagnosis of the antisocial tendency as the basic problem behind the Delinquency Syndrome (19).

woman. It is necessary to think of these changes in psychological terms and this in spite of the fact that there may be endocrinological factors which can be affected by medication.

No doubt the physiological changes sensitize the woman to the more subtle psychological changes that follow.

Soon after conception, or when conception is known to be possible, the woman begins to alter in her orientation, and to be concerned with the changes that are taking place within her. In various ways she is encouraged by her own body to be interested in herself.[1] The mother shifts some of her sense of self on to the baby that is growing within her. The important thing is that there comes into existence a state of affairs that merits description and the theory of which needs to be worked out.

The analyst who is meeting the needs of a patient who is reliving these very early stages in the transference undergoes similar changes of orientation; and the analyst, unlike the mother, needs to be aware of the sensitivity which develops in him or her in response to the patient's immaturity and dependence. This could be thought of as an extension of Freud's description of the analyst as being in a voluntary state of attentiveness.

A detailed description of the changes in orientation in a woman who is becoming or who has just become a mother would be out of place here, and I have made an attempt elsewhere to describe these changes in popular or non-technical language (Winnicott, 1949a).

There is a psycho-pathology of these changes in orientation, and the extremes of abnormality are the concern of those who study the psychology of puerperal insanity. No doubt there are many variations in quality which do not constitute abnormality. It is the degree of distortion that constitutes abnormality.

By and large mothers do in one way or another identify themselves with the baby that is growing within them, and in this way they achieve a very powerful sense of what the baby needs. This is a projective identification. This identification with the baby lasts for a certain length of time after parturition, and then gradually loses significance.

In the ordinary case the mother's special orientation to the infant carries over beyond the birth process. The mother who is not distorted in these matters is ready to let go of her identification with the infant as the infant needs to become separate. It is possible to provide good initial care, but to fail to complete the process through an inability to let it come to an end, so that the

[1] For a more detailed statement on this point see 'Primary Maternal Preoccupation' (1956).

mother tends to remain merged with her infant and to delay the infant's separation from her. It is in any case a difficult thing for a mother to separate from her infant at the same speed at which the infant needs to become separate from her.[1]

The important thing, in my view, is that the mother through identification of herself with her infant knows what the infant feels like and so is able to provide almost exactly what the infant needs in the way of holding and in the provision of an environment generally. Without such an identification I consider that she is not able to provide what the infant needs at the beginning, which is *a live adaptation to the infant's needs*. The main thing is the physical holding, and this is the basis of all the more complex aspects of holding, and of environmental provision in general.

It is true that a mother may have a baby who is very different from herself so that she miscalculates. The baby may be quicker or slower than she is, and so on. In this way there may be times when what she feels the baby needs is not in fact correct. However, it seems to be usual that mothers who are not distorted by ill-health or by present-day environmental stress do tend on the whole to know accurately enough what their infants need, and further, they like to provide what is needed. This is the essence of maternal care.

With 'the care that it receives from its mother' each infant is able to have a personal existence, and so begins to build up what might be called *a continuity of being*. On the basis of this continuity of being the inherited potential gradually develops into an individual infant. If maternal care is not good enough then the infant does not really come into existence, since there is no continuity of being; instead the personality becomes built on the basis of reactions to environmental impingement.

All this has significance for the analyst. Indeed it is not from direct observation of infants so much as from the study of the transference in the analytic setting that it is possible to gain a clear view of what takes place in infancy itself. This work on infantile dependence derives from the study of the transference and counter-transference phenomena that belong to the psycho-analyst's involvement with the borderline case. In my opinion this involvement is a legitimate extension of psycho-analysis, the only real alteration being in the diagnosis of the illness of the patient, the etiology of whose illness goes back behind the Oedipus complex, and involves a distortion at the time of absolute dependence.

[1] Case-material to illustrate one type of problem that is met with clinically and relates to this group of ideas is presented in an earlier paper (1948).

Freud was able to discover infantile sexuality in a new way because he reconstructed it from his analytic work with psychoneurotic patients. In extending his work to cover the treatment of the borderline psychotic patient it is possible for us to reconstruct the dynamics of infancy and of infantile dependence, and the maternal care that meets this dependence.

Summary

(i) An examination is made of infancy; this is not the same as an examination of primitive mental mechanisms.

(ii) The main feature of infancy is dependence; this is discussed in terms of the holding environment.

(iii) Any study of infancy must be divided into two parts:

(a) Infant development facilitated by good-enough maternal care;

(b) Infant development distorted by maternal care that is not good enough.

(iv) The infant ego can be said to be weak, but in fact it is strong because of the ego support of maternal care. Where maternal care fails the weakness of the infant ego becomes apparent.

(v) Processes in the mother (and in the father) bring about, in health, a special state in which the parent is orientated to the infant, and is thus in a position to meet the infant's dependence. There is a pathology of these processes.

(vi) Attention is drawn to the various ways in which these conditions inherent in what is here termed the holding[1] environment can or cannot appear in the transference if at a later date the infant should come into analysis.

---

[1] Concept of 'holding' in case work: Cf. Winnicott, Clare [1954].

4

EGO INTEGRATION IN CHILD
DEVELOPMENT
(1962)

The term ego can be used to describe that part of the growing human personality that tends, under suitable conditions, to become integrated into a unit.

In the body of an anencephalic infant functional events, including instinctual localizations, may be taking place, events that would be called experiences of id-function if there were a brain. It could be said that if there had been a normal brain there would have been an organization of these functions, and to this organization could have been given the label ego. But with no electronic apparatus there can be no experience, and therefore no ego.

But id-functioning is normally not lost; it is collected together in all its aspects and becomes ego-experience. There is thus no sense in making use of the word 'id' for phenomena that are not covered and catalogued and experienced and eventually interpreted by ego-functioning.

In the very early stages of the development of a human child, therefore, ego-functioning needs to be taken as a concept that is inseparable from that of the existence of the infant as a person. What instinctual life there may be apart from ego-functioning can be ignored, because the infant is not yet an entity having experiences. There is no id before ego. Only from this premise can a study of the ego be justified.

It will be seen that the ego offers itself for study long before the word self has relevance. The word self arrives after the child has begun to use the intellect to look at what others see or feel or hear and what they conceive of when they meet this infant body. (The concept of the self will not be studied in this chapter.)

The first question that is asked about that which is labelled ego is this: is there an ego from the start? The answer is that the start is when the ego starts.[1]

Then *the second question* arises: is the ego strong or weak? The answer to this second question depends on the actual mother and

[1] It is well to remember that the beginning is a summation of beginnings.

56

her ability to meet the absolute dependence of the actual infant at the beginning, at the stage before the infant has separated out the mother from the self.

In my terminology the good-enough mother is able to meet the needs of her infant at the beginning, and to meet these needs so well that the infant, as emergence from the matrix of the infant-mother relationship takes place, is able to have a brief *experience of omnipotence*. (This has to be distinguished from *omnipotence*, which is the name given to a quality of feeling.)

The mother can do this because of her having temporarily given herself over to the one task, that of the care of this one infant. Her task is made possible by the fact that the baby has a capacity, when this matter of the mother's supportive ego-function is operative, to relate to *subjective objects*. In this respect the baby can meet the reality principle here and there, now and then, but not everywhere all at once; that is, the baby retains areas of subjective objects along with other areas in which there is some relating to objectively perceived objects, or 'not-me' ('non-I') objects.

So much difference exists between the beginning of a baby whose mother can perform this function well enough and that of a baby whose mother cannot do this well enough that there is no value whatever in describing babies in the earliest stages except in relation to the mother's functioning. When there is not-good-enough mothering the infant is not able to get started with ego-maturation, or else ego-development is necessarily distorted in certain vitally important respects.

It must be understood that when reference is made to the mother's adaptive capacity this has only a little to do with her ability to satisfy the infant's oral drives, as by giving a satisfactory feed. What is being discussed here runs parallel with such a consideration as this. It is indeed possible to gratify an oral drive and by so doing to *violate* the infant's ego-function, or that which will later on be jealously guarded as the self, the core of the personality. A feeding satisfaction can be a seduction and can be traumatic if it comes to a baby without coverage by ego-functioning.

At the stage which is being discussed it is necessary not to think of the baby as a person who gets hungry, and whose instinctual drives may be met or frustrated, but to think of the baby as an immature being who is all the time *on the brink of unthinkable anxiety*. Unthinkable anxiety is kept away by this vitally important function of the mother at this stage, her capacity to put herself in the baby's place and to know what the baby needs in the general management of the body, and therefore of the person. Love, at this stage, can only be shown in terms of body-care, as in the last stage before full-term birth.

Unthinkable anxiety has only a few varieties, each being the clue to one aspect of normal growth.

(1) Going to pieces.
(2) Falling for ever.
(3) Having no relationship to the body.
(4) Having no orientation.

It will be recognized that these are specifically the stuff of the psychotic anxieties, and these belong, clinically, to schizophrenia, or to the emergence of a schizoid element hidden in an otherwise non-psychotic personality.

From here it is necessary to interrupt the sequence of ideas in order to examine the fate of the baby who misses good-enough care in the early stage before the baby has separated off the 'not-me' from the 'me'. This is a complex subject because of all the degrees and varieties of maternal failure. It is profitable, first, to refer to:

(1) distortions of the ego-organization that lay down the basis for schizoid characteristics, and

(2) the specific defence of self-holding, or the development of a caretaker self and the organization of an aspect of the personality that is false (false in that what is showing is a derivative not of the individual but of the mothering aspect of the infant-mother coupling). This is a defence whose success may provide a new threat to the core of the self though it is designed to hide and protect this core of the self.

The consequences of defective ego support by the mother can be very severely crippling, and include the following:

A. *Infantile Schizophrenia or Autism*

This well-known clinical grouping contains disorder secondary to physical brain lesions or deficiency, and also includes some degree of every kind of failure of the earliest maturational details. In a proportion of cases there is no evidence of neurological defect or disease.

It is a common experience in child psychiatry for the clinician to be unable to decide between a diagnosis of primary defect, mild Little's disease, pure psychological failure of early maturation in a child with brain intact, or a mixture of two or all of these. In some cases there is good evidence of a reaction to failure of ego-support of the kind I am describing in this chapter.

B. *Latent Schizophrenia*

There are many clinical varieties of latent schizophrenia in children who pass for normal, or who may even show special brilliance of intellect or precocious performance. The illness shows in the brittleness of the 'success'. Strain and stress at later stages of development may trigger off an illness.

C. *False Self-defence*

The use of defences, especially that of a successful false self, enables many children to seem to give good promise, but eventually a breakdown reveals the fact of the true self's absence from the scene.

D. *Schizoid Personality*

Commonly there develops personality disorder which depends on the fact that a schizoid element is hidden in a personality that is otherwise sane. Serious schizoid elements become socialized in so far as they can hide in a pattern of schizoid disorder that is accepted in a person's local culture.

These degrees and kinds of personality defects can be related, in investigations of individual cases, to various kinds and degrees of failure of holding, handling and object-presenting at the earliest stage. This is not to deny the existence of hereditary factors, but rather to supplement them in important respects.

Ego development is characterized by various trends:
(1) The main trend in the maturational process can be gathered into the various meanings of the word *integration*. Integration in time becomes added to (what might be called) integration in space.
(2) The ego is based on a body ego, but it is only when all goes well that the person of the baby starts to be linked with the body and the body-functions, with the skin as the limiting membrane. I have used the term *personalization* to describe this process, because the term depersonalization seems at basis to mean a loss of firm union between ego and body, including id-drives and id-satisfactions. (The term depersonalization has gathered to itself a more sophisticated meaning in psychiatric writings.)
(3) The ego *initiates object-relating*. With good-enough mothering at the beginning the baby is not subjected to instinctual gratifications except in so far as there is ego-participation. In this respect it is not so much a question of giving the baby satisfaction

as of letting the baby find and come to terms with the object (breast, bottle, milk, etc.).

When we attempt to assess what Sechehaye (1951) did when she gave her patient an apple at the right moment (symbolic realization) it is of but little moment whether the patient ate the apple, or just looked at it, or took it and kept it. The important thing was that the patient was able to create an object, and Sechehaye did no more than enable the object to take apple-shape, so that the girl had created a part of the actual world, an apple.

It would seem to be possible to match these three phenomena of ego-growth with three aspects of infant and child-care:

Integration matches with holding.
Personalization matches with handling.
Object-relating matches with object-presenting.

This leads to a consideration of two problems associated with the idea of integration:

(1) *Integration from what?*

It is useful to think of the material out of which integration emerges in terms of motor and sensory elements, the stuff of primary narcissism. This would acquire a tendency towards a sense of existing. Other language can be used to describe this obscure part of the maturational process, but the rudiments of an imaginative elaboration of pure body-functioning must be postulated if it is to be claimed that this new human being has started to be, and has started to gather experience that can be called personal.

(2) *Integration with what?*

All this tends towards the establishment of a unit self, but it cannot be over-emphasized that what happens at this very early stage depends on the ego-coverage given by the mother of the infant-mother coupling.

It can be said that good-enough ego-coverage by the mother (in respect of the unthinkable anxieties) enables the new human person to build up a personality on the pattern of a continuity of going-on-being. All failures (that could produce unthinkable anxiety) bring about a reaction of the infant, and this reaction cuts across the going-on-being. If reacting that is disruptive of going-on-being recurs persistently it sets going a pattern of fragmentation of being. The infant whose pattern is one of fragmentation of the line of continuity of being has a developmental task that is, almost from the beginning, loaded in the direction of psychopathology. Thus there may be a very early factor (dating from the first days or hours of life) in the aetiology of restlessness, hyperkinesis, and inattentiveness (later called inability to concentrate).

It is pertinent here to state that, whatever the external factors, it is the individual's view (fantasy) of the external factor that counts. Alongside this it is necessary to remember, however, that there is a stage before the individual has repudiated the not-me. So that there is, at this very early stage, no external factor; the mother is part of the child. At this stage the infant's pattern includes the infant's experience of the mother, as she is in her personal actuality.

The opposite of integration would seem to be disintegration. This is only partly true. The opposite, initially, requires a word like unintegration. Relaxation for an infant means not feeling a need to integrate, the mother's ego-supportive function being taken for granted. The understanding of unexcited states requires further consideration in terms of this theory.

The term disintegration is used to describe a sophisticated *defence*, a defence that is an active production of chaos in defence against unintegration in the absence of maternal ego-support, that is, against the unthinkable or archaic anxiety that results from failure of holding in the stage of absolute dependence. The chaos of disintegration may be as 'bad' as the unreliability of the environment, but it has the advantage of being produced by the baby and therefore of being non-environmental. It is within the area of the baby's omnipotence. In terms of psycho-analysis, it is analysable, whereas the unthinkable anxieties are not.

Integration is closely linked with the environmental function of holding. The achievement of integration is the unit. First comes 'I' which includes 'everything else is not me'. Then comes 'I am, I exist, I gather experiences and enrich myself and have an introjective and projective interaction with the NOT-ME, the actual world of shared reality'. Add to this: 'I am seen or understood to exist by someone'; and, further, add to this: 'I get back (as a face seen in a mirror) the evidence I need that I have been recognized as a being.'

In favourable circumstances the skin becomes the boundary between the me and the not-me. In other words, the psyche has come to live in the soma and an individual psycho-somatic life has been initiated.

The establishment of a state of I AM, along with the achievement of psycho-somatic indwelling or cohesion, constitutes a state of affairs which is accompanied by a specific anxiety affect that has an expectation of persecution. This persecutory reaction is inherent in the idea of the repudiation of the 'not-me', which goes with the limitation of the unit self in the body, with the skin as the limiting membrane.

In psycho-somatic illness of one kind there is in the symptomatology an insistence on the interaction of psyche and soma, this being maintained as a *defence* against threat of a loss of psycho-somatic union, or against a form of depersonalization.

Handling describes the environmental provision that corresponds loosely with the establishment of a psycho-somatic partnership. Without good-enough active and adaptive handling the task from within may well prove heavy, indeed it may actually prove impossible for this development of a psycho-somatic inter-relationship to become properly established.

The initiation of object-relating is complex. It cannot take place except by the environmental provision of object-presenting, done in such a way that the baby creates the object. The pattern is thus: the baby develops a vague expectation that has origin in an unformulated need. The adaptive mother presents an object or a manipulation that meets the baby's needs, and so the baby begins to need just that which the mother presents. In this way the baby comes to feel confident in being able to create objects and to create the actual world. The mother gives the baby a brief period in which omnipotence is a matter of experience. It must be emphasized that in referring to the initiating of object-relating I am not referring to id-satisfactions and id-frustrations. I am referring to the preconditions, internal to the child as well as external, conditions which make an ego-experience out of a satisfactory breast feed (or a reaction to frustration).

Summary

My object is to make a bare-bone statement of my conception of the beginnings of the ego. I use the concept of ego-integration and the place of ego-integration in the initiation of emotional development in the human child, in the child who is all the time moving from absolute dependence to relative dependence, and towards independence. I also trace the beginnings of object-relating within the framework of a baby's experience and growth.

Further, I attempt to assess the importance of the actual environment at the earliest stage, that is, before the baby has separated out the not-me from the me. I contrast the ego-strength of the baby who gets ego-support from the mother's actual adaptive behaviour, or love, with the ego-weakness of the baby for whom environmental provision is defective at this very early stage.

5

PROVIDING FOR THE CHILD IN HEALTH AND IN CRISIS[1]

(1962)

The subject is a wide one. I propose therefore to select certain features that can be stated easily and that can be put forward as significant, noting in particular those aspects of this general question that belong to the present age.

1. When we think of providing for health we nowadays think in terms of mental health. It is the emotional development of the child that concerns us, and the laying down of the foundations of a lifetime of mental health. The reason for this is that in paediatrics the developments on the physical side have been so great that we know where we are. There is bodily development that takes place, given good heredity, as a result of good food and good physical conditions. We understand the meaning of the words 'good food', and deficiency diseases are now rare. Also, when starvation or poor housing conditions are a feature, we have a social conscience, and we know what to do. In Great Britain this has crystallized out into the welfare state, which with all its drawbacks and the new problems it creates makes us rather pleased as well as annoyed when we pay heavy taxes.

In considering this subject, then, let us take it for granted either that the children we refer to are as healthy physically as modern physical prophylaxis and therapy can ensure; or else that any physical disease that is present is under paediatric control, and that our aim is to study the mental health of the child with that illness. For simplicity's sake we start with the mental health of the physically healthy child.

Of course, if a child suffers from anorexia nervosa the starvation that results is not to be attributed to physical neglect. If there is a so-called 'problem family', then it is not the local authority that can be wholly blamed for the slum conditions in which a child is being brought up. Physical care is affected by the child's or the parents' ability to receive care, and we see that all around the edge of the area that we call physical care there is

[1] Presented in a Panel Discussion organized by the Extension Division Workshop of the San Francisco Psychoanalytic Institute, October 1962.

the complex territory of emotional disorder in the individual, or in groups of individuals, or in society.

2. Providing for the child is therefore a matter of providing the environment that facilitates individual mental health and emotional development. We really do know today a great deal about the way adults grow out of children and children out of infants, and a first principle is that health is maturity, maturity at age.

Emotional development takes place in the individual child if good-enough conditions are provided, and the drive to development comes from within the child. The forces towards living, towards integration of the personality, towards independence, are immensely strong, and with good-enough conditions the child makes progress; when conditions are not good enough these forces are contained within the child, and in one way or another tend to destroy the child.

We have a dynamic view of childhood development, and we see this becoming converted (in healthy conditions) into the family and social drives.

3. If health is maturity, then immaturity of any kind is mental ill health, and is a threat to the individual and a drain on society. For whereas society can use individual aggressive tendencies it cannot use individual immaturities. If we consider what we must provide here we see that we must add:

(i)   toleration of individual immaturity and mental ill-health;
(ii) therapy;
(iii) prophylaxis.

4. Immediately I want to put in a word to counteract any impression I may have given that health is enough. We are not only concerned with individual maturity and with the freedom of individuals from mental disorder or from psycho-neurosis; we are concerned with the richness of individuals in terms not of money but of inner psychic reality. Indeed, we often forgive a man or woman for mental ill-health or for some kind of immaturity because that person has so rich a personality that society may gain much through the exceptional contribution he or she can make. May I say that Shakespeare's contribution was such that we would not mind much if we found that he was immature, or homosexual, or antisocial in some localized sense. This principle can be applied in a broad way and I need not labour the point. A research project, for instance, might show by significant statistics that infants who are bottle-fed are physically healthier

and even, perhaps, less liable to mental disorder than those who are not. But we are concerned also with the richness of the breast-feeding experience in comparison with its alternative, if this affects the richness of the personality potential of the infant now grown to childhood and to adult life.

It is enough if I have made it clear that we aim at providing more than healthy conditions to produce health. Richness of quality rather than health is at the top of the ladder of human progress.

5. We discuss providing for the child—and for the child in the adult. The mature adult is in fact taking part in the providing. In other words, childhood is a progression from dependence to independence. We need to examine the changing needs of the child as dependence changes over into independence. This leads us to a study of the very early needs of small children and of infants, and to the extremes of dependence. We can think of the degrees of dependence as a series:

(a) *Extreme dependence.* Here conditions must be good enough, otherwise the infant cannot start the development that is born with him.
    Environmental failure: Mental defect non-organic; childhood schizophrenia; liability to mental-hospital disorder at a later date.

(b) *Dependence.* Here conditions that fail do in fact traumatize, but there is already a person there to be traumatized.
    Environmental failure: Liability to affective disorders; antisocial tendency.

(c) *Dependence-independence mixtures.* Here the child is making experiments in independence, but needs to be able to re-experience dependence.
    Environmental failure: Pathological dependence.

(d) *Independence-dependence.* This is the same, but with the accent on independence.
    Environmental failure: Defiance; outbreaks of violence.

(e) *Independence.* Implying an internalized environment: an ability on the part of the child to look after himself or herself.
    Environmental failure: Not necessarily harmful.

(f) *Social sense.* Here it is implied that the individual can identify with adults and with a social group, or with society, without too great a loss of personal impulse and originality, and without too much loss of the destructive and aggressive impulses that have, presumably, found satisfactory expression in displaced forms.

Environmental failure: Partly the responsibility of the individual, himself or herself a parent, or a parent-figure in society.

6. It is of course a gross over-simplification to say that health is maturity (at age). The story of the emotional development of a child is tremendously complicated, and it is more complex even than we know. We cannot put what we know into a few words, and we cannot agree exactly in regard to details. But that does not matter. Infants and children have been growing and developing satisfactorily for centuries, that is, apart from progress in our intellectual understanding of childhood. But we do need to try to get at a theory of normal growth so as to be able to understand illness and the various immaturities, since we are now no longer contented unless we can cure and prevent. We do not accept childhood schizophrenia any more than we accept poliomyelitis or the condition of the spastic child. We try to prevent, and we hope to be able to lead the way to cure wherever there is abnormality, which means suffering for someone.

It is necessary to say, however, that if one first accepts heredity, then:

(a) Good-enough environmental provision really does tend to prevent psychotic or schizophrenic disorder; but

(b) with all the good care in the world the individual child is liable to the disturbances associated with conflict arising out of the instinctual life.

In regard to (b): the child who is healthy enough to reach the triangular situations as between whole people at the toddler age, when (as later at adolescence) the instinctual life is at its nodal point of intense expression, such a child is subject to conflicts, and to some extent these show clinically as anxiety and in the form of defences organized against anxiety. These defences occur in health, but when rigid they constitute the symptom-formations of psycho-neurotic (not psychotic) illness.

So in health personal difficulties have to be resolved within the child, and cannot be prevented by good management. Earlier distortions, on the other hand, can be prevented.

It is difficult to state this without being misunderstood. Whatever stage of development one is considering it is always the individual baby's or child's personal conflicts that are the central theme. It is the innate tendencies towards integration and growth that produce the health, not the environmental provision. Yet good-enough provision is necessary, absolutely at the beginning, and relatively at later stages, at the stage of the Oedipus complex, in the latency period, and also at adolescence. I have tried to find words that indicate a lessening degree of dependence on environmental provision.

7. In order to avoid overloading this section with a statement of the theory of emotional development, it is convenient to refer to the essential stages in the following way:

(i) Development in terms of the instinctual life (*id*), i.e. in terms of object relationships.

(ii) Development in terms of personality structure (*ego*), i.e. in terms of what exists for experiencing instinctual drives and the object relationships that have the instinctual drives as a basis.

(i) In the theory by which we work there is a now well-known progression from an alimentary instinctual life to a genital instinctual life. The latency period marks the end of a growth period which will be resumed at puberty. In health the four-year-old child has it in him or her to experience an identification with both parents in their instinctual relationships, but this experience is complete only in play and in dreams, and through the use of symbolism. At puberty the child's growth adds to all this the physical capacity for genital experience and also for actual killing. This is the central theme of personal childhood development.

(ii) Certain tendencies in personality growth are characterized by the fact that they can be discerned from the very beginning, and they never reach completion. I refer to such things as:

(*a*) Integration, including time-integration.

(*b*) What might be called 'in-dwelling': the achievement of a close and easy relationship between the psyche and the body, and body functioning.

(*c*) The development of a capacity to make relationships with objects in spite of the fact that in one sense, and an important sense, the individual is an isolated phenomenon and defends this isolation at all costs.

(*d*) Tendencies that gradually reveal themselves in health, such as the tendency towards independence (to which I have already referred); the capacity for a sense of concern and guilt; the capacity to love and to like the same persons; and the capacity for happiness at appropriate times.

In discussing provision for mental health it is more profitable to give consideration to (ii) than to (i). The vitally important details of (i) can be left to take care of themselves, and if they go awry then the child needs a psychotherapist. In regard to the processes grouped together in (ii), however, what we provide goes on being important as the child grows, and indeed never ceases, and joins up with the provisions that concern those who care for the aged. In other words, it will profit us to look at the needs of infants, and then to translate these needs into language that is appropriate at all ages.

To make my meaning clear, when we provide a swimming pool and all that goes with it, this provision links with the care with which a mother baths her infant, and with which she generally caters for the infant's need for bodily movement and expression, and for muscle and skin experiences that give satisfactions. It also links with the provision that is appropriate in the therapeutics of certain illnesses. On the one hand it links with the occupational therapy that has great value at certain stages in the treatment of the mentally ill; and, on the other, it links with the physiotherapy that is appropriate, for instance, in the care of spastic children.

In all these cases—the normal child, the infant, the mentally ill person, and the spastic or handicapped—the provision is facilitating the child's innate tendency to inhabit the body and to enjoy the body's functions, and to accept the limitation that the skin provides, a limiting membrane, separating me from not-me.

8. While we try to understand all this we also want to try to understand why a mother (I include father) does not have to have an intellectual understanding of the infant's needs. An intellectual understanding of such needs is of no use to her, and throughout the ages mothers have met their infants' needs adequately, by and large.

In my writings I have made a special feature of this. I think we must allow for a feature of motherhood which finds a reflection in our own need to become preoccupied with any task if we are to do it well. In concentrating or in becoming preoccupied, we can be said to become withdrawn, moody, anti-social, or just irritable, according to our pattern. I think that this is a pale reflection of the thing that happens to mothers, if they are well enough (as most are) to surrender to motherhood. They become more and more closely identified with the baby, and this they retain when the baby is born, but they gradually lose it in the few months following the baby's birth. Because of this identification with the baby they more or less know what the baby needs. I refer to vital things like being held, being turned over, being put down and taken up, being handled, and of course being fed in a sensitive way which involves more than the satisfaction of an instinct. All these things facilitate the early stages of the infant's integrative tendencies and the beginning of ego structuring. One might say that the mother makes the baby's weak ego into a strong one, because she is there, reinforcing everything, like power-assisted steering on a motor-bus.

I have spent some time on this because I think that any mother, if she knew it (and I do not much want her to), has something to teach us in our efforts to go on providing for the needs of individuals, so that their natural processes can develop momentum. The pattern is that by some degree of capacity to identify with the individual we can provide what an individual needs at any one moment. It is only we who know that there exists something that can meet this need.

I remember when I was four years old I woke up on Christmas morning and found I possessed a blue cart made in Switzerland, like those that the people there use for bringing home wood. How did my parents know that this was exactly what I wanted? Certainly I did not know that such heavenly carts existed. Of course, they knew because of their capacity to feel my feelings, and they knew about the carts because they had been to Switzerland. This leads on to Sechehaye's 'symbolic realization', the central feature in the treatment of schizophrenia of the kind in which inability to make object relationships is a main feature.[1] Sechehaye knew about the patient's need and she also knew where to find a ripe apple. It is the same as the mother's presenting a breast to the infant and, later on, introducing hard objects to the infant, and the fruits of the earth, and father, not creating the infant's needs, but meeting these needs at the right moment.

We, like the mother, must know the importance of:

continuity of the human environment, and likewise of the non-human environment, which helps with the integration of the individual personality;
reliability, which makes mother's behaviour predictable;

[1] Sechehaye, M. A. (1951), *Symbolic Realization*. New York: International Universities Press.

graduated adaptation to the changing and expanding needs of the child, whose growth processes impel him or her towards independence and adventure;
provision for realizing the child's creative impulse.

Further, the mother knows she must keep alive and allow the baby to feel and hear her aliveness. She knows she must postpone her own impulses until the time when the child is able to use her separate existence in a positive way. She knows she must not leave her child for more minutes, hours, days than the child is able to keep the idea of her alive and friendly. If she must be away too long she knows that for some time she will have to change from a mother into a therapist, that is to say, she will have to 'spoil' her child in order to turn the child back (if it is not too late) to a state in which he or she takes the mother for granted again. This links with the provision that we make in meeting crisis—that is apart from supplying psycho-analysis, which is quite another subject.

In this context I go back to 5(*b*) above, which covers the point that separation of a one- or two-year-old child from the mother, beyond the capacity of the child to keep alive the idea of her, produces a state that may later appear as an antisocial tendency. The inner working of this is complex, but the continuity of the child's object relationships has been broken, and development is held up. When the child tries to reach back over the gap this is called stealing.

To do her job well the mother needs outside support; usually the husband shields her from external reality and so enables her to protect her child from unpredictable external phenomena to which the child must react; and it must be remembered that each reaction to an impingement breaks the continuity of the child's personal existing, and goes against the process of integration.

But, broadly speaking, to study what we provide in health and in crisis we can best study the mother (always, I include the father), and what comes naturally to her to provide for her infant. We find that the main feature is that she knows about the infant's needs *through her identification with the infant.* In other words, we find that she does not have to make a sort of shopping list of things she must do tomorrow; she feels what is needed at the moment.

In the same way we do not have to plan the details of what we must provide for children in our care. *We do have to organize ourselves so that in every case there is someone who has time and inclination to know what the child needs.* This can be known on the basis of someone knowing the child. The identification with the child does not have to be as deep as that of the mother with the new-born baby, except of course when the child under consideration is ill—emotionally immature or distorted, or under handicap because of a physical disorder. When the child is ill, then there is a crisis, and the therapy that is needed involves the therapist personally, and the work cannot be done on any other basis.

Summary

I have attempted to relate the needs of children to those of babies, and to relate the needs of children in crisis to those of babies, and to relate what we provide in child care to that which is provided naturally by parents (that is, unless they are too ill to respond to the call of parenthood). We need not think then of being clever, or even of knowing all the complex theory of the emotional development of the individual. Rather, we need to give opportunity for the right kind of people to get to know the children themselves and so to feel their needs. One could use the word 'love' here, at risk of sounding sentimental.

And this leads on to a final observation: often, without leaving the area covered by the word love, we shall find that a child needs firm management, needs to be treated as the child he or she is, and not as an adult.

6

THE DEVELOPMENT OF THE CAPACITY
FOR CONCERN[1]
(1963)

The origin of the capacity to be concerned presents a complex problem. Concern is an important feature in social life. Psycho-analysts usually seek origins in the emotional development of the individual. We want to know the aetiology of concern, and the place where concern appears in the child's development. We also are interested in the failure of the establishment of an individual's capacity for concern, and in the loss of concern that has to some extent been established.

The word 'concern' is used to cover in a positive way a phenomenon that is covered in a negative way by the word 'guilt'. A sense of guilt is anxiety linked with the concept of ambivalence, and implies a degree of integration in the individual ego that allows for the retention of good object-imago along with the idea of a destruction of it. Concern implies further integration, and further growth, and relates in a positive way to the individual's sense of responsibility, especially in respect of relationships into which the instinctual drives have entered.

Concern refers to the fact that the individual *cares*, or *minds*, and both feels and accepts responsibility. At the genital level in the statement of the theory of development, concern could be said to be the basis of the family, where both partners in inter-course—beyond their pleasure—take responsibility for the result. But in the total imaginative life of the individual, the subject of concern raises even wider issues, and a capacity for concern is at the back of all constructive play and work. It belongs to normal, healthy living, and deserves the attention of the psycho-analyst.

There is much reason to believe that concern—with its positive sense—emerges in the earlier emotional development of the child at a period before the period of the classical Oedipus complex, which involves a relationship between three persons, each felt to be a whole person by the child. But there is no need to be precise about timing, and indeed most of the processes that start

[1] Presented to The Topeka Psychoanalytic Society, 12 October 1962, and first published in the *Bulletin of the Menninger Clinic*, **27**, pp. 167–76.

up in early infancy are never fully established, and continue to be strengthened by the growth that continues in later childhood, and indeed in adult life, even in old age.

It is usual to describe the origin of the capacity for concern in terms of the infant-mother relationship, when already the infant is an established unit, and when the infant feels the mother, or mother-figure, to be a whole person. It is a development belonging essentially to the period of a two-body relationship.

In any statement of child-development, certain principles are taken for granted. Here I wish to say that the maturation processes form the basis of infant- and child-development, in psychology as in anatomy and physiology. Nevertheless, in emotional development it is clear that certain external conditions are necessary if maturation potentials are to become actual. That is, development depends on a good-enough environment, and the earlier we go back in our study of the baby, the more true it is that without good-enough mothering the early stages of development cannot take place.

A great deal has happened in the development of the baby before we begin to be able to refer to concern. The capacity to be concerned is a matter of health, a capacity which, once established, presupposes a complex ego-organization which cannot be thought of in any way but as an achievement, both an achievement of infant- and child-care and an achievement in terms of the internal growth-processes in the baby and child. I shall take for granted a good-enough environment in the early stages, in order to simplify the matter that I wish to examine. What I have to say, then, follows on complex maturational processes dependent for their becoming realized on good-enough infant- and child-care.

Of the many stages that have been described by Freud and the psycho-analysts who have followed him, I must single out one stage which has to involve the use of the word 'fusion'. This is the achievement of emotional development in which the baby experiences erotic and aggressive drives toward the same object at the same time. On the erotic side there is both satisfaction-seeking and object-seeking, and on the aggressive side, there is a complex of anger employing muscle erotism, and of hate, which involves the retention of a good object-imago for comparison. Also in the whole aggressive-destructive impulse is contained a primitive type of object relationship in which love involves destruction. Some of this is necessarily obscure, and I do not need to know all about the origin of aggression in order to follow my argument, because I am taking it for granted that the baby has become able to combine erotic and aggressive experience, and in relation to one object. Ambivalence has been reached.

By the time that this becomes a fact in the development of a child, the infant has become able to experience ambivalence in fantasy, as well as in body-function of which the fantasy is originally an elaboration. Also, the infant is beginning to relate himself to objects that are less and less subjective phenomena, and more and more objectively perceived 'not-me' elements. He has begun to establish a self, a unit that is both physically contained in the body's skin and that is psychologically integrated. The mother has now become—in the child's mind—a coherent image, and the term 'whole object' now becomes applicable. This state of affairs, precarious at first, could be nicknamed the 'humpty-dumpty stage', the wall on which Humpty Dumpty is precariously perched being the mother who has ceased to offer her lap.

This development implies an ego that begins to be independent of the mother's auxiliary ego, and there can now be said to be an inside to the baby, and therefore an outside. The body-scheme has come into being and quickly develops complexity. From now on, the infant lives a psychosomatic life. The inner psychic reality which Freud taught us to respect now becomes a real thing to the infant, who now feels that personal richness resides within the self. This personal richness develops out of the simultaneous love-hate experience which implies the achievement of ambivalence, the enrichment and refinement of which leads to the emergence of concern.

It is helpful to postulate the existence for the immature child of two mothers—shall I call them the object-mother and the environment-mother? I have no wish to invent names that become stuck and eventually develop a rigidity and an obstructive quality, but it seems possible to use these words 'object-mother' and 'environment-mother' in this context to describe the vast difference that there is for the infant between two aspects of infant-care, the mother as object, or owner of the part-object that may satisfy the infant's urgent needs, and the mother as the person who wards off the unpredictable and who actively provides care in handling and in general management. What the infant does at the height of id-tension and the use thus made of the object seems to me very different from the use the infant makes of the mother as part of the total environment.[1]

In this language it is the environment-mother who receives all

[1] This is a theme that has recently been developed in a book by Harold Searles (1960).

that can be called affection and sensuous co-existence; it is the object-mother who becomes the target for excited experience backed by crude instinct-tension. It is my thesis that concern turns up in the baby's life as a highly sophisticated experience in the coming-together in the infant's mind of the object-mother and the environment-mother. The environmental provision continues to be vitally important here, though the infant is beginning to be able to have that inner stability that belongs to the development of independence.

In favourable circumstances, when the baby has reached the necessary stage in personal development, there comes about a new fusion. For one thing, there is the full experience of, and fantasy of, object-relating based on instinct, the object being used without regard for consequences, used ruthlessly (if we use the term as a description of our view of what is going on). And alongside this is the more quiet relationship of the baby to the environment-mother. These two things come together. The result is complex, and it is this that I especially wish to describe.

The favourable circumstances necessary at this stage are these: that the mother should continue to be alive and available, available physically and available in the sense of not being preoccupied with something else. The object-mother has to be found to survive the instinct-driven episodes, which have now acquired the full force of fantasies of oral sadism and other results of fusion. Also, the environment-mother has a special function, which is to continue to be herself, to be empathic towards her infant, to be there to receive the spontaneous gesture, and to be pleased.

The fantasy that goes with full-blooded id-drives contains attack and destruction. It is not only that the baby imagines that he eats the object, but also that the baby wants to take possession of the contents of the object. If the object is not destroyed, it is because of its own survival capacity, not because of the baby's protection of the object. This is one side of the picture.

The other side of the picture has to do with the baby's relation to the environment-mother, and from this angle there may come so great a protection of the mother that the child becomes inhibited or turns away. Here is a positive element in the infant's experience of weaning and one reason why some infants wean themselves.

In favourable circumstances there builds up a technique for the solution of this complex form of ambivalence. The infant experiences anxiety, because if he consumes the mother he will lose her, but this anxiety becomes modified by the fact that the baby has a contribution to make to the environment-mother. There is a growing confidence that there will be opportunity for contributing-in, for giving to the environment-mother, a confidence which makes the infant able to hold the anxiety. The anxiety held in this way becomes altered in quality and becomes a sense of guilt.

Instinct-drives lead to ruthless usage of objects, and then to a guilt-sense which is held, and is allayed by the contribution to the environment-mother that the infant can make in the course of a few hours. Also, the opportunity for giving and for making reparation that the environment-mother offers by her reliable presence, enables the baby to become more and more bold in the experiencing of id-drives; in other words, frees the baby's instinctual life. In this way, the guilt is not felt, but it lies dormant, or potential, and appears (as sadness or a depressed mood) only if opportunity for reparation fails to turn up.

When confidence in this benign cycle and in the expectation of opportunity is established, the sense of guilt in relation to the id-drives becomes further modified, and we then need a more positive term, such as 'concern'. The infant is now becoming able to be concerned, to take responsibility for his own instinctual impulses and the functions that belong to them. This provides one of the fundamental constructive elements of play and work. But in the developmental process, it was the opportunity to contribute that enabled concern to be within the child's capacity.

A feature that may be noted, especially in respect of the concept of anxiety that is 'held', is that integration *in time* has become added to the more static integration of the earlier stages. Time is kept going by the mother, and this is one aspect of her auxiliary ego-functioning; but the infant comes to have a personal time-sense, one that lasts at first only over a short span. This is the same as the infant's capacity to keep alive the imago of the mother in the inner world which also contains the fragmentary benign and persecutory elements that arise out of the instinctual experiences. The length of the time-span over which a child can keep the imago alive in inner psychic reality depends partly on maturational processes and partly on the state of the inner defence organization.

I have sketched some aspects of the origins of concern in the early stages in which the mother's continued presence has a specific value for the infant, that is, if the instinctual life is to have freedom of expression. But this balance has to be achieved over and over again. Take the obvious case of the management of adolescence, or the equally obvious case of the psychiatric patient, for whom occupational therapy is often a start on the road towards a constructive relation to society. Or consider a doctor, and his needs. Deprive him of his work, and where is he? He needs his patients, and the opportunity to use his skills, as others do.

I shall not develop at length the theme of lack of development of concern, or of loss of this capacity for concern that has been almost, but not quite, established. Briefly, failure of the object-mother to survive or of the environment-mother to provide reliable opportunity for reparation leads to a loss of the capacity for concern, and to its replacement by crude anxieties and by crude defences, such as splitting, or disintegration. We often discuss separation-anxiety, but here I am trying to describe what happens between mothers and their babies and between parents and their children when there is *no* separation, and when external continuity of child-care is *not* broken. I am trying to account for things that happen when separation is avoided.

To illustrate my communication I shall give a few examples from clinical work. I do not want, however, to suggest that I am referring to anything rare. Almost any psycho-analysis would provide an example in the course of a week. And it must be remembered that in any clinical example taken from an analysis there is a host of mental mechanisms that the analyst needs to be able to understand which belong to later stages of the individual's development, and to the defences that are called psycho-neurotic. These can be ignored only when the patient is in a state of severe regression to dependence in the transference, and is, in effect, a baby in the care of a mother-figure.

Example I: First I cite the case of the boy of twelve whom I was asked to interview. He was a boy whose *forward* development led him to depression, which included a vast quantity of unconscious hate and aggression, and whose *backward* development, if I may use the phrase, led him to seeing faces, to experiences that were horrible because they represented dreams dreamed in the waking state, hallucinosis. There was good evidence of ego-strength in this boy, as witness his depressive moods. One way that this ego-strength showed in the interview was as follows:

He drew a nightmare, with a huge horned male-creature threatening a tiny self, an 'ant'-self. I asked if he had ever dreamed of himself as the huge horned male, with the ant as someone else, his brother, for instance, at the time of the brother's infancy. He allowed this. When he did not reject my interpretation of his hatred of his brother, I gave him an opportunity to tell me of his reparative potential. This came quite naturally through his description of his father's job as a refrigeration mechanic. I asked him what he himself might want one day to be. He 'had no idea', and he was distressed. He then reported 'not a sad dream, but what a sad dream would be: his father dead'. He was near tears. In this phase of the interview there was a long period of nothing much happening. At length the boy said, very shyly, that he would like to be a scientist.

Here, then, he had shown that he could think of himself as contributing. Though he may not have had the requisite ability, he had the idea. Incidentally, this pursuit would bring him right ahead of his father because, as he said, his father's job was not at all that of a scientist, it was 'just being a mechanic'.

I then felt the interview could end in its own time; I felt the boy could go away without being disturbed by what I had done. I had interpreted his potential destructiveness, but it was true that he had it in him to be constructive. His letting me know he had an aim in life enabled him to go, without feeling he had made me think he was only a hater and a destroyer. And yet, I had not reassured him.

Example II: A patient of mine doing psychotherapy started off a session by telling me that he had been to see one of his patients performing; that is to say, he had gone outside the role of a therapist dealing with the patient in the consulting room, and had seen this patient at work. The work of my patient's patient was highly skilled, and he was very successful in a particular job in which he used quick movements which in the therapeutic hour made no sense, but moved him around on the couch as if he were possessed. Although doubtful about having seen this man at work, my patient felt that probably it was a good thing. He then referred to his own activities in the holidays. He had a garden, and he very much enjoyed physical labour and all kinds of constructive activity, and he liked gadgets, which he really used.

I had been alerted to the importance of his constructive activities by his report of his having gone to see his patient at work. My patient returned to a theme which had been important in the recent analysis in which various kinds of engineering tools were important. On his way to the analytic session he often stopped and gazed at a machine tool in a shop window near my house. The tool had the most splendid teeth. This was my patient's way of getting at his oral aggression, the primitive love-impulse with all its ruthlessness and destructiveness. We could call it 'eating in the transference relationship'. The trend in his treatment was towards this ruthlessness and primitive loving, and the resistance against getting to the deep layers of it was tremendous. Here was a new integration and a concern about the survival of the analyst.

When this new material came up relating to primitive love and to the destruction of the analyst, *there had already been* some reference to constructive work. When I made the interpretation that the patient needed from me, about his destruction of me (eating), I could have reminded him of what he had said about construction. I could have said that just as he saw his patient performing, and the performance made sense of the jerky movements, so I might have seen him working in his garden, using gadgets in order to improve the property. He could cut through walls and trees, and it was all enjoyed tremendously. If such activity had come apart from a report of the constructive aim it would have been a senseless maniacal episode, a transference madness.

I would say that human beings cannot accept the destructive aim in their very early loving attempts. The idea of destruction of the object-mother in loving can be tolerated, however, if the individual who is getting towards it has evidence of a constructive aim already at hand, and of an environment-mother ready to accept.

Example III: A man patient came into my room and saw a tape-recorder. This gave him ideas, and he said as he lay down and as he gathered himself together for the work of the analytic hour, 'I would like to think that when I have finished treatment, what has happened here with me will be of value to the world in some way or other.' I said nothing, but I made a mental note that this remark *might* indicate that the patient was near to one of those bouts of destructiveness with which I had had to deal repeatedly in two years of his treatment. Before the end of the hour, the patient had truly reached a new awareness of his envy of me, an envy which was the outcome of his thinking I was a good analyst. He had the impulse to thank me for being good, and for being able to do what he needed me to do. We had had all this before, but he was now more than on previous occasions in touch with his destructive feelings towards what might be called a good object, his analyst.

When I linked these two things, he said that this felt right, but he added how awful it would have been if I had interpreted on the basis of his first remark. He meant, if I had taken up his wish to be of use and had told him that this indicated an unconscious wish to destroy. He had to reach to the destructive urge before I acknowledged the reparation, and he had to reach it in his own time and in his own way. No doubt it was his capacity to have an idea of ultimately contributing that was making it possible for him to get into more intimate contact with his destructiveness. But constructive effort is false and meaningless unless, as he said, one has first reached to the destruction.

Example IV: An adolescent girl was having treatment from a therapist who was also taking care of the girl at the same time in the therapist's home, along with her own children. This arrangement had advantages and disadvantages.

The girl had been severely ill, and at the time of the incident I shall recount she was emerging from a long period of regression to dependence and to an infantile state. She is no longer regressed in her relation to the home and the family, but is still in a very special state in the limited area of the treatment sessions which occur at a set time each day.

A time came when the girl expressed the deepest hate of the therapist (who is both caring for her and doing her treatment). All was well in the rest of the twenty-four hours, but in the treatment area the therapist was destroyed utterly, and repeatedly. It is difficult to convey the degree of the girl's hate of the therapist and, in fact, the annihilation of her. Here it was not a case of the therapist going out to see the patient at work, for the therapist had charge of the girl all the time, and there were two separate relationships going on between them simultaneously. In the day, all sorts of new things began to happen: the girl began to want to help clean the house, to polish the furniture, to be of use. This helping was absolutely new, and had never been a feature in this girl's personal pattern in her own home, even before she became acutely ill. And it happened silently (so to speak) alongside the utter destructiveness that the girl began to find in the primitive aspects of her loving, which she reached in her relation to the therapist in the therapy sessions.

You see the same idea repeating itself here. Naturally, the fact that the patient was becoming conscious of the destructiveness, made possible the constructive activity which appeared in the day. *But it is the other way round that I want to make plain here and now.* The constructive and creative experiences were making it possible for the child to get to the experience of her destructiveness. And thus, in the treatment, conditions were present that I have tried to describe. The capacity for concern is not only a maturational node, but it also depends for its existence on an emotional environment that has been good enough over a period of time.

Summary

Concern, as the term has been used here, describes the link between the destructive elements in drive-relationships to objecst, and the other positive aspects of relating. Concern is presumed to belong to a period prior to the classical Oedipus complex, which is a relationship between three whole persons. The capacity for concern belongs to the two-body relationship between the infant and the mother or mother-substitute.

In favourable circumstances, the mother by continuing to be alive and available is both the mother who receives all the fullness of the baby's id-drives, and also the mother who can be loved as a person and to whom reparation can be made. In this way, the anxiety about the id-drives and the fantasy of these drives becomes tolerable to the baby, who can then experience guilt, or can hold it in full expectation of an opportunity to make reparation for it. To this guilt that is held but not felt as such, we give the name 'concern'. In the initial stages of development, if there is no reliable mother-figure to receive the reparation-gesture, the guilt becomes intolerable, and concern cannot be felt. Failure of reparation leads to a losing of the capacity for concern, and to its replacement by primitive forms of guilt and anxiety.

7

FROM DEPENDENCE TOWARDS INDEPENDENCE IN THE DEVELOPMENT OF THE INDIVIDUAL[1]

(1963)

I have chosen in this chapter to describe emotional growth in terms of the journey from dependence to independence. If you had asked me to perform this task thirty years ago I should almost certainly have referred to the changes by which immaturity gives place to maturity in terms of progression in the individual's instinctual life. I would have referred to the oral phase, and to the anal phase, and to the phallic phase and the genital. I might have divided these phases up—first oral, preambivalent, second oral, oral sadistic, and so on. Some authors have very much divided up the anal phase; others have been content to have the idea of a pregenital phase that is based generally on the functioning of the organs of ingestion, absorption, and elimination. All this is good. It is as true now as it was, and it has started off our thinking and the structure of the theory by which we steer our course. Nevertheless, it is now in our bones, so to speak. We take it for granted, and we look to other aspects of growth when we find ourselves in the position I am in just now, where I am expected to say something that is not exactly common knowledge, or that takes into consideration the later developments in theory and attitude.

If I have chosen to look at growth in terms of dependence changing gradually towards independence you will agree, I hope, that this does not in any way invalidate the statement I might have made of growth in terms of erotogenic zones, or of object relating.

Socialization

Maturity of the human being is a term that implies not only personal growth but also socialization. Let us say that in health, which is almost synonymous with maturity, the adult is able to identify with society without too great a sacrifice of personal spontaneity; or, the other way round, the adult is able to attend

[1] Talk given at the Atlanta Psychiatric Clinic, October 1963.

to his or her own personal needs without being antisocial, and indeed, without a failure to take some responsibility for the maintenance or for the modification of society as it is found. We get left with certain social conditions, and this is a legacy we have to accept, and, if necessary, alter; it is this that we eventually hand down to those who come after us.

Independence is never absolute. The healthy individual does not become isolated, but becomes related to the environment in such a way that the individual and the environment can be said to be interdependent.

The Journey

There is nothing new about the idea of a journey from dependence to independence. Each human being must start on this journey, and many arrive somewhere not far from this destination, and arrive at independence with a built-in social sense. Here psychiatry is looking at healthy growth, a matter which is often left to the educationalist or to the psychologist.

The value of this approach is that it enables us to study and discuss at one and the same time the personal and the environmental factors. In this language health means both health of the individual and health of society, and full maturity of the individual is not possible in an immature or ill social setting.

Three Categories

In planning this brief statement on a very complex theme I find I need three rather than two categories, not simply dependence and independence. It is helpful to think separately of:

absolute dependence;
relative dependence;
and   towards independence.

Absolute Dependence

I will first draw your attention to the very early stages of the emotional development of every infant. At the beginning the infant is entirely dependent on the physical provision of the live mother and her womb or her infant care. But in terms of psychology we have to say that the infant is at one and the same time dependent and independent. It is this paradox that we need to examine. There is all that is inherited, including the maturational processes, and perhaps pathological inherited trends, and these have a reality of their own, and no one can alter these; at the same time, the maturational processes depend for their evolution on the environmental provision. We can say that the facilitating environment makes possible the steady progress of the maturational processes. But the environment does not make the child. At best it enables the child to realize potential.

This term 'maturational process' refers to the evolution of the ego and of the self, and includes the whole story of the id, of instincts and their vicissitudes, and of defences in the ego relative to instinct.

In other words, a mother and father do not produce a baby as an artist produces a picture or a potter a pot. They have started up a developmental process which results in there being a lodger in the mother's body and then in her arms and then in the home provided by the parents, and what this lodger will turn out to be like is outside anyone's control. The parents are dependent on the infant's inherited tendencies. It may well be asked: 'What then can they do if they cannot make their own child?' They can of course do a great deal. I shall say that they can provide for a child who is healthy, in the sense of being mature according to what maturity means at any moment for that child. If they succeed in making this provision then the infant's maturational processes are not blocked but are met and enabled to become part of the child.

It turns out that this adapting to the infant's maturational processes is a highly complex thing, one that makes tremendous demands on the parents, and at first it is the mother herself who is the facilitating environment. She needs support at this time, which is best given by the child's father (let us say her husband), her mother, the family and the immediate social environment. This is terribly obvious but none the less true and needing to be said.

I like to give this special state of the mother a special name, because I think its importance is not appreciated. Mothers recover from this state and forget. I call it 'primary maternal preoccupation'. This is not necessarily a good name, but the point is that towards the end of the pregnancy and for a few weeks after the birth of a child the mother is preoccupied with (or better, 'given over to') the care of her baby, which at first seems like a part of herself; moreover she is very much identified with the baby and knows quite well what the baby is feeling like. For this she uses her own experiences as a baby. In this way the mother is herself in a dependent state, and vulnerable. It is to describe this stage that I use the words *absolute dependence* in referring to the state of the baby.

In this way natural provision is made in nature for what the infant needs, which is a high degree of *adaptation*. I will explain what I mean by this word.

In early psycho-analytic days adaptation could only mean one thing, meeting the infant's instinctual needs. A great deal of misconception has arisen out of the slowness of some to understand that an infant's needs are not confined to instinct tensions, important though these may be. There is the whole of the infant's ego development that has its own needs. The language here is that the mother 'does not let her infant down', though she may and must frustrate in the sense of meeting instinct needs. It is amazing how well mothers do meet the ego-needs of their own infants, even mothers who are not good at giving the breast but who quickly substitute the bottle and the formula.

There are always a few who cannot fully commit themselves in the way that is needed at this very early stage, although the stage only lasts a few months towards the end of pregnancy and at the beginning of the infant's life.

I shall describe ego-needs, since these are multifarious. The best example would be the simple matter of holding. No one can hold a baby unless able to identify with the baby. Balint (1951, 1958) has referred to the oxygen in the air, of which the infant knows nothing. I could remind you of the temperature of the bathwater, tested by the mother's elbow; the infant does not know that the water might have been too hot or too cold, but comes to take for granted the body temperature. I am still talking about absolute dependence. It is all a matter of impingement, or no impingement, on the infant's existence, and I want to develop this theme.

All the processes of a live infant constitute a *going-on-being*, a kind of blue-print for existentialism. The mother who is able to give herself over, for a limited spell, to this her natural task, is able to protect her infant's going-on-being. Any impingement, or failure of adaptation, causes a reaction in the infant, and the reaction breaks up the going-on-being. If reacting to impingements is the pattern of an infant's life, then there is a serious interference with the natural tendency that exists in the infant to become an integrated unit, able to continue to have a self with a past, present, and future. With a relative absence of reactions to impingements the infant's body-functions give a good basis for the building up of a body-ego. In this way the keel is laid down for future mental health.

You see how it is that the sensitive adaptation to an infant's ego-needs only lasts a little while. Soon the infant begins to get a kick out of kicking, and to get something positive out of being angry because of what could be called minor failures of adaptation. But by this time the mother is beginning to restart her own life that eventually becomes relatively independent of her infant's needs. Often the child's growing up corresponds quite accurately with the mother's resumption of her own independence, and you would agree that a mother who cannot gradually *fail* in this matter of sensitive adaptation is failing in another sense; she is failing (because of her own immaturity or her own anxieties) to give her infant reasons for anger. An infant that has no reason for anger, but who of course has in him (or her) the usual amount of whatever are the ingredients of aggressiveness, is in a special difficulty, a difficulty in fusing aggression in with loving.

So in absolute dependence the infant has no means of awareness of maternal provision.

Relative Dependence

Just as I call the first stage 'absolute dependence', so I call the next stage 'relative dependence'. In this way one can distinguish between dependence that is quite beyond the infant's ken, and dependence that the infant can know about. A mother does a vast amount in meeting her infant's ego-needs, all of which goes unrecorded in the infant mind.

The next stage, that of relative dependence, turns out to be a stage of adaptation with a gradual failing of adaptation. It is part of the equipment of the great majority of mothers to provide a graduated de-adaptation, and this is nicely geared to the rapid developments that the infant displays. For instance, there is the beginning of intellectual understanding, which develops as a vast extension of simple processes, such as conditioned reflexes. (Think of an infant expecting a feed. The time comes when the infant can wait a few minutes because noises in the kitchen indicate that food is about to appear. Instead of simply being excited by the noises, the infant uses the news item in order to be able to wait.)

Naturally infants vary very much in their capacity to use intellectual understanding early, and often the understanding they might have had is delayed by the existence of a muddle in the way reality is presented. There is an idea for emphasis here, for the whole procedure of infant-care has as its main characteristic a steady presentation of the world to the infant. This is something that cannot be done by thought, nor can it be managed mechanically. It can only be done by continuous management by a human being who is consistently herself. There is no question of perfection here. Perfection belongs to machines; what the infant needs is just what he usually gets, the care and attention of someone who is going on being herself. This of course applies to fathers too.

A special point needs to be made of this 'being herself' because one should separate out the person from the man or woman, mother or nurse, who is *acting* the part, perhaps acting it quite well at times, and perhaps acting it well because of having learned how to care for infants from books or in a class. But this acting is not good enough. The infant can only find an unmuddled presentation of external reality by being cared for by a human being who is devoted to the infant and to the infant-care task. The mother will grow up out of this state of easy devotion, and soon she will be back to the office desk, or to writing novels, or to a social life along with her husband, but for the time being she is in it up to the neck.

The reward at the first stage (absolute dependence) is that the infant's process of development is not distorted. The reward at this stage of relative dependence is that the infant begins to be in some way *aware of dependence*. When the mother is away for a moment beyond the time-span of his (or her) capacity to believe in her survival, anxiety appears, and this is the first sign that the infant knows. Before this, if the mother is away the infant simply fails to benefit from her special ability to ward off impingements, and essential developments in ego structure fail to become well established.

The next stage beyond that at which the infant in some way feels a need for the mother is one in which the infant begins to *know in his mind* that mother is necessary.

Gradually the need for the actual mother (in health) becomes fierce and truly terrible, so that mothers do really hate to leave their children, and they sacrifice a great deal rather than cause distress and indeed produce hatred and disillusionment during this phase of special need. This phase could be said to last from (roughly) six months to two years.

By the time an infant is two years old there have begun new developments, and these equip the child to deal with loss. It will be necessary to refer to these. Along with these personality developments in the child there are important though variable environmental factors to be taken into consideration. For instance there may be the mother-nurse team, itself an interesting subject for study. There may be suitable aunts and grandparents or special friends of the parents who by their constant presence qualify as mother-substitutes. Then also the mother's husband may be an important person in the home, helping to create a home, and he may be a good mother-substitute, or he may be important in a more masculine way by giving his wife support and a feeling of security, which she can pass on to the infant.

It will not be necessary to deal fully with these rather obvious and yet highly significant details. It will be seen, however, that these details vary greatly, and the infant's own growth-processes are pulled this way and that according to what obtains.

Case Material:

I had the chance to observe a family of three boys at the time of their mother's sudden death. The father acted in a responsible way, and the mother's friend who knew the boys well took over their care, and after a period of time she became their step-mother.

The baby boy was four months old when his mother suddenly disappeared from his life. His development proceeded satis-factorily and there was no clinical sign indicating a reaction. In my language the mother was 'a subjective object' for this baby boy, and the mother's friend stepped into the mother's position. Later he thought of his stepmother as his mother.

When this the youngest boy was four years he was brought to me, however, because he was starting to show various person-ality difficulties. In play in the psychotherapeutic interview he invented a game which had to be repeated very many times. He hid, and I made a very slight alteration in, say, the position of a pencil on the table. He then came in, found the slight alteration, and became very angry indeed and killed me. He would have persisted with this game for hours.

Applying what I had learned I told his stepmother to be ready to talk to him about death. That very evening, for the first time in his life, he gave the stepmother a chance to talk about death, and this led on to his needing to know exactly all the facts about the mother whose inside he came out of, and of her death. This then gathered momentum in the next few days, and everything had to be repeated and repeated. He continued with his good relationship with his stepmother whom he continued to call mother.

The oldest of the three children was six years old when his mother died. He simply mourned her as a person who was loved. The mourning process took about two years, and as he emerged from it he had a bout of stealing. He accepted the stepmother as a stepmother, and he remembered his real mother as a person sadly lost.

The middle boy was three at the time of the tragedy. He was

strongly in a positive relationship with his father at the time, and he became a psychiatric casualty, needing psychotherapy (about seven sessions over a period of eight years). The oldest boy said of this one: 'We didn't tell him of father's remarriage because he thinks marriage means "killing".'

This middle boy was in a muddle, and unable to cope with the guilt that he needed to be able to experience because of his mother's dying when he was in the homosexual phase with special attachment to his father. He said: 'I don't mind, it was —— (the older brother) who loved her.' Clinically he became hypomanic. His extreme restlessness lasted a long time, and it was clear that a depression was threatening. His play showed a degree of muddle, but he was able to organize his play sufficiently to convey to me in the psychotherapeutic sessions what were the specific anxieties that made him restless.

There are still signs of residual psychiatric disorder in this boy who is now thirteen—that is, ten years after the tragedy which for this one boy proved traumatic.

One important development in the infant comes under the heading 'identification'. Quite early an infant may be able to show a capacity to identify with the mother. There are primitive reflexes that may be said to form a basis for these developments, as when a baby responds to a smile with a smile. Quickly the baby becomes capable of more complex forms of identification, implying the existence of an imagination. An example of this would be the infant who may wish to find the mother's mouth and feed her with his or her finger while taking the breast. I have seen this happen at three months; but dates should not worry us. Sooner or later these things happen to all infants (except to some ill infants) and we know that a great relief from dependence follows the development in an infant of a capacity to step into the mother's shoes. Out of this comes the full development of an understanding of the mother's personal and separate existence, and *eventually* the child comes to be able to believe in the parents' coming together which in fact led to his or her own conception. This is a long way ahead and never achieved at deepest levels.

The effect of these new mental mechanisms on the subject of dependence is that the infant can allow for events that are outside his or her control, and because of being able to identify with the mother or the parents the infant can side-track some of the very great hatred that is felt towards that which challenges the infant's omnipotence.

Then speech becomes understood and perhaps used. This

tremendous development in the human animal enables the parents to give every opportunity for the infant to co-operate, through intellectual understanding, even though *in deep feelings* the infant may feel grief, hatred, disillusionment, fear and impotence. The mother can say: 'I am going out to get some bread.' This may work unless, of course, she is away beyond the time-span of the infant's capacity to keep the idea of her alive, in feeling.

I wish to mention a form of development that especially affects the infant's capacity for making complex identifications. This has to do with the stage at which the integrating tendencies of the infant bring about a state in which the infant is a unit, a whole person, with an inside and an outside, and a person living in the body, and more or less bounded by the skin. Once outside means 'not-ME' then inside means ME, and there is now a place in which to store things. In the child's fantasy the personal psychic reality is located inside. If it is located outside there are good reasons.

Now the infant's growth takes the form of a continuous interchange between inner and outer reality, each being enriched by the other.

The child is now not only a potential creator of the world, but also the child becomes able to populate the world with samples of his or her own inner life. So gradually the child is able to 'cover' almost any external event, and perception is almost synonymous with creation. Here again is a means by which the child gains control over external events as well as over the inner workings of his or her own self.

Towards Independence

Once these things are established, as they are in health, the child is able gradually to meet the world and all its complexities, because of seeing there more and more of what is already present in his or her own self. In ever-widening circles of social life the child is identified with society, because local society is a sample of the self's personal world as well as being a sample of truly external phenomena.

In this way a true independence develops, with the child able to live a personal existence that is satisfactory, while involved in society's affairs. Naturally there are big possibilities for setback in this development of socialization, right up to the late stages beyond puberty and adolescence. Even a healthy individual may meet a social tension which is beyond what that individual could allow for, in advance of the individual's personal broadening of the basis of tolerance.

In practice you can watch your adolescents graduating from one grouping to another, all the time widening the circle, all the time embracing new and more and more strange phenomena that society throws up. Parents are very much needed in the management of their own adolescent children who are exploring one social circle after another, because of their ability to see better than their children can when this progression from the limited social circle towards the unlimited social circle is too rapid, perhaps because of dangerous social elements in the immediate neighbourhood, or because of the defiance that belongs to puberty and to a rapid development in the sexual capacity. They are needed especially because of the instinct tensions and patterns that reappear and which were first laid down at the toddler age.

'Towards independence' describes the strivings of the toddler child and of the child at puberty. In the latency period children are usually contented with whatever dependence that they are lucky to be able to experience. Latency is the period of school playing a role as a substitute for home. This is not always true, but there is no place for a further development of this special theme here.

Adults must be expected to be continuing the process of growing and of growing up, since they do but seldom reach to full maturity. But once they have found a niche in society through work, and have perhaps married or have settled in some pattern that is a compromise between copying the parents and defiantly establishing a personal identity, once these developments have taken place, adult life can be said to have started, and the individuals one by one climb out of the area covered by this brief statement of growth in terms of dependence towards independence.

8

MORALS AND EDUCATION[1]

(1963)

The title of my lecture gives me scope to develop the theme not so much of society that changes as of human nature that does not change. Human nature does not change. This is an idea that could be challenged. Nevertheless, I shall assume its truth, and build on this foundation. It is true that human nature evolved, just as human bodies and beings evolved, in the course of hundreds of thousands of years. But there is very little evidence that human nature has altered in the short span of recorded history; and comparable with this is the fact that what is true about human nature in London today is also true in Tokyo, in Accra, in Amsterdam and Timbuktoo. It is true for whites and blacks, for giants and pygmies, for the children of the Harwell or Cape Canaveral scientist and for the children of the Australian aboriginal.

Applied to the subject that is under discussion (moral education today) this means that there is an area for study that may be called the capacity of the human child to be morally educated. What I am referring to in this lecture is limited to this area, the human child's development of a capacity for having a moral sense, for experiencing a sense of guilt and for the setting up of an ideal. Analogous would be an attempt to get behind such an idea as 'belief in God' to the idea of 'belief', or (as I would prefer to say) 'belief in'. To a child who develops 'belief in' can be handed the god of the household or of the society that happens to be his. But to a child with no 'belief in', god is at best a pedagogue's gimmick, and at worst a piece of evidence for the child that the parent-figures are lacking in confidence in the processes of human nature and are frightened of the unknown.

Professor Niblett in the opening lecture of this series referred to the headmaster Keate who said to a child: 'You will believe in the Holy Ghost by 5 o'clock this afternoon or I will beat you till you do,' and in this way Professor Niblett led on to the idea of the futility of teaching values or religion by force. I am trying to

[1] Lecture given in a series at University of London Institute of Education, 1962, and first published (under the title 'The Young Child at Home and at School') in *Moral Education in a Changing Society*, ed. W. R. Niblett. (London: Faber, 1963.)

93

open up this important theme and to examine the alternatives. My main point is that there does exist a good alternative, and that this good alternative is not to be found in a more and more subtle teaching of religion. The good alternative has to do with the provision of those conditions for the infant and child that enable such things as trust and 'belief in', and ideas of right and wrong, to develop out of the working of the individual child's inner processes. This could be called the evolution of a personal superego.

Religions have made much of original sin, but have not all come round to the idea of original goodness, that which by being gathered together in the idea of God is at the same time separated off from the individuals who collectively create and re-create this God concept. The saying that man made God in his own image is usually treated as an amusing example of the perverse, but the truth in this saying could be made more evident by a restatement, such as: man continues to create and re-create God as a place to put that which is good in himself, and which he might spoil if he kept it in himself along with all the hate and destructiveness which is also to be found there.

Religion (or is it theology?) has stolen the good from the developing individual child, and has then set up an artificial scheme for injecting this that has been stolen back into the child, and has called it 'moral education'. Actually moral education does not work unless the infant or child has developed in himself or herself by natural developmental process the stuff that, when it is placed up in the sky, is given the name God. The moral educator depends for success on there being that development in the individual child that enables the child to accept this God of the moral educator as a projection of the goodness that is part of the child and of his actual experience of life.

We are reduced in practice, therefore, whatever our theological system, to a dependence in the case of each new child on the way the child is being or has been enabled to make the grade developmentally. Has the child been able to pass, so to speak, his or her entrance examination in moral sense, or to acquire this thing that I am calling *belief in*? I cling to this ugly, incomplete phrase, belief in. In order to complete that which has been started up, someone must let the child know what we in this family and in this bit of society at the present time happen to believe in. But this completing process is of secondary importance, because if 'belief in' has not been reached then the teaching of morals or religion is mere Keatean pedagogy, and is generally accepted as objectionable or ludicrous.

I feel dissatisfied with the idea that is often expressed by other-wise well-informed persons that Freud's mechanistic approach to psychology or his reliance on the theory of the evolution of men from animals interferes with the contribution psycho-analysis might make to religious thought. It might even turn out that religion could learn something from psycho-analysis, something that would save religious practice from losing its place in the civilization processes, and in the process of civilization. Theology, by denying to the developing individual the creating of whatever is bound up in the concept of God and of goodness and of moral values, depletes the individual of an important aspect of creativeness.

Surely Mrs Knight in the controversy of some years ago was not devaluing God by comparing God with Father Christmas; she was saying or trying to say that you can put some parts of a child into the witch of the fairy story, some of the child's belief and generosity can be handed out to Father Christmas, and all sorts of feelings and ideas of goodness that belong to the child and his or her inner and outer experiences can be put out there and labelled 'God'. In the same way, nastiness in the child can be called 'the devil and all his works'. The labelling socializes the otherwise personal phenomenon. Practising psycho-analysis for thirty years has made me feel that it is the ideas bound up with the organization of moral education that deplete the individual of individual creativeness.

There are reasons why the ideas of the moral educationalist die hard. An obvious one is that there do exist wicked people. In my language, this means that there are persons in all societies and in all ages who in their emotional development did not reach to a stage of believing in, nor did they reach a stage of innate morality involving the total personality. But moral education that is designed for these ill persons is unsuitable for the vast majority of persons who, in fact, are not ill in this respect. I shall refer to wicked people again later.

So far I have spoken as an amateur theologian, but I have been asked to speak as a professional child psychiatrist. To contribute usefully I must now be able to give a brief story of the emotional development of the human infant and child. You know of course that this is an extremely complex subject and a story that can-not be briefly told. There are many ways of approaching the subject of emotional growth and I shall attempt to use various methods.

The basis of child-development is the physical existence of the infant along with his or her inherited tendencies. These inherited tendencies include the maturational drives to forward development. Let us say, an infant tends to use three words at one year and tends to walk by fourteen months or so, and tends to reach the same shape and height as one of the parents, and tends to be clever or stupid or moody or to have allergies. In more hidden ways there starts in the infant and continues in the child a tendency towards integration of the personality, the word integration tending to have a more and more complex meaning as time goes on and as the child gets older. Also the infant tends to live in his or her body and to build the self on a basis of bodily functioning to which belong imaginative elaborations that quickly become extremely complex and constitute the psychic reality specific to that infant. The infant becomes established as a unit, feels an I AM feeling, and bravely faces the world with which he or she is already becoming able to form relationships, affectionate relationships and (by contrast) a pattern of object-relationships based on the instinctual life. And so on. All this, and much much more, is true and always has been true of human infants. Here is human nature unfolding itself. BUT, and this but is a big one, maturational processes depend for their becoming actual in the child, and actual at the appropriate moments, on a good enough environmental provision.

This is the old argument of nature and nurture. I suggest that this problem is not incapable of statement. The parents do not have to make their baby as the artist has to make his picture or the potter his pot. The baby grows in his or her own way if the environment is good enough. Someone has referred to the good enough provision as 'the average expectable environment'. The fact is that throughout the centuries mothers, and parents, and parent-substitutes, have in fact usually provided exactly those conditions that the infant and small child do in fact need at the beginning, at the stage of their greatest dependence, and this continues even a little later when, as children, the infants are becoming somewhat separate from the environment and relatively independent. After this things tend to be not so good, but at the same time this fact matters less and less.

It will be noted that I am referring to an age at which verbal teaching does not apply. Neither Freud nor psycho-analysis was needed to tell mothers and parents how to provide these conditions. These conditions start with a high degree of adaptation on the part of the mother to the infant's needs, and gradually become a series of failures of adaptation; these failures are again a kind of adaptation because they are related to the growing need of the child for meeting reality and for achieving separation and for the establishment of a personal identity. (Joy Adamson describes all this beautifully in terms of her upbringing of Elsa the lioness, and of the cubs who are now Forever Free.)

It seems that although most religions have tended to recognize the importance of family life it fell to psycho-analysis to point out to the mothers of babies and to the parents of the very young the value—no, the essential nature—of their tendency to provide for each infant that which each infant absolutely needs by way of nurture.

The mother (I do not exclude the father) adapts so well that it can only be said that she is closely identified with her baby, so that she knows what is needed at any one moment, and also in a general way. The infant, of course, is at this first and earliest stage in a state of mergence, not yet having separated out mother and 'not-me' objects from the 'me', so that what is adaptive or 'good' in the environment is building up in the infant's storehouse of experience as a self quality, indistinguishable at first (by the infant) from the infant's own healthy functioning.

At this early stage the infant does not register what is good or adaptive, but reacts to, and therefore knows about and registers each failure of reliability. Reacting to unreliability in the infant-care process constitutes a trauma, each reaction being an interruption of the infant's 'going-on-being' and a rupture of the infant's self.

To sum up this first stage of my simplified scheme for describing the developing human being: the infant and small child is usually cared for in a reliable way, and this being cared for well enough builds up in the infant to a belief in reliability; on to this a perception of the mother or father or grandmother or nurse can be added. To a child who has started life in this way the idea of goodness and of a reliable and personal parent or God can follow naturally.

The child who is not having good enough experiences in the early stages cannot be given the idea of a personal God *as a substitute for infant-care*. The vitally important subtle communicating of the infant-mother kind antedates the stage at which verbal communication can be added. This is a first principle of moral education, that *moral education is no substitute for love*. At the beginning love can only be expressed effectually in terms of infant- and child-care, which means for us the provision of a facilitating or good-enough environment, and which means for the infant a chance to evolve in a personal way according to the steady gradation of the maturational process.

How can I go on to develop this theme, taking into account the rapidly increasing complexity of the individual child's inner reality and the expanding storehouse of the child's internal and external experiences remembered, or for economy forgotten?

At this point I must try to say something about the origin in the infant or small child of those elements which the words good and bad can describe and be apposite. It is not necessary of course that words should be offered at this stage, and indeed approval and disapproval can be conveyed to the deaf, and to infants at a stage long before verbal communication has begun. There do develop in the infant certain opposed feelings, apart altogether from the approval and disapproval which is conveyed to the child by the parent, and it is these that must be noted and perhaps tracked down to their source.

In the developing storehouse of personal memories and of the phenomena that constitute the inner psychic reality of the individual child there appear elements which are at first simply opposed. They may be called supportive and disruptive elements, or friendly and hostile elements, or benign and persecutory elements; these arise partly out of the infant's satisfactions and frustrations in the living experience, which includes excitements, and partly this build-up of positive and negative elements depends on the infant's capacity to avoid the pain of ambivalence by not joining up the objects that feel to be either good or bad.[1]

I cannot avoid using the words good and bad here even though to do so defeats my own object, which is to describe phenomena prior to the use of words. The fact is that these important things that are going on in the developing infant and small child demand description in terms of good and bad.

All this is closely intertwined with the perception of maternal approval and disapproval, but here as everywhere the internal and personal factor is more important than the external or environmental factor, a precept which is at the very heart of my communication. If I am wrong in this respect then my thesis is faulty. If my thesis is faulty, then infants and small children do depend on having right and wrong injected into them. This means that parents must approve and disapprove instead of loving, and in fact they must be moral educators instead of parents. How they would hate this!

The child does need to meet with approval and disapproval, but parents on the whole find themselves waiting, refraining from showing approval and disapproval until they have found in their infant the elements of a sense of values and of good and bad and

[1] This primitive state of affairs becomes employed as a defence against the pain of ambivalence and is then called 'splitting' the object.

of right and wrong, that is, in the particular area of child-care which is significant at the moment.

It is now necessary to take a glimpse at the inner psychic reality of the infant and child. This becomes a rapidly growing personal world that is localized by the child both inside and outside the self, the self that is but newly established as a unit with a 'skin'. What is inside is part of the self though not inherently so, and it can be projected. What is outside is not part of the self, but again not inherently so, and it can be introjected. In health, a constant interchange goes on as the child lives and collects experiences, so that the external world is enriched by the inner potential, and the inner is enriched by what belongs outside. The basis for these mental mechanisms is clearly the functioning of incorporation and elimination in bodily experience. Ultimately it may be perceived by the child, who is by then becoming a mature individual, that there does exist that which is truly environmental, and this (the environmental) includes the inherited tendencies as well as the environmental provision and the world past and future, and the universe as yet unknown.

It is evident that as the child grows in this way the content of his personal self is not only he. The self becomes increasingly shaped by the environmental provision. The baby who adopts an object as almost part of the self could not have adopted it unless it had been lying round for adoption. In the same way all the introjects are not only exports reimported, they are also truly foreign goods. The infant cannot know this until considerable maturation has taken place, and the mind has become able to deal intellectually and intelligently with phenomena that have no meaning in terms of emotional acceptance. In terms of emotional acceptance the self, at its core, is always personal, isolated and unaffected by experience.

This way of looking at emotional development is important for my argument, for as the infant grows in this way the stage becomes set for those engaged in infant- and child-care to leave lying round not only objects (such as golliwogs or teddy bears or dolls or toy engines) but also moral codes. These moral codes are given in subtle ways by expressions of acceptance or by threats of the withdrawal of love. In fact, the phrase 'sphincter morality' has been used to describe the way that ideas of right and wrong can be conveyed to infants and small children in terms of the way in which incontinence turns into socialized self-control. Control over excretions is only one rather obvious instance in a host of comparable phenomena. However, in terms of sphincter morality, it is easy to see that parents who expect the small child to comply with the regulations before reaching the stage in which self-control has meaning are depriving the child of the sense of achievement and of faith in human nature that comes from a natural progress towards sphincter control. This sort of mistaken attitude to 'training' ignores the child's maturational processes, and ignores the child's wanting to be like the other persons and animals who are in the child's world.

No doubt there are and always will be those who by nature and nurture prefer to implant morals, just as there are also those who by nature and nurture prefer to wait, and perhaps to wait a long time, for natural developments. Nevertheless such matters can be discussed.

In these matters the answer is always that there is *more to be gained from love than from education*. Love here means the totality of infant- and child-care, that which facilitates maturational processes. It includes hate. Education means sanctions and the implantation of parental or social values *apart from* the child's inner growth or maturation. Education in terms of the teaching of arithmetic has to wait for that degree of personal integration in the infant that makes the concept of *one* meaningful, and also the idea contained in the first pronoun singular. The child who knows the I AM feeling, and who can carry it, knows about one, and then immediately wants to be taught addition, subtraction and multiplication. In the same way moral education follows naturally on the arrival of morality in the child by the natural developmental processes that good care facilitates.

Sense of Values

Soon the question arises: what about a sense of values generally? What is the parents' duty here? This more general issue follows on the management of the more specific issues of infant behaviour. Again there are those who fear to wait, and who implant, just as there are those who wait, and keep ready for presentation the ideas and expectations that the child can use on his arrival at each new developmental stage of integration and capacity for objective consideration.

In regard to religion, and the idea of a god, there are clearly the extremes of those who do not know that the child has a capacity to create a god so that they implant the idea as soon as possible, and there are those who wait and see the results of their efforts to meet the needs of their developing infant. These latter, as I have already said, will introduce the family gods to the child when the child has reached to the stage for their acceptance. In the latter case, there is the minimum of set pattern; in the first case the set pattern is what is wanted, and the child can only accept or reject this essentially foreign thing, the implanted god concept.

Advocates could be found for not leaving any cultural phenomena lying round for the child to catch hold of and to adopt. I even knew a father who refused to allow his daughter to meet any fairy story, or any idea such as that of a witch or a fairy, or of a prince, because he wanted his child to have only a personal personality; the poor child was being asked to start again with the building up of the ideas and the artistic achievements of the centuries. This scheme did not work.

In the same way it is no answer to the problem of moral values to expect a child to have his or her own, and for the parents to have nothing to offer that comes from the local social system. And there is a special reason why a moral code should be available, namely, that the infant's and the small child's innate moral code has a quality so fierce, so crude, and so crippling. Your adult moral code is necessary because it humanizes what for the child is subhuman. The infant suffers talion fears. The child bites in an excited experience of relating to a good object, and the object is felt to be a biting object. The child enjoys an excretory orgy and the world fills with water that drowns and with filth that buries. These crude fears become humanized chiefly through each child's experiences in relation to the parents, who disapprove and are angry but who do not bite and drown and burn the child in retaliation related exactly to the child's impulse or fantasy.

By experience of life and living the child in health becomes ready to believe in something that can be handed over in terms of a personal god. But the personal god idea has no value to a child who has not had the experience of human beings, persons humanizing the terrifying superego formations that relate directly to the infantile impulse and to the fantasy that goes with body functioning and with crude excitements involving instinct.[1]

This principle affecting the handing on of moral values applies likewise to the handing on of the whole torch of culture and civilization. Give a child Mozart and Haydn and Scarlatti from the beginning and you may get precocious good taste, something that can be shown off at parties. But the child probably has to start with noises blown through toilet paper over a comb, and then to graduate to drumming on a saucepan and blowing into

[1] Erikson has written on this theme in terms of the concept of virtue (Erikson, 1961).

an old bugle; the distance from screaming and from vulgar noises to *Voi che Sapete* is vast, and an appreciation of the sublime should be a personal achievement, not an implant. Yet no child can write or perform his or her own Mozart. You must help him to find this and other treasures. In the area of living this implies that you provide your child with an example, not better than you really are, not dishonest, but tolerably decent.

The fiercest morality is that of early infancy, and this persists as a streak in human nature that can be discerned throughout an individual's life. Immorality for the infant is *to comply at the expense of the personal way of life*. For instance, a child of any age may feel that to eat is wrong, even to the extent of dying for the principle. Compliance brings immediate rewards and adults only too easily mistake compliance for growth. The maturational processes can be by-passed by a series of identifications, so that what shows clinically is a false, acting self, a copy of someone perhaps; and what could be called a true or essential self becomes hidden, and becomes deprived of living experience. This leads many people who seem to be doing well eventually to end their lives which have become false and unreal; unreal success is morality at its lowest ebb as compared with which a sexual misdemeanour hardly counts.

One stage in the child's development has especial importance, and I must refer to it, although it is only a new and much more complex example of the environmental provision facilitating maturational processes.

At this stage to which I refer now there is a gradual build-up in the child of a capacity to feel a sense of responsibility, that which at base is a sense of guilt. The environmental essential here is the continued presence of the mother or mother-figure over the time in which the infant and child is accommodating the destructiveness that is part of his make-up. This destructiveness becomes more and more a feature in the experience of object relationships, and the phase of development to which I am referring lasts from about six months to two years, after which the child may have made a satisfactory integration of the idea of destroying the object and the fact of loving the same object. The mother is needed over this time and she is needed because of her survival value. She is an environment-mother and at the same time an object-mother, the object of excited loving. In this latter role she is repeatedly destroyed or damaged. The child gradually comes to integrate these two aspects of the mother and to be able to love and to be affectionate with the surviving mother at the same time. This phase involves the child in a special kind of anxiety which is called a sense of guilt, guilt related to the idea of destruction where love is also operating. It is this anxiety that drives the child towards constructive or actively loving behaviour in his limited world, reviving the object, making the loved object better again, rebuilding the damaged thing. If the mother-figure is not able to see the child through over this phase then the child fails to find or loses the capacity to feel guilt, but instead feels crudely anxious and this anxiety is merely wasteful. (I have described this elsewhere and more thoroughly than I can do it here, and of course the chief work leading to this part of our understanding of the child's development comes from Melanie Klein, and is to be found in her writings under the heading 'The Depressive Position'.)

Provision of Opportunity

Here is an essential stage in child-development, and it has nothing to do with moral education except that if this stage is successfully negotiated then the child's own and personal solution to the problem of destruction of what is loved turns into the child's urge to work or to acquire skills. It is here that the provision of opportunity, and this includes the teaching of skills, meets the child's need. But the need is the essential factor, and the need arises out of the child's establishment within the self of a capacity to stand feeling guilt in regard to destructive impulses and ideas, to stand feeling generally responsible for destructive ideas, because of having become confident in regard to reparative impulses and opportunities for contributing in. This reappears in a big way at the period of adolescence, and it is well known that the provision of opportunity for service for young people is of more value than moral education in the sense of teaching morals.

Earlier I indicated that I would return to the idea of wickedness and the wicked. For the psychiatrist the wicked are ill. Wickedness belongs to the clinical picture produced by the antisocial tendency. It ranges from bed-wetting to stealing and telling lies and includes aggressive behaviour, destructive acts and compulsive cruelty, and perversions. For an understanding of the oetiology of the antisocial tendency there exists a vast literature, and only a short statement can be allowed here. Briefly the antisocial tendency represents the hopefulness in a deprived child who is otherwise hopeless, hapless and harmless; a manifestation of the antisocial tendency in a child means that there has developed in the child some hopefulness, hope that a way may be found across a gap. This gap is a break in the continuity of environmental provision, experienced at a stage of relative dependence. In every case there has been experienced a break in the continuity of the environmental provision, and one that resulted in a hold-up of maturational processes and a painful confusional clinical state in the child.

Often the child psychiatrist is able, in a case seen before the development of secondary gain, to help the child back over the gap, so that instead of stealing there appears a return of an old good relationship with mother or a mother-figure or parent. The wickedness goes if the gap is bridged. This is an over-simplification but it must suffice. Compulsive wickedness is about the last thing to be cured or even stopped by moral education. The child knows in his bones that it is *hope* that is locked up in the wicked behaviour, and that *despair* is linked with compliance and false socialization. For the antisocial or wicked person the moral educator is on the wrong side.

The understanding that psycho-analysis can offer has importance although its application-value is limited. Modern thinking, largely based on psycho-analysis, makes it possible to see what is important in infant- and child-care, and relieves the parents of the burden that they feel when they think they have to make their children good. It evaluates the maturational processes in individual growth, and relates these to the facilitating environment. It examines the development of moral sense in the individual, and demonstrates the way in which a capacity for feeling a sense of personal responsibility belongs to health.

What the psycho-analyst leaves unsolved has to do with the moral education of individuals in so far as they have not matured in essential respects, and in so far as they have no capacity for moral evaluation or for feeling responsibility. The psycho-analyst simply says that these people are ill, and in some cases he is able to give treatment that is effective. But there remains the moral educator's effort to deal with these individuals, whether they are ill or not. Here the psycho-analyst can only ask that the educator shall not spill over his methods designed for these ill persons so that they affect the well persons. The vast majority of people are not ill, though indeed they may show all manner of symptoms. Strong or repressive measures, or indoctrination even, may suit society's need in the management of the antisocial individual, but these measures are the worst possible thing for healthy persons, for those who can grow from within, given the facilitating environment especially in the early stages of growth. It is these latter, the healthy, who grow into the adults who constitute society, and who collectively establish and maintain the moral code for the next decades, till their children take over from them.

As Professor Niblett said again in the first lecture of the series, we cannot meet out adolescents with the words: over to you. We have to provide them in infancy and childhood and adolescence, in home and in school, with the facilitating environment in which each individual may grow his or her own moral capacity, develop a superego that evolved naturally from crude superego elements of infancy, and find his or her own way of using or not using the moral code and general cultural endowment of our age.

By the time the child is growing up towards an adult state the accent is no longer on the moral code that we hand on; the accent has passed over to that more positive thing, the storehouse of man's cultural achievement. And, instead of moral education we introduce to the child the opportunity for being creative that the practice of the arts and the practice of living offers to all those who do not copy and comply but who genuinely grow to a way of personal self-expression.

Part Two

THEORY AND TECHNIQUE

ON THE CONTRIBUTION OF DIRECT CHILD OBSERVATION TO PSYCHO-ANALYSIS[1]

(1957)

I wish to deal with the confusion that I think may arise through an acceptance of the word 'deep' as synonymous with the word 'early'. I have published two contributions specifically in the field of direct observation; these concern (a) the infant's way of coming to terms with an object (Winnicott, 1941), and (b) the use of objects and phenomena during the time of the infant's transition from a purely subjective life to the next stage (Winnicott, 1951).

Each of these will provide useful material for the examination of my main thesis, which is that 'deep' in the analytic sense is not the same as 'early' in the sense of infant development.

The Observation of Infants in a Set Situation

(I will call this Action Research, to give it modern dress and to link it with Kris.)

It is possible to see three main stages in the approach of an infant to an object (one presented in a formal way, as described).

First Stage   Initial reflex grasp;
withdrawal;
tension covering renewed voluntary grasp and slow passage of object to mouth.

Here the mouth becomes suffused, saliva flows.

Second Stage   Mouthing of the object;
carefree use of the object in experimental exploration, in play and as something with which to feed others.

Here the object drops by mistake. Let us assume that it is picked up and returned to the infant.

Third Stage   Riddance.

In considering these matters with reference to an example one

[1] Read at the 20th International Psycho-Analytical Congress, Paris, July 1957, and first published (in French) in the *Revue française de Psychanalyse*, **22**, pp. 205-11.

immediately needs to be given the age of the infant. Typical is eleven months. At thirteen and fourteen months infants have developed so many other interests that the main issue is likely to be obscured.

At ten months or nine months most infants will pass through the phases normally, though the younger they are the more they need some measure of that subtle co-operation which sensitive mothers can give, which supports yet does not dominate. It is not common in my experience for a six-months-old baby to show clearly the whole physical performance. Immaturity at that age is such that it is an achievement that the object has been grasped and held, and perhaps mouthed. Direct observation shows that the baby must have a physical and psychological maturity of a certain degree before being able to enjoy the full emotional experience.

When these phenomena appear in psycho-analysis, whether in a session or in a phase lasting days or weeks, it is not possible for the analyst to date what is observed or deduced. For the analyst who reviews the material presented in analysis it may seem as if the phenomena I have described were applicable to the patient's early infancy, even to the first weeks and days. This material may appear in the analysis mixed up with details that do actually belong to earliest infancy, even to the post-birth state. This the analyst must learn to allow for. Nevertheless it is in analysis that the full significance of the infant's play becomes recognized, play which indicates the whole of the fantasy of incorporation and elimination, and of the growth of the personality through imaginative eating.

Transitional Objects and Phenomena

In the simplest case, a normal baby adopts a piece of cloth or a napkin and becomes addicted to it, and the date is perhaps six months to a year or later. Examination of this phenomenon in analytic work makes it possible for us to refer to the capacity for symbol formation in terms of the use of a transitional object. In analytic work, however, it would seem possible to allow these ideas to apply in earliest infancy, in rudimentary form. Yet the fact remains that there is an age before which the transitional object cannot exist, on account of the immaturity of the infant. Also, animals have transitional objects. Even the thumb-sucking of earliest infancy cannot have the significance for the infant at birth that it can have for the infant of a few months, and certainly not the whole of the significance that compulsive thumb-sucking has for a psychotic child of ten years.

Deep is not synonymous with early, because an infant needs a degree of maturity before becoming gradually able to be deep. This is obvious, almost trite, yet I think it has not been given sufficient attention.

At this point it would be helpful if I could define the word 'deep'. James Strachey (1934), faced with this same problem, wrote:

The ambiguity of the term, ('deep' interpretation) however, need not bother us. It describes, no doubt, the interpretation of material which is either genetically early and historically distant from the patient's actual experience or which is under an especially heavy weight of repression—material, in any case, which is in the normal course of things exceedingly inaccessible to his ego and remote from it.

He seems to accept the words as synonymous.

On looking into the matter we see that 'deep' is a matter of variable usage and 'early' is a matter of fact; which makes a comparison of the two difficult and of temporary significance. It is deeper to refer to infant-mother relationships than to triangular relationships, to refer to internal persecutory anxiety than to refer to the sense of external persecution; splitting mechanisms, disintegration, an incapacity to make contact, seem to me to be deeper than is anxiety in a relationship.

I think that when we use the word 'deep' we always imply deep in the patient's unconscious fantasy or psychic reality; that is to say, the patient's mind and imagination are involved.

In the course of his 'Opening Remarks on Psychoanalytic Child Psychology' Kris (1951) remarked: 'By extrapolating from psychotic mechanism to early childhood . . .' He was examining critically the relationship between the depth of interpretation in analyses and the earliness of the applicability of psychotic mechanisms to infant psychology. In our analytic work, with the help of our developing concepts, we get deeper and deeper. We are able to see and to use transference phenomena that relate to deeper and deeper elements in the emotional development of our patients. To some extent 'deeper and deeper' does of course imply 'earlier and earlier', but only to a limited extent. We have to take into account the fact that in our analytic patients there has been a fusion of early with later elements.

We have become accustomed to formulating ideas about childhood through what we find in analysis. This came from the work of Freud himself. When applying Freud's work on the origin of psycho-neuroses to the psychology of the child at the toddler age we were not involved in much difficulty, although even here psycho-analysts were liable to say things which were true in analysis and yet untrue when applied in a crude way to the psychology of childhood.

As we use ideas that take us deeper we take much more of a risk when we apply what we find to the psychology of infancy. Let us consider the Klein concept that is referred to under the title 'the depressive position in emotional development'. It goes deeper, in one sense, and also earlier. Study of ego development would make us unable to accept so complex a matter as the depressive position in an infant younger than six months, and indeed it would be safer to give a later date. If we found references to the depressive position as something that might be found in infants of a few weeks, this would be absurd. What is called by Melanie Klein the 'paranoid position', however, is surely a much more crude thing, almost a matter of talion, and could be perhaps found before integration is a fact. History-taking in the paediatric clinic would indicate that the expectation of retaliation can date from the first days of life. I would therefore refer to the paranoid position as early rather than deep.

As for splitting mechanisms, are these a matter of early or of deep psychology? I suggest that it is important to know the answer because the answer would indicate the ego development and the part played by the mother. We can refer to what is deep as part of the infant, but when we refer to what is early we must take into account the ego-supportive environment that is an important feature at the early stages of extreme dependence.

Now, the direct observer of infants must be prepared to allow the analyst to formulate ideas about very early infancy, ideas which may be psychically true and yet which cannot be demonstrated; indeed it may be possible sometimes by direct observation to prove that what has been found in analysis could not in fact exist at the time claimed because of the limitations imposed by immaturity. What is found repeatedly in analysis is not annulled by being proved to be wrong through direct observation. Direct observation only proves that the patients have been antedating certain phenomena and therefore giving the analyst the impression that things were happening at an age when they could not have happened.

Certain concepts ring true from my point of view when I am doing analysis, and yet ring false when I am looking at infants in my clinic. Kris (1951) goes on to say: 'Observations . . . carried out in a large number of setups confirmed the view of those who stressed the importance of the child's concrete environment for its development.' There is a subtle way in which the concrete environment may be underrated by many analysts who do nevertheless carefully state that they know and allow for the environmental factor. It is very difficult to get at the bone of contention, yet in a discussion like this we must try to get to it. If deeper and deeper as formulated through analytic work meant earlier and earlier, then it would be necessary to assume that the immature infant of a few weeks could be aware of the environment. We know, however, that the infant is not aware of the environment as environment, especially when the environment is good or good-enough. The environment induces reactions indeed when it fails in some important respect, but what we call a good environment is something which is taken for granted. The infant in the early stages has no knowledge of the environment, knowledge, that is, which could be brought forward and presented as material in analysis. The conception of the environmental has to be added by the analyst.

When an analyst takes us deeper in the understanding of the material presented by the analytic patient, it is not enough for that analyst to state that the external factor is recognized as having its importance. If a formulation of a complete child psychology is being made, one that can be tested by direct observation, the analyst must imaginatively clothe the earliest material presented by the patient with the environment, the environment *that is implied* but which the patient cannot give in analysis because of never having been aware of it. I have illustrated this in my published case description in which the patient had the feeling of being curled up and revolving, in a moment of withdrawal, and I interpreted a medium which was implied but which could not be reported. There is no emotional or physical survival of an infant minus environment. To start with, minus environment the infant would fall infinitely. The infant who is held or who is lying in a cot is not aware of being preserved from infinitely falling. A slight failure of holding, however, brings to the infant a sensation of infinite falling. In analysis a patient may report a sense of falling, dating from earliest days, but can never report being held at this early stage of development.

Deeper and deeper takes us to the instinctual roots of the individual, but this gives no indication of ordinary dependence and dependence which has left no trace on the individual, although these characterize early life.

I would suggest that if this essential difference between depth and earliness be recognized it may be easier for direct observers and analysts to come to terms with each other. It will always be the direct observers who are telling the analysts that they have made too early an application of their theories. The analysts will continue to tell the direct observers that there is much more in human nature than can be observed directly. In a way there is no difficulty here except a series of interesting theoretical points for discussion. In practice, however, there are certain ways in which it is very important for us to know what is and what is not applicable to earliest infancy.

Psycho-analysis has much to learn from those who make direct observations of infants, and of mothers and infants together, and of small children in the environment in which they naturally live. Also direct observation is not able of itself to construct a psychology of early infancy. By constantly co-operating analysts and direct observers may be able to correlate what is deep in analysis with what is early in infant development.

In two words: a human infant must travel some distance from early in order to have the maturity to be deep.

CHILD ANALYSIS IN THE LATENCY PERIOD[1]

(1958)

The subject under discussion is the treatment of the latency child. I have been invited to refer to *psycho-analytic treatment*, and to balance this a colleague has been invited to refer to *individual psychotherapy*. I expect we both start off with the same problem: how to distinguish between the two? Personally I am not able to make this distinction. For me the question is: has the therapist had an analytic training or not?

Instead of contrasting our two subjects each with the other, we might more profitably contrast our two subjects with that of child psychiatry. In my practice I have treated thousands of children of this age group by child psychiatry. I have (as a trained analyst) given individual psychotherapy to some hundreds. Also I have had a certain number of children of this age group for psycho-analysis, more than twelve and less than twenty. The borders are so vague that I would be unable to be exact.

For me, therefore, this discussion should be one between colleagues who are doing the same work, but who are prepared for their work by various training schemes. We would not do well to argue here about the training schemes, though some of these (it will be admitted) are less adequate than others.

It does not surprise me when investigations show that psychotherapy and child analysis give very much the same appearance when written up, regardless of the school from which the therapist derives. If the therapist is suitable by temperament and is able to be objective and to become concerned with the need of the child then the therapy will become adapted to the needs of the case as these present themselves in the course of the treatment.

In this conference I believe we may leave out consideration of therapy based on the various attitudes that are at variance with our own, of which the following would be examples: educational, moralistic, persuasive, punitive, magical, physical.

I must repeat, in order to make it clear, that I feel that there

[1] Read at the 14th International Congress of Child Psychiatry, Lisbon, June 1958, and first published in *A Criança Portuguesa*, **17**, pp. 219–29.

need be no contrast between psycho-analysis and individual psychotherapy. The words can mean the same thing and often do.

As it is my job to speak as one trained in the school of psycho-analysis I must refer, though very briefly, to the nature of psycho-analysis. After this I shall proceed to the discussion of the treatment of the latency child.

The Nature of Psycho-Analysis

It is not thought to be necessary here to do more than to give a reminder of some main principles. Psycho-analysis of children is not different from that of adults. The basis of all psycho-analysis is a complex theory of the emotional development of the infant and child, a theory which Freud initiated and which is constantly being extended and enriched and emended.

The advances in the understanding of the emotional development of the individual have been so rapid in the past twenty or thirty years that it is difficult for the outsider to keep up with these changes through a study of the literature.

The theory assumes a genetic tendency in the individual towards emotional development as towards physical growth; it assumes a continuity from the time of birth (or just before) onwards; it assumes a gradual growth of ego-organization and strength, and the individual's gradual acceptance of the personal instinctual life, and of responsibility for its real and imagined consequences.

Freud established the importance of the repressed unconscious, and in his study of psycho-neurosis he arrived at a central point, undoubtedly the most difficult one in terms of general acceptance, that which he named the Oedipus complex, with castration anxiety as an inherent complication. Freud drew attention to the instinctual life of the individual human child and to the fact that it is in relation to the instinctual life along with the total fantasy of instinct that the main difficulties arise in healthy individuals, that is to say, children who have passed through the essential early stages of emotional development without too much distortion. Psycho-neurosis therefore can be stated as evidence of the strain of ambivalence in relationships between relatively normal 'whole' persons.

Gradually, as is well known, the study of the child led to a formulation of the stages of childhood and infancy development prior to the Oedipus complex, the pregenital roots of genitality. The ego eventually became subjected to study, and so, at last, analysts began to look at the self of the infant, the infant as a person, a person dependent on someone else.

Melanie Klein (among other things) enabled us to deal with a vitally important stage in the relationship between the child and the mother, that at which a capacity for concern is reached; she also drew attention to the mechanisms that characterize earliest infancy in which the object or the subject itself is split in such a way that ambivalence is avoided. Anna Freud helped to clarify ego defence mechanisms. The work of various (mainly) American analysts has taken us to the study not simply of the mechanisms that are characteristic of earliest infancy but to the young child, the child as a person dependent on child-care. I myself have played some part in the attempt to make a statement of the earliest phases in which the infant is merged in with the mother and (by a complex and precarious mechanism) emerges, and consequently must deal with the relationship to objects that are not part of the self.

All these developments make the study of psycho-analysis very exciting and highly significant for the student of mental disorder and its prevention.

Diagnosis

Psycho-analysis as a treatment cannot be described without reference to the diagnosis. The classical psycho-analytic setting is related to the diagnosis of psycho-neurosis, and it might be convenient to speak only of psycho-neurosis. Here indeed is a big enough subject for many conferences, but what is expected today is a comprehensive statement in a few words of psycho-analysis, whatever the diagnosis, including the normal. It must be emphasized, though the theme cannot be developed in this setting, that in the technique of psycho-analysis there are very big differences according to whether the child is neurotic or psychotic or anti-social.

It should be added, for completeness, that the difference between the child and the adult is that the child often plays rather than talks. This difference, however, is almost without significance, and indeed some adults draw or play.

The Transference

It is characteristic of psycho-analysis that the analyst does not waste the valuable material that comes up for analysis in terms of the emotional relationship between patient and analyst. Here in the unconscious transference appear samples of the personal pattern of the patient's emotional life, or psychic reality. The analyst learns to detect these unconscious transference phenomena and, by using the clues supplied by the patient, is able to interpret that which is just ready for conscious acceptance at any one session. The most fruitful work is that which is done in terms of transference.

Our discussion here could usefully aim at describing the transference as it appears characteristically in the latency period.

Psycho-Analytic Technique Adapted to the Latency Child

It is now necessary to consider the peculiarities of psychoanalysis when this form of treatment is adapted to the age group under discussion. It is generally conceded that the most rewarding age group for the analyst, especially for the beginner, is the first group, in which the child is two, three or four years old. After the passing of the Oedipus complex, there develop tremendous defences.

Nature of Latency

It is not yet certain what constitutes the latency period. Biologically it would seem necessary to assume that in these few years, 6-10, the development of instinct ceases, so that for the time being the child is left with an instinctual life based on what has been built up in the earlier period. Changes will begin to occur again at puberty, and then again the child will be needing to organize against an altering state of affairs; to be on the alert against new anxieties and to have the excitement of enjoying new experiences and new satisfactions, and new degrees of satisfaction.

Whatever else may be said about the latency period it seems fairly clear that there are big defences organized and maintained. Here we find agreement between the two main writers on this subject, Melanie Klein and Anna Freud. In her chapter on the latency period in *The Psycho-Analysis of Children* (1932) Melanie Klein starts by referring to the special difficulties of the latency period. 'Unlike the small child', she says, 'whose lively imagination and acute anxiety enable us to gain an easier insight into its unconscious and make contact there, they (latency children) have a very limited imaginative life, in accordance with the strong tendency to repression which is characteristic of their age: while, in comparison with the grown-up person, their ego is still undeveloped and they neither understand that they are ill nor want to be cured, so that they have no incentive to start analysis and no encouragement to go on with it.'

Anna Freud's book, *The Psycho-Analytical Treatment of Children*

(1946) is concerned in the first chapter with the discussion of an introductory phase which is necessary in the analysis of children. From the examples given it can be seen that Miss Freud is referring chiefly to children of the latency period, although not entirely so.

If one reads these two books, each of which is full of infinite richness and indicates vast clinical experience which we can well envy, one can either see similarities or differences. Similarities certainly there are and they concern this matter of the altered technique which is necessary for the latency child. What is not made clear is that many of the differences concern diagnosis.

In regard to other differences, and it is these that we wish to study, we can note immediately that Melanie Klein finds it good to interpret the unconscious conflicts and the transference phenomena as they arise, and to form a relationship with the child on the relief given by such interpretations; by contrast Miss Freud tends to build up a relationship with the child on a conscious level and she describes how she gets gradually to the work of the analysis with the conscious co-operation of the patient. The difference is largely a matter of *conscious or unconscious co-operation*.

It would seem to me to be possible to exaggerate the differences here, although they may be real enough in certain instances. In my opinion, the sooner the analyst interprets the unconscious the better, because this orientates the child towards analytic treatment, and the first relief undoubtedly gives the first indications to the child that there is something to be got out of analysis. On the other hand, it is possible to lose latency patients in the initial stages through not gaining their conscious co-operation. We may hand over to the parents the introduction of the child to an intellectual understanding of the need for treatment, and in this way may escape responsibility for the introductory phase in the child's analysis. But it makes a great deal of difference how the parents or the guardians of a child give an idea to the child of what is to be expected from this daily treatment session. Miss Freud deliberately takes over the burden of explaining to the child what is happening, and Mrs Klein leaves this to those who are bringing the child, hoping to be able to do without explanations on a conscious level by getting quickly to the unconscious co-operation, that is, co-operation that is based on the work of the analysis.

It is necessary for us to deal with the situation as we find it in each case that we treat. With very intelligent children we need to be able to talk to their intelligence, to feed their intelligence. It is sometimes a complication when we are doing work with a child and the child feels that something is going on, and yet has no intellectual understanding of what it is all about. In any case it would seem to be a pity to waste the intellectual understanding of the child, which can be a very powerful ally, although of course in certain cases the intellectual processes may be used in defence, making the analysis more difficult.

To some extent at this point we are again talking about diagnosis. Where there is anxiety of psychotic intensity, there is a great need for help and help must be given immediately, and yet even so the intellect can be met. I am thinking at the moment of a boy of ten. As I came into the room when I first met him he was saying to his mother: 'But you don't understand, it's not the nightmare I'm frightened of; the trouble is that *I'm having a nightmare while I'm awake.*' In these words he was giving a true description of his illness and I was able to start at this point, working both with his very fine intellect and also giving interpretations at all levels, including the deepest.

In trying to sort out the various opinions which are expressed and which I personally feel, I find myself wishing to quote Berta Bornstein, from her paper 'On Latency' (1951). She starts: 'From the standpoint of the intellectual ability of the child in latency, we could expect the child to associate freely. The factors responsible for the child's failure to do so create a general limitation of child analysis. There are several reasons for his inability to associate. In addition to those well known to us, I will mention only one which has not been stressed yet: *Free association is experienced by the child as a particular threat to his ego organization*' (my italics).

I find this way of looking at the latency period very helpful. I have no time here to refer to Berta Bornstein's division of the latency period into phases. In a general way, however, it seems to be important that we should realize when we are treating children of this age that they have achieved a sanity and they have left the primary process. Their ego achievement must not be broken into. This same chapter ends with the following words: 'The utmost care has to be exercised in the analysis of latency to strengthen weak structures and to modify those which interfere with normal development. The selection of material for interpretation and the form of interpretation itself must be geared to these ends.' For this reason we co-operate with the child in all sorts of activities while gathering material for the mutative interpretation.

Berta Bornstein also refers to Freud's (1905a) 'ideal of latency', that is to say, the successful warding off of instinctual demands.

I am thinking of an exercise book that I have in my possession. Each page of this book represents very constructive work done by a girl in the latency period. Hers is one of those difficult cases in which one can say that almost her only symptom was bed-wetting. Behind this lay a character disorder that was only too successfully dove-tailed in with the mother's own homosexual repression. The characteristic of this exercise book as one looks at it is that it is mainly composed of very well-constructed pictures done with coloured chalks. The analysis was extremely boring for me. The girl seemed to blot me out. Of the fifty or so pictures only two or three in the middle lose the characteristic of organized defence. These two or three show every kind of breakdown, a mess and a muddle, disintegration; and, in one of them, a breast-like object is cut out with scissors and left separate lying between the leaves. Here is oral sadism and also incontinence and a fantasy of incontinence. If this child had been three years old it would have been much easier to have got at the *child* incontinent or disintegrated; but because she was in the latency group I had to be contented with reaching to an *illustration* of her hidden madness. Whereas a small child is often 'mad' and yet healthy, because naturally controlled by those in care, a latency child who is 'mad' is very seriously ill, and needs nursing.

My contribution here is a development of the accepted theme of the latency period as the period in which the ego comes into its own, so to speak. In health the latency child is not compelled to bow to id-demands, though id-drives maintain force and appear in all manner of indirect forms.

Of all that could be said I choose to say here that in the latency period:

(1) The child is in one sense alone, though needing to be with others who are similarly placed. Relationships between healthy latency children can be intimate over long periods, without becoming sexualized in a manifest sense. The sexual symbolism holds. The manifest sexual elements of deprived children disturb play and ego-relatedness.

(2) The latency child is ready for introjecting, but not for incorporating—ready to take in whole elements from chosen persons but not ready to eat or be eaten, or to merge in an intimate relationship involving instinct.

(3) The latency child is a specialist in the display of inner phenomena without becoming directly involved in the full life. Persistence of the latency phase may show in an adult's capacity for ego achievement at the expense of id-freedom.

(4) Sanity is essential in the latency phase, and the child in this

phase who cannot maintain sanity is clinically very ill. The ego-organization carries the drive which both earlier and later is partly carried by id-impulse.

Time to Interpret

I think that it is the earliest possible moment that is the right moment for an interpretation, that is to say *the earliest moment at which the material makes it clear what to interpret.* But I am economical in my interpretations, and if I am not sure what to interpret I have no hesitation in playing for time. In playing for time I find myself involved in an introductory or preparatory phase, playing, constructing with the child, or just being blotted out, wasted. I would be concerned, however, with only one thing, the search for the clue which makes possible the interpretation that is the appropriate one at the moment, the interpretation that brings about a shift of emphasis in the unconscious transference.

Perhaps a statement such as this one could meet with general acceptance. Some analysts are more quick than others to pick up the clue, and there is room for the quick and the slow in this work. What matters to the patient is not the accuracy of the interpretation so much as the willingness of the analyst to help, the analyst's capacity to identify with the patient and so to believe in what is needed and to meet the need as soon as the need is indicated verbally or in non-verbal or pre-verbal language.

The End of the Treatment

Finally I will ask you to consider the ending of analysis. Of course it is always necessary to think in terms of the individual case and the diagnosis, but there is something of general significance that can be said. In the analysis of small children the analyst is considerably helped by the tremendous changes that take place naturally in the child of five, six, or seven years of age. At the time when the early analysis is ending these growths are taking place, facilitated no doubt by the success of the analysis. Any improvement due to analysis is in this way *exaggerated* by the natural course of events. Especially in regard to the socialization of the child it is often easy for those who are in charge of the child to be pleased with the result, because the child loses the wildness and changeability of the pre-latency era and becomes more happy in groups. By contrast the *latency analysis tends to end at a very awkward time.*

It would be interesting to hear this matter discussed. Typically the analysis is ending when the child is eleven or twelve and the complications of pre-puberty and of puberty itself are appearing.

It is perhaps advisable to plan analyses so that they either end before the onset of puberty or else in such a way that they may continue right on through the first years of the new developments. It may be that some analysts, in following the latter course, see their patients at relatively infrequent intervals, keeping in touch with them, and expecting to be needed five times a week over certain periods of time during the puberty era. Apart from the actual changes of puberty, there may so easily be incidents, traumatic friendships, grand passions, seductions, masturbation anxieties, which lead to exacerbations of defences or to frank anxiety.

The question arises: what place is there for the analysis confined to the latency age, for instance, from six to ten? How far during this period of relative calm in the instinctual world can the analyst claim to know the child? How far can the analyst deduce from what happens in such an analysis what the child was like at three or predict what the child will be like at thirteen? I am not sure of the answers to these questions but I know that I personally have been deceived, sometimes making a prognosis too favourable and sometimes not favourable enough. It is probably more easy to know what to do when the child is ill because then the obvious illness dominates the scene and treatment is not considered to be finished while the child's illness remains. When the child is relatively well then it is not lightly that anyone will put his or her latency child in analysis.

One analyst cannot have enough cases to cover all contingencies, and it is therefore necessary for us to pool experiences, not being afraid to make suggestions which turn out to be stupid when examined by a group. Each analyst builds up a highly specialized experience, rich indeed, but needing to be related to the experiences of colleagues doing the same work, but with other children.

CLASSIFICATION:
IS THERE A PSYCHO-ANALYTIC CONTRIBUTION TO PSYCHIATRIC CLASSIFICATION?[1]
(1959–1964)

This chapter is intended as a preliminary contribution calling attention to the importance of the subject, given in the hope that it will lead to a discussion in which analysts with various types of experience will take part.

Before making my own specific contribution, in which I indicate why I do believe that psycho-analysis has a contribution to make to classification, I must attempt an historical sketch. This sketch will be inadequate and perhaps inaccurate, but if I omit this task I have no background against which to give my opinion as to the profound effect that recent psycho-analytic developments have had on our attitude to psychiatric classification. The recent developments that I refer to are the concept of the false self, the linking of psychopathy with deprivation, and the understanding that psychosis takes origin at a stage at which the immature human being is truly dependent on environmental provision. These three ideas have been chosen because they have interested me personally.

Historical

In the early days of psycho-analysis Freud concerned himself with three aspects of psychiatric illness. One was behaviour, the patient's relation to reality. The second was symptom-formation, which Freud established as a *communication*, this concept being part of his new understanding of the unconscious. The third was aetiology, which Freud transformed by introducing the idea of the developmental process. Freud studied the development of the instinctual life and this involved him in the theory of childhood sexuality, which eventually led to the theory of the pregenital instinctual life of the human infant and to the concept of the fixation points. The aetiology of psychiatric disorder now demanded of the clinician an interest in history-taking. In this way the

[1] Read at Scientific Meeting of the British Psycho-Analytical Society, 18 March 1959.

psycho-analysts became pioneers in psychiatric history-taking, and it is they who have recognized that the most important part of history-taking derives from the material arrived at in the course of psycho-therapy.

In a classification based on those areas of interest which Freud covered in the early years of his work the patients were either psychotic or hysterical. I should say in passing that Freud was always interested in the constitutional factors.

At the beginning of the second decade of the century Freud began to develop his structural view of the personality. The ego, the id, and the censor were concepts which led to a clearer study of intrapsychic conflict, and intrapsychic equilibrium was taken as evidence of successful defence. The quality as well as the quantity of the processes in the ego became significant. The concept of the superego eventually became formulated and was at first thought to be a result of massive introjections and identifications, dating from the two- to five-year-old period, and from the time of the full-blown Oedipus complex. The story of pregenital instinctual development led to an elaboration of the idea of regression to fixation points. Fixation points were points of origin of illness-types. They indicated that anxiety (being intolerable) had involved the individual in the organization of defences of pathological degree or kind with the result that further progress in instinctual development was hampered. Classification became related to these fixation points, as well as to the ego mechanisms of defence, which were eventually to become stated exhaustively in psycho-analytic terms by Anna Freud (1936). At the centre of all this is castration anxiety and the Oedipus complex. The disorders are the psycho-neuroses.

Already Freud had introduced the idea of dependence (anaclitic object-love) (Freud, 1914) and the matter of ego-weakness and -strength became significant in psycho-analytic metapsychology. In this way a language was found for the description of the borderline case and of character disorders. Narcissistic elements in the patient were all the time considered to be indications of an ego disorder making psycho-analysis unlikely to be effective because of the weakening of the capacity of the patient for the development of a transference neurosis (Freud, 1937).

Gradually and in the course of time the study of psychosis began to make more sense. Ferenczi (1931) contributed significantly by looking at a failed analysis of a patient with character disorder not simply as a failure of selection but as a deficiency of psycho-analytic technique. The idea implied here was that psycho-analysis could learn to adapt its technique to the character disorder or the borderline case without turning over into management, and indeed without losing the label psycho-analysis. Eventually Melanie Klein (1932, 1948) made her specific contributions showing that in the analysis of children psychotic disorders must be encountered, and that these could be dealt with if met by adequate technique, so that failure to deal with psychotic manifestations in childhood meant for her (as for Ferenczi) a failure of technique, not a failure of selection.

Then the concept of the setting of the analysis began to widen. Already Aichhorn (1925) had shown that special technical adaptations must be made when the patient is an antisocial case. At first Aichhorn's work may have given some alarm because he was acting in a way which would be 'bad analysis' in the treat-ment of a case of hysteria or a case of obsessional neurosis It is now possible to see that Aichhorn was a pioneer and initiated a genuine movement towards an adaptation of the psycho-analytic technique to meet the needs of the psychopath or of the deprived child with an antisocial tendency.

All these developments tended to make the early history of each case more and more important. Just here a dichotomy seemed to arise in psycho-analytic circles. I would say that Melanie Klein represents the most vigorous attempt to study the earliest processes of the developing human infant *apart from the study of child-care*. She has always admitted that child-care is im-portant but has not made a special study of it. On the other hand there have been those who developed an interest in the child-care and infant-care techniques. Those who did this always ran the risk of being considered traitors to the cause of the internal pro-cesses. The work of Miss Freud and Mrs Burlingham in the Hampstead War Nursery (Burlingham and Freud, 1944) led to a development of the study of external conditions and their effect. It is clear that this dichotomy between those who almost confine their researches to a study of the internal processes and those who are interested in infant-care is a temporary dichotomy in psycho-analytic discussion, one which will eventually dis-appear by natural processes (cf. Hartmann, 1939; James, 1962; Kris, 1950).

Now we see the ego of the infant as something dependent at first on ego-support, something which derives structure and strength from a highly complex and subtle system of adaptation to need, this adaptation being supplied by the mother or mother-figure. Also we see the interesting process of the absorption into the individual child of the child-care elements, those which could be called 'supporting ego' elements. The relationship between this absorption of the environment and the introjection processes with which we are already familiar provides great interest. Along with all this goes a study of the mechanisms by which the infant emerges from a state of being merged in with the mother, a process that demands of the mother a capacity to hate as well as to love. In the theory of the emotional development of the child the gradual establishment of the individual as a separate person becomes a matter of central importance, and these matters belong to present-day research. Classification must be affected by these theoretical formulations.

As a result of these new developments narcissism in the clinical condition is seen in a new light. It is as if in looking at narcissistic illness the clinician is liable to be caught up with the absorbed, or internalized, environment, and to mistake this (unless well prepared) for the real individual, who in fact is hidden and is secretly loved and cared for by the self within the self. It is the true individual that is hidden.

These developments lead to a reconsideration of other concepts. The concept of the death instinct seems to disappear simply through being unnecessary. Aggression is seen more as evidence of life. Under favourable conditions, fusion occurs between the erotic and the motility impulses, and then the term oral sadism becomes applicable, followed by all the developments of this theme. This is matched by the mother's wish to be imaginatively eaten. Failure of fusion, or loss of fusion that has been achieved, produces a potential element of pure destructiveness (i.e. without guilt-sense) in the individual, but even this destructiveness remains a lifeline in the sense of its being the basis of object relationships that feel real to the patient.

Fusion of the two roots of instinctual impulses (aggressive and erotic) belongs to a stage in infant development in which there is very great dependence. There is no possibility whatever that an infant whose environment is insufficiently adapted to the needs of an infant near the beginning may reach to a state of fusion of the aggressiveness (which makes object relationships feel real, and makes objects external to the self) and of the erotic desires (which carry a capacity for libidinal satisfaction).

Furthermore, the concept of regression has changed its meaning in psycho-analytic metapsychology. For many years the term carried with it an implication of a return to earlier phases of the instinctual life, and regression was to a fixation point. This belongs to the view of primitive instinctual elements in the individual, with child-care taken for granted. In the study of the *actual* infant it is no longer possible to avoid taking into account the environment, so that in speaking of an actual infant one must mention dependence and the nature of the environment. The term regression therefore has now a clinical application in *regression to dependence*. It is a tendency towards a re-establishment of dependence and therefore the behaviour of the environment becomes something that cannot be ignored if the word regression is used. The term regression continues to contain the idea of regression to primary process. The tendency to regression in a patient is now seen as part of the capacity of the individual to bring about self-cure. It gives an indication from the patient to the analyst as to how the analyst should behave rather than how he should interpret. Associated with this subject is the clinical fact of self-cure through a process of regression which is very commonly met with outside psycho-analytic treatment.

Psychosis is no longer to be ascribed to a reaction to anxiety associated with the Oedipus complex, or as a regression to a fixation point, or to be linked specifically with a position in the process of the individual's instinctual development. Instead it could be postulated that the regressive tendency in a psychotic case is part of the ill individual's *communication*, which the analyst can understand in the same way that he understands the hysterical symptom as a communication. The regression represents the psychotic individual's hope that certain aspects of the environment which failed originally may be relived, with the environment this time succeeding instead of failing in its function of facilitating the inherited tendency in the individual to develop and to mature.

In the course of the vast expansion of theory which I have sketched here there came a development which enabled the clinician to begin to be able to relate mood disorder to the general scheme of psycho-analytic metapsychology. Early formulations had made possible a statement of health in negative terms, as an absence of rigid defence or as an absence of fixations, and in positive terms as a matter of ego-strength. There now appeared something which made it possible for the first time in psycho-analytic metapsychology to speak of *value* in the personality. This came through Freud's development of an idea of Abraham's in 'Mourning and Melancholia', and the elaboration of this theme by Klein. Now the affective disorders began to fall into place, and the way was prepared for a statement of the relationship between depression and concern. Here Melanie Klein made her most significant contribution, enriching our ideas of the superego, and introducing the idea of primitive superego elements derived from the instinctual life of the infant. Such superego elements take origin prior to the phase of the full-blown Oedipus complex, or the ambivalencies associated with the inter-relationships between three 'whole' personalities.

This is not the place for a restatement of the very considerable metapsychological developments that follow from this work of Melanie Klein. This work relates the contending forces that operate within the self to the instinctual life, and relates the pat-terns of defences that organize within the self to mood. There follows a vast extension of the understanding of the representa-tions of an individual's inner psychic reality in his or her mental life.

Melanie Klein's work has altered psychiatric classification by separating out two kinds of depression the one from the other. One kind represents an achievement in emotional development almost synonymous with the acquisition of a capacity to be re-sponsible, or a capacity to feel a sense of guilt, and the other (with depersonalization and other features that could be referred to as 'schizoid') represents a failure initiated at an early stage, before the establishment of what Melanie Klein calls the 'depres-sive position' in emotional development.

From this work one naturally turns to hypomania as a clinical expression of the manic defence, a denial of depression that is a fact; and also to the manic-depressive swing, which implies a dis-sociation, a dissociation in the patient between control of unfused aggression and of introjected omnipotent elements, and pos-session by these elements.

On the basis of this statement it is possible to glance at the large subject of classification today.

Psycho-Neurosis and Psychosis

It is probably a matter of general agreement among analysts that there is value in the use of the two words *psycho-neurosis and psychosis*.[1] Here is a simple classification of all mental disorders.

I am, of course, referring to disorders of emotional develop-ment and not to such illnesses as primary mental defect, post-encephalitis states, arteriosclerotic brain, G.P.I., etc., etc. Where there is disease or disorder of the brain itself there is naturally a secondary disorder of the personality, but this complication need not be included in this preliminary contribution. It is the psycho-analysts who have put forward and developed the psycho-genic theory of the psycho-neuroses and the psychoses; or perhaps one should say psycho-analysts have retained some of the view of

[1] I deliberately leave out 'actual neurosis' in this context.

mental disorder which was prevalent before the more mechanistic view which reached the climax half a century ago and which still dominates non-analytic psychiatry generally.

The term psycho-neurosis implies to analysts that the patient as an infant and child reached to a certain stage of emotional development and that, genital primacy and the stage of the Oedipus complex having been achieved, certain defences against castration anxiety have become organized. These defences constitute psycho-neurotic illness, and the degree of illness is reflected in the degree of rigidity of the defence. This is of course a gross over-simplification, but psycho-analysts have found that castration anxiety is central in psycho-neurotic illness, although it is recognized that the pattern of the illness is variable according to the pregenital experiences of the individual. Where annihilation anxiety, not castration anxiety, is found as an important feature, then on the whole the psycho-analyst will consider that the patient's diagnosis is not psycho-neurosis but psychosis. It is to some extent a matter of whether the threat is in terms of part object or whole object.

The various types of psycho-neurotic illness are best grouped around the types of defence, the central being repression. I shall not enumerate these. Psycho-analysis as we teach it is primarily based on the treatment of psycho-neurosis and we attempt to choose cases for our students which are suitable for this kind of teaching although we recognize that with the best possible selection some cases will have disturbances that go deeper (i.e. notably depression appears either in the quality of the anxiety or as a mood disorder).

The psychology of psycho-neurosis leads the student immediately to the repressed unconscious and to the instinctual life of the individual. The instinctual life has to be considered both in terms of the bodily functions and of the imaginative elaboration of these functions. (By instinctual one means what Freud called sexual, i.e. the whole range of local and general excitements which are a feature of animal life; in the experience of these there is a period of preparation, an act with climax, an aftermath.)

Further treatment of this theme would lead to a repetition of a large part of classical Freudian theory. In using the term psycho-neurosis there is an implication that the individual's personality is intact, or, in terms of development, that the personality has been constructed and is being maintained and that a capacity for relationships to objects is intact. (Also it is implied that the individual's character is not markedly distorted by resentment or by more organized psychopathic trends.)

Leaving out mood disorder, for the moment, I now refer to psychosis[1] in order to reach to the points of contrast.

The term *psychosis* is used to imply either that as an infant the individual was not able to reach to the degree of personal health which makes sense of the concept of the Oedipus complex, or alternatively that the organization of the personality had weaknesses which became revealed when the maximal strain of the Oedipus complex had to be borne. It will be seen that there is a very thin line between this second type of psychosis and psycho-neurosis. In the extreme of the first type of psychosis there is but little resemblance to psycho-neurosis, since no significant Oedipus stage has ever been reached, and castration anxiety was never a major threat to an intact personality.

In some cases of clinical psychosis what we see represents a *breakdown of defences*; new defences may come to be set up of a yet more primitive kind but the clinical picture is dominated by a breakdown in defences, at any rate temporarily; this is what is ordinarily meant by mental breakdown; defences have become unsatisfactory, and the patient has to be nursed while new defences are being organized.[2] In the organization of defences the individual is affected by all manner of environmental factors, and also hereditary tendencies may sometimes have specific importance. Behind all mental breakdown is theoretically a state of chaos but complete breakdown must be rare clinically, even if it is possible, as it would indicate an irreversible change away from personal growth towards fragmentation.

Just as a study of *psycho-neurosis* leads the student to the Oedipus complex and to the triangular situations that reach their height in the child at the toddler age and again in adolescence, so the study of psychosis leads the research worker to the earliest stages of infant life. This implies the infant-mother relationship since no infant can develop outside such a relationship. (It involves the idea of dependence prior to the establishment of the operation of the mechanisms of projection and introjection.)

[1] I realize that the word 'psychosis' presents all manner of difficulties. In a way I am claiming a meaning for the word at a time when there are many who would like to see the word dropped. I suggest, however, that there is still a use for this term to cover emotional disorder that is not included in the terms psycho-neurosis or neurotic depression. I am aware that in psychiatry the term psychosis is used to describe various syndromes which have a physical basis. Here is another source of confusion. I cannot see, however, that anything can be gained from inventing a new word.

[2] See a later note on the subject of mental breakdown, given at the end of this chapter.

General Comment

Probably the most important contribution from psycho-analysis to psychiatry and to psychiatric classification is the destruction of the old idea of disease entities. Here the psycho-analyst is right at the other end of the pole from the kind of psychiatrist who thinks that there is a disease, schizophrenia, and another disease, manic-depressive psychosis, and so on (cf. Menninger *et al.*, 1963).

The psycho-analyst, as I have already said, can be looked upon as a specialist in history-taking. It is true that this history-taking is a very involved process. A psycho-analytic case description is a series of case histories, a presentation of different versions of the same case, the versions being arranged in layers each of which represents a stage of revelation. The analyst gets a view of mental disorder which is very different from that of the psychiatrist who makes a very careful examination of a patient at a certain moment in the history of the case, as for instance when there has been a breakdown or when hospitalization has occurred.

It is possible to trace a disorder in a patient from childhood through adolescence and through early and late adult life, and to see the way in which there has been a transmutation all along the line from one type of disorder to another. In this way it is impossible for the analyst to retain any idea he may have had from his formal psychiatric training that there are definite psychiatric diseases. In fact it becomes evident to the analyst in the course of his analytic work that in so far as psychiatry concerns diagnosis it is making a tremendous attempt to do the impossible, since a patient's diagnosis not only becomes clearer as analysis proceeds but also the diagnosis alters. An hysteric may reveal underlying schizophrenia, a schizoid person may turn out to be the healthy member of an ill family grouping, an obsessional may turn out to be a depressive.

Practising psycho-analysts would agree that there is a gradation from normality not only into psycho-neurosis but also into psychosis, and the close connexion between depression and normality has already been stressed. It may be true that there is a closer link between normality and psychosis than between normality and psycho-neurosis; that is to say, in certain respects. For instance, the artist has an ability and the courage to be in touch with primitive processes which the psycho-neurotic cannot bear to reach, and which healthy people may miss to their own impoverishment.

I can now come to the positive suggestions which I wish to make for discussion at this preliminary stage. Let it be understood that I recognize the immense value of classical psychiatric classifications.

My concern is with the effect on classification of some of the newer ideas (or perhaps these are old ideas given new emphasis, or wrapped up in new language?). I shall choose matters which I personally have studied and have tried to elucidate in various papers. The same ideas have been introduced independently into the literature by other analysts, but it would confuse the issue if I were to attempt to quote, or to compare the various terms used by these other writers with those used by myself.

I give special consideration to:

(i) The idea of the true and the false self.

(ii) The idea of delinquency and psychopathy as derivations of perceived, actual emotional deprivation.

(iii) The idea of psychosis as related to emotional privation at a stage before the individual could perceive a deprivation.

(i) *False Self*

The concept of the false self (as I call it) is not a difficult one. The false self is built up on a basis of compliance. It can have a defensive function, which is the protection of the true self.

A principle governing human life could be formulated in the following words: only the true self can feel real, but the true self must never be affected by external reality, must never comply. When the false self becomes exploited and treated as real there is a growing sense in the individual of futility and despair. Naturally in individual life there are all degrees of this state of affairs so that commonly the true self is protected but has some life and the false self is the social attitude. At the extreme of abnormality the false self can easily get itself mistaken for real, so that the real self is under threat of annihilation; suicide can then be a reassertion of the true self.

Only the true self can be analysed. Psycho-analysis of the false self, analysis that is directed at what amounts to no more than an internalized environment, can only lead to disappointment. There may be an apparent early success. It is being recognized in the last few years that in order to communicate with the true self where a false self has been given pathological importance it is necessary for the analyst first of all to provide conditions which will allow the patient to hand over to the analyst the burden of the internalized environment, and so to become a highly dependent but a real, immature, infant; then, and then only, the analyst may analyse the true self. This could be a present-day statement of Freud's *anaclitic dependence* in which the instinctual drive leans on the self-preservative. Dependence of the schizoid patient or of the borderline case on the analyst is very much a reality, so much so that many analysts prefer to avoid the burden and they select cases carefully. In selecting cases for analysis analysts must therefore take into account the common existence of a false self. Selection requires in the clinician an ability to detect the false-self defence, and when this is detected the clinician must then decide whether this is likely to be a positive help in the analysis, or whether in a particular case it is pathologically powerful and indicates so severe an initial handicap in emotional development that psycho-analysis had better be left out of consideration.

I suggest that 'false self' is a valuable classificatory label, one that almost absolves us from further diagnostic effort. It is in this type of case, not uncommon, that psycho-analysis can be dangerous, that is if the analyst is taken in. The defence is massive and may carry with it considerable social success. The indication for analysis is that the patient asks for help because of feeling unreal or futile in spite of the apparent success of the defence.

A special case of the false self is that in which the intellectual process becomes the seat of the false self. A dissociation between mind and psyche-soma develops, which produces a well-recognized clinical picture. In many of these cases there is probably an especially high intellectual endowment, and this may contribute to the building up of the syndrome although the high I.Q. on test may result from the dissociation.

(ii) *Psychopathy*

First, I must try to define the word psychopathy. I am using the term here (and I believe I am justified in doing so) to describe an adult condition which is an uncured delinquency. A delinquent is an uncured antisocial boy or girl. An antisocial boy or girl is a deprived child. A deprived child is one who had something good-enough, and then no longer had this, whatever it was, and there was sufficient growth and organization of the individual *at the time of the deprivation* for the deprivation to be perceived as traumatic. In other words, in the psychopath and the delinquent and the antisocial child there is logic in the implied attitude 'the environment owes me something'. I personally believe that in every case of antisocial organization there was a point at which a change occurred, with the individual able to appreciate the fact. This appreciation of course is not usually conscious, but the point of deprivation may be remembered, unless it has become lost among innumerable successive deprivations.

The main thesis here is that the maladjustment and all the derivatives of this type of disorder consist essentially in an original maladjustment of the environment to the child, the maladjustment not having occurred early enough to produce psychosis. The accent is on environmental failure and the pathology is therefore primarily in the environment and only secondarily in the child's reaction. The classification of delinquents and psychopaths ought logically to be in terms of the classification of environmental failure. It is for this reason that there is a confusion immediately if an attempt is made to bring psychopathy and recidivism and the antisocial tendency into line with other labels such as neurosis and psychosis.

This argument leads to:

(iii) *The Question of Psychosis and Classification*

If it be true that the disorders which come under the wide heading of psychosis (and which comprise the various types of schizophrenia) are produced by environmental deficiency at a stage of maximal or double dependence, then the classification has to be adapted in order to meet this idea. Such a development would certainly have surprised psycho-analysts of thirty years ago, most of whom, in considering psychosis, would have started off with an assumption that very primitive mechanisms were aetiologically significant in such illness. Today, I suggest, we are coming round to the view that in psychosis it is very primitive *defences* that are brought into play and organized, *because of environmental abnormalities*. We can of course see the very primitive mechanisms at work in psychotics as also in our 'normal' patients, and indeed in all people. We cannot diagnose psychotic illness by finding primitive mental mechanisms. Of course, in psychotic illness it is the primitive defences that we meet with, defences which do not have to be organized if in the earliest stages of near-absolute dependence the good-enough environmental provision does in fact exist. Justice can be done to all the factors by the statement that the individual's maturational processes (including all that is inherited) require a facilitating environment, especially in the very early stages. Failure of the facilitating environment results in developmental faults in the individual's personality development and in the establishment of the individual's self, and the result is called schizophrenia. Schizophrenic breakdown is the reversal of the maturational processes of earliest infancy.

I am suggesting that in a study of psychosis the attempt must be made to classify the environment and the types of environmental abnormality, and the point in the development of the individual at which these abnormalities operate, and that to attempt to classify sick individuals on the basis of the clinical pictures that they present leads to no useful result. I repeat: the environmental deficiencies which produce psychosis belong to the stage prior to that at which the developing individual has the equipment to be aware of either the environmental provision or its failure (cf. the antisocial tendency). It will be seen that in attempting to date the onset of psychosis I am therefore referring to the degree of the individual's dependence and not to the individual's pregenital instinctual life, nor to the stage of the infant's erotogenic zone primacy.

The argument has been developed here on the basis of extremes. In our clinical work we meet mostly with patients who are to some extent or under certain conditions healthy, but who can be ill, so that it can be said that they bring their illness to us for treatment as a mother might bring a sick child.

Inherent Conflict

Let us now look at the internal factors, those which concern us as analysts. Apart from the study of healthy persons, it is perhaps only in *psycho-neurosis* and *reactive depression* that one may get near to the truly *internal* illness, the illness that belongs to intolerable *conflict* which is inherent in life and in living as whole persons. It might be a definition of relative psychiatric health that in the healthy one can genuinely carry the difficulties that the individual encounters back to the inherent struggle of individual life, the (unconscious) attempt of the ego to manage the id and to use id-impulse in the fullest possible way in relationship with reality. It is important for me to make this clear because some may feel that in putting forward a method of classifying which includes a classification of environment I am leaving aside all that psychoanalysis has gained in the study of the individual.

Without attempting to review the literature I wish to refer to the writings of two of my teachers, Rickman and Glover. Rickman's 1928 lectures had a big influence on the development of my thought but I am not aware that Rickman dealt with the importance of dependence.

In Edward Glover's *On the Early Development of Mind* (1956) there are many references to classification. I think there are only two references in this book to the environment of the kind that I am developing into a main theme. On page 174 there is the sentence: 'An instinct that requires a true external object, such as the mother's nipple, is unmasterable unless with the collusion of the real object.' This is from a 1932 lecture, entitled 'A Psycho-Analytic Approach to the Classification of Mental Disorders'. The other reference comes in his 1949 statement in the *British Medical Bulletin* on 'The Position of Psycho-Analysis in Great Britain' (Glover, 1949). After painting rather a gloomy picture of the state of affairs in the British Society he puts forward the following comment: 'But when all is said, the present is an interesting phase in the history of psycho-analysis. However absurd some of the hypotheses recently advanced may have been, there is no doubt that the focusing of interest on problems of early ego-development and on the organization of mind during the phase of "primary identification" (i.e. at the stage before the "self" and the "not-self" are accurately differentiated), will in the long run produce results of value both diagnostically and therapeutically.'

I wish also to refer to Ackerman (1953), who however does not seem to concern himself with the special feature of dependence at a very early date.

Classification According to Environmental Distortion

I think it might be valuable to classify according to the degree and quality of the environmental distortion, or deficiency, that which can be recognized as aetiologically significant. It is necessary to look at this point of view, even if only to reject it.

In the case of any individual at the start of the process of emotional development there are three things: At one extreme there is heredity; at the other extreme there is the environment which supports or fails and traumatizes; and in the middle is the individual living and defending and growing. In psycho-analysis we deal with the individual living, defending and growing. In classification, however, we are accounting for the total phenomenology and the best way to do this is first to classify the environmental states; then we can go on to classify the individual's defences, and finally attempt to look at heredity. Heredity, in the main, is the individual's inherent tendency to grow, to integrate, to relate to objects, to mature.

Classification in terms of environment would require a more

accurate knowledge than at present exists, as far as I know, of the stages of dependence. For the time being I find it valuable to use the concepts which I have put forward in other papers, of independence arising out of dependence, which in turn arises out of double dependence. By double dependence I mean dependence which could not at the time be appreciated even unconsciously by the individual, and which therefore cannot be communicated to an analyst in a patient's analysis. As I have said elsewhere (Chapter 9), the analyst has to reclothe the patient's material, using his or her imagination in so doing.

Summary

By my way of looking at things at the beginning we see a concentration of environmental phenomena in which there crystallizes out a person, a mother, and it is in the mother that the infant begins to appear first as an anatomical and a physiological unit, and then gradually, at about the birth date, becomes a male or a female person. This infant member of 'the nursing couple' develops in his or her own right *in so far as the environment does not fail in its various essential functions*, functions which change in their emphasis and develop in their quality as the growth of the individual proceeds.

Under the most favourable conditions, where continuity is preserved externally and the facilitating environment allows the maturational process to act, the new individual really starts and eventually comes to feel real, and to experience life appropriate to his or her emotional age. This individual can be described and typed, defences can be classified, and value or lack of value in the personality can be noted. In such cases we may find depressive or psycho-neurotic defences or we may find a normality. If we like we may attempt to group individuals according to types, and according to the ways the hereditary elements gather together in individuals in relation to specific environments; and (in maturity) we may go on to take note of the capacity of the individual to take part in the creation and maintenance of the local environment.

All this assumes a good enough beginning, with the true self operative, protected by a false self which is no more than a social manner.

The alternative is psychotic illness, with organization of primitive defences. Here the illness is aetiologically secondary to environmental failure, although the illness shows clinically in a more or less permanent distortion in the personality structure of an individual. In between these two is the antisocial tendency, in which the environment fails at a later stage, a stage of relative dependence, a stage at which the individual child has the equipment to perceive the fact of an actual deprivation.

In our therapeutic work we may choose to study and isolate the distortion that takes place in the personality structure. Our immediate need, however, is for a classification and a re-evaluation of the environmental factor in so far as this affects in a positive or negative way the maturational development and the integration of the self.

Postscript 1964:

A Note on Mental Breakdown

Some patients have a fear of mental breakdown. It is important for the analyst to keep in mind the following axiom:

Axiom

The breakdown that is feared has already been. What is known as the patient's illness is a system of defences organized relative to this past breakdown.

Breakdown means a failure of defences, and the original breakdown ended when the new defences were organized which constitute the patient's illness pattern. The patient can remember the breakdown only in the special circumstances of a therapeutic setting, and because of ego-growth.

The patient's fear of breakdown has one of its roots in the patient's need to remember the original breakdown. Memory can only come through re-experiencing. Hence the positive use that can be made of a breakdown if its place in the patient's tendency towards self-cure be recognized and used practically.

The original breakdown took place at a stage of dependence of the individual on parental or maternal ego-support. For this reason work is often done in therapeutics on a later version of the breakdown—say a breakdown in the latency period, or even in early adolescence; this later version occurred when the patient had developed ego-autonomy and a capacity to be a person-having-an-illness. Behind such a breakdown there is always, however, a failure of defences belonging to the individual's infancy or very early childhood.

Often, the environmental factor is not a single trauma but a pattern of distorting influences; the opposite, in fact, of the facilitating environment which allows of individual maturation.

EGO DISTORTION IN TERMS OF
TRUE AND FALSE SELF
(1960)

One recent development in psycho-analysis has been the increasing use of the concept of the False Self. This concept carries with it the idea of a True Self.

History

This concept is not in itself new. It appears in various guises in descriptive psychiatry and notably in certain religions and philosophical systems. Evidently a real clinical state exists which deserves study, and the concept presents psycho-analysis with an aetiological challenge. Psycho-analysis concerns itself with the questions:

(1) How does the False Self arise?
(2) What is its function?
(3) Why is the False Self exaggerated or emphasized in some cases?
(4) Why do some persons not develop a False Self system?
(5) What are the equivalents to the False Self in normal people?
(6) What is there that could be named a True Self?

It would appear to me that the idea of a False Self, which is an idea which our patients give us, can be discerned in the early formulations of Freud. In particular I link what I divide into a True and a False Self with Freud's division of the self into a part that is central and powered by the instincts (or by what Freud called sexuality, pregenital and genital), and a part that is turned outwards and is related to the world.

Personal Contribution

My own contribution to this subject derives from my working at one and the same time

(a) as a paediatrician with mothers and infants and
(b) as a psycho-analyst whose practice includes a small series of borderline cases treated by analysis, but needing to experience

in the transference a phase (or phases) of serious regression to dependence.

My experiences have led me to recognize that dependent or deeply regressed patients can teach the analyst more about early infancy than can be learned from direct observation of infants, and more than can be learned from contact with mothers who are involved with infants. At the same time, clinical contact with the normal and abnormal experiences of the infant-mother relationship influences the analyst's analytic theory since what happens in the transference (in the regressed phases of certain of his patients) is a form of infant-mother relationship.

I like to compare my position with that of Greenacre, who has also kept in touch with paediatrics while pursuing her practice of psycho-analysis. With her too it seems to be clear that each of the two experiences has influenced her in her assessment of the other experience.

Clinical experience in adult psychiatry can have the effect on a psycho-analyst of placing a gap between his assessment of a clinical state and his understanding of its aetiology. The gap derives from an impossibility of getting a reliable history of early infancy either from a psychotic patient or from the mother, or from more detached observers. Analytic patients who regress to serious dependence in the transference fill in this gap by showing their expectations and their needs in the dependent phases.

Ego-needs and Id-needs

It must be emphasized that in referring to the meeting of infant needs I am not referring to the satisfaction of instincts. In the area that I am examining the instincts are not yet clearly defined as internal to the infant. The instincts can be as much external as can a clap of thunder or a hit. The infant's ego is building up strength and in consequence is getting towards a state in which id-demands will be felt as part of the self, and not as environmental. When this development occurs, then id-satisfaction becomes a very important strengthener of the ego, or of the True Self; but id-excitements can be traumatic when the ego is not yet able to include them, and not yet able to contain the risks involved and the frustrations experienced up to the point when id-satisfaction becomes a fact.

A patient said to me: 'Good management' (ego care) 'such as I have experienced during this hour is a feed' (id-satisfaction). He could not have said this the other way round, for if I had fed him he would have complied and this would have played into his False Self defence, or else he would have reacted and rejected my advances, maintaining his integrity by choosing frustration.

Other influences have been important for me, as for instance when periodically I have been asked for a note on a patient who is now under psychiatric care as an adult but who was observed by myself when an infant or small child. Often from my notes I have been able to see that the psychiatric state that now exists was already to be discerned in the infant-mother relationship. (I leave out infant-father relationships in this context because I am referring to early phenomena, those that concern the infant's relationship to the mother, or to the father as another mother. The father at this very early stage has not become significant as a male person.)

Example

The best example I can give is that of a middle-aged woman who had a very successful False Self but who had the feeling all her life that she had not started to exist, and that she had always been looking for a means of getting to her True Self. She still continues with her analysis, which has lasted many years. In the first phase of this research analysis (this lasted two or three years), I found I was dealing with what the patient called her 'Caretaker Self'. This 'Caretaker Self':

(1) found psycho-analysis;
(2) came and sampled analysis, as a kind of elaborate test of the analyst's reliability;
(3) brought her to analysis;
(4) gradually after three years or more handed over its function to the analyst
(this was the time of the depth of the regression, with a few weeks of a very high degree of dependence on the analyst);
(5) hovered round, resuming caretaking at times when the analyst failed (analyst's illness, analyst's holidays, etc.);
(6) its ultimate fate will be discussed later.

From the evolution of this case it was easy for me to see the defensive nature of the False Self. Its defensive function is to hide and protect the True Self, whatever that may be. Immediately it becomes possible to classify False Self organizations:

(1) At one extreme: the False Self sets up as real and it is this that observers tend to think is the real person. In living relationships, work relationships, and friendships, however, the False Self begins to fail. In situations in which what is

expected is a whole person the False Self has some essential lacking. At this extreme the True Self is hidden.

(2) Less extreme: the False Self defends the True Self; the True Self is, however, acknowledged as a potential and is allowed a secret life. Here is the clearest example of clinical illness as an organization with a positive aim, the preservation of the individual in spite of abnormal environmental conditions. This is an extension of the psycho-analytic concept of the value of symptoms to the sick person.

(3) More towards health: The False Self has as its main concern a search for conditions which will make it possible for the True Self to come into its own. If conditions cannot be found then there must be reorganized a new defence against exploitation of the True Self, and if there be doubt then the clinical result is suicide. Suicide in this context is the destruction of the total self in avoidance of annihilation of the True Self. When suicide is the only defence left against betrayal of the True Self, then it becomes the lot of the False Self to organize the suicide. This, of course, involves its own destruction, but at the same time eliminates the need for its continued existence, since its function is the protection of the True Self from insult.

(4) Still further towards health: the False Self is built on identifications (as for example that of the patient mentioned, whose childhood environment and whose actual nannie gave much colour to the False Self organization).

(5) In health: the False Self is represented by the whole organization of the polite and mannered social attitude, a 'not wearing the heart on the sleeve', as might be said. Much has gone to the individual's ability to forgo omnipotence and the primary process in general, the gain being the place in society which can never be attained or maintained by the True Self alone.

So far I have kept within the bounds of clinical description. Even in this limited area recognition of the False Self is important, however. For instance, it is important that patients who are essentially False Personalities shall not be referred to students of psycho-analysis for analysis under a training scheme. The diagnosis of False Personality is here more important than the diagnosis of the patient according to accepted psychiatric classifications. Also in social work, where all types of case must be accepted and kept in treatment, this diagnosis of False Personality is important in the avoidance of extreme frustration associated with therapeutic failure in spite of seemingly sound social work based on analytic principles. Especially is this diagnosis important in the *selection* of students for training in psycho-analysis or in psychiatric social work, that is to say, in the selection of case-work students of all kinds. The organized False Self is associated with a rigidity of defences which prevents growth during the student period.

The Mind and the False Self

A particular danger arises out of the not infrequent tie-up between the intellectual approach and the False Self. When a False Self becomes organized in an individual who has a high intellectual potential there is a very strong tendency for the mind to become the location of the False Self, and in this case there develops a dissociation between intellectual activity and psycho-somatic existence. (In the healthy individual, it must be assumed, the mind is not something for the individual to exploit in escape from psycho-somatic being. I have developed this theme at some length in 'Mind and its Relation to the Psyche-Soma', 1949c.)

When there has taken place this double abnormality, (i) the False Self organized to hide the True Self, and (ii) an attempt on the part of the individual to solve the personal problem by the use of a fine intellect, a clinical picture results which is peculiar in that it very easily deceives. The world may observe academic success of a high degree, and may find it hard to believe in the very real distress of the individual concerned, who feels 'phoney' the more he or she is successful. When such individuals destroy themselves in one way or another, instead of fulfilling promise, this invariably produces a sense of shock in those who have developed high hopes of the individual.

Aetiology

The main way in which these concepts become of interest to psycho-analysts derives from a study of the way a False Self develops at the beginning, in the infant-mother relationship, and (more important) the way in which a False Self does not become a significant feature in normal development.

The theory relative to this important stage in ontogenetic development belongs to the observation of infant-to-mother (regressed patient-to-analyst) living, and it does not belong to the theory of early mechanisms of ego-defence organized against id-impulse, though of course these two subjects overlap.

To get to a statement of the relevant developmental process it is essential to take into account the mother's behaviour and attitude, because in this field dependence is real, and near absolute. *It is not possible to state what takes place by reference to the infant alone.*

In seeking the aetiology of the False Self we are examining the stage of first object-relationships. At this stage the infant is most of the time unintegrated, and never fully integrated; cohesion of the various sensori-motor elements belongs to the fact that the mother holds the infant, sometimes physically, and all the time figuratively. Periodically the infant's gesture gives expression to a spontaneous impulse; the source of the gesture is the True Self, and the gesture indicates the existence of a potential True Self. We need to examine the way the mother meets this infantile omnipotence revealed in a gesture (or a sensori-motor grouping). I have here linked the idea of a True Self with the spontaneous gesture. Fusion of the motility and erotic elements is in process of becoming a fact at this period of development of the individual.

The Mother's Part

It is necessary to examine the part played by the mother, and in doing so I find it convenient to compare two extremes; by one extreme the mother *is a good-enough mother* and by the other the mother *is not a good-enough mother*. The question will be asked: what is meant by the term 'good-enough'?

The good-enough mother meets the omnipotence of the infant and to some extent makes sense of it. She does this repeatedly. A True Self begins to have life, through the strength given to the infant's weak ego by the mother's implementation of the infant's omnipotent expressions.

The mother who is not good enough is not able to implement the infant's omnipotence, and so she repeatedly fails to meet the infant gesture; instead she substitutes her own gesture which is to be given sense by the compliance of the infant. This compliance on the part of the infant is the earliest stage of the False Self, and belongs to the mother's inability to sense her infant's needs.

It is an essential part of my theory that the True Self does not become a living reality except as a result of the mother's repeated success in meeting the infant's spontaneous gesture or sensory hallucination. (This idea is closely linked with Sechehaye's idea contained in the term 'symbolic realization'. This term has played an important part in modern psycho-analytic theory, but it is not quite accurate since it is the infant's *gesture or hallucination* that is made real, and the capacity of the infant *to use a symbol* is the result.)

There are now two possible lines of development in the scheme of events according to my formulation. *In the first case* the mother's adaptation is *good enough* and in consequence the infant begins to believe in external reality which appears and behaves as by magic (because of the mother's relatively successful adaptation to the infant's gestures and needs), and which acts in a way that does not clash with the infant's omnipotence. On this basis the infant can gradually abrogate omnipotence. The True Self has a spontaneity, and this has been joined up with the world's events. The infant can now begin to enjoy the *illusion* of omnipotent creating and controlling, and then can gradually come to recognize the illusory element, the fact of playing and imagining. Here is the basis for the symbol which at first is *both* the infant's spontaneity or hallucination, *and also* the external object created and ultimately cathected.

In between the infant and the object is some thing, or some activity or sensation. In so far as this joins the infant to the object (viz. maternal part-object) so far is this the basis of symbol-formation. On the other hand, in so far as this something separates instead of joins, so is its function of leading on to symbol-formation blocked.

In the second case, which belongs more particularly to the subject under discussion, the mother's adaptation to the infant's hallucinations and spontaneous impulses is deficient, *not good enough*. The process that leads to the capacity for symbol-usage does not get started (or else it becomes broken up, with a corresponding withdrawal on the part of the infant from advantages gained).

When the mother's adaptation is not good enough at the start the infant might be expected to die physically, because cathexis of external objects is not initiated. The infant remains isolated. But in practice the infant lives, but lives falsely. The protest against being forced into a false existence can be detected from the earliest stages. The clinical picture is one of general irritability, and of feeding and other function disturbances which may, however, disappear clinically, only to reappear in serious form at a later stage.

In this second case, where the mother cannot adapt well enough, the infant gets seduced into a compliance, and a compliant False Self reacts to environmental demands and the infant seems to accept them. Through this False Self the infant builds up a false set of relationships, and by means of introjections even attains a show of being real, so that the child may grow to be just like mother, nurse, aunt, brother, or whoever at the time dominates the scene. The False Self has one positive and very important function: to hide the True Self, which it does by compliance with environmental demands.

In the extreme examples of False Self development, the True Self is so well hidden that spontaneity is not a feature in the infant's living experiences. Compliance is then the main feature, with imitation as a speciality. When the degree of the split in the infant's person is not too great there may be some almost personal living through imitation, and it may even be possible for the child to act a special role, that of the True Self *as it would be if it had had existence.*

In this way it is possible to trace the point of origin of the False Self, which can now be seen to be a defence, a defence against that which is unthinkable, the exploitation of the True Self, which would result in its annihilation. (If the True Self ever gets exploited and annihilated this belongs to the life of an infant whose mother was not only 'not good enough' in the sense set out above, but was good and bad in a tantalizingly irregular manner. The mother here has as part of her illness a need to cause and to maintain a muddle in those who are in contact with her. This may appear in a transference situation in which the patient tries to make the analyst mad (Bion, 1959; Searles, 1959). There may be a degree of this which can destroy the last vestiges of an infant's capacity to defend the True Self.)

I have attempted to develop the theme of the part the mother plays in my paper on 'Primary Maternal Preoccupation' (1956a). The assumption made by me in this paper is that, in health, the mother who becomes pregnant gradually achieves a high degree of identification with her infant. This develops during the pregnancy, is at its height at the time of lying in, and it gradually ceases in the weeks and months after the confinement. This healthy thing that happens to mothers has both hypochondriacal and secondary narcissistic implications. This special orientation on the part of the mother to her infant not only depends on her own mental health, but also it is affected by the environment. In the simplest case the man, supported by a social attitude which is itself a development from the man's natural function, deals with external reality for the woman, and so makes it safe and sensible for her to be temporarily in-turned, self-centred. A diagram of this resembles the diagram of an ill paranoid person or family. (One is reminded here of Freud's (1920) description of the living vesicle with its receptive cortical layer. . . .)

The development of this theme does not belong here, but it is important that the function of the mother should be understood. This function is by no means a recent development, belonging to civilization or to sophistication or to intellectual understanding. No theory is acceptable that does not allow for the fact that mothers have always performed this essential function well enough. This essential maternal function enables the mother to know about her infant's earliest expectations and needs, and makes her personally satisfied in so far as the infant is at ease. It is because of this identification with her infant that she knows how to hold her infant, so that the infant starts by existing and not by reacting. Here is the origin of the True Self which cannot become a reality without the mother's specialized relationship, one which might be described by a common word: devotion.[1]

The True Self

The concept of 'A False Self' needs to be balanced by a formulation of that which could properly be called the True Self. At the earliest stage the True Self is the theoretical position from which come the spontaneous gesture and the personal idea. The spontaneous gesture is the True Self in action. Only the True Self can be creative and only the True Self can feel real. Whereas a True Self feels real, the existence of a False Self results in a feeling unreal or a sense of futility.

The False Self, if successful in its function, hides the True Self, or else finds a way of enabling the True Self to start to live. Such an outcome may be achieved by all manner of means, but we observe most closely those instances in which the sense of things being real or worth while arrives during a treatment. My patient to whose case I have referred has come near the end of a long analysis *to the beginning of her life.* She contains no true experience, she has no past. She starts with fifty years of wasted life, but at last she feels real, and therefore she now wants to live.

The True Self comes from the aliveness of the body tissues and the working of body-functions, including the heart's action and breathing. It is closely linked with the idea of the Primary Process, and is, at the beginning, essentially not reactive to external stimuli, but primary. There is but little point in formulating a True Self idea except for the purpose of trying to understand the False Self, because it does no more than collect together the details of the experience of aliveness.

Gradually the degree of sophistication of the infant becomes such that it is more true to say that the False Self hides the infant's inner reality than to say that it hides the True Self. By this time the infant has an established limiting membrane, has an inside

[1] On account of this I called my series of talks to mothers, 'The Ordinary Devoted Mother and Her Baby' (Winnicott, 1949a).

and an outside, and has become to a considerable extent dis-entangled from maternal care.

It is important to note that according to the theory being for-mulated here the concept of an individual inner reality of objects applies to a stage later than does the concept of what is being termed the True Self. The True Self appears as soon as there is any mental organization of the individual at all, and it means little more than the summation of sensori-motor aliveness.

The True Self quickly develops complexity, and relates to external reality by natural processes, by such processes as develop in the individual infant in the course of time. The infant then comes to be able to react to a stimulus without trauma because the stimulus has a counterpart in the individual's inner, psychic reality. The infant then accounts for all stimuli as projections, but this is a stage that is not necessarily achieved, or that is only partially achieved, or it may be reached and lost. This stage having been achieved, the infant is now able to retain the sense of omnipotence even when reacting to environmental factors that the observer can discern as truly external to the infant. All this precedes by years the infant's capacity to allow in intellectual reasoning for the operation of pure chance.

Every new period of living in which the True Self has not been seriously interrupted results in a strengthening of the sense of being real, and with this goes a growing capacity on the part of the infant to tolerate two sets of phenomena: These are:

(1) Breaks in continuity of True Self living. (Here can be seen a way in which the birth process might be traumatic, as for instance when there is delay without unconsciousness.)

(2) Reactive or False Self experiences, related to the environ-ment on a basis of compliance. This becomes the part of the infant which can be (before the first birthday) taught to say 'Ta', or, in other words, can be taught to acknowledge the existence of an environment that is becoming intellectually accepted. Feelings of gratitude may or may not follow.

The Normal Equivalent of the False Self

In this way, by natural processes, the infant develops an ego-organization that is adapted to the environment; but this does not happen automatically and indeed it can only happen if first the True Self (as I call it) has become a living reality, because of the mother's good-enough adaptation to the infant's living needs. There is a compliant aspect to the True Self in healthy living, an ability of the infant to comply and not to be exposed. The ability to compromise is an achievement. The equivalent of the False Self in normal development is that which can develop in the child into a social manner, something which is adaptable. In health this social manner represents a compromise. At the same time, in health, the compromise ceases to become allowable when the issues become crucial. When this happens the True Self is able to override the compliant self. Clinically this constitutes a recurring problem of adolescence.

Degrees of False Self

If the description of these two extremes and their aetiology is accepted it is not difficult for us to allow in our clinical work for the existence of a low or a high degree of the False Self defence, ranging from the healthy polite aspect of the self to the truly split-off compliant False Self which is mistaken for the whole child. It can easily be seen that sometimes this False Self defence can form the basis for a kind of sublimation, as when a child grows up to be an actor. In regard to actors, there are those who can be themselves and who also can act, whereas there are others who can only act, and who are completely at a loss when not in a role, and when not being appreciated or applauded (acknowledged as existing).

In the healthy individual who has a compliant aspect of the self but who exists and who is a creative and spontaneous being, there is at the same time a capacity for the use of symbols. In other words health here is closely bound up with the capacity of the individual to live in an area that is intermediate between the dream and the reality, that which is called the cultural life. (See 'Transitional Objects and Transitional Phenomena', 1951.) By contrast, where there is a high degree of split between the True Self and the False Self which hides the True Self, there is found a poor capacity for using symbols, and a poverty of cultural living. Instead of cultural pursuits one observes in such persons extreme restlessness, an inability to concentrate, and a need to collect impingements from external reality so that the living-time of the individual can be filled by reactions to these impingements.

Clinical Application

Reference has already been made to the importance of a recognition of the False Self personality when a diagnosis is being made for the purposes of the assessment of a case for treatment, or the assessment of a candidate for psychiatric or social psychiatric work.

Consequences for the Psycho-Analyst

If these considerations prove to have value, then the practising psycho-analyst must be affected in the following ways:

(a) In analysis of a False Personality the fact must be recognized that the analyst can only talk to the False Self of the patient about the patient's True Self. It is as if a nurse brings a child, and at first the analyst discusses the child's problem, and the child is not directly contacted. Analysis does not start until the nurse has left the child with the analyst, and the child has become able to remain alone with the analyst and has started to play.

(b) At the point of transition, when the analyst begins to get into contact with the patient's True Self, there must be a period of extreme dependence. Often this is missed in analytic practice. The patient has an illness, or in some other way gives the analyst a chance to take over the False Self (nursemaid) function, but the analyst at that point fails to see what is happening, and in consequence it is others who care for the patient and on whom the patient becomes dependent in a period of disguised regression to dependence, and the opportunity is missed.

(c) Analysts who are not prepared to go and meet the heavy needs of patients who become dependent in this way must be careful so to choose their cases that they do not include False Self types.

In psycho-analytic work it is possible to see analyses going on indefinitely because they are done on the basis of work with the False Self. In one case, a man patient who had had a considerable amount of analysis before coming to me, my work really started with him when I made it clear to him that I recognized his non-existence. He made the remark that over the years all the good work done with him had been futile because it had been done on the basis that he existed, whereas he had only existed falsely. When I had said that I recognized his non-existence he felt that he had been communicated with for the first time. What he meant was that his True Self that had been hidden away from infancy had now been in communication with his analyst in the only way which was not dangerous. This is typical of the way in which this concept affects psycho-analytic work.

I have referred to some other aspects of this clinical problem. For instance, in 'Withdrawal and Regression' (1954a) I traced in the treatment of a man the evolution in the transference of my contact with (his version of) a False Self, through my first contact with his True Self, to an analysis of a straightforward kind. In this case withdrawal had to be converted into regression as described in the paper.

A principle might be enunciated, that in the False Self area of our analytic practice we find we make more headway by recognition of the patient's non-existence than by a long-continued working with the patient on the basis of ego-defence mechanisms. The patient's False Self can collaborate indefinitely with the analyst in the analysis of defences, being so to speak on the analyst's side in the game. This unrewarding work is only cut short profitably when the analyst can point to and specify an absence of some essential feature: 'You have no mouth', 'You have not started to exist yet', 'Physically you are a man, but you do not know from experience anything about masculinity', and so on. These recognitions of important fact, made clear at the right moments, pave the way for communication with the True Self. A patient who had had much futile analysis on the basis of a False Self, co-operating vigorously with an analyst who thought this was his whole self, said to me: 'The only time I felt hope was when you told me that you could see no hope, and you continued with the analysis.'

On the basis of this one could say that the False Self (like the multiple projections at later stages of development) deceives the analyst if the latter fails to notice that, regarded as a whole functioning person, the False Self, however well set up, lacks something, and that something is the essential central element of creative originality.

Many other aspects of the application of this concept will be described in the course of time, and it may be that in some ways the concept itself will need to be modified. My object in giving an account of this part of my work (which links with the work of other analysts) is that I hold the view that this modern concept of the False Self hiding the True Self *along with the theory of its aetiology* is able to have an important effect on psycho-analytic work. As far as I can see it involves no important change in basic theory.

STRING: A TECHNIQUE OF
COMMUNICATION[1]
(1960)

A boy aged seven years was brought to the Psychology Department of the Paddington Green Children's Hospital by his mother
and father in March 1955. The other two members of the family
also came: an M.D. girl aged ten, attending an E.S.N. school,
and a rather normal small girl aged four. The case was referred
by the family doctor because of a series of symptoms indicating a
character disorder in the boy. For the purposes of this description
all details that are not immediately relevant to the main theme
of this paper are omitted. An intelligence test gave this boy an
I.Q. of 108.

I first saw the parents in a long interview in which they gave a
clear picture of the boy's development and of the distortions in
his development. They left out one important detail, however,
which emerged in the interview with the boy.

It was not difficult to see that the mother was a depressive
person, and she reported that she had been hospitalized on
account of depression. From the parents' account I was able to
note that the mother cared for the boy until the sister was born
when he was 3 years 3 months. This was the first separation of
importance, the next being at 3 years 11 months when the mother
had an operation. When the boy was 4 years 9 months the
mother went into a mental hospital for two months, and during
this time he was well cared for by his mother's sister. By this
time everyone looking after this boy agreed that he was difficult,
although showing very good features. He was liable to change
suddenly and to frighten people by saying, for instance, that he
would cut his mother's sister into little pieces. He developed
many curious symptoms such as a compulsion to lick things and
people; he made compulsive throat noises; often he refused to
pass a motion and then made a mess. He was obviously anxious
about his elder sister's mental defect, but the distortion of his
development appears to have started before this factor became
significant.

[1] First published in the *Journal of Child Psychology and Psychiatry*, **1**, pp. 49–52.

After this interview with the parents I saw the boy in a personal interview. There were present two psychiatric social workers and two visitors. The boy did not immediately give an abnormal impression and he quickly entered into a squiggle game with me. (In this squiggle game I make some kind of an impulsive line-drawing and invite the child whom I am interviewing to turn it into something, and then he makes a squiggle for me to turn into something in my turn.)

The squiggle game in this particular case led to a curious result. The boy's laziness immediately became evident, and also nearly everything I did was translated by him into something associated with string. Among his ten drawings there appeared the following:

> lasso,   whip,   crop,
> a yo-yo string,
> a string in a knot,
> another crop,
> another whip.

After this interview with the boy I had a second one with the parents, and asked them about the boy's preoccupation with string. They said they were glad that I had brought up this subject, but they had not mentioned it because they were not sure of its significance. They said that the boy had become obsessed with everything to do with string, and in fact whenever they went into a room they were liable to find that he had joined together chairs and tables; and they might find a cushion, for instance, with a string joining it to the fireplace. They said that the boy's pre-occupation with string was gradually developing a new feature, one which had worried them instead of causing them ordinary concern. He had recently tied a string round his sister's neck (the sister whose birth provided the first separation of this boy from his mother).

In this particular kind of interview I knew I had limited opportunity for action: it would not be possible to see these parents or the boy more frequently than once in six months, as the family lived in the country. I therefore took action in the following way. I explained to the mother that this boy was dealing with a fear of separation, attempting to deny separation by his use of string, as one would deny separation from a friend by using the telephone. She was sceptical, but I told her that should she come round to finding some sense in what I was saying I would like her to open up the matter with the boy at some convenient time, letting him know what I had said, and then developing the theme of separation according to the boy's response.

I heard no more from these people until they came to see me about six months later. The mother did not report to me what she had done, but I asked her and she was able to tell me what had taken place soon after the visit to me. She had felt that what I had said was silly, but one evening she had opened the subject with the boy and found him to be eager to talk about his relation to her and his fear of a lack of contact with her. She went over all the separations she could think of with him with his help, and she soon became convinced that what I had said was right, because of his responses. Moreover, from the moment that she had this conversation with him the string play ceased. There was no more joining of objects in the old way. She had many other conversations with the boy about his feeling of separateness from her, and she made the very important comment that she felt the most important separation to have been his loss of her when she was seriously depressed: it was not just her going away, she said, but her lack of contact with him because of her complete preoccupation with other matters.

At a later interview the mother told me that a year after she had her first talk with the boy there was a return to playing with string and to joining together objects in the house. She was in fact due to go into hospital for an operation, and she said to him: 'I can see from your playing with string that you are worried about my going away, but this time I shall only be away a few days, and I am having an operation which is not serious.' After this conversation the new phase of playing with string ceased.

I have kept in touch with this family and have helped with various details in the boy's schooling and other matters. Now, four years after the original interview, the father reports a new phase of string preoccupation, associated with a fresh depression in the mother. This phase lasted two months, and cleared up when the whole family went on holiday, and when at the same time there was an improvement in the home situation (the father having found work after a period of unemployment). Associated with this was an improvement in the mother's state. The father gave one further interesting detail relevant to the subject under discussion. During this recent phase the boy had acted out something with rope which the father felt to be significant, because it showed how intimately all these things were connected with the mother's morbid anxiety. He came home one day and found the boy hanging upside down on a rope. He was quite limp and acting very well as if dead. The father realized he must take no notice, and he hung around the garden doing odd jobs for half an hour, after which the boy got bored and stopped the game. This was a big test of the father's lack of anxiety. On the following day, however, the boy did the same thing from a tree which could easily be seen from the kitchen window. The mother rushed out severely shocked and certain that he had hanged himself.

The following additional detail might be of value in the understanding of the case. Although this boy, who is now eleven, is developing along 'tough-guy' lines, he is very self-conscious and easily goes red in the neck. He had a number of teddy bears which to him are children. No one dares say that they are toys. He is loyal to them, expends a great deal of affection over them, and makes trousers for them which involves careful sewing. His father says that he seems to get a sense of security from his family, which he mothers in this way. If visitors come he quickly puts them all into his sister's bed, because no one outside the family must know that he has this family. Along with this is a reluctance to defaecate, or a tendency to save up his faeces. It is not difficult to guess, therefore, that he has a maternal identification based on his own insecurity in relation to his mother, and that this could develop into homosexuality. In the same way the preoccupation with string could develop into a perversion.

Comment

The following comment seems to be appropriate.

(1) String can be looked upon as an extension of all other techniques of communication. String joins just as it also helps in the wrapping up of objects and in the holding of unintegrated material. In this respect string has a symbolic meaning for everyone; an exaggeration of the use of string can easily belong to the beginnings of a sense of insecurity or the idea of a lack of communication. In this particular case it is possible to detect abnormality creeping into the boy's use of string, and it is important to find a way of stating the change which might lead to its use becoming perverted.

It would seem possible to arrive at such a statement if one takes into consideration the fact that the function of the string is changing from a joining into a *denial of separation*. As a denial of separation spring becomes a thing in itself, something which has dangerous properties and has to be mastered. In this case the mother seems to have been able to deal with the boy's use of spring just before it was too late, when the use of it still contained hope. When hope is absent and string represents a denial of separation, then a much more complex state of affairs has arisen—one which becomes difficult to cure, because of the secondary gains which arise out of the skill that develops whenever an object has to be handled in order to be mastered.

This case therefore presents special interest if it makes possible the observation of the development of a perversion.

(2) It is also possible to see from this material the use that can be made of parents. When parents can be used they can work with great economy, especially if the fact is kept in mind that there will never be enough psychotherapists to treat all those who are in need of treatment. Here was a good family that had been through a difficult time because of the father's unemployment; that had been able to take full responsibility for a backward girl in spite of the tremendous drawbacks, socially and within the family, that this entails; and that had survived the bad phases in the mother's depressive illness, including one phase of hospitalization. There must be a great deal of strength in such a family, and it was on the basis of this assumption that the decision was made to invite these parents to undertake the therapy of their own child. In doing this they learned a great deal themselves, but they did need to be informed about what they were doing. They also needed their success to be appreciated and for the whole process to be verbalized. The fact that they have seen their boy through an illness has given the parents confidence with regard to their ability to manage the other difficulties which arise from time to time.

Summary

A case has been briefly described in order to illustrate a boy's compulsion to use string, at first in an attempt to communicate symbolically with his mother in spite of her withdrawal during depressive phases, and then as a denial of the separation. As a symbol of the denial of separation, string became a thing that was frightening and that had to be mastered, and its use then became perverted. In this case the mother herself did the psychotherapy, her task being explained to her by the psychiatrist.

14

COUNTER-TRANSFERENCE[1]
(1960)

What I want to say can be briefly stated.

I think that the use of this word counter-transference should now be brought back to its original use. We can use words as we like, especially artificial words like counter-transference. A word like 'self' naturally knows more than we do; it uses us, and can command us. But counter-transference is a term that we can enslave, and a perusal of the literature makes me think that it is in danger of losing its identity.

There is now quite a literature around the term, and I have tried to study it. In my paper 'Hate in the Counter-transference' (1947) (which is chiefly about hate), I said that one use of the word counter-transference would be to describe 'abnormality in counter-transference feelings, and set relationships and identifications that are under repression in the analyst. The comment on this is that the analyst needs more analysis. . . .'

For the purposes of that paper I then gave two other possible meanings.

A discussion based on the failures of the analysts' own analyses must be futile. In a sense, this ends the debate.

The meaning of the word counter-transference can be extended, however, and I think we have all agreed to extend it a little so that we may take this opportunity to look at our work afresh. I shall return, however, to this idea that I have already expressed. Before I proceed I must go back to a remark made by Michael Fordham at the beginning of his paper, in which he quotes Jung as protesting against the idea that transference is the product of psycho-analytic technique, emphasizing that it is a general transpersonal or social phenomenon. Apart from the fact that I do not know what 'transpersonal' means, I think that confusion could arise here by a distortion of the use of the term transference as I think Freud introduced it. The characteristic of psycho-analytic technique is this use of transference and of the

---

[1] Presented in the second part of a Symposium on Counter-Transference held by the Medical Section of the British Psychological Society, London, 25 November 1959, and first published in the *British Journal of Medical Psychology*, **33**, pp. 17–21.

transference neurosis. Transference is not just a matter of rapport, or of relationships. It concerns the way in which a highly subjective phenomenon repeatedly turns up in an analysis. Psycho-analysis very much consists in the arranging of conditions for the development of these phenomena, and in the interpretation of these phenomena at the right moment. The interpretation relates the specific transference phenomenon to a bit of the patient's psychic reality, and this in some cases means at the same time relating it to a bit of the patient's past living.

In a typical example, a patient is gradually working round to suspicion and hate in the relation to the analyst, which can be seen to have a correlation with the danger of meeting another patient, or with the breaks due to week-ends and holidays. In the course of time an interpretation makes sense of all this in terms not of the present but of the dynamic structure of the patient's personality. Following this work the patient loses the specific transference neurosis and begins to boil up for another. (Often the work is not done in such a clear way, but for teaching purposes this might be a fair description of a basic principle.)

Michael Fordham (1960) gave a good example of this in the patient who asked questions. Eventually she said: 'You are like my father, you never answer questions.' Often a patient will have given clues so that the analyst may interpret fruitfully, but here a little bit (but an important bit) of the interpretation was arrived at by the patient, and no doubt the analyst was then able to weigh in with a more complete interpretation.

It is necessary for me to take up time in this way because if we do not agree about the term transference we must not start discussing counter-transference.

Incidentally, may I remind Dr Fordham that some of the terms he uses are not of any value to me because they belong to the jargon of Jungian conversation. He in turn can tell me which of my words are useless to him. I refer to: transpersonal, transpersonal unconscious, transpersonal analytic ideal, archetypal, the contra-sexual components of the psyche, the animus and anima, animus-anima conjunction.

I cannot be communicated with in this language. For some in this hall these are household words, and for the rest they have no precise meaning.

We must also be careful over the use of words that are used in different ways by various groups of workers: ego, unconscious, illusory, syntonic (react syntonically), analysis, etc.

I can now return to the subject of transference-counter-transference phenomena and examine what happens in professional work generally. Professional work is quite different from ordinary life, is it not?

All this started up with Hippocrates. He perhaps founded the professional attitude. The medical oath gives a picture of a man or woman who is an idealized version of the ordinary man or woman in the street. Yet *that is how we are* when professionally engaged. Included in the oath is the promise that we do not commit adultery with a patient. Here is a full recognition of one aspect of the transference, the patient's need to idealize the doctor, and to fall in love with him, to dream.

Freud allowed for the development of a full range of subjective phenomena in the professional relationship; the analyst's own analysis was in effect a recognition that the analyst is *under strain in maintaining a professional attitude*. It is on purpose that I use this wording. I am not saying that the analyst's analysis is to free him from neurosis; it is to increase the stability of character and the maturity of the personality of the worker, this being the basis of his or her professional work and of our ability to maintain a professional relationship.

A professional attitude may, of course, be built up on a basis of defences and inhibitions and obsessional orderliness, and I suggest that it is here that the psychotherapist is particularly under strain, because *any structuring of his ego-defences lessens his ability to meet the new situation*. The psychotherapist (analyst, or analytical psychologist) must remain vulnerable, and yet retain his professional role in his actual working hours. I guess that the well-behaving professional analyst is easier to come by than the analyst who (while behaving well) retains the vulnerability that belongs to a flexible defence organization. (Fordham refers to this same idea in his own language.)

There is a much fuller use of transference phenomena in psycho-analysis than in social work, for instance. This gives a therapeutic advantage to the analyst over the social worker, but it is necessary to remember the advantages that remain with the more general case-worker who, working in with the patient's ego-functions, is in a better position to relate the individual's ego-needs to social provision. As analysts we are often hampered in this which is not our function.

In analysis the transference neurosis is characteristically id-derived. In social work a man may say to the worker, 'You remind me of my mother.' Nothing need be done about this, except for the worker to believe in it. In analysis the analyst will be given the clues so that he can interpret not only the transference of feelings from mother to analyst, but also the unconscious instinctual elements that underlie this, and the conflicts that are aroused, and the defences that organize. In this way the unconscious begins to have a conscious equivalent and to become a living process involving people, and to be a phenomenon that is acceptable to the patient.

What the patient meets is surely the professional attitude of the analyst, not the unreliable men and women we happen to be in private life.

I want to make this clear observation first, although later I shall modify what I am now saying.

I want to state that the working analyst is in a special state, that is, *his attitude is professional*. The work is done in a professional setting. In this setting we assume a freedom of the analyst from personality and character disorder of such a kind or degree that the professional relationship cannot be maintained, or can only be maintained at great cost involving excessive defences.

The professional attitude is rather like symbolism, in that it assumes a *distance between analyst and patient*. The symbol is in a gap between the subjective object and the object that is perceived objectively.

It will be seen that here I am disagreeing with a statement of Fordham's although a little later I shall agree with him. The statement I am disagreeing with is the following: 'He [Jung] compares the analytic relation to a chemical interaction, and continues that treatment can "by no device . . . be anything but the product of mutual influence, in which the whole being of the doctor as well as the patient plays a part".' Later he is very emphatic that it is futile for the analyst to erect defences of a professional kind against the influence of the patient, and continues: 'By doing so he only denies himself the use of a highly important organ of information.'

I would rather be remembered as maintaining that in between the patient and the analyst is the analyst's professional attitude, his technique, *the work he does with his mind*.

Now I say this without fear because I am not an intellectual and in fact I personally do my work very much from the body-ego, so to speak. But I think of myself in my analytic work working with easy but conscious mental effort. Ideas and feelings come to mind, but these are well examined and sifted before an interpretation is made. This is not to say that feelings are not involved. On the one hand I may have stomach ache but this does not usually affect my interpretations; and on the other hand I may have been somewhat stimulated erotically or aggressively by an idea given by the patient, but again this fact does not usually affect my interpretative work, what I say, how I say it or when I say it.

The analyst is objective and consistent, for the hour, and he is not a rescuer, a teacher, an ally, or a moralist. The important effect of the analyst's own analysis in this connexion is that it has strengthened his own ego so that he can remain *professionally* involved, and this without too much strain.

In so far as all this is true the meaning of the word counter-transference can only be the neurotic features *which spoil the professional attitude* and disturb the course of the analytic process as determined by the patient.

In my opinion this holds except in so far as the diagnosis of the patient is of a certain kind, and I now want to describe the kinds of diagnosis which to my mind alter the whole problem and make me wish to agree with the statement that I have just disagreed with. The subject under discussion is now: *the role of the analyst*; and this role must vary according to the diagnosis of the patient. Neither speaker had time to refer more than briefly to the matter of diagnosis (although Fordham quoted Jung: 'It is clear, however, that he is sure the patient can have very drastic effects on the analyst and that this can induce pathological manifestations in him. He states that this is particularly the case when cases of borderline schizophrenia are being treated; and Jung developes this theme in an interesting way).

I am now, therefore, speaking from a different position, and the change comes from the fact that I now refer to the management and treatment of borderline cases for which the word psychotic is more appropriate than the word neurotic. But the vast majority of people who may come to us for psycho-analysis are not psychotic and students must be first taught the analysis of non-psychotic cases.

You might expect me to use words like psycho-neurosis, psychosis, or hysteria, affective disorder and schizophrenia, but I shall not do so in classifying cases for our purposes here.

Two types of case seem to me to completely alter the therapist's professional attitude. One is the patient who has *an antisocial tendency*, and the other is the patient *who needs a regression*. The first, the patient with more or less antisocial tendency, is permanently reacting to a deprivation. The therapist is compelled by the patient's illness, or by the hopeful half of the patient's illness, to correct and to go on correcting the failure of ego-support which altered the course of the patient's life. The only thing the therapist can do, apart from getting caught up, is to use what happens in an attempt to get down to a precise statement of the original deprivation or deprivations, as perceived and felt by the patient as a child. This may or may not involve work with the patient's unconscious. A therapist wholly engaged in work with patients who display an antisocial tendency would not be in a good position to understand the psycho-analytic technique or the operation of the transference, or the interpretation of the transference neurosis. We try to avoid giving our psycho-analytic students antisocial cases, precisely because we cannot teach psycho-analysis on these cases. They are better dealt with in other ways, though psycho-analysis can sometimes be usefully added. I shall leave aside further consideration of the antisocial tendency.

In the other type of patient to which I refer a regression will be needed. If a significant change is to be brought about the patient will need to pass through a phase of infantile dependence. Here again psycho-analysis cannot be taught, though it can be practised in modified form. The difficulty here is in diagnosis, in the spotting of the falseness of the false personality which hides the immature true self. If the hidden true self is to come into its own in such a case the patient will break down as part of the treatment, and the analyst will need to be able to play the part of mother to the patient's infant. This means giving ego-support in a big way. The analyst will need to remain orientated to external reality while in fact being identified with the patient, even merged in with the patient. The patient must become highly dependent, even absolutely dependent, and these words are true even when there is a healthy part of the personality that acts all along as an ally of the analyst and in fact tells the analyst how to behave.

You will note that I am now using phrases that are in line with phrases used by Fordham.

Now here again it can be said that analysts who work chiefly with patients who become very fully dependent in this way can fail to understand and learn the psycho-analytic technique which is based on work with the vast majority of patients, those whose own infantile dependence was successfully managed by their own mothers and fathers. (I cannot too strongly emphasize the fact that most people, if analysed, do need the classical psycho-analytic technique, with the analyst's professional attitude in between the patient and the analyst.)

Per contra, the classical analyst, the one who has learned his job and who is confident in his ability to deal with the transference neurosis as it develops and repeatedly redevelops, has a great deal to learn from those who care for and who attempt to do psycho-therapy of the patients who need to go through the stages of emotional development that properly belong to infancy.

From this changed position, therefore, with the patient diagnosed as psychotic or schizophrenic, and the transference dominated by the patient's need to regress to infantile dependence, I find I am able to join up with a whole lot of Dr Fordham's observations, which, however, I think he did not properly link with the classification of the patients because he had not time.

The borderline psychotic gradually breaks through the barriers that I have called the analyst's technique and professional attitude, and forces a direct relationship of a primitive kind, even to the extent of merging. This is done in a gradual and orderly manner, and recovery is correspondingly orderly, except where it is part of the illness that chaos must reign supreme both without and within.

In the training of psycho-analysts and the like we must not place the students in the position of being related to the primitive needs of psychotic patients, because few will be able to stand it, and few will be able to learn anything from the experience. On the other hand, in a properly organized psycho-analytic practice there is room for some patients who force their way across the professional borderline, and who make these special tests and demands which we seem to be including under the term counter-transference in this discussion. I could take up the subject of the analyst's responses. In fact I find it difficult to miss this opportunity for discussing all kinds of things that I have experienced and which link up with ideas put forward by Dr Fordham. For instance, I got hit by a patient. What I said is not for publication. It was not an interpretation but a reaction to an event. The patient came across the professional white line and got a little bit of the real me, and I think it felt real to her. But a reaction is not counter-transference.

Would it not be better at this point to *let the term counter-transference revert to its meaning* of that which we hope to eliminate by selection and analysis and the training of analysts? This would leave us free to discuss the many interesting things that analysts can do with psychotic patients who are temporarily regressed and dependent for which we could use Margaret Little's term: the analyst's total response to the patient's needs. Under this or a similar title there is much to be said about the use that the analyst can make of his or her own conscious and unconscious reactions to the impact of the psychotic patient or the psychotic part of the patient on his or her self, and the effect of this on the analyst's professional attitude. I am one of those who have already written a little and said much on this subject which interests Jungians and Freudians alike. This could form and must indeed form a basis for future discussions, but I think that only muddle can come from stretching to cover all this the word which is in the title of this symposium: counter-transference.

15

THE AIMS OF PSYCHO-ANALYTICAL TREATMENT[1]

(1962)

In doing psycho-analysis I aim at:

> Keeping alive
> Keeping well
> Keeping awake

I aim at being myself and behaving myself.

Having begun an analysis I expect to continue with it, to survive it, and to end it.

I enjoy myself doing analysis and I always look forward to the end of each analysis. Analysis for analysis' sake has no meaning for me. I do analysis because that is what the patient needs to have done and to have done with. If the patient does not need analysis then I do something else.

In analysis one asks: how *much* can one be allowed to do? And, by contrast, in my clinic the motto is: how *little* need be done?

But these are surface matters. What are the deeper aims? What does one do in the professional setting that is so carefully prepared and maintained?

I do adapt quite a little to individual expectations at the very beginning. It is unhuman not to do so. Yet I am all the time manœuvring into the position for standard analysis. What I must try to state is the meaning for me of the term *standard analysis*.

For me this means communicating with the patient from the position in which the transference neurosis (or psychosis) puts me. In this position I have some of the characteristics of a transitional phenomenon, since although I represent the reality principle, and it is I who must keep an eye on the clock, I am nevertheless a subjective object for the patient.

Most of what I do is of the nature of a verbalization of that which the patient brings for me to use today. I make interpretations for two reasons:

[1] Presented to the British Psycho-Analytical Society, 7 March 1962.

(1) If I make none the patient gets the impression that I understand everything. In other words, I retain some outside quality by not being quite on the mark—or even by being wrong.

(2) Verbalization at exactly the right moment mobilizes intellectual forces. It is only a bad thing to mobilize the intellectual processes when these have become seriously dissociated from psycho-somatic being. My interpretations are economical, I hope. One interpretation per session satisfies me if it has referred to the material produced by the patient's unconscious co-operation. I say one thing, or say one thing in two or three parts. I never use long sentences unless I am very tired. If I am near exhaustion point I begin teaching. Moreover, in my view an interpretation containing the word 'moreover' is a teaching session.

The stuff of the secondary process is applied to the stuff of the primary process, as a contribution to growth and integration.

What does the patient bring to me today? This depends on unconscious co-operation which is set up at the time of the first mutative interpretation, or earlier. It is axiomatic that the work of the analysis is done by the patient, and that this is called unconscious co-operation. It includes such things as dreaming, the remembering of dreams and the reporting of them in a useful way.

Unconscious co-operation is the same as resistance, but the latter belongs to a negative transference element. The analysis of resistance releases the co-operation which belongs to positive transference elements.

Although psycho-analysis may be infinitely complex, a few simple things may be said about the work I do, and one is that I expect to find a tendency towards ambivalence in the transference and away from more primitive mechanisms of splitting, introjection and projection, object retaliation, disintegration, etc. I know that these primitive mechanisms are universal and that they have positive value, but they are defences in so far as they weaken the direct tie to the object through instinct, and through love and hate. At the end of endless ramifications in terms of hypochondriacal fantasy and persecutory delusion a patient has a dream which says: I eat you. Here is stark simplicity like that of the Oedipus complex.

Stark simplicity is only possible as a bonus on top of the ego-strengthening that analysis brings about. I would like to make special reference to this but first I must refer to the fact that in many cases the analyst displaces environmental influences that are pathological, and we gain insight of the kind that enables us to know when we have become modern representatives of the parent figures of the patient's childhood and infancy, and when by contrast we are displacing such figures.

In so far as we come through this, we see ourselves affecting the patient's ego in three phases:

(a) We expect a kind of ego-strength in the early stages of an analysis, because of the ego-support that we give simply by doing standard analysis and by doing it well. This corresponds to the ego-support of the mother which (in my theorizing) makes the infant ego strong if and only if the mother is able to play her special part at this time. This is temporary and belongs to a special phase.

(b) Then follows a long phase in which the patient's confidence in the analytic process brings about all kinds of experimenting (on the part of the patient) in terms of ego independence.

(c) In the third phase the now independent ego of the patient begins to show and to assert its own individual characteristics, and the patient begins to take for granted a feeling of existing in his or her own right.

It is this ego-integration that particularly concerns me, and gives me pleasure (though it must not be for my pleasure that it takes place.) It is very satisfactory to watch the patient's growing ability to gather all things into the area of personal omnipotence, even including the genuine traumata.

Ego-strength results in a clinical change in the direction of a loosening up of the defences which become more economically employed and deployed, with the result that the individual feels no longer trapped in an illness, but feels free, even if not free from symptoms. In short, we see growth and emotional development that had become held up in the original situation.

What about modified analysis?

I find myself working as a psycho-analyst rather than doing standard analysis when I meet certain conditions that I have learned to recognize.

(a) Where fear of madness dominates the scene.

(b) Where a false self has become successful, and a façade of success and even brilliance will be destroyed at some phase if analysis is to succeed.

(c) Where in a patient an antisocial tendency, either in the form of aggression or of stealing or of both, is the legacy of a deprivation.

(*d*) Where there is no cultural life—only an inner psychic reality and a relationship to external reality—the two being relatively un-linked.

(*e*) Where an ill parental figure dominates the scene.

These and many other illness-patterns make me sit up. The essential thing is that I do base my work on diagnosis. I continue to make a diagnosis of the individual and a social diagnosis as I go along, and I do definitely work according to diagnosis. In this sense I do psycho-analysis when the diagnosis is that this individual, in his or her environment, wants psycho-analysis. I might even try to set going an unconscious co-operation, when conscious wish for analysis is absent. But by and large, analysis is for those who want it, need it, and can take it.

When I am faced with the wrong kind of case I change over into being a psycho-analyst who is meeting the needs, or trying to meet the needs, of that special case. I believe this non-analytic work can usually be best done by an analyst who is well versed in the standard psycho-analytic technique.

Finally, I would like to say this:

I have based my statement on the assumption that all analysts are alike in so far as they are analysts. But analysts are not alike. I am not like what I was twenty or thirty years ago. Some analysts undoubtedly work best in the simplest and most dynamic area where the conflict between love and hate, with all its ramifications in conscious and unconscious fantasy, constitutes the main problem. Other analysts work as well or better when they are able to deal with more primitive mental mechanisms in the transference neurosis or transference psychosis. In this way by interpreting part object retaliations, projections and introjections, hypochondriacal and paranoid anxieties, attacks on linkages, thinking disturbances, etc., etc., they extend the field of operation and the range of the cases they can tackle. This is research analysis, and the danger is only that the patient's needs in terms of infantile dependence may be lost in the course of the analyst's performance. Naturally as we come to gain confidence in the standard technique through our use of it in suitable cases we like to feel that we can tackle the borderline case without deviating, and I see no reason why the attempt should not be made, especially as the diagnosis may alter in our favour as the result of our work.

In my opinion our aims in the practice of the standard technique are not altered if it happens that we interpret mental mechanisms which belong to the psychotic types of disorder and to primitive stages in the emotional stages of the individual. If our aim continues to be to verbalize the nascent conscious in terms of the transference, then we are practising analysis; if not, then we are analysts practising something else that we deem to be appropriate to the occasion. And why not?

A PERSONAL VIEW OF THE
KLEINIAN CONTRIBUTION[1]
(1962)

In the course of your explorations outside Freud's own writings you will already have come across other important names, and you will have met analysts who have contributed in an original way, and whose contributions have been found generally acceptable. For instance, you will have met Anna Freud, who had a unique position in her father's life during the last two decades, and who cared for him with fortitude when he was ill, and you will be familiar at least with her classic summary of psychoanalytic theory in her *Ego and the Mechanisms of Defence* (1936). In any case, Anna Freud has had an immense influence on the way psycho-analysis has developed in the United States, and her stimulating interest in what others are doing has been responsible for much research that is published under other names.

Now Anna Freud was not so important in England as she has been in the United States, simply because of the very great developments that took place in London in the twenty years after the end of World War I, before Miss Freud came over with her father, refugees from Nazi persecution. It was during this period that my own psycho-analytic growth was making root and stem, and it might interest you therefore to hear from me something of the soil in which I had become planted.

You see, there developed a Melanie Klein–Anna Freud controversy, and this has not yet resolved itself. But this was not important for me in my early and formative years, and it is only important to me now in so far as it hampers free thought. In fact Melanie Klein and Anna Freud had a relationship in the Vienna days but this had no meaning for me.

From my point of view psycho-analysis in England was an edifice whose foundation was Ernest Jones. If any man earned my gratitude it was Ernest Jones, and it was Jones to whom I went when I found I needed help in 1923. He put me in touch with James Strachey, to whom I went for analysis for ten years,

[1] A talk given to the Candidates of the Los Angeles Psychoanalytic Society, 3 October 1962.

but I always knew that it was because of Jones that there was a Strachey and a British Psycho-Analytical Society for me to use.

So I came to psycho-analysis ignorant of personality clashes between the various analysts, and only too pleased to get effective help for the difficulties that were mine.

I was starting up as consultant paediatrician at that time, and you can imagine how exciting it was to be taking innumerable case histories and to be getting from uninstructed hospital-class parents all the confirmation that anyone could need for the psycho-analytic theories that were beginning to have meaning for me through my own analysis. At that time no other analyst was also a paediatrician, and so for two or three decades I was an isolated phenomenon.

I mention these facts because by being a paediatrician with a knack for getting mothers to tell me about their children and about the early history of their children's disorders, I was soon in the position of being astounded both by the insight psychoanalysis gave into the lives of children and by a certain deficiency in psycho-analytic theory which I will describe. At that time, in the 1920s, everything had the Oedipus complex at its core. The analysis of the psycho-neuroses led the analyst over and over again to the anxieties belonging to the instinctual life at the 4–5-year period in the child's relationship to the two parents. Earlier difficulties that came to light were treated in analyses as regressions to pregenital fixation points, but the dynamics came from conflict at the full-blown genital Oedipus complex of the toddler or late toddler age, that is just before the passing of the Oedipus complex and the onset of the latency period. Now, innumerable case histories showed me that the children who became disturbed, whether psycho-neurotic, psychotic, psycho-somatic or antisocial, showed difficulties in their emotional development in infancy, even as babies. Paranoid hypersensitive children could even have started to be in that pattern in the first weeks or even days of life. Something was wrong somewhere. When I came to treat children by psycho-analysis I was able to confirm the origin of psychoneurosis in the Oedipus complex, and yet I knew that troubles started earlier.

I gave many tentative and frightened papers to colleagues from the mid-twenties onwards pointing out these facts, and eventually my point of view boiled up into a paper (1936) which I called 'Appetite and Emotional Disorder'. In this I gave samples of the case histories that had to be reconciled somehow with the theory of the Oedipus complex as the point of origin of individual conflicts. Babies could be emotionally ill.

It was an important moment in my life when my analyst broke into his analysis of me and told me about Melanie Klein. He had heard about my careful history-taking and about my trying to apply what I got in my own analysis to the cases of children brought to me for every kind of paediatric disorder. I especially investigated the cases of children brought for nightmares. Strachey said: 'If you are applying psycho-analytic theory to children you should meet Melanie Klein. She has been enticed over to England by Jones to do the analysis of someone special to Jones; she is saying some things that may or may not be true, and you must find out for yourself for you will not get what Melanie Klein teaches in my analysis of you.'

So I went to hear and then to see Melanie Klein, and I found an analyst who had a great deal to say about the anxieties that belong to infancy, and I settled down to working with the benefit of her help. I took her a case written up in great detail, and she had the goodness to read it right through, and on the basis of this one pre-Klein analysis that I did on the basis of my own Strachey analysis I went on to try to learn some of the immense amount that I found she knew already.

This was difficult for me, because overnight I had changed from being a pioneer into being a student with a pioneer teacher. Melanie Klein was a generous teacher, and I counted myself lucky. I remember on one occasion going to her for a supervision, and of a whole week's work I could remember nothing at all. She simply responded by telling me of a case of her own.

I now learned psycho-analysis from Melanie Klein, and I found other teachers comparatively rigid. For one thing, she had an amazing memory. On Saturday evening, if she so wished, she could go over every detail of the week's work with each patient, without reference to notes. She remembered my cases and my analytic material better than I did myself. Later she entrusted me with the analysis of someone near and dear to her, but it should be made clear that I never had analysis by her, or by any of her analysands, so that I did not qualify to be one of her group of chosen Kleinians.

Now I must try to specify what I did get from Melanie Klein. This is difficult because at the time I simply worked on the material of my cases, and on cases she told me about, and I had no idea that what was being taught me was highly original. The thing was that it made sense, and joined up my case-history details with psycho-analytic theory.

For Melanie Klein child analysis was exactly like adult analysis. This was never a trouble from my point of view as I started with the same view, and I hold this view now. The idea of a preparatory period belongs to the type of case, not to a set technique belonging to child analysis.

Then Melanie Klein used sets of very small toys. These I found truly valuable, as they are easily manipulated and they join up with the child's imagination in a special way. It was an advance on talking and also on the drawing which I always used because of the convenience of one's having the drawings to keep to remind one of the nightmare or sample of playing.

Melanie Klein had a way of making inner psychic reality very real. For her a specific play with the toys was a projection from the child's psychic reality which is localized by the child, localized inside the self and the body.

In this way I grew up thinking of the child's manipulation of the little toys, and other special and circumscribed playing as glimpses into the child's inner world, and one saw that psychic reality can be referred to as 'inner' because it does belong to the child's concept of himself (or herself) as having an inside that is part of the self and an outside that is not-me and that is repudiated.

So in this way there was a close connexion between the mental mechanisms of introjection and the function of eating. Also projection had a relation to the bodily functions that are excretory—saliva, sweat, faeces, urine, screaming, kicking, etc.

In this way the material of an analysis either had to do with the child's object relationship or with the mechanisms of introjection and projection. Also the term object relationship could mean relationship to inner or to external objects. The child thus grew in a world, both the child and the world all the time being enriched by projection and introjection. The material for projection and introjection had a pre-history, however, for at basis what is in and of the child was at first taken in in relation to the bodily function of eating. In this way, while one could analyse for ever in terms of projection and introjection, the changes came about in relation to the eating, that is the oral erotism and sadism.

Following this, angry biting in the transference in relation to a week-end or a holiday would lead to an increase in the strength of the internal objects that had a persecutory quality. In consequence of this the child had a pain, or felt threatened within, or was sick, or else by the mechanisms of projection the child felt threatened from outside, developed phobias or had threatening fantasies either awake or asleep, or became suspicious. And so on.

Thus a very rich analytic world opened up for me, and the

material of my cases confirmed the theories and did so repeatedly. In the end I came to take it all for granted. In any case these ideas are adumbrated in Freud's 'Mourning and Melancholia' (1917); and Abraham (1916) (Klein's teacher in Berlin) opened up the new territory which Melanie Klein so much enjoyed pegging out.

The important thing for me was that while none of the impact of the Oedipus complex was lost, work was now being done on the basis of anxieties related to pregenital drives. One could see that in the more or less pure psycho-neurotic case the pregenital material was regressive and the dynamics belonged to the four-year-old period, but on the other hand, in many cases, there was illness and an organization of defences belonging to the earlier times in the infant's life, and many infants never in fact arrived at so healthy a thing as an Oedipus complex at toddler age.

In my second child training case in the early thirties I was lucky in that I had a girl of three who had started her illness (anorexia) on her first birthday. The material of the analysis was Oedipal, with reactions to the primal scene, and the child was in no way psychotic. Moreover she got well and she is now married happily and rearing her own family. But her Oedipus conflict started on her first birthday when she for the first time sat at table with her two parents. The child, who had shown no symptoms previously, reached out for food, solemnly looked at her two parents, and withdrew her hand. Thus started a severe anorexia, at exactly one year. In the material of the analysis the primal scene appeared as a meal, and sometimes the parents ate the child, whereas at other times the child upset the table (bed) and destroyed the whole set-up. Her analysis was finished in time for her to have a genital Oedipus complex before the onset of the latency period.

But this was an old-fashioned case. Melanie Klein's approach enabled me to work on the infantile conflicts and anxieties and primitive defences whether the patient was child or adult, and gradually threw light on the theory of reactive depression (started by Freud) and the theory of some states characterized by persecutory expectation, and made sense of such things as the clinical alternations to and fro between hypochondria and delusions of persecution, and between depression and the obsessional defence.

All the time working with Klein I found that there was no variation on the strict application of Freudian principles of technique. There was a careful avoidance of stepping outside the analyst's role, and the main interpretations were transference interpretations. This was natural for me because my own analyst was strictly orthodox. [Later I had a second analyst: Mrs Joan Riviere.]

What I did find was a much enriched understanding of the material presented, and in particular I found it to be valuable to be in a position to localize the item of psychic reality, inside or outside, and to get free of the use of the phrase 'weaker fantasy', even spelt with a 'ph'.

Working along Klein lines one came to an understanding of the complex stage of development that Klein called the 'depressive position'. I think this is a bad name, but it is true that clinically, in psycho-analytic treatments, arrival at this position involves the patient in being depressed. Here being depressed is an achievement, and implies a high degree of personal integration, and an acceptance of responsibility for all the destructiveness that is bound up with living, with the instinctual life, and with anger at frustration.

Klein was able to make it clear to me from the material my patients presented, how the capacity for concern and to feel guilty is an achievement, and it is this rather than depression that characterizes arrival at the depressive position in the case of the growing baby and child.

Arrival at this stage is associated with ideas of restitution and reparation, and indeed the human individual cannot accept the destructive and aggressive ideas in his or her own nature without experience of reparation, and for this reason the continued presence of the love object is necessary at this stage since only in this way is there opportunity for reparation.

This is Klein's most important contribution, in my opinion, and I think it ranks with Freud's concept of the Oedipus complex. The latter concerns a three-body relationship and Klein's depressive position concerns a two-body relationship—that between the infant and the mother. The main ingredient is a degree of ego-organization and strength in the baby or young child, and for this reason it is difficult to place the beginnings of the depressive position earlier than 8–9 months, or a year. But what does it matter?

All this belongs to the era between the wars, when there was rapid growth in the British Society and when Klein was the fertilizing agent. Paula Heimann and Susan Isaacs were in support, and also Joan Riviere, my second analyst.

Since those days a great deal has happened, and I do not claim to be able to hand out the Klein view in a way that she would herself approve of. I believe my views began to separate out from hers, and in any case I found she had not included me in as a Kleinian. This did not matter to me because I have never been able to follow anyone else, not even Freud. But Freud was easy to criticize because he was always critical of himself. For instance, I simply cannot find value in his idea of a Death Instinct.

Well, Klein has done a great deal more that we cannot afford to ignore. She has gone deeper and deeper into the mental mechanisms of her patients and then has applied her concepts to the growing baby. I think it is here that she has made mistakes because deeper in psychology does not always mean earlier.

It has become an important part of the Klein theory to postulate a paranoid-schizoid position which dates from the very beginning. This term paranoid-schizoid is certainly a bad one, but we nevertheless cannot ignore the fact that we meet, in a vitally important way, the two mechanisms

(1) talion dread
(2) splitting of the object into 'good' and 'bad'.

Klein seemed to think at the end that infants start in this way, but this seems to ignore the fact that with good-enough mothering the two mechanisms may be relatively unimportant until the ego-organization has made the baby capable of using projection and introjection mechanisms in gaining control over objects. If there is not good-enough mothering, then the result is chaos rather than talion dread and a splitting of the object into 'good' and 'bad'.

In regard to good and bad, I think it doubtful whether these words can be used before the infant has become able to sort out benign from persecutory internal objects.

So much of what Klein wrote in the last two decades of her fruitful life may have been spoilt by her tendency to push the age at which mental mechanisms appear further and further back, so that she even found the depressive position in early weeks; also she paid lip-service to environmental provision, but would never fully acknowledge that along with the dependence of early infancy is truly a period in which it is not possible to describe an infant without describing the mother whom the infant has not yet become able to separate from a self. Klein claimed to have paid full attention to the environmental factor, but it is my opinion that she was temperamentally incapable of this. Perhaps there was a gain in this, for certainly she had a powerful drive to go further and further back into the personal individual mental mechanisms that constitute the new human being who is at the bottom rung of the ladder of emotional development.

The main point is that whatever criticism we may want to

make of Klein's standpoint in her last two decades, we cannot ignore the very great impact her work had in England, and will have everywhere, on orthodox psycho-analysis.

As for the controversy between Klein and Anna Freud, and between the followers of each, this has no importance to me, nor will it have to you, because it is a local matter, and a strong wind will blow it away. The only important thing is that psycho-analysis, firmly based on Freud, shall not miss Klein's contribution which I shall now attempt to summarize:

Strict orthodox technique in psycho-analysis of children.

Technique facilitated by use of tiny toys in initial stages.

Technique for analysis of two-and-a-half-year-old children and all ages older.

Recognition of fantasy as localized by the child (or adult), i.e. inside or outside the self.

Understanding of internal benign and persecutory forces or 'objects' and their origin in satisfactory or unsatisfactory instinctual experiences (originally oral and oral sadistic).

Importance of projection and introjection as mental mechanisms developed in relation to the child's experience of the bodily functions of incorporation and excretion.

Emphasis on the importance of destructive elements in object relationships, i.e. apart from anger at frustration.

Development of a theory of the individual's attainment of a capacity for concern (depressive position).

Relationship of constructive play
             work
             potency and child-bearing
   to the depressive position.

Understanding of denial of depression (manic defence).

Understanding of threatened chaos in inner psychic reality and defences related to this chaos (obsessional neurosis or depressive mood).

Postulation of infantile impulses, talion fears and the splitting of the object prior to attainment of ambivalence.

Always an attempt to state the infant's psychology without reference to the quality of the environmental provision.

Then come certain more *doubtful* contributions:

Retaining a use of the theory of the Life and Death Instincts.

An attempt to state infantile destructiveness in terms of
   (a) heredity
   (b) envy.

COMMUNICATING AND NOT COMMUNICATING LEADING TO A STUDY OF CERTAIN OPPOSITES[1]

(1963)

Every point of thought is the centre of an intellectual world
(Keats)

I have started with this observation of Keats because I know that my paper contains only one idea, a rather obvious idea at that, and I have used the opportunity for re-presenting my formulations of early stages in the emotional development of the human infant. First I shall describe object-relating and I only gradually get to the subject of communicating.

Starting from no fixed place I soon came, while preparing this paper for a foreign society, to staking a claim, to my surprise, to the right not to communicate. This was a protest from the core of me to the frightening fantasy of being infinitely exploited. In another language this would be the fantasy of being eaten or swallowed up. In the language of this paper it is *the fantasy of being found*. There is a considerable literature on the psycho-analytic patient's silences, but I shall not study or summarize this literature here and now. Also I am not attempting to deal comprehensively with the subject of communication, and in fact I shall allow myself considerable latitude in following my theme wherever it takes me. Eventually I shall allow a subsidiary theme, the study of opposites. First I find I need to restate some of my views on early object-relating.

Object-Relating

Looking directly at communication and the capacity to communicate one can see that this is closely bound up with relating to objects. Relating to objects is a complex phenomenon and the development of a capacity to relate to objects is by no means a matter simply of the maturational process. As always, *maturation*

[1] Differing versions of this paper were given to the San Francisco Psycho-analytic Society, October 1962, and to the British Psycho-Analytical Society, May 1963.

(in psychology) *requires and depends on the quality of the facilitating environment.* Where neither privation nor deprivation dominates the scene and where, therefore, the facilitating environment can be taken for granted in the theory of the earliest and most formative stages of human growth, there gradually develops in the individual a change in the nature of the object. The object *being at first a subjective phenomenon becomes an object objectively perceived.* This process takes time, and months and even years must pass before privations and deprivations can be accommodated by the individual without distortion of essential processes that are basic to object-relating.

At this early stage the facilitating environment is giving the infant the *experience of omnipotence*; by this I mean more than magical control, I mean the term to include the creative aspect of experience. Adaptation to the reality principle arises naturally out of the experience of omnipotence, within the area, that is, of a relationship to subjective objects.

Margaret Ribble (1943), who enters this field, misses, I think, one important thing, which is the mother's identification with her infant (what I call the temporary state of Primary Maternal Preoccupation). She writes:

The human infant in the first year of life should not have to meet frustration or privation, for these factors immediately cause exaggerated tension and stimulate latent defense activities. If the effects of such experiences are not skillfully counteracted, behavior disorders may result. For the baby, the pleasure principle must predominate, and what we can safely do is to bring balance into his functions and make them easy. Only after a considerable degree of maturity has been reached can we train an infant to adapt to what we as adults know as the reality principle.

She is referring to the matter of object-relating, or of id-satisfactions, but I think she could also subscribe to the more modern views on ego-relatedness.

The infant experiencing omnipotence under the aegis of the facilitating environment *creates and re-creates the object,* and the process gradually becomes built in, and gathers a memory backing.

Undoubtedly that which eventually becomes the intellect does affect the immature individual's capacity to make this very difficult transition from relating to subjective objects to relating to objects objectively perceived, and I have suggested that that which eventually gives results on intelligence testing does affect the individual's capacity to survive relative failures in the area of the adapting environment.

In health the infant creates what is in fact lying around waiting to be found. But in health *the object is created, not found.* This fascinating aspect of normal object-relating has been studied by me in various papers, including the one on 'Transitional Objects and Transitional Phenomena' (1951). A good object is no good to the infant unless created by the infant. Shall I say, created out of need? Yet the object must be found in order to be created. This has to be accepted as a paradox, and not solved by a restatement that, by its cleverness, seems to eliminate the paradox.

There is another point that has importance if one considers the location of the object. The change of the object from 'subjective' to 'objectively perceived' is jogged along less effectually by satisfactions than by dissatisfactions. The satisfaction to be derived from a feed has less value in this respect of the establishment of object-relating than when the object is, so to speak, in the way. Instinct-gratification gives the infant a personal experience and *does but little to the position of the object*; I have had a case in which satisfactions eliminated the object for an adult schizoid patient, so that he could not lie on the couch, this reproducing for him the situation of the infantile satisfactions that eliminated external reality or the externality of objects. I have put this in another way, saying that the infant feels 'fobbed off' by a satisfactory feed, and it can be found that a nursing mother's anxiety can be based on the fear that if the infant is not satisfied then the mother will be attacked and destroyed. After a feed the satisfied infant is not dangerous for a few hours, has lost object-cathexis.

Per contra, the infant's experienced aggression, that which belongs to muscle erotism, to movement, and to irresistible forces meeting immovable objects, this aggression, and the ideas bound up with it, lends itself to the process of placing the object, to placing the object separate from the self, in so far as the self has begun to emerge as an entity.

In the area of development that is prior to the achievement of fusion one must allow for the infant's behaviour that is reactive to failures of the facilitating environment, or of the environment-mother, and this may look like aggression; actually it is distress.

In health, when the infant achieves fusion, the frustrating aspect of object behaviour has value in educating the infant in respect of the existence of a not-me world. Adaptation failures have value *in so far as the infant can hate the object*, that is to say, can retain the idea of the object as potentially satisfying while recognizing its failure to behave satisfactorily. As I understand it, this is good psycho-analytic theory. What is often neglected in statements of this detail of theory is the immense development that takes place in the infant for fusion to be achieved, and for environmental failure therefore to play its positive part, enabling the infant to begin to know of a world that is repudiated. I deliberately do not say external.

There is an intermediate stage in healthy development in which the patient's most important experience in relation to the good or potentially satisfying object is the refusal of it. The refusal of it is part of the process of creating it. (This produces a truly formidable problem for the therapist in anorexia nervosa.)

Our patients teach us these things, and it is distressing to me that I must give these views as if they were my own. All analysts have this difficulty, and in a sense it is more difficult for an analyst to be original than for anyone else, because everything that we say truly has been taught us yesterday, apart from the fact that we listen to each other's papers and discuss matters privately. In our work, especially in working on the schizoid rather than the psycho-neurotic aspects of the personality, we do in fact wait, if we feel we know, until the patients tell us, and in doing so creatively make the interpretation we might have made; if we make the interpretation out of our own cleverness and experience then the patient must refuse it or destroy it. An anorexia patient is teaching me the substance of what I am saying now as I write it down.

Theory of Communication

These matters, although I have stated them in terms of object-relating, do seem to affect the study of communication, because naturally there comes about a change in the purpose and in the means of communication *as the object changes over* from being subjective to being objectively perceived, in so far as the child gradually leaves the area of omnipotence as a living experience. In so far as the object is subjective, *so far is it unnecessary for communication with it to be explicit.* In so far as the object is objectively perceived, communication is either explicit or else dumb. Here then appear two *new* things, the individual's use and enjoyment of modes of communication, and the individual's non-communicating self, or the personal core of the self that is a true isolate.

A complication in this line of argument arises out of the fact that the infant develops two kinds of relationships at one and the same time—that to the environment-mother and that to the object, which becomes the object-mother. The environment-mother is human, and the object-mother is a thing, although it is also the mother or part of her.

Intercommunication between infant and environment-mother is undoubtedly subtle to a degree, and a study of this would involve us in a study of the mother as much as of the infant. I will only touch on this. Perhaps for the infant there is communication with the environment-mother, brought into evidence by the experience of her *unreliability*. The infant is shattered, and this may be taken by the mother as a communication if the mother can put herself in the infant's place, and if she can recognize the shattering in the infant's clinical state. When her *reliability* dominates the scene the infant could be said to communicate simply by going on being, and by going on developing according to personal processes of maturation, but this scarcely deserves the epithet communication.

Returning to object-relating: as the object becomes objectively perceived by the child so does it become meaningful for us to contrast communication with one of its opposites.

The Objectively Perceived Object

The objectively perceived object gradually becomes a person with part objects. Two opposites of communication are:

(1) A simple not-communicating.
(2) A not-communicating that is active or reactive.

It is easy to understand the first of these. Simple not-communicating is like resting. It is a state in its own right, and it passes over into communicating, and reappears as naturally. To study the second it is necessary to think in terms both of pathology and of health. I will take pathology first.

So far I have taken for granted the facilitating environment, nicely adjusted to need arising out of being and arising out of the processes of maturation. In the psycho-pathology that I need for my argument here the facilitation has failed in some respect and in some degree, and in the matter of object-relating the infant has developed a split. By one half of the split the infant relates to the presenting object, and for this purpose there develops what I have called a false or compliant self. By the other half of the split the infant relates to a subjective object, or to mere phenomena based on body experiences, these being scarcely influenced by an objectively perceived world. (Clinically do we not see this in autistic rocking movements, for instance; and in the abstract picture that is a cul-de-sac communication, and that has no general validity?)

In this way I am introducing the idea of a communication with subjective objects and at the same time the idea of an active non-communication with that which is objectively perceived by the infant. There seems to be no doubt that for all its futility from the observer's point of view, the cul-de-sac communication (communication with subjective objects) carries all the sense of real. *Per contra*, such communication with the world as occurs from the false self does not feel real; it is not a true communication because it does not involve the core of the self, that which could be called a true self.

Now, by studying the extreme case we reach the psychopathology of severe illness, infantile schizophrenia; what must be examined, however, is the pattern of all this in so far as it can be found in the more normal individual, the individual whose development was not distorted by gross failure of the facilitating environment, and in whom the maturational processes did have a chance.

It is easy to see that in the cases of slighter illness, in which there is some pathology and some health, there must be expected an active non-communication (clinical withdrawal) because of the fact that communication so easily becomes linked with some degree of false or compliant object-relating; silent or secret communication with subjective objects, carrying a sense of real, must periodically take over to restore balance.

I am postulating that in the healthy (mature, that is, in respect of the development of object-relating) person there is a need for something that corresponds to the state of the split person in whom one part of the split communicates silently with subjective objects. There is room for the idea that significant relating and communicating is silent.

Real health need not be described only in terms of the residues in healthy persons of what might have been illness-patterns. One should be able to make a positive statement of the healthy use of non-communication in the establishment of the feeling of real. It may be necessary in so doing to speak in terms of man's cultural life, which is the adult equivalent of the transitional phenomena of infancy and early childhood, and in which area communication is made without reference to the object's state of being either subjective or objectively perceived. It is my opinion that the psycho-analyst has no other language in which to refer to cultural phenomena. He can talk about the mental mechanisms of the artist but not about the experience of communication in art and religion unless he is willing to peddle in the intermediate area whose ancestor is the infant's transitional object.

In the artist of all kinds I think one can detect an inherent dilemma, which belongs to the co-existence of two trends, the urgent need to communicate and the still more urgent need not to be found. This might account for the fact that we cannot conceive of an artist's coming to the end of the task that occupies his whole nature.

In the early phases of emotional development in the human being, silent communicating concerns the subjective aspect of objects. This links, I suppose, with Freud's concept of psychic reality and of the unconscious that can never become conscious. I would add that there is a direct development, in health, from this silent communicating to the concept of inner experiences that Melanie Klein described so clearly. In the case descriptions of Melanie Klein certain aspects of a child's play, for instance, are shown to be 'inside' experiences; that is to say, there has been a wholesale projection of a constellation from the child's inner psychic reality so that the room and the table and the toys are subjective objects, and the child and the analyst are both there in this sample of the child's inner world. What is outside the room is outside the child. This is familiar ground in psycho-analysis, although various analysts describe it in various ways. It is related to the concept of the 'honeymoon period' at the beginning of an analysis, and to the special clarity of certain first hours. It is related to dependence in the transference. It also joins up with the work that I am doing myself on the full exploitation of first hours in the short treatments of children, especially antisocial children, for whom full-scale analysis is not available and not even always advisable.

But my object in this paper is not to become clinical but to get to a very early version of that which Melanie Klein referred to as 'internal'. At the beginning the word internal cannot be used in the Klein sense since the infant has not yet properly established an ego boundary and has not yet become master of the mental mechanisms of projection and introjection. At this early stage 'inner' only means personal, and personal in so far as the individual is a person with a self in process of becoming evolved. The facilitating environment, or the mother's ego-support to the infant's immature ego, these are still essential parts of the child as a viable creature.

In thinking of the psychology of mysticism, it is usual to concentrate on the understanding of the mystic's withdrawal into a personal inner world of sophisticated introjects. Perhaps not enough attention has been paid to the mystic's retreat to a position in which he can communicate secretly with subjective objects and phenomena, the loss of contact with the world of shared reality being counterbalanced by a gain in terms of feeling real.

A woman patient dreamed: two women friends were customs officers at the place where the woman works. They were going through all the possessions of the patient and her colleagues with absurd care. She then drove a car, by accident, through a pane of glass.

There were details in the dream that showed that not only had these two women no right to be there doing this examining, but also they were making fools of themselves by their way of looking at everything. It became clear that the patient was mocking at these two women. They would not in fact get at the secret self. They stood for the mother who does not allow the child her secret. The patient said that in childhood (nine years) she had a stolen school book in which she collected poems and sayings, and she wrote in it 'My private book'. On the front page she wrote: 'What a man thinketh in his heart, so is he.' In fact her mother had asked her: 'Where did you get this saying from?' This was bad because it meant that the mother must have read her book. It would have been all right if the mother had read the book but had said nothing.

Here is a picture of a child establishing a private self that is not communicating, and at the same time wanting to communicate and to be found. It is a sophisticated game of hide-and-seek in which *it is joy to be hidden but disaster not to be found.*

Another example that will not involve me in too deep or detailed a description comes from a diagnostic interview with a girl of seventeen. Her mother worries lest she become schizophrenic as this is a family trait, but at present it can be said that she is in the middle of all the doldrums and dilemmas that belong to adolescence.

Here is an extract from my report of the interview:

X. then went on to talk about the glorious irresponsibility of childhood. She said: 'You see a cat and you are with it; it's a subject, not an object.'

I said: 'It's as if you were living in a world of subjective objects.'

And she said: 'That's a good way of putting it. That's why I write poetry. That's the sort of thing that's the foundation of poetry.'

She added: 'Of course it's only an idle theory of mine, but that's how it seems and this explains why it's men who write poetry more than girls. With girls so much gets caught up in looking after children or having babies and then the imaginative life and the irresponsibility goes over to the children.'

We then spoke about bridges to be kept open between the imaginative life and everyday existence. She kept a diary when she was 12 and again at 14, each time apparently for a period of seven months.

She said: 'Now I only write down things that I feel in poems; in poetry something crystallizes out,'—and we compared this with autobiography which she feels belongs to a later age.

She said: 'There is an affinity between old age and childhood.'

When she needs to form a bridge with childhood imagination it has to be crystallized out in a poem. She would get bored to write an autobiography. She does not publish her poems or even show them to anybody because although she is fond of each poem for a little while she soon loses interest in it. She has always been able to write poems more easily than her friends because of a technical ability which she seems to have naturally. But she is not interested in the question: are the poems really good? or not? that is to say: would other people think them good?

I suggest that in health there is a core to the personality that corresponds to the true self of the split personality; I suggest that this core never communicates with the world of perceived objects, and that the individual person knows that it must never be communicated with or be influenced by external reality. This is my main point, the point of thought which is the centre of an intellectual world and of my paper. Although healthy persons communicate and enjoy communicating, the other fact is equally true, that *each individual is an isolate, permanently non-communicating, permanently unknown, in fact unfound.*

In life and living this hard fact is softened by the sharing that belongs to the whole range of cultural experience. At the centre of each person is an incommunicado element, and this is sacred and most worthy of preservation. Ignoring for the moment the still earlier and shattering experiences of failure of the environment-mother, I would say that the traumatic experiences that lead to the organization of primitive defences belong to the threat to the isolated core, the threat of its being found, altered, communicated with. The defence consists in a further hiding of the secret self, even in the extreme to its projection and to its endless dissemination. Rape, and being eaten by cannibals, these are mere bagatelles as compared with the violation of the self's core, the alteration of the self's central elements by communication seeping through the defences. For me this would be the sin against the self. We can understand the hatred people have of psycho-analysis which has penetrated a long way into the human personality, and which provides a threat to the human individual in his need to be secretly isolated. The question is: how to be isolated without having to be insulated?

What is the answer? Shall we stop trying to understand human beings? The answer might come from mothers who do not communicate with their infants except in so far as they are subjective objects. By the time mothers become objectively perceived their infants have become masters of various techniques for indirect communication, the most obvious of which is the use of language. There is this transitional period, however, which has specially interested me, in which transitional objects and phenomena have a place, and begin to establish for the infant the use of symbols.

I suggest that an important basis for ego development lies in this area of the individual's communicating with subjective phenomena, which alone gives the feeling of real.

In the best possible circumstances growth takes place and the child now possesses three lines of communication: communication that is *for ever silent*, communication that is *explicit*, indirect and pleasurable, and this third or *intermediate* form of communication that slides out of playing into cultural experience of every kind.

Is silent communication related to the concept of primary narcissism?

In practice then there is something we must allow for in our work, the patient's non-communicating as a positive contribution. We must ask ourselves, does our technique allow for the patient to communicate that he or she is not communicating? For this to happen we as analysts must be ready for the signal: 'I am not communicating', and be able to distinguish it from the distress signal associated with a failure of communication. There is a link here with the idea of being alone in the presence of someone, at first a natural event in child-life, and later on a matter of the acquisition of a capacity for withdrawal without loss of identification with that from which withdrawal has occurred. This appears as the capacity to concentrate on a task.

My main point has now been made, and I might stop here. Nevertheless I wish to consider what are the opposites of communication.

Opposites

There are two opposites of communication, simple non-communication, and active non-communication. Put the other way round, communication may simply arise out of not-communication, as a natural transition, or communication may be a negation of silence, or a negation of an active or reactive not-communicating.

In the clear-cut psycho-neurotic case there is no difficulty because the whole analysis is done through the intermediary of verbalization. Both the patient and the analyst want this to be so. But it is only too easy for an analysis (where there is a hidden schizoid element in the patient's personality) to become an infinitely prolonged collusion of the analyst with the patient's negation of non-communication. Such an analysis becomes tedious because of its lack of result in spite of good work done. In such an analysis a period of silence may be the most positive contribution the patient can make, and the analyst is then involved in a waiting game. One can of course interpret movements and gestures and all sorts of behavioural details, but in the kind of case I have in mind the analyst had better wait.

More dangerous, however, is the state of affairs in an analysis in which the analyst is permitted by the patient to reach to the deepest layers of the analysand's personality because of his position as subjective object, or because of the dependence of the patient in the transference psychosis; here there is danger if the analyst interprets instead of waiting for the patient to creatively discover. It is only here, at the place when the analyst has not changed over from a subjective object to one that is objectively perceived, that psycho-analysis is dangerous, and the danger is one that can be avoided if we know how to behave ourselves. If we wait we become objectively perceived in the patient's own time, but if we fail to behave in a way that is facilitating the patient's analytic process (which is the equivalent of the infant's and the child's maturational process) we suddenly become not-me for the patient, and then we know too much, and we are dangerous because we are too nearly in communication with the central still and silent spot of the patient's ego-organization.

For this reason we find it convenient even in the case of a straightforward psycho-neurotic case to avoid contacts that are outside the analysis. In the case of the schizoid or borderline patient this matter of how we manage extra-transference contacts becomes very much a part of our work with the patient.

Here one could discuss the purpose of the analyst's interpreting. I have always felt that an important function of the interpretation is the establishment of the *limits* of the analyst's understanding.

Individuals as Isolates

I am putting forward and stressing the importance of the idea of the *permanent isolation of the individual* and claiming that at the core of the individual there is no communication with the not-me world either way. Here quietude is linked with stillness. This leads to the writings of those who have become recognized as the world's thinkers. Incidentally, I can refer to Michael Fordham's very interesting review of the concept of the Self as it has appeared in Jung's writings. Fordham writes: 'The over-all fact remains that the primordial experience occurs in solitude.' Naturally this that I am referring to appears in Wickes's *The Inner World of Man* (1938), but here it is not always certain that a distinction is always drawn between pathological withdrawal and healthy central self-communication (cf. Laing, 1961).

Among psycho-analysts there may be many references to the idea of a 'still, silent' centre to the personality and to the idea of the primordial experience occurring in solitude, but analysts are not usually concerned with just this aspect of life. Among our immediate colleagues perhaps Ronald Laing is with most de- liberation setting out to state the 'making patent of the latent self' along with diffidence about disclosing oneself (cf. Laing, 1961, p. 117).

This theme of the individual as an isolate has its importance in the study of infancy and of psychosis, but it also has importance in the study of adolescence. The boy and girl at puberty can be described in many ways, and one way concerns *the adolescent as an isolate*. This preservation of personal isolation is part of the search for identity, and for the establishment of a personal technique for communicating which does not lead to violation of the central self. This may be one reason why adolescents on the whole eschew psycho-analytic treatment, though they are interested in psycho-analytic theories. They feel that by psycho-analysis they will be raped, not sexually but spiritually. In practice the analyst can avoid confirming the adolescent's fears in this respect, but the analyst of an adolescent must expect to be tested out fully and must be prepared to use communication of indirect kind, and to recognize simple non-communication.

At adolescence when the individual is undergoing pubertal changes and is not quite ready to become one of the adult com- munity there is a strengthening of the defences against being found, that is to say being found before being there to be found. That which is truly personal and which feels real must be defended at all cost, and even if this means a temporary blindness to the value of compromise. Adolescents form aggregates rather than groups, and by looking alike they emphasize the essential loneliness of each individual. At least, this is how it seems to me.

With all this is bound up the crisis of identity. Wheelis, who has struggled with identity problems, states (1958) clearly and crudely the problem of the analyst's vocational choice, and links this with his loneliness and need for intimacy which, in analytic work, is doomed to lead nowhere. The analyst who seems to me to be most deeply involved in these matters is Erik Erikson. He discusses this theme in the epilogue of his book, *Young Man Luther* (1958), and he reaches to the phrase 'Peace comes from the inner space' (i.e. not from outer space exploration and all that).

Before ending I wish to refer once more to the opposites that belong to negation. Melanie Klein used negation in the concept of the manic defence, in which depression that is a fact is negated. Bion (1962a) referred to denials of certain kinds in his paper on thinking, and de Monchaux (1962) continued with the theme in her comment on Bion's paper.

If I take the idea of liveliness, I have to allow for at least two opposites, one being deadness, as in manic defence, and the other being a simple absence of liveliness. It is here that silence is equated with communication and stillness with movement. By using this idea I can get behind my rooted object to the theory of the Life and Death Instincts. I see that what I cannot accept is that Life has Death as its opposite, except clinically in the manic-depressive swing, and in the concept of the manic defence in which depression is negated and negatived. In the development of the individual infant living arises and establishes itself out of not-living, and being becomes a fact that replaces not-being, as communication arises out of silence. Death only becomes meaningful in the infant's living processes when hate has arrived, that is at a late date, far removed from the phenomena which we can use to build a theory of the roots of aggression.

For me therefore it is not valuable to join the word death with the word instinct, and less still is it valuable to refer to hate and anger by use of the words death instinct.

It is difficult to get at the roots of aggression, but we are not helped by the use of opposites such as life and death that do not mean anything at the stage of immaturity that is under consideration.

The other thing that I wish to tie on to the end of my paper is an altogether different opposite to aliveness or liveliness. This opposite is not operative in the majority of our cases. Usually the mother of an infant has live internal objects, and the infant fits into the mother's preconception of a *live* child. Normally the mother is not depressed or depressive. In certain cases, however, the mother's central internal object is dead at the critical time in her child's early infancy, and her mood is one of depression. Here the infant has to fit in with a role of *dead* object, or else has to be lively to counteract the mother's preconception with the idea of the child's deadness. Here the opposite to the liveliness of the infant is *an anti-life factor* derived from the mother's depression. The task of the infant in such a case is to be alive and to look alive and to communicate being alive; in fact this is the ultimate aim of such an individual, who is thus denied that which belongs to more fortunate infants, the enjoyment of what life and living may bring. To be alive is all. It is a constant struggle to get to the starting point and to keep there. No wonder there are those who make a special business of existing and who turn it into a religion. (I think that Ronald Laing's (1960, 1961) two books are attempting to state the predicament of this nature that many must contend with because of environmental abnormalities.) In healthy development the infant (theoretically) starts off (psychologically) without life and becomes lively simply because of being, in fact, alive.

As I have already said at an earlier stage, this being alive is the early communication of a healthy infant with the mother-figure, and it is as unselfconscious as can be. Liveliness that negates maternal depression is a communication designed to meet what is to be expected. The aliveness of the child whose mother is depressed is a communication of a reassuring nature, and it is unnatural and an intolerable handicap to the immature ego in its function of integrating and generally maturing according to inherited process.

You will have observed that I have brought the subject back to that of communication, but I do recognize that I have allowed myself a great deal of freedom in following trains of thought.

Summary

I have tried to state the need that we have to recognize this aspect of health: the non-communicating central self, for ever immune from the reality principle, and for ever silent. Here communication is not non-verbal; it is, like the music of the spheres, absolutely personal. It belongs to being alive. And in health, it is out of this that communication naturally arises.

Explicit communication is pleasurable and it involves extremely interesting techniques, including that of language. The two extremes, explicit communication that is indirect, and silent or personal communication that feels real, each of these has its place, and in the intermediate cultural area there exists for many, but not for all, a mode of communication which is a most valuable compromise.

18

TRAINING FOR CHILD PSYCHIATRY[1]
(1963)

I have found it very difficult to write this paper. The reason, I believe, is that in this discussion we are concerned neither with scientific nor with poetic truth.

Indeed, what I have to say *must* be affected by the history of my own development, it *must* be prejudiced according to my feelings about certain key matters, and it *must* be a sub-total statement in accordance with the limited scope of one man's experience.

Quite simply, I wish to state that the work we do which is at present called child psychiatry is a speciality on its own. If we retain the term 'child psychiatry', we must be quite clear that it is not a part of general psychiatry.

I shall explore the relationship of our work to the work of neighbouring specialities, and I shall make a few positive suggestions.

The training of child psychiatrists depends on our views on the nature of the work we do, and I shall put in a plea for the retention of variety in the matter of portals of entry. In particular let no overhead planning exclude the possibility of entry into child psychiatry through paediatrics.

I shall assume that at the Child Guidance Training Centre and at the Tavistock Clinic and the Maudsley Child Psychiatry Department the same questions are being asked that I am asking in this paper. Recently there was a discussion on this subject at the Tavistock Clinic, and those who were present will agree that the ground was pretty well covered on that occasion.

What is Child Psychiatry?

The question that must be asked first is: what is child psychiatry? In child psychiatry the work is essentially practical. In respect of each case we meet a challenge. In terms of bringing about clinical improvement we may fail, and we often succeed. Real failure can only be stated in terms of *a failure to meet the*

[1] Contribution to Symposium first published in the *Journal of Child Psychology and Psychiatry*, 4, pp. 85–91.

challenge of the case. For this reason the part of our work that is done privately and apart from team-work shows us more than team-work does that the need in each case is for someone to meet someone at a deep level. It is generally accepted that the case conference is of no value unless afterwards someone carries over into a personal relationship the new understanding that discussion has brought. New understanding does nothing by itself.

The basis of much of the work of the child psychiatrist is the psycho-therapeutic interview with the child. If he has not the skill for this, or is not a suitable person to make contact with the child in this way, he cannot even make a diagnosis, let alone know how to alter a fixed situation, or understand what the other members of his team are doing. A training scheme must take this into account.

Likewise the child psychiatrist is engaged in working with the parents. Or it may be that he is in search of a plan that would enable the mother, or the father, or someone *in loco parentis*, to provide a suitable environment for a child during a phase of difficulty. The theory behind this is that suitable environmental provision facilitates the internal maturational process.

Often we find we are making a diagnosis of health, or normality, in face of the undoubted existence of symptoms in the child's developing relationship to the self, to the parents, to the family unit, and to the environment generally. Health is almost synonymous with maturity—maturity at age.

A Classification

It is not possible, I find, to make a comprehensive statement of our work, but instead I shall attempt a rough classification:

Cases Manifesting:
(a) Inherent difficulties in the emotional development of the individual.
    Environmental factors that are unhelpful or actually harmful.
    Symptomatology based on defence organizations relative to inherent difficulties interwoven with environmental failures.
    Illness based on the failure of defences and the reorganization of new defences.
(b) Illness associated with or secondary to physical disease.
(c) Problems that take us to the borderline (paediatrics, neurology, adult psychiatry, obstetrics).
(d) Illness involving society: The antisocial tendency.
    Co-operation with legal procedure.
(e) Problems at the borderline of the educational specialist.

A child psychiatrist must be medically qualified, and should have *practised* as a doctor, because he will need to take responsibility for life and death, and for the occasional suicide that must certainly come his way. What does he need in addition? The first answer is, of course, that he needs opportunity for experience. (Here I was lucky, because as physician in my own right at The Queen's (now Queen Elizabeth) Hospital for Children for ten years, and at Paddington Green Children's Hospital from 1923 till now, I had a medical department of my own that I could exploit as I wished. Hector Cameron had just this. But it must be rare for anyone to have such an opportunity to come to child psychiatry slowly and naturally.) The moral here is that we must plan to allow those who wish to specialize our way to have the chance to develop at a natural pace. If, on the other hand, the child psychiatrist who is starting is immediately asked to do teaching, then he must teach what others have said and not what he himself has discovered, which is a pity.

The Backing for Child Psychiatry

But my main theme needs to be stated. I will approach it this way. The educational psychologist has the backing of education, and I am glad; it supports his learning process, it gives him status, and it looks after his finances. Now, who shall back those who are clinically involved? The universities are suspicious of the practical application of psychology in terms of human affairs, especially where individual human beings are being helped; also the universities are suspicious of psychology unless it keeps on the academic rails and eschews working with the dynamic unconscious.

The social workers of various kinds are struggling to establish themselves as professional workers. What about the child psychiatrists? Who shall give them backing (except that which they automatically get by being medically qualified)?

We need only consider two types of backing, paediatrics and psychiatry, and we can say that in each case we have been so badly let down that we now cannot consider anything but autonomy. The fact that our chairman is a paediatrician can rightly be taken to indicate that there exist enlightened paediatricians now who are not only friendly but who are actively supportive. Also at Paddington Green and then (since we became absorbed) at St Mary's, I have been treated generously, and with great friendliness. But I cannot allow my own good fortune to blind me to the general position. Paediatrics has failed as a parental figure for child psychiatry, and so has psychiatry.

I will first refer to adult psychiatry and then to paediatrics, and then attempt to formulate something positive.

Psychiatry

How far can general psychiatry be trusted with the task of representing child psychiatry at planning level? I suggest that the general psychiatrist is not usually aware of what a child psychiatrist does and is. If this be so, how can he represent child psychiatry? There are of course vast areas of overlap between general psychiatry and child psychiatry. Who could say whether mental defect is psychiatric, neurological or paediatric? No need to decide. Also adolescence gradually merges into adulthood, and so child psychiatry overlaps with adult psychiatry when patients get stuck at the time when their teenage doldrums normally resolve. Also, parents and parent figures are frequently to be recognized as ill in a psychiatric sense; and adult type psychiatric syndromes do periodically appear in the child psychiatry clinic. There will always be a proportion of those entering child psychiatry who graduate first in adult psychiatry, and I have no wish to see this altered. In any case we need the adult psychiatrist to look after us when we ourselves go ungracefully into a decline. But I do wish to express the opinion that, for us, adult psychiatry is concerned with alien problems. If your son wishes to enter child psychiatry, if you advise him first to become a psychiatrist you are advising him to waste a great deal of time which he could be better spending in paediatrics.

Is it not true that adult psychiatry grew out of a concern for people who had diseased brains or who were thought to have a physical or inherited disorder? Is it not true that adult psychiatry has clung on to the biochemistry and the neurophysiology of mental disorder, at the expense, in this country, of a study of the contribution that could be made through co-operation with dynamic psychology? This is understandable in view of the fact that the adult psychiatrist has to cope with the enormous burden of the degenerated insane and with the almost insoluble problem of their nursing needs. But these same considerations make it necessary for child psychiatry to separate itself off from adult psychiatry, especially in respect of training.

Areas of Concern

Adult psychiatry is concerned with two sets of problems:

(a) Disorder of the mind secondary to inherited tendencies, to brain tissue deficiency, to brain tissue disease, to general degenerative diseases, such as arteriosclerosis, which incidentally affect the brain.

(b) Disorders of the mind which are *late* evidence of *early* emotional distress.

In this second category may come the majority of adult psychiatric cases, and here the adult psychiatrist *always comes too late* to the field. In all these latter cases, the time at which the illness started was in the patient's infancy or early childhood. The paediatrician was the doctor who was naturally involved at the time of maximum stress, but fortunately for his peace of mind the paediatrician did not know. If he did, then he may have called for help from the child psychiatrist, and a proportion of the adult psychiatrist's cases are therapeutic failures of the combined paediatric and child psychiatric departments. Our successes manage to avoid coming to the department of adult psychiatry.

Child psychiatry is concerned with:

(a) The development of the personality and the character of the individual *in health*, and in various family and social patterns.

(b) The disorders of emotional development at their beginning, and in the early stages, when the defences are in process of hardening into syndromes, and as these interweave with the environmental provision and reaction.

The vast majority of our cases can be dealt with satisfactorily (as clinical problems) and every improvement we initiate is expanded into a larger improvement because our patients are immature and growth-process can be set free. We scarcely meet with disorders due to degeneration of tissues, and this distinguishes us from the adult psychiatrist. Moreover, we can usually rely on the parents to provide the patient's nursing home or mental hospital by their adaptation to the ill child's needs at home.

Psychiatry and the Theory of Personality Development

While I am exploring this area I want to say that I personally am not impressed when I look at the contribution made by adult psychiatry to the understanding of the developmental processes that lead to the growth of the personality and to the establishment of character. It is said that the practice of psychiatry has greatly advanced in the last thirty years, but on the debit side a few things could be said also. Here I definitely let myself go in expression of some personal opinions. With the passing of the word asylum it has become almost impossible for an ill patient

to find asylum, unless perhaps in a religious house. Also, treatment by fits has produced clinical improvement in very many
cases, but has it added anything at all to the understanding of
the way illness develops or treatment produces change? Perhaps
by giving fits the psychiatrist helps the patient to commit suicide
without dying? And in a course of convulsion therapy, the hatred
of the treatment that the patient develops, that is to say, hatred
without murder, may produce valuable integration in a disintegrated personality. But if these theories have truth in them they
do not come from psychiatry. Lastly, in my series of personal
complaints, treatment by leucotomy *really shocked me*, and gave
me a suspicion of adult psychiatry from which I shall not hope to
recover. In leucotomy, which has now mercifully gone out, I can
only see the patient's insane delusion being met by a delusion on
the part of the doctor.

Perhaps but few share these, my personal prejudices. There is a
reluctance on the part of dog to eat dog and on the part of
medical men and women to criticize colleagues. There are
moments, however, when we must criticize and expect to be
criticized, and we can do this within a framework of respect for
one another as persons.

I am glad I never did work in a mental hospital where I
would have had to do these bad things. I could not have done
them, and I should have reverted to physical paediatrics, where
I could have enjoyed myself immensely. But I would then have
missed much that I value in the practice of child psychiatry.

Paediatrics

I now come to the subject of paediatrics. As is well known, my
bias is towards paediatrics as the natural training ground for
child psychiatry. Paediatrics gives the student and the doctor the
very best opportunity for really getting to know the child patients
and the parents. If paediatricians wish, they can be child psychiatrists without even knowing it. The paediatrician has to be
fully equipped to deal with physical emergencies and this puts
him in a very strong position in the management of doctor-
parent relationships; in the guise of infant-feeding, the paediatrician can, if he is so minded, work in with the mother in her
very delicate task of introducing the world to the baby, and
therefore of laying down for the child the mental health which is
the negative of the mental hospital disorders. It was as a practising paediatrician that I found the therapeutic value of history-
taking, and discovered the fact that this provides the best

opportunity for therapeutics, provided that the history-taking is not done for the purpose of gathering facts. Psycho-analysis for me is a vast extension of history-taking, with therapeutics as a by-product.

I have continued throughout my career to believe in paediatrics as the proper root of child psychiatry, and the main thing that I wish to say in this paper is that in any planning that is to be made, the way must be left open for the doctor who wishes to come to child psychiatry through paediatrics. I mean the practice of paediatrics, over a decade. If he is to be compelled to go through the adult psychiatry training, if he is to take the D.P.M.,[1] then he must inevitably cease to be a practising paediatrician in the true sense of the term. There is so much to be learned and *experienced in the practice* of paediatrics that it is not possible to embrace another speciality such as psychiatry, which has so much in it that in no way concerns infants or children.

I hold this view very strongly in spite of the fact that paediatrics has failed to play the part that it was destined to play in relation to child psychiatry. Twenty-five years have been wasted now since those who are responsible for paediatrics in this country were introduced to the idea that child psychiatry is one half of paediatrics. Official paediatrics has avoided the issue quite deliberately, and there is now nothing to be gained by waiting longer for child psychiatry to become a twin with physical paediatrics. This could have been done, but it has not been done.

Child Psychiatry in its Own Right

But it is open to child psychiatry to give preference to paediatricians, and to ask for paediatric training and experience. The only solution is for child psychiatry to become a thing in its own right and to devise its own training. I would like to ask, has the Professor of Paediatrics ever met the Professor of Psychiatry to discuss this question of there being one day a Professor of Child Psychiatry?

But, and here is a very big but, sometimes paediatricians tend to think they can simply switch over to child psychiatry, as by changing the name from 'paediatrics' to 'child health'. This of course is not possible. If they come over to child psychiatry they must be prepared to re-orientate and to drop much of the power that they wield as physical paediatricians.

[1] Diploma of Psychological Medicine.

Place of Psycho-Analysis

This leads on to the matter of the relationship between child psychiatry and psycho-analysis and I will be brief because I believe this is not intended to become a main issue at this meeting. But I cannot avoid the issue. Committed as I am to the idea that paediatrics is the best of the various possible preparations for child psychiatry, I have to go quickly on to an assertion that the really necessary preparation for child psychiatry (whether of paediatrician or psychiatrist) is in *the psycho-analytic training*. It is an important thing for me that what I have to say about this is now generally recognized, whereas a few years ago it was quite revolutionary. It is now in my experience an *asset* when a candidate applies for a child psychiatry post if he is an analyst or if he has been accepted as a student at the Institute of Psycho-Analysis. (For the purposes of this discussion I must here include the Jungian training, in spite of the important differences which we can find between the two disciplines if we are looking for differences.) Many child psychiatrists in charge of clinics today have completed one of these trainings. This does not mean of course that the psycho-analytic training equips the candidate for child psychiatry; it concerns only the training in the psycho-analysis of adults and of children. But it does include the teaching of a theory of child development which is dynamic and which can be applied. Some institutions which go further and train in child psychiatry, e.g. the Tavistock Clinic, more or less insist on a psycho-analytic training; at others it is quite common, and Miss Freud's Hampstead Clinic, where lay psychotherapists can receive training, is of course orientated to psycho-analysis and the theories that belong to psycho-analysis.

My point is that a paediatrician who is capable of taking responsibility for his cases has a very good opportunity for developing into a child psychiatrist if, at the same time that he is gaining experience on the physical side, he is able to take the psycho-analytic training.

Selection

All this links up with the idea of selection.

The important thing in the psycho-analytic training is the personal analysis of the candidate. For the purpose of this paper I would like to take this personal analysis as being a part of selection. The psycho-analytic training is given after *selection*, and selection procedure is taken very seriously. First there is self-selection; then there is selection; and then there is further self-selection which goes with the patient's own analysis. In regard to child psychiatry, it is essential that careful selection according to personality and according to health and maturity should be made by a responsible body. The crux of the matter is: who shall select and continue to select and have the right to reject the child psychiatry aspirant? This is an important contribution that could be made by The Institute of Psycho-Analysis. It is not at all certain, for instance, that the doctor that you would certainly call in to look after your own infant in a physical emergency, or the psychiatrist to whom you would send your mother or brother, would be the one you would select for practice in child psychiatry. This is a matter that is fraught with difficulties, but the idea that there should be an entry into child psychiatry that is free from selection is a much worse prospect than that there should be child psychiatrists who have not got the D.P.M., or have not worked in a mental hospital.

Conclusion

First let us establish child psychiatry as a thing in its own right; then let adult psychiatrists continue to enter the child psychiatry field, if they are willing to study the physical and emotional development of the infant and child and to undergo a psychoanalytic training which includes a selection procedure and a personal analysis. Also, allow the paediatrician the same chance with the same proviso. But these things cannot be done without the active co-operation of official psychiatry and official paediatrics, since financial help must be found for the analytic training. Also there should be a willing facilitation of the paediatrician's, or the psychiatrist's, or the child's psychiatrist's, valiant effort to fit an analytic training in with the whole-time job that provides the basic security which is necessary for the founding of a home and family.

Summary

Child psychiatry is a speciality on its own account, whereas general psychiatry is concerned with degenerative processes and with neurological phenomena that are not important in the average child psychiatry department. Child psychiatry is concerned with the emotional development of the individual child and with the interferences with maturational processes that come from the environment and from conflict within the child. This makes child psychiatry akin to paediatrics.

The general psychiatrist or the paediatrician needs additional training of the kind provided by Psycho-Analysis and Analytical Psychology. These Institutes also provide machinery for selection.

There will always be those who come to child psychiatry from general psychiatry, but it is important to keep open the route through paediatric practice.

PSYCHOTHERAPY OF CHARACTER DISORDERS[1]

(1963)

Although the title chosen for this paper is the 'Psychotherapy of Character Disorders', it is not possible to avoid a discussion of the meaning of the term 'Character Disorder'. As Fenichel (1945, p. 539) remarks,

> The question may be raised whether there is any analysis that is not 'character analysis'. All symptoms are the outcome of specific ego attitudes, which in analysis make their appearance as resistances and which have been developed during infantile conflicts. This is true. And to a certain degree, really, all analyses are character analyses.

And again,

> Character disorders do not form a nosological unit. The mechanisms at the basis of character disorder may be as different as the mechanisms at the basis of symptom neuroses. Thus a hysterical character will be more easily treated than a compulsive one, a compulsive one more easily than a narcissistic one.

It is clear that either the term is too wide to be useful, or else I shall need to use it in a special way. In the latter case I must indicate the use I shall make of the term in this paper.

First, there must be confusion unless it be recognized that the three terms: character, a good character, and a character disorder, bring to mind three very different phenomena, and it would be artificial to deal with all three at one and the same time, yet these three are inter-related.

Freud wrote (1905b) that 'a fairly reliable character' is one of the prerequisites for a successful analysis (Fenichel, 1945, p. 537); but we are considering *unreliability* in the personality, and Fenichel asks: can this unreliability be treated? He might have asked: what is its aetiology?

When I look at character disorders I find I am looking at *whole persons*. There is in the term an implication of a degree of integration, itself a sign of psychiatric health.

[1] Read at the 11th European Congress of Child Psychiatry, Rome, May–June 1963.

The papers that have preceded mine have taught us much, and have strengthened me in the idea of character as something that belongs to integration. Character is a manifestation of successful integration, and a disorder of character is a distortion of the ego structure, integration being nevertheless maintained. It is perhaps good to remember that integration has a time factor. The child's character has formed on the basis of a steady developmental process, and in this respect the child has a past and a future.

It would seem to be valuable to use the term character disorder in description of a child's attempt to accommodate his or her own developmental abnormalities or deficiencies. Always we assume that the personality structure is able to withstand the strain of the abnormality. The child needs to come to terms with the personal pattern of anxiety or compulsion or mood or suspicion, etc., and also to relate this to the requirements and expectations of the immediate environment.

In my opinion the value of the term belongs specifically to a description of personality distortion that comes about *when the child needs to accommodate some degree of antisocial tendency*. This leads immediately to a statement of my use of this term.

I am using these words which enable us to focus our attention not so much on behaviour as on those roots of misbehaviour that extend over the whole area between normality and delinquency. The antisocial tendency can be examined in your own healthy child who at the age of two takes a coin from his mother's handbag.

The antisocial tendency always arises out of a *deprivation* and represents the child's claim to get back behind the deprivation to the state of affairs that obtained when all was well. I cannot develop this theme here, but this thing that I call the antisocial tendency must be mentioned because it is found regularly in the dissection of character disorder. The child in accommodating the antisocial tendency that is his or hers may hide it, may develop a reaction formation to it, such as becoming a prig, may develop a grievance and acquire a complaining character, may specialize in day-dreaming, lying, mild chronic masturbating activity, bedwetting, compulsive thumb-sucking, thigh-rubbing, etc., or may periodically manifest the antisocial tendency (that is his or hers) in a *behaviour disorder*. This latter is always associated with hope, and it is either of the nature of stealing or of aggressive activity and destruction. It is compulsive.

Character disorder, then, according to my way of looking at things, refers most significantly to the distortion of the *intact* personality that results from the antisocial elements in it. It is the antisocial element that determines society's involvement. Society (the child's family and so on) must meet the challenge, and must *like or dislike* the character and the character disorder.

Here then is the beginning of a description:

Character disorders are not schizophrenia. In character disorder there is hidden illness in the intact personality. Character disorders in some way and to some degree actively involve society.

Character disorders may be divided according to:

Success or failure on the part of the individual in the attempt of the total personality to hide the illness element. Success here means that the personality, though impoverished, has become able to socialize the character distortion to find secondary gains or to fit in with a social custom.
Failure here means that the impoverishment of the personality carries along with it a failure in establishment of a relation to society as a whole, on account of the hidden illness element.

In fact, society plays its part in the determination of the fate of a person with character disorder, and does this in various ways. For example:

Society tolerates individual illness to a degree.
Society tolerates failure of the individual to contribute-in.
Society tolerates or even enjoys distortions of the mode of the individual's contributing-in.
or Society meets the challenge of the antisocial tendency of an individual, and its reaction is being motivated by:
   (1) Revenge.
   (2) The wish to socialize the individual.
   (3) Understanding and the application of understanding to prevention.

The individual with character disorder may suffer from:

   (1) Impoverishment of personality, sense of grievance, unreality, awareness of lack of serious purpose, etc.
   (2) Failure to socialize.

Here then is a basis for psychotherapy, because psychotherapy relates to individual *suffering* and need for help. But this suffering in character disorder only belongs to the early stages in the individual's illness; the secondary gains quickly take over, lessen the suffering, and interfere with the drive of the individual to seek help or to accept help offered.

It must be recognized that in respect of 'success' (character disorder hidden and socialized) *psychotherapy makes the individual ill*, because illness lies between the defence and the individual's health. By contrast, in respect of 'unsuccessful' hiding of character disorder, although there may be an initial drive in the individual to seek help at an early stage, because of society's reactions, this motive does not necessarily carry the patient through to the treatment of the deeper illness.

The clue to the treatment of character disorder is given by the part the environment plays in the case of *natural cure*. In the slight case the environment can 'cure' because the cause was an environmental failure in the area of ego-support and protection at a stage of the individual's dependence. This explains why it is that children are regularly 'cured' of incipient character disorder in the course of their own childhood development simply by making use of home life. Parents have a second and third chance to bring their children through, in spite of failures of management (mostly inevitable) in the earliest stages when the child is highly dependent. Family life is the place therefore that offers the best opportunity for investigation into the aetiology of character disorder; and indeed it is in the family life, or its substitute, that the child's *character* is being built up in positive ways.

Aetiology of Character Disorder

In considering the aetiology of character disorder it is necessary to take for granted both the maturational process in the child, the conflict-free sphere of the ego (Hartmann), also forward movement with anxiety drive (Klein), and the function of the environment which facilitates the maturational processes. Environmental provision must be 'good' enough if maturation is to become a fact in the case of any one child.

With this in mind, one can say that there are two extremes of distortion, and that these relate to the stage of maturation of the individual at which environmental failure did actually overstrain the ego's capacity for organizing defences:

At one extreme is the ego hiding *psycho-neurotic* symptom-formations (set up relative to anxiety belonging to the Oedipus complex). Here the hidden illness is a matter of conflict in the individual's personal unconscious.

At the other extreme is the ego hiding *psychotic* symptom-formations (splitting, dissociations, reality side-slipping, depersonalization, regression and omnipotent dependencies, etc.). Here the hidden illness is in the ego structure.

But the matter of society's essential involvement does not depend on the answer to the question: is the hidden illness psycho-neurotic or psychotic? In fact, in character disorder there is this other element, *the individual's* correct perception at a time in early childhood that at first all was well, or well enough, and then that all was not well. In other words, that there happened at a certain time, or over a phase of development, an actual failure of ego-support that held up the individual's emotional development. A reaction in the individual to this disturbance took the place of simple growth. The maturational processes became dammed up because of a failure of the facilitating environment.

This theory of the aetiology of character disorder, if correct, leads to a new statement of character disorder at its inception. The individual in this category carries on with two separate burdens. One of these, of course, is the increasing burden of a disturbed and in some respects stunted or postponed maturational process. The other is the hope, a hope that never becomes quite extinguished, that the environment may acknowledge and make up for the specific failure that did the damage. In the vast majority of cases the parents or the family or guardians of the child recognize the fact of the 'let-down' (so often unavoidable) and by a period of special management, spoiling, or what could be called mental nursing, they see the child through to a recovery from the trauma.

When the family does not mend its failures the child goes forward with certain handicaps, being engaged in

(1) arranging to live a life in spite of emotional stunting, and
(2) all the time liable to moments of hope, moments when it would seem to be possible to force the environment to effect a cure (hence: acting-out).

Between the clinical state of a child who has been hurt in the way that is being described here and the resumption of that child's emotional development, and all that that means in terms of socialization, there is this need to make society acknowledge and repay. Behind a child's maladjustment is always a failure of the environment to adjust to the child's absolute needs at a time of relative dependence. (Such failure is initially a failure of nurture.) Then there can be added a failure of the family to heal the effects of such failures; and then there may be added the failure of society as it takes the family's place. Let it be emphasized that in this type of case the initial failure can be shown to have happened at a time at which the child's development had made it just possible for him or her to perceive the fact of the failure and to perceive the nature of the environment's maladjustment.

The child now displays an antisocial tendency, which (as I have said) in the stage before the development of secondary gains is always a manifestation of hope. This antisocial tendency is liable to show in two forms:

(1) The staking of claims on people's time, concern, money, etc. (manifested by stealing).
(2) The expectation of that degree of structural strength and organization and 'comeback' that is essential if the child is to be able to rest, relax, disintegrate, feel secure (manifested by destruction which provokes strong management).

On the basis of this theory of the aetiology of character disorder I can proceed to examine the matter of therapy.

Indications for Therapy

Therapy of character disorder has three aims:

(A) A dissection down to the illness that is hidden and that appears in the character distortion. Preparatory to this may be a period in which the individual is invited to become a patient, to become ill instead of hiding illness.
(B) To meet the antisocial tendency which, from the point of view of the therapist, is evidence of hope in the patient; to meet it as an S.O.S., a *cri de cœur*, a signal of distress.
(C) Analysis that takes into consideration both the ego distortion and the patient's exploitation of his or her id-drives during attempts at self-cure.

The attempt to meet the patient's antisocial tendency has two aspects:

The allowance of the patient's claims to rights in terms of a person's love and reliability.
The provision of an ego-supportive structure that is relatively indestructible.

As this implies, the patient will from time to time be acting-out, and as long as this has a relation to the transference it can be managed and interpreted. The troubles in therapy come in relation to antisocial acting-out which is outside the total therapeutic machinery, that is to say, which involves society.

In regard to the treatment of hidden illness and of ego distortion, the need is for psychotherapy. But at the same time the antisocial tendency must be engaged, as and when it appears. The aim in this part of the treatment is to arrive at the original trauma. This has to be done in the course of the psychotherapy, or if psychotherapy is not available, in the course of the specialized management that is provided.

In this work the failures of the therapist or of those managing the child's life will be real and they can be shown to reproduce the original failures, in token form. These failures are real indeed, and especially so in so far as the patient is either regressed to the dependence of the appropriate age, or else remembering. The acknowledgement of the analyst's or guardian's failure enables the patient to become appropriately angry instead of traumatized. *The patient needs to reach back through the transference trauma to the state of affairs that obtained before the original trauma.* (In some cases there is a possibility of quick arrival at deprivation trauma in a first interview.) The reaction to the current failure only makes sense in so far as the current failure *is* the original environmental failure from the point of view of the child. Reproduction in the treatment of examples as they arise of the original environmental failure, along with the patient's experience of anger that is appropriate, frees the patient's maturational processes; and it must be remembered that the patient is in a dependent state and needing ego-support and environmental management (holding) in the treatment setting, and the next phase needs to be a period of emotional growth in which the character builds up positively and loses its distortions.

In a favourable case the acting-out that belongs to these cases is confined to the transference, or can be brought into the transference productively by interpretation of displacement, symbolism, and projection. At one extreme is the common 'natural' cure that takes place in the child's family. At the other extreme are the severely disturbed patients whose acting-out may make treatment by interpretation impossible because the work gets interrupted by society's reactions to stealing or destructiveness.

In a moderately severe case the acting-out can be managed provided that the therapist understands its meaning and significance. It can be said that acting-out is the alternative to despair. Most of the time the patient is hopeless about correcting the original trauma and so lives in a state of relative depression or of dissociations that mask the chaotic state that is always threatening. When, however, the patient starts to make an object relationship, or to cathect a person, then there starts up an anti-social tendency, a compulsion either to lay claims (steal) or by destructive behaviour to activate harsh or even vindictive management.

In every case, if psychotherapy is to be successful, the patient must be seen through one or many of these awkward phases of manifest antisocial behaviour, and only too often it is just at these awkward points in the case that treatment is interrupted. The case is dropped not necessarily because the situation cannot be tolerated, but (as likely as not) because those in charge do not know that these acting-out phases are inherent, and that they can have a positive value.

In severe cases these phases in management or treatment present difficulties that are so great that the law (society) takes over, and at the same time psychotherapy goes into abeyance. Society's revenge takes the place of pity or sympathy, and the individual ceases to suffer and be a patient, and instead becomes a criminal with a delusion of persecution.

It is my intention to draw attention to *the positive element in character disorder*. Failure to achieve character disorder in the individual who is trying to accommodate some degree of antisocial tendency indicates a liability to psychotic breakdown. Character disorder indicates that the individual's ego structure can bind the energies that belong to the stunting of maturational processes and also the abnormalities in the interaction of the individual child and the family. Until secondary gains have become a feature the personality with character disorder is always liable to break down into paranoia, manic depression, psychosis or schizophrenia.

To sum up, a statement on the treatment of character disorder can start with the dictum that such a treatment is like that of any other psychological disorder, namely, psycho-analysis if it be available. There must follow the following considerations:

(1) Psycho-analysis may succeed, but the analyst must expect to find *acting-out* in the transference, and must understand the significance of this acting-out, and be able to give it positive value.

(2) The analysis may succeed but be difficult because the hidden illness has psychotic features, so that the patient must become ill (psychotic, schizoid) before starting to get better; and all the resources of the analyst will be needed to deal with the primitive defence mechanisms that will be a feature.

(3) The analysis may be succeeding, but as acting-out is not con-

fined to the transference relationship the patient is removed from the analyst's reach because of society's reaction to the patient's antisocial tendency or because of the operation of the law. There is room for great variation here, owing to the variability of society's reaction, ranging from crude revenge to an expression of society's willingness to give the patient a chance to make late socialization.

(4) In many cases incipient character disorder is treated and treated successfully in the child's home, by a phase or by phases of special management (spoiling) or by especially *personal* care or strict control by a person who loves the child. An extension of this is the treatment of incipient or early character disorder without psychotherapy by management in groups designed to give what the child's own family cannot give in the way of special management.

(5) By the time the patient comes to treatment there may already be a fixed antisocial tendency manifest, and a hardened attitude in the patient fostered by secondary gains, in which case the question of psycho-analysis does not arise. Then the aim is to provide firm management by understanding persons, and to provide this as a *treatment* in advance of its being provided as a *corrective* by court order. Personal psychotherapy can be added if it is available.

Finally,

(6) The character disorder case may present as a court case, with society's reaction represented by the probation order, or by committal to an approved school or a penal institution.

It can happen that early committal by a court proves to be a *positive* element in the patient's socialization. This corresponds again to the natural cure that commonly takes place in the patient's family; society's reaction has been, for the patient, a practical demonstration of its 'love', that is of its willingness to 'hold' the patient's unintegrated self, and to meet aggression with firmness (to limit the effects of maniacal episodes) and to meet hatred with hatred, appropriate and under control. This last is the best that some deprived children will ever get by way of satisfactory management, and many restless antisocial deprived children change from ineducable to educable in the strict regime of a remand home. The danger here is that because restless antisocial children thrive in an atmosphere of dictatorship this may breed dictators, and may even make educationalists think that an atmosphere of strict discipline, with every minute of the child's day filled, is good educational treatment for normal children, which it is not.

Girls

Broadly speaking, all this applies equally to boys and girls. At the stage of adolescence, however, the nature of the character disorder is necessarily different in the two sexes. For example, at adolescence girls tend to show their antisocial tendency by prostitution, and one of the hazards of acting-out is the production of illegitimate babies. In prostitution there are secondary gains. One is that girls find they contribute-in to society by being prostitutes, whereas they cannot contribute-in by any other means. They find many lonely men, who want a relationship rather than sex, and who are ready to pay for it. Also, these girls, essentially lonely, achieve contacts with others of their kind. The treatment of adolescent antisocial girls who have started to experience the secondary gains of the prostitute, presents *insuperable difficulties*. Perhaps the idea of treatment does not make sense in this context. In many cases it is already too late. It is best to give up all attempts to cure prostitution, and instead to concentrate on giving these girls food and shelter and opportunity for keeping healthy and clean.

Clinical Illustrations

A Common Type of Case

A boy in later latency (first seen at ten years) was having psycho-analytic treatment from me. His restlessness and liability to outbreaks of rage started from a very early date, soon after his birth and long before he was weaned at eight months. His mother was a neurotic person and all her life more or less depressed. He was a thief and given to aggressive outbursts. His analysis was going well, and in the course of a year of daily sessions much straightforward analytic work was accomplished. He became very excited, however, as his relationship to me developed significance, and he climbed out on to the clinic roof and flooded out the clinic and made so much noise that the treatment had to stop. Sometimes there was danger to me; he also broke into my car outside the clinic and drove off in bottom gear by using the self-starter, thus obviating the need for a car key. At the same time he started stealing again and being aggressive outside the treatment setting, and he was sent by the Juvenile Court to an approved school just at a time when the treatment by psycho-analysis was in full spate. Perhaps if I had been much stronger

CHARACTER DISORDERS (1963)

than he I might have managed this phase, and so have had opportunity to complete the analysis. As it was I had to give up.

(This boy did moderately well. He became a lorry driver, which suited his restlessness. He had kept his job fourteen years at the time of the follow-up. He married and had three children. His wife divorced him, after which he kept in touch with his mother, from whom the details of the follow-up were obtained.)

Three Favourable Cases

A boy of eight started stealing. He had suffered a relative deprivation (in his own good home setting) when he was two, at the time his mother conceived, and became pathologically anxious. The parents had managed to meet this boy's special needs and had almost succeeded in effecting a natural cure of his condition. I helped them in this long task by giving them some understanding of what they were doing. In one therapeutic consultation when the boy was eight it was possible for me to get this boy into feeling-contact with his deprivation, and he reached back to an object relationship to the good mother of his infancy. Along with this the stealing ceased.

A girl of eight years came to me because of stealing. She had suffered a relative deprivation in her own good home at the age of 4–5 years. In one psychotherapeutic consultation she reached back to her early infantile contact with a good mother, and at the same time her stealing disappeared. She was also wetting and messing and this minor manifestation of the antisocial tendency persisted for some time.

A boy of thirteen years, at a public school a long way from his good home, was stealing in a big way, also slashing sheets and upsetting the school by getting boys into trouble and by leaving obscene notes in lavatories, etc. In a therapeutic consultation he was able to let me know that he had been through a period of intolerable strain at the age of six when he went away to boarding school. I was able to arrange for this boy (middle child of three) to be allowed a period of 'mental nursing' in his own home. He used this for a regressive phase, and then went to day school. Later he went to a boarding school in the neighbourhood of his home. His antisocial symptoms ceased abruptly after his one interview with me and follow-up shows that he has done well. He has now passed through a university, and is establishing himself as a man. Of this case it is particularly true to say that the patient brought with him the understanding of his case, and what he needed was for the facts to be acknowledged and for an attempt to be made to mend, in token form, the environmental failure.

Comment

In these three cases in which help could be given when secondary gains had not become a feature the general attitude of myself as psychiatrist enabled the child in each case to state a specific area of relative deprivation, and the fact that this was accepted as real and true enabled the child to reach back over the gap and make anew a relationship with good objects that had been blocked.

A Case on the Borderline between Character Disorder and Psychosis

A boy has been under my care over a period of years. I have only seen him once, and most of my contacts have been with the mother at times of crisis. Many have tried to give direct help to the boy, who is now twenty, but he quickly becomes uncooperative.

This boy has a high I.Q. and all those whom he has allowed to teach him have said that he could be exceptionally brilliant as an actor, a poet, an artist, a musician, etc. He has not stayed long at any one school but by self-tuition has kept well ahead of his peers, and he did this in early adolescence by coaching his friends in their school-work, then keeping in touch.

In the latency period he was hospitalized and diagnosed schizophrenic. In hospital he undertook the 'treatment' of the other boys, and he never accepted his position as a patient. Eventually he ran away and had a long period without schooling. He would lie in bed listening to lugubrious music, or lock himself into the house so that no one could get to him. He constantly threatened suicide, chiefly in relation to violent love affairs. Periodically he would organize a party, and this would go on indefinitely, and damage was sometimes done to property.

This boy lived with his mother in a small flat and he kept her constantly in a state of worry, and there was never any possibility of an outcome since he would not go away, he would not go to school or to hospital, and he was clever enough to do exactly as he wanted to do, and he never became criminal, and so kept out of the jurisdiction of the law.

At various times I helped the mother by putting her in touch with the police, the probation service, and other social services, and when eventually he said he would go to a certain grammar school I 'pulled strings' to enable him to do this. He was found to be well ahead of his age group, and the masters gave him great encouragement because of his brilliance. But he left school before time, and obtained a scholarship for a good college of acting. At this point he decided that he had the wrong-shaped nose, and eventually he persuaded his mother to pay a plastic surgeon to alter it from retroussé to straight. Then he found other reasons why he could not go forward to any success, and yet he gave no one any opportunity to help him. This continues, and at present he is in the observation ward of a mental hospital, but he will find a way of leaving this and will settle in at home once more.

This boy has an early history that gives the clue to the anti-social part of his character disorder. In fact he was the result of a partnership that foundered soon after its unhappy start, and the father soon after separating from the mother himself became a paranoid casualty. This marriage followed immediately after a tragedy, and was doomed to failure because the boy's mother had not yet recovered from the loss of her much-loved fiancé whom, as she felt, was killed by the carelessness of this man whom she married and who became the father of the boy.

This boy could have been helped at an early age, perhaps six, when he was first seen by a psychiatrist. He could then have led the psychiatrist to the material of his relative deprivation, and he could then have been told about his mother's personal problem, and the reason for the ambivalence in her relationship to him. But instead the boy was placed in a hospital ward, and from this time on he hardened into a case of character disorder, becoming a person who compulsively tantalizes his mother and his teachers and his friends.

I have not attempted to describe a case treated by psycho-analysis in this series of short case-descriptions.

Cases treated by management alone are innumerable and include all those children who when deprived in one way or another are adopted, or fostered out, or placed in small homes that are run as therapeutic institutions and on personal lines. It would be giving a false impression to describe one case in this category. It is indeed necessary to draw attention to the fact that incipient character disorder is being treated successfully all the time, especially in the home, in social groups of all kinds, and quite apart from psychotherapy.

Nevertheless, it is intensive work with the few cases that throws light on the problem of character disorder as of other types of psychological disorders, and it is work of the psycho-analytic groups in various countries that has laid the basis for a theoretical statement and has begun to explain to the specialized therapeutic groups what it is that is being done in such groups that so often succeeds in the prevention or treatment of character disorder.

THE MENTALLY ILL IN YOUR CASELOAD[1]
(1963)

Since the beginning of the century there has been a crescendo of attempts to rescue psychiatry from stagnation. Psychiatrists have had a big task in changing the care and treatment of mentally ill persons from mechanical restraints to a human and humane method. Then came the application of dynamic psychology to psychiatry. It is the *psychology* of mental illness that is of interest to psycho-analysts and to those who work on the basis of dynamic psychology, and this category includes many social workers. My task will be to make this link between mental illness and the stages of individual emotional development and I shall go ahead without being in a position to offer positive proof of the details of my thesis.

First, I must remind you of the psychiatrist's classification of mental disorder. I shall deal summarily with the mental disorders that arise from physical abnormality of the brain, which is the electronic apparatus upon which the mind depends for functioning. The apparatus can be faulty in various ways, hereditarily, congenitally, through infectious disease, because of a tumour, or through degenerative processes such as arteriosclerosis. Also certain general physical disorders affect the electronic apparatus, such as myxoedema, and hormone unbalance associated with the menopause. We must brush aside these considerations, important though they are, in order to get towards the area of mental disorder that is a matter of psychology, of dynamic psychology, of emotional immaturity.

I shall also have to take for granted your knowledge of the effect on mental states of bodily illness, and the threat of bodily illness. It certainly does affect a person's mentality to have cancer or heart disease. Only the psychology of these effects can concern us here now.

A classification starts, then, with these three categories:

(a) Diseases of the brain with consequent mental disorder.
(b) Diseases of the body affecting mental attitudes.
(c) Mental disorders proper, that is, disorders that are not dependent on brain or other physical disease.

[1] Talk given to the Association of Social Workers, London, and published in *New Thinking for Changing Needs*, by the Association of Social Workers, 1963.

From this we start to divide mental disorder into psycho-neurosis and psychosis. You will not jump to the conclusion that psycho-neurotic persons are necessarily less ill than psychotic persons. The word 'ill' needs to be examined at this point. Let me use my friend the late John Rickman's definition: 'Mental illness consists in not being able to find anyone who can stand you.' In other words, there is a contribution from society into the meaning of the word 'ill', and certainly some psycho-neurotic persons are maximally difficult to live with. Yet they are not usually certifiable. This presents a difficulty to which I will refer later.

Health is emotional maturity, emotional maturity of the individual person. Psycho-neurosis relates to the state of the person as a child of toddler age; to the positive or negative family provision; to the way in which the latency period relieved or accentuated the tensions that were operative in the individual; and to the reassembly in the various stages of adolescence of the changes in the instinctual drives, and the new organization of defences against anxiety that came to blue-print in the early childhood of the individual.

Psycho-neurosis is the term used to describe the illness of persons who became ill at the stage of the Oedipus complex, at the stage of the experience of relationships as between three *whole* people. The conflicts arising out of these relationships lead to defensive measures which, if they become organized in a relatively rigid state, qualify for the title psycho-neurosis. These defences have been listed and clearly stated. Obviously the way in which they build up and become fixed depends to some extent, perhaps to a great extent, on the history of the individual prior to his or her arrival at the stage of triangular relationships as between whole persons.

Now psycho-neurosis involves repression, and the repressed unconscious, which is a special aspect of the unconscious. Whereas the unconscious generally is the storehouse of the richest areas of a person's self, the repressed unconscious is the bin in which is held (at great cost in terms of the mental economy) that which is intolerable and beyond the capacity of the individual to accommodate as part of the self and of personal experience. The unconscious proper can be reached in dreams and contributes fundamentally to all the most significant experiences of the human individual; by contrast, the repressed unconscious is not freely available for use, and appears only as a threat or as a source of reaction formation (for example, sentimentality indicating repressed hatred). All this is the stuff of dynamic psychology.

Repression belongs to psycho-neurosis just as splitting of the personality belongs to psychosis.

Psycho-neurotic illness can be severe indeed. Moreover, this type of illness makes the social worker despair, because the repressed unconscious is the province of the psycho-analyst. By contrast, as I shall try to show, the areas of illness named psychosis, or madness, offer more scope for the social worker, and this partly because such disorders offer less scope for the psycho-analyst, unless, indeed, he steps outside his role at appropriate moments and himself becomes a social worker. (This theme will develop gradually as I proceed.)

As I have said, in psycho-neurosis one of the defences has to do with regression. The person who is ill is found to have retreated from genital sexuality and from the triangular relationships as between whole people and to have taken up certain positions that belong to his or her life prior to the stage of the heterosexual and homosexual positions in interpersonal matters. To some extent the fixation points, the points used in these regressive defences, depend on good and bad experiences in the individual's earlier developmental stages, and of course on the corresponding good and bad environmental factors relative to these stages.

Psychosis may be looked at as illness that has more to do with the experiences in the earlier phases than with the tensions at the level of interpersonal relationships which lead to repressive defences. In the extreme case there has been no true Oedipus complex because the individual was so much caught up in an earlier stage of development that true and full-blooded triangular relationships never became a fact.

Of course you will find cases to describe in which there can be demonstrated a mixture of normality in terms of the Oedipus complex and of psychosis in terms of being stuck at a phase of early emotional development. However, these mixed cases need not concern us here, where we are trying to state an extremely complex matter in simple terms.

Psycho-neurosis, then, belongs to the defences organized around the anxieties and conflicts of relatively normal persons, that is persons who at any rate have reached the stage of the Oedipus complex. In a treatment by psycho-analysis the analyst makes it possible for the quantity of repression to lessen, and at the end of the treatment the interpersonal relationships come to fuller expression and experience, and there is a lessening of the pregenital component of sexuality.

All the rest of mental illness (other than psycho-neurosis)

belongs to the build-up of the personality in earliest childhood and in infancy, along with the environmental provision that fails or succeeds in its function of facilitating the maturational processes of the individual. In other words, mental illness that is not psycho-neurosis has importance for the social worker because it concerns not so much the individual's organized defences as the individual's failure to attain the ego-strength or the personality integration that enables defences to form.

I can now return to classification of psychiatric types more happily because I think I may have conveyed to you the idea that madness is your province just as psycho-neurosis is the province of the orthodox Freudian analyst. Moreover madness has a relation to ordinary life. In madness we find instead of repression the processes of personality establishment and self-differentiation in reverse. This is the stuff of madness and it is this which I am principally trying to describe. Failures in the maturational process (itself a matter of heredity) are of course often associated with pathological hereditary factors, but the point is that these failures are very much associated with failures of the facilitating environment. You will see that it is here that the social worker comes in, since the environmental factor has a specific significance in the *aetiology* of madness. The basic assumption here is that the mental health of the individual is held down in the area of infant-care and child-care and both infant- and child-care reappear in the social worker's casework. In the psychotherapy of psycho-neurosis, which is essentially a disorder of inner conflict (that is to say, conflict within the intact integrated personalized and object-related self), these phenomena that derive from infant- and child-care turn up in that which is called the transference neurosis.

Let us go back then to my attempt to assemble the illnesses other than psycho-neurosis in the psychiatric classification. It would be simpler from the point of view of my presentation if I could take the two extremes and refer to psycho-neurosis at one extreme and to schizophrenia at the other. I cannot do this, however, because of the affective disorders. Between psycho-neurosis and schizophrenia lies the whole territory covered by the word depression. When I say between I really do mean that in the aetiology of these disorders the points of origin of depression lie between the points of origin of psycho-neurosis and of schizophrenia. I also mean that there is every degree of overlap, that there are no clear-cut distinctions and that in psychiatric illness it is false to label disorders as if they were diseases in the way that is characteristic of classification in physical medicine. (Here of course I am excluding brain diseases which are really physical diseases with secondary psychological effects.)

The depressions constitute a very wide concept of mental disorder. Developments in psycho-analysis have elucidated much of the psychology of depressive illness and also have related depression to that which is essentially healthy, namely the capacity to mourn and the capacity to feel concerned. The depressions therefore range from near-normal to near-psychotic. At the normal end of the depressions come those depressive illnesses which imply maturityi n the individual and imply a degree of integration of the self. Here, as in psycho-neurosis, the psycho-analyst rather than the social worker is needed, but there is one thing which can be of great importance to the social worker, namely the tendency for depression to lift. Without doing any psychotherapy the social worker can do a great deal on the basis of allowing a depression to take its course. What is needed here is an assessment of the individual as one whose past history gives evidence that the personality integration can stand the strain of the depressive illness in which a certain type of conflict is working through. This conflict in depression roughly-speaking has to do with the individual's personal task of accommodating his or her own aggression and destructive impulses. When someone who is loved dies, the mourning process belongs to the working-through within the individual of the feeling of personal responsibility for the death because of the destructive ideas and impulses that accompany loving. Depression at this end of the scale is formed on this pattern that is more obvious in mourning, the difference being that in depression there is a higher degree of repression and the processes take place at a level which is more unconscious (in the sense of being repressed) than in mourning.

From the psycho-analyst's point of view the psychotherapy of depression of this kind is not unlike that of psycho-neurosis except that in the transference the most powerful dynamic is in the two-body relationship based on that which was originally infant and mother. The important part of the analyst's therapeutic in the treatment of depression is his survival over a period in which destructive ideas dominate the scene, and here again the social worker who sees a depressed person through a depression is doing therapy simply by continuing to exist in person and by survival.

Allied to depressive illness of this reactive kind is that which is associated with menopausal and other types of contraction of opportunity for construction and creative contribution.

At the other extreme of this grouping of the depressions is

psychotic depression in which there are associated features which link illness with schizophrenia. There may be some degree of depersonalization or of unreality feelings. Depression here is also associated with loss but the loss is of a more obscure kind than is the case with reactive depression and derives from an earlier date in the development of the individual. For example, the loss might be that of certain aspects of the mouth which disappear from the infant's point of view along with the mother and the breast when there is a separation at a date earlier than that at which the infant had reached a stage of emotional development which would provide the infant with the equipment for dealing with loss. The same loss of the mother a few months later would be a loss of object without this added element of a loss of part of the subject.

It is necessary therefore to categorize two forms of depression: *reactive depression* and *schizoid depression*. In extreme cases of the latter the clinical picture resembles that of schizophrenia, and in fact there can be no clear line of demarcation between any form of mental illness and the other forms. And in an individual's illness any kind of mixture and alternation must be expected. And alternations occur in one individual between a psycho-neurotic manifestation and a more psychotic illness (e.g. obsessional neurosis breaking down into a phase of agitated depression, and recovering to obsessional neurosis, etc.). For mental illnesses are not diseases like phthisis, or rheumatic fever, or scurvy. They are patterns of compromise between success and failure in the state of the individual's emotional development. Thus health is emotional maturity, maturity at age; and mental ill-health always has behind it a hold-up of emotional development. The tendency towards maturation persists, and it is this that provides the drive towards cure, and towards self-cure if no help is available. It is this that is at the back of the *process* that can be relied on to appear if there can be provided a facilitating environment, nicely adjusted to the immediate needs of the person's maturational stage. It is here that the social worker becomes involved in a constructive way, and in fact the social worker has power that is not available to the psycho-analyst in so far as the latter is confining his work to interpreting the nascent conscious elements in the transference neurosis, appropriate in the treatment of psycho-neurosis.

Let me emphasize the point that mental illnesses are not diseases; they are compromises between the individual's immaturity and the actual social reactions, both helpful and avenging. In this way the clinical picture of a mentally-ill person varies according to the environmental attitude, even when the illness in the patient remains fundamentally unaltered; for example, a thirteen-year-old girl was dying at home, through refusing food, but normal and even happy in an alternative environment.

At the end of the scale beyond schizoid depression is schizophrenia proper. Here the accent is on certain failures of personality construction. These will be listed, but first it must be made clear that clinically there may be a normally functioning area of the personality even in a severe schizoid case, so that the unwary may be deceived. This complication will be dealt with below under the term false self.

To understand schizophrenia-type illness it is necessary to examine the maturational processes as they carry the infant and the small child along in the early stages of emotional development. In this early time, when so much development is starting and nothing is being completed, the two trends are described by the words *maturation* and *dependence*. The environment is essential and gradually becomes less essential, so that one could speak of double dependence, changing into simple dependence.

The environment does not make the infant grow, nor does it determine the direction of growth. The environment, when good enough, facilitates the maturational process. For this to happen the environmental provision in an extremely subtle manner adapts itself to the changing needs arising out of the fact of maturation. Such subtle adaptation to changing need can only be given by a person, and one who has for the time being no other preoccupation, and who is 'identified with the infant' so that the infant's needs are sensed and met, as by a natural process.

In a facilitating environment the infant person is engaged in making various grades, three of which can be described as:

Integration
Personalization
Object-relating

Integration rapidly becomes complex, and soon includes the concept of time. The reverse process is that of disintegration, and this is a word used to describe a type of mental illness: disintegration of the personality. In lesser degree the reverse of integration is splitting, and it is this feature, splitting, that characterizes schizophrenia, hence its name.

Personalization is a word that can be used to describe the achievement of a close relationship between the psyche and the body. Freud said that the ego is essentially built up on a basis of body-functioning; the ego is essentially a body-ego (that is to say, not a matter of the intellect). In the present context we are looking at the achievement in each individual person of the linkage of psyche and soma. Psycho-somatic disease is sometimes little more than a stressing of this psycho-somatic link in face of a danger of a breaking of the link; this breaking of the link results in various clinical states which receive the name 'depersonalization'. Here again, the reverse of the development that we see in the dependent infant is a state that we recognize as a mental illness, namely depersonalization, or psycho-somatic disorder hiding this.

The same will be found if we examine object-relating, and the instinctual life. The infant becomes able to relate to an object and to join up the idea of the object with a perception of the whole person of the mother. This capacity to relate to an object develops only as a result of a maternal adaptation that is good enough; the theory of this is complex and I have tried to describe its complexity elsewhere (Winnicott, 1951). This capacity cannot develop by maturational process alone; the good-enough adaptation of the mother is essential, and this must last over a long enough period, and a capacity for relating to objects can be lost, in part or wholly. At first the relationship is to a subjective object, and it is a long journey from here to the development and establishment of a capacity to relate to an object that is objectively perceived and that is allowed a separate existence, an existence outside the omnipotent control of the individual.

Success in this field of development is closely linked with the person's capacity to feel real; this, however, has to be brought into line with the idea of feeling real in the world and feeling that the world is real. It has to be acknowledged that the normal person cannot achieve a feeling of reality in the world comparable with the schizophrenic's feeling of reality in the absolutely private world of the schizophrenic's relation to subjective objects. For normal persons the only approach that can be made to this quality of feeling is in the cultural field. The opposite to the maturational trend towards object-relating is de-realization and loss of contact with (shared) reality, and here again are words that describe mental illness.

Added to all this there is a whole category of illness, paranoia and the persecutory elements that may complicate depression, and which, when contained within the personality, bring about the state of hypochondria. It is not possible to include a description of this here, because paranoia is not an illness in itself, but it is a complication of either depression or schizophrenia. In

the last analysis the origin of the persecutory elements that complicate depressive illness takes the patient and the analyst to oral
sadism that has not been accepted by the individual, along with
its results in the patient's imaginative concept of the psycho-
somatic self. But there can be a deeper origin to paranoia, which
may be associated with integration and the establishment of a
unit self: I AM.

Here could be brought in the concept of the true and the false
self. It is essential to include this concept in the attempt to
understand the deceptive clinical picture presented in most cases
of schizophrenic-type illness. What is presented is a false self,
adapted to the expectations of various layers of the individual's
environment. In effect the compliant or false self is a pathological
version of that which is called in health the polite, socially
adapted aspect of the healthy personality. (I have described elsewhere (Winnicott, 1952) the point of origin of the false self, in
relation to a not-quite-good-enough adaptation in the process in
the infant of relating to objects.

In the pathological form of this the individual eventually destroys the false self, and attempts to reassert a true self, although
this may not be compatible with living in the world, or with life.
A mental breakdown is often a 'healthy' sign in that it implies a
capacity of the individual to use an environment that has become
available in order to re-establish an existence on a basis that feels
real. Naturally such a device does not by any means always succeed, and it is very puzzling to society to see a compliant and
perhaps valuable false self destroy good prospects by a renun-
ciation of every obvious advantage simply for the hidden advantage of gaining a feeling of reality.

One other type of illness, psychopathy, must be described. In
order to do this it is necessary to get on to another track and to
look at the emotional growth of the individual in terms of dependence.

It will be observed that there is no place, in my way of stating
these matters, for a mental illness that is not related to a developmental immaturity, perhaps with distortions due to the attempt
of the individual to use the environment for the purpose of
self-cure.

In terms of dependence it can be stated that there are for comparison two extremes and an area in between. At one extreme,
where dependence is adequately met, the child achieves interpersonal
relationships as between whole people, and is healthy or mature
enough to suffer from, and to deal with, the conflicts that are
personal and that belong to the individual's own psychic reality,

or that are in the person's own inner world. Illness here is called psycho-neurosis and is measured by the degree of rigidity of the personal defences organized to deal with anxiety in the personal dream.

At the other extreme is mental illness of mental hospital type, psychosis, that is aetiologically linked with environmental failure, failure to facilitate the maturational processes, at the stage of double dependence. The term double dependence implies that the essential provision was completely outside the perception and comprehension of the infant at the time. Failure here is called *privation*.

In between is failure on top of success, failure of the environment that was perceived by the child as such at the time that the failure occurred. For such a child there was good-enough environmental provision, and then this stopped. The going-on-living that belonged to taking for granted a good-enough environment became replaced by a reaction to environmental failure, and this reaction broke up the sense of going-on-living. The name given to this state of affairs is *deprivation*.

This is the point of origin of the antisocial tendency, and here begins that which takes hold of the child whenever he or she feels hopeful, and compels activity that is antisocial until someone acknowledges and attempts to correct the failure of the environment. A failure really did happen in the child's history and there really was a significant maladjustment to the child's essential needs. Ironically, the child who is compelled to state and restate this claim on society is called maladjusted.

This antisocial tendency is naturally very common in its minor manifestations, since to some extent parents must fail to meet even essential needs often; but these minor failures of adjustment are corrected by the parents with the child living a home life in the family. The more serious examples of letting a child down (failure of ego-support), however, give the child an antisocial tendency and lead to character disorder and to delinquency. When the defences have become hardened and disillusionment is complete the child who has been affected in this way is destined to be a psychopath, specializing in violence or theft or in both together; and the skill that goes into the antisocial act provides secondary gains, with the result that the child loses the drive to become normal. But in many cases, had treatment been given at an early stage, before secondary gains had complicated matters, it would have been possible to find in the manifestations of the child's antisocial tendency an S.O.S. to society to acknowledge its debt and to re-establish for the child an environment in which impulsive action was once more safe and acceptable, as it had been before the environmental maladjustment.

The field of psychiatry having been covered in this psychological way, in terms of the emotional development of the individual, it is possible for me to pass over to a description of mental illness in terms of response to help. We need to acknowledge that there are cases that are outside remedy. We may die straining to give help where help cannot be given. Apart from this, I do know that psychiatrists and psycho-analysts constantly hand over cases to the care of the psychiatric social worker for no better reason than that they can do nothing themselves. I do this. What sense does it make?

Well, in my view, there are reasons why you might accept the position as it is. First I would call attention to Clare Winnicott's (1962) statement of agency function. For instance, the fact that you represent the Mental Health Act, or the Home Office, or society's genuine concern in regard to its deprived children, really does put you in a position that is unique in each case. This gives you special scope, especially in respect of the mentally ill who are not psycho-neurotic and in respect of the early cases displaying an antisocial tendency.

Your function can logically be reviewed in terms of infant-care, that is in terms of the facilitating environment, the facilitation of maturational processes. Integration is vitally important in this connexion, and your work is quite largely counteracting disintegrating forces in individuals and in families and in localized social groups.

I think of each social worker as a therapist, but not as the kind of therapist who makes the correct and well-timed interpretation that elucidates the transference neurosis. Do this if you like, but your more important function is therapy of the kind that is always being carried on by parents in correction of relative failures in environmental provision. What do such parents do? They exaggerate some parental function and keep it up for a length of time, in fact until the child has used it up and is ready to be released from special care. Special care becomes irksome once the need for it has passed.

For instance, think of casework as providing a human basket. Clients put all their eggs into one basket which is you (and your agency). They take a risk, and first they must test you to see if you may be able to prove sensitive and reliable or whether you have it in you to repeat the traumatic experiences of their past. In a sense you are a frying-pan, with the frying process played backwards, so that you really do unscramble the scrambled eggs.

Infant-care can almost be described in terms of holding, holding that starts off immensely simple and that steadily becomes extremely complex, yet remains, just the same, a holding. In other words, social work is based on the environmental provision that facilitates the individual's maturational process. It is simple and at the same time it is as complex as this environmental provision rapidly becomes in infant- and child-care. It is even more complex because it continues the provision to cover family care and the care of the small social unit. Always it has as its aim not a directing of the individual's life or development, but an enabling of the tendencies that are at work within the individual, leading to a natural evolution based on growth. It is emotional growth that has been delayed and perhaps distorted, and under proper conditions the forces that would have led to growth now lead to a disentanglement of the knot.

One of the difficulties you encounter may be singled out for special consideration. I refer to the clients who become clinically ill *because they find in you and your care the environment which is reliable,* and which, for them, practically invites a mental breakdown. In the area of delinquency (antisocial tendency related to deprivation) this means that when the client gains confidence in you there comes stealing, or destruction that uses your capacity to act strongly, backed by your agency. In the area of madness, what happens is that your client uses your special provision in order to become disintegrated or uncontrolled or dependent in the way that belongs to the period of infancy (regression to dependence). The client goes mad.

This has the germ of healing in it. It is a process of self-cure that needs your help; and in some cases it works. It is relaxation that is not possible except in the setting you have shown you can provide, in a limited professional area. All the same, you may find this difficult to distinguish from the willy-nilly breakdowns of those who cannot wait for good conditions but who simply fail to maintain the integration and emotional growth which they have attained or have seemed to have attained. Usually it is not impossible to make the distinction.

You will see why it is that I spoke first of psycho-neurosis and the repressed unconscious. On the whole repression is not relieved by environmental provision, however skilled and constant. Here the psycho-analyst is needed.

However, the more psychotic or insane disorders are formed in relation to failures in environmental provision, and they can be treated, sometimes successfully, by new environmental provision and this may be your psychiatric social work, casework. What you find yourself providing in your work can be described in the following ways:

You apply yourself to the case.
You get to know what it feels like to be your client.
You become *reliable* for the limited field of your professional responsibility.
You behave yourself professionally.
You concern yourself with your client's problem.
You accept being in the position of a subjective object in the client's life, while at the same time you keep both your feet on your ground.
You accept love, and even the in-love state, without flinching and without acting-out your response.
You accept hate and meet it with strength rather than with revenge.
You tolerate your client's illogicality, unreliability, suspicion, muddle, fecklessness, meanness, etc. etc., and recognize all these unpleasantnesses as symptoms of distress. (In private life these same things would make you keep at a distance.)
You are not frightened, nor do you become overcome with guilt-feelings when your client goes mad, disintegrates, runs out in the street in a nightdress, attempts suicide and perhaps succeeds. If murder threatens you call in the police to help not only yourself but also the client. In all these emergencies you recognize the client's call for help, or a cry of despair because of loss of hope of help.

In all these respects you are, in your limited professional area, a person deeply involved in feeling, yet at the same time detached in that you know that you have no responsibility for the fact of your client's illness, and you know the limits of your powers to alter a crisis situation. If you can hold the situation together the possibility is that the crisis will resolve itself, and then it will be because of you that a result is achieved.

PSYCHIATRIC DISORDER IN TERMS
OF INFANTILE MATURATIONAL PROCESSES[1]
(1963)

My aim is to follow up the main trend in Freud's general thesis, that for the aetiology of psycho-neurosis we must look to the Oedipus complex, and therefore to the interpersonal relationships as between three persons belonging to the child's toddler age. I do thoroughly believe in this theory. I have worked on the basis of this theory for forty years, and I believe, as most psychoanalysts do, that the training in the psycho-analytic technique should be done in respect of cases that can be treated by classical technique, that is, a technique devised for precisely this: the analysis of the psycho-neurotic.

As supervisors of students we find ourselves at our best when the student analyst has a good case, and indeed good analysis can only be done on a good case. If the case is not good (psychoneurotic) we cannot tell whether the student is doing well or badly in his or her effort to learn the basic technique of our craft.

Types of Case Available

We all know, however, that in our practical work, once we are qualified as analysts, we cannot restrict our work to the analysis of psycho-neurotics. To start with, as our work gets deeper and more thorough we discover the psychotic (may I use the word?) elements in our psycho-neurotic patients. To jump ahead with my thesis, the pregenital fixations of our psycho-neurotic patients turn out sometimes to be there in their own right, not simply as regressive phenomena organized in defence on account of anxieties belonging to the Oedipus complex proper.

We cannot always make a correct diagnosis at the beginning. Some reactive depressions turn out to be more severe than we could have guessed; especially does hysteria tend eventually to show psychotic features as analysis proceeds. And there is the very real bugbear of the as-if personality—that which I person-

[1] Dorothy Head Memorial Lecture given to the Philadelphia Psychiatric Society at the Institute of the Pennsylvania Hospital, Philadelphia, October 1963.

ally call the *False Self*, which presents well to the world, but our treatment must get behind it to the breakdown that is negated. In these False Self cases our treatment makes successful people ill, and sometimes we just have to leave them ill; who is to know that without us they would not have been worse—perhaps would have killed themselves or perhaps would have become even more successful but more and more unreal to themselves. And then it also happens that as psychotherapists we get asked to treat frankly psychotic persons, and we may accept them as research cases. But what do we do? Can we apply the psycho-analytic technique?

Wider Application of Psycho-Analytic Technique

I personally believe we can, provided that we accept a change in the theory of the aetiology of the disorder. We shall not always produce cures, but at any rate we shall be able to feel we are doing honest work.

The Deepening of Interpretative Work

There is a very big complication which I must surmount if I am to present my view in a brief statement, and this is that it is possible to do deeper and deeper work using the classical technique, by knowing more and more about mental mechanisms and applying this knowledge. I could talk just simply about this extension of psycho-analytic work but instead I wish to explain what I mean.

Classical psycho-analysis can be done on a well-chosen psycho-neurotic case simply by the interpretation of ambivalence as and when it turns up in the transference neurosis. (This type of case is getting rare, at any rate in England, because it seems that patients have already done this work on themselves through reading and through absorbing the general cultural trend, as expressed openly and in novels and plays and in the modern reassessment of the old masters (Shakespeare, Leonardo da Vinci, Beethoven, etc. etc.).)

Then comes the analysis of depression. By diagnosing depression we are taking for granted ego organization and strength. The analysis of depression involves an understanding of the mental mechanisms of introjection, and the theory of an inner psychic reality, localized (in the patient's fantasy) in the belly or in the head, or in some way or other within the self. The lost object is taken into this inside place and there subjected to hate, till hate is expended; and recovery from mourning or depression takes place, spontaneously in mourning and often spontaneously in reactive depression. This extension of theory leads in practice to developments that arise out of the study of the world of inner phenomena. And the end of a depression may come as the passage of a dark faecal lump, or by surgical removal of a tumour, or in some dream form that reaches to this in symbolic form.

Personal Psychic Reality Located Inside

Analysis of depression and hypochondria leads then to an extension based on the study of the whole body functioning, including that of the bowels, and introjection and projection become mental mechanisms that originate as elaborations of ingestion and elimination.

Freud, Abraham and Klein opened up a new world here for the practising analyst. The technique of analysis was not affected.

The analyst is now involved in a study of not only hate and aggression, but also of the results of these in the patient's inner psychic reality. These results can be labelled as benign and persecutory elements, that need management in this unget-at-able inside world, and in fact the mood depression becomes a clinical feature indicating a temporary blanketing of all inner phenomena; recovery from depression becomes a carefully controlled lifting of the fog, where here and there in the inner world benign and persecutory elements can be safely allowed to meet and contend.

Projection and Introjection Mechanisms

Now a new area for interpretative work is opened up because of the interchange of the elements that accrue in the inner psychic reality and in the external (or shared) reality. This forms an important aspect of the individual's relationship to the world, and has to be accepted as comparable in importance with the object relationships that have id-functioning as their basis.

Moreover the clinical alternative between hypochondria and delusions of persecutory factors becomes manageable as a concept, representing introjected and projected forms of the same thing, namely, the attempt to control and the failure to control the persecutory elements in the personal inner world of the individual.

From here the analyst, keeping within the classical technique, finds he can interpret the way benign and persecutory internal factors depend for their origin on instinctual experiences in their satisfactory and unsatisfactory aspects respectively.

Relating to Objects

In the same way the analyst goes deeper in his interpretations of the individual's relating to objects. There are primitive aspects of such relating, and these include a splitting of the object, so that ambivalence is avoided, and also splitting in the personality itself to match the splitting of the object. Also relating with instinctual drive to a part-object, or what cannot be conceived of except as a part-object, gives rise to crude talion fears, which make the individual withdraw from relating to objects. All these things can be seen in analytic material, and especially when the patient is dealing with psychotic material and is a 'borderline' case.

It is necessary to try to get all these things into the scope of one's understanding, using the classical analytic technique, so that interpretation may be made if the patient is ready for interpretations of this kind.

The State of the Patient's Ego

At this stage in my exposition you may be feeling, as clinicians, some kind of a strain. I hope you are, because there is a reason for this that can be given.

At this point the question does arise: *in what state is the patient's ego? What dependence is there on ego-support?* How can the analyst know what degree of intellectual—rather than feeling—response will be evoked by interpretations of this kind at a particular moment? If the interpretation is incomprehensible then, whatever the reason, the patient feels hopeless, and may feel attacked, destroyed and even annihilated.

From here we go on to a study of ego psychology, to an assessment of the ego-structuring and ego-strength or rigidity or flexibility, and of ego-dependence.

The Infant in Care

It may be that in analysis of borderline cases we can interpret in a way that could be called deeper and deeper, but in doing so we are becoming more and more divorced from the state of affairs of the patient as an infant. For an infant is an infant in care, a dependent being, absolutely dependent at first; and it is not possible to talk about an infant without at the same time talking about infant-care and the mother.

Infant-care and Mental Health

This leads directly to my main point, which is that *I think we follow Freud when we make a direct link between early infancy* (that is, the infant in care, in a state of absolute dependence) *and the more primitive psychiatric disorders*, those grouped under the word schizophrenia. The aetiology of the schizophrenic takes us back not to the Oedipus complex (which was never properly or wholly reached) but to the two-body relationship, the relationship of the infant to the mother before father or any other third body came on the scene.

In fact, we come to the life of the infant related to part-objects, and the infant who is dependent but not able to know about dependence. The mental health of the individual in respect of freedom from psychotic illness is being laid down by the infant and mother together in the very early stages of infant growth and infant-care.

The Ego in Infancy

What are the main things that take place in the emotional growth of the infant in the early weeks and months (consolidated at later stages)?

Three of these are: Integration
Personalization
Relating to objects.

The ego of the infant is very strong, but only so because of the ego-support given by a good-enough mother who is able to throw her whole self into adapting to the needs of her infant, gradually withdrawing from this position as the infant needs her to adapt less and less closely. Without this ego-support the infant's ego is unformed, weak, easily disrupted, and incapable of making growth along the lines of the maturational process.

The Nature of Psychiatric Disorder

Psychiatric illness is commonly described in language that indicates specific failures on the part of the patient to establish these and other infantile positions. Personalities become 'disintegrated', patients 'lose the capacity to dwell in their bodies' and to accept their skin-boundary, and patients become 'unable to relate to objects'. They 'feel unreal' in relation to the environment and they 'feel that the environment is unreal'.

The point is: how far do psychiatrists feel it is a fair statement that the disorders they are dealing with are relative failures exactly where achievements characterize the life of every healthy infant?

Sources of My Personal Ideas

This way of looking at development derives from a con-fluence of several types of experience. For my part, I have had much opportunity as a paediatrician to observe infants with their mothers, and have made a point of getting innumerable mothers to describe their infants' way of life in the early stages before the mother has got out of touch with these intimate things. (If I had my time again I would work with premature infants, but this has not been possible.) Then I have had a personal analysis which took me back into the forgotten territory of my own infancy. This was followed by the psycho-analytic training, and my basic training cases took me to early infantile mental mechanisms as displayed in dreams and in symptoms. Child analysis gave me a child's view of infancy.

Then I came to the analysis of patients who proved to be borderline, or who came to have the mad part of them met and altered. It is work with borderline patients that has taken me (whether I have liked it or not) to 'the early human condition, and here I mean to the early life of the individual rather than to the mental mechanisms of earliest infancy.

Clinical Illustration

(The characteristic of the Monday session, the one before the session that I am reporting for discussion, was that my young female patient came loaded up with groceries. She had dis-covered the shops near my consulting room, and she was de-lighted with them. This was a natural development of her gradual discovery of the relationship to me in the transference of what she calls her greed. She has even said that coming to analysis is coming to a meal. There has been a long preparation for this in reports of her anorexia which alternates with an extreme degree of libidinization of a really good well-cooked and well-served meal.)

On Tuesday Miss X lay on the couch and, as usual, covered herself with the rug from neck to toe, and lay on her side facing me. (I sit, in her analysis, at the side, but at the level of the cushions.) Nothing happened. She was not anxious, nor was I. We talked about a few things in a desultory manner, but there was no development of any theme. At the end Miss X was contented to go, and she had enjoyed her session.

This is an analysis with a very steady development in the analytic process, and I was by no means at sea, although I did not and could not know exactly what was happening.

The next day, Wednesday, Miss X covered herself over as

usual, and this day she talked a lot, half apologizing that there seemed to be no material for analysis. We had a conversation about horse-jumping, and as it happened we had each watched the same horse-jumping competition on TV. I took part naturally in the conversation, not knowing what was going on. She said that the English just let the horse jump, and when there is success, as there often is, it's just that the horse is a very good one. The Germans, on the other hand, calculate everything, including the number of steps the horse will need to take before each hurdle. In the end it emerged that what impressed her most in horse-jumping was the training of the horses.

Now, I pricked up my ears here, because I know that Miss X has a vested interest in the training of analysts. She had several years with one before finding out that he wasn't trained, and she did a great deal of reading before risking a second analysis, and choosing me. I found that she had read me pretty thoroughly, and once she had decided on me she had waited a considerable time rather than go to anyone else.

So now the session was three-quarters through, and the work was done in the last few minutes, as often happens in her case.

She now reported a dream about a painter whose work she had told me about a week earlier. His paintings are very good indeed and he is not recognized yet. In the dream she went to buy a picture, perhaps one of those she saw in the original exhibition, but he had now painted many pictures, and had changed. His original pictures were like those of a child. She would rather buy a child's picture. But all the later pictures were calculated and sophisticated and the artist couldn't even remember the original pictures. She even drew one of them but he couldn't remember.

When I said that this dream continued the theme of the technique for horse-jumping, and the matter of training and loss of spontaneity, she immediately saw that this was so, and she was pleased. She elaborated the theme. It was a question of the early promise and the practical technique producing a finished product.

This opened up the whole idea of yesterday's session which she went on to say had been important and indeed crucial. In the evening she had been thinking about it, and she now remembered. This was how it was.

In the previous analysis she had quickly reached to the point where she is with me now in this analysis. However, the previous analyst could not let things develop. When she lay quiet, for instance, he might tell her to sit up, or he might adopt some other procedure, and she quickly lost touch with the process that had started up in her. It took some years for her to recognize that it was the analyst's technique that was not suitable for her type of case, and eventually she discovered that he was not a trained analyst. And if he had been a trained analyst he might not have been able to meet her needs which were those of a psychotic patient (this in spite of the fact that she is not as ill as many schizophrenics she had known and lived with and tried to help).

In the quiet session yesterday she had reached to this point and had got through a difficulty. On the one hand she would be relieved to find that her analysis with me, which also started well, would fail too; that would be too bad, and it would end in suicide, but that is what she knows about from experience, and she can become numb and avoid pain in experiencing this which is what she expects. She can even feel power here by knowing the truth in advance.

What took place in the hour was that she came to know that the analysis was not going to fail in the usual way, and that she would go ahead and take all the risks and let feelings develop, and perhaps suffer deeply. In this way she found this Tuesday hour extremely satisfying, and she felt grateful.

She now went on to do what she sometimes does and can do because of her special insight, and she gave me a useful hint about the analyst's role in the treatment of patients whose fear is of disintegration. She pointed out that such patients absolutely need the analyst to be omnipotent. Here they are unlike psychoneurotics. They need the analyst to know and to tell them what they fear. They themselves know all the time, but the thing is that the analyst must know and say it. The patient may say and do things to put the analyst off the scent, in a further test of his ability to see the main point without being told.

Together we added the explanation that it is the patient's own omnipotence and omniscience that the analyst must take over so that the patient may with relief break down, break up, and experience the worse degree of disintegration or sense of annihilation.

As a corollary, a schizoid patient is gullible. Anyone may come along, a quack, a faith-healer, a wild analyst—he (or she) has only to say: I know what you are like and I can cure you, and the patient must fall for it. This is the first phase, and the person who says this may be wholly untrained and in fact may be an ignorant fool, or a charlatan. Then comes the testing, and the patient's disillusionment and withdrawal to a new hopelessness, which is so familiar that it is almost welcomed. To get the patient through to the next phase the analyst must be trained or must have a structured theory and a mature personality and a steady attitude towards the patient and the treatment. Some analysts may not like this aspect of their work because what is not called for is cleverness.

The next day, Thursday, Miss X came a quarter of an hour late, a very rare thing in her analysis. The car had not come in time, but Miss X said this was not a satisfactory explanation because she had dreamed that she was late for today's session. I interpreted here that something had changed so that she now showed ambivalence in her relation to me and the analysis. She agreed and said that in fact she was especially eager to come because she felt very pleased indeed with the last few days' analysis. Obviously there must be some other factor going counter to her wish to come.

What happened in the hour was a new statement of the difficulties ahead. It would be found that she could be exceedingly greedy. We discussed this, and I interpreted that this meant that there exists a compulsive element in her appetite. (We have already done work on this.) What she knows will be difficult will be for me to manage the analysis when she reaches to her full capacity to lay claim to me and all that is mine. Stealing comes in here, and on Monday, I remembered, she had borrowed a book.

On the other hand, and I pointed this out, she had yesterday paid me on the spot by giving me a useful hint on the analyst's role in the analysis of schizoid patients.

We had plenty of material available that had to do with eating the analyst (the grocer's shop, etc.) and I was glad I had not interpreted oral sadism in these earlier stages because the significant interpretation, now becoming acceptable, was of the compulsive greed of the antisocial tendency. This relates to deprivation.

The Dependent Infant

Reformulating the infancy experience I find I must speak in terms of dependence, and in fact I am now suspicious of all statements about early mental mechanisms that do not take into account the infant caught up in the behaviour and attitude of the mother.

The Inherited Tendencies

This brings me to a statement of early infancy. In infancy the growth-process belongs to the infant, and is the sum of inherited tendencies, and this includes the *maturational process*. The maturational process only takes effect in an individual infant in so far as there is a *facilitating environment*. The study of the facilitating environment is almost as important at the beginning as the study of the individual maturational process. The characteristic of the maturational process is the drive towards *integration*, which comes to mean something more and more complex as the infant grows. The characteristic of the facilitating environment is *adaptation*, starting almost at 100 per cent and turning in graduated doses towards de-adaptation according to the new developments in the infant which are part of the gradual change towards independence.

When the facilitating environment is good enough (this always means that there is a mother who is at first given over to her job of infant-care, gradually, and only gradually, reasserting herself as an independent person) then the maturational process has its chance. The result is that the infant personality achieves some degree of integration, at first under the umbrella of ego-support (the mother's adaptation) and in time more and more an achievement that stands on its own legs.

As I have said, in the course of these early weeks, months, years, the infant also becomes able to relate to objects, becomes a dweller in his own body and body-functioning, and experiences an I AM feeling, and is ready to meet all-comers.

These developments in the individual that are based on the maturational processes constitute mental health. It is to the opposite or the reversal of these same processes that we must look if we are to understand personality disturbance of schizoid kind.

Modifications of Technique

The important thing left over for me to describe is the modification of technique needed when it is a borderline case that is being treated. The basis of the treatment is the classical technique, but things taken for granted in psycho-analysis of the psycho-neurotic become the cornerstone of the modified technique.

In psycho-analysis the setting is taken for granted. The analyst behaves himself, gives himself over to the patient's interests in the analytic hour, ignores all but the essentials which are the details of the transference neurosis. He believes in the patient, and when there are deceptions he believes in the motives the patient has for deceiving the analyst.

When the psycho-neurotic patient refers to these matters the analyst knows he or she is finding in the analytic setting reliable elements that have already been experienced in the past. The psycho-neurotic has a capacity to believe in the analysis based on experience, and his suspicions are due to his ambivalences.

What has been said here of psycho-neurotics is also true of the depressives, except in so far as these have schizoid characteristics included in them.

When a psycho-analyst is working with schizoid persons (call it psycho-analysis or not) the insightful interpretation becomes less important, and the maintenance of an ego-adaptive setting is essential, The reliability of the setting is a primary experience, not something remembered and re-enacted in the analyst's technique.

The Risks of Dependence

Dependence takes on a form that is exactly like that of the infant in the infant-mother relationship, only the patient may take a long time to get there because of all the tests that have to be made by the patient who has become wary because of previous experiences. It is, one can well understand, very painful to the patient to be dependent unless one is actually an infant, and the risks that have to be taken in regression to dependence are very great indeed. The risk is not that the analyst will die so much as that the analyst will suddenly be unable to believe in the reality and the intensity of the patient's primitive anxiety, a fear of disintegration, or of annihilation, or of falling for ever and ever.

The Holding Function

You will see that the analyst is *holding* the patient, and this often takes the form of conveying in words at the appropriate moment something that shows that the analyst knows and understands the deepest anxiety that is being experienced, or that is waiting to be experienced. Occasionally holding must take a physical form, but I think this is only because there is a delay in the analyst's understanding which he can use for verbalizing what is afoot.

There are times when you carry round your child who has earache. Soothing words are no use. Probably there are times when a psychotic patient needs physical holding, but eventually it will be understanding and empathy that will be necessary.

Techniques Compared

With the *psycho-neurotic* case the analyst must interpret love and hate as it appears in the transference neurosis, and this means taking what is going on back to childhood. This concerns the patient's relating to objects.

With the *depressive* case the analyst must survive the aggression that goes with loving. Reactive depression is much like psycho-neurosis and needs interpretation of the transference. But depression needs the survival of the analyst, and this gives the patient time to reassemble the elements in his or her inner reality so that the inner analyst also survives. This is a task that can be done since *depression implies ego-strength,* and our diagnosis of depression implies that we think that the patient can cope with guilt and ambivalence and accept personal aggressive drives without disruption of the personality, given time.

In treatment of *schizoid* persons the analyst needs to know all about the interpretations that might be made on the material presented, but he must be able to refrain from being sidetracked into doing this work that is inappropriate because the main need is for an unclever ego-support, or a holding. This 'holding', like the task of the mother in infant-care, acknowledges tacitly the tendency of the patient to disintegrate, to cease to exist, to fall for ever.

Adaptation and the Satisfaction of Id-drives

A source of misunderstanding here is the idea (that some analysts have) that the term 'adaptation to need' in treatment of schizoid patients and in infant-care means meeting id-drives. In this setting it is not a question of meeting id-drives or of frustrating id-drives. There are more important things going on, and these are of the nature of giving ego-support to ego processes. It is only under conditions of ego adequacy that id-drives, whether satisfied or frustrated, become experiences of the individual.

Summary

The processes that constitute schizophrenic mental illness are the processes of early infantile maturation, but in reverse.

HOSPITAL CARE SUPPLEMENTING
INTENSIVE PSYCHOTHERAPY
IN ADOLESCENCE[1]
(1963)

Adolescence, which means becoming an adult, is a phase in healthy growth. It covers the period of the individual's puberty. It also includes the socialization of the boy or girl. Here, the word socialization does not mean adaptation and conformity. When in health the individual becomes a mature adult, this implies that he or she is able to identify with parent-figures and with some aspect of society without too great a sacrifice of personal impulse, or alternatively, be essentially himself or herself without needing to be antisocial. In health the boy or girl becomes able to take responsibility, and to help to maintain, or modify, or even to alter completely the legacy of the last generation. Inevitably he and she will eventually, as adults, hand on a legacy to the next generation in the eternal series.

Adolescence, then, is a phase in the growth-process of every boy or girl. In our theoretical considerations and practical work we have to keep this in mind while we are dealing with that other thing: psychiatric illness in a boy or girl who happens to be in the age group of the adolescent or young adult.

Sketch of Adolescence

Adolescence itself can be a stormy time. Defiance mixed with dependence, even at times extreme dependence, makes the picture of adolescence seem mad and muddled. Parents, who are much needed over this phase, find themselves confused as to their role. They may find themselves paying out dollars to enable their own children to flout them. Or they may find themselves being necessary as people to be wasted, while the adolescent goes for friendship and advice to aunts and uncles and even to strangers. Where the family is absent or ill some aspect

[1] Lecture given at The McLean Hospital, Belmont, Massachusetts, U.S.A., as part of a Clinical Symposium: 'The Individual and the Community: Current Perspectives in Rehabilitation', on the occasion of the formal opening of the new Rehabilitation Building, October 1963.

of society must take over the family function. On top of all this is the complication that adolescents have adult techniques at their command. The boy of four years, who is in the throes of Oedipus conflicts, dreams of his father's death, but now at fourteen he has the power to kill. Suicide is now possible. Drugs can be obtained. The girl, who at four years was identified with mother and also jealous of her mother's power to conceive, dreaming of burglars or of her mother's death, now at fourteen can become pregnant or may offer her body for money. The adolescent girl can become pregnant although not at the stage of wanting to give a baby to someone she loves or of wanting to devote herself to a baby's care. This is only to remind you, though you need no such reminder, that adolescence itself is no easy thing in the world of affairs (cf. Winnicott, 1962).

If it be agreed that the adolescent boy has a special problem with his aggressive drives (and so the girl, too, indirectly), it will be agreed also that the problem is altered for the worse by advances in thermonuclear physics. Most of us believe that there will be no sub-total wars since any war becomes total war and total war is unthinkable. We are here driven to an assessment of the value of war in its function of giving a licence to kill. I put 'value' in inverted commas, because I suppose everyone hates war and prays for peace; but as psychiatrists or social psychologists we are forced to measure the effect of permanent peace on the mental health of the community. The effect of the idea of permanent peace puts a severe strain on everything except emotional maturity, which is rather a rare achievement. Can adolescence in general gather all its aggression into the competitive or dangerous sport? Will not society clamp down on dangerous sport and make even this unrespectable or even anti-social? We do not know the answer to this broad question yet, but we do know that a localized war, with all its immense tragedy, used to do something positive for the relief of individual tensions, enabling paranoia to remain potential and giving a sense of REAL to persons who do not always feel real when peace reigns supreme. Especially in boys, violence feels real, while a life of ease brings a threat of depersonalization.

You will have given much thought to these problems that are inherent in the growing-up process, and you will have found ways of stating the important part that the child's own home can play if it is still a going concern. Your institution is in part an organized substitute for the home, which is often satisfactory enough and yet not quite able to stand the specific strain of caring for an ill member over a long period.

Continuing my sketch of adolescence, dogmatically stated for brevity's sake: there is only one cure for adolescence, and this is the passage of time and the passing on of the adolescent into the adult state. We must not try to cure adolescents as if they were suffering from a psychiatric disorder. I have used the phrase 'adolescent doldrums' to describe the few years in which each individual has no way out except to wait and to do this without awareness of what is going on. In this phase the child does not know whether he or she is homosexual, heterosexual or narcissistic. There is no established identity, and no certain way of life that shapes the future and makes sense of working for graduation exams. There is not yet a capacity to identify with parent figures without loss of personal identity.

Then again, the adolescent has a fierce intolerance of the false solution. We contribute something to the adolescent if we as adults offer no false solutions, but if instead we meet the localized challenges and deal with acute needs as they arise. We expect defiant independence to alternate with regression to dependence, and we hold on, playing for time instead of offering distractions and cures.

Illness during Adolescence

Naturally we find any and every disorder in this phase of development:

Psychoneurosis proper.

Hysteria, with some psychosis hidden away causing trouble but never showing up clearly as madness.

Affective disorders, with depression at the base. These include:

Manic-depressive swings.

Manic-defence (denial or negation of depression).

Elation, and paranoid and hypochondriacal complications.

The false-self personality that threatens to break down at the period of examinations.

The schizoid group of disorders. These involve the undoing of integration and of the maturational processes generally. Clinical manifestations include lack of contact with reality, depersonalization, splitting, and loss of sense of identity.

We find ourselves dealing with these disorders in patients who are at the puberty period of growth and who are adolescent in so far as they can be. It is difficult to sort out the ill from the normal at this stage; also it is difficult to know in these cases whether to offer treatment in terms of care and management or in terms of psychotherapy. Roughly speaking, we offer psychotherapy to those patients who feel a need for it, or who can easily be helped to see that psychotherapy is relevant; here we watch out for the moment when institutional care or special mental nursing becomes necessary, necessary because the treatment has enabled the patient to reach a point at which breaking down becomes constructive. For the others who have no insight we try to provide care or mental nursing, and expect regressive phenomena to appear eventually; and we may wait to be able to add psychotherapy in some cases.

If in this new hospital building the intention is to facilitate the interaction of care and psychotherapy, this is to be providing just exactly what is necessary and also just what is difficult to provide. Why difficult? Briefly: not only do the care- and the therapy-personnel become jealous of each other, each unable to see the other's value, but also some patients tend to foster a split between these two groups. There is often a reflection here of the tensions between the patient's parents, and we see in displaced form the patient's fear of allowing the parents to come together (in the unconscious fantasy system).

There is much that could be said about the management or care of boys and girls who have these various disorders. Let me choose to pick out one thing for special mention. *There will be suicides*. Management Committees must learn to reconcile themselves to suicides, to truancy, and the occasional maniacal outburst with something in it very like murder, and broken windows and destruction of things. Psychiatrists who are blackmailed by these disasters are unable to do what is best for the rest of the community in their care. And the same applies to the blackmail of the psychiatrist by the antisocial tendency in patients. Of course actual destruction is not helpful, and prevention of actual destruction or suicide is the aim; but it is *human* prevention that is needed, and mechanical restraint is not valuable. This means that there will be failures of prevention since human beings have human limits to what they can and are willing to do.

You will have noticed that I have left out of my rough classification one important grouping, namely, the antisocial tendency, which can lead a boy or girl to delinquency and eventually to recidivism.

The term 'antisocial tendency' has a use because it links this type of disorder with the normal, and with what it is at its inception, a reaction to deprivation. This tendency can become a futile compulsion and the child is then to be labelled delinquent.

Here is a disorder that is not to be classified along with the psycho-neuroses and the affective disorders and with schizophrenia; and it is a disorder that links very easily with the disorders that are inherent in the adolescent growth syndrome. Special management problems belong to work in this area. Here the theme cannot be developed but the main idea is that the antisocial tendency in a child represents (unconscious) hope related to the mending of a deprivation trauma (Winnicott, 1956).

Interaction of Maturational and Pathological Processes

I now come to the great difficulty which confronts all who are engaged in preventive and curative work. At this phase of individual growth, it is surely very difficult to diagnose health and normality and to distinguish it from psychiatric disorder. Adolescence alters the shape of psychiatric illness.

Here are twenty adolescents. They are isolated personalities but they group together loosely because of common interests: pop singers, the twist, jazz, a way of dressing, a state of doldrums which it would be dishonest to try to avoid. On the fringe of any group there is a depressive boy or girl who attempts suicide. Now the whole group displays a depressed mood, and is 'with' the one who makes the attempt. Another breaks a glass window for no reason at all. Now all the group is with this one who breaks the glass window. Another, along with some who are nearby, breaks into a shop and steals some cigarettes, or does something that arouses the law's attention. Now all the group is with this law-breaker.

Yet it can be said that on the whole the boys and girls comprising this group will come through without suicide, without murder, without violence and without theft.

In other words, adolescents in the doldrums phase seem to me to use the ill individuals on the fringe of the group to give reality to their own potential symptomatology. Let me now give an example to illustrate the problems of diagnosis and management.

Note on the Case of a Boy

I will refer to the case of a boy first referred to me at the age of eight years. It was possible at that age to see in him an organized sense of grievance which dated from a phase in his early childhood management and was related to the continued severe mental illness of his mother. Therapy was attempted at that stage but it was not successful partly because of the mother's illness.

The boy was sent to me again at the age of fifteen. In consultation at this age he was able to give me a vital clue relating to his attacks of violence. In actual fact he had been in danger of attempting to kill his father. The enlightenment came in the form of a dream which he illustrated with a drawing. The drawing showed his hand reaching towards the hand of his girl friend. In between the two hands in the dream was a barrier made of glass. The violence that he feared had to do with an attempt to break through the barrier between him and the actual world, a barrier which became more real the more his instincts were involved in object-relating.

I referred this boy to a colleague who is in charge of a mental hospital and who admitted the boy with my diagnosis of schizophrenia. This boy was dealt with well in hospital and he soon managed to fit into the community. A notable thing was that he temporarily found asylum from his mother's severe mental illness. Undoubtedly the immediate change in this boy was chiefly due to his finding an alternative home, one however which could not last long. Soon after he had settled into the hospital he was able to sever his tie with his particular girl friend on whom he was excessively dependent. Before coming into hospital he had constantly been found weeping after interminable conversations with this girl, the telephone and the wires representing the same as the glass frame between himself and the girl in the dream. Because of the fact of the thing in between him and the girl he was able to feel the full intensity of his love and his dependence. This girl had been needed to displace the ill mother. He improved after he had given up his addiction to this girl friend and he became more easy with the other members of the group and with the staff.

It is here that the case of this boy seems apposite in an address given to this hospital[1] at this moment. It illustrates the difficulties. In hospital the boy was able to use the excellent occupational therapy and art therapy departments. He settled in to very creative and original work both in modelling and in painting. Everything he did had striking significance. So often psychotic and near-psychotic patients prove to be deeply rewarding when they undertake original work in one of the departments of rehabilitation. The trouble was that this boy improved so much and he so much enjoyed the new relationship to the world that he formed in this small community that the doctors altered his diagnosis. They decided now that he was hysterical and somewhat antisocial, and that the external factor of his home conditions

[1] The McLean Hospital, Belmont, Massachusetts, U.S.A.

was the chief cause of his being thought to be ill. The boy was therefore discharged but not before the physician had found a good school for him where the whole of the boy's difficulties were plainly set before the headmaster. After a few months at the new school the boy began to show again the symptoms for which he was sent into hospital; he became violent and destructive and was unable to settle down to work. The diagnosis of schizophrenia was now reapplied; he was quickly removed from the school and at present the parents are trying to deal with the difficult situation by arranging for him to have an unlimited journey round the world in the hope that by the time he gets back home he will have grown up out of his difficulties. By then he may of course have got into serious trouble, or even may have done harm to someone.

This unsuccessful case can be used to illustrate the fact that a successful rehabilitation department can alter the clinical picture and make it seem that a patient has got well so that the original diagnosis is lost sight of. You and the department here will be aware of these dangers and will not easily be deceived. You will not be deceived, for instance, by excellent artistic productions which can indeed denote potential health in the patient but which do not stand for health itself.

Summary

Some characteristics of adolescence have been sketched and the relationship has been discussed of these characteristics to the symptomatology of psychiatrically ill children at the age of puberty. A case is given that illustrates some of the difficulties that belong to the management of patients of this age-group, and to the provision of rehabilitation facilities such as these that are being formally initiated on the day of this meeting.

DEPENDENCE IN INFANT-CARE, IN CHILD-CARE, AND IN THE PSYCHO-ANALYTIC SETTING[1]

(1963)

There is nothing new in the idea of dependence, either in the early life of the individual or in the transference which develops force as a psycho-analytic treatment gets under way. What I feel may need restating from time to time is the relationship between these two examples of dependence.

I need not quote from Freud. Dependence of the patient on the analyst has always been known and fully acknowledged, and for instance shows in the reluctance of an analyst to take on a new patient within a month or two of a long summer holiday. The analyst rightly fears that the patient's reaction to the break will involve deep changes that are not yet available for analysis. I will start with a development of this theme.

A young woman patient had to wait for a few months before I could start, and then I could see her only once a week; then I gave her daily sessions just when I was due to go abroad for a month. The reaction to the analysis was positive and developments were rapid, and I found this independent young woman becoming, in her dreams, extremely dependent. In one dream she had a tortoise, but its shell was soft so that the animal was unprotected and would therefore certainly suffer. So in the dream she killed the tortoise to save it the intolerable pain that was coming to it. This was herself and indicated a suicide tendency, and it was to cure this tendency that she had come for treatment.

The trouble was that she had not yet had time in her analysis to deal with reactions to my going away, and so she had this suicidal dream, and clinically she became physically ill, though in an obscure way. Before I went I just had time, but only just, to enable her to feel a connexion between the physical reaction and my going away. My going away re-enacted a traumatic episode or series of episodes of her own babyhood. It was in one

[1] A paper read to the Boston Psychoanalytic Society, October 1962, and first published in the *Int. J. Psycho-Anal.*, **44,** pp. 339-44.

language as if I were holding her and then became preoccupied with some other matter so that she felt *annihilated*. This was her word for it. By killing herself she would gain control over being annihilated while dependent and vulnerable. In her healthy self and body, with all her strong urge to live, she has carried all her life the memory of having at some time had a total urge to die; and now the physical illness came as a localization in a bodily organ of this total urge to die. She felt helpless about this until I was able to interpret to her what was happening, whereupon she felt relief, and became able to let me go. Incidentally her physical illness became less of a threat and started to heal, partly of course because it was receiving appropriate treatment.

If illustration were needed this might show the danger of underestimating transference dependence. The amazing thing is that an interpretation can bring about a change, and one can only assume that understanding in a deep way and interpreting at the right moment is a form of reliable adaptation. In this case, for instance, the patient became able to cope with my absence because she felt (at one level) that she was now not being annihilated, but in a positive way was being kept in existence by having a reality as the object of my concern. A little later on, in more complete dependence, the verbal interpretation will not be enough, or may be dispensed with.

You will have observed that I could go in either of two directions, starting from such a fragment from an analysis. One direction would take us to the analysis of reaction to loss and so to the main part of that which we learn in our psycho-analytic training. The other direction takes us to that which I wish to discuss in this paper. This other direction takes me to the understanding we have in us that makes us know that we must avoid going away just after starting an analysis. It is an awareness of the vulnerability of the patient's ego, the opposite of ego-strength. In innumerable ways we meet our patient's needs because we know what the patient is feeling like, more or less, and we can find the equivalent of the patient in ourselves. What we have in ourselves we can project, and find in the patient. All this is done silently, and the patient usually remains unaware of what we do well, but becomes aware of the part we play when things go wrong. It is when we fail in these respects that the patient reacts to the unpredictable and suffers a break in the continuity of his going-on-being. I wish to take up this point in particular later on in this paper, in discussing Zetzel's Geneva Congress paper (1956).

My general objective is to relate dependence in the psycho-

analytic transference to dependence at various stages of infant-
and child-development and care. You will see that I am involved in an attempt to evaluate the external factor. May I
be allowed to do this without being thought to be going back on
what psycho-analysis has stood for over the past forty years in
child psychiatry. Psycho-analysis has stood for the personal
factor, the mechanisms involved in individual emotional growth,
the internal strains and stresses that lead to the individual's
defence organization, and the view of psycho-neurotic illness as
evidence of intrapsychic tension that is based on id-drives that
threaten the individual ego. But here we return to ego vulnerability and therefore to dependence.

It is easy to see why it is that psycho-analysts have been
reluctant to write about the environmental factor, since it has
often been true that those who wished to ignore or deny the
significance of the intrapsychic tensions chiefly stressed the bad
external factor as a cause of illness in child psychiatry. However,
psycho-analysis is now well established, and we can afford to
examine the external factor both bad and good.

If we accept the idea of dependence, then we have already
started to examine the external factor, and indeed when we say
an analyst should be trained we are saying that an essential for
orthodox psycho-analysis is an external factor, that is to say the
good-enough analyst. All this is self-evident, yet I can still find
those who *either* never mention this external factor as if it were
really important, *or else* talk about it all the time, ignoring the
internal factors in the process. As Zetzel said in a seminar
recently: first Freud thought all neurotic persons had had sexual
traumata in childhood, and then he found that they had had
wishes. And then for several decades it was assumed in analytic
writings that there was not such a thing as a real sexual trauma.
Now we have to allow for this too.

In a deliberate examination of the external factor, I am thus
far engaged in relating the analyst's personality, capacity for
identifying with the patient, technical equipment, and so on,
to the multifarious details of child-care, and then in a more
specific way to the special state that a mother is in (perhaps father
also, but he has less opportunity to show it) in the short time-
space covering the later stages of pregnancy and the first months
of the infant's life.

Psycho-analysis as we learn it is not at all like child-care. In
fact, parents who interpret the unconscious to their children are
in for a bad time. But in the part of our work as analysts that
I am referring to there is nothing wc do that is unrelated to

child-care or to infant-care. In this part of our work we can in fact learn what to do from being parents, from having been children, from watching mothers with very young babies or babies un-born, from correlating parental failures with subsequent clinical states of ill children. While we know that psycho-neurotic illness is not caused by parents, we also know that the mental health of the child cannot become established without good-enough paren-tal or maternal care. We also know that a corrective environ-mental experience does not directly cure the patient any more than a bad environment directly causes the illness structure. I refer to this again at the end of this paper.

I now wish to refer back to my fragment of clinical material. Very early in the analysis this patient had become represented in her dream material by frail and often maimed creatures, and now she had dreamed of the tortoise with a soft shell.[1] You will have noted that this points the way to a regression to dependence that is bound to come. The patient had had several years of analysis along ordinary lines by an analyst who disallowed re-gression if this threatened to become acted out and to involve dependence on the analyst. She was therefore over-ripe for this part of the total analytic procedure, though of course needing as much as anyone else does the usual interpretations that become appropriate from day to day, or from minute to minute.

If I go a little further into the interpretative problem in the analysis of this fragment, I think I can show how interwoven are these two things: the intrapsychic mechanisms and dependence, which by definition involves the environment and its behaviour.

I had plenty of material in this case for the interpretation of the patient's reaction to my going away in terms of oral sadism belonging to love reinforced by anger—anger with me and all the others in her life who have gone away, including the mother who weaned her. I could have weighed in, fully justified in terms of what the patient had told me, but then I should have been a bad analyst making good interpretations. I should have been a bad analyst because of the way the material had been given me. All the time in our analytic work we are assessing and reassessing the ego-strength of the patient. The material had been given me in a way that indicated that the patient knew she could trust me not to use it brusquely. She is hypersensitive to all drugs and to all illnesses and to slight criticisms, and I must expect her to be sensitive to any mistake I make in my estimation of the strength of her ego. Something central in her personality only too easily

---

[1] By the way, she could also be a horse that had to be shot, else it would have kicked its way out of an aeroplane.

feels the threat of annihilation; clinically of course she becomes tough and extremely independent, well defended, and along with this goes a sense of futility and of being unreal.

In fact her ego is not able to accommodate any strong emotion. Hate, excitement, fear—each equally separates off, like a foreign body, and all too easily becomes localized in a bodily organ which goes into spasm and tends to destroy itself by a perversion of its physiological functioning.

The reason why the regressive and dependence dreams have appeared has to do chiefly with her finding that I do not use every bit of material for interpretation, but that I store everything up for use at the right moment and content myself for the present with making preparation for meeting the dependence that is coming up. This dependence phase will be very painful for the patient, and she knows it, and a risk of suicide goes with it, but, as she says, there is no other way. There *is* another way, for if her analyst is not able to meet her dependence so that the regression becomes a therapeutic experience, she will break down into psychosomatic illness, which produces the much-needed nursing but not the insight or the mental care that can really make a difference. The analyst needs to know why the patient would rather kill himself or herself than live under threat of annihilation.

By looking at this bit of material in this way, we reach a point where we are discussing both analysis and the meeting of dependence needs. A string of 'good' interpretations relative to the general content of the session would produce anger or excitement, and it is not yet possible for this patient to deal with these all-out emotional experiences. It would therefore be bad in the sense of my present statement of analytic procedure to interpret the very things that are relative to the premature separation.

In the course of a talk in which we made plans for the future and discussed the nature of her illness and the risks that are inherent in going on with the treatment, I said:[1] 'So here is yourself ill, and we can see that the physical illness hides an extreme reaction to my going away, although you are not able to reach to a direct feeling-awareness of this. So that you could say that I have caused your illness, just as others have caused you to be ill when you were a baby, and you could be angry.' She said: 'But I'm not.' (Actually she holds me in an idealized position at present, and tends to find doctors of the body to be persecutors.) So I said: 'The path is there, wide open for your hatred and anger, but anger refuses to walk down the path.'

[1] I was clearly affected by the intellectual level of her method of presenting material.

The patient told me that the main thing that brought about the very swift, involuntary development towards dependence was the fact that I let things be, and wanted to see what each hour would bring. Actually the pattern had been that she would start almost as if the hour were a social visit. She would lie down and display very clear intellectual awareness of herself and of her surroundings. I played in with all this, and there was much silence. Near the end of each hour she would quite unexpectedly remember a dream, and she would then get my interpretation. The dreams presented in this way were not very obscure, and the dream resistance could usually be seen to reside in the forty-five minutes of material that preceded it and that was not good material for interpretation. That which has been dreamed and remembered and presented is within the capacity of the ego-strength and structure.

So this patient will be very dependent on me over a phase; the hope is that for her sake, as well as for mine, this dependence will be kept within the confines of the transference and of the analytic setting and sessions. But how can one tell in advance? How can one make this sort of diagnosis that is concerned with assessment of needs?

In terms of *child-care*, I would like to exemplify regression in the service of the ego by looking at the phases of spoiling which parents find one child needs from time to time—parents, that is, who do not spoil their child because of their own anxieties. Such phases of spoiling bring many a child through without any involvement of a doctor or a child guidance clinic. It is difficult to give a case without making it sound rare, and these are matters of common experience in family life, when parents care for their own children. For a few hours, or days, or weeks, in a special context, a child is treated as if of a younger age than is in fact true chronologically. Sometimes it happens when a child bangs his head or cuts his finger; he goes in a moment from four to two, and is screaming and consoling himself with his head in his mother's lap. Then in no time, or after a sleep, he is again very grown up, and more so than his own age warrants.

Here is a boy of two (Winnicott, 1963). He reacted very badly at twenty months to the mother's anxiety which she experienced when she conceived. It is part of her pattern to become extremely anxious at conception. He stopped using the pot and stopped using words, and his forward progress was held up. When the baby was born he was not hostile to the baby, but he wanted to be bathed like the baby. At breast-feeding time he started thumb-sucking, which had not previously been a feature. He made special claims on the parents' indulgence, needing to sleep in their bed for many months. His speaking was delayed.

The parents met all these changes and demands in a satisfactory way, but the neighbours said that they were spoiling the boy. Eventually the boy emerged from his regression or withdrawal and the parents were able to finish with spoiling him when he was eight years old, after he had had a phase in which he was stealing money from them.[1]

This is a common type of case in child psychiatry, as I know it, especially in private practice when children are brought for symptoms that in child guidance might be considered to be insignificant. It has been an important part of my child psychiatry orientation to recognize that in such a case one does not immediately think of psycho-analysis; one thinks of supporting these parents in their management of their child's babyishness. One may be in a position, of course, to give psycho-analytic help, while the parents are carrying out the mental nursing of the patient, but it is a formidable matter to treat such a case by psycho-analysis if there is not a parental provision that will meet the mental nursing needs. Without the parents' mental nursing the psycho-analyst doing psycho-analysis must find the patient not only dreaming of being taken over by the analyst and into his or her home, but also actually needing to be taken in.

A corollary of this is that when an orthodox psycho-analysis of a child is successful there is an acknowledgement to be made by the psycho-analyst that the parents' home, relations, helpers, friends, etc., did nearly half the treatment. We do not have to make these acknowledgements out loud, but we need to be honest about these matters of the patient's dependence when we are theory-building.

Now I come to the earlier *infant-mother relationship*. A great deal has been written about this. I want to draw your attention to the part the mother plays at the time of her baby's very great dependence at the beginning. Although I believe readers are fully aware of these matters, I wish to go over the argument again so that it can be discussed.

Here I wish to refer to a paper by Zetzel (1956). I need not gather together all the threads that went to the making of this very valuable review of Current Concepts of Transference. I only want to take out of her paper the paragraphs in which she refers to my own work. She writes: 'Other analysts—Dr Winnicott, for example—attribute psychosis mainly to severe traumatic

[1] Miss Freud has taken up the subject of ego-regression in a paper published in the Menninger Bulletin (1963).

experiences, particularly of deprivation in early infancy. According to this point of view, profound regression offers an opportunity to fulfil, in the transference situation, primitive needs which had not been met at the appropriate level of development. Similar suggestions have been proposed by Margolin and others . . .'

It is valuable to me to have the opportunity to take up this description of my attitude to this subject, a subject that has great importance because of the fact that one of the growing points of psycho-analysis is in the treatment of the borderline case and in the attempt to formulate a theory of psychotic illness, especially schizophrenia.

Firstly, do I attribute psychosis mainly to severe traumatic experiences, partly of deprivation in early infancy? I can well understand that this is the impression that I have given, and I have changed the way I present my view in the course of the past decade. It is necessary, however, to make some corrections. I have definitely stated that in the aetiology of psychotic illness and particularly of schizophrenia (except in so far as hereditary elements are operative) there has to be noted a failure in the total infant-care process. In one paper I went so far as to state: 'Psychosis is an environmental deficiency disease.' Zetzel uses the term 'severe traumatic experiences', and these words imply bad things happening, things that look bad from the observer's point of view. The deficiencies that I am referring to are failures of basic provision—like my going away to the U.S.A. when my patient is not ready for the reactions that occur in her to my going. In other papers I have explored in great detail the kinds of failure that constitute failure of basic provision. The main point is that these failures are unpredictable; they cannot be accounted for by the infant in terms of projection, because the infant has not yet reached the stage of ego-structuring that makes this possible, and they result in the *annihilation* of the individual whose going-on-being is interrupted.

Mothers who are not themselves ill do in fact avoid this type of failure of care of an infant.

Under the heading 'Primary Maternal Preoccupation' I have referred to the immense changes that occur in women who are having a baby, and it is my opinion that this phenomenon, whatever name it deserves, is essential for the well-being of the infant. It is essential because without it there is no one who is sufficiently identified with the infant to know what the infant needs, so that the basic ration of adaptation is missing. It will be understood that I am not just referring to adaptation in terms of the satisfying of id-drives.

A basic ration of environmental provision facilitates the very important *maturational developments* of the earliest weeks and months, and any failure of early adaptation is a traumatic factor interfering with the integrative processes that lead to the establishment in the individual of a self that goes on being, that achieves a psychosomatic existence, and that develops a capacity for relating to objects.

So a statement of my view would include the following:

(i) It is in psycho-neurotic illness that we find the conflicts that are truly personal to the individual, and relatively free from environmental determinants. One needs to be healthy enough at the toddler age to achieve psycho-neurotic illness, let alone health in this area.

(ii) It is in the earlier stages that the basis of the mental health of the individual is being laid down. This involves:

(*a*) maturational processes, which are inherited tendencies, and

(*b*) the environmental conditions that are needed if the maturational processes are to become actual.

In this way, failure of early basic environmental provision disturbs maturational processes, or prevents their contributing to the individual child's emotional growth, and it is this failure of the maturational processes, integration, etc., that constitutes the ill-health that we call psychotic. This failure of the environmental provision (privation) is not usually referred to by the word 'deprivation', hence my need to correct the words of Zetzel's reference to my work.

(iii) A complication in the making of this statement is the fact that there is an intermediate position, one in which environmental provision is at first good, and then fails. It succeeds in that it allows of ego-organization of considerable degree, and then it fails at a stage before the individual has become able to establish an internal environment—that is, to become independent. This is what is usually called a 'deprivation', and it does not lead to psychosis; it leads to a development in the individual of an 'antisocial tendency', which may in turn force the child into having a character disorder and becoming a delinquent and a recidivist.

All these over-simplifications need elaboration which I have given them elsewhere but which I cannot gather together here. I wish, however, to refer briefly to a few of the effects of this attitude to mental disorder on our way of thinking.

(i) One is that it is in the psychoses—not in the psycho-neuroses —that we must expect to find examples of self-cure. Some environmental happening, perhaps a friendship, may provide a correction of a failure of basic provision, and may unhitch the catch that prevented maturation in some respect or other. In any case, it is sometimes the very ill child in child psychiatry who can be enabled to start growing by snack-bar psychotherapy, whereas in the treatment of psycho-neurosis one always wants to be able to provide a psycho-analytic treatment.

(ii) The second is that a corrective experience is not enough. Certainly no analyst *sets out to provide* a corrective experience in the transference, because this is a contradiction in terms; the transference in all its details comes through the patient's unconscious psycho-analytic process, and depends for its development on the interpreting that is always relative to material presented to the analyst.

Of course, the practising of a good psycho-analytic technique *may* in itself be a corrective experience, and for instance in analysis a patient may for the first time get full attention from another person, limited though it be to the reliably established fifty-minute session; or may for the first time be in contact with someone who is capable of being objective. And so on.

But even so, the corrective provision is never enough. What is it that may be enough for some of our patients to get well? In the end the patient uses the analyst's failures, often quite small ones, perhaps manœuvred by the patient, or the patient produces delusional transference elements (Little, 1958) and we have to put up with being in a limited context misunderstood. The operative factor is that the patient now hates the analyst for the failure that originally came as an environmental factor, outside the infant's area of omnipotent control, but that is *now* staged in the transference.

So in the end we succeed by failing—failing the patient's way. This is a long distance from the simple theory of cure by corrective experience. In this way, regression can be in the service of the ego if it is met by the analyst, and turned into a new dependence in which the patient brings the bad external factor into the area of his or her omnipotent control, and the area managed by projection and introjection mechanisms.

Finally, in regard to the patient to whom I have referred, I must not fail in the child-care and infant-care aspects of the treatment until at a later stage when *she will make me fail* in ways.

determined by her past history. What I fear is that by giving myself the experience of a month abroad I may have already failed prematurely and have joined up with the unpredictable variables of her infancy and childhood, so I may have truly made her ill now, as indeed the unpredictable external factors did make her ill in her infancy.

BIBLIOGRAPHY I

BOOKS AND PAPERS REFERRED TO
IN THE TEXT

ABRAHAM, KARL (1916). 'The First Pregenital Stage of the Libido.' *Selected Papers of Karl Abraham.* (London: Hogarth, 1927)
— (1924). 'A Short Study of the Development of the Libido, Viewed in the Light of Mental Disorders.' *ibid.*
ACKERMAN, N. (1953). 'Psychiatric Disorders in Children—Diagnosis and Aetiology in our Time.' In: *Current Problems in Psychiatric Diagnosis*, ed. Hoch and Zubin. (New York: Grune & Stratton)
AICHHORN, A. (1925). *Wayward Youth.* (New York: Viking, 1935)
BALINT, M. (1951). 'On Love and Hate.' In: *Primary Love and Psycho-Analytic Technique.* (London: Hogarth, 1952)
— (1958). 'The Three Areas of the Mind.' *Int. J. Psycho-Anal.,* **39.**
BION, W. (1959). 'Attacks on Linking.' *Int. J. Psycho-Anal.,* **40.**
— (1962a). 'The Theory of Thinking.' *Int. J. Psycho-Anal.,* **43.**
— (1962b). *Learning from Experience.* (London: Heinemann)
BORNSTEIN, B. (1951). 'On Latency.' *Psychoanalytic Study of the Child,* **6.**
BOWLBY, J. (1958). 'Psycho-Analysis and Child Care.' In: *Psycho-Analysis and Contemporary Thought*, ed. J. D. Sutherland. (London: Hogarth)
— (1960). 'Separation Anxiety.' *Int. J. Psycho-Anal.,* **41.**
BURLINGHAM, D., and FREUD, A. (1944). *Infants without Families.* (London: Allen & Unwin; New York: Int. Univ. Press)
ERIKSON, E. (1950). *Childhood and Society.* (London: Imago; New York: Norton)
— (1958). *Young Man Luther.* (London: Faber)
— (1961). 'The Roots of Virtue.' In: *The Humanist Frame*, ed. J. Huxley. (London: Allen & Unwin)
FENICHEL, O. (1945). *The Theory of Neurosis.* (New York: Norton)
FERENCZI, S. (1931). 'Child Analysis in the Analysis of Adults.' In: *Final Contributions to Psycho-Analysis.* (London: Hogarth, 1955)
FORDHAM, M. (1960). Contribution to Symposium on 'Counter-Transference'. *Brit. J. med. Psychol.,* **33.**
FREUD, A. (1936). *The Ego and the Mechanisms of Defence.* (London: Hogarth, 1937)
— (1946). *The Psycho-Analytical Treatment of Children.* (London: Imago)
— (1953). 'Some Remarks on Infant Observations.' *Psychoanalytic Study of the Child,* **8.**
— (1963). 'Regression as a Principle in Mental Development.' *Bull. Menninger Clinic,* **27.**
FREUD, S. (1905a). *Three Essays on the Theory of Sexuality. Standard Edition,* **7.**
— (1905b). 'On Psychotherapy.' *Standard Edition,* **7.**
— (1909). 'The Analysis of a Phobia in a Five-Year-Old Boy.' *Standard Edition,* **10.**
— (1911). 'Formulations on the Two Principles of Mental Functioning.' *Standard Edition,* **12.**
— (1914). 'On Narcissism.' *Standard Edition,* **14.**
— (1915). 'Some Character-Types met with in Psycho-Analytic Work.' *Standard Edition,* **14.**

261

FREUD, S. (1917). 'Mourning and Melancholia.' *Standard Edition*, **14.**
   (1920). *Beyond the Pleasure Principle. Standard Edition*, **18.**
   (1926). *Inhibitions, Symptoms and Anxiety. Standard Edition*, **20.**
   (1937). 'Analysis Terminable and Interminable.' *Standard Edition*, **23.**
GILLESPIE, W. (1944). 'The Psychoneuroses.' *J. ment. Sci.*, **90.**
GLOVER, E. (1949). 'The Position of Psycho-Analysis in Great Britain.'
   British Medical Bulletin, **6.**
   (1956). *On the Early Development of Mind.* (London: Imago)
GREENACRE, P. (1958). 'Early Physical Determinants in the Development of
   the Sense of Identity.' *J. Amer. Psychoanal. Assoc.*, **6.**
GUNTRIP, H. (1961). *Personality Structure and Human Interaction.* (London:
   Hogarth)
HARTMANN, H. (1939). *Ego Psychology and the Problem of Adaptation.* (London:
   Imago, 1958)
   (1954). Contribution to Discussion of 'Problems of Infantile Neurosis'.
   Psychoanalytic Study of the Child, **9.**
HOCH, P., and ZUBIN, J. (1953). *Current Problems in Psychiatric Diagnosis.* (New
   York: Grune & Stratton)
HOFFER, W. (1955). *Psychoanalysis: Practical and Research Aspects.* (Baltimore:
   Williams & Wilkins)
JAMES, H. M. (1962). 'Infantile Narcissistic Trauma.' *Int. J. Psycho-Anal.*, **43.**
KLEIN, M. (1932). *The Psycho-Analysis of Children.* (London: Hogarth)
   (1935). 'Contribution to the Psychogenesis of Manic Depressive States.'
   In: *Contributions to Psycho-Analysis, 1921–1945.* (London: Hogarth)
   (1940). 'Mourning and its Relation to Manic Depressive States.' *ibid.*
   (1946). 'Notes on Some Schizoid Mechanisms.' In: *Developments in Psycho-
   Analysis*, ed. J. Riviere. (London: Hogarth)
   (1948). *Contributions to Psycho-Analysis, 1921–1945.* (London: Hogarth)
   (1961). *Narrative of a Child Analysis.* (London: Hogarth)
KRIS, E. (1950). 'Notes on the Development and on Some Current Problems
   of Psychoanalytic Child Psychology.' *Psychoanalytic Study of the Child*, **5.**
   (1951). 'Opening Remarks on Psychoanalytic Child Psychology.' *Psycho-
   analytic Study of the Child*, **6.**
LAING, R. D. (1960). *The Divided Self.* (London: Tavistock)
   (1961). *The Self and Others.* (London: Tavistock)
LITTLE, M. (1958). 'On Delusional Transference (Transference Psychosis).'
   Int. J. Psycho-Anal., **39.**
MENNINGER, K., *et al.* (1963). *The Vital Balance.* (New York: Basic Books)
MONCHAUX, C. DE (1962). 'Thinking and Negative Hallucination.' *Int. J.
   Psycho-Anal.*, **43.**
RIBBLE, M. (1943). *The Rights of Infants.* (New York: Columbia Univ.
   Press)
RICKMAN, J. (1928). *The Development of the Psycho-Analytical Theory of the
   Psychoses, 1893–1926.* Int. J. Psycho-Anal. Suppl. 2. (London: Baillière)
SEARLES, H. F. (1959). 'The Effort to Drive the Other Person Crazy—An
   Element in the Aetiology and Psychotherapy of Schizophrenia.' *Brit. J.
   med. Psychol.*, **32.**
   (1960). *The Nonhuman Environment.* (New York: Int. Univ. Press)
SECHEHAYE, M. (1951). *Symbolic Realisation.* (New York: Int. Univ. Press)
STRACHEY, J. (1934). 'The Nature of the Therapeutic Action of Psycho-
   Analysis.' *Int. J. Psycho-Anal.*, **15.**
WHEELIS, A. (1958). *The Quest for Identity.* (New York: Norton)
WICKES, F. G. (1938). *The Inner World of Man.* (New York: Farrar & Rine-
   hart; London: Methuen, 1950)

WINNICOTT, C. (1954). 'Casework Techniques in the Child Care Services.' *Child Care and Social Work.* (Codicote Press, 1964)

(1962). 'Casework and Agency Function.' *ibid.*

WINNICOTT, D. W. (1936). 'Appetite and Emotional Disorder.' *Collected Papers.*

(1941). 'The Observation of Infants in a Set Situation.' *ibid.*

(1945). 'Primitive Emotional Development.' *ibid.*

(1947). 'Hate in the Counter-Transference.' *ibid.*

(1948). 'Reparation in Respect of Mother's Organized Defence against Depression.' *ibid.*

(1949a) *The Ordinary Devoted Mother and her Baby.* Nine Broadcast Talks. Republished in: *The Child and the Family.* (London: Tavistock, 1957)

(1949b) 'Birth Memories, Birth Trauma, and Anxiety.' *Collected Papers.*

(1949c) 'Mind and its Relation to the Psyche-Soma.' *ibid.*

(1951). 'Transitional Objects and Transitional Phenomena.' *ibid.*

(1952). 'Psychoses and Child Care.' *ibid.*

(1953). 'Symptom Tolerance in Paediatrics: A Case History.' *ibid.*

(1954a). 'Withdrawal and Regression.' *ibid.*

(1954b). 'The Depressive Position in Normal Emotional Development.' *ibid.*

(1954c) 'Metapsychological and Clinical Aspects of Regression within the Psycho-Analytical Set-up.' *ibid.*

(1956a). 'Primary Maternal Preoccupation.' *ibid.*

(1956b). 'The Antisocial Tendency.' *ibid.*

(1958). *Collected Papers: Through Paediatrics to Psycho-Analysis.* (London: Tavistock)

(1962). 'Adolescence.' *The Family and Individual Development.* (London: Tavistock, 1965)

(1963). 'Regression as Therapy Illustrated by the Case of a Boy whose Pathological Dependence was Adequately Met by the Parents.' *Brit. J. med. Psychol.*, **36**.

ZETZEL, E. (1956). 'Current Concepts of Transference.' *Int. J. Psycho-Anal.*, **37**.

BIBLIOGRAPHY II

PUBLICATIONS BY D. W. WINNICOTT
1926-1964

EDITORIAL NOTE. This bibliography details the complete list of Winnicott's writings. Items are listed under year of first publication. An earlier date in brackets refers to the time of first *presentation*. Republications and translations of articles are listed under year of first publication and are not repeated. *Reviews* are included whenever possible. There are others whose data are not available. Figures in heavy type are volume numbers. The bibliography is divided into two sections: Section A is books only and Section B is the complete bibliography.

M. M. R. K.

Section A

Clinical Notes on Disorders of Childhood. (London: Heinemann, 1931)

The Child and the Family: First Relationships. (London: Tavistock, 1957) includes:

A Man Looks at Motherhood (1949)
Getting to Know your Baby (1944)
The Baby as a Going Concern (1949)
Infant Feeding (1944)
Where the Food Goes (1949)
The End of the Digestive Process (1949)
The Baby as a Person (1949)
Close-Up of Mother Feeding Baby (1949)
Why Do Babies Cry? (1944)
The World in Small Doses (1949)
The Innate Morality of the Baby (1949)
Weaning (1949)
Knowing and Learning (1950)
Instincts and Normal Difficulties (1950)
What About Father? (1944)
Their Standards and Yours (1944)
Young Children and Other People (1949)
What Do We Mean by a Normal Child? (1946)
The Only Child (1945)
Twins (1945)
Stealing and Telling Lies (1949)

Visiting Children in Hospital (1951)
On Adoption (1955)
First Experiments in Independence (1955)
Support for Normal Parents (1944)
The Mother's Contribution to Society (1957)

The Child and the Outside World: Studies in Developing Relationships.
(London: Tavistock, 1957)
includes:
Needs of the Under-Fives in a Changing Society (1954)
The Child's Needs and the Role of the Mother in the Early Stages (1951)
On Influencing and Being Influenced (1941)
Educational Diagnosis (1946)
Shyness and Nervous Disorders in Children (1938)
Sex Education in Schools (1949)
Pitfalls in Adoption (1954)
Two Adopted Children (1953)
Children in the War (1940)
The Deprived Mother (1940)
The Evacuated Child (1945)
The Return of the Evacuated Child (1945)
Home Again (1945)
Residential Management as Treatment for Difficult Children (1947)
Children's Hostels in War and Peace (1948)
Towards an Objective Study of Human Nature (1945)
Further Thoughts on Babies as Persons (1947)
Breast Feeding (1945)
Why Children Play (1942)
The Child and Sex (1947)
Aggression (1939)
The Impulse to Steal (1949)
Some Psychological Aspects of Juvenile Delinquency (1946)

Collected Papers: Through Paediatrics to Psycho-Analysis. (London: Tavistock; New York: Basic Books, 1958)
includes:
A Note on Normality and Anxiety (1931)
Fidgetiness (1931)
Appetite and Emotional Disorder (1936)
The Observation of Infants in a Set Situation (1941)
Child Department Consultations (1942)
Ocular Psychoneuroses of Childhood (1944)
Reparation in Respect of Mother's Organized Defence against Depression (1948)
Anxiety Associated with Insecurity (1952)
Symptom Tolerance in Paediatrics: a Case History (1953)
A Case Managed at Home (1955)
The Manic Defence (1935)
Primitive Emotional Development (1945)
Paediatrics and Psychiatry (1948)

Birth Memories, Birth Trauma, and Anxiety (1949)
Hate in the Counter-Transference (1947)
Aggression in Relation to Emotional Development (1950)
Psychoses and Child Care (1952)
Transitional Objects and Transitional Phenomena (1951)
Mind and its Relation to the Psyche-Soma (1949)
Withdrawal and Regression (1954)
The Depressive Position in Normal Emotional Development (1954)
Metapsychological and Clinical Aspects of Regression within the Psycho-Analy-
    tical Set-Up (1954)
Clinical Varieties of Transference (1955)
Primary Maternal Preoccupation (1956)
The Antisocial Tendency (1956)
Paediatrics and Childhood Neurosis (1956)

The Child, the Family, and the Outside World. (Harmondsworth: Penguin
Books, 1964. Pelican Book A668)
includes:
A Man Looks at Motherhood (1949)
Getting to Know your Baby (1944)
The Baby as a Going Concern (1949)
Infant Feeding (1944)
Where the Food Goes (1949)
The End of the Digestive Process (1949)
Close-Up of Mother Feeding Baby (1949)
Breast Feeding (1945)
Why Do Babies Cry? (1944)
The World in Small Doses (1949)
The Baby as a Person (1949)
Weaning (1949)
Further Thoughts on Babies as Persons (1947)
The Innate Morality of the Baby (1949)
Instincts and Normal Difficulties (1950)
Young Children and Other People (1949)
What About Father? (1944)
Their Standards and Yours (1944)
What Do We Mean by a Normal Child? (1946)
The Only Child (1945)
Twins (1945)
Why Children Play (1942)
The Child and Sex (1947)
Stealing and Telling Lies (1949)
First Experiments in Independence (1955)
Support for Normal Parents (1944)
Needs of the Under-Fives (1954)
Mother, Teacher, and the Child's Needs (1953)
On Influencing and Being Influenced (1941)
Educational Diagnosis (1946)

Shyness and Nervous Disorders in Children (1938)
Sex Education in Schools (1949)
Visiting Children in Hospital (1951)
Aspects of Juvenile Delinquency (1946)
Roots of Aggression (1964)

The Family and Individual Development. (London: Tavistock, 1964)
includes:

The First Year of Life: Modern Views on the Emotional Development (1958)
The Relationship of a Mother to Her Baby at the Beginning (1960)
Growth and Development in Immaturity (1950)
On Security (Broadcast 1960)
The Five-Year-Old (Broadcast 1962)
Integrating and Disruptive Factors in Family Life (1957)
The Family Affected by Depressive Illness in one or both Parents (1958)
The Effect of Psychotic Parents on the Emotional Development of the Child (1959)
The Effect of Psychosis on Family Life (1960)
Adolescence (1961)
The Family and Emotional Maturity (1960)
Theoretical Statement of the Field of Child Psychiatry (1958)
The Contribution of Psycho-Analysis to Midwifery (1957)
Advising Parents (1957)
Casework with Mentally Ill Children (1959)
The Deprived Child and How He Can Be Compensated for Loss of Family Life (1950)
Group Influences and the Maladjusted Child: The School Aspect (1955)
Some Thoughts on the Meaning of the Word Democracy (1950)

The Maturational Processes and the Facilitating Environment (this volume).

Section B

1926

(1) Varicella Encephalitis and Vaccinia Encephalitis. *Brit. J. Children's Dis.*, **23.**

1928

(2) The Only Child. In: *The Mind of the Growing Child* (Lectures to the National Society of Day Nurseries) ed. Viscountess Erleigh. (London: Faber)

1930

(3) Short Communication on Enuresis. *St Bartholomew's Hosp. J.*, April 1930.
(4) Pathological Sleeping (Case History). *Proc. Roy. Soc. Med.*, **23.**

1931

(5) Pre-Systolic Murmur, Possibly Not Due to Mitral Stenosis (Case History). *Proc. Roy Soc. Med.*, **24.**

(6) *Clinical Notes on Disorders of Childhood.* (London: Heinemann) (See Section A)

(7) Fidgetiness. In (6), (116).

(8) A Note on Normality and Anxiety. In (6), (116).

1934

(9) The Difficult Child. *J. State Medicine*, **42.**

(10) Papular Urticaria and the Dynamics of Skin Sensation. *Brit. J. Children's Dis.*, **31.**

1936

(11) Discussion (with R. S. Addis and R. Miller) on Enuresis. *Proc. Roy. Soc. Med.*, **29.**

1938

(12) Skin Changes in Relation to Emotional Disorder. *St John's Hosp. Derm. Soc. Report*, 1938.

(13) Shyness and Nervous Disorders in Children. *The New Era in Home and School*, **19.** Also in (108), (158).

(14) Notes on a Little Boy. *The New Era in Home and School*, **19.**

(15) Review: *Child Psychiatry* by Leo Kanner (Baltimore, Md: Thomas, 1935; London: Baillière, 1937). *Int. J. Psycho-Anal.*, **19.**

1939

(16) The Psychology of Juvenile Rheumatism. In: *A Survey of Child Psychiatry* ed. R. G. Gordon. (London: Oxford Univ. Press)

1940

(17) Children in the War (Broadcast 1939). *The New Era in Home and School*, **21.** Also in (108).

(18) The Deprived Mother (Broadcast 1939). *The New Era in Home and School*, **21.** Also in (108).

(19) Children and their Mothers. *The New Era in Home and School*, **21.**

1941

(20) The Observation of Infants in a Set Situation. *Int. J. Psycho-Anal.*, **22.** Also in (116).

(21) On Influencing and Being Influenced. *The New Era in Home and School*, **22.** Also in (108), (158).

1942

(22) Child Department Consultations. *Int. J. Psycho-Anal.*, **23.** Also in (116).

(23) Why Children Play. *The New Era in Home and School*, **23.** Also in (108), (158).

1943

(24) Delinquency Research. *The New Era in Home and School*, **24.**

(25) The Magistrate, the Psychiatrist and the Clinic (Correspondence with R. North). *The New Era in Home and School*, **24.**

1944

(26) (with Clare Britton) The Problem of Homeless Children. *Children's Communities* Monograph No. 1. Also in: *The New Era in Home and School*, **25**.

(27) Ocular Psychoneuroses. *Trans. Ophthalmological Soc.*, **44**.

1945

(28) *Getting to Know Your Baby* (Six Broadcast Talks). (London: Heinemann) Also in: *The New Era in Home and School*, **26**; and in (100), (158).

(29) Getting To Know Your Baby. In (28), (100), (158).

(30) Why Do Babies Cry? In (28), (100), (158).

(31) Infant Feeding. In (28), (100), (158).

(32) What about Father? In (28), (100), (158).

(33) Their Standards and Yours. In (28), (100), (158).

(34) Support for Normal Parents. In (28), (100), (158).

(35) Talking about Psychology. *The New Era in Home and School*, **26**. Reprinted under the title 'What is Psycho-Analysis?' *The New Era in Home and School* (1952), **33**. Also under the title 'Towards an Objective Study of Human Nature' in (108).

(36) Thinking and the Unconscious. *The Liberal Magazine*, March 1945.

(37) Primitive Emotional Development. *Int. J. Psycho-Anal.*, **26**. Also in (116). Spanish trans: 'Desarrollo emocional primitivo'. *Rev. de Psicoanal.* (1948), **5**.

(38) *Five Broadcast Talks* in (108).

(39) The Evacuated Child. In (38), (108).

(40) The Return of the Evacuated Child. In (38), (108).

(41) Home Again. In (38), (108).

(42) The Only Child. In (38), (100), (158).

(43) Twins. In (38), (100), (158).

1946

(44) What Do We Mean by a Normal Child? *The New Era in Home and School*, **27**. Also in (100), (158).

(45) Some Psychological Aspects of Juvenile Delinquency. *The New Era in Home and School*, **27**. Also in (108) and as 'Aspects of Juvenile Delinquency' in (158).

(46) Educational Diagnosis. *Nat. Froebel Foundation Bull.* No. 41. Also in (108), (158).

1947

(47) The Child and Sex. *The Practitioner*, **158**. Also in (108), (158).

(48) Babies Are Persons. *The New Era in Home and School*, **28**. Reprinted as 'Further Thoughts on Babies as Persons' in (108), (158).

(49) Physical Therapy of Mental Disorder. *Brit. med. J.*, May 1947.

(50) (with Clare Britton) Residential Management as Treatment for Difficult Children. *Human Relations*, **1**. Also in (108).

1948

(51) Children's Hostels in War and Peace. *Brit. J. med. Psychol.*, **21**. Also in (108).

(52) Obituary: Susan Isaacs. *Nature*, **162**.

(53) Pediatrics and Psychiatry. *Brit. J. med. Psychol.*, **21**. Also in (116).

1949

(54) Sex Education in Schools. *Medical Press*, **222**. Also in (108), (158).

(55) Hate in the Counter-Transference. *Int. J. Psycho-Anal.*, **30**. Also in (116).

(56) Young Children and Other People. *Young Children*, **1**. Also in (100), (158).

(57) Leucotomy. *Brit. med. Students' J.*, **3**.

(58) *The Ordinary Devoted Mother and Her Baby* (Nine Broadcast Talks. Privately published). Reprinted in (100), (158).

(59) Introduction to (58). Republished as 'A Man Looks at Motherhood' in (100), (158).

(60) The Baby as a Going Concern. In (58), (100), (158).

(61) Where the Food Goes. In (58), (100), (158).

(62) The End of the Digestive Process. In (58), (100), (158).

(63) The Baby as a Person. In (58), (100), (158). Also in *Child-Family Dig.*, Feb. 1953.

(64) Close-Up of Mother Feeding Baby. In (58), (100), (158).

(65) The World in Small Doses. In (58), (100), (158).

(66) The Innate Morality of the Baby. In (58), (100), (158).

(67) Weaning. In (58), (100), (158).

(68) Review: *Art versus Illness* by Adrian Hill (London: Allen & Unwin). *Brit. J. med. Psychol.*, **22**.

1950

(69) Review: *Infancy of Speech and the Speech of Infancy* by Leopold Stein (London: Methuen, 1949). *Brit. J. med. Psychol.*, **23**.

(70) Some Thoughts on the Meaning of the Word Democracy. *Human Relations*, **3**. Also in (163).

1951

(71) The Foundation of Mental Health. *Brit. med. J.*, June 1951.

(72) Review: *Papers on Psycho-Analysis* by Ernest Jones, 5th edn
     (London: Baillière, 1948). *Brit. J. med. Psychol.*, **24**.
(73) Review: *Infant Feeding and Feeding Difficulties* by P. R. Evans and
     R. MacKeith (London: Churchill). *Brit. J. med. Psychol.*, **24**.
(74) *The Times* Correspondence on Care of Young Children. *Nursery
     Journal*, **41**.
(75) Critical Notice: *On Not Being Able to Paint* by Joanna Field
     (London: Heinemann, 1950). *Brit. J. med. Psychol.*, **34**.

                              1952
(76) Visiting Children in Hospital (Two B.B.C. Broadcasts, 1951).
     Child-Family Digest, Oct. 1952; *The New Era in Home and
     School*, **33**. Also in (100), (158).

                              1953
(77) Psychoses and Child Care. *Brit. J. med. Psychol.*, **26**. Also in
     (116).
(78) Symptom Tolerance in Paediatrics. *Proc. Roy. Soc. Med.*, **46**.
     Also in (116).
(79) Transitional Objects and Transitional Phenomena. *Int. J.
     Psycho-Anal.*, **34**. Also in (116). French trans.: 'Objets tran-
     sitionnels et phénomènes transitionnels'. In: *La Psychanalyse*,
     Vol. 5 (Paris: Presses Univ., 1959)
(80) Review: *Psycho-Analysis and Child Psychiatry* by Edward Glover
     (London: Imago). *Brit. med. J.*, Sept. 1953.
(81) Review: *Maternal Care and Mental Health* by John Bowlby
     (Geneva: W.H.O., 1951). *Brit. J. med. Psychol.*, **26**.
(82) Review: *Direct Analysis* by John N. Rosen (New York: Grune &
     Stratton). *Brit. J. Psychol.*, **44**.
(83) Review: *Twins: A Study of Three Pairs of Identical Twins* by
     Dorothy Burlingham (London: Imago, 1952). *The New Era
     in Home and School*, **34**.
(84) Review (with M. M. R. Khan): *Psychoanalytic Studies of the Per-
     sonality* (London: Tavistock, 1952). *Int. J. Psycho-Anal.*, **34**.
(85) (with other members of the group) The Child's Needs and the
     Role of the Mother in the Early Stages (UNESCO No. 9 in
     series 'Problems in Education'). Also in (108) and as 'Mother,
     Teacher and the Child's Needs' in (158).

                              1954
(86) Review: *Aggression and its Interpretation* by Lydia Jackson (Lon-
     don: Methuen). *Brit. med. J.*, June 1954.
(87) Pitfalls in Adoption. *Medical Press*, **232**. Also in (108).
(88) Two Adopted Children (Talk given to Assoc. Child Care
     Officers 1953). *Case Conference*, **1**. Also in (108).

(89) Mind and its Relation to the Psyche-Soma. *Brit. J. med. Psychol.*, **27.** Also in (116).

(90) The Needs of the Under-Fives in a Changing Society. *The Nursery Journal*, **44.** Also in (108) and as 'The Needs of the Under-Fives' in (158).

(91) Review: *Clinical Management of Behavior Disorders in Children* by H. and R. M. Bakwin (Philadelphia: Saunders, 1953). *Brit. med. J.*, Aug. 1954.

1955

(92) Régression et repli. *Rev. franç. psychanal.*, **19.** German trans.: 'Zustände von Entrückung und Regression'. *Psyche* (1956), **10.** In English, 'Withdrawal and Regression', in (116).

(93) Foreword to *Any Wife or Any Husband* by Joan Graham Malleson. (London: Heinemann)

(94) Metapsychological and Clinical Aspects of Regression within the Psycho-Analytical Set-Up. *Int. J. Psycho-Anal.*, **36.** Also in (116).

(95) Childhood Psychosis: A Case Managed at Home. *Case Conference*, **2.** Also in (116).

(96) The Depressive Position in Normal Emotional Development. *Brit. J. med. Psychol.*, **28.** Also in (116).

(97) Adopted Children in Adolescence. (Address to Standing Conference of Societies Registered for Adoption.) *Report of Residential Conference*, July 1955.

1956

(98) On Transference. *Int. J. Psycho-Anal.*, **37.** Republished ¿ 'Clinical Varieties of Transference' in (116).

1957

(99) The Contribution of Psycho-Analysis to Midwifery. *Nursing Mirror*, May 1957. Also in (163).

(100) *The Child and the Family. First Relationships.* (London: Tavistock) (See Section A.) American edition: *Mother and Child (A Primer of First Relationships)*. (New York: Basic Books)

(101) Knowing and Learning (Broadcast 1950). In (100).

(102) Instincts and Normal Difficulties (Broadcast 1950). In (100), (158).

(103) Stealing and Telling Lies (1949). In (100), (158).

(104) On Adoption (Broadcast 1955). In (100).

(105) First Experiments in Independence (1955). In (100), (158).

(106) The Mother's Contribution to Society. In (100).

(107) Health Education through Broadcasting. *Mother and Child*, **28.**

(108) *The Child and the Outside World. Studies in Developing Relationships.* (London: Tavistock) (See Section A.)

(109) The Impulse to Steal (1949). In (108).

(110) Breast Feeding (1945—revised 1954). In (108), (158).

(111) Aggression (1939). In (108).

1958

(112) Twins (Broadcast 1945). *Family Doctor*, Feb. 1958.

(113) Review: *The Doctor, His Patient and The Illness* by Michael Balint (London: Pitman, 1957). *Int. J. Psycho-Anal.*, **39**.

(114) Child Psychiatry. In: *Modern Trends in Paediatrics* ed. A. Holzel and J. P. M. Tizard. (London: Butterworth). Modified as 'Theoretical Statement of the Field of Child Psychiatry.' In (163).

(115) The Capacity to be Alone. *Int. J. Psycho-Anal.*, **39**. Also in (176). German trans.: 'Über die Fähigkeit, allein zu sein'. *Psyche* (1958), **12**. Spanish trans.: 'La capacidad para estar solo'. *Rev. de Psicoanal.* (1959), **16**; *Rev. Uruguaya de Psicoanal.* (1963), **5**.

(116) *Collected Papers. Through Paediatrics to Psycho-Analysis.* (London: Tavistock; New York: Basic Books) (See Section A.)

(117) Appetite and Emotional Disorder (1936). In (116).

(118) Reparation in Respect of Mother's Organized Defence against Depression (1948—revised 1954). In (116).

(119) Anxiety Associated with Insecurity (1952). In (116).

(120) The Manic Defence (1935). In (116).

(121) Birth Memories, Birth Trauma, and Anxiety (1949). In (116).

(122) Aggression in Relation to Emotional Development (1950–55). In (116).

(123) Primary Maternal Preoccupation (1956). In (116). German trans.: 'Primäre Mutterlichkeit'. *Psyche* (1960), **14**.

(124) The Antisocial Tendency (1956). In (116).

(125) Paediatrics and Childhood Neurosis. In (116).

(126) Ernest Jones. *Int. J. Psycho-Anal.*, **39**.

(127) New Advances in Psycho-Analysis. Turkish trans.: 'Psikanalizde Ilerlemeler'. *Tipta Yenilikler*, **4**.

(128) Child Analysis. *A Criança Portuguesa*, **17**. Also, under the title 'Child Analysis in the Latency Period', in (176).

(129) Modern Views on the Emotional Development in the First Year of Life. *Medical Press*, March 1958. Republished as 'The First Year of Life' in (163). Ital. trans.: 'Il Primo Anno di Vita'. *Infanzia Anormale* (1959), **30**. German trans.: 'Über die emotionelle Entwicklung im ersten Lebensjahr'. *Psyche* (1960), **14**. French trans.: 'La Première année de la vie'. *Rev. franç. psychanal.* (1962), **26**. Turkish trans.: 'Hayatin Ilk Yili'. *Tipta Yenilikler* (1962), **7**. Spanish trans.: 'Primeiro Ano

de Vida—Desenvolvimento Emocional'. *J. de Pediatria* (1961), **7.**

(130) Discussion sur la contribution de l'observation directe de l'enfant à la psychanalyse. *Rev. franç. psychanal.*, **22.** In English: 'On the Contribution of Direct Child Observation to Psycho-Analysis' in (176).

(131) Psycho-Analysis and the Sense of Guilt. In: *Psycho-Analysis and Contemporary Thought* ed. J. D. Sutherland. (London: Hogarth) Also in (176).

1959

(132) Review: *Envy and Gratitude* by Melanie Klein. (London: Tavistock, 1957) *Case Conference*, **5.**

1960

(133) Counter-Transference. *Brit. J. med. Psychol.*, **33.** Also in (176).

(134) String. *J. Ch. Psychol. Psychiat.*, **1.** Also, as 'String: A Technique of Communication', in (176).

(135) The Theory of the Parent-Infant Relationship. *Int. J. Psycho-Anal.*, **41.** Also in (176). French trans.: 'La Théorie de la relation parent-nourisson'. *Rev. franç. psychanal.* (1961), **25.**

1961

(136) Integrating and Disruptive Factors in Family Life. *Canad. Med Assoc. J.*, April 1961. In (163).

(137) Review: *The Purpose and Practice of Medicine* by Sir James Spence (London: Oxford Univ. Press, 1960). *Brit. med. J.*, Feb. 1961.

(138) The Effect of Psychotic Parents on the Emotional Development of the Child. *Brit. J. Psychiatric Soc. Work*, **6.** In (163).

(139) The Paediatric Department of Psychology. *St Mary's Hosp. Gaz.*, **67.**

1962

(140) Review: *Psychologie du premier age* by M. Bergeron (Paris: Presses Univ., 1961). *Arch. Dis. Childhood*, **37.**

(141) Review: *Un Cas de psychose infantile* by S. Lebovici and J. McDougall (Paris: Presses Univ., 1960). *J. Ch. Psychol. Psychiat.*, **3.**

(142) The Child Psychiatry Interview. *St Mary's Hosp. Gaz.*, **68.**

(143) The Theory of the Parent-Infant Relationship: Further Remarks. *Int. J. Psycho-Anal.*, **43.** French trans.: 'La Théorie de la relation parent-enfant: remarques complémentaires'. *Rev. franç. psychanal.* (1963), **27.**

(144) Review: *Letters of Sigmund Freud 1873–1939* ed. E. Freud (London: Hogarth). *Brit. J. Psychol.*, **53.**

(145) Adolescence. *The New Era in Home and School*, **43.** Also in (163). Republished in modified form under title 'Struggling through the Doldrums', *New Society*, April 1963.

1963

(146) Review: *Schizophrenia in Children* by William Goldfarb (Cambridge, Mass.: Harvard Univ. Press, 1961). *Brit. J. Psychiatric Soc. Work*, **7.**

(147) Dependence in Infant-Care, in Child-Care, and in the Psycho-Analytic Setting. *Int. J. Psycho-Anal.*, **44.** Also in (176).

(148) The Young Child at Home and at School. In: *Moral Education in a Changing Society* ed. W. R. Niblett. (London: Faber) Also in (176) as Morals and Education.

(149) The Development of the Capacity for Concern. *Bull. Menninger Clin.*, **27.** Also in (176).

(150) Regression as Therapy Illustrated by the Case of a Boy whose Pathological Dependence was Adequately Met by the Parents. *Brit. J. med. Psychol.*, **36.**

(151) The Mentally Ill in Your Caseload. In: *New Thinking for Changing Needs.* (London: Assoc. Social Workers) Also in (176).

(152) A Psychotherapeutic Consultation: a Case of Stammering, wrongly named: 'The Antisocial Tendency Illustrated by a Case'. *A Criança Portuguesa*, **21.**

(153) Training for Child Psychiatry. *J. Ch. Psychol. Psychiat.*, **4.** Also in (176).

(154) Review: *The Nonhuman Environment* by Harold F. Searles (New York: Int. Univ. Press, 1960). *Int. J. Psycho-Anal.*, **44.**

1964

(155) Review: *Heal the Hurt Child* by Hertha Riese (Chicago Univ. Press, 1963). *New Society*, Jan. 1964.

(156) Correspondence: Love or Skill? *New Society*, Feb. 1964.

(157) Review: *Memories, Dreams, Reflections* by C. G. Jung (London: Collins and Routledge, 1963). *Int. J. Psycho-Anal.*, **45.**

(158) *The Child, The Family, and the Outside World.* (Harmondsworth: Penguin Books. Pelican Book A668) (See Section A.)

(159) The Roots of Aggression (1964). In (158).

(160) The Value of Depression (1963). *Brit. J. Psychiatric Soc. Work*, **7.** (Shortened version entitled: Strength out of Misery, *The Observer*, 31.5.64.)

(161) Youth Will not Sleep. *New Society*, 28.5.64. *Atlas* **8.**

(162) Deductions drawn from a Psychotherapeutic Interview with an Adolescent. *Report of the 20th Child Guidance Inter-Clinic Conference, 1964.* National Association for Mental Health.

1965)
(163) *The Family and Individual Development.* (London: Tavistock, 1965) (See Section A.)
(164) The Relationship of a Mother to Her Baby at the Beginning (1960). In (163).
(165) Growth and Development in Immaturity (1950). In (163).
(166) On Security (1960). In (163).
(167) The Five-Year-Old (1962). In (163).
(168) The Family Affected by Depressive Illness in one or both Parents (1958). In (163).
(169) The Effect of Psychosis on Family Life (1960). In (163).
(170) The Family and Emotional Maturity (1960). In (163).
(171) Theoretical Statement of the Field of Child Psychiatry (1958). In (163).
(172) Advising Parents (1957). In (163).
(173) Casework with Mentally Ill Children (1959). In (163).
(174) The Deprived Child and how he can be Compensated for Loss of Family Life (1950). In (163).
(175) Group Influences and the Maladjusted Child: The School Aspect (1955). In (163).
(176) *The Maturational Processes and the Facilitating Environment.* (This volume) (See Section A).
(177) Ego Integration in Child Development (1962). In (176).
(178) Providing for the Child in Health and Crisis (1962). In (176).
(179) From Dependence towards Independence in the Development of the Self (1963). In (176).
(180) Classification: Is there a Psycho-Analytic Contribution to Psychiatric Classification? (1959). In (176).
(181) Ego Distortion in Terms of True and False Self (1960). In (176).
(182) The Aims of Psycho-Analytical Treatment (1962). In (176).
(183) A Personal View of the Kleinian Contribution to the Theory of Emotional Development at Early Stages (1962). In (176).
(184) Communicating and Not Communicating Leading to a Study of Certain Opposites (1963). In (176).
(185) Psychotherapy of Character Disorders (1963). In (176).
(186) Psychiatric Disorder in Terms of Infantile Maturational Processes (1963). In (176).
(187) Hospital Care Supplementing Intensive Psychotherapy in Adolescence (1963). In (176).
(188) Child Therapy. In: *Modern Perspectives in Child Psychiatry.* Ed. J. Howells. (Oliver & Boyd).
(189) The Value of the Therapeutic Consultation. In: *Foundations of Child Psychiatry.* Ed. E. Miller. (Pergamon Press).
(190) The Antisocial Tendency. In: *Criminal Behaviour and New Directions in Criminal Law Administration.* (Ed. R. Slovenko. (Charles Thomas Publishing Co, U.S.A.)

INDEX

N.B. Italicized page numbers refer to case histories.

A

ABRAHAM, K., 128, 175, 232
Absolute dependence in infancy, and mother's role, 84-6
Absorption of environment, 126-7
Acceptance female, 31
Achievement silence in session as, 20
ACKERMAN, N., 137
Acting out
and antisocial tendency, 207-9
repeats original trauma through transference trauma, 209-11
Actors and 'false self', 150
ADAMSON, J., 97
Adaptation
and satisfaction of id-drives, 241
by mother to infant's ego-needs, 86-7
characteristic of facilitating environment, 239
graduated, 71
mother's gradual failure of, 87-9
mother's, to infant's need, 54
Adolescence
and antisocial tendency, 245-6
and environmental provision, 68
and intolerance of false solution, 244
definition of, 242
doldrum phase in, 246

group-formation in, 246
illness during, 244-6
in girls, 212
isolation in, 246
psychodynamics of, 242-4
psychotherapy of, 242-8
suicide in, 245
violence in, *246-8*
Adolescents, 92
and dread of analysis, 190
as isolates, 190
Aggression, 17
and mother's gradual failure in adaptation, 87-9
and placing of objects, 181
as evidence of life, 127
defusion of, 45
in adolescence, 243
Klein on, 42
vs 'death instinct', 127
AICHHORN, A., 126
'Alone'
as immature state, 32
as infant with mother, 30
capacity to be, 29-36
capacity to be, and anaclitic relationship, 29
capacity to be, and good internal objects, 31-2
capacity to be, and intercourse, 31
capacity to be, and primal scene, 31
child, in latency, 121
Ambivalence
and guilt, 16-17, 21, 75-8
and splitting, 98

role of, in psycho-neurosis, 116
Anaclitic dependence and analyst, 134
Anaclitic object love, 125
Anaclitic relationship and capacity to be alone, 29
Anatomy of Melancholy, 17-18
Anger
repetition in analysis appropriate to environmental failure, 209
Annihilation
and failures of holding environment, 77
from impingements in infancy, 52
through break in analysis, *250, 253*
through exploitation of 'true self', 147
through failure in infant-care, 256
vs 'castration anxiety', 41
Anorexia nervosa, 64, *175*
and refusal of satisfying object, 182
Anti-life factor in mother's depression, 192
Antisocial tendency
and acting out, 208-10
and Aichhorn, 126
and awareness of deprivation, 134-5
and crime, 27
and environmental failure, 52
and need for physical climax, 35
and wickedness, 103-4

277

Stanwyck

A Biography

AXEL MADSEN

HarperPaperbacks
A Division of HarperCollins*Publishers*

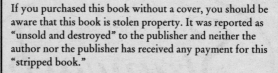

HarperPaperbacks   *A Division of* HarperCollins*Publishers*
10 East 53rd Street, New York, N.Y. 10022

A hardcover edition of this book was published in 1994 by HarperCollins*Publishers*

Cover photo © Neal Peters Collection

First HarperPaperbacks printing: October 1995

Printed in the United States of America

HarperPaperbacks and colophon are trademarks of HarperCollins*Publishers*

❖ 10 9 8 7 6 5 4 3 2 1

She has played five gun molls, two burlesque queens, half a dozen adulteresses and twice as many murderers. When she was good, she was very, very good. And when she was bad, she was terrific.

WALTER MATTHAU

Contents

CONTENTS

Acknowledgments

M y interest in Barbara Stanwyck goes back to the ten years I was a Hollywood writer and journalist. I interviewed Stanwyck on the set of "The Big Valley" and later in connection with her work on "The Colbys" television series. After her death in 1990, I realized that the Stanwyck story had never really been told. I wrote this book to help fill the gap and to satisfy my curiosity about a golden age.

I am indebted to many people who helped me with this project. Some contributors are no longer living; others asked for confidentiality. My respect and thanks extend to everyone, including, in Los Angeles, Iris Adrian, William Aldrich, Maggy Maskel Ferguson, Nina Foch, Michael Hargraves, Dr. Robert J. Kositchek, Frank McCarthy, Nolan Miller, Terry Sadler, Viege Traub, Gertrude Walker, and Billy Wilder.

In New York, Joan Benny, Tracy Devine, and Tom Miller; in Detroit, Shirley Eder; in Paris, Alain LéGrignou, and in Carversville, Pennsylvania, David Greenwald.

I also want to extend special thanks to Dana Harrington and to my agent, Jane Jordan Browne.

1

"I Hope She Lives"

To get up in the morning and, on a soundstage, to become more intense and riveting than the reflection in the bathroom mirror fulfilled her deepest existential need. To crawl into fictional skins, to step into the pool of fused, dedicated light and hear a director's call for action suspended the banality of living. To assume made-up characters more raffish, witty, and lovely than her own self made hurts and failings go away.

She was an orphan when she was three. In her daydreams her parents had been rich, but somebody had got it all mixed up. It was all a big mistake. *She* was the princess on the pea. Not that it led to any *folie de grandeur*. "I just wanted to survive and eat, and have a nice coat," she'd say late in life. The norm of her childhood was struggle, confusion, and pain, but she learned not to blame anybody. Pop psychology wants us to understand Bette Davis in terms of her stage mother, Katharine Hepburn by explaining her doctor father. There is nobody to explain Barbara Stanwyck. She found it a bit embarrassing herself and in self-defense made her childhood a taboo subject for much of her life. In her eighties, she relented. "All right, let's just say I had a terrible childhood. Let's say that 'poor' is something I understand." She thought there was something second-rate about not having a mother, that she wasn't good enough—not altogether the woman she should be, not quite the actress people kept telling her she was.

A movie role was a nice coat to slip into, to disguise, not reveal, who she was. The lines were written in advance, and saying them masked the lack of education she knew was the reason she had a hard time expressing herself. From fifteen to eighty she was the perpetual overachiever and an exception to the rule that artistic temperament rarely goes hand in hand with financial smarts. She kept as firm a grip on herself as she did on her money.

A streak of bitterness ran deep in her. It made her earthy, instinctive, sarcastic, weary of sophisticates, and not very good at the games of love. Her orphan childhood made her deny her soft, caring, and vulnerable sides. She was too straightforward, too headstrong for romance, and couldn't believe a partner would want the relationship any other way. Men and women were equal, she believed, because character has nothing to do with gender.

She was a woman of allure, dogged calculation, and repressed emotions. She possessed a keen native intelligence, had a tongue as sharp as a rapier, yet her orphan's powerlessness left a hollow core in her that she hated. She was easily bored with herself and, to flesh out her existence, took any role. She taught her adopted son to take the knocks on the chin and to forget to cry. Her scrapper's mettle, her emotional reserve and cheeky pluck gave her a gravity that directors realized they could capture with a camera. Frank Capra embarrassed her when he told her that her austere beauty, wide thin mouth, straight brows, and classical nose projected purity, a kind of lonely gallantry and self-assurance that gave the scripted wisecracks contrast. In her fifties, *The Barbara Stanwyck Show* failed because as a TV host she had to open the show by standing there, stripped of a part, and be herself.

The conflict that shaped her life—and made her so interesting to watch on the screen—was the struggle between her wish to give of herself and her need to be in control. Too special and too identifiable to play Everywoman, she was wrong for many of her parts. Prestigious films eluded her as she aged, yet she survived the cameras for an astonishing fifty-five years.

She did not burst onto the scene. She eased on and eased off even more leisurely. Frank Capra's *Ladies of Leisure* was her breakthrough, but it was already her fourth movie. *The Night Walker* was her eighty-eighth and last, but it was followed by twenty years of television, much of it unworthy of her talent.

She played a rich mix of characters, many of them gutsy, self-reliant women, faith leaders and chiselers, gold diggers and saps, burlesque queens and cardsharps. When movies got fewer and shabbier in the 1950s and '60s, she let go playing high-ridin' women engaged in brutal mating games. Her sexuality in *The Furies* and *Forty Guns* is so arrogant that to win her the gunfighters in love with her practically have to kill her. There were also portrayals of victims, of course. Barbara did her share of movies in which a woman sacrifices herself for her man, her child, for other women, and she excelled at that other movie staple—the tough reporter who goes mushy in the fadeout. She was attracted to roles that required her to annihilate herself in another, invented woman and knew how to endow both her victims and hard-as-nails dames with *faux-naïf* cunning and dramatic sense. She was fearless when it came to fleshing out swindlers, gun molls, dupes, and sentimental masochists. "Some of my most interesting roles have been completely unsympathetic," she said. "Actresses welcome such parts, knowing that vitriol makes a stronger impression than syrup." She talked a good game, but lost her nerve when Joseph Mankiewicz offered her *All About Eve*. Playing an actress on the skids terrified her.

To be a star is to live in a glass house, yet Stanwyck eluded just about everyone. She knew how to choke off subjects she didn't want to talk about, how to close doors behind her, even to friends. Insiders were surprised when Malcolm Byron Stevens died in 1964. They didn't know she had a brother.

A lot was never known about her.

She grew up afraid of trusting anyone, afraid of people finding out she didn't belong to anybody. Her insecurity gave her tough veneer. It also gave her the kind of discipline that helps a person hang on to dazzling success. She longed for acceptance and stability, but the first man who paid attention died when she was twenty-one. She rushed into the arms of a riveting charm-pot and had to learn all over again that the only person she could count on was herself.

People who met her for the first time were surprised by how small she was. She stood all of 5' 3" and most of her life weighed under 115 pounds. In her teens her voice was already deep and husky and made her sound like someone with a secret. Her alto was all-business, and it deepened over the years into a voice whose throaty undertone warned of the scam to come. In many of her films, there is a suggestion of zingy, smutty sex, of a woman enjoying her perversity and control. She saw life as a poker game. You play the hand life deals you. If men lose, it's their problem. Instead of seeing the glint in her eyes they should watch the cards in their hands.

She was the incarnation of grace and save-your-ass resilience that defined an era. While remaining the least mannered and pretentious of the stars of her period, she was up there with Bette Davis, Joan Crawford, and Katharine Hepburn. Her uncanny way of looking at herself as if she were a third person appealed to both male and female audiences. Lesbians in search of role models adopted her as one of their own. They admired the qualities she projected, her inscrutability to the opposite sex in her films, the way she related to men. Fear of her own feelings and of society's reaction made her surround her intimate life with discretion. People could never wrest from her anything she didn't want them to know.

She maintained an easy camaraderie with her strong directors—William Wellman, Howard Hawks, Preston Sturges, and Billy Wilder. Capra wanted to tumble into bed with her, but discovered a greater rush in the way she goaded his talent. There is a measure of irony in the fact that her all-round good sport, "director's actress" reputation robbed her of choice roles. Self-respecting legends are supposed to throw tantrums, to knife fellow actors in the back, to intimidate employers. The scheming of her friend Joan Crawford to get the *Mildred Pierce* title role so awed its producer that the casting of Stanwyck was rescinded. Barbara could never convince David O. Selznick she was perfect for the good-time girl dying of a brain tumor in *Dark Victory* or Jack Warner that *The Fountainhead*'s woman between two men was her.

She was famously married to actors for periods of her life. Frank Fay was a one-man vaudeville act who sank in direct proportion to her rise. She felt guilty and responsible for his failure and veered from wanting to lose herself in the marriage to being fiercely independent, deepening her fears of intimacy. Their seesaw relationship became so much a model for *A Star Is Born* that Selznick hired lawyers to make sure the screenplay wasn't liable to court action. Growing up shifting for herself may have tempered maternal instincts, but to save the marriage she conned Fay into adopting a baby. She was never close to the boy. When he was six she banished him to a succession of boarding schools.

She married Robert Taylor on her terms. She treated the matinee idol as an adolescent and humiliated him in front of the macho friends he so desperately needed to reinforce his masculinity. Their sex life, such as it was, lasted only months, but the marriage turned out to be a clever career move. They were a fulsomely correct couple during World War II and the Hollywood witch-hunt years when, politically, they swung sharply to the right. He loathed his own screen-lover image and hated the pretty-boy roles that made women swoon. Upholding the image, however, was all-important. When challenged by Ava Gardner, he climbed into bed with her. In old age Stanwyck's passion for him turned morbid. Twenty years after he died, she became convinced his ghost was visiting her, that he had returned to guide her into the afterlife.

Stanwyck walked too fast, talked too fast, and made too many pictures. She made no excuses for her clunkers with Ronald Reagan, Barry Sullivan, and Joel McCrea. She told interviewers that if she didn't have fun working, she wouldn't be doing it. When people suggested such sentiments were typically associated with actors like James Cagney and Spencer Tracy, she answered, "Maybe we're just more used to these traits in men, so that we associate them with masculinity instead of character."

Barbara worked tirelessly to improve herself. Because she realized she lacked education and social graces, she read, studied, and, to deal with people smarter than she, built an armor plate of one-of-the-boys wisecracks. She detested people who felt pity for themselves. She hated hats, flattery, feathers, and conversationalists who began their sentences with "Listen . . . " She never veered out of control, never suffered tortured brooding or chemical dependencies. Acting was a job. She put on lipstick without a mirror and when people asked, "What if it smears?" she said, "Then the makeup man fixes it. That's his job. We all have jobs." She refused to watch the dailies or to be technical. "Don't teach me, take care of me," she told her cinematographers, who over the years ranged from studio journeymen to "name" cameramen like George Barnes, Rudolph Maté, and James Wong Howe. Not to have a role lined up in some movie made her restless. When married to Taylor she agreed with him that she should have some other interests, but went right ahead signing up for film after film. Fellow actors both admired and resented her self-punishing exactness. She was never late on a shoot, never forgot her lines. They paid her a lot to do what she liked best, she thought. The least she could do was get there on time.

Stanwyck was a homebody who traveled only under duress. She visited Europe only three times and, feeling out of her depth, lapsed into a caricature of the American yahoo abroad. For half her long life she lived alone and called herself a bachelor woman. In her later years she spent long, solitary nights drinking herself into a stupor. Like many movie stars of her generation, she smoked herself to death.

Bad health plagued her old age, but she refused to let the public see her fall apart. She had the memory of an elephant. It took her from thirty to sixty, she said, to sort out and jettison the clutter in her mind. "I think living in the past, clinging to memories and souvenirs of days long gone, treating the present as a sort of hazy, second-rate competitor of the 'good old days,' is an anesthetic for those who have too little to do, and too much time in which to do it," she proclaimed.

Being a loner gave her otherworldly insights that astonished even her. "I see things, I have instincts," she said on her eightieth birthday. "Many times before somebody says something, I know what they'll say. A couple of times people said, 'You're weird.'" Nancy Sinatra, Sr., her best friend during her later years, thought she was reincarnated, that she had been on this earth before. To which Barbara cracked, "Other people say senility is setting in."

She was of a period that wasn't all-knowing about show business. Her stardom didn't rely on finding an angle or a spin. She never "did" Barbara Walters, or *The Tonight Show*, or a book tour (or a book). Her best friend was her publicist, who saw to it that the Stanwyck-Taylor marriage fell apart according to sanitized Hollywood standards. Nobody quoted

Barbara on her conservative politics during the Red Scare or interviewed her brother or her sisters back in Brooklyn.

In today's ever-recycled entertainment world of short and shallow screen careers and video-rental accessibility, she is an intriguing personality of a fabled age, the orphan as ready vessel into which roles are poured. Hollywood's pinnacle decades were her busiest, and happiest, years. The all-powerful studios and the most gifted directors wanted her. She was married to the top studio's handsomest leading man, was a pro's pro, and earned scads of money.

Her long career offers insight into the trajectory of women in pop culture. In the 1930s, she was, with Joan Blondell and Carole Lombard, a favorite of male audiences. Nobody played a saucy dame better than she. Women movie-goers didn't quite know how to accept the tart, direct females in wisecracking comedies or the tough ladies in the action movies and often preferred to see Bette Davis, Helen Hayes, and Ruth Chatterton give up "everything" for the man they loved.

Today's young women see Stanwyck as one of them, as someone who challenged the notions of what a woman could be and do long before society thought of redefining feminine parameters. Today, Madonna tries to capture the Stanwyck allure that made the screen sizzle with carnality and cynicism. In *Hero*, Geena Davis reprises Stanwyck's classic tough gal reporter, Bette Midler remakes *Stella Dallas*, and Dyan Cannon stars in a TV remake of *Christmas in Connecticut*.

Barbara talked about the women she played in the third person and, once a shoot was over, how she hoped she had breathed life into them. "It's gone and done and you did it and you feel a little bit of emptiness after it's over. You thought it had left you, but it hadn't. You say to yourself, 'I hope she lives.'"

2

Brooklyn

S he was born Ruby Stevens.

Her place of birth was 246 Classon Avenue, Brooklyn, the date July 16, 1907. She was the fifth, and last, child of Byron and Catherine McGee Stevens, both working-class natives of Chelsea, Massachusetts. Catherine was the daughter of Irish emigrants, Byron of English parents. As an adult Stanwyck played up the Irish heritage. She knew how to glide like the leprechauns, she said, and besides the Irish brashness also possessed the Irish quietude. Ernest Hemingway said she had "a good tough Mick intelligence."

Catherine had raven-black hair and violet eyes. She was twenty when she married Byron, a handsome, red-haired part-time fisherman and construction worker. Children followed in quick succession. They all had names beginning with M— Maud, Mabel, Mildred, and Malcolm Byron.

Chelsea offered few opportunities. When Stevens heard bricklayers were making fifty cents an hour erecting row houses in New York's expanding boroughs, he ran off one night in 1905. By questioning the men he had worked with, Catherine managed to find her husband. She packed her four children and their possessions and in Brooklyn found Byron. The family lore would have it that he was less than pleased when Cathy showed up with the kids. But bricklaying was a trade in demand and the family settled at 246 Classon Avenue, a long street running north-south from Myrtle Avenue to Prospect Park, where their last child—Ruby Katherine—was born.

Maud and Mabel were teenagers, Mildred eight, Malcolm

Byron six, and little Ruby going on three during the winter of 1909–10, when their mother became pregnant again. Cathy was stepping off a streetcar when a drunkard lurched forward and knocked her to the ground. Her head struck the curb. A month later she was dead.

Ruby walked behind the coffin with her father, three sisters, and brother. Two weeks after the burial, Byron enlisted to join a work crew digging the Panama Canal. His children never saw him again.

The two eldest daughters shifted for themselves and soon married. It eventually fell to the third daughter, Mildred, to bring up Byron, as Malcolm Byron was always called, and Ruby. Little more than a child herself, Mildred became a showgirl. When she went on the road, she shuttled Byron and Ruby from pillar to post, farming them out to a shifting cast of relatives and neighbors. She couldn't always "place" the two siblings together. Each time little Ruby ran away from a foster home, Byron knew where to find her—on the stoop on Classon Avenue, where she'd be sitting "waiting for Mama to come home."

In order not to hurt Byron and Ruby, Mildred never mentioned their mother and father, but only talked about "the family." In one year, Ruby boarded with four different households. Her fear was that if she made the wrong move the people who took her in would send her to an orphanage. Adopted children grew up being told, "You're lucky." The message Ruby grew up with was that inside hurts didn't really matter, that the outside appearance—looking good and having nice clothes—is what counts. She was keenly aware that she was different. She told herself she was an orphan. "I'll always be an orphan," she'd say until her fighting spirit snapped. Then she'd sniffle and say, "Cats and dogs are orphans, and who has more fun—kids or cats?"

For the next eight years, Byron and Ruby clung to each other. Being boarded out meant that they were never part of anybody. Trust and distrust became exaggerated. One way little Ruby learned to handle people was not to get too close to them. A little bundle of rejection, she shut out her feelings and made sure she showed her disinterest before anybody had a chance to abandon her. Late in life, she would say, "At least nobody beat me. Where I grew up, kids existed on the brink of domestic or financial disaster." She chose to remember that as a result, the children were "alert, precocious and savage." She would remember little of her parents, but imagined she had her mother's eyes, that her father was someone who "squared his shoulders against circumstances, too young, despairing sometimes." She never talked about how she felt. Memory and fantasy remained intertwined and hard to differentiate. Ambivalence colored her recollections of childhood. Being poor led both to the idea that it was all a big mistake and to I'll-show-you spunk and motivation. Maybe it wasn't her mother who had died. Maybe their father would come home. Millie knocked the bottom out of Ruby's daydreams when she pointed out that the Panama Canal had been opened to shipping since 1914.

A hard-nosed view of life counterbalanced the yearnings of her daydreaming, which she came to regard as utter folly. Teeming immigrant Brooklyn sent forth a robust generation ready to bend the American Dream in its direction. She later chose to remember her neighborhood's and her generation's swagger and optimism. "Growing up in one foster home after another didn't give me any edge on the other kids or any excuse for whining, protesting, demanding. Besides, why whine? Too many neighborhood kids were already making it big. Their accomplishments were inspiring facts—the promise and proof that we weren't puppets. Hapless, maybe, but not helpless, not hopeless. We were free to work our way out of our surroundings, free to work our way up—up as far as we could dream of."

Mildred didn't want her kid sister to become a showgirl. Quick on her feet, Ruby nevertheless learned Millie's show routine by heart. Byron didn't approve. To annoy him, Ruby scrawled her name in chalk on the neighborhood sidewalks, "to show everybody how it's going to look in electric lights." During the summer of 1916 and 1917, Millie took her kid sister with her on tour. Ruby watched every show from the wings and picked up more routines.

Teachers in P.S. 15 didn't tolerate children out of control, kids cursing and fighting. Ruby was defiant and resentful. She hated to do what she was told, picked arguments, teased classmates. For want of attention, she was alternately seductive and aggressive, provocative and infuriating, always quick to lose her temper. "I didn't relish the disciplines of my childhood," she would say when she was sixty, "I hated them." Her grades were appalling, and she would admit she was "the stupidest little brat in school." Threats from the principal that misbehavior would get her in trouble left her indifferent because things couldn't possibly get any worse.

She wanted to be like the other girls who had mommies and daddies who came home after work. Why had it happened to her? She was resentful, took everything personally. Why her? She couldn't bring herself to make friends with anybody, and the neighborhood kids in turn were suspicious of her. In school, she learned never to volunteer information about the people with whom she lived, never to invite classmates home. Girls didn't care for Ruby, and she had no close friends. For a while her brother made the boys on the block tolerate her in their games.

When Ruby was going on twelve, Millie was in the chorus of *Glorianna*, the 1918–19 musical starring Eleanor Painter. James Buck McCarthy, known professionally as James "Buck" Mack, was one half of the show's song-and-dance team. He became Millie's boyfriend and soon got to know her kid sister. Ruby called him "Uncle" Buck. She loved to sneak into the wings of the Liberty Theatre and watch rehearsals. Invariably, when Buck came to work, she'd stop him in the hallway and shout, "Hey, Uncle Buck, watch this." Oblivious to chorus girls and musicians rushing to get ready for the first performance, Ruby launched into a tap routine she had watched in the afternoon and learned to perfection.

Ruby's biggest disappointment was that Millie refused to take her with her when *Glorianna* went on tour. Ruby couldn't go, Millie decided, because it was in the middle of the school year. Left with a family in the Flatbush section, Ruby flirted with religion as a calling. The inspiration was the Reverend William Carter, pastor of the Dutch Reformed Church on the corner of Flatbush and Church avenues, who inscribed a page of a book to "Rubie [sic] Katharine Stevens: In all the ways acknowledge Him. Prov. 3:6," and dated it January 5, 1919. "No one in my family was Dutch Reformed, but he was very kind and their church was the prettiest I had ever seen. I heard tales about the gallant women who were making enormous sacrifices for the heathen. That, I decided, was for me."

Religion was to remain peripheral to her life, however.

Twelve years later, she played an evangelist and a missionary in a pair of Frank Capra movies and came to hate the hypocrisy of a churchgoing husband. During the McCarthy era, she talked up the wholesomeness of godly beliefs, but she never became a practicing Christian herself.

Ruby quit P.S. 15 when she was thirteen, although early biographical thumbnail sketches had her attend Brooklyn's Erasmus Hall High School. Still a small person, she looked older than her years and was quick to lie about her age. By fourteen she had mastered every dance step she had ever seen. Her first job, however, was as a wrapper of packages at Brooklyn's Abraham & Straus department store. "The plain wrapping, not the fancy," she would specify. Next she answered a newspaper ad for a girl to file cards at the Brooklyn telephone office on Dey Street. The job paid $14 a week and became an early milestone because she never again depended on her family for financial support.*

"I knew that after fourteen I'd have to earn my own living, but I was willing to do that," she would say in 1937. "I've always been a little sorry for pampered people, and of course, they're *very* sorry for me."

Escape was going to the movies and reading trashy novels. "Once in a while my sister Millie would take me to a stuffy little movie theater to see Pearl White in her *Perils of Pauline*. It was not money wasted. Pearl White was my goddess and her courage, her grace and her triumphs lifted me out of this world. I read nothing good, but I read an awful lot. Here was escape! I read lurid stuff about ladies who smelled sweet and looked like flowers and were betrayed. I read about gardens and ballrooms and moonlight trysts and murders. I felt a sense of doors opening. And I began to be conscious of myself, the way I looked, the clothes I wore. I bought awful things at first, pink shirtwaist, artificial flowers, tripe."

---

*All figures are given in vintage dollars. To get a sense of money, the reader should multiply 1920s figures by twelve; $14 a week is the equivalent of about $168 in 1994 dollars. It should be kept in mind that federal and state taxes averaged a mere 3 percent on high incomes and were nonexistent on low incomes (source: Federal Reserve Library of Research).

Ruby followed telephone card filing with work as a dress pattern cutter. She persuaded *Vogue* that she was the right person to help customers cut material. For the first time she found herself in a situation she couldn't handle. Complaints of paper patterns for sleeves laid sideways on material with up-down designs, of ruined fabric, piled up. She was fired.

She went to live with Maude in Flatbush while she looked for another job.

She had hated selling patterns as much as she had hated wrapping packages and filing cards. "I gave up trying to follow the 'sensible' advice of my sister, who knew all the hazards and heartaches of show business and tried to save me from them," she would say forty years later. "I hated those three little jobs. I knew there was no place but show business that I wouldn't hate." Millie, however, won one last time. They needed whatever steady money Ruby could make, and she applied for a typist's job in Manhattan.

The moment Ruby walked into the Jerome H. Remick Music Company on Twenty-eighth Street she felt a surge of excitement. Several pianos were going at once as song pluggers and vocalists tried out for auditions. It was at Remick's that fifteen-year-old George Gershwin had found a job as piano demonstrator; it was Remick's that published his first song, "When You Want 'Em, You Can't Get 'Em." The manager, Will Von Tilzer, sent Ruby upstairs to the business office. She was hired and quickly learned that the company's all-time hit was "Till We Meet Again" and that Von Tilzer's brother Albert provided the music for the current Broadway musical hit, *The Gingham Girl.*

Typing letters above the bedlam was the next best thing to being on Broadway.

Ruby spent her free time with Millie and Uncle Buck. Perhaps at his urging, Millie gave up trying to shelter her kid sister from show business. He taught Ruby the rudiments of the business, how to try for a job on Broadway.

Uncle Buck and showbiz became her family—for life. From the mid-1930s, he would live on her ranch and various estates and run her household. When old age and emphysema prevented him from climbing stairs, she would sell her house and buy a one-story bungalow.

* * *

Either Uncle Buck or Von Tilzer got her an audition with Earl Lindsay, the manager of the Strand Roof, a nightclub over the Strand Theatre in Times Square. A few months short of sixteen, Ruby borrowed her sister's dress, rouged her face, painted her lips, and presented herself at the Strand audition. She already had a deep, experienced voice, but Lindsay was more amused than convinced by her grown-up airs. "I'll always love Earl Lindsay, though there was nothing gentle about the bawling out he gave me when I was fifteen and working in my first job," she would say thirty years later. "I owe everything to his teaching. It made me a professional. I started in the back row of the chorus where it was easy to give something less than your best. He never let me get away with that. 'You'll never get ahead if you're sloppy, out of the spotlight or in it,' he said."

Lindsay hired her at the princely salary of $35 a week. She was as elastic as a rubber band, could kick higher than anyone in the chorus, and made a point of doing it. "My idea was that everybody would say, 'Look at that girl who can kick higher than everybody.' I very nearly kicked myself out of a job. Lindsay pulled me out of the line and told me off in blistering terms. 'You'd better learn right now that if you can't learn to be part of a team, you better get off the stage. You're spoiling everybody's work by thinking of yourself and not the show.'"

Ruby loved it. Lindsay's scolding meant he cared. To be a dancer made her feel confident, and to repeat the routine and to see Lindsay watching in the wings every night gave her a sense of stability. Frank Capra would remember her telling how gangsters controlled New York's nightlife, how being an underage chorus girl was tough. Her own memories, however, mellowed over the years: "Some people call night spots a pretty bad environment; maybe they are. I had to earn my living and I was grateful for work I loved as much as dancing.

"Then pretty soon I heard that there were better salaries in road shows, so I went after a job in a road show . . . and got it. The day we left New York for Columbus, I had a new suitcase. I think I packed and unpacked it fifty times. I'd never been on a train before. I sat up all night in the Pullman just to see the towns and the country go by."

3

"Stark Naked, I Swear"

S he was sixty and sure there was no age she would want to be again, when she remembered her days as a chorus girl and relented. "I might, just might, be tempted to be fifteen again—but if I were fifteen again, I couldn't get the jobs I got then. What with work permits, compulsory education, union wages, that whole carefree, on-your-own adventure is not attainable. But how my memories of those three years sparkle! My chorine days may not have seemed perfect to anyone else, but they did to me."

She was only a few weeks from her sixteenth birthday when she obtained a bit in the 1922 edition of the *Ziegfeld Follies*.

The 1922 *Follies* at the New Amsterdam Theatre headlined Gilda Gray, the new shimmying sexpot attuned to the pace of the dizzy, jazzy Roaring Twenties. The breezy Mary Eaton, who the next year would be Eddie Cantor's costar in *Kid Boots*, contributed the glamour, and Vivienne Segal was the show's vivacious ingenue. Ruby was in the first-act finale that had the young women on a golden staircase, marching through golden gates.

The *Follies* gave an opulent illusion of sin. As Brooks Atkinson, the dean of theater critics, would put it, "For a quarter of a century, the *Follies* represented the businessman's ideal of a perfect harem. Everything about the *Follies* was beautiful, plump, mysterious, and equivocally erotic. Ziegfeld created the formula; no one could make it work after he went."

Rivals, however, were crowding in on the legendary

showman. Earl Carroll and Ziegfeld's former employee, George White, made him testy with copycat shows. To sustain his notoriety, Ziegfeld resorted to increasingly silly publicity stunts. A showgirl's complaint to the press that she would rather have dinner with a pig than with some of the men she knew led to a Central Park dinner at the Casino, where a select group of authors, actors, and society people dined with the showgirl and a white pig tied to a highchair. To launch the shimmying Gilda Gray, Ziegfeld arranged for an employee, pretending to be a Texas oil tycoon, to toss a $100,000 necklace into her lap on the stage.

The dressing rooms in the New Amsterdam were peculiar because the theater was the only one in New York allowed by fire laws to be sheathed in an office building. Offstage on the ground floor was a single star's dressing room. The floor above was for Ziegfeld's showgirls—the tall beauties who did not dance but paraded across the stage in elaborate costumes or stood immobile and naked to the waist in various tableaus.* The principals dressed on the third floor. As a chorus girl, Ruby belonged on the fourth floor.

Ruby's only school was the backstage, her teachers other performers. She learned quickly and worked hard. Her memory would be selective. "I was in the 16th row of the chorus and wore a beaded thing and occasionally sat on an elephant," she would say in 1949. No mention of riding the elephant in a scanty costume or, in a famous Ziegfeld Shadowgraph tableau, standing naked to the waist behind a white screen.

For young Ruby, hypocrisy, repressed sexuality, and the power of real acting came together in Jeanne Eagels's brilliant acting in *Rain*. The stage adaptation of Somerset Maugham's short story was a sensation when it opened on Broadway in November 1922. Eagles was an actress of irresistible freshness and strangely corrupt beauty, who electrified audiences for the four-year run of the play. Any actress with a brain and a figure wanted to repeat the performance, and Tallulah Bankhead went to London to persuade Maugham she was the

---

*A loophole in the law allowed nudity on the stage if the naked woman did not move. Powdered and rouged from head to toe, Kay Laurell, Ziegfeld's statuesque beauty, was the center of these tableaus.

actress for the West End version. We do not know what Ruby thought of Sadie Thompson and the missionary who, after reducing her to misery, shame, and repentance, falls prey to her vitality, commits suicide, and leaves her scornfully calling all men dirty pigs. We do know that Ruby was so fascinated by Eagles that she returned four times to see her play.

R uby shared her first apartment with two fellow chorines. Mae Clarke and Walda Mansfield were also in the *Follies* lineup, and together the trio took a cold-water flat on Forty-sixth Street between Fifth and Sixth avenues.

"We lived over a laundry, which could be steamy at times and especially hot in the summer," she would recall. "The heat seemed to come through every crack in the floor and ceiling. Then there was the noisy Sixth Avenue El that shook the walls. Sometimes we felt we could reach out and touch the trains."

Walda was a skinny girl with a small mousy face. Mae was born Mary Klotz in Philadelphia, the daughter of a movie theater organist, and had danced in amateur musicals in Atlantic City, where she had caught the eye of Earl Lindsay.

As chorus girls, Ruby, Walda, and Mae managed as many as thirty-eight routines a night. Ruby would remember working a restaurant job on West Forty-eighth Street and rushing from there to the Shubert Theatre on West Forty-fourth Street at 8:15 every night with nothing on but a coat and a pair of shoes—"stark naked, I swear, in freezing weather, and the coats were not so hot either," she'd say in 1943. "Ask Mae Clarke—she used to do the run with me every night. I tell you we worked like dogs, were strong as horses. But don't ask your baby Duses to do that now, they're worrying about their psyches."

From midnight to 7:00 A.M., Ruby and Mae worked shows in the succession of nightclubs that Mary Louise "Texas" Guinan opened—and police closed. By serving booze, the zany, wisecracking queen of nightclubs broke the law nightly in her many elegantly designed clubs. Guinan paid police a fortune to stay open. But, as one cop put it, "Temperance crackpots had to be appeased," and her clubs were regularly raided. Federal agents who pretended to be customers so they could be served and pour the contents of their drinks into small bottles as evidence usually waited for the girls to finish their act before standing up and announcing, "Okay, everybody, stay where you are. This is a raid!"

Guinan billed herself as "God's Masterpiece and the Most Fascinating Actress in America" and was famous for greeting her rich male patrons with "Hello, suckers" before singing a few songs and browbeating her audience with insolent remarks that everyone adored. Following blues and torch singers, Ruby and six other girls danced a furious Charleston for three hundred revelers. Guinan's clientele ranged from fun-loving Mayor Jimmy Walker to newspaper columnists, stellar figures of the underworld, W. C. Fields, Ann Pennington, Al Jolson, and—her lifeblood—blue-chip suckers. She ordered her waiters to shout risqué words to the dancers and to refill customers' glasses without being asked. "Give the girls a great big hand," Texas demanded in her trademark comment at the end of the act. With winks toward the big spenders, Texas had the young women run through the cramped table area and do short shimmies in front of sugar daddies to encourage them to stuff banknotes into their scanty costumes.

Ruby and Mae were also on call as dance instructors at a speakeasy for gays and lesbians owned by Guinan's less-renowned brother. Jimmy Guinan's lover was a New York City cop who made it his business to know when a police raid was planned. On nights when police activity appeared imminent, Jimmy borrowed several of his sister's girls and transformed his nightclub into a dance studio. Ruby later neglected to remember her tours of duty as teacher at Jimmy Guinan's, but Sheldon Dewey, who wrote a society column under the pen name Harry Otis, would recall taking impromptu tango lessons from the future Barbara Stanwyck during a vice squad raid.

Stage-door johnnies were a fact of life, and when Mae, Walda, or Ruby accepted a date they had their swains drop them off at one of the theater-district hotels, both to pretend they could afford to live there and also not to let their admirers know their real address. Even in the early 1920s, $40 a week only covered the necessities and sometimes not even that, she would remember. Chorines usually had three choices when it came to men—musicians, gangsters, or millionaires. The musicians, who were in the pit every night and rubbed shoulders with the girls backstage and in the hallways, usually won out. Bea Palmer, one of Ruby's colleagues, managed all three. She had married a banker from Baltimore, left him to marry a banjo player from the George Olsen band, and, after curtain time every night, was escorted by the enforcer for the Yellow Cab Company. A blue-eyed Shubert chorine named Lucille LeSueur married James Welton, a saxophone player in the pit orchestra of *The Passing Show of 1924*. Two years later, Metro-Goldwyn-Mayer gave her a screen test, shipped her to California, and changed her name to Joan Crawford.

Ruby left no written memories of her time as a Ziegfeld and George White chorine, but a young woman who joined the 1924 edition of White's *Scandals* did. Long after she had flamed out as an icon of film history, Louise Brooks would paint a lively picture of backstage life in the *Scandals* lineup in her autobiographical novel, *Naked on My Goat*.

Eligible bachelors in their thirties were eager to escort showgirls to places like the Colony and "21." Finding debutantes a threat, [they] turned to pretty girls in the theater, whose mothers weren't husband hunting. Café society developed about this time. The theater, Hollywood, and society mingled in the monthly Mayfair danced at the Ritz, where society women could monitor their theatrical enemies and snub them publicly.

All the rich men were friends who entertained one another in their perfectly appointed Park Avenue apartments and Long Island homes. The extravagant sums given to the girls for clothes were part of the fun—part of competing to see whose girl would win the Best-Dressed title. Sexual submission was not a condition of this arrangement, although many affairs grew out of it.

In self-defense against lechers in tuxedos and ballroom rakes, Ruby, Mae, and Walda made the caustic Oscar Levant their "mascot." The boyfriend of an Irish chorus girl, Levant was a pianist and knew everybody. He played in orchestras in the smartest nightclubs, at social functions in private homes, in jazz dives, and had recorded George Gershwin's *Rhapsody in Blue* for Brunswick records. He knew LeRoy Pierpont Ward, for whom speakeasy doors flew open and who called most of New York society by first name, and he played for Jimmy Walker, who wrote lyrics for *Tin Pan Alley*, kept showgirls on the side, and took seven vacations during his first two years in office.

Levant took Ruby, Mae, and Walda to Harlem, where the after-theater limousine crowd looked for new thrills. The "class white-trade" nightclubs like the Cotton Club on Lenox and 142nd Street featured jazz, chorus lines, comedians, singers like Ethel Waters, and marvelous dancers like Bill "Bojangles" Robinson. Louis Armstrong performed at Connie's Inn on 131st Street and Bessie Smith at the Lafayette on Seventh Avenue and 132nd Street. The Park Avenue sophisticated also frequented the mixed basement speakeasies like the Drool Inn and the Clam House, where transvestites performed and lesbians flaunted themselves. Bessie Smith's lesbian interests were well known, and her mentor, Ma Rainey, was just out of jail for arranging a lesbian orgy in her home involving the women in her chorus. One night Ruby was introduced to Jeanne Eagels, high on opium and clinging to the butchy singer Libby Holman.

Levant would remember Ruby as "wary of sophisticates and phonies." She was fascinated by the gritty realities of backstage life, but for the most part remained aloof. It was provocative for an entertainer to admit to a "touch" of lesbianism, but most dancers expected to marry and live as heterosexuals. As Mae West said, the theater was full of odd men and odd women. Ruby knew show business couldn't exist without them.

Ruby was one of the sixteen "Keep Kool Cuties" in the *Keep Kool* revue when the show opened at the Morosco, May 22, 1924. *Variety* said of them, "The sixteen girls are pips, lookers and dancers, kicking like steers and look like why-men-leave-home in their many costume flashes." Hazel Dawn was the star. Ruby had a number with Johnny Dooley called "A Room Adjoining a Boudoir." When the show closed in August, Ziegfeld decided to take some of the sketches on his *Follies* road show. Ruby was invited to go on tour. In an imitation of the deleted "Comic Supplement" number, she did a striptease behind a white screen in a Ziegfeld Shadowgraph tableau. Her salary jumped to $100 a week.

Back in New York, she had no trouble finding jobs. In April 1925, she and Mae Clarke danced in the chorus in Anatole Friedland's Club on Fifty-fourth Street. They never went to bed before dawn.

After the nightclub stint, Lindsay offered both girls parts in the Shuberts' *Gay Paree* at the Winter Garden. The show satirized the folks of an imaginary Hicksville, and not one song dealt with Paris. The score was by J. Fred Coots, the former Chicago song plugger and *Sally, Irene and Mary* composer who, in 1931, would write "I Still Get a Thrill Thinking of You" for Bing Crosby. Most of the comedy fell to Chic Sale, who portrayed an announcer at a church social. Ruby and Mae danced in lavish production numbers that had chorus beauties parading in "Glory of Morning Sunshine" and shimmying to "Florida Mammy."

The thirteen-year period between 1924–37 has been called the golden age of the Broadway musical, and the 1925–26 season was enthralling. George and Ira Gershwin, Lorenz Hart, and Cole Porter gave new sophistication to their rhymes. The world hummed "Oh, Lady, Be Good!" and *No, No, Nanette* ran for 321 performances after a year in Chicago while *The Desert Song* and *Rio Rita* nearly topped five hundred shows.

Ruby danced in the 1926 version of *George White's Scandals*. White had danced with Ann Pennington in Ziegfeld's dazzling war shows and in 1919 had become the producer of a lavish new revue, *Scandals*. The 1926 edition at the Apollo ran for 424 performances, almost double the series' previous record. Pennington led the dancers, Eugene and Willie Howard headed the clowns. The McCarthy Sisters were joined by an eye-filling chorus line dressed by Erté. Ruby danced the black bottom.

The city elders were uneasy about the morals of Broadway people. Jimmy Walker threatened managers with punitive action unless they cleaned up their acts. Mae West spent ten days in the workhouse and was fined $500 for her play *Sex*, and New York's district attorney closed down *The Captive* and hauled away cast and management in paddy wagons because the heroine in Edouard Bourdet's play was seduced (offstage) by another woman.

Ruby, Walda, and Mae moved in together at the Knickerbocker Hotel on Forty-fifth Street. Walda was the first to go steady. Her boyfriend was Irving Berlin's partner, Walter Donaldson. A large, ruddy man at home in the knockabout world of Tin Pan Alley, Walter had been a piano demonstrator when he wrote his first hit song, "Back Home in Tennessee," without ever having visited the state. As a composer, he had followed up with Al Jolson's "My Mammy," "Carolina in the Morning," and Eddie Cantor's new hit, "Yes Sir, That's My Baby." It is not known whether Walda was the inspiration for Walter's most famous song, "My Blue Heaven," but in 1935 they got married.

Mae married Fanny Brice's brother, Lew, who was twice her age.

Ruby went out with a boy named Edward Kennedy. She would have little to say about this first boyfriend except that he wanted them to get married. She told him they should wait.

A photo of Ruby, Mae, and Walda shows three young women in a theatrical pose on a sofa, Ruby and Walda revealing long, silk-stocking legs. The blond Mae is in black, sitting on the armrest, strumming a guitar. Walda and Ruby sit below Mae, chiseled-faced Walda in profile looking at Ruby with one hand on her shoulder. Ruby's face is fuller than in her 1930s movie stills, but with her clear, straight gaze she is unmistakably the future Barbara Stanwyck.

The roommates generally paid for their own dinners, usually at The Tavern, Billy LaHiff's Forty-eight Street hangout for show people. LaHiff liked to have attractive girls sprinkled about in his restaurant and let showgirls between jobs eat on credit. On occasion, he served as self-appointed talent scout and go-between.

One night, LaHiff came over and said, "Ruby, I've got a chance for you."

He introduced her to Willard Mack, producer, director, playwright, screenwriter and actor, and husband of the strikingly beautiful actress Marjorie Rambeau.

Twenty years later she would remember:

Mr. Mack was a director of legitimate plays. He was more famous than anyone I'd ever met, up to that moment. When I'm frightened, even now, I try to act bold. I was really scared then. So I looked at Willard Mack with impudent assurance, just to keep from turning around and running away.

Billy [LaHiff] said, "Mr. Mack, you said one of your characters in the new play is a chorus girl. Why not cast a real one in the part?"

Ruby would have two versions of what happened next. In one, Mack said, "All right, Ruby. I'll give you a try." Emboldened, she said she lived with two other girls. "We all need jobs. All of us, or nobody."

"Mack looked furious. Then he burst out laughing. 'So you won't walk out on your friends?' he said. 'Well, you're quite a girl, Ruby.' So he gave us all jobs."

In her seventies, she would not mention Mae and Walda, only Mack telling her the part had already been cast for New York but she could have it out of town.

4

Rex

"I was a dancer, not a great one, but I knew left from right," Barbara would sum up her apprentice years. "But I was no actress. It never occurred to me that I could make the grade as an actress. I didn't even try. It was as a chorus girl that I was signed for a very small part in Mack's play. All I did was dance on stage in the second act. I did have six lines to say, but they were incidental. Mack just began training me."

Little is known today of Willard Mack (né Charles Willard McLaughlin). In the teens and early twenties when the commercial stage was at its zenith and the twin mechanical entertainment sources, radio and films, were in their infancy, the Canadian actor-playwright was a significant presence in the popular theater. He wrote thirty-four plays, twenty-six of which were produced on Broadway, acted in many of them, and moved to Hollywood to become a writer-director. A native of Morrisburg, Ontario, he was married four times to noted actresses. *Kick In*, his first Broadway play, was an expanded version of the vaudeville skit that brought him from San Francisco to New York in 1913 and starred John Barrymore. Three years later, David Belasco, Broadway's premier impresario, produced a Mack drama. As an actor, Mack created the part of Captain Bartlett in Eugene O'Neill's *Gold* in 1921. Oscar Levant called Mack a "Belasco hack," one of the dramatists writing plays to order for Belasco and his contract stars.

When Mack met Ruby at LaHiff's, he was forty-eight, a man with expressive, almost bulging eyes, who combed his dark hair forward over his high forehead to cover a receding hairline. He was married to his fourth wife, Marjorie Rambeau.

Mack's new play, *The Noose*, was a death-row drama. It told the story of Nickie Elkins, a young man whose involvement with bootleggers has led to him being convicted of murder. As the curtain rises on the first act, Nickie is awaiting execution and two women, a society lady and a chorus girl, are in love with him. Helen Flint would play the female lead, the society lady. Mack cast George Nash as the bad guy, and for the Governor chose Lester Lonergan. His choice for the leading role of the noble convict was Rex Cherryman, an exciting young face on Broadway who had made his New York debut two seasons earlier in *The Valley of Content* opposite Rambeau. The handsome Cherryman came to *The Noose* fresh from *Downstream*, a little-remembered play that nevertheless established him as a promising newcomer. Before that he had made a noted impression as the young lawyer opposite Carroll McComas in a revival of the 1908 drawing-room drama *Madame X*.

Walda and Mae got to go to Pittsburgh for out-of-town tryouts with Ruby. The three friends spent Ruby's nineteenth birthday competing for the part of Dot, the chorus girl with the six lines in the third act. Walda didn't make it and returned to New York. Ruby got the part, and Mae was cast as a second chorus girl in the second-act bootleg cabaret.

Ruby was happy with her walk-on and with watching Rex Cherryman rehearse. Later in life she would tell how her Brooklyn accent made her insecure, how she went around saying she wasn't sure she had the voice for acting. In fact, she had already declaimed it on radio. In 1922, Marcus Loew had decided that if he owned one of those new radio stations, vaudeville players performing in Loews theaters could advertise their acts. He bought WHN and had headliners like Eddie Cantor and Mae West perform on radio. With airtime to fill, aspiring actors were invited to go on the air. Ruby Stevens recited poetry.

Ruby thought *The Noose* was wonderful. Mack liked what she tried to do and began showing her how to take advantage of entrances and exits. "I was temperamental, but I was scared," she would recall. "I told him I couldn't act, that it was hopeless. I couldn't and what's more, I wouldn't. Then Mr. Mack did a turnabout and in front of the entire company said I was a chorus girl and would always be a chorus girl, would live like a chorus girl, so to hell with me! It worked, I yelled back that I could act."

Ed Kennedy was sure she was in love with Mack. Her eyes were not on their playwright-director, however, but on the leading man. Cherryman looked older than his twenty-eight years. Ruby thought he was full of talent. She loved his matinee-idol looks and sense of humor, but, she soon realized, so did other women. Besides, he was married and had a son, although his wife was trying to divorce him.

The Pittsburgh tryout was a disaster. The society woman's third-act plea with the Governor didn't go over with the preview audience. The *Pittsburgh Gazette* review mentioned that "Barbara Stanwyck, as Dot, did an unexpected bit of genuine pathos." The *Pittsburgh Press* called the play "overworked" and never mentioned her. Clearly, there would be no New Haven engagement en route to New York.

Instead of giving up, however, Mack opted for extensive changes. The preview audience—and perhaps the *Gazette*'s critic—made him realize the pathos would be more riveting if it is the chorus girl who pleads with the Governor. "It's got to be the chorus girl who pleads with the Governor," he told the cast and the less-than-enthusiastic financial backers. "She's got to carry the third act."

This was bad news for Ruby. "Naturally the expanded part called for a real actress. I could manage six lines, but carry a big scene through a whole act? No one thought I could possibly do it. No one but Bill Mack."

The backers agreed to give Mack two days to whip the play into shape.

Mack wrote an emotional monologue in which Ruby admits to the Governor that Nickie doesn't love her. She hopes she will be allowed to bury Nick in a little cemetery and tell his deaf ears all the things she hasn't dared tell him. Moved, the Governor tells her Nickie isn't dead, that there has been a stay of execution. Dot begs the Governor not to ever, ever tell Nickie of her visit.

She would recall the forty-eight hours as living hell. "Bill Mack was going over and over and over the new third act with me. Except for catnaps backstage, I didn't sleep at all. He hammered every line, every inflection, every gesture of the part into my memory. I was too tired and too terrified to think for myself. All I could do was go, like a robot, through the part as he told me to. Toward the end I broke down and wept from exhaustion and nerves and fright." It was no use, she told him. He couldn't expect her to learn to act in forty-eight hours. It was all right when he was there, but what would happen on opening night when she'd be all alone on the stage?

"You'll do it when the time comes because you'll have to," he answered.

The rehearsals continued. "He taught me how to walk, taught me nuances, taught me tricks to use and not to use." Satisfied with the rewrites and recasting the heroine, Mack and his backers aimed for a mid-October Broadway opening.

There are at least two versions of how Ruby became Barbara Stanwyck. In one account, Mack decided to change her stage name because Ruby Stevens, he told her, sounded too much like a stripper. After glancing at an old poster hanging in the green room of the Belasco Theatre advertising the English actress Jane Stanwyck waving her rebel flag in *Barbara Frietchie*, Mack coupled the last name of the actress and the first name of the title to make a stage name for Ruby. In her own retelling, she would remember coming into the green room and seeing Mack talking to a white-haired person she thought was a clergyman.

Mack introduced her.

"Yes, I've been watching you," said David Belasco. "I'll give you a new name as a gift. 'Barbara' from *Barbara Frietchie*—on that program there. And 'Stanwyck' after Jane Stanwyck, a mighty good actress." It was the only time Ruby met the then seventy-two-year-old Belasco, who thrust the American theater toward greater emotionalism and realism.

Ruby liked her stage name and thought it sounded elegant.

The Noose opened October 20, 1926, at the Hudson Theatre on Forty-fourth Street and Broadway. The new Barbara Stanwyck sent a wire to Mildred to come and see her at the first matinee. The telegram, which was signed

Ruby, failed to mention that she didn't appear until the third act. Since the program listed no Ruby Stevens and her sister didn't appear in the first two acts, Mildred left the theater just before Barbara/Ruby made her entrance. In another version of the story, Barbara invited several people from her old Brooklyn neighborhood. Tickets were waiting for them at the box office, her telegrams said. When she came onstage and saw strangers in the seats she had paid for, she felt utterly forlorn. The explanation was her new name. Her friends had shown up, but when they didn't see Ruby Stevens on the playbill, they thought they had blundered into the wrong theater or that they had got tickets meant for someone else. They quickly sold the tickets on the sidewalk.

The *New York Times* called *The Noose* "melodrama of a slightly older model." The play occasionally lingered too long over situations, the paper said, "but it is good entertainment when it gets going, and is further to be recommended for several good performances." Dorothy [sic] Stanwyck was mentioned in the last paragraph for her "good work." The *New York Telegram* was more generous: "There is an uncommonly fine performance by Barbara Stanwyck, who not only does the Charleston step of a dancehall girl gracefully, but knows how to act, a feature which somehow with her comely looks, seems kind of superfluous. After this girl breaks down and sobs out her unrequited love for the young bootlegger in that genuinely moving scene in the last act, of course, there was nothing for the Governor to do but to reprieve the boy. If he hadn't, the weeping audience would probably have yelled till he did." The *New York Telegraph* published a production photo of Cherryman and Stanwyck. The *New York Sun* and the *Newark Telegraph* gave it all to the leading man. The *Sun* called Cherryman's portrayal of the convict "warm and sympathetic," and the *Telegraph* said, "Cherryman runs away with every part of the play that he appears in despite the sentimental treatment he must give his lines." Elisha Cook, Jr., who became a "perennial juvenile" on stage and screen, would never forget the new Barbara Stanwyck in *The Noose*: "She had a scene—she made me vomit—they were going to electrocute her husband [sic], and she had a scene with the Governor, that she could have the guy's body. I went down to the bathroom and vomited, she was so great in that scene. I'll never forget it. If anybody influenced me, she did."

Love is a leap of faith, a risk not always welcomed by very young women all on their own. Every night the new Barbara Stanwyck declaimed her love for a condemned man who couldn't return it. Every night Rex Cherryman stood in the wings and listened to her beg the Governor never to let him know the depth of her feelings. Offstage she knew nothing about permanence and everything about ad-libbed happiness and hedged bets. Edward Kennedy wanted to marry her, but *The Noose* made acting too important for her to consider marriage. Without ever quite saying Rex was her first lover, she would remember him as the first man who understood her, the first man she loved.

"It was my first chance at dramatic acting and everything enchanted me," she would remember. "Rex was handsome and young and had great talent and good humor. Ed Kennedy hadn't quite given me up. He was jealous of Willard Mack, but he was wrong there. If he had to be jealous of anyone, he should have focused on Rex. I adored him."

The Noose ran for nine months; 197 performances.

Barbara and Rex spent a busy autumn together while Rex's wife, Esther, obtained a divorce. Rex was from Grand Rapids, Michigan. He owed his love of the theater to his mother, Myrtle Koon Cherryman, who was a dramatic reader in Grand Rapids. Barbara thought everything about Rex was vital and convincing. Her childhood had taught her that getting close to someone was difficult. But Rex was everything little Ruby had wanted, someone to trust, to depend on. To her he was confidence and energy personified. The ovation that swept up over them when they stood hand in hand and took bows carried her to heights she had never dreamed of.

Both were eager to please, to see their careers flourish. Rex told her how he had acted in Hollywood movies before being signed to a four-year contract by a San Francisco stock company. His breakthrough had come in Chicago, where he appeared in *Topsy and Eva* for one year. Rex had met Esther Lamb when he was twenty-two, and he worked in a bank briefly before deciding to become an actor and take off for Los

Angeles. The marriage had been a mistake, but he and Esther remained on friendly terms.

Mack set to work writing his next play, telling Barbara she could have the lead. *A Free Soul* would be about a young woman who falls in love with her attorney father's criminal client. The new drama wasn't ready when *The Noose* closed in June 1927, so Barbara went back to the chorus line, this time in *A Night in Spain*. In August, Rex got the costarring role in *The Trial of Mary Dugan* opposite silver-blond Texan Ann Harding. His performance of the young brother who successfully defends his sister from a murder charge was called outstanding when the Bayard Veiller drama opened in September.

Film companies tested Barbara. One was First National, soon to be taken over by Warner Brothers. She reported to director Joseph C. Boyle for a screen test for *Broadway Nights*, a silent movie filming at William Randolph Hearst's Cosmopolitan studio at Second Avenue and 125th Street. Sam Hardy had been chosen to play the leading man, a gambling Tin Pan Alley tunesmith.

The scenario of this obscurity-to-fame programmer was by Forrest Halsey, Gloria Swanson's favorite screenwriter, and the first openly gay man Barbara knew. The *Broadway Nights* story was a portent of Barbara's relationship with men. Sam Hardy's character was named Johnny Fay. Johnny and his wife, Fanny, live a roller-coaster relationship of unfulfilled needs and mutual dependence. Fanny constantly implores her Johnny to give up his addiction to dice, and various characters make comments on whether Fanny is a nobody without Johnny or she is everything and he nothing more than a stupid gambler. Where would he be without her beauty and dancing talent? Where would she be without his tuneful music?

Boyle explained the role demanded that Barbara cry. Would she please cry when he yelled "Action"? In *The Noose*, she had cried every night on cue, but after the director disappeared behind the camera and yelled "Action," she was unable to get the tears to flow.

"Cut," Boyle shouted.

Would she please try by holding raw onion under her eyes?

Nothing helped.

Stanwyck didn't get the part. Lois Wilson, famous for the 1923 epic *The Covered Wagon*, did. Barbara, however, accepted the smaller role of the heroine's backstage pal. Sylvia Sidney, the quintessential proletarian princess of the 1930s, also made her film debut in *Broadway Nights*.

Four months after the electrifying premiere of Warner Brothers' *Jazz Singer*, studios tried to dispose of millions of dollars' worth of silent merchandise by adding sound in some form so that theater owners could advertise that their attraction talked. Fans quickly became adept at deducing from the ads the degree to which silents were being made audible. "Sound effects and music" meant recorded orchestral accompaniments plus various bell ringings and door knockings. "With sound and dialogue" usually meant that the players remained silent for five reels, became briefly loquacious in the sixth, only to relapse into silence in the final reel.

Broadway Nights was released June 28, 1927, with sound effects and background music. Stanwyck never mentioned the picture. Her screen debut, she felt, was in sound films.*

Besides, why care about *Broadway Nights* when the real Broadway theater was so much more exciting? Two hundred and sixty-eight attractions were produced on Broadway in 1927—the highest number ever—over two hundred and fifty productions opened in 1928, and the road was in a healthy condition. Cut-rate ticket agencies allowed new plays to attain moderate runs, and promising young players elbowed each other to assure the theater's future. Ironically, it was *Broadway Nights* that gave the twenty-year-old Stanwyck her stage triumph.

Playwright George Manker Watters had seen the new Barbara Stanwyck in *The Noose* and suggested her for the feminine lead in the play he and Arthur Hopkins were writing together. Hopkins was the producer of the decade's most electrifying play—Maxwell Anderson's and Laurence Stalling's antiwar drama *What Price Glory?* Its frank presentation of the profanity and brutality of soldiers had made it the

*See Filmography (page 434) for detailed credits and thumbnail summary of all Barbara Stanwyck movies.

sensation of 1924. With new plays by Sidney Howard, Elmer Rice, John Howard Lawson, and George S. Kaufman, Hopkins proved that "new" drama could be produced commercially on Broadway. His greatest feat was putting on a cycle of classical plays, including Tolstoy's *Redemption*, Shakespeare's *Hamlet* and *Richard III*, which firmly established John Barrymore as the greatest actor of his generation.

Hopkins leased the Plymouth Theatre on Forty-fifth Street from Lee and J. J. Shubert. A short, plump man with a round, red face, he summoned Stanwyck to his drab cubbyhole of an office off the mezzanine. When she entered he was seated behind a rolltop desk wearing his trademark derby and bow tie.

> "I sat down and waited," she would remember. "Had I not been told he was a man of few words, I might have walked out. But he finally leaned back in his swivel chair and told me the name of the play was *Burlesque*, a backstage drama he had written himself with George Manker Watters. He gave me a copy of the script. He didn't actually *offer* me the part, but told me his terms and his production schedule. Apparently, it was up to me to find out when the rehearsals started and to show up on the first day."

The heroine of the play-within-a-play is Bonny, the leading lady in *Parisian Widows* going into rehearsals in a Midwestern burlesque theater. Bonny is married to Skid, the show's premiere comedian, but when he gets a job in a big Broadway musical, his ardor for his wife begins to wane. Without Bonny, he falls prey to bootleggers and after one notorious party loses his engagement. In the last act, he returns to the burlesque show and is reunited with Bonny. A beefy cattleman puts up the money to revive *Parisian Widows*, and with the road company's stage manager, company manager, songwriter, and a fireman, Bonny and Skid whip the show into shape and end up performing it in Paterson, New Jersey.

Rehearsals had started when Hopkins hired Hal Skelly to play Skid. Skelly was a gangly song-and-dance man who had studied for the priesthood in Davenport, Iowa, before running off with a musical comedy company. He was a screwy, skinny

Falstaff with an enormous appetite for fun and frolics. He had toured Hawaii, Japan, and the Philippines and made his Broadway breakthrough in *Orange Blossoms*.

Hopkins liked the Stanwyck-Skelly chemistry of the funny hoofer and his proud faithful wife. Barbara knew lots of women in show business like Bonny, women looking after men who badly needed to be looked after. Hopkins thought Barbara had the "tough poignancy" Bonny needed. Later, he would say she expressed emotions more easily than any actress since Pauline Lord.

Barbara's old escort Oscar Levant was hired to play the company's songwriter and quickly talked Hopkins into letting him score the second act. Since Barbara and her friends had made him their mascot, Oscar had been to London, accompanying the classical saxophonist Rudy Wiedoeft. Besides cutting records and partying with the Mayfair crowd, he had made a brief appearance in fellow American Frank Fay's vaudeville act at the Palladium. London and a side trip to Paris had given the already caustic Oscar added brilliance. *Burlesque* was his first try at acting.

Burlesque opened September 1, 1927, at the Plymouth Theatre. The *New York Times*'s Brooks Atkinson was favorable. "None of the details of dialogue or background matches the resourcefulness of the acting," he wrote. "As the comedian in question, Mr. Skelly gives a glowing performance of fleeting character portrayal and a whirl of eccentric makeup and bits of hoofing and clowning. Miss Stanwyck, as his wife, plays with genuine emotion and kicks her way skillfully through the chorus numbers." In his *New York World* review, Alexander Woollcott called her performance "touching and true."

Barbara worked hard to improve herself. Hopkins coached her for interviews that made her sound mature and introspective. In a *New York Review* interview she not only analyzed Bonny's love for Skid, but marveled at the power of stagecraft that could sharpen the acuity of playgoers and make them realize that "life holds a great deal more for us than we thought."

She looked good in a body stocking and modeled a home exercise machine advertisement. With the Health Builder's oscillator belt around her svelte buttocks for a "massage-vibratory treatment better than a skilled masseur," the ad identified the model as "Barbara Stanwyck, leading actress in the well-known New York success 'Burlesque.'" She was insecure when the cast was invited to parties and often begged off. "If we were invited to a chic party such as Jules Glaenzer gave in those days, Barbara couldn't abide going," Levant would remember. "Glaenzer would have George Gershwin, Dick Rodgers, half a dozen piano players, all the popular show girls in New York and a generous smattering of Society. They appalled Stanwyck."

She was not the first young woman who tried to please by being different, who assigned to herself the role of buddy, chum, and sidekick because she didn't want to be dependent on men, on their appetites, their whims, their money. In any case, *Burlesque*'s leading lady and second-banana piano man had plenty of time to get to know each other. The musical ran for 332 performances.

The Trial of Mary Dugan opened a week after *Burlesque*, and critics called Rex Cherryman's performance sensational. His role as the younger brother who defends his sister from a murder charge in Bayard Veiller's courtroom drama vaulted him to the rank of Broadway's best-known new actors. Ann Harding received Hollywood offers. Rex had already tried the movies. He wanted to bide his time and settled in for a long run.

Rex and Barbara were a popular twosome. He found her scrappy, streetwise gumption stimulating and different; she thought of herself as awkward and was flattered by his adult consideration for her. Theater folk assumed they would get married. But as if to undercut her feelings for Rex she would later say that although "everything about him was so vivid," the reason she fell in love with him was perhaps his ability to act, to project.

The Trial of Mary Dugan was a hit, and Rex signed on for the season. He agreed to consider producer Sam H. Harris's offer to go on tour with the play in the fall. Rex turned thirty during the summer of 1928, when illness forced him to skip a few performances of *Mary Dugan*. Doctors said he needed complete rest and recommended a sea voyage. He settled on a quick trip to Paris. Barbara went to see Hopkins about getting time off after Harris gave Rex a three-week vacation and Rex signed on to resume his role in Chicago on August 31.

Barbara accompanied Rex to the French Line pier. He was suffering a cold, but decided to sail aboard the S.S. *De Grasse* as planned. See you in Paris, they said as they hugged. Rex ran up the gangplank, and Barbara waved as the huge ocean liner slid into the Hudson River.

Rex died aboard the *De Grasse* August 10, shortly before the ship docked at Le Havre. Septic poisoning was ruled the cause of death.

One hundred and ninety-seven times she had declared her love for Rex and begged the Governor to be allowed to bury the man she loved. There was no repeat of *The Noose*. Cherryman's manager, A. H. Woods, had his European representative carry out Rex's wish to be cremated. Internment would be in France. Cast members of *Burlesque* rallied around Barbara, told her it was tough luck.

She screwed on her other face, the one that said she could handle it, that she was in charge, dammit. She overcame her shock by doing what she had always done—rely on herself. She riveted her concentration on the one thing that soothed and made her forget—work. Finding deliverance by digging deeper into her career was to become a lifelong characteristic when adversity struck.

5

Faysie

"Bring Stanwyck," said Frank Fay. "I'll leave two seats at the door." Oscar Levant grinned. The two of them might be friends of sorts, but Oscar only knew Fay as a tightwad. Fay was Irish Catholic. He ritualistically crossed himself whenever he spent any money or passed a church. Levant was Jewish and irreverent to the point of saying Judaism had its lamentable sides. Fay disliked Jewish comedians.

The Great Faysie, as he styled himself, was a cocky, conceited, and outstanding wit of vaudeville. A week at New York's Palace Theatre was every vaudevillian's dream, two weeks an accomplishment. Fay was the only song-and-dance man to play ten successive weeks at the Palace, at $17,500 a week in 1925 dollars. Fay had an acute sense of people and developed the role of master of ceremonies into an art of repartee and humor. His specialty was the studied insult, the raised eyebrow followed by a suggestive double entendre or a cutting quip. His parody of the song "Tea for Two" (who wants to bake a cake at three in the morning) was a classic.

Levant and Fay had met in London in 1926 when Frank had a monthlong engagement at the Palladium and Oscar appeared in Fay's act, accompanying his songs on the piano. At the end of the engagement, Frank and Oscar flew to Paris. This was one year before Charles Lindbergh's transatlantic flight—and Frank, according to Oscar, had crossed himself all the way across the English Channel. Some thirty thousand Americans were living in Paris, painters, writers, composers, and plain loafers. Obligatory stops on the American-in-Paris circuit included Harry's Bar in the Rue Daunou, the Ritz, the elegant and aristocratic dance hall owned by Harry Pilcer where Josephine Baker performed as a favor to the new American manager, Elsa Maxwell, and the Café du Dôme, where Oscar wanted to meet George Antheil, the most avant-garde of the American expatriate composers. Fay had Levant pay for every theater they attended, although one night Oscar outfoxed Frank and treated himself to a performance of *Die Walküre* at the Opéra. Oscar loved the racy Left Bank Bohemia and called Frank a Babbitt for being hopelessly motherhood and apple pie despite his bluster. "There was an aura of shabby worldliness about Frank," Levant would write. "Frank was so strictured, both in his devotion to Catholicism and right-wing political beliefs, that even in later years the mention of Helen Hayes—an arch-Republican herself—brought forth a contumacious volley of: 'She's a Red . . . she's a Pink.'" When Oscar ran out of money, they had sailed home—Frank, with money remaining, in first class on a fast ocean liner, Oscar on a slower ship.

Levant brought Stanwyck to Fay's show. The pianist would remember the performance as being one of Fay's Palace shows; Barbara would say Oscar took her to Texas Guinan's newest supper club, where Fay was the headliner.

After the show, Oscar took Barbara backstage.

It was, on Stanwyck's part, infatuation, if not love, at first sight. She felt so utterly lost, so totally alone in the world that, to the amazement of Levant, she threw herself at Fay. "Barbara fell madly in love with him," Levant would write in his memoirs. "She went for Fay in such a complete way—I never saw anything to equal it."

What vulnerable twenty-one-year-old Barbara saw in the thirty-one-year-old Frank she saw without misgivings. What she saw was a natural take-charge temperament, a mesmerizing, complicated guy who never missed a beat. Frank was fun to be with. He was a guy who could bolster her, who might care for her, support her. What overwhelmed her was his cocksure grin, his barbs, and his loud humor. What he saw was a flattering mirror soaking him up, a lovely chorine sharp enough to match his gab, hungry enough for love to be swept off her feet.

It was "Hi there, Frankie" and "Hello, Mr. Fay!" from

every corner on Broadway. Frank saw something to laugh at in everything and never let anyone close enough to criticize him. And he was a charmer. He had two marriages behind him—to Frances White, a popular torch singer, and Gladys Lee Buchanan, an actress. His romances and escapades were part of the gossip of the day, as was his Irish gab.

Born November 17, 1897, in San Francisco, Francis Anthony Donner was the son of a vaudeville couple. He had been in show business from the age of four, and, like Buster Keaton and John Huston, his first stage appearance was as a prop in his parents' act. He had played a potato bug, an elf, or a teddy bear—he claimed he couldn't remember which—in Victor Herbert's *Babes in Toyland*. Joe Frisco, a little dancer and comic, taught him step routines. Fay did road shows in the Midwest and made his Broadway debut in *The Passing Show of 1918*, in which he starred with Fred and Adele Astaire, Charles Ruggles, and Nita Naldi.

Fay married torch singer and *Ziegfeld Follies* headliner Frances White. The wedding took place while he starred with Joe E. Brown in *Jim Jam Jems* and she was a gorgeous, short-haired flapper in *The Hotel Mouse*. She was famous for "knocking down a grand a week" singing "Mississippi." They divorced in 1919. Her name made a blip in the press in 1930 when she was arrested for not having $3.50 to pay a New York cabdriver. Fay married his second wife, Gladys Lee Buchanan, on the road. He claimed he attended mass every day, wore a Saint Christopher's medal, and always tipped his hat when he passed a church, which didn't prevent him from divorcing three wives and fathering at least one illegitimate child. As a young man Fred Astaire was mad about the famous *Follies* girl Eleanor Holm. "Lay off that one," Fay admonished the dancer, "she's Faysie's." Astaire was so scared he never went near Holm again.

Drinking and gambling were part of Fay's bravado. Being either flush or dead broke went with the persona. In 1921, he had filed a voluntary petition for bankruptcy, declaring his only asset to be $100 worth of clothes. Two years later, he bounced back in the Shuberts' Artists and Models.

Frank gloried in praise and was resentful of criticism, which he considered carping or enviousness. He wasn't much liked by other comedians. "Fay's friends could be counted on the missing arm of a one-armed man," said Milton Berle. But they admired his gall and told the story of his day in court on a business matter. His attorney coached him to answer only what was asked of him, not to volunteer anything.

When the opposing attorney had Fay on the stand and asked for his profession, Frank answered, "I'm the greatest comedian in the world."

Later, Fay's attorney said, "Frank, I told you to answer simply. The other lawyer asked, 'What's your profession?' How could you answer, 'I'm the greatest comedian in the world'?"

Said Fay, "I was under oath, wasn't I?"

Anything for a laugh. Comedy came first for Faysie, ahead of friends, family, or peace of mind.

Barbara would admit she trailed after Frank Fay like a stray pup after the news of Rex's death—and got about as much attention. He took her to lunch at Sardi's. Frank took bows, Frank said howdy all around, and Frank held court. He was everything she imagined her father would have been. In Frank's company her lack of education didn't matter. Before *Burlesque* closed on Broadway and went on the road, Levant realized Fay had enough ascendancy over her to dictate her career moves.

Hollywood scouts were combing stage doors and the offices of actors' agents. The switch to talkies had Hollywood studio executives coming to New York to scout for actors with voices for dialogue who were willing to sign lush contracts and come to California. Everybody heard stories of soundmen with earphones plugged into black magic boxes lording over the talkie movie sets and of film stars from Gloria Swanson to Greta Garbo hesitating to face the new microphones. But everybody also heard the money being offered promising young players with stage-trained voices. Stanwyck's fellow actors of the 1928 Broadway season about to head west included Ann Harding and her husband, Harry Bannister, Claudette Colbert, Clark Gable, Spencer Tracy, Archie Leach (Cary Grant), Muni Weisenfreund (Paul Muni), Miriam Hopkins, Lee Tracy, Chester Morris, Mae West, and Aline MacMahon.

After seeing *Burlesque* one night Louis B. Mayer, the big boss at Metro-Goldwyn-Mayer, decided Stanwyck had picture potential. As Mayer's wife, Margaret, was related to Levant's mother and the Mayers were staying with Oscar's aunt and uncle, Levant took them to Texas Guinan's supper club, where, after the last *Burlesque* curtain call, Barbara could be found every night.

When the pianist introduced the movie mogul to Stanwyck, Fay became irate. Sensing that the physical Mayer had a terrible temper when provoked, Frank waited until Mayer left before threatening to punch Oscar's nose for even introducing Barbara to the MGM boss. Stanwyck's introduction to movie acting in *Broadway Nights* had not been the most thrilling experience. She told Levant to tell his distant relative she wasn't interested.

Famous Players–Lasky Paramount Pictures bought the rights to *Burlesque* and invited Stanwyck, Skelly, and Levant to test for the screen version. Hal and Oscar jumped at the chance to go to Hollywood. Barbara said no. She didn't want to be three thousand miles from Frank. His whirlwind courtship of her was flattering and persistent, and she wanted to make a big sacrifice for him. She was ready to give up what she loved most—acting. He left New York for an engagement in St. Louis as emcee at the Missouri Theatre at the same time *Burlesque* went on the road.

By telegram, he proposed.

Frank's allure and intuition would turn into dangerous attributes, but Barbara got on a train to St. Louis. Frank was what she wanted—family, home, security, someone who would take care of her. Less than four weeks after she had waved au revoir to Rex at New York's French Line pier, she married Frank in St. Louis. The August 26, 1928, wedding took place in the early afternoon at the home of the St. Louis recorder of deeds, William Tamme. At 5:00 P.M., Mrs. Frank Fay boarded a train taking her back to Newark, New Jersey, to begin the *Burlesque* tour. Frank stayed with his St. Louis engagement.

Six months later they were on their way to Hollywood.

"Pretty little Barbara Stanwyck, who walked right out of a night club into a spectacular stage success in *Burlesque*, has been signed by United Artists," the *New York Times* reported on February 28, 1929. "Miss Stanwyck first came into notice when *Burlesque* was hailed as a sensational hit. At the time Famous Players–Lasky bought *Burlesque*. Hundreds of people suggested Little Miss Stanwyck for the role that she created on the stage, but Famous Players had its own rising star, Nancy Carroll, so why import a new face?"

Joseph Schenck had seen Barbara in *Burlesque* and had come backstage to say, "If you ever want to do a movie part, just telephone me." The new Mrs. Frank Fay did because now her husband was also being courted by Hollywood. Schenck signed her for *The Locked Door*, the film adaptation of Channing Pollock's popular 1919 play *The Sign on the Door*. With the advent of sound, Hollywood scouts also combed Broadway for filmable properties. Pollock was a prolific playwright and critic, librettist, and comedy writer. The role was a stock character Barbara would impersonate many times—a woman with a past.

She was to play Anne, a young secretary who accepts the invitation of her boss's son Frank to dine with him. Police are watching the private supper club he chooses, and before the dessert the place is raided. A flash photo catches Anne and Frank as they are arrested. Eventually, they jump bail. Five years later Anne is married to a widower with an attractive eighteen-year-old daughter. Frank reappears, in pursuit this time, of Anne's stepdaughter. Hearing the girl in danger alone in her room with Frank, Anne barges in. As the daughter flees, Anne's husband is announced. Anne hides and overhears her husband storm in, already incensed at Frank for having seduced the wife of a friend. The men scuffle and Frank is killed.

Placing the gun in the dead man's hand, the husband hangs a DO NOT DISTURB sign on the door and leaves. He locks the door from the outside, inadvertently locking his wife in with the dead man. Police arrive. Anne is arrested and exposure seems imminent, when, by a lucky twist, she is saved.

Barbara and Frank traveled west with the plain, oafish-looking Schenck, who insisted his surname was pronounced "Skenk." The four-and-a-half-day train ride allowed her to promote Frank with the United Artists boss. Fay undermined her efforts, however, playing the smart-ass know-it-all. "We're not exactly broke coming out," he grinned in an oft-repeated joke of his. "In fact, I have $8 or $9 in my wallet." Turning serious, he said he was going to take Hollywood by storm. If the talkies needed people with stage presence, how could the studios afford *not* to hire Broadway's favorite son? Yes, he would be negotiating with the studios from a position of strength. We have no record of what Schenck answered to Fay's braggadocio. If only Fay had shut up, he might have learned something about the picture business he was sure he would conquer.

D. W. Griffith, Charles Chaplin, Mary Pickford, and her husband, Douglas Fairbanks, and the two newest investors, Gloria Swanson and Samuel Goldwyn, were the artist-owners of United Artists. As head of UA, Schenck was the real power, just as his brother Nicholas was the ultimate authority behind MGM's corporate parent, Loews Inc. The Schenck brothers had come from Russia at the age of twelve and ten and climbed from drugstore clerks to drugstore owners to controlling partners of an amusement park and aides to Marcus Loew. In 1917, they had gone separate ways—Nick to become Loew's heir apparent, Joe to produce Fatty Arbuckle slapsticks. Like Irving Thalberg and Samuel Goldwyn, Joe had married an actress—Norma Talmadge.

Joe and Norma were the first mogul-star couple, the first to build on the Santa Monica beach. They now had Jesse and Bess Lasky, he the monocled studio boss of Famous Players–Lasky Paramount Pictures, as neighbors. William R. Hearst and Margaret and Louis B. Mayer lived further down the road near Irving Thalberg and Norma Shearer. Joe casually invited the great and the raffish, his wife asked whomever she pleased, and neither cared about the mix.

It was Fairbanks who had convinced Schenck to become the administrative head of UA. Fairbanks was the only one of the "united artists" besides Goldwyn to know anything about cost, distribution deals, options, loan guarantees, film rentals. The talkies demanded actors with stage experience, and the coming of sound was shaking up the industry, but the fundamentals were the same. Low-budget westerns, action pictures, and stunt thrillers were still the bread and butter of the picture business. Movies had a life expectancy of half a week, as most theater owners changed their playbills on Mondays and Fridays. More interesting from a financial point of view were two other classifications: "Rialto specials," films that ran as long as the public wanted them, and the several annual "road-show" pictures that lent prestige and goodwill to the industry.

Moviegoing had become a worldwide obsession in the mid-twenties, when almost every one of the 740 films made each year in Hollywood earned fat profits in the world's fifty thousand movie theaters (nearly a third of the cinemas were in the United States and Canada). Two years after the sensational debut of *The Jazz Singer*, sound was both a fact of life and a frightfully expensive upgrade of technology and talent. The April issue of *Photoplay* counted 1,600 theaters wired for sound, and its poll of moviegoers showed 90 percent favored talkies. If exhibitors faced huge expenditures—installing sound cost as much as $20,000 per cinema—the studios faced even bigger outlays, from soundproofing stages to retraining technicians and on-screen talent.

Barbara thought Schenck was returning from a yearlong absence when the welcoming throng at Union Station included, besides his wife and the press, Mary Pickford, Douglas Fairbanks, and Irving Thalberg. When one of the VIPs asked Schenck if he had enjoyed his trip and he replied, "Three weeks is a short time to enjoy New York," Barbara realized she was in a land of new rituals. Here, the natives paid tribute to a returning king even if he had been gone only three weeks.

6

Hollywood

The Fays arrived in Los Angeles in early March 1929. A United Artists publicist met them at Union Station and piled them into a studio car that took them up long straight streets lined with shady trees. Hollywood was sparkling and sunny. Between private residences, the first office buildings were lining Hollywood Boulevard. Frank and Barbara came down with a severe case of longing for midtown Manhattan. He felt California was the end of the world. She was ready to take the first train back.

She was up early the next morning, however. Her first meeting was with Arthur Lyons, a talent agent Frank had lined up before they left New York. Lyons proved to be a resourceful agent. Before he took her to the United Artists lot, he told her he would demand a radio clause for her. That way, he explained, if she was ever suspended she could pick up pocket money working on "Silver Theatre" or "Lux Radio Theatre."

UA was located at the former Pickford-Fairbanks Studio on Santa Monica Boulevard, and Lyons was smartly whisked through the main entrance on Formosa Avenue. No one at UA had a radio clause, but Schenck agreed to Lyons's demand.

"Someone will take you over to meet George," Schenck told Barbara, dismissing her and her agent. Lyons wished her good luck and climbed into his automobile. Five minutes later Barbara met her director, who immediately plunged into a lengthy discourse on the enormous difficulties of filmmaking with microphones.

The forty-four-year-old George Fitzmaurice and his camera operator, Ouida Bergère, were a husband-and-wife team, French immigrants who always worked together. Fitzmaurice was convinced audiences demanded more than action, that filmmakers had to know psychology. "To incorporate human nature into a picture you must understand the science of mental phenomena, for it is this science that is the guiding hand of realistic action," he said in 1916. He had directed two films in Islington, London, in 1922, and his attention to character analysis enormously impressed his young assistant, Alfred Hitchcock.

Fitzmaurice had misgivings about sound. He was no more eager to "go sound" and risk his reputation than D. W. Griffith, Charlie Chaplin, Cecil B. DeMille, Erich von Stroheim, Allan Dwan, Henry King, William Wellman, and King Vidor. Chaplin positively hated sound, and Dwan wanted to believe talkies were just a fad. Directors sensed that sound created a new dynamic on the screen, and many of them issued brave statements that soon proved either wrongheaded or downright silly. Like the stars and writers, directors had to prove their talents all over again.

To Barbara, Fitzmaurice was the director of Pola Negri in *The Cheat* and Rudolph Valentino in *The Son of the Sheik*, the man who had worked with all the beauties of the silents—Norma Talmadge, Vilma Banky, Billie Dove. How would he make her beautiful? "He kept arranging all kinds of drapery and tapestries behind me, and finally he shook his head and screamed, 'Dammit, I can't make you beautiful no matter what I do. I put tapestries and draperies behind you and nothing helps.' So I said, 'They sent for me. I didn't send for them.'"

The Locked Door was no low-budget programmer. Rod La Rocque, a Latin lover type from Quebec who was taller than Rudolph Valentino, had top billing as Frank. La Rocque had attracted notice in DeMille's 1923 spectacular, *The Ten Commandments*, as Gloria Swanson's costar and lover the following year, and as Joan Crawford's husband in *Our Modern Maidens*. He had made his talkie debut opposite Norma Shearer and Marie Dressler in *Let Us Be Gay* and was happily married to Samuel Goldwyn's star Vilma Banky. William "Stage" Boyd—so named so as not to be confused with the

William Boyd who became Hopalong Cassidy—was cast as Stanwyck's husband, and Betty Bronson, who had played the title role in *Peter Pan* in 1924, as her stepdaughter. Mack Swain and Zasu Pitts, who dated from the birth of the movies, rounded out the cast.

Fitzmaurice's reputation rested on his knack for unearthing promising scripts and for his way with actors, but on *The Locked Door* he had little time for his leading lady. "I staggered through it," Barbara would recall. "It was all one big mystery to me." The free-flowing action and continuity that had become second nature to Fitzmaurice during fifty-nine movies was abruptly replaced by a static, stagelike technique because the cameras had to be immured in soundproof booths and the microphone—"King Mike" and "Terrible Mike" to chafing studio crews—was at first immovable and all action had to be geared to its location. Fitzmaurice tore his hair in frenzy when his dramatic efforts were vetoed by the sound engineer, a new despot trained by the telephone companies. The sound engineer's only concern was that all conversations be conducted at one voice level.

The Hungarian accent of Vilma Banky made her an early casualty of the microphone; Milton Sills the first suicide. The list of stars playing the waiting game included Greta Garbo, Lillian Gish, and Norma Talmadge. To take the plunge, Gloria Swanson signed Laura Hope Crews, a former Broadway actress, to a $1,000-a-week contract to teach her diction. The opportunities represented by Hollywood stars with uncultured and untrained vocal cords resulted in a second Gold Rush as Crews's Broadway colleagues hurried west as coaches.

The Locked Door sound engineer concealed microphones in flowerpots, dictated where actors could stand to record, and yelled "Cut!" if any actor so much as turned his head away from the mike. Since sound film ran at twenty-four frames per second instead of sixteen, twice as much light was needed to expose the same strip of celluloid. Already nervous actors were soaked to the skin under the heat of the added kilowatts.

The picture was awful. Barbara "projected" too much, and Fitzmaurice was too new to talkies to tone down her stage delivery. When *The Locked Door* was released in January 1930, the film was seen for what it was, an early "all-talker," that is, a statically filmed play about a husband and wife trying to save each other by assuming guilt for a murder. The reviews were generally devastating, and Barbara quipped, "They never should've unlocked that damned thing!"

But *The Locked Door* made one thing clear—Stanwyck's throaty voice and her alluring, all-business delivery were made for the talkies.

Warner Brothers signed Frank Fay. Ann Harding, who had been Rex Cherryman's costar in *The Trial of Mary Dugan*, was signed by Radio-Keith-Orpheum (RKO), and a postcard from Mae Clarke announced *her* signing with Warner Brothers. Hollywood would pay anything to borrow Broadway's zip and smarts because showy talkies were what moviegoers wanted. MGM had set the pace in February by releasing *The Broadway Melody*, its first talkie, to rave reviews and standing-room-only performances. Warner Brothers came out with a two-color Technicolor *The Gold Diggers of Broadway*, Paramount had a plotless extravaganza simply called *Paramount on Parade*, and Fox had *Fox Movietone Follies*. Warners lured Texas Guinan from her supper club, added her to the roster, and planned to release several musicals under the title *The Show of Shows*. Fay was to play the master of ceremonies presenting Warners' artists.

Frank loved being the on-screen emcee, introducing the cast of seventy-seven stars and musical numbers that in one segment included two hundred dancers. John Barrymore delivered the Duke of Gloucester's soliloquy from *Henry VI*, the first time his "voice has come from the shadow." Fay cued in Ted Lewis and his band. He introduced veterans H. B. Warner, Monte Blue, Lupino Lane, and Ben Turpin, stage players Chester Morris and Beatrice Lillie, and, among the new faces, Irene Bordoni, Myrna Loy, Douglas Fairbanks, Jr., and Betty Compton. The director was John G. Adolfi, a veteran of thirty-five silents, who had to struggle not only with sound technicians but with Technicolor engineers. Part of *The Show of Shows* was filmed in the garish new color process.

Frank and Barbara rang in the New Year of 1930 at the Mayfair party at the Biltmore Hotel. Six footmen in white jackets and red satin knee britches greeted the three hundred and fifty guests, who all seemed to arrive at the same time.

The evening was the film colony's copycat affair emulating
Southern California's blueblood society events, and every-
body was there, the stars—Douglas Fairbanks and Mary
Pickford, Dolores Del Rio, Gloria Swanson, Claudette
Colbert, Constance Bennett, Ann Harding, Harold Lloyd,
Buster Keaton, Loretta Young, and the studio bosses—Louis
B. Mayer, Jack Warner, B. P. Schulberg, the diminutive Carl
Laemmle, and William LeBaron. The Mayfair benefited the
Motion Picture Relief Fund, and it had its own built-in snob
appeal. To be invited signaled to a newcomer that he or she
had "arrived."

As Warners' new contractee, Fay and wife were assigned
to the WB table, a few tables from the William Randolph
Hearst–Marion Davies party, which included the Hearst
papers' formidable gossip columnist Louella Parsons. As soon
as they and everybody else had found their seats, the men
crowded into one end of the ballroom and the women came
together in the other end, all to gossip without the restraints
of mixed company. After sitting alone for a while, Barbara
joined the women and, as a newcomer, waited for someone to
initiate a conversation. There was a clock on the mantel. Out
of curiosity, she timed her loneliness. It was exactly forty minutes before anyone spoke to her.

If Frank could use his stage-honed emcee talent to make it in
the movies, why couldn't she? Her wish to sacrifice everything on the altar of marriage was fading. She regretted her
decision not to try for the screen version of *Burlesque* along
with Hal Skelly and Oscar Levant, especially after she learned
she was director John Cromwell's choice.

Cromwell was another relocated Broadway whiz, an actor
turned stage director with only one film under his belt. Their
mutual friend was Helen Flint, who after playing the society
lady in *The Noose* had been Cromwell's leading lady in
Gentlemen of the Press. Cromwell liked Barbara's earthiness
and told her to campaign hard for the role with the
Paramount front office. Too late. Studio chief Jesse Lasky
now wanted Nancy Carroll, who had just scored in the film
Abie's Irish Rose, to star.

The studio retitled the film version of Barbara's stage
success. Because of its association with bawdy songs,

striptease, suggestive dancing, and scantily clad females, the title *Burlesque* was ruled inadmissible by Hollywood's censorship czar Will Hays. Paramount owned *The Dance of Life*, Havelock Ellis's shocking—and then unfilmable—study of sexuality and simply slapped that title on the movie version of the long-running Arthur Hopkins–George Manker Watters show.

Columbia Pictures' feared and fearsome Harry Cohn offered Barbara a one-picture deal to play a bordertown temptress in *Mexicali Rose*. To make up for missing out on *Dance of Life*, she let Arthur Lyons convince her to say yes to the low-budget B picture. The agent insisted that for a new actress *any* footage was good.

Cohn represented shirt-sleeved "Gower Gulch" B-picture filmmaking. Located on Gower Street, Columbia was small, cheap, and dingy, and its boss took pleasure in being mean, rude, and, when he could get away with it, a cheat. A few blocks east on Sunset Boulevard was Warner Brothers, a film factory that had started out as modestly as Columbia. A family business run by Harry and Albert in New York and Jack in Los Angeles, the brothers Warner tried to hire only a few important stars. With the Vitaphone "talking pictures," they vaulted themselves into the major league.

A short, broad man with sharp-cut features and intense blue eyes, Cohn resisted the bigger studios' impulse to move to more spacious quarters. Until his death in 1958, Columbia stayed on Gower Street, swallowing adjacent lots until it occupied the long block between Sunset Boulevard and Fountain Avenue. Cohn, his older brother, Jack, and their friend Joe Brandt were the founding fathers, but by 1929 Harry had wrested control of Columbia from his partners. Except for program westerns, Columbia movies were, as a matter of economics, filmed on interior sets. They were also usually contemporary because Harry felt insecure when he ventured into historical periods. He couldn't afford the list of stars that Paramount and MGM had under contract, but he knew top people could be lured by good scripts. His improvised style and chutzpah were the opposite of the obsessive second-guessing of Irving Thalberg, the boy wonder with a weak heart who was Mayer's number-two man and the

Hollywood producer incarnate. There were no producers at Columbia. And Mayer had to answer to Nicholas Schenck in New York. Cohn answered to no one.

Frank Capra was one director who preferred to work on Gower Street because Cohn was desperate enough to tolerate a young director's bustling ambitions. Harry let his staff make their pictures with much of the freedom the pioneers had enjoyed.

Capra had stumbled into the movies and worked himself up through apprenticeship as a gag writer for Mack Sennett to become Harry Langdon's collaborator. In 1926, he made a promising feature debut as a director with *The Strong Man*, Langdon's second feature. Cohn hired Capra to direct action-adventure quickies for a flat $1,000 a picture. No fewer than seven Capra films were released in 1928. Cohn's attitude toward less ambitious directors ranged from indifferent to brutal. Oddly, his opinion of writers was charitable. The reason, some said, was Dorothy Howell, who had been with him since the beginning when she and a telephone operator were Columbia Pictures' only two employees. From selecting rented costumes for actresses, Dorothy had progressed to cutting and editing celluloid. By 1925, she was the writer of fifteen of the seventeen stories Cohn produced that year. Sound had made her head scenarist and a sane influence on the fresh, young writers—mostly apprentice playwrights—Harry imported from New York on very short-term contracts.

Jo Swerling was one of Cohn's imports, a squat, heavyset, Russian-born reporter and magazine writer who chain-smoked White Owl cigars. His output matched Capra's. During his first eleven months at Columbia, Swerling wrote thirteen produced scripts. Robert Riskin was another. At seventeen, this native New Yorker had sold original screen stories to Paramount. As Capra's chief collaborator, Riskin introduced the director to urban cynicism and helped tighten the narrative of Capra movies. Riskin wrote his screenplays in longhand, usually sitting on the porch of the Writers Building. If a director was less than happy with a scene, Swerling would return an hour later with four different variations. Riskin never reread or rewrote himself. Among them, Howell, Swerling, and Riskin would write eight movies starring Stanwyck.

Barbara didn't get to work for Capra on *Mexicali Rose*. Her director was Erle C. Kenton, another Sennett crossover who was to reach a measure of fame as the director of Frankenstein and Dracula movies. The story was credited to Gladys Lehman—one of Howell's noms de plume.

Barbara continued to find acting in pictures disconcerting.

On the newly padded stage that became sweltering in the afternoon, Kenton started by shooting the ending, then jumped around in the script, filming scenes in no particular order. Barbara found it hard to snap into the right mood. She decided the only way to survive in the movies was to learn the entire screenplay. As a nine-year-old, she had watched all of Millie's shows from the wings and learned *all* her sister's routines. "You memorize the script, the whole thing, so you can think of any place in it, then work backward or forward from there—like a sailor boxing the compass," she would remember. Kenton filmed her bare-legged to the crotch as the perfidious Sam Hardy slips a necklace around her left ankle. She wasn't equipped to play a vengeful bordertown belle, and her director offered little help. The critics mocked her flat, nasal Brooklyn accent, and in her own mind, *Mexicali Rose* was worse than *The Locked Door*. "I made a frightful thing for Columbia called *Mexicali Rose*," she told the *New York Times* a year later.

She was certain the movies were a big mistake.

Her husband wanted her to drop acting. She wanted to go back to the stage. Ten months into the marriage their rivalry was still below the surface. She was torn between standing on her own two feet as she had done since she was fourteen and relying on her husband. Frank was persuasive. He was under a two-year contract to Warners, and, he told her, he was enough of a success for both of them. Having her at home suited him fine. Saying yes to screen tests when Art Lyons convinced a studio to ask her became a neat way of *not* making up her mind.

A test she did at Warners was particularly mortifying. She arrived at the appointed hour at the assigned soundstage only to find it deserted. A monocled cameraman with a heavy Hungarian accent eventually appeared and introduced himself as Alexander Korda. The future movie tycoon was also a newcomer to Hollywood and he, too, hated the place. He had directed films in Berlin and had just finished *The Squall* with Alice Joyce and Myrna Loy. He made it perfectly clear he considered this screen test assignment the ultimate indignity.

After setting up a couple of lights, Korda put her in front of tapestries and screens. She tensed up, remembering Fitzmaurice doing the same thing and telling her he couldn't make her beautiful no matter what. Sure enough, nothing worked for Korda either. He dropped his head in despair and told her, "I have tried everything, but look at the way you look. It's hopeless." She exploded in anger. She wasn't here begging for a chance, the goddamn studio had sent for her. Korda had no material, no script she could read from. She decided to do a three-minute scene from *The Noose*, reading both her own lines and those of Rex Cherryman.

Frank Fay may have been the perfect bright-eyed emcee in *The Show of Shows*—with billing second to John Barrymore—but the picture was a flop. Stiffly directed by John Adolfi from what appeared to be fifth-row-center, the elaborate musical was a mixture of songs, production numbers, and comedy sketches that included a skit on the French Revolution and the guillotine and a succession of real-life sister acts with songs for each pair.

If low-budget Warners excelled in anything, it was in making movies that looked at life from an underdog's point of view. Headlines about gangsters, unemployment, corruption, and juvenile delinquency were fodder for the studio's hard-hitting dramas. Following the takeover of First National, Warners owned nearly a quarter of North America's movie screens. The driving force behind the studio was former gag writer Darryl Zanuck.

As second in command to Jack Warner, the twenty-eight-year-old Zanuck was a fantastic worker, staying at the studio every night and in general making sure directors, writers, and actors all contributed to the violence, tension, big-city cynicism, and knockout action audiences loved. *Little Caesar*, filmed under the First National banner, was the first and most famous of WB's gangster flicks. It was directed by Mervyn LeRoy, the slight and dapper cousin of Paramount's studio boss, Jesse Lasky, and starred Edward G. Robinson in a daring caricature of Al Capone. With his squat build, frog mouth, and heckling voice, Robinson was the kind of actor no studio would have put in a starring role in a silent. Warners' "working-girl" programmers—and the actresses Warner and Zanuck put under contract—were fast, hip, contemporary, and urban expressions of self-affirmation. Showgirls were on the lam, spouting wiseass slang, in WB's shopgirl-princess vehicles. Robinson, James Cagney, Adolphe Menjou, George Brent, and George Arliss fought and loved Ruth Chatterton, Ruby Keeler, Kay Francis, and, soon to outshine them all, Bette Davis. "Women love bums" was the way Zanuck put it.

Zanuck was the only mogul who wasn't Jewish. A Midwesterner who had started as a writer, he possessed a busy mind bubbling with story ideas cribbed from tabloid front pages and cocktail-party chatter. He had dashed off scripts under a number of pen names, but when he became production chief he hired others to flesh out his ideas. Although his opinion usually prevailed, he was a great listener with an open mind. He watched every wardrobe test of every star and could remember that he didn't like a spotted tie on a man in test number three or he didn't like the cut of a skirt on Barbara in test number four.

Frank Fay's talent was too peculiar to hold the production chief's attention. But since Frank was under contract, Zanuck decided he should play foreigners. The studio barber changed Frank's tousled red hair to sleek, oily black so he could play a Frenchman in *The Matrimonial Bed* and a Mexican in *Under a Texas Moon*. Adopted from a farce that ran in London under the title *What's His Name*, the complicated *Matrimonial Bed* had Fay as a boulevardier who, because of a train crash, is amnesiac. After five years he doesn't recognize his wife, who, anyhow, has since married someone else. Fay hadn't been on a horse in twenty years, but they hoisted him up on one and put him through *Under a Texas Moon*. The picture had him as a redoubtable Don Juan who, at the sight of a pair of pretty eyes and ruby lips, forgets an apparently dangerous mission. Myrna Loy played one of the distracting damsels.

Both B pictures were directed by Mihaly Kertész, who, since coming to Hollywood from his native Budapest, had changed his name to Michael Curtiz. This tall, flamboyant

Hungarian, who married Zanuck's favorite screenwriter, Bess Meredyth, was famous for his command of lighting, mood, and action and for his vigorous mangling of the English language (Bette Davis, he said, "is a flea in the ointment and a no good sexless sonofabitch"). As a director, he was ruthless. No matter what, he'd finish on time and within budget.

Frank didn't want to play a Mexican or a Frenchman. He wanted to play himself, Broadway's Favorite Son. But he *was* the star of *Under a Texas Moon*, heading a cast of twenty that besides Myrna Loy, Raquel Torres, and Mona Maris included Noah Berry, George Cooper, Fred Kohler, and Tully Marshal. And movie stars were America's aristocracy. What they wore, on and off the screen, set fashions. Their lifestyles and opinions—invented or merely improvised by studio publicists—were chronicled in every tabloid and a score of fan magazines. As Warners' director of publicity, Hal Wallis saw to it that the Fays—Frank more than Barbara—got their share of attention. Wallis had been the publicist on *The Jazz Singer* and was currently concentrating on the studio's expensive musicals. "This was before the days of the gossip column when stories were simple, bland, and devoid of scandal," the future producer would remember. "The public worshiped the stars, loving them as though they were personal friends. They wanted to hear about their lavish homes, luxurious gardens, parties, automobiles, and clothes." The Fays had no lavish home to show off, but they looked good in bathing suits, and Wallis sent a studio photographer to Malibu to shoot them clowning on the sand.

Frank and Barbara liked the informality of Malibu so much they rented a beach house.

In contrast to the Santa Monica beach homes that Louis B. Mayer, Irving Thalberg, Joe Schenck, and William Randolph Hearst built twenty miles to the south, the Malibu colony was a collection of bungalows owned or rented by lesser picture people.

Adeline Schulberg, the wife of Paramount studio boss B. P. Schulberg, built the first Cape Cod on a ninety-foot oceanfront lot and filled it with Early American furniture. Warner Baxter, John Gilbert and his new wife, Ina Claire, Clara Bow and her boyfriend, Rex Bell, the ageless Gloria Swanson and her French marquis husband, Henri de la Falaise, followed, owning or renting cottages for the summer.

George Cukor, the recently transplanted Broadway director, shared a rented beach house with Alex Tiers, an independently rich young man making a halfhearted stab at acting. Cukor was discreetly homosexual and threw memorable parties. The Fays' immediate neighbor was Joseph Santley; Barbara's first friend was Adela Rogers St. Johns. Like Barbara, Santley was a former Broadway dancer induced to come west to be in talkies. With Robert Florey, he had been hired to direct the Marx Brothers in *The Coconuts*. Adela was the Hearst chain's most famous newspaperwoman, the star reporter of the Lindbergh kidnapping trial. The daughter of Earl Rogers, California's celebrated trial lawyer, she shared her beach house with an Italian heavyweight champion.

Going out in Los Angeles meant different places on different nights. The place to be Sunday nights was the Cotton Club in Culver City, where the Fays saw the ravishing Jean Harlow with Howard Hughes, the orphaned Texas millionaire who was vaulting into national prominence as the producer-director of *Hell's Angels*. One Tuesday night, Barbara and Frank ran into Oscar Levant at the Club Montmartre, where songwriters gathered. Oscar was in Hollywood to play his original part in *The Dance of Life*. He was thinking of staying on to write songs for Radio Pictures, RCA's newly formed production subsidiary. For Barbara, the success of *The Dance of Life* hurt. The "all-talking, all-dancing, all-star production of stagedom's hit of hits" could have been hers. If only she had traveled to California with Hal back in August 1928 when Paramount invited Hal Skelly, Oscar Levant, and her to come out and test for the *Burlesque* screen version. The Skelly–Nancy Carroll musical with Levant at the piano even featured a musical number filmed in two-color Technicolor.

Fay went to church Sunday mornings, but insisted on having open house in the afternoon. Anybody and everybody dropped in, the women in fluttering beach pajamas, the men in white duck trousers and striped shirts. Frank drank too much.

Capra

The director who, with King Vidor, personified American optimism, the virtues of common people, and sophisticated comedy was a man who proved you could be creative and successful in Hollywood without going crazy. At thirty-three, Frank Capra was a recently divorced charmer who was converting from Catholicism to Christian Science to please his fiancée, Lucille Warner Reyburn.

Born in the hills above Palermo, Francesco Capra had arrived in America at the age of six, and, in Los Angeles, spent a traditional Sicilian immigrant childhood and youth, hawking newspapers while attending the new Manual Arts High School on Vermont Avenue and becoming a door-to-door-salesman to help his family and send himself through college. In 1923, he had married the sharp-witted actress Helen Howell (no relation to Cohn's formidable senior writer Dorothy Howell) because she could help him get into the movies. Emotional and stubborn streaks in his character made him an ideal director.

His success as a gagman and director for Harry Langdon allowed him to buy a home in the Hollywood Hills and with Helen start a family. When Helen suffered a miscarriage, she went to pieces and Capra became distant and hostile toward her. Helen began to drink, and by 1927 the marriage was over. By the first year of the Depression, Capra was a conspicuous success story, an ambitious thirty-three-year-old, both attracted to and deeply suspicious of money—and women. His obsession with corruption and loss of innocence that would make him a household word for urban romances, comedies, and social commentaries was all in the future.

Ladies of Leisure would be his fifth talker and his first "woman's picture." The source material was Milton Herbert Gropper's play *Ladies of the Evening*. The story was derivative of George Bernard Shaw's 1913 *Pygmalion*—itself an update of Ovid's rewrite of the Greek legend of the sculptor king of Cyprus who, although he hated women, fell in love with his own statue of Aphrodite. The heroine of Gropper's play, produced on Broadway by David Belasco in 1924, was Kay Arnold, a prostitute who longs to be loved, but is too proud to believe it can happen. Capra was less than happy with the play. After sending a first-draft screenplay to Dorothy Howell, Jo Swerling, Robert Riskin, and ten other creative people on the lot, Capra got everybody together in Cohn's office for a brainstorming session.

"Capra doesn't want to hear what you *like* about the script," Cohn told the new people. "He's looking for knocks. Understand?"

Puffing on his White Owl, Swerling jumped up: "You want knocks, Mr. Cohn. That's my cue. I don't like Hollywood, I don't like you, and I certainly don't like this putrid piece of Gorgonzola somebody gave me to read." He called the script inane, vacuous, pompous, unreal, and incredibly dull. Capra challenged the cigar-chomping critic to come up with a rewrite that was less inane, vacuous, pompous, unreal, and dull.

Three days later, Swerling delivered forty pages.

To give Jerry Strange, the story's wealthy hero, something to *do*, Swerling turned him into a society painter and updated Kay Arnold to a professional escort, a "party girl." For a "meeting-cute" opening, he had both escape from wild parties. Jerry abandons his snooty fiancée and a party in his Park Avenue penthouse and drives out into the country only to blow a tire on a shoreline road. A white-gowned Kay jumps from the clutches of a guy aboard a yacht and rows herself to shore. Hair disheveled and mascara smudged, Kay scrambles up a hill and comes upon Jerry changing his tire. Before prompting him to offer her a ride back to town, she asks, "Hey, don't you tote a flask—you know, first aid to the nearly injured?"*

---

*Swerling's line was a swipe at Prohibition. The repeal of the Volstead Act was still two years away.

Jerry loads her into his automobile and wraps her in his topcoat. As Kay draws it over her shoulders, she registers the fatness of the wallet in the pocket. She doesn't swipe it though. She returns it with the borrowed coat when she shows up for her first sitting as his model.

Capra called the forty pages "magnificent, human, witty, poignant" and sent the writer back to the typewriter with the admonition not to forget the theme. "It's all in two words, 'Look up!' That's what the boy *must* say to this tart—'Look up at the stars.'"

Swerling complied.

"Look up!" says Jerry to the Eliza Doolittle he is sketching for a canvas he wants to call *Hope*. Swerling's script had her snap back that he should entitle his painting *The Lost Zeppelin*.

Capra cast his former boss at Mack Sennett's as the mon-eyed artist Jerry Strange. Ralph Graves was an aloof and ami-able actor who in the Keystone Kop two-reelers Capra wrote for Sennett had played college men or clumsy go-getters. Graves had become a director for Cohn in 1927, and it was Graves who had brought his former gag writer to Cohn's attention. Since then, Graves had starred in two of Capra's sound pictures. While looking for the actress to play Kay Arnold, Capra filled out the rest of the cast by signing the frizzy-haired Marie Prevost as Kay's roommate and stage actress Nance O'Neil to play Kay's mother. Lowell Sherman was given the role of Jerry's best friend.

Frank Fay and Harry Cohn would both claim responsibility for introducing Stanwyck to Frank Capra. Everyone agrees, however, that Barbara was a terrible snob who refused to meet Capra, let alone read for the part in his new picture.

One version has Frank, forever the emcee, hosting a ben-efit sponsored by the *Los Angeles Examiner*, the powerful Hearst paper no one said no to. Onstage, Barbara joined her husband in a sketch that prompted one man in the audience to seek her out afterward.

"Capra is going to do *Ladies of Leisure*," Cohn told her. "Why don't you test for it?"

"No thanks," she answered. "I've had my experience with tests. I made one at Warner Brothers. If you want to see me on film, send for it."

In another account the various rejections had sent Barbara into such a funk that Fay sought out Cohn and offered to pay back whatever salary Columbia agreed to pay his wife for starring in *Ladies of Leisure*. Both Fay and Cohn were notorious tightwads, and we can only guess who was more discomfited—Frank in bribing the studio boss or Harry in refusing an under-the-table payback. In the end, it seemed, Cohn insisted Capra see the new actress. Under duress, Capra did.

To please her husband, Barbara agreed to the meeting. She walked into the director's office with defeat written all over her face, and a bored Capra kept the interview to a polite minimum. Signaling the end of the meeting, he said that in any case she would have to do a test.

She got up and crossed to the door. "Oh hell, you don't want any part of me!" she yelled in tears and left.

Capra picked up the phone and dialed Cohn. "Harry, forget Stanwyck. She's not an actress. She's a porcupine."

Seeing Barbara arrive home in tears, Fay called Columbia, got Capra on the phone, and asked what the hell the director had done to his wife.

"Do to her? I couldn't even talk to her."

Fay got huffy, but Capra cut him off. "I don't want any part of your wife or of *you*. She came in here with a chip on her shoulder and went out with an ax on it."

Fay mellowed. Since they got to California, his wife had been kicked around. Maybe Capra should just look at Barbara's big third-act screen test from *The Noose*.

Capra said okay. Fay tore off in a taxi with the can of *The Noose* test under his arm. It was 9:00 P.M. before a screening room was available. Cohn and Capra slumped down in executive recliners, and Fay nodded to the projectionist to roll the three-minute test. Capra was certain that nothing in the world was going to make him like the test, but he recalled, "after only thirty seconds I got a lump in my throat as big as an egg."

Writing his autobiography forty years later, Capra got *The Noose* relationship wrong, but his own reaction to the Stanwyck screen test right. "She was pleading with the governor to pardon her convicted husband [sic]," he would remember. "Never had I seen or heard such emotional sincerity. When it was over I had tears in my eyes. I was stunned."

Cohn huffed that Capra was "crazy" when the director begged to be allowed to cast the bristling twenty-three-year-old he had dismissed hours earlier. Cohn let himself be persuaded—after all, Stanwyck was already under contract and not exactly the most expensive choice Capra could come up with.

Shooting began January 14, 1930, ten days after Swerling finished the rewrite. For director and star the shoot was a mutual discovery. Capra got to play his own Henry Higgins, molding near-virgin clay. Barbara brought to the part her Brooklyn directness, her intuition and honesty, that both coarsened and softened the heroine. Her severe beauty and wounded pride muted the character's impertinence and made Swerling's wise-cracking party girl both earthy and contemporary.

"Naive, unsophisticated, caring nothing about makeup, clothes or hairdos, this chorus girl could grab your heart and tear it to pieces," Capra would write. "She knew nothing about camera tricks, how to 'cheat' her looks so her face could be seen, how to restrict her body movements in close shots. She just turned it on—and everything else on the stage stopped."

Stanwyck was at her best the first time they filmed a scene. Capra noted that in her multiple-take scenes, she got worse and worse while her opposite actor often got better and better. To avoid tensions, the director rehearsed the cast without Barbara and filmed her closeups with several cameras so she would only have to do the scene once.

The cameraman on *Ladies of Leisure* was Joseph Walker, a heavyset miner's son from Denver who designed and ground his own custom lenses for each female star he worked with and held twelve patents for motion picture devices. Capra would do twenty movies with Walker, Barbara six. Walker's camera caught her hard little chin, full cheeks, gum-chewing, fast-talking funny face. But multiple-camera setups were time-consuming—and demanding of Walker. Graves and the others grumbled that it was not fair to them. Capra was adamant. Stanwyck was to stay in her dressing room until every camera angle was in place and rehearsed. When he brought her out, he told his leading lady, "No matter what the other actors do, whether they stop or blow their lines, *you* continue your scene right to the end."

Capra told his crew they were working for the actors and

not the other way around. "It put a helluva burden on every-body," said Edward Bernds, who started with Capra as a sound mixer on *Ladies of Leisure* and worked on nearly all his other Columbia pictures. "My God, we were all on our toes to get it the first time. That first take with Stanwyck was sacred."

Did Svengali fall in love with his Trilby? Capra was aware that Fay's drinking and jealousy were getting on Barbara's nerves and claimed he would marry her if she divorced Fay. "I fell in love with Stanwyck, and had I not been more in love with Lucille Reyburn I would have asked Barbara to marry me after she called it quits with Frank Fay," Capra would write in 1971, when he and Lucille were about to celebrate their fortieth anniversary.

When Barbara, Lucille, and the two Franks were all dead, biographer Joseph McBride would claim Capra and Stanwyck were lovers for nearly two years, that it was Barbara who in the end rejected the director. Without saying outright he was Barbara's lover, Capra would admit he was very close to her, that their relationship was both important and rewarding: "I wish I could tell you more about it, but I can't, I shouldn't, and I won't, but she was delightful."

Barbara never admitted to any affair. Sentiments aside, a liaison stretching into the fall of 1931 seems unlikely. If any-thing, Barbara was trying to save her marriage. Frank Fay had walked out on wives twice before and probably would have done so again if his interest in Barbara had dwindled. However morbid his resentment of her success would eventu-ally become, his intense jealousy demonstrated his wish to keep her. As it was, it was Barbara who would compromise her movie career to help Frank recapture his Broadway celebrity.

But that was a year away when Capra rented a beach house in the Malibu Colony across from Clara Bow's house. Frank Capra and Lucille were a sane presence, symbols of moderation and rationality for whom all-night drinking and gambling were unthinkable. Fay, Capra, Barbara, and Lu saw a good deal of each other and of Jack Gilbert. Ina Claire had left Gilbert, and the actor was leasing a beach house again and living alone with his Scotch terrier. His latest picture, *The Phantom of Paris*, was a success, and seemed to end the curse of his voice registering too high.

Columbia released *Ladies of Leisure* in May 1930. In the first months of the Depression, audiences loved this sentimental story of a party girl ("Well, brother, that's my racket. I'm a party girl") who unintentionally falls in love with the society artist. "It is a really fine picture because of the astonishing performance of a little tap-dancing beauty who has in her the spirit of a great artist," raved *Photoplay*. "Her name is Barbara Stanwyck. Go and be amazed by this Barbara girl!" Capra was sure *Ladies of Leisure* would win Academy Awards for himself, Stanwyck, and perhaps even Best Picture. When the film failed to get a single nomination (MGM's *Grand Hotel* won Best Picture; Helen Hayes won for *The Sin of Madelon Claudet*, a sob story notably teary even by Hollywood standards; and Frank Borzage won for directing *Bad Girl*), Capra and Cohn sent angry letters to the Academy of Motion Picture Arts and Sciences, Capra demanding to become a member, his boss wanting to know why Columbia's star director had been snubbed. The Academy quickly made Capra its four-hundred-and-forty-ninth member. Still not satisfied, he lobbied to become a member of the Academy board of governors and was elected to a three-year appointment.

Barbara loved acting, loathed being "in pictures." She hated Los Angeles and the social life of the movie colony. She considered herself a misfit in California and called Hollywood "the papier-mâché town."

"It isn't what you do or have done that counts here," she told the *Los Angeles Times*'s Muriel Babcock a year after *Ladies of Leisure* established her with moviegoers. "It's what happens. That's why I have never understood the minds of the picture brains. And never will. The same thing is true nowhere else. On the stage if an actress is great she is always great. Alice Brady hasn't had a good play in five years in New York, but Alice Brady is still considered a splendid actress by the producers. If they have what they think is a fine play, they will call Miss Brady and not somebody unknown and unskilled."

Barbara learned that if acting onstage is a matter of mannerism, screen acting is done with the eyes. "Mr. Capra taught me that. I mean, sure, it's nice to say very nice dialogue, if you can get it. But great movie acting ... Watch the eyes." Range is a matter of looks, in the way an actor makes an audience *read* his or her thoughts. Acting, her own and other people's performances, became a lifelong source of satisfaction. Acting means becoming someone else, usually someone quicker, handsomer, and smarter than the Barbara Stanwyck who reported to makeup at 6:30 A.M. and tooled home along Sunset Boulevard ten hours later.

Earl Lindsay and Willard Mack had given her lessons in professional honesty and taught her that acting was teamwork, that success was something to be earned. Arthur Hopkins didn't so much direct her in *Burlesque* as he told her stories and let her imagine how she should feel in various situations. In his review of *Burlesque*, Alexander Woollcott applauded the twenty-year-old Stanwyck for bringing "much to those little aching silences in a performance of which Mr. Hopkins knows so well the secret and the sorcery."

She was surprised by how good she looked on the screen. Capra told her not to go to the dailies or rushes, the screenings of the previous day's footage. "You never really look at yourself," he told her. "You're always looking at the veins sticking out of your neck or how you hold your hands. So never look at yourself while you are working. Only go later, when the thing is done." She felt he was right because what she had noticed when she did attend rushes was the "dainty things, the *feminine* things, and missing the larger picture." Not looking at rushes became a lifelong habit. Over the years, she would find a distance to her screen image that gave her an uncanny ability to look at herself almost in the third person. Her deadpan honesty with herself made her see herself, other actors, the movies, the business not only with objectivity but with a grain of salt. She never forgot where she came from. "When I was a chorus girl, I made people sit up." The years of her debut were very much an integral part of her.

Her Kay Arnold in *Ladies of Leisure* was the first role that allowed her acting to hint at unexpected substance under the brassy, wised-up veneer that 1930s audiences wanted. In a quintessential Stanwyck scene, she tells pal Marie Prevost she isn't falling in love with her Pygmalion portrait painter. But a soft tremolo in her voice negates her denials. Much of the delight of seeing Stanwyck act is to see her play a woman who has no idea how alluring she is. "She can give out that burst of emotion," Capra would recall decades later. "She played parts that were a little tougher, yet at the same time you could sense that this girl could suffer from her toughness."

Stanwyck's 1930s roles demanded this kind of double-edged acting. The characters she was asked to play are social mavericks, women armored up in carnality, cynicism, crass logic, and steely confidence. The heroines she incarnated step outside conventions to survive. They dodge bullets and rich men's mothers, have children out of wedlock, wield power in bank boardrooms, fight their own urges but know what to do next. With her dancer's figure and sassy demeanor she was perfect casting for down-on-their-luck-but-with-hearts-of-gold Depression characters. In the "weepies" Warner Brothers put her in, her acting movingly bared grief and loneliness beneath her tough and efficient facade. Her women often have to keep their feelings in check because they know men are no good. Typically, the hard-as-nails lady she plays has no parents, but the moment she gets involved with an upper-class chap, his father or, more often, his mother swoops down to beseech her not to ruin the son's life. By the 1940s, when more mature sophistication enters the mix, the Stanwyck heroine is more surefooted. Men are either heels or suckers, and the trick is to elude the former and take the latter to the cleaners. When she is typecast as a tough broad, she seems to promise men as much pain as pleasure. Her dance-hall belle with criminal connections in *This Is My Affair* is totally different from her *Ball of Fire* stripper on the run from the mob and her *File on Thelma Jordan* murder suspect.

"If the part calls for a glamorous appearance, then I want to look the very best that a cameraman can make me look," she said. "If I'm supposed to be an old bag, then fine, let's go. I'll do anything at all to make it real."

8

Low-budget Life

The golden era was a time when actresses' menstrual periods were tracked on a posted chart, when MGM maintained an in-house abortionist, Clark Gable's false teeth and Gary Cooper's impaired hearing were closely guarded secrets, and the studios knew whose hair was truly straw-colored. To prove herself an authentic blonde, Carole Lombard—along with Jean Harlow—reportedly bleached their pubic hair.

The studios taught, groomed, and managed new faces with the efficiency of prime-rib stock breeders and endlessly molded and manipulated careers. If box-office returns justified a thrust in a certain direction, a studio chief had at his fingertips the pool of writers, directors, and stars to put the hunch on film. The bosses easily persuaded themselves that they had some mysterious insights into public tastes. Although Irving Thalberg often guessed wrong—he felt talkies would never catch on and took longer than most to realize the stage was often a poor source for screen material—he was the first administrator with a craving for "creative input," a precedent that David Selznick would carry to Byzantine extremes. The studio system was ruthless. Studios loaned out contractees to each other no matter what the actors, directors, or cameramen under contract might say. Such "loanouts" sometimes worked in the performers' favor. To punish Clark Gable for refusing a silly picture with Joan Crawford, Louis B. Mayer farmed him out to Columbia. The loanout picture was *It Happened One Night*, the Capra classic that gave Clark his first Oscar.

Before *Ladies of Leisure* was released, Cohn loaned Barbara to Warner Brothers' Darryl Zanuck for a sophisticated love story. *Illicit* followed *Little Caesar* and, like the gangster classic, expressed contemporary smarts spiked with a touch of sentiment and a heart tug of honesty. Zanuck liked ticklish propositions, and *Illicit* told the story of a lover who foolishly insists on becoming a husband. The source material was a play by Robert Riskin and his lover and writing partner Edith Fitzgerald. Warners publicity called it "a smart, sophisticated story of ultra moderns."

Zanuck assigned Archie Mayo to direct *Illicit*. Mayo was a rude, fat man, who, despite a somewhat redeeming sense of humor, was in the habit of pinching the buttocks of his leading ladies. Dolores Del Rio, it was said, turned right around and slapped his face; Barbara grabbed his arm the first time he tried.

Movies were made fast and cheap at Warners. "I don't want it good, I want it Tuesday" was Jack Warner's oft-repeated order. Like Columbia's Cohn, Jack Warner operated as a "totalitarian godhead"—one observer called him "a bargain-basement dictator," others called him the "Clown Prince." He was vain, ignorant, conceited, pretentious, and fond of telling bad jokes and flipping ashes from an extravagantly long cigar. He had risen above his brothers by pushing the Vitaphone sound system to its phenomenal breakthrough. WB might be in its nouveau riche phase, but the studio retained its under-dog culture. There was no coddling of talents—even the brightest stars were made to punch time cards.

In *Illicit*, Barbara played Anne Vincent, a girl deeply in love with James Rennie. While agreeing to live with him, she nevertheless refuses to marry him. They share an apartment, although society drunk and best friend Charles Butterworth tells them that isn't done. Anne isn't keen to tie the knot with her roommate, but he is persuasive. Marriage, inevitably, means spats and misunderstandings. The appearance of Joan Blondell as his former flame and Ricardo Cortez as Anne's former swain complicates matters. Bruised egos lead to a planned trip to Bermuda by the wrong twosome followed by more misunderstanding and a cliffhanger reconciliation.

Blondell and Stanwyck became fast friends. The blond, apple-cheeked Joan with her chesty voice, china-blue eyes, and self-deprecating humor was the daughter of itinerant actors. She had lived on the road till she was nineteen and knew all about sawdust, bare stages, back alleys, and hard work. She belonged to WB's stock company as much as the first bread-and-butter talents of Rin-Tin-Tin and Wesley Barry, dog and boy. She had married a cameraman, George Barnes, and, like Barbara, she was less than happy with her husband and Hollywood. Unlike Barbara, however, she had little ambition. "This town hasn't got into my blood," she said. "I like it—it has been good to me—but I'm my father's child, and if the callboard for happiness ever indicated any other place, well, a Blondell has never yet been afraid of 'the big hike.'"

A few stages from *Illicit*, Frank Fay was filming *Bright Lights* with the beautiful Dorothy Mackaill. Mixed reviews and box-office returns had greeted Fay's back-to-back pictures during the spring and summer of 1930. Frank was praised for the humor he lent to *Under a Texas Moon*, but *The Matrimonial Bed* was considered a mess. He had not wanted to play the foreign-type lover; he wanted to play himself, a red-headed, red-blooded Irish American, so Zanuck gave him *Bright Lights*, the story of a vaudevillian whose success goes to his head. Warners still thought Fay was a promising discovery. Playing on Elinor Glyn's famous pronouncement that Clara Bow was the "It Girl" supreme, the studio dubbed Fay the "It Man" and billed him as "the 1932 model lover—built for speed, style and endurance." Frank hated every minute of *Bright Lights* because Michael Curtiz never took breaks. The director paced the stage floor while his actors and crew went to lunch, devising what he should have them do when they got back, and at the end of the day, hated to go home. "They were squeezing as much out of us as they could—eleven-, twelve-hour days—frequently working nights right through to sunup," James Cagney would remember of the early 1930s WB days. As Curtiz and Mayo never finished a day's shooting simultaneously, Barbara and Frank returned home separately at all hours.

To Frank's dismay, the studio teamed him with Curtiz again before *Bright Lights* was even released. The new picture was *God's Gift to Women*, and the title said it all. Frank played a Frenchman again, a boulevardier with a gift for separating pretty women from their better judgment. His ladies were Blondell, Louise Brooks, and Laura La Plante.

The Fays had Louise Brooks out for a Sunday at the beach. Frank knew her from her Ziegfeld chorus days. She came with a dress designer, plunked herself down in a deck chair, and made everybody understand she longed for Germany and her silent triumph in *Pandora's Box*. The Fays found her lazy and arrogant and didn't invite her again.

Frank kept talking about *his* Broadway, but the news from back east was disturbing. The legitimate theater suffered far more than the movies during the 1930–31 season, the first real winter of the Depression. Theaters were so empty that Joe Frisco coined the joke, "Do you have change for a match?" Investors had disappeared with the Wall Street crash, sending the Shubert organization, the giant of the theater operators, into receivership. The Palace Theatre was losing $4,000 a week, and one by one the playhouses along Forty-second Street were converting to movie theaters. For as little as a quarter, cinemas offered a main attraction, a newsreel, an animated cartoon, and possibly a second feature. Frank was sure, however, that it would be SRO if *he* returned to the Palace.

Barbara thought they should stay right where they were. Five thousand theater people were out of work on Broadway. At least the picture business seemed immune to the recession. We do not know what the Warner contract paid Frank, but Columbia had paid Barbara $1,000 a week in period dollars for the five weeks they filmed *Ladies of Leisure*. The box-office result spoke for itself, and Cohn offered her a new, three-picture contract. Now that her name had box-office allure, Art Lyons drove a hard bargain. Cohn agreed to pay Stanwyck $12,000 for the first film of the three-picture deal. Barbara never stopped working and Frank never stopped grumbling, but they lived nonchalantly in Malibu. So nonchalantly that the Internal Revenue Service attached a $6,102 lien to her wages for nonpayment of income tax.

A week after Barbara finished *Illicit*, Cohn had the first picture of the new contract ready to go. *Ten Cents a Dance* got its title from a Richard Rodgers–Lorenz Hart song that former *Ziegfeld Follies* star Ruth Etting had made a hit. The script concocted by Dorothy Howell and Jo Swerling told the story of a dance-hall hostess and her lustful employer who will forgo pressing charges against her embezzling husband if she surrenders to him. Howell and Swerling laced the script with punchy lines for Barbara: When a man asks what he has to do to get to dance with a taxi girl, Barbara snaps: "All ya need is a ticket and some courage." *Ten Cents a Dance* teamed Barbara with Ricardo Cortez again.

Their director was Lionel Barrymore. In his early fifties and looking his years, the once swaggering oldest sibling of the Ethel, Lionel, and John Barrymore dynasty was seeing sound renew his career. Barrymore liked Barbara's Brooklyn accent, which came in handy for the taxi dancer role. He also liked her vitality and took pains directing her. During the shooting, she suffered a fractured pelvis and was partially paralyzed for several hours. She was out of the hospital in two days and back on the set. She hated being passive, had no physical fears, and repeatedly refused to use a double. Over the years, she was seriously injured in several filming accidents.

Warner Brothers had no picture for Fay after *God's Gift to Women*. On weekdays, Frank sat brooding and drinking in the beach house, waiting for Barbara to come home. On Sundays, he went to church in the morning and invited at least twenty people for the afternoon. Their bootlegger's bill soared.

Cohn sent Stanwyck back to Warner Brothers to do *Night Nurse* opposite WB's own Joan Blondell and another loanout—MGM's Clark Gable.

The director was William "Wild Bill" Wellman, a tempestuous charmer with a sharp eye, a keen ear, and a quick fist. Actresses often found him too intent on creating a personality, but Barbara—and Ida Lupino—adored him and felt secure on his sets. The former flying ace with curly hair, piercing blue eyes, and checkered career was fun to be with. When Barbara first met him he sat in an enormous chair, feet on the desk, his hair windblown as if he just landed an open cockpit plane. A wound in a Great War dogfight had resulted in the implantation of a steel plate in his forehead. People called him Wild Bill because they believed the steel plate made him crazy. He possessed strength of character, quickness of mind, and a crooked sense of perspective and as a director was a jack-of-all-trades who did adventures, weepies, swash-bucklers, thrillers, and comedies. His first wife, Helene Chadwick, was a former Goldwyn Studios ingenue, and he was a friend of Barbara's *Burlesque* costar Hal Skelly.

"Directors are very vain, and I admire them for it," Barbara would remember. "Of course, as soon as a director became powerful or established, the producers started thinking of ways to get rid of him, but not Bill Wellman. He was too smart for them, a wonderful man. Never thought he was a genius, like Cecil B. DeMille or King Vidor. I don't know what ruined him, but I don't think it was booze."

Ben Lyon and Stanwyck had top billing in *Night Nurse*, with, in descending order, Joan Blondell, Clark Gable, Blanche Frederici, and Charlotte Merriam. Gable was not yet the biggest thing to hit the movies since Garbo, but he was the busiest. He appeared in twelve films in 1931—three pictures with Joan Crawford—and in movies with Fay Wray, Norma Shearer, Constance Bennett, Madge Evans, Dorothy Jordan, Jean Harlow, and Garbo. *Night Nurse* did a lot for the big-eared lumberjack whose crackling voice and takeover style made him the new screen lover. Moviegoers suddenly found the stylized romanticism of the silents' Lotharios passé. MGM had just released *A Free Soul*, for which Lionel Barrymore would win an Oscar, but it was Gable's shoving Norma Shearer back into a chair that gave the picture its charge. Men cheered and women loved to see a poor guy making a dishonest buck and giving it to a rich dame. In *Night Nurse*, Wellman dressed Gable in black and had him punch Barbara in the nose and steal food from two little girls.

As soon as *Night Nurse* was finished, MGM put Gable into *Sporting Blood* with Madge Evans and Marie Prevost. Nineteen years later, when Stanwyck teamed with Clark in *To Please a Lady*, she would tell how Gable's next picture came out a few days before *Night Nurse*. Confusing *Sporting Blood* with *China Seas*, a picture Gable made in 1935, Stanwyck would remember how, back in March 1931, people went from Gable-conscious to Gable-crazy: "Our dandy little opus hit Broadway the first day billed as Ben Lyon and Barbara Stanwyck in *Night Nurse*. The second day it was Ben Lyon, Barbara Stanwyck and Clark Gable in *Night Nurse*. And the fourth day all you could see were black letters three feet high which simply said 'Clark Gable' and left poor Ben and me out completely."

When *Bright Lights* didn't do well, Frank drowned his disappointment in drink. The blow to his ego was compounded by his wife's soaring popularity. Tensions mounted. The press sniffed marital trouble. In March 1931, the Fays denied they were separating. Frank referred questions to his wife. Barbara tried to make light of it. She was in the middle of baking a cake, she told reporters phoning for her comment. "Does this sound like we're separated?" she asked. "Would any wife do that much for a husband she was mad at?" Fay and Zanuck couldn't agree on Frank's next picture. In June, Warners canceled Frank's contract.

Barbara faced the press alone. Her husband had not liked the scripts the studio proposed, but had offers from two major companies "and will sign with one or the other." She asserted that Warner Brothers had almost killed him with poor material and tried to be cynical about her own success. "I'm a star now," she said, "but give me one or two bad pictures and Hollywood will consider me a flop again. Frank did a couple of bad films, but so what? The same thing could happen to me. I've been through it."

She insisted her husband was responsible for her success. As proof she told reporters how Frank's rushing her screen test to Capra had resulted in her getting the starring role in *Ladies of Leisure*. Yes, she had to admit he would prefer if she didn't work. "He's old-fashioned. He thinks that a woman's place is at home. But he wants me to be happy and he knows I am happier doing something."

She fibbed when she said two other studios were making overtures to Frank. Nobody wanted to sign him. Ego and survival instinct made him decide to return to New York. The stage was where he belonged. He insisted that she follow. She didn't refuse, but reminded him that she still owed Harry Cohn another picture. She'd retire once he reestablished himself on Broadway, and in any event, she'd come as soon as possible. Perhaps to keep an eye on her, Frank had his father move in with them in Malibu. Francis Donner had given up vaudeville the year before and was happy to move in with his son and daughter-in-law. Before Frank boarded the Santa Fe Super Chief, he told his wife to tell Cohn she needed a vacation.

* * *

The Academy snub of *Ladies of Leisure* still rankled Capra. To show he was a first-class director, Capra wanted to do a prestige picture starring Barbara Stanwyck. *Illicit* not only proved a smart follow-up to *Ladies of Leisure* for Barbara, it made Robert Riskin a hot writer. At Capra's urging, Cohn bought *Bless You, Sister*, the controversial 1927 Broadway play Riskin had written with John Meehan, in which Alice Brady had starred.

Bless You, Sister was inspired by the Aimee Semple McPherson scandal. "Sister" Aimee had packed the five-thousand-seat Angelus Temple near Glendale Boulevard and showed the Midwesterners who filled the Los Angeles tract homes that worship could be fun. She and her flock praised the Lord with music and dance. In her famous throw-out-the-lifeline number, the former Ontario farm girl had a dozen imperiled maidens cling to a storm-lashed Rock of Ages while special effects men worked heroically with thunder, lightning, and wind machines. Just when all seemed lost, Sister Aimee in an admiral's uniform appeared and ordered a squad of lady sailors to the rescue. The Angelus Temple boasted a huge choir, a brass band, and a pipe organ. A "miracle room" at the Glendale Boulevard temple displayed crutches, wheelchairs, and braces abandoned after faith cures. A radio station broadcast the Foursquare gospel.

Aimee's apparent suicide by drowning off the California coast in 1926 was a mystery; her reappearance thirty-seven days later a national sensation. Stumbling out of the Arizona desert, she claimed a trio of kidnappers had taken her to a shack in the Mexican desert. Los Angeles gave her a tumultuous welcome, and her flock greeted her as someone risen from the dead. Had she not insisted on bringing her alleged abductors to justice, the affair might have blown over. Police found notes in Aimee's handwriting showing she and the operator of her temple's radio station had enjoyed many a tryst in hotels and that they had spent the five weeks she was kidnapped in a seaside cottage together. Aimee set out on a rehabilitation tour. In cities where crowds had thronged to hear her, the halls were now empty. Capra believed an exposé of a woman evangelist fleecing the faithful was a daring career move and that Stanwyck would make a helluva Aimee.

Cohn was jittery, but gave *Bless You, Sister* the go-ahead

on condition Dorothy Howell help Riskin write the script. Her levelheadedness, Cohn figured, would keep the satire in check. Riskin didn't want to have anything to do with the project. He warned Cohn, Capra, and Howell that if Broadway's sophisticates had found it offensive, what would Bible Belt moviegoers say?

Capra got his way. With Jo Swerling and Dorothy Howell, he wrote an opening scene that was nothing if not powerful: A congregation that has already decided to replace its aging, old-fashioned preacher with an up-and-coming "modernist" minister gathers for one last sermon by the old man. Instead of the outgoing minister, it is his daughter, Florence Fallon, who mounts the pulpit to announce that her father has just died in her arms. She lashes out at the worshipers, telling them that they killed her father. "For thirty years he tried to touch your stony hearts with the mercies of God—and *failed*. Why? Because you don't want God." As they flee the church, she shouts, "And you're right! There is no God." Here director and screenwriters lost their nerve.

What Capra originally had in mind—and Broadway audiences had objected to—was a lady evangelist milking the faithful. The script was softened by introducing a con man, a carny promoter who manipulates Sister Florence into becoming the big-money revivalist, and a good guy, a blind war veteran who is saved from suicide by her preaching on the radio.

Director and star worked smoothly, and Barbara knew how to illuminate both Sister Fallon's early cynicism and her pangs of conscience when she realizes not only the promoter's lack of scruples but the amount of deception in her own preaching. On the script level, however, Sister Fallon's motivations are neither clear nor persuasive.

Because Capra had seen a Lon Chaney movie about faith healing in 1919 called *The Miracle Man*, the picture was released in July 1931 under the title *The Miracle Woman*. It was a failure. In his memoirs, Capra would blame himself. "I weaseled," he wrote. "I insisted on a 'heavy' to take the heat off Stanwyck the evangelist. *He* cons her into it. *He* gets wealthy. She becomes his flamboyant stooge. Did she or did she not herself believe those 'inspiring' sermons delivered in diaphanous robes, with live lions at her side? I didn't know. Stanwyck didn't know, and neither did the audience.

The next six months were sheer hell. On the long-distance telephone, Frank Fay thundered that she was Mrs. Fay first, an actress second. At the studio, the long-engaged Frank Capra told her to divorce the bastard and marry him. A smarmy "plant" with a newspaper columnist called Barbara Stanwyck "one movie star who is happily married" and quoted Capra's coy rejoinder that "she was so pleased with her last wedding that she can hardly wait for the next one."

Capra wanted to do another film with Stanwyck. "Confession" or "cry" pictures about good girls gone astray, unwed mothers, and love that cannot end in marriage were big box office. Universal had bought Fannie Hurst's 1930 bestseller *Back Street* for Irene Dunne. Capra figured he could beat Universal to the punch. In *Forbidden* Stanwyck would sacrifice everything for her married lover *and* their illegitimate baby.

Practically the entire Columbia writing staff worked on *Forbidden*, although Swerling got the screenplay credit and Capra gave himself the original story credit. They invented a barking city editor, a suave district attorney, and Lulu Smith, who loves the D.A. but marries the editor. Adolphe Menjou was cast as the district attorney and father of Lulu's child. They can't marry because he won't leave his crippled wife (Dorothy Peterson). To give the illegitimate daughter a home and a future, Lulu gives up her baby girl to Menjou and his wife. Lulu marries Al, the editor, played by Ralph Bellamy, and becomes the tabloid's writer of advice to the lovelorn. Al discovers his wife's secret and makes the downfall of the district attorney his sole ambition. To save the reputation of the father of her child from Al, Lulu shoots her husband. Menjou is elected governor and pardons her. He is taken ill and on his deathbed hands Lulu a will that admits their affair and leaves her half his estate. In the fadeout, Lulu destroys the will. Nobody will ever know.

The two Franks kept tearing at Barbara. Her husband's long-distance demands that she get herself to New York matched Capra's entreaties that she stay. She was his inspiration, the director told her; they would top *Ladies of Leisure* with this one. Barbara went to Cohn. She needed a breather. She needed a little time off so she could go to New York and appease her husband. Cohn wouldn't hear of it. He was paying her $2,000 a week, but only when she was working. Frank apparently needed the Western Union money orders she sent him every week more than he needed her wifely presence. He relented temporarily and *Forbidden* was set to start in late April 1931, then delayed to mid-May.

It was not a happy shoot. A photograph of Lulu murdering her husband shows Barbara, haggard and distant, in the doorway limply holding a gun. Barbara asked Cohn to let her make a quick trip to New York. Life would be so much easier, she told Cohn, if she and Frank could spend their third anniversary together. Cohn refused, convinced the real motive was to get Barbara away from Capra, that once in New York Fay would delay his wife's return to California.

Barbara shifted tactics. Cohn might yield, she decided, if she made a sufficiently outrageous demand. She had received $12,000 for *Ten Cents a Dance* and $16,000 for *The Miracle Woman*. She telephoned the studio and said she wouldn't work unless she got $50,000 for *Forbidden*. Cohn offered her $20,000. She said in that case she could not report to work. On July 17, 1931, the trade press reported she had "failed to put in an appearance at the Columbia studio" and that production was suspended.

Charles Cradick, her lawyer, decided he should go public while she remained in seclusion. Everybody agreed Stanwyck had signed a contract to do three films for Columbia, Cradick told a news conference. Where the disagreement came in was over which one was the third. The studio claimed *Forbidden* was the last picture; Barbara considered *Illicit*, the "loan picture" she had made for Warners and for which she had been paid $35,000, the third and final commitment of her Columbia contract.

"The trouble is," Cradick said, "that while Miss Stanwyck's pictures, those made for Warner Brothers under arrangement with Columbia, and those made for Columbia, have all been tremendously successful, and while Columbia has seen fit to exercise all its options on my client's services, the concern has not seen fit to give her any added compensation. This she feels is unjust." In a play for journalistic sympathy, the lawyer told how, after a fall during the shooting of *Ten Cents a Dance*, Stanwyck had been required to return to work while still suffering.

Cohn's answer came in the form of a court petition demanding that she be barred from working anywhere until she honored her Columbia contract. To make sure she understood the gravity of her situation, the studio first told the press *Forbidden* was canceled, then announced the existing footage of Stanwyck might be reshot with Helen Hayes in the lead. The papers Barbara was served demanded that she go back to work on *Forbidden* and asked the court to issue an injunction barring her from fulfilling whatever contracted arrangements she had made with Warners. Fay rushed back to Los Angeles to escort his wife to Superior Court.

Columbia lawyers told Judge Douglas L. Edmunds the studio was "incurring $8,000 a day losses while Miss Stanwyck withholds her services." Cradick countered that she considered *Illicit*, the "loan" film she had made for Warners, the third and last picture of her Columbia contract. Pending trial, Judge Edmunds issued an injunction forbidding Stanwyck to work for Warners, or anyone else, until she completed her Columbia Pictures contract.

Four days later, Cohn and Stanwyck kissed and made up.

Once she knuckled under and reported to work, Cohn called her in to talk things over. He offered her more money, and the studio publicity department laid on flattering interviews. "You didn't argue with him," she would recall. "He was a bully toward everybody, or tried to be."

Forbidden resumed, but Capra was furious. During the three-week court fight, Cohn had put him to work on *Platinum Blonde*, a Riskin–Swerling–Dorothy Howell programmer that established Jean Harlow's stardom. The tension on the *Forbidden* set could have been cut with a knife. Frank Fay showed up on the stage, belligerent and suspicious. "I can remember vividly how the crew would separate and make way for him," Bellamy would say. "He was a very unpopular guy—and worked at it. Barbara told me afterward that he thought I was having something to do with her."

Fresh disasters struck. Horseback riding didn't come natural to a Brooklyn street kid. Barbara was not comfortable on horses, but managed to ride one. On October 4, she and

Menjou galloped through the surf in a night scene near Laguna Beach when her horse reared at the glare of a suddenly turned on reflector. Barbara's head hit the horse's. A second later, the horse threw her. In panic, the animal kicked her before falling on top of her. Somewhere, Capra shouted, "Cut!" Assistants came running and, with Menjou's help, pulled Barbara unconscious from under the horse.

When she came to, she said they'd have to finish the scene immediately because her legs were getting stiff. Capra ordered an ambulance. She refused to go to the hospital. To clear her head for a retake, she walked into the surf, followed by Menjou, came back, and fainted again. Crew members carried her to a nearby cottage. She woke up in the hospital, where X rays showed her tailbone had been dislocated.

Sprained legs kept her hospitalized for several days. To complete the filming, doctors allowed her to be released during daytime hours. She returned to the hospital after each day's shooting to spend the night in traction. The crew built a slanted board so she could rest her back between takes. "It hurt," she would say in 1984. "It still hurts."

The Fays were at a party three weeks later when Frank's father called from Malibu to say the beach house was on fire. Fanned by an onshore breeze, the flames had started two beach houses away, destroyed Joseph Santley's house next door, and torched theirs. When Frank and Barbara got there, the house was a smoking ruin. Among the losses were almost all of the photographs of Barbara's childhood and early career.

Forbidden wrapped in late October, and Capra decided to take a long vacation, his first since 1927. To his biographer, Joseph McBride, Capra would suggest the reason he went to Europe was to sort out his feelings for Lu and Barbara. Before he left in mid-December, Lu asked when they were going to get married. He avoided a direct answer, but once in Paris panicked when she informed him by telegram that she had decided to marry someone else. Two weeks later Capra was in New York marrying Lucille. Barbara wired her congratulations and when they returned thought they made a handsome couple. "Those people were clones," she would say.

Beating Universal's *Back Street* to the box office by

seven months, *Forbidden* was Columbia's top moneymaker of 1932.

Shopworn was Columbia's next Stanwyck vehicle. While Swerling and Riskin finished the hard-luck waitress story, Cohn allowed Barbara to go to New York—after all, he didn't pay when she wasn't working—for Fay's two-week engagement at the Palace. Hollywood's columnists and celebrity reporters didn't like movie stars who had anything but Hollywood on their mind, but Barbara was too busy trying to save marriage and career to court the press. Fan magazines complained that Barbara Stanwyck wasn't seen at the social centers where film celebrities gathered. The reason, *Photoplay* announced, was that she believed the industry had given her husband a raw deal. "She just doesn't like the town, nor the people, not the climate, not anything about it. Maybe you don't like olives—well, Barbara doesn't like Hollywood. As a result she is called temperamental and hard to manage. But that's only because she is indifferent." If she didn't mingle the reason was that she feared Frank would humiliate them. She watched a string of celebrity suicides and was particularly affected when Jeanne Eagels killed herself with a deliberate overdose of heroin. What was happening to Frank and her?

At the Palace, Barbara joined Frank in a skit. To help boost the box office, she added scenes from *Ladies of Leisure*, *The Miracle Woman*, and *Forbidden* to the repertoire. If she had limited herself to doing slapstick onstage with her husband, nobody would have objected. Advertising her screen career on the stage was considered very poor taste.

Her name on the marquee increased the box office. Frank took all the credit. *Photoplay* dispatched its East Coast correspondent to critique her in *Christmas*, a playlet written and directed by Frank. The review was devastating:

> Let us draw a kindly charitable veil over the next ten minutes. It is Christmas in a department store, and Babs has been caught snitching tin soldiers for her "little crippled buvver." Stanwyck labors on—it is like setting Lionel Barrymore to play a conventional English butler named Meadows. And so the afternoon wears on—paper thin. Fay holds the stage for half an hour

with the aid of assistant buffoons, but it is easy to sense he is not gripping and mowing down his audience as he did when he was Crowned Prince of Seventh Avenue, ere the Hollywood gold fields lured him away. And Barbara? She darts on and darts off—displaying the rich Hollywood wardrobe at Frankie's laughing behest. The bill winds up with a Grand Afterpiece in which the gorgeous one is surrounded by eight clowns, counting Fay, in outlandish states of undress, red noses and fake mustaches. Alas—it is as funny as a plane crash.

Barbara fled to California and slipped happily into *Shopworn*'s waitress-turned-star role. Playing someone else gave her identity and made her forget Frank's whining, boozing, and jealousy. *Shopworn* was a cry picture bringing little credit to those involved in it, but Barbara didn't care. She is a hard-luck waitress who becomes an actress and marries man-about-town Regis Toomey only to be railroaded on a morals charge by her wealthy mother-in-law (Clara Blandick). Fresh from eight years with MGM, director Nick Grinde tried his best to make the story believable, that is, to make the waitress-turned-star's setbacks engrossing without telegraphing her faithful love of Toomey that, halfway through, the audience guesses anyway. The *Hollywood Herald* called *Shopworn* "tawdry and cheap."

Warners provided a desperately needed boost. After first borrowing Stanwyck for *Jewel Robbery*, Darryl Zanuck decided to cast her instead opposite George Brent and Bette Davis in the film version of Edna Ferber's 1925 Pulitzer Prize winner and bestseller *So Big*. Twenty-four-year-old Davis was furious when her own studio made her play second banana to loanout Stanwyck's starring role.

So Big was Stanwyck's first A movie and her second picture with Bill Wellman. For star, director, and even Warner Brothers, doing Ferber's big, sprawling novel as an eighty-minute movie was a big leap. Barbara's role demanded that she age from a young girl to a woman in her mid-fifties. Wellman saw to it that she matured believably, and Warners had its celebrated new dress designer, Orry-Kelly, do her wardrobe. John Orry-Kelly had come from Australia via theatrical design in New York and quickly established himself as WB's versatile, if temperamental, costume designer.

Bette Davis was intensely jealous of Barbara. The two had few scenes together, but Bette's tense mannerisms and constant wiggling struck Barbara as affected and designed to steal scenes. "She had the kind of creative ruthlessness that made her success inevitable," Barbara would remember. Over the years Stanwyck and Davis would compete for many roles, but, as Bette said, there was "nevah" a fight between them.

So Big established Stanwyck as an actress with a brilliant emotional range. Critics deplored cramming the events of the heroine's lifetime into eighty minutes, but applauded Barbara's performance. In New York, Frank talked the owner of the Strand Theatre, which was playing *God's Gift to Women*, into letting him appear in person before each screening. Despite the presence of the gorgeous Louise Brooks, the seasoned La Plante, and WB house diva Blondell, the picture was "exclusively Fay's show," said *Variety*, adding, "When a two-reeler plot is stretched to feature length, it is no gift to audiences."

God's Gift to Women was yanked after three days.

9

What Price Hollywood?

Frank Fay returned to Los Angeles, where all eyes were on his wife. His downward slide and her steady rise increased his jealousy, suspicion, and resentment. No amount of reasoning on her part could dislodge his belief that she, Zanuck, Cohn, Capra, and Hollywood had robbed him of his talent, that her fame was filched and misbegotten. To calm him down, she told interviewers she was either about to retire or, if the movies didn't want her, she'd be going back to the stage. To herself, she denied anything was wrong and met hints by acquaintances that Frank might have a drinking problem with a blank look on her face.

To stay out of Frank's hair, she agreed to do a third picture with Bill Wellman. *The Purchase Price*, a standard action picture, started filming during the winter of 1931–32. Between setups she confided the details of her marital troubles to her director. Because he understood "fellers" better than "gals," as he said, Wellman was better at explaining Frank to her than anyone. We do not know whether Wild Bill could explain delusion, tenaciously held, irrational beliefs or whether she heeded his grousing, plainspoken advice. We do know that when he turned in the first draft of *A Star Is Born* three years later, David O. Selznick pronounced it too close to the Fays' real-life drama.

The thirty-year-old Selznick was the youngest studio chief, head of the newly merged RKO and Pathé pictures. Selznick believed Hollywood was a refuge for life's misfits. He was intrigued by the way movie fame can shunt a husband or a wife, however happily married, into obscurity, how one partner's identity can be destroyed by the other's radiance. With Constance Bennett playing a waitress and Lowell Sherman a brilliant but alcoholic director, Selznick made *What Price Hollywood?* one of RKO's big 1932 releases. The original story was by someone who knew the Fays all too well, Adela Rogers St. Johns. George Cukor directed the star-crossed romance between the young ingenue and the talented but self-destructive filmmaker who, to avoid becoming a hindrance to her rise, ends up committing suicide. Sherman used his brother-in-law John Barrymore as a role model, and the result was a realistic and not unsympathetic screen drunkard. However, neither director nor producer nor producer's wife was happy with *What Price Hollywood?* Cukor called it "a mixed bag"; Selznick said that it went off in too many directions. Irene Selznick thought it was phony. As Louis B. Mayer's daughter, she knew something about growing up in real Hollywood. Her husband promised he'd make a true inside Hollywood movie.

When Selznick set up his own production company, he decided to redo the story of a seesaw Hollywood marriage and to get it right. To help Wellman write a script, he hired an untried youngster, Robert Carson. Within two weeks Wellman and Carson submitted a detailed story line that Selznick found so close to the Fay-Stanwyck marriage that he asked attorneys specializing in invasion-of-privacy litigation to go over it. The lawyers came back with a twenty-page brief, listing similarities in incidents and situations between the script and Frank and Barbara Fay. Wellman and Carson decided one way to distance their plot line from the Fays was to make the husband a dejected and humorless person. Selznick, who was never content with letting writers develop a script on their own, ordered another rewrite. In the new version the husband was more comic in tone, that is, more like Fay. Selznick still wasn't happy with the script. He signed *What Price Hollywood?* writer-director Rowland Brown to work on the continuity and dialogue, fired Brown a week later, and replaced him with Dorothy Parker and her gay husband, Alan Campbell. Budd Schulberg and Ring Lardner, Jr., whom Selznick had hired as "junior writers," also had some influence on the finished script. Rewrites continued through 1934 and 1935, even after Wellman started the Technicolor film with Fredric March and Janet Gaynor. "It was a story based on things that happened," Wellman would say defensively of *A Star Is Born*, which earned him his only Oscar and became a film classic.

The May 1932 issue of *Photoplay* called Stanwyck "the most promising young star in pictures" and Fay a has-been with an attitude. Frank refused to accept the industry's thumbs-down verdict of his talent or *Photoplay*'s unctuous hope that Frank would "find a niche in pictures." He had never endeared himself to the Hollywood press, and columnists and reporters blamed him for Barbara's reluctance to play the movie star.

Photoplay's top columnist Cal York said: Stanwyck would sacrifice her career for her husband. The columnist, who knew Fay from Broadway, intimated that if Warner Brothers had given Frank a second chance it was his wife's doing:

> Suddenly Broadway's favorite son was no longer the big shot in the family. Did this make any difference to Stanwyck? None—except that she seemed more devoted to her red-haired spouse than ever.
>
> No Frankie, no fame—she announced it proudly while Hollywood wondered and sighed. Suddenly Fay was really through on the Warner pasture. Barbara announced her independence from Hollywood and all its weird works and ways. Due to start work on a picture at Columbia, she simply failed to show up at camera-time.
>
> Some people in the know may say it's money trouble. But the knowing ones will tell you, in all honesty, that the heart is talking and not the checkbook. Barbara Stanwyck will have no part of a world where Frank Fay isn't chairman of the board of directors.

For the love of her husband, York predicted, she would give it all up so that someday people would recognize her in a theater lobby or a restaurant and someone would exclaim, "Look! There's Barbara Stanwyck!" To which another would reply, "Gosh—how beautiful. Do you remember?"

It was the age of the press columns and fan magazines. The

Fays were not the only ones to try to hide the turmoil of their relationship while pretending to "confide" in columnists they invited to their home. Stars and executives cringed before the peephole columnists while wooing them with corruptive flattery and self-destructive cooperation. The ears of Hedda Hopper, her sister columnist Louella Parsons, Cal York, and a host of lesser gossips were always perked, and to be sure they were always au courant, they employed networks of informants while affecting a stewardship of public morality. Nothing was more provocative than the misdemeanors of the privileged. To see them spanked in print was both edifying and entertaining.

The Purchase Price was shot during Frank's worst behavior. Barbara laughed off persistent newspaper hints at a breakup. She invited *Los Angeles Times* columnist Harrison Carroll to interview her at home. In the movies, she said, an actress only had a few good years. She intended to make the most of hers. "Either that or I'll quit pictures."

The columnist described how Frank sat in on the interview, "the man of this house, and no mistaking," saying he and his wife were homebodies. "We don't have all those fireside pictures taken; we don't believe in it," said Frank. "But we like each other's company. Don't party much."

Frank added that he had never wanted his wife to be in the movies. "On our way out here, we each said, 'Well, I wonder how long we'll stick together in Hollywood.' Here we are." In his syndicated column, Carroll described how Barbara smiled and nodded, lit a cigarette, and took it over to her husband in a "domestic scene that was very convincing."

The Fays could project homely bliss for a visiting columnist, but there were ugly fights in nightclubs that beat reporters picked up from waiters and parking attendants. After accusing Barbara of drinking too much, Frank knocked her down and got into a fistfight with intervening bystanders. One of their evenings out hit the police blotter when Frank was arrested for drunk driving, injuring a woman visiting from San Francisco, and leaving the scene of an accident. Barbara posted bail. Charles Cradick got the municipal court to postpone Fay's court appearance for the hit-and-run accident until the woman, who didn't want to return to Los Angeles to testify, dropped charges.

At home, their fights grew increasingly ugly. Neighbors

complained to police of screamed obscenities and door slamming at all hours. Even if no gory headlines reached the newspapers, friends and acquaintances knew what was going on. Nina Foch, who costarred with Stanwyck in *Executive Suite* twenty-two years later, was to speculate that Barbara's lifelong back problems were caused by Fay's beatings, not the result of her fall from a horse during the *Forbidden* shoot. "She did one odd thing during *Executive Suite*," Foch would recall of the 1953 filming. "She had a very emotional scene in which she had to walk up to a desk. She kept hitting the desk, bruising herself. She showed off the bruises. It was as if she was proud of the pain."

Actors often like to measure a performance's veracity according to the emotional strain and physical damage it inflicts, but the bruised thigh, hit again and again at the same spot during successive takes, offers a clue to a latent streak of masochism in Barbara. Better to be used than to feel a pit of emptiness. As much as she shrewdly presented herself at work as the pro always in control of herself, she stepped into the loyal wife character at home. Becoming famous not only meant living in a glass house, it required a level of conformity. To keep the marriage respectable, she took her husband's abuse, sometimes rearing up and fighting back, but always letting him win in the end. She wasn't sure she could change things, but was certain she could overcome both his sway and her own acquiescence. However, his domination was, in Oscar Levant's phrase, "suffocating and total." Still, she preferred pain to neglect, misery to indifference.

To escape the crowds they had once sought in Malibu, Frank and Barbara bought a three-acre property in the fashionable new Brentwood area of West Los Angeles. The walled, block-long estate was at 441 North Bristol Avenue between San Vicente and Sunset boulevards. Willard Mack lived at 12805 Sunset Boulevard with his new wife, Beatrice Banyard. Cole and Linda Porter owned a beautiful house one street over, and comedy producer Hal Roach was a few houses down. Joan Crawford, newly divorced from Douglas Fairbanks, Jr., lived in a ten-room Georgian-style manor across the street. Frank and Lucille Capra moved to Brentwood a few years later.

Over the next two years, the Fays struggled to keep the

facade of their marriage, lavishing attention on the house, pouring money and devotion into it, enlarging, changing, and rebuilding for months at a time. James E. Dolena, the architect who created some of the most elegant neoclassical houses in Southern California, built a gymnasium, and added a swimming pool and bath-bungalow. He insisted on the finest craftsmanship and angrily rejected work that didn't meet his standards. Barbara paid for the remodeling—and for Frank's Catholic charities. Barbara's new Rolls-Royce became the grand prize at Frank's parish church bazaar.

The cost of the mansion was fuel for the smoldering rumors that Barbara was fighting with Warner Brothers because of the studio's treatment of her husband and the recurring speculation about divorce. Frank and Barbara played it cute by making fun of their own nouveau riche status. Now that they had finished the house in Spanish style, they would not be surprised if they rebuilt it in English Tudor, they told *Photoplay*'s Ruth Biery. If any bright morning, Frank would wake up and say, "What I really wanted was an English house," Barbara was sure there would be seventy-five workmen on the premises by noon.

"Sure," said Frank, "that will give us something to do."

"See?"

Biery described Barbara's laugh floating over "the Spanish balcony to the Spanish swimming pool, bungalow dressing room and gymnasium" and quoted their banter verbatim:

BARBARA: I just know it was coming. Then I might want Italian.
FRANK: Then, we'd do it again, darling.
BARBARA: We'll probably end by starving.
FRANK: But we'll starve in a nice house, honey.

More seriously, Barbara told the fan magazine there wasn't a picture over which she didn't fight with Zanuck. Recently, Zanuck had showed her a note from an important theater owner criticizing Warners for making an inferior picture like *The Purchase Price*. "I chose that picture," she said. "I just *knew* it would make a good picture. There is no one to blame but me." Frank called the film business a crap game:

"You may take a trip to Palm Springs. The butler will ask for your name at your own door when you return. Whenever you leave Hollywood you are forgotten."

They were rarely invited anywhere. Perhaps they knew they were out of their depth among the film colony's slightly less nouveau new rich. The wives of studio executives were as alien to Barbara as the Manhattan rakes Oscar Levant had wanted her to meet. Barbara and Frank tried to break the ice by inviting fifty people to a big party. Two hundred and seventy-five showed up. Frank ridiculed the Charlie Chaplin fetes, the Douglas Fairbanks–Mary Pickford soirees that were de rigueur for anyone bidden to Pickfair or to the Santa Monica Art Deco home of MGM art director Cedric Gibbons and his beautiful wife, Dolores Del Rio. Frank might be a gambler, but there were no invitations from Joe and Norma Schenck to the Sunday crap games or the rival card games Irving Thalberg played at his and Norma Shearer's Santa Monica beach house. On Sundays, Frank liked to lend their home to his church, much to the annoyance of Crawford and Tone next door, who objected to the people and the traffic.

Nevertheless, Barbara and Joan became fast friends. They talked about happy coincidences, people they both knew. Willard Mack was the screenwriter of Joan's first all-talkie, *Untamed*. They had both had Marie Prevost as a fellow actress in the pictures that launched them in films. Less happily, they both had men who weren't cutting it. Joan's new love interest was Franchot Tone. Newly arrived from New York's eminent Group Theatre, Tone came from an elegant family and, until he met Crawford, was not interested in movie fame. After she fell in love with him and got MGM to renegotiate his contract, the studio gave him several opportunities. However, he was quickly typecast as the stuffed-shirt second fiddle who usually lost Crawford to Gable. Like Fay, he disdained Hollywood society, hit the bottle, and, after he married Joan, his wife. Like Frank and Barbara, Joan and Franchot were childless. Joan told friends she had seven miscarriages while married to Tone.

Joan and Barbara had a lot more in common than jealous, alcoholic husbands. Both were products of tawdry childhoods. They shared chorus girl beginnings and showbiz names picked by others. Both were more ambitious than their men.

Crawford, of course, was already a glamour queen. The saying around her studio, MGM, was that Norma Shearer got the productions, Garbo supplied the art, and Crawford made the money to pay for both.

Joan used tantrums, tears, and intimidation to advance her career. Barbara's toughness was less mannered, less posed, but both were totally self-invented, always trying harder. Joan used sex to land plum roles and preferred treatment; Barbara was less crude. She had a way of manipulating the weaknesses of the opposite sex, of appealing to men's chivalry. Three years older than Barbara, Joan had a knack for dramatizing herself, for communicating with her fans and, in blue language, for speaking the truth. She had long since forgotten her saxophone player and cast off her second husband, Douglas Fairbanks, Jr. With Clark Gable, she was MGM's favorite proletarian. Their rough manner together—in such contrast to the Broadway and British actors imported for talkies—fit perfectly the mood of the Depression. Louis B. Mayer recognized the Crawford-Gable potency. If Gable was a mobster and Crawford an impoverished heiress in *Dance, Fools, Dance,* he was a Salvation Army captain, she the owner of a clip joint in *Laughing Sinners.* Theater owners clamored for more Gable-Crawford fare, and MGM rushed the pair into two more pictures. Since MGM had given Joan a screen test in 1924, she had been in thirty-four movies. Studio designer Gilbert Adrian was fast making padded shoulders, ruffles, and wide collars her glamour trademark. Joan believed in physical fitness. Besides going to dance classes, taking swimming lessons and exercising, she had her body rubbed with ice cubes every day.

Crawford was also a bisexual who not only had a torrid affair with Gable under her husband's nose but seduced young women when they were available. More than one young reporter would tell of interviews at the Crawford residence at which the star, under the pretext of needing to change, invited the journalist to continue the conversation while she dressed for dinner. Once in the bedroom, Crawford made remarks about the color coordination of the reporter's clothes and, picking designer dresses from her own closet, suggested the visitor slip out of her dress and try on several outfits. At nineteen, she had appeared in a pornographic movie that, in

1935, led blackmailers to extort a reputed $100,000 from MGM in return for the negative. Photos of a reclining naked Crawford, eyes heavenward in real or fake ecstasy, a woman between her spread-eagled legs, circulated in the pornographic underground. Christina Crawford, Joan's adopted daughter, would say that her mother tried to sleep with a hired nurse. "I knew about my mother's lesbian proclivities," Christina would write in *Mommie Dearest*, "and this only added to what I had already figured out for myself."

Evidence of lesbianism among Hollywood's stars would always remain elusive. While homosexuality, real or supposed, was a topic of gossip, the film colony's gays lived double lives, hiding part of themselves from blackmailers, tabloid columns, and guardians of conformity and decency. The rules were not the same for lesbians and homosexual men. As long as a woman could show she was married or occasionally available to men, lesbian affairs were more acceptable in some circles than avant-garde art. At the same time, lesbians were more protective of each other than gay men. Women who dared perceive themselves as gay rarely risked admitting their lesbianism, even among women they were all but certain were also lesbian. Since childhood, Stanwyck had known how to hide her innermost feelings. Stardom had taught her pretense and how to resort to one-of-the-boys chumminess, elaborate surfaces, and campy disguises. Throughout her life, she would erase and deny all areas of intimacy. She would never define herself by her feelings for Helen Ferguson.

Sex is often a minor part of lesbian attraction, rated below respect, loyalty, and trust, and Stanwyck's lifelong friendship with Ferguson was framed within the public bounds of a working relationship that no one would question. Helen was Barbara's publicist.

An actress turned press agent and career counselor, Ferguson for nearly thirty years remained Barbara's friend. She had married and divorced an actor, and, on a second try, married a banker. Helen was as hard-driving and hard-swearing as Barbara, and her racy cussing was much admired by Barbara and by Helen's other clients—Clark Gable, Loretta Young, Henry Fonda, Nelson Eddy, Jeanette MacDonald, and Robert Taylor. Helen charged Barbara $400 a month and for twenty-seven years never varied her price. She claimed she was a publicist who never told the press a lie. When pressed on the point, she conceded, "We certainly present the facts as dramatically as the facts allow."

Born in Decatur, Illinois, Helen had started playing bit parts at thirteen in Essanay two-reelers in Chicago and made her stage debut the same year as Barbara. Jesse Lasky and Samuel Goldwyn brought her to Hollywood. Her first husband was the actor William "Big Bill" Russell, her second spouse Russell's best friend, Robert L. Hargreaves. Helen quit acting for public relations in 1930 and, with Jewel Smith as her associate, managed the Helen Ferguson Publicity Agency at 321 South Beverly Drive in Beverly Hills. Barbara and Helen had a lot in common. Neither of Helen's two marriages had produced a child. Both women struggled with feelings of uneasiness and inadequacy in their marriages. Helen was good company, if at times a bit overwhelming. By the mid-1930s their friendship was something of a joke to Jack Benny's wife, Mary Livingstone. "Why do you always bring that maid of yours?" Mary would ask. To which Barbara would pretend offense and reiterate that her friend was no maid. When they traveled together and Helen insisted too much on the star treatment for Stanwyck, Barbara was brutal. To Helen's "You are entitled" in front of hotel front desks or limousine drivers, Barbara would sneer, "Oh, shut up, Helen."

Helen Ferguson came into Stanwyck's life at a time when Barbara's faith in her marriage was floundering, when she felt she no longer knew how to set things right, when she no longer believed she could keep a lid on what her husband was doing to himself and to them. Helen was dependable where Frank was unreliable. She was a good person, fun and assertive, where Frank was a strain. Barbara reached out to Helen, but resented Helen for meeting a lot of her needs. We do not know whether the two women physically consummated their relationship—and psychiatrists of a later period would argue that the question was immaterial—but their affection for each other was lasting. Helen would live on and off at the successive Stanwyck estates, always present at critical moments in her life.

Intricate checks and balances marked their relationship. Stanwyck never mixed or confused her on-screen persona with her offscreen self. As much as she willingly bared herself for a camera, she hated revealing her private life. It was Helen's job to tell the world about Stanwyck, to tout the luminous performer. Golden-age Hollywood demanded glitter, and Helen knew earthiness didn't lend itself to star worship. Barbara didn't mix with the smart set. She wasn't quotable. Helen limited access to Barbara, imposed a distance as if she were afraid members of the press would discover there was *less* to Stanwyck than they expected. Although Barbara occasionally resented Helen for mothering her, she trusted her not only to pick the journalists she should see, but to sit in on the few interviews they both found unavoidable, steering questions away from what would have made the Barbara Stanwyck story more than the prosaic little-girl-lost, up-from-the-bottom saga. Copy from the Helen Ferguson Agency described Stanwyck's sincerity, loyalty, and intrinsic honesty and turned her head-over-heels falling for Fay into reticence. "It wasn't love at first sight," said a 1938 Helen Ferguson Agency ten-page biography. "Barbara was on top, she didn't need any help, didn't want to marry." The "bio" postponed the St. Louis wedding by a year. In a digression that perhaps reflected Barbara's adult marital trouble more than a memory of parental discord since she was three when her mother died and her father disappeared, she was quoted as saying the reason she had hesitated to marry Fay was that she "remembered what marriage meant from her childhood days."

Stanwyck was never inside, or "in the life," as the lesbian bar phrase of the period had it, but the screen image of gutsy, self-reliant, and self-assured woman she developed combined with her reticence to tell the world about herself made her a lifelong icon of gay women. Unearthing the truth about her sexuality would remain impossible, not only because Helen never quite trusted us with the real Barbara, but because Tinseltown's anything-goes myth encouraged prurient conjecture. People would swear that she was, with Greta Garbo, Hollywood's most famous closeted lesbian, that "everybody" knew. Some would say they were friends of so-and-so who had been her lover. Such informants, however, would shy away from giving the name of the woman or retreat into generalities. The Fays were never thought of as "twilight tandems," nor was their marriage a "lavender" cover-up. Barbara enjoyed people—men—as long as they didn't come too close.

Catholicism and Judaism—the predominant faiths of showbiz people—are explicitly antagonistic to same-sex love. Although Hollywood was more tolerant of drinking, drugs, cohabitation, and avant-garde politics than the rest of the country, homosexuality was a deadly proclivity that, if found out, usually meant instant ruin. Since it was hardly in any studio's interest if word got out that its leading man was faking it when he kissed the leading lady, homosexuals lived behind the wall of silence. Arm-twisted by the studios that had them under contract, suspected lesbian actresses routinely married, many of them husbands who were homosexuals. Gay and lesbian couples like Vincente Minnelli and Judy Garland produced children when they had to.

To heterosexual males Stanwyck was provocative, to women in love with women she was affirming. To lesbians growing up in loneliness, lacking contacts with other lesbians, fearing parental shock and despairing of finding examples to emulate, the Barbara Stanwyck screen image defined her as "one of us." The reason was not any coded message in gestures or delivery, but the way the screen characters to which she gave life defined themselves in their own terms and were comparatively independent of men and of household expectations. What made lesbians sit up and notice was that when Stanwyck confronted men there was no subliminal I'm-Jane-you're-Tarzan glint of the kind Bette Davis, Katharine Hepburn, and Rosalind Russell used. Stanwyck was mocking and emotionally honest, and the way she related to the opposite sex was different from that of the screen's other tough ladies.

To a majority of lesbians of her day who saw marriage as the safest front and therefore the only viable choice, she was someone who arranged her life in such a way as to avoid public censure yet, on the screen, luminously defied respectability. In the dark anonymity of a movie theater, lesbians didn't care that the plot demanded Stanwyck be attracted to a man. They told each other the characters she played in *Ladies of Leisure*, *Ten Cents a Dance*, *Ladies They Talk About*—much lesbian slang came from women's prisons—and *Baby Face* "worked" for them. They watched every new Stanwyck movie and projected their sexual instincts onto the screen and read their yearnings into Barbara's straight gaze and pulsating voice.

Her sexual ambivalence was buried deep in her private nature. She grew up without focused attention, knowing she didn't really matter to anybody. Accepting herself became a lifelong undertaking. She didn't believe private behavior could reveal public character, but turning made-up parts into full-blooded women was the essential rush of her life. The camera was never a threat, the curiosity of strangers was.

The "gay lib" of the 1970s and '80s made Stanwyck uncomfortable. When a gay activist asked about her sexual preference, he was nearly thrown out of her house. Her marginal childhood made her want to conform. Anything borderline was risky. Her politics were right of center, not so much because of Frank's conservatism but because of her deep-seated need to be in control. Others might liberate themselves, in Virginia Woolf's phrase, from "unreal loyalties," including loyalties to accepted sexual norms. But Barbara never considered her relationships with Helen Ferguson, Crawford, and others as having anything to do with the attachments between "real lesbians."

Despite his risqué stage repertoire and rogue swagger, Fay was a prude. He had worked with Eva Le Gallienne, an actress who was candid about her lesbianism, but he was convinced Katharine Cornell was more applauded because she concealed her sexual inclination in her long-term marriage to bisexual producer Guthrie McClintic. When Frank said he wanted his wife to stay home, he expressed prevailing women's magazine convictions that a woman holding down a professional position was in danger of losing her womanly qualities. With Barbara, he avoided discussing matters that might prove embarrassing to either of them.

Stanwyck's only public brush with convoluted morals charges came in 1934 when a private nurse sued her. Stanwyck had hired Elizabeth Curtis in New Jersey and brought her to Los Angeles. Claiming she was owed $3,500 in wages, the nurse alleged that Stanwyck had wanted her to live with Frank's father and in a deposition hinted that sexual favors had been expected of her. In the absence of specifics, everyone assumed it was Francis Donner's libido, not his daughter-in-law's, that Nurse Curtis had been expected to stroke. Charles Cradick handled the damage control as he had done in Barbara's contractual dispute with Harry Cohn two years earlier. Hinting that the young woman's character was more suspect than her pay claim suggested, the lawyer told the press that Stanwyck would not dignify the allegation with an answer. "If persons engaged in the motion-picture business made public statements each time unwarranted demands were made on them for money and such statements were published in the press, there would be little, if any, space for other news."

Curtis's Superior Court suit was filed March 9, 1934, naming Stanwyck, Frank Fay, and his father as defendants. Frank and Barbara spirited Francis Donner to Arizona so he couldn't be subpoenaed to testify and, through Cradick, let it be known they were visiting Donner in Arizona themselves. When District Attorney Burton Fitts began checking the nurse's allegation, she dropped charges of sexual impropriety. In an amended complaint filed three weeks later, she withdrew her statement that Stanwyck had induced her to stay with Donner Sr., and reduced her complaint to compensation for services as "private nurse, companion, maid and cook." Her $3,500 suit was settled out of court.

Although Stanwyck and Crawford were sometime rivals for juicy roles over the years, they remained lifelong friends, on occasion comforting each other. Joan would recall how Barbara climbed over the wall one night, saying she was leaving Frank and asking if she could spend the night. "Their fights were dreadful," Joan would remember. "He hit her often. Franchot hit me, too. When it goes that far, the time has come to call it quits. Barbara and Frank might have made a success of their marriage if they'd gone back to New York." Crawford believed her friend stayed married—and in Hollywood—because the sacrifices on the way up had been too hard. "Like Barbara, I was challenged by Hollywood. We fought and starved and begged. How could we give it up even for a good marriage?"

The deepest contradiction in Joan and Barbara was a need both to be in control and to be taken care of. Marriage, even a cracked marriage, gave both a sense of belonging and stability. It was par for the course. Besides Crawford and Tone, Barbara's old roommate Mae Clarke had suffered the same indignities trying to keep her husband in gambling money. Mae had played the heroine in Universal's *Waterloo Bridge*, portrayed Lionel Barrymore's daughter in *This Side of Heaven*, and come close to stardom when James Cagney pushed half a grapefruit into her face in *Public Enemy*. Her husband, Lew Brice, never got anywhere in pictures, and after years of being known as Fanny Brice's brother, he instead become known as Mae Clarke's husband. When she came home after a day's work at the studio, Lew would demand, "Who the hell have you been flirting with today?" and rough her up. After he roughed her up one day she spent the night at her sister-in-law's. They had divorced by the time of the Cagney grapefruit scene, and Lew made it doubly famous in New York by entering the Strand Theatre just before Cagney shoved the grapefruit in Mae's face. Lew sat and gloated, left, and returned for the next screening. Mae starred with Cagney again in *Lady Killer*, and critics had fun with Cagney picking on her again, this time dragging her around by the hair. In 1936, Cagney and Clarke were teamed a third time in *Great Guy*, but the routine mercifully had become repetitious.

Frank couldn't cope with a life beneath his abilities. He had what Barbara called a "wounded animal" attitude toward bad luck. In his own mind, there was nothing irrational in believing that for him the movies were jinxed. So firmly did he accept this that there was nothing to explain. Hollywood was out to get him.

While he began negotiating with Broadway impresarios about another return, Barbara tried a new tack—involving him in *her* career. She told him Jack Warner and Darryl Zanuck agreed she could have some say in the choice of films. For each of her remaining three commitments, Zanuck would submit six possible stories for her consideration. If she wasn't sure, Zanuck, she, *and* Frank would make the final choice.

Both Columbia and Warner Brothers publicists tried to deflect newspaper inquiries into the state of the Fay marriage, but Frank foiled their best efforts by acting up in nightclubs. Friends excluded them, and when Frank realized invitations had dried up he blamed her. Barbara ignored the blows Frank administered, refused to see anything terribly wrong. She went along with whatever he wanted, covered for him. She let him tell people *he* was the star and his wife merely fulfilling a contract. On nights out, she drank with him. She had never found life to be fair, and she took Frank's abuse. He was no longer the man she had looked up to, but she couldn't give him up. If she did, she would be back to the worst aspects of her unconnected, empty childhood.

Frank got a movie. *Stars Over Broadway* was his first in four years, a tongue-in-cheek opera movie starring Pat O'Brien. Fay played the master of ceremonies at a comic amateur hour against O'Brien's manager of the Metropolitan Opera and tenor James Melton's classical singer.

Their fights continued. Few personal mementos would survive a fire at her house in 1938, but one undated letter, written to Frank after one of their brawls, told of her desperation to hang on to him, to somehow make it all come out right, even if it meant the end of her career.

> I love you just as much as it is possible for a woman to love a man. If I were born with anything fine in me, and I choose to think I was from what I know of my father and mother, you have brought that fineness to the surface.
>
> I cannot imagine life without you and I am not being melodramatic.
>
> I probably do not give you the impression at any time—that of not being able to imagine life without you, I mean. However, that is due to my lack of education and not being able to express myself clearly in speech.
>
> I can write it, however. You are always right about everything so you must be right about what you want to do. Please, Frank, love me—whatever you do. And wherever you go, take me. For there I shall be content.
>
> Pain rather than indifference.

10

Depression Blues

A few years ago they talked about her as 'Frank Fay's poor talented little wife who couldn't seem to get a start in pictures,'" wrote columnist Thomas Reddy. "Today they talk about her as a picture star in her own right who goes on to the stage to act as 'stooge' for the wisecracks of her comedian husband. Barbara didn't worry about the sympathy that was wasted on her three or four years ago, but she objects rather strenuously to the 'talk' occasioned by her devotion to the career of Frank Fay." She insisted they were going to be happy despite the gossip.

Living with Frank was a roller-coaster ride of good times and pain, fun and disillusions, and desperate attempts at making up. The relationship chewed them up. There were moments when she found it hard to believe it was she talking. She wanted the two of them to make it and made herself believe it was her duty to get Frank to stop drinking because she was married to him and marriage was supposed to anchor their existence and last forever. She was angry with herself because he didn't succeed in making his career rebound. Was a child the solution?

Not that she was expecting. During her teenage years and early twenties, she had avoided stag parties but shimmied in speakeasies, danced in chorus lines on Broadway and on the road, cadged meals at LaHiff's, impressed Willard Mack and Arthur Hopkins, and fallen in love with Rex Cherryman, all without getting pregnant. Or had she? Contraception was crude in the 1920s. Barbara would never admit to an abortion, nor would she ever bear a child. An unwanted pregnancy was the chorus girl's curse—her friend Crawford admitted to four abortions—and for Barbara and Rex enjoying their first flush of success, a pregnancy would have been devastating. There can be no doubt that she would have done whatever it took not to let the brass ring slip from her grasp, including a back-alley abortion.

Frank didn't want to adopt a child—to him fatherhood had to be biological. But Barbara insisted. Two weeks before Christmas 1932, they adopted a ten-month-old boy from the Children's Home Society. Court papers showed John Charles Greene to be the son of Vivian Greene, whose written consent was obtained for the file. No father was mentioned.

Once home on Bristol Avenue, Barbara and Frank named their son Anthony Dion and happily played house. For a brief time they bent over the crib in awe and self-congratulation, but within weeks, the infant was left in the care of a succession of nurses and nannies. Stanwyck talked of baby Dion as a fulfillment and reminded reporters that she had been an orphan herself. She would like to adopt a slew of orphans and surround them with love, she told *Photoplay*. When the press asked to take pictures of Dion in her arms, she refused. "Too much attention will make him unhappy, too," she said. "We want him to have a normal, happy childhood. We all just want to be left alone, please."

It was all a facade. Barbara put in long days, six days a week at the studio, and her husband's brooding and drinking didn't stop. Frank whined that he was sacrificing his career for hers. She couldn't stand to see Frank unhappy and, against her better judgment, all too often gave in to him. After he threw Dion into the swimming pool in a drunken rage, the nanny locked herself and the toddler into the nursery when he was home. Frank's father was so ill at ease he talked of moving out.

In his rages and self-pity Frank conveniently forgot who earned the money that paid for the mansion and the staff and kept him in booze. Frank had voted for Herbert Hoover, but Franklin D. Roosevelt won on the promise of intervening directly to redress the economic situation. Hollywood was among the last businesses to feel the Depression. Cinema admissions were pushing a hundred million a week in 1930, and going to the movies remained the cheapest and, for many, the only entertainment. All-night movie houses at ten cents a seat were crowded with homeless snorers. Many people couldn't afford even dimes for entertainment or comfort, however, and attendance began to slip. By 1932, Paramount, Metro-Goldwyn-Mayer, Warners, Fox, and RKO were losing money. The need to turn out sparkling entertainment—and to complete the costly switch to sound—kept even a pacesetter like MGM (and cost-conscious outfits like Warners and Universal) dependent on a few sources of big money. It was, of course, the moviemen's experience that bankers first made suggestions, later imposed restrictions, and finally gave orders.

Sure enough. A month after Roosevelt had won the election, creditors forced Loews Inc. and its subsidiary MGM to temporarily cut the salaries of everybody earning more than $1,500 a week. Paramount, Fox, and RKO were on the brink of receivership. The industry imposed a 50 percent across-the-board salary cut for all personnel in a scramble to contain costs. To make everybody swallow, the studios agreed that the Academy of Motion Picture Arts and Sciences and the Price Waterhouse accounting firm—not the studios themselves—would decide when a company must end its cuts.

Since *Ladies of Leisure* Stanwyck had made four pictures for Columbia, four for Warners, and in the process turned herself into a recession-proof asset. As a girl with a past, dance-hall hostess, tent-show evangelist, unwed mother, night nurse, waitress on the make, Edna Ferber heroine, and torch singer turned mail-order bride she had become the throaty-voiced stand-up dame that Depression audiences loved. In *The Bitter Tea of General Yen*, she got to play a brash and virginal missionary tempted by unseemly desire for a man of another race. Capra got to veil her in the most erotic camerawork of his career.

The original novel was by Grace Zaring Stone, an author of spare prose and cosmopolitan views. *The Bitter Tea of General Yen* had been published to glowing reviews in 1930—a year before Pearl S. Buck's *Good Earth*. "A remarkable picture of white people in China, and wherever Miss Stone deals with them she is extraordinarily effective," wrote *The Nation*. The book told the story of a young American woman who comes to

Shanghai to marry a medical missionary and finds herself, through stress of civil war and circumstance, an uninvited guest in the spy-infested residence of General Yen, a Kuomintang leader fighting the Communists. For three days Megan Davis is in intimate contact with the cultured, brilliant, cynical general. She tries to save his concubine from the inevitable penalty for treason and to save Yen from the encircling Communists. An American named Jones counterbalances Megan as a Machiavellian figure whose chosen vocation is to bankroll the civil war and advise General Yen.

When a railway car stashed with money to pay his mercenary army is waylaid by Yen's enemies, the general finds himself powerless. Aware that Megan has fallen in love with him, he nevertheless commits suicide by poisoning his own tea. Megan and Jones escape to Shanghai by boat, she much less sure of herself and of Christian ethics as a cure-all for the world. As Jones tells her, "Yen was a great guy. He said we never really die, only change. Maybe he's the wind that's pushing the sail now and playing around your hair."

Capra not only fell in love with Stone's story of people from alien cultures coming together, clashing, and falling in love, but saw its screen version as a chance finally to earn a Best Director Academy Award. Constance Bennett, who had starred in Capra's latest film, American Madness, was set to play Megan, when he cast Stanwyck. "The missionary was a well-bred, straightlaced New England young lady, externally frigid but internally burning with her 'call,'" he would write in his autobiography. "Casting this part was easy—Barbara Stanwyck." So was the role of Jones. In a New York play, Capra had seen Walter Connolly and immediately decided he should play the fat, wheezy cynic who sells his deadly talents to the highest bidder.

General Yen was another matter.

The realism of sound aroused fierce demands for stricter censorship. The transplanted playwrights, short-story writers, and novelists writing talkies were accustomed to the freedom of the stage and of publishing and tended to write screenplays with much of the same freedom. But sound gave ammunition to procensorship pressure groups. What had been a pantomime of hints, winks, and allusions in silent movies was shockingly amplified when words matched the action.

The detailed listing of "don'ts" and "be carefuls" of the revised 1930 Production Code included miscegenation. If the studios pledged that their movies would never show "any licentious or suggestive nudity—in fact or in silhouette, any inference of sex perversion, white slavery, sex hygiene and venereal diseases, and children's organs," they also agreed not to show love relationships between people of different races. While the code was more often honored in the breach than in the observance, this was one taboo that nobody dared infringe. Miscegenation statues forbidding and declaring invalid marriages between persons of different color were on the books in thirty states, including California.

In 1916, DeMille had starred Fannie Ward and Sessue Hayakawa in *The Cheat*, the story of a society woman who gambles away Red Cross funds entrusted to her, borrows $10,000 from a wealthy Japanese, and is forced by the exigencies of the plot to behave for most of the film like a vamp. But that was before Mary Pickford's Nevada "quickie" divorce from Owen Moore and her marriage to Douglas Fairbanks without waiting the full year required by California law shocked the country. It was before Charlie Chaplin was caught with underage girls, before the California State Board of Pharmacy revelation that over five hundred film personalities were on its rolls as drug addicts, and before the 1924 sex-orgy-with-murder-trial of Fatty Arbuckle that gave churchmen, clubwomen, schoolteachers, and editorial writers the chance to inveigh against the new Sodom on the Pacific.

In self-defense, the studio chiefs had hired Will Hays, the Presbyterian elder and Indiana politician, and created the Association of Motion Picture Producers and Distributors of America—better known as the Hays Office. Howard Hawks was forced to cast Myrna Loy as a Chinese woman in *A Girl in Every Port* so Victor McLaglen could kiss her. As Capra tried to decide how to shape *The Bitter Tea of General Yen*, the newly organized Catholic Legion of Decency pushed for a tougher code.

As Barbara knew from her tough-dames flicks, the trick for producers and directors was to walk right up to the *don't* line while suggesting in their advertising that they were crossing it. Capra protested that what he didn't want was a well-known star made up as an Asian while knowing a Caucasian in makeup *was* the only solution. After seeing several actors, he chose Nils Asther, a tall, blue-eyed Swedish homosexual whose impassive good looks usually had him cast as exotic, often royal, romantic figures.

Almost deported six months earlier for working on a tourist visa, Asther conveniently married Vivian Duncan of the Duncan Sisters, divorcing her several months later. He was a portrait painter on his days off, and had been Greta Garbo's leading man in *The Single Standard*. To the delight of the film crew, Garbo told him during a kissing scene, "Don't kiss me so hard! I'm not one of your sailors!" Asther spoke a slightly pedantic English that as much as his imperturbable face pleased Capra.

Blue eyes photographed steel-gray in black-and-white. Working with the studio makeup artist, Capra and Joe Walker covered Asther's upper eyelids with smooth, round, false "skin" and clipped his eyelashes to one-third their natural length. The stiff upper eyelids kept his eyes in a permanent, half-closed position. On the screen, he looked strange and decisively not Caucasian. Wearing a uniform or a Mandarin wardrobe and adapting a long, slow walk with arms moving back and forth parallel with each stride, the handsome Swede was metamorphosed into a stunningly cultured, mysterious, and ruthless General Yen.

Exposing his denuded eyes to the glare of studio lights, however, nearly blinded him. Studio doctors ordered him locked up in a dark dressing room between shots and insisted that he wear dark glasses during rehearsals. Despite the precautions, he suffered acute pain throughout the filming. Doctors administered compresses, eyedrops, and painkillers after each exposure of Asther's nearly eyelashless eyes to the sun arcs. Capra and Cohn congratulated themselves on their own cleverness. Who could object when what anyone would *see* on the screen was Barbara Stanwyck kissing a white man in makeup?

The Megan Stanwyck and Capra created on the screen hovers disturbingly between missionary rectitude and unseemly yearnings. Megan is both repelled and attracted to Yen, and, in Capra's changed ending, the general commits suicide rather than live with the humiliation of sexual rejection. "Any revulsion would be within herself," said Barbara of

Megan. "At least that is how I felt—how could I be attracted. How *could* I?"

It was only a year earlier that Capra had taken off for Europe after Barbara had refused to divorce and marry him, and, on the rebound, had married Lucille. To show her attraction to the general, Capra invented a disturbing sexual dream sequence that didn't exist in the novel. Caught in Joe Walker's most sensuous camera movements, Megan dreams that a handsome, masked stranger comes to her bed. For a quick cut Yen turns into a westernized lover. A second later, her erotic dream turns into nightmare as she realizes the clawed and diabolic stranger is General Yen. Was Capra exorcising his own passions for Barbara? The dream-hallucination scene would remain a unique attempt at illustrating unconscious desire in his career.

The Bitter Tea of General Yen was the only Capra film until *Lost Horizon* in 1937 not set in America. The film inaugurated New York's Radio City Music Hall as a movie theater on January 11, 1933. Over 10 million Americans were out of work—there would be 14.5 million unemployed by midsummer—and in its review of the picture the *New York Times* noted how the Music Hall management was agreeably surprised at the throngs for the initial performance: "Most of the lower-priced seats were filled before 1 o'clock in the afternoon, and later there were lines in the grand foyer and along the 50th Street side of the house awaiting admission. Even the loge chairs were well patronized." Critics praised Capra for the sensuous atmospherics, Stanwyck for her portrayal of the prim Miss Megan, and Asther for his exotic Yen, but called the story of forbidden love and suicide as implausible as it was entertaining. *Variety* warned that "seeing a Chinaman attempting to romance with a pretty and supposedly decent young American white woman is bound to evoke adverse reaction."

The film was not a success, and Capra would have to wait until *It Happened One Night* before he won his first Oscar. Scheduled for at least a two-week run, *Bitter Tea* was pulled from Radio City after one week.

"The story was far ahead of its time in that the missionary comes to respect the 'heathen' attitudes of the Oriental," Barbara would say forty years later. "Before the General drinks his poisoned tea, she touches him in farewell—and worse—actually kisses his hand. His hand! Women's groups all over the country protested, wrote letters to exhibitors, saying we were condoning miscegenation." Barbara was under the impression that *Bitter Tea* was banned in Britain and the Commonwealth, when it fact it was passed by the British Board of Censors after a few cuts were made and also approved by the Commonwealth Film Censorship Board. Barbara no doubt got the impression of racial censorship after Columbia passed along an Australian scandal sheet's attack on the film. Calling it a "detestable" story of "a loathsome Chinese bandit pawing and mauling a white woman," *Truth* deplored the fact that it had been passed "by the Commonwealth Film Censorship Board without the slightest misgiving, apparently."

Zanuck assigned Stanwyck to star in a women's prison yarn that stands the woman-redeeming-the-man conventions on its head. In her tough, no-nonsense style, Barbara plays a gorgeous bank robber and Preston Foster a reformer-evangelist she gets even with. After she accuses him of frustrating a jailbreak in which two of her friends are killed, she loses her temper, pulls a gun from her handbag, and shoots him. *Ladies They Talk About* had two directors—Howard Bretherton and William Keighley. Bretherton made over a hundred B movies between 1926 and 1952 and reached a measure of fame as William (Hopalong Cassidy) Boyd's favorite director. Keighley was a painstaking company craftsman who spent his twenty-year career at Warners. Together or separately, they surrounded Stanwyck with a motley crew of sashaying, conceited, jealous fellow prisoners and added domestic touches to life in the "Big House." The convicts' frank man-hunger got *Ladies They Talk About* into trouble with the Hays Office.

Feminist film historians would come to see Barbara Stanwyck as a victim of the Depression screen smut and cite *Baby Face*, a nervy Zanuck programmer, as the most exploitative of the string of early 1930s Stanwyck movies. But Barbara was an inventive partner in the sleaze.

Notes kept by writer Howard Smith of a November 1932 story conference show how he, Zanuck, and Stanwyck decided to start the movie with a zinger: Baby Face's father should force her to have sex with different men.

Smith wrote to Zanuck:

> Following the conference with contract star Barbara Stanwyck, I am sending you this note to remind you of the things she suggested, and which you suggested during this conference, for amplification and improvement of the story.
>
> The idea of [sic] Baby Face's father beats her and forces her into a room where he knows a guy is waiting to spend the night with her—forces her into the room and turns the key in the lock after her. This is planted to definitely establish dialogue at the scene where the young banker asks Barbara Stanwyck to let him have the money he had given her in order to save him from prison.

Roosevelt took office on March 4, 1933, a month after Adolf Hitler became reich chancellor of Germany. The next day, the new president informed *The Nation* he was calling for a special session of Congress and that the next four days were to be holidays for all banks and financial institutions. By June FDR's National Industrial Recovery Act was helping Hollywood by sanctioning certain monopoly practices. Darryl Zanuck was sure Warners had weathered the Depression. When the Academy and Price Waterhouse told the company to restore salaries, however, Harry Warner refused.

Zanuck was furious. He had promised his people to restore their salaries on the date designated by the Academy and Price Waterhouse and in a violent confrontation with Harry Warner refused to renege. It was a rude awakening. Zanuck had come to believe he was the crown prince. Now Harry told him he was just another studio employee.

Zanuck's fight with the brothers Warner over restoring studio salaries came to a head during the filming of *Baby Face*. Stanwyck was teamed again with George Brent and directed by Alfred E. Green. Lily Powers is an ambitious working woman who uses her wiles to climb the corporate ladder in a New York bank. Brent is the bank president, Donald Cook the nice young man she tosses aside, and Robert Barrat plays her father, the owner of a shady speakeasy. A big, shy new-comer from Winterset, Iowa, whose name had only recently been changed from Marion Morrison to John Wayne, played the assistant bank manager.

Lily uses the young cashier engaged to marry the first vice president's daughter to attract the attention of the vice president and, later, the president himself. After she threatens to sell her story to the tabloids, she is shipped to Paris to work at the bank's branch office. When President Brent comes to Paris, he becomes sufficiently smitten to marry her. Back in New York, he embezzles funds to keep her in cash, jewelry, and furs. Although she knows she must hand back the $500,000 in cash if her husband is to avoid being discovered and convicted, she decided to leave for Paris again. In post-production, *Baby Face* ran into demands for stricter censor-ship rules.

Zanuck was working on the picture when he tore up his contract in his dispute with Harry Warner. Afraid of taking sides, gossip columnists suggested the Warner-Zanuck row was over *Baby Face*. Cuts and a rewritten ending allowed *Baby Face* to slip under the wire before a revised Production Code went into effect.

Zanuck walked out cold on his $5,000-a-week WB job. Everybody wanted him. Louis B. Mayer invited him to join MGM, Harry Cohn cornered him at a preview, but it was the canny Joe Schenck who came up with the offer Zanuck couldn't refuse. "You and I will start a producing company," said Schenck, who was also becoming restless as United Artists president. They'd call their new company Twentieth Century. To sign the deal, Schenck handed Zanuck a check for $100,000. Barbara would have loved to follow, but she couldn't walk out of her Warners contract—if nothing else her fights with Cohn had taught her that lesson. She had fought with Zanuck over *Illicit*, *So Big*, *The Purchase Price*, and *Ladies They Talk About*, but with him gone she lost her best front-office support.

Stanwyck changed agents during the summer of 1933. After four years with Arthur Lyons, she opted for Zeppo Marx, who after serving as his brothers' butt decided being a talent agent was more fun.

Adolph (Harpo), Leonard (Chico), Julius (Groucho), Milton (Gummo), and young Herbert (Zeppo) had honed their madcap humor in vaudeville and in 1929 switched to movies and made five moderately popular Paramount comedies, including *Monkey Business*, *Horse Feathers*, and the now classic *Duck Soup*. Chico specialized in Italian dialect routines, Harpo performed in pantomime and played the harp, and Groucho was the leering, bushy-browed, fast-quipping, wisecracking leader, leaving little for Gummo and Zeppo to do. Taking pity on Gummo, the brothers had made him their business manager.

In 1928, Zeppo married Marion Benda, née Bimberg. He was getting less money than any of the brothers, and yet Marion and he lived better than any of them. Zep had none of Groucho's needs for racing to New York for intellectual stimulus. He had none of Chico's womanizing habits, but all of his gambling addiction. Zep's aggressive card sense made him a terror of the studio bosses; in one all-night poker game he won $22,000 from Paramount's studio chief, B. P. Schulberg. Claiming he was "sick and tired of being the stooge," the youngest son of Minnie and Simon "Frenchy" Marx's sons left the team after *Duck Soup*.

Zep got the idea of becoming a talent agent by watching Myron Selznick wheel and deal for the Marx Brothers. Selznick handled writers, directors, stars—even Paramount's costume designer Travis Banton—and exploited *any* advantage to negotiate lucrative deals that made his client and him rich and the studios less so.

Myron and his younger brother, David, were sons of a Russian Jewish emigrant who made a shaky fortune in the chaotic early years of the picture business. When Lewis J. Selznick lost it all, his boys vowed vengeance on the studio heads who had contributed to their father's downfall. Revenge and proving everybody wrong were what motivated much of Myron's meteoric career as a superagent and David's as a movie tycoon. Zep could think of no greater thrill than to become an agent of Myron Selznick's class. In 1933, Zep bought a partnership in the Bren-Orsatti Agency. There was no Bren, only the Orsatti brothers, Victor and Frank. Victor was on the phone all day doing the contracts his feisty brother initiated over cobb salads at studio commissaries and the

Brown Derby. Their father, Morris Orsatti, was serving a twenty-year sentence for attempting bribery of a federal agent, and Frank was a former bootlegger and real-estate agent rumored to have connections with the Mafia. Budd Schulberg called Frank Orsatti the characteristic "agent pimp with a touch of *Little Caesar.*"

Georges Kaufman and Moss hart gave Zep permission to use their names as clients so that other writers would consider signing up with him. Two years later, Gummo became his kid brother's East Coast representative when Bren-Orsatti opened a New York office and made plans to represent stage talents. Learning a few tricks from Myron Selznick, Zeppo threatened MGM's Irving Thalberg with joining Chico, Harpo, and Groucho in the upcoming *A Night at the Opera* unless the studio chief hired one of his clients. It is not known whether the prospect of Zep as a straight man so ruined Thalberg's hopes for the new Marx Brothers films that he gave in, but the threat improved Zep's aura as a talent agent.

Compared to his brothers, Zep was good-looking. Barbara would remember him as a bodybuilding enthusiast showing off his bulging, rippling muscles and his wife as a vivacious brunette of exquisite taste. Both were fierce tennis players and robust social drinkers who indulged themselves by buying a yacht and, under Marion's supervision, redecorating their ranch on the far side of the San Fernando Valley. "It was the prettiest house I've ever seen," Chico's daughter Maxine recalled. "Marion designed it from a movie she saw. It wasn't ostentatious, but the house was totally charming."

Stanwyck was a coup for Marx and the Orsatti brothers. Frank Orsatti convinced Barbara she needed a permanent stand-in and insisted the studios use a young actress named Jean Chatburn as Stanwyck's double and that she be part of each contract. Next, he married Chatburn. Shortly after Barbara signed up, a saxophone player who didn't think he could act also became a client. In less than six years, Stanwyck and Fred MacMurray would be the highest-paid Hollywood stars.

Without Zanuck in her corner and without any input from Frank, Barbara made five movies for Warners over the next year and a half. In *Ever in My Heart*, she played a patriot who marries a German spy. The story was by Beulah Marie

Dix, a historian and screenwriter who with William DeMille, Cecil B's brother, had founded the Famous Players–Lasky scenario department in 1916. Directed by Archie Mayo, this heavy romantic drama had Otto Kruger as a German-born college professor deported during World War I. Barbara is his American wife who discovers he is a spy, kills him, and, to prevent secrets from reaching the enemy, commits suicide.

Eight years later when versatility was paying off and Edith Head created twenty-five gowns for her for *The Lady Eve*, Barbara would have little use for *Ever in My Heart* and other "women programmers" of the deep Depression years. "Only once did I seem to be setting into a groove and that was in the days when I was under regular contract at Warners," she would say in 1944 when she was the highest-paid woman in the United States. "I played a series of parts that were much alike—women who were suffering and poor, and living amid sloppy surroundings."

She lost a pair of plum parts in film versions of top Broadway plays. George S. Kaufman and Moss Hart had satirized Hollywood in their 1930 smash hit, *Once in a Lifetime*, and when Universal Pictures bought the screen rights, Stanwyck tried for the movie version. Aline MacMahon, the actress Warners considered among the ten smartest, in a class with Katharine Hepburn and Helen Hayes, got the part in the razor-sharp, mad comedy about the havoc the coming of sound wreaked on Hollywood. Next, Cohn announced Stanwyck would be loaned to Paramount to star in the screen adaptation of the S. N. Behrman play *Brief Moment*. The leading lady's role as a nightclub singer was right up Barbara's alley. But Carole Lombard, who was hitting her stride as the stylish, wisecracking heroine of screwball comedies, got the part.

Frank conjured up a scheme to rebound on Broadway, convinced that what his wife and the movie people didn't understand was his need for a live audience. His comedy routines fed on audience reactions, his phrasing, looks, and timing on laughter and applause. Humor was delicate. A titter in the tenth row could string out a line, belly laughs in the balcony sent him off in new ad-libbing. Jokes wilted on a soundstage, where a director commanded dead silence by yelling

"Action!" or asked for a tenth take of the quip. To help save his and her own sanity, Barbara sank her first important money into *Tattle Tales*, a musical revue Fay could star in.

The timing was wrong. Audiences with money to spend deserted vaudeville for the all-talking, all-singing, all-dancing movies. But Frank was sure that, like Eddie Cantor and Sophie Tucker, he could still pull them in.

Tattle Tales went on its pre-Broadway tour in April 1933. Fay and Nick Copeland wrote twenty-nine scenes, Copeland performing in some of them. The show featured eighteen performers and, in a spoof on Hollywood, a song called "I'll take an Option on You." The road reviews were not unacceptable, and *Tattle Tales* was scheduled for a June 11 New York opening at the Broadhurst Theater on Forty-fourth Street. To give the opening a lift, and despite the earlier criticism for capitalizing on her film success, Barbara joined the *Tattle Tales* cast with a scene from *The Miracle Woman*. The premiere audience and critics suggested a summer-long run was in store for *Tattle Tales*. Two weeks later, *Baby Face* opened at New York's Strand Theatre to sensational reviews. "Any hotter than this for public showing would call for an asbestos audience blanket," winked *Variety*.

The month of July turned out to be the hottest on record in New York, and *Tattle Tales* wilted as the heat drove audiences from the non-air-conditioned Broadhust. The Frank Fay show closed after twenty-eight days. As if it wasn't humiliating enough for Frank to see *Tattle Tales* fold, his wife's other Warner Brothers quickie, *Ever in My Heart*, opened three weeks later. "Barbara Stanwyck demonstrated that she is one of the first—the very first—actresses among the more exalted leading ladies in Hollywood," wrote the *New York World-Telegram*.

In Barbara's mind, the point of adopting little Dion had been to save the marriage. The point of *Tattle Tales* had been to save Frank's career and her marriage. Since it did neither, she decided that from now on she would stay in California.

Stanwyck was also hitting her stride as an independent businesswoman. Disciplined and hardworking, she was the exception to the star system. No actress free-lanced as she did during the golden era. In the seven years since United Artists had brought her to Hollywood for *The Locked Door*, she had made seven films for Columbia, seven for Warners, and was soon to sign one- and two-picture deals with MGM, RKO, Twentieth Century-Fox, and Paramount. She counted on Zep Marx for contractual fine points, Helen Ferguson for public relations, but she was her own judge on what to accept. Her assertiveness and business acumen would grow throughout her life, and in 1933 she found a revealing way of making a mark of her own. Nobody would have been astonished if she devoted her spare energies to the adoption of orphans or other studio-approved worthy causes. Bess Lasky, her former Malibu neighbor, worked to maintain a home where the many eager young women lured west by shady talent schools could escape the casting couches her husband and other producers so diligently set up in their offices. What interested Barbara, however, was not safeguarding the virtue of would-be actresses, but the advancement of young women in business. If businessmen had their Rotary Clubs, why couldn't professional women have their support groups? Women in the professions shouldn't hang back like privileged wives of successful businessmen, but try to extend their influence by seizing opportunities. Stanwyck became the founder of the Athena National Sorority, an organization for young businesswomen named after the Greek goddess of war, handicraft, and practical reason. Seven years later, the Athena Sorority boasted more than four hundred members.

Single

Stanwyck made four Warner Brothers programmers back-to-back to pay for *Tattle Tales*. She was a fashion model in love with an older man in *A Lost Lady* and, like Crawford, got to change clothes every few minutes. The *Baby Face* writers, Gene Markey and Kathryn Scola, were responsible for the empty-headed adaptation of Willa Cather's 1923 novel, Alfred E. Green for the direction. The film so outraged Cather that she wrote a clause into her will in 1943 forbidding any future dramatization of her novels.

Gambling Lady was Stanwyck's first film with Joel McCrea. McCrea was twenty-nine, a tall, golden, athletic hunk with boyish charm and a winning personality. Born on Hollywood Boulevard, the "All-American Boy," as William Hearst labeled him, was married to Frances Dee. Barbara and Joel liked each other and thought the chemistry between them was one of bread and butter rather than champagne and caviar. In *Gambling Lady*, directed by fanny-pinching Archie Mayo, she played the daughter of a professional cardsharp. The cinematographer was George Barnes, Joan Blondell's husband and future cameraman of a pair of Alfred Hitchcock's classics, *Rebecca* and *Spellbound*. The fast-paced *Gambling Lady* was smart entertainment for 1934.

The Secret Bride was spun from the same cloth as *Forbidden* and told the story of a district attorney secretly married to the daughter of a politician he is trying to impeach. Warren William played the D.A., Barbara the title role. There are three murders before she proves her father's innocence. The director was William Dieterle, a refugee from Nazi

Germany, former *jeune premier* and disciple of Max Reinhardt at the Deutsches Theater. Reduced to making schlock for Warners, Dieterle was the busiest director on the lot, turning out an astonishing fifteen films in four years. Whether he was shooting interiors or location work, he wore white gloves and never made a move unless his wife approved it astrologically.

The Woman in Red, a triumph of mise-en-scène over plot, completed her contract with Warner Brothers. Fresh from *I Am a Thief*, a Mary Astor–Ricardo Cortez programmer about murder on the Orient Express, Robert Florey, who was something of a specialist in chillers (*Murders in the Rue Morgue*), directed the trite tale of love overcoming caste and scandal with bracing excitement. Members of the horsy set of Long Island and California raise plucked eyebrows when Stanwyck manages to marry Gene Raymond of a poor but polo-playing family. Things turn tricky when the new bride will either have to remain quiet and see a friend convicted of murder or, by admitting she was, however innocently, the woman in red who was on his yacht on the fatal night, clear him but risk wrecking her marriage. Despite Florey's enthusiasm, Barbara's heart was not in it. The shooting coincided with her worst fights with Frank.

Humiliated by his own stumbling, Frank lashed out. In November 1934, the press reported Frank's altercation with MGM's general studio manager Eddie Mannix over a table at the Brown Derby. Barbara was mortified.

Barbara might tell Frank she couldn't imagine life without him, but his drinking and rages were sapping her strength. Making work her escape led to new brawls. Frank upbraided her for leaving at dawn, returning after dinner, and learning scripts until all hours of the night. He swore he would put an end to it and started calling Jack Warner to complain about the hours his wife was forced to put in. Whether Frank's ultimate revenge was to see her fired or the studio had enough of his interfering, she was let go. "Frank Fay was causing so much trouble that the studio dropped me," she would say forty-five years later. "There was a period when nothing came my way."

Depriving her of work, of what made her feel alive, broke the camel's back. Laid-off Barbara, Frank, little Dion, and the nanny were at the pool when Frank became enraged because

Barbara admitted she had gone to Minsky's burlesque show with Zeppo and Marion Marx. Dion's cries drove Frank wild, and he struck Barbara. She hit the ground.

That night she told him she wanted a divorce.

In August 1935, Barbara left Frank. Taking Dion and his nanny with her, she found refuge near Zeppo and Marion Marx. She moved into a ranch in the Northridge area of the San Fernando Valley, thirty miles from Hollywood. The house was small, built in rough gray stone. The porch, with its rust-red flagstone floor, was as long as the house. The Marxes were a reassuring presence next door.

Barbara had never lived in the country, and there were days when the 160 acres of brush and rustling eucalyptus and nights of cicadas seemed to provide too much serenity. But it was what she needed. To columnists who asked why she was holed up in Northridge, she said, "Right now I don't want people staring at me."

The Marxes had horses. She could imagine her own stables, paddocks, and barns and Dion, going on four, learning to ride on his own little pony.

Zep and Marion were the kind of friends any woman divorcing after seven years would wish for. They were considerate without being overwhelming, solicitous without being intrusive, and by interesting her in the business of horse breeding took her mind off herself. They made her take up riding in a serious fashion. When, after an arduous weekend of training, Zep gave her a ring with a horseshoe of diamonds, she was so touched she wore it to work until directors asked her to take it off.

To have something to do while she sorted out her life, Barbara accepted when independent producer Edward Small offered her a part in a picture called *Red Salute*. Small worked with Joseph Schenck and had a hot little gangster flick called *Let 'Em Have It* in release. He sent Barbara the script. *Red Salute*, she realized, was another facsimile of Capra's *It Happened One Night*.

A mixture of screwball farce and radical politics, this early road movie was Stanwyck's first screen comedy. The director was Sidney Lanfield, a former jazz musician and gag writer whose claim to fame would be the Basil Rathbone ver-

sion of *The Hound of the Baskervilles*. In *Red Salute*, Barbara is
the leftist daughter of an archconservative general. To bring
her to her senses and cool her passion for a college pacifist,
the general (Purnell Pratt) arranges to have her kidnapped
and dropped off in Mexico. There, she meets Robert Young,
an American soldier on leave. The two of them get passably
drunk. By the time the soldier has come to his sober senses,
he has unwittingly deserted, smashed a government car, run
the border back into the United States, and finds himself
driving toward California with a girl whose politics he can't
stand, who loathes the sight of a uniform, and can't wait to
get back to her campus agitator boyfriend. Hardie Albright,
who in *The Purchase Price* had filled the role of Barbara's son,
was her boyfriend.

The "Red" in the title intimidated some distributors,
and when the film was released in October 1935 it was
banned in several cities for the way it made fun of politics.
United Artists changed the title and rereleased it as
Runaway Daughter. The picture found one enthusiastic
reviewer in Britain. Graham Greene was *The Spectator*'s new
film critic. *Red Salute*, or *Arms and the Girl* as it was titled in
England, was "one of the best comedies of the screen since *It
Happened One Night*," the novelist wrote. "Miss Stanwyck as
the malicious-tongued aristocratic Red and Mr. Robert
Young as the reckless irritated private soldier give admirable
performances."

On November 9, 1935, Barbara filed for divorce. Still protective of Frank's fragile ego, she charged him with
harassing her about "trivial matters." She asked for custody of
Dion and in her complaint said a property settlement had
been reached.

The Fays signed a predivorce settlement December 31.
The New Year's Eve agreement gave Barbara full custody of
Dion and Frank twice-a-week visiting rights. Frank relinquished all claims to the house in Brentwood. The divorce
was granted six weeks later.

Six months later the Internal Revenue Service garnisheed
her wages for nonpayment of her and Frank's joint taxes. They
had been a married couple, filing joint returns when Frank had
neglected to pay the taxes she had set aside and told him to

pay on her considerable earnings. Since he was unemployed in 1936, the government attached her earnings.

Comedians had their fun with the divorce.

Ed Wynn said, "The second nicest thing Frank Fay ever did was to marry Barbara Stanwyck. The nicest thing he ever did was to divorce Barbara Stanwyck." At the 1936 Friars Club roundtable, Jackie Gleason roasted Humphrey Bogart for his performance of the vicious, inhuman Duke Mantee in *The Petrified Forest* by saying, "Bogart played a real creep, he must have studied Frank Fay for weeks." When Bogart, Milton Berle, and Frank discussed a new play and Fay knocked every performance, Bogey turned to him and said, "Frank, the way you find fault, you'd think there was a reward for it."

In a postmortem to the divorce, the *Hollywood Citizen* reported that Frank had ordered his attorney, Hy Schwartz, to hire three private detectives to tail his wife. Frank's jealousy didn't end with the divorce. He began using his visitation rights to Dion to call at odd hours. When he was drunk in New York, he would call and plead with Barbara to forgive him. Harry Golden, the cigar-chomping wit and ghostwriter for politicians, would recall agreeing to let Fay dial Stanwyck in Los Angeles and pay for the call later. "He would go on binges, work himself into a crying jag, and then beg to use the phone to see if she would take him back." After a while Barbara refused to so much as speak to her former husband. "She loathed him," Oscar Levant would remember, adding that he always felt guilty about having been the catalyst to the Fay–Stanwyck romance.

Barbara felt empty, second-rate. Divorce was so common. She had allowed Frank to dictate her behavior and feelings, allowed herself to be bullied and misused. She was too angry, too proud, and too rich to ask for child support. Fay only called when he was drunk. Barbara refused to let him see Dion. When Frank was out of town and called to talk to Dion, she handed the phone to the boy. Fay complained to Schwartz: "All I get for a hundred bucks a call is 'Hello, Dad' and dead air!" His lawyer contacted Barbara's attorney, who retorted that Frank was always inebriated when he called and therefore a threat to the child's welfare. She sold the Brentwood house for $80,000 and moved permanently to

Northridge. She barred Frank from the ranch and was eventually hauled to court to show cause why her former husband should not see their son.

Her early life had been struggles and suspended hopes. She had trained herself to look for the positive side. Now, at twenty-eight, she was alone but able to be herself for the first time, in charge of her life and her career. She was not over-anxious about her adopted son and easily convinced herself that what the boy needed most was stability. She was more than happy to leave him in the care of his nannies. Uncle Buck McCarthy came with her to the ranch, and for a while Byron came to stay. Her brother had grown into a quiet, handsome man, whose hair turned snow-white when he was twenty-six. Something of a daydreamer, he had little of his sister's ambition and eventually found a career as a film extra. When attending social functions was mandatory, she went with Byron—a mystery man in her life to columnists until their sibling relationship was explained.

The abutting Marx and Stanwyck ranches totaled 140 acres of dry California grasslands, and Barbara and Zeppo went into business together to breed thoroughbreds. Their corporate name was Marwyck. Knowing that Uncle Buck would look after her interests, Barbara made him the boss of the ranch hands and stable boys.

Zeppo was doing well as a talent agent. William Wilkinson, publisher of the *Hollywood Reporter*, took sixteen-year-old Julia Turner to Marx, who, after changing her first name to Lana, got her a walk-on in Mervyn LeRoy's *They Won't Forget*, the film that turned her into "The Sweater Girl." Zep and Marion took it upon themselves to arrange dates for Barbara. She told them she wasn't interested. They kept trying, setting up dates with Moss Hart, newly arrived in Hollywood, and others.

RKO, the "biggest little major of them all," offered Stanwyck movies that promised to be of a higher caliber than the Warner Brothers quickies. Under the flaring lightning bolts and flaming radio beacons of the RKO logo, the Gower Street studio announced a procession of "big pictures," guaranteed to "electrify the industry," including Fred Astaire and Ginger Rogers in *Top Hat* and Barbara Stanwyck in *Annie Oakley*. The publicity release didn't mention that Stanwyck got the part in the sunny costume picture because Jean Arthur had turned it down. Barbara didn't care.

Constance Bennett was RKO's brightest star, and its stable of contractees included Ann Harding, who seven years ago had shared the stage with Rex Cherryman in *The Trial of Mary Dugan*. Barbara knew Hermes Pan, the choreographer of the studio's song-and-dance shows, from her chorus-girl days. Pan never worked out routines on paper, just remembered everything in his head and told directors what angles to shoot from. Barbara sneaked in on the double soundstages where he was rehearsing *Top Hat*. The sight took her breath away. In the huge white Art Moderne recreation of Venice with canals and danceable bridges, Astaire, Pan, and Rogers went through "The Piccolino" number. Pan rehearsed with a huge mirror instead of a camera. Hermes, who danced as well as Astaire, shaped the ensemble numbers while Astaire worked out his dances with Rogers. Then with a playback of Irving Berlin's tunes, the two men refined the numbers together. With Fred, Pan was Ginger; with Ginger he was Fred.

Barbara's feet were tingling. At the commissary, she and the choreographer agreed they would try to work together if either of them had a chance to recommend the other.

Annie Oakley was the saga of Phoebe Anne Oakley Mozee, who learned to shoot with a muzzle-loader in the Ohio backwoods in the 1860s and whose story was set to music by Irving Berlin and immortalized in *Annie Get Your Gun*. Annie was still in her teens when she beat Frank Butler, the celebrated marksman, in an all-comers challenge match in Cincinnati. Frank and Phoebe married and toured with Buffalo Bill's Original Wild West Show. *Annie Oakley*'s director was George Stevens, RKO's fair-haired boy who had honed his talents on shoestring productions and was enjoying his first hit—*Alice Adams* with Katharine Hepburn and Fred MacMurray.

Stanwyck's Annie is no gawky, pigtailed yahoo, but an intelligent farm girl competing in a male world. The screenplay by Joel Sayre and John Twist had her win Buffalo Bill's sharpshooting "Male Against Female Titanic Battle" contest without losing her man. Says Melvyn Douglas sweetly: "I don't care anymore who wins. I know you can beat me, and I'm proud of you." The script was only partly finished when Stevens started shooting. The director improvised as he went along—and drove Barbara crazy with his slow, thoughtful work method and his long silences before he answered a question. If the final film paid too much attention to Annie's romantic problems, Chief Sitting Bull, played with comic virility by a superbly surly Indian billed as Chief Thunderbird, stole the picture and had 1935 audiences screaming with laughter.

None of Stanwyck's 1936 films were as good as *Annie Oakley*, but they kept her working at Century-Fox, RKO, and MGM. *A Message to Garcia* was one of Darryl Zanuck's sillier endeavors after he merged Twentieth Century with Fox Film. The capital foundation of the merger gave Zanuck financial clout—and a salary of $260,000 a year. Instead of making himself production chief as he had been at Warners, he made himself a full-sized mogul, and the films he produced or wrote under one or another of his pseudonyms made money. To feed its National Theaters and Fox West Coast chains with thirty-five movies a year, the new company hired stars left and right to supplement its few in-house contractees, Alice Faye, Henry Fonda, John Boles, and Shirley Temple. Stanwyck was quickly signed, along with Loretta Young and newcomer Tyrone Power.

Zanuck's fondness for directors who were "absolute bastards" made him keep a pair of Fox's no-nonsense craftsmen, the boozing John Ford and the cheerful George Marshall. Both knew how to knock out three or four films a year. Marshall was assigned to *A Message to Garcia*.

Barbara read Retired Lieutenant Andrew S. Rowan's bestselling memoirs of his adventures as presidential emissary and spy in Cuba in 1898. John Boles was cast as Rowan, Barbara as a Cuban nobleman's daughter who falls in love with Rowan, Wallace Beery as the soldier of fortune, and Enrique Acosta as General Garcia. Harry Brand, the studio's publicity chief, waxed effusively about Stanwyck's beautiful spy. Known as the "herald of hyperbole" for his enthusiastic news releases, Brand invited the Hollywood press corps to the set to see Barbara crawl through the backlot jungle. Soldier of fortune Beery, however, ran away with the picture.

Barbara was back at RKO to star with Gene Raymond and Robert Young in an affable marital comedy that promised more than it delivered. Leigh Jason, who directed several agreeable but negligible comedies, was in charge of *The Bride Walks Out*. Boy (Raymond) and girl (Stanwyck) are married and trying to live on his $35-a-week salary. Girl likes pretty clothes and buys them, so first thing you know they're in trouble and headed for divorce. Rich man (Young) is ready to lead our young lady into the lap of luxury when husband starts off on a dangerous mission to South Africa. Wife sees the light. Reunion. Fadeout. *Variety* said Stanwyck was a little hard to believe, but called *The Bride Walks Out* "a homey picture in which nothing happens but there's a lot of pleasant chatter about it all."

Barbara signed a one-picture deal with MGM to star in *His Brother's Wife* with Robert Taylor. Taylor was Metro's new matinee idol, and Zep and Marion took it upon themselves to have Barbara meet her new costar in a more congenial atmosphere than a studio office. They invited Barbara to a dinner dance at the Café Trocadero, the new Sunset Strip supper club. They had someone they wanted her to meet.

Who?

R.T., they said.

The gorgeous young actor with the coal-black hair, blue eyes, and double eyelashes was seated at their reserved table when the Marxes and Barbara got there. Zeppo and Marion soon made themselves scarce so the two stars could chat. When Taylor stood up to invite her to dance, she realized how short he was. She declined, saying she was waiting for a Mr. Artique. He sat down again, puzzled. She said perhaps she wasn't pronouncing the name right.

"Artique . . . Artique," he repeated. His face lit up. "That's me," he laughed. "R.T. Get it?"

The next morning, she received a box of long-stemmed roses with a card from Taylor thanking her for "a thoroughly delightful evening."

12

Arly

Stardom had come to Robert Taylor in *Magnificent Obsession*, his ninth movie, in which he played the doctor he had once wanted to be. Directed by the urbane John Stahl and costarring Irene Dunne, the movie version of Lloyd Douglas's international bestseller had Taylor as a physician questioning his own values after accidentally blinding the story's heroine. "We have abandoned the dangerous sheik and the man who socks women and the sophisticated lover," wrote Adela Rogers St. Johns in the first magazine assessment of the twenty-four-year-old prince charming. "Our girls and women have declared for Robert Taylor, and that is as important an indication of our return to old-fashioned femininity as was the return of the trailing skirt, the soft girls, and the picture hat." What charmed St. Johns when she met him in person was the fact that his terrific success hadn't spoiled him. "You wish instantly that he was your younger brother or your son or your sweetheart or something. Dick Barthelmess had that same tug at your heartstrings. No one has had it since, until young Taylor came along."

Summing up, she said Taylor was someone for young women to hang their dreams upon: "He is the young man they hope to meet some day, and marry and set up housekeeping for and with. I think they must be rather nice clean fine dreams somehow, or Robert Taylor wouldn't fit into them. For he belongs to romance, not to the day of sex drama and melodrama." Overseas, he was becoming so big so fast that the *London Observer* declared, "1936 will go down as the year of Edward VIII, the Spanish war and Robert Taylor."

If anyone typified the Hollywood golden age it was this matinee idol whose name had been changed from Spangler Brugh the moment he signed with Metro-Goldwyn-Mayer in February 1934 and who remained under contract to MGM longer than anyone else. Except for loanouts, Robert Taylor never worked for another studio until 1960. The so-called standard seven-year studio contract was the norm and only Charles Boyer, Cary Grant, and a few others insisted on signing for just one picture at a time. The contract, with options, gave the studio all the advantages. It allowed the studio both to terminate the relationship every six months and, if the newcomer was promising, to lock him or her in for seven years. The studio usually renewed its option twice a year, usually with an increase in salary. "Talent"—actors, directors, and any other people considered valuable enough to be under contract—benefited from the security of continual employment. The advantage for the studios was that the system allowed management to favor those who behaved. Free-lancing was not without its downside for an actor. No one studio, for example, had a vested, long-term interest in building up hop-scotching Stanwyck.

Barbara may have been troubled in her relationships with others, uncomfortable with intimacy, but she was never assailed by profound, existential self-doubt, never questioned her ability to survive. Bob Taylor was different. As much as she liked being in charge of her own momentum, Bob's temperament was suited to the strictures of the studio system. He was a mama's boy who was comfortable with being told what to do. Still, if there was one thing he admired in Stanwyck, it was her free-lancing. He was not alone. Joan Crawford, under contract to MGM since 1925, admired Barbara's independence. Conveniently forgetting she was getting $100,000 per picture, Joan complained to Barbara, "It's like a one-sided marriage. What the hell do I get out of it?"

A few actresses were leading the rebellion against what all contractees hated most—the self-perpetuating nature of the studio contracts.

Following a few poor decisions by several stars, the studio chiefs had become frightened and proclaimed that no artist, no matter how big, had the right to decide what films he or she wanted to work in. The penalty for disobedience was, as always, suspension, which meant the particular artist was declared persona non grata on his or her home lot and forbidden employment elsewhere. The suspended person's salary was stopped and the number of weeks or months of suspension tagged to the end of the running contract. At Warner Brothers, "doing solitary" meant suspension plus roles in "triple B pictures."

Shooting *The Secret Bride* two stages away from the Bette Davis–Humphrey Bogart starrer *Marked Woman* in 1935, Stanwyck had been eyewitness and cheerleader to Davis's mutiny. After being denied better scripts and cast as a lady lumberjack, Bette Davis had revolted.

Despite dire warnings from fellow contractees, agents, and lawyers, Bette had fled to Vancouver with her husband, Harmon Nelson, Jr., crossed Canada to Montreal, and sailed for England, all to avoid being served injunctions by Warners' lawyers. In London, she signed with Anglo-Italian producer Ludovico Toeplitz, who caved in when pressure built from Hollywood and reneged on his contract with her. Warners served her with an injunction forbidding her from rendering her services anywhere and prepared for a court battle.

Jack Warner came to London with William Randolph Hearst, whose newspapers treated Davis as a wayward schoolgirl in need of a spanking. Warner had Alexander Korda testify on his behalf, and the court turned down Davis's argument that the self-perpetuating nature of industry contracts made them into "life sentences." Warners won a three-year injunction which, if the studio chose to pick up all the options, put Bette into golden bondage until 1942. The injunction was valid in Britain only, but Bette knew when she was defeated.

Like Harry Cohn had done after Stanwyck's insurrection five years earlier, Jack Warner bent over backward to forget and forgive when Bette returned. The publicity of her fight, however, paved the way for other court contests. But it would be 1944 before Olivia de Havilland won, on appeal, a California Superior Court ruling that time lost by a player put on suspension could not be added to a term contract after its expiration date.

On their second date, Bob took Barbara and Dion to the Santa Monica pier. Barbara found Bob to be surprisingly normal, a small-town boy who took life as easily as it took him. Going out with the respectful and courteous Bob, four years younger than she, was such a change from her years with Frank Fay that she enjoyed their dates. She took him to meet Joan, still married to Franchot Tone and still living in regal splendor on Bristol Avenue in Brentwood. The country might be in the depths of the Depression, but Joan forcefully defended her lavish lifestyle. "I believe in the dollar, everything I have, I spend," she said. The evenings on Bristol Avenue followed the same timetable—cocktails and dinner followed by a movie at Joan's private screening room, nightcaps and chat around Bob on the piano.

Music was something that was part of him. He had started on the piano when he was twelve, had tried the saxophone, and settled on the cello in school. If anybody besides his parents had molded his life, he told Barbara, it was his music teacher, Hubert Gray, at Doane College in Crete, Nebraska. Taylor came to California to pursue music when Gray transferred to Pomona College in Claremont.

Spangler Arlington Brugh, born in Filley, Nebraska, August 5, 1911, was the only son of a merchant turned country doctor and a woman with a weak heart. His father, Andrew Spangler Brugh, was a twenty-nine-year-old grain merchant of Pennsylvania Dutch stock who had come west and, in Filley, met eighteen-year-old Ruth Stanhope. The birth of their son almost cost Ruth her life. It revealed the fact that she had an incurable heart ailment. When doctors decided nothing could be done for her, Andrew decided to study medicine himself. At thirty, the grain merchant sold his successful business, moved his family to Kirksville, Missouri, and entered medical school. What takes most people eight years, he did in three. As a physician he specialized in heart diseases.

Arly, as everybody called their son, grew up ruled and cuddled by his debilitated mother. Ruth domineered both her husband and her son. She dressed Arly in velvet and soft white shirts that made classmates ridicule him. She was often too ill to care for her son, and Arly spent many quiet hours sitting in on lectures with his father.

"There are so many great men who are just country

doctors, smalltown doctors," he told Adela Rogers St. Johns. "They have so much understanding, so much strength. They give so much and help so many in trouble. My father was like that. I asked him one time what was the greatest study I could follow. And he just smiled at me and said, 'Human nature.'"

At twelve, Arly decided he wanted to be a doctor—a surgeon if possible—and to specialize in childhood diseases. A year later, he was smitten by music, but never quite abandoned the idea of going to medical school. When Gray moved to Claremont, Arly persuaded his parents to give him a car so he could attend college there.

"I remember the day the professor told me he was accepting a teaching job at Pomona College in Claremont, California, and my whole world fell apart," he told Barbara. Arly persuaded his mother to make the three-thousand-mile round-trip journey to the Los Angeles suburb with him and, once she had inspected the Pomona College campus, to allow him to enroll.

It was the first time Arly had been away from home. At eighteen, he was terribly handsome. His dark good looks made his classmates nickname him "The Sheik." He was homesick, slow to make friends, and didn't know anyone besides Gray.

The teacher was a stern taskmaster, quick to berate Arly for showing interest in anything but the cello. "He can be a concert performer," said Gray. "He has tremendous talent. But he must stop monkeying around with this acting business. Dramatics! Such a waste of time." MGM publicity would wax on the way young Robert Taylor struggled with himself, hard-pressed to decide whether he should make the cello his life or yield to the siren call of acting. His first school play role, in his senior year, was that of the once idealistic hero in R. C. Sherriff's *Journey's End*, a play set in the British trenches of the Great War. Bob would never forget seeing the printed program, which coincidentally combined his mother's maiden name with his:

Captain Stanhope Spangler Brugh

The Robert Taylor studio bio would tell how studio scout Ben Piazza was in the Pomona College auditorium that night and how a surprised Spangler Brugh was called to the phone the next day and asked to come to Hollywood for a screen test. In reality, it was Arly who pulled all the wires to get an audition. Joel McCrea was the most famous graduate of Pomona's drama department, and Arly's teacher wrote a letter of introduction. "I took Arlington out to MGM, where he made a test for a crime short with Virginia Bruce," McCrea would remember.

Arly spent another year at Pomona. His parents came to California for his graduation in June 1933. Four months later, Dr. Brugh died.

Ruth buried her husband in Nebraska, moved to Los Angeles, and set up housekeeping for her son. Arly was twenty-two with a widow's peak and a face so handsomely regular it looked as if he had undergone plastic surgery. He made a second screen test, this time at the Goldwyn Studios and, while he waited for a casting call, tried to enrich his acting skills at the Pasadena Playhouse, Southern California's most exciting theater venue.

The Biltmore, El Capitan, Hollywood Playhouse, Mayan, Belasco, and, in season, the Hollywood Bowl were the locales for touring Broadway productions, the Pasadena Playhouse the home for experimental and avant-garde drama. Besides reviving classics the Playhouse regularly offered new plays by unknown playwrights and conducted an acclaimed acting school. Its founder and director was Gilmor Brown, recently made California state supervisor for the Roosevelt administration's Federal Theatre Project. The forty-six-year-old Brown was a notorious homosexual who immediately found an opening for Arly in his acting class, and in his experimental Playbox showcase. "Every year Gilmor Brown had a particular favorite, and during the early 1933–34 season Arlington Brugh was the one," fellow neophyte actor Harry Hay would recall. "We all understood what it meant to be his protegée. A year later it was Tyrone Power."

The Playhouse was an exciting place—seven hundred actors performed there over the years—but it didn't pay. Brugh and Hay wanted to be in the movies. Harry, who was a few months younger than Arly and had come to Los Angeles at the age of seven, knew Hollywood was a party town. They got themselves invited to dance parties, costume parties, theme parties, pajama parties, and come-as-your-favorite-character parties. "We had no money, but an elderly gentleman took us to a gay and lesbian party at Mercedes De Acosta's huge house in Brentwood," Hay would remember. "She was the lover to the stars, Garbo and Dietrich were among her conquests, and was notorious for wearing pants and slicking back her black hair with brilliantine." Arthur Treacher, the Englishman who had made his screen debut in a minor role opposite Stanwyck in *Gambling Lady* and between film jobs was active on the local stage, introduced them to the lively British colony. Arlington could recite Hugh Walpole's poem "Make Me a Man" ("Blessed be all Sorrows, Torments, Hardships, Endurance that demand Courage . . . Blessed be these things; for of those things cometh the making of Man") and blushed when Treacher introduced him to the famous homosexual poet and novelist. Being Gilmor Brown's fair-haired boy meant rehearsing at the director's home, where the Playbox Theatre was showcased. The day before rehearsals were to begin, however, Arly was asked to come to Culver City to meet Louis B. Mayer. The MGM boss studied the young man with a talent man's shrewd eye and ordered a screen test.

Arly's startling good looks photographed handsomely. In February 1934, Metro signed him to a $35-a-week, seven-year contract. Ida Koverman, Mayer's secretary and confidante, changed Arly's name—although Arly thought "Robert Taylor" terribly common for someone named Spangler Arlington Brugh. The studio put him in Oliver Tinsdell's acting school and loaned him out to Fox for a role in *Handy Andy*, a star vehicle for Will Rogers full of cracker-barrel folk wisdom. When the studio bought the rights to S. J. and Laura Perelman's Americans-in-Paris play *All Good Americans* a month later, Bob and fellow-newcomer Betty Furness starred in it in a summer charity production.

Bob was acutely conscious of his looks and couldn't wait for rugged, brawny parts. The studio supervisors, if not L.B. himself, said, Yes sure, after the next one. Realizing that his well-bred, clean-cut persona made women swoon, they cast him in supporting roles in weepers like *There's Always Tomorrow* and *Society Doctor* and romantic dramas like *Times Square Lady*, designed as a test for young talent.

Bob might have resented the pretty-boy image, but Howard Strickling, MGM's formidable publicity chief, capitalized on it, creating celluloid romances with Virginia Bruce, his leading lady in *Society Doctor* and *Times Square Lady*, and with Metro's new Hungarian import, Hedy Lamarr. Pairing new male hopefuls with their leading ladies or starlets was part of the publicity machine. With *His Brother's Wife* in production, Strickling jumped at the chance to link Taylor and Stanwyck.

Strickling was something of a rarity in the movie business, a native of Los Angeles. A high school dropout who had worked as a sports reporter, he found his true métier in the new field of movie public relations. His work methods were not dissimilar to those at the other studios. Golden age press agentry of course, was invented not only to blow the horn but to act as a giant veil. "We told stars what they could say, and they did what we said because they knew we knew best," Strickling would say in a rare candid moment. He rewrote the lives of Metro's stars in free translation and, as the guardian angel of Metro's galaxy of stars, made sure each performer's reputation remained unsullied.

L.B., as Mayer was called, believed the public should never hear of the screen idols' failings. "Talent is like a precious stone, like a diamond or a ruby," the boss told Strickling. "You take care of it. You put it in a safe, you clean it, polish it, look after it. Who knows the value of a star?" To which Strickling added that film studios were the only companies where the assets walked out the gate every night. "In other businesses it's different, like if an editor gets drunk too often you hire another one. Well, if you got John Barrymore in a picture you can't say throw the bum out. Okay, you've got Gable and Taylor and Garbo, but there's only one of each so you work things out."

Strickling realized the press could be neutralized by cooperation. With one hundred press agents under his command, he developed the technique of continued coverage from the inception of a script through every phase of production to release. By making himself indispensable to the stars, they came to rely on him and eventually to heed his advice. He also attached spies to willful stars, making his publicist, Betty

Asher, the personal press agent to twenty-year-old Judy Garland. Asher became Garland's lover, encouraged the young star's drinking, and, unstable herself, eventually committed suicide. "MGM created a certain name, but they didn't prepare you for life," Lena Horne would recall. "I mean, what do you say when Howard Strickling wasn't around and you had to get an abortion." Strickling said that by helping Gable or Taylor or Harlow, he became important to them. "And in that way I could get them to do things. My relationship with Clark and Bob Taylor—maybe Jean Harlow and Norma Shearer—was different, because I was closer to them than to some of the others."

Protecting the celebrities from themselves was no easy job, but Strickling could count on MGM's own police force headed by Whitey Hendry, a former chief of police of Culver City, who had been lured to the studio for a lot of money. If, during one of his boozy nights out, Spencer Tracy was picked up for wrecking a hotel room in Beverly Hills, Hendry would call the Beverly Hills police chief and Tracy wouldn't be booked. When a very drunk Gable smashed up his car and himself in Brentwood one night, police on the scene called the West Los Angeles Division, which called downtown.

"The accident scene was roped off," Strickling would remember. "Gable was hustled away to a private hospital, and the incident never reported on the police blotter—or in the press. For multiple-problem people like Tracy, we devised an even more elaborate technique. We kept an official-looking ambulance on call at the studio. Every bar owner and hotel manager in the area knew what to do if Tracy showed up drunk and began causing a problem. They'd phone me, and I'd phone Whitey, and the ambulance would take off with a couple of our security men dressed as paramedics. They'd go to the scene, strap Tracy to a stretcher, and then rush him away in the ambulance before too many people could recognize Tracy as the troublemaker."

Strickling's worry in Robert Taylor's case was how to contain rumors of homosexuality. Gays lusted as much after Bob as Adela Rogers St. Johns and a million women moviegoers did, and he was not always as careful as Strickling wanted him to be. Bob insisted he was not gay but had a hard time pretending he desired any woman in the flesh. "Taylor was careless because he thought he had the cleanest image of any of Metro's male stars, onetime Strickling publicist Rick Ingersoll would recall. "Whispers that his intense, dashing virility was a sham never went away." Each attestation to Taylor's heterosexuality—usually offered by women—would be matched by an equally convincing denial. Hedda Hopper couldn't believe Taylor was a homosexual. "We're always in costume," said Harry Hay of the industry's homosexual executives, producers, writers, agents, and actors. "Whether we groom our physiques, go to a party, or look for a job, we turn on attitudes."

A sexy, heterosexual image was crucial, and Strickling linked Taylor to several actresses, even though none of these relationships ever became a full-fledged romance. Bob was defensive about his personal feelings. Gilmor Brown, Harry Hay, and Forman Brown of the Hollywood Turnabout Theatre knew him as a homosexual. He was a friend of John Gilbert and cruised gay parties with the silent-screen idol. Gilbert was sixteen years older than Bob, but they were both from small western towns (Gilbert was born in Logan, Utah), and both knew the only reason they were in the movies was their looks. Gilbert was drinking himself to death. "I have been on the screen for twenty years and I have managed to squeeze out of it complete unhappiness," he told Bob. In 1930, he had made $250,000 a picture; now he couldn't get a job at $25 a week. Bob accompanied Gilbert to a gay party in Hollywood. While Gilbert was dancing, his toupee fell off. Bob gallantly retrieved it from under a dancer's feet, only to see Gilbert flee the party.

In concert with Mayer, Strickling planted stories about Bob's growing up in rugged Big Sky country, his affection for firearms and hunting. At the studio commissary, Strickling got Bob seated at the directors' table, a large table on a screened-in porch off the main dining room. Some thirty people, a handful of directors, Gable, Tracy, plus a coterie of writers and department heads lunched at this ultimate symbol of macho status. No actress ever sat at the table.

At Fox, Harry Brand worked as diligently to coarsen that studio's too handsome new star Tyrone Power. Two years younger than Bob, the handsome Ty was another repressed homosexual who lived with his mother and was discovered at

Gilmor Brown's workshop. He was fascinated with people as famous as he and enjoyed the excitement and danger of liaisons with gay celebrities. While Fox linked him with Loretta Young, Janet Gaynor, and Sonja Henie, he went to bed with the composer Lorenz Hart, Errol Flynn, and several other stars. When he was on the verge of becoming Fox's top male star, ahead of Henry Fonda and John Payne, Darryl Zanuck arm-twisted him into marrying Annabella (née Suzanne Charpentier), an athletic older French actress with an eight-year-old daughter.

During the first week of the shooting of *His Brother's Wife*, press releases from the Strickling office described how Taylor lunched with Stanwyck every day in her dressing room or his, how he never let her begin a day without a basket of flowers.

L.B., who called Taylor "son," doubted there was anything in the Taylor-Stanwyck relationship. It was all right if Strickling invented a little setside romance to sell *His Brother's Wife*, but it was out of the question for Bob to be serious about a woman who was not only four years older than he but a divorcée with a young son. Besides, women wanted their matinee idol single.

Private Lives

Barbara's earthiness and unaffectedness was as fetching as her ranch living, where she appeared at the stables in red flannel shirt, corduroy riding britches, and hair tucked under a scarf. Her chin-up, keep-busy style, her wry sense of humor and one-of-the-boys aplomb covered a lot of bitterness. Her gift for turning chores into challenges covered her fear of being had again, of losing control over herself and her carefully reconstructed world and its inhabitants.

She wasn't sure she understood men. Love was not the vital center of her existence. Work was. *His Brother's Wife* was her second picture in 1936—two more would follow before the year was out. She had played a Cuban señorita in *A Message to Garcia* and was now set to frolic with Bob Taylor, Jean Hersholt, and Joseph Calleia in MGM's back-lot jungle. Work gave her freedom to live according to her own rules, and divorce allowed her to pick up where she had been at twenty-one. Now, however, she would be in charge of herself, be well beyond the girl she had been in 1928, who, after Rex Cherryman's death, had been too alone and too willing to believe Frank Fay's snake oil. She now lived with people of her choosing. She was paid unheard-of sums to get herself to a studio in the morning and, in the company of pros she valued, plunge into make-believe.

His Brother's Wife was Barbara's first for MGM. The sprawling film factory in Culver City was hitting its stride and laying down the standards by which Hollywood measured prestige, glamour—and earnings. Metro's profits in 1935 had been $7.5 million in period dollars, more than the rest of

Hollywood's Big Seven movie companies combined. For 1936, profits surpassed $10 million.

Barbara had danced for Florenz Ziegfeld, but visiting Stage 34 made her wish she was eighteen again and dancing all night. *The Great Ziegfeld* was fast becoming MGM's most expensive production since *Ben Hur* and was planned as a three-hour extravaganza. Three cameramen were filming Dennis Morgan singing Irving Berlin's "A Pretty Girl Is Like a Melody" on a giant wedding cake topped with a sweep of chorus girls. Even at his most extravagant, Ziegfeld had never matched the opulence Metro lavished on his movie biography. William Powell incarnated the great showman, and the two Mrs. Ziegfelds were played by Myrna Loy, as Billie Burke, and Luise Rainer, as Anna Held. Fanny Brice was herself.

His Brother's Wife was not quite *Magnificent Obsession*, but it, too, had a fateful plot line. Robert Taylor is a medical researcher and Barbara Stanwyck a nightclub hostess. He goes to the tropics to investigate spotted fever. Why she should decide to show her love for him by marrying his brother, played by John Eldredge, is never explained. But in the last reel, she has spotted fever, Taylor gets her, and director W. S. "Woody" Van Dyke had another of his seemingly endless hits.

Woodbridge Strong Van Dyke II liked to shoot fast. This son of an actress had been a lumberjack, gold miner, railroader, and mercenary before finding work as an assistant to D.W. Griffith. "One-take Woody" was responsible for the first talkie *Tarzan* and the first William Powell–Myrna Loy *Thin Man*. It was rumored that he got a large extra sum for each day he brought in a picture ahead of schedule, and he was impatient with any assignment that took more than twenty days to shoot. He had not seen the script of *His Brother's Wife* until the first day of shooting. When somebody objected that the swamp effects of the back-lot tropics were not geographically correct, he snapped, "Fine, kid, that's how it is, and this is how it's going to be."

Bob Taylor provided pleasant offscreen interludes. He was such an attentive date that Barbara found herself saying yes to his invitations. Going out with an inexperienced young man carried little risk of evenings ending with clammy invitations to a backseat tumble or messy front-porch good-night kisses that insisted on more. Stanwyck and Taylor were seen at Palomar's, the huge nightclub on the corner of Vermont and Third streets that was packed every night, where a year earlier Benny Goodman had soared to fame. Barbara danced with Jackie Cooper, Bob with Bette Davis and Martha Raye.

Barbara enjoyed teaching Bob the showbiz ropes. When his latest picture, *Private Number*, came out, he was so thrilled at seeing his name above Loretta Young's that he took Barbara to Hollywood Boulevard to see his name in lights at Grauman's Chinese Theatre marquee. "The trick," Barbara told him, "is to keep it there."

His meteoric rise at MGM was so overpowering, he told her, it made him as bewildered as if he had failed. "Most of the time you don't know *where* you stand," he said one evening at the Venice amusement park. Mayer and Strickling encouraged and destroyed romances according to what they decided the worldwide box offices of Loews movie houses wanted, and Bob was sure the press-agent fiction had a way of becoming fact. Studio photographers snapped the two of them smoking, talking, even standing in front of Bob's roadster. Picking up the story, press photographers caught the new twosome dancing to the tunes of the Artie Shaw and Glenn Miller bands at the Palladium, near Sunset and Vine.

Van Dyke finished *His Brother's Wife* in his usual double time. The *New York Times*'s Frank Nugent called it "a triumph of machine-made art that will succeed no matter how we, in our ivory tower, rail against it for its romantic absurdity." Nugent called Taylor the "crown prince of charm and heir apparent to Clark Gable" and reported that at the screening he attended the dialogue was almost drowned out by the coos of women in the audience.

To his mother's ongoing distress, Bob saw altogether too much of Barbara. He had moved into his own apartment, but was in the habit of looking in on his mother every day. To show him how deeply his relationship with Barbara wounded her, Ruth stopped dyeing her hair. "Arly likes it natural," Ruth said when people asked why she was suddenly silver-haired.

Barbara had been around; Bob was inexperienced. He was well educated; she was not. She had been in charge of herself since she was fourteen; he heeded his mother, his teachers, Louis B. Mayer. She hated a lie and never trusted anyone who failed her a first time. He was bad at fibbing, and hated picking up a ringing telephone for fear he wouldn't be able to say no. If invited by mail, he sent telegrams to beg off, knowing he was too easily persuaded to reconsider if he talked to the would-be host by phone.

He was tactful where Barbara was brutally frank. He admired the way she never forgot those who had rankled or hurt her. He understood her drive but had little of it himself. He didn't see the point of quarreling endlessly with studio bosses. Besides being chain smokers and disliking displays of temperament, Barbara and Bob had little in common. They overlapped in their caustic humor, emotional ambivalence, and hatred of crowds. He loved to cook, she was hopeless with pots and pans. He loved hunting, she loathed guns. He liked nonthreatening women in soft blouses and flounce skirts; she dressed in tailored suits, sports outfits, and slacks made of men's fabric. His classic line to reporters eager to know more about the romance was "Miss Stanwyck is not the sort of woman I'd have met in Nebraska."

Louis B. put him in *The Gorgeous Hussy*, the spurious retelling of the mildly scandalous love affair of President Andrew Jackson and Peggy O'Neal, an innkeeper's daughter who became the president's confidante. Joan Crawford played O'Neal. Lionel Barrymore was President Jackson, and Taylor joined Melvyn Douglas and James Stewart in the opulent $1.1 million production. Without telling Crawford, Mayer cast Franchot Tone as the hussy's suitor. Crawford exploded when she realized her husband only had eleven lines.

Mayer asked her to be patient and supportive of the new boy, James Stewart.

"What about Robert Taylor," she snarled. "Do I change his diapers, too?"

A week into production, Joan realized *The Gorgeous Hussy* was a mistake for her. To Bob's dismay, there was more tension on the set than in the movie they were shooting. Joan thought Bob had a complex because he was so damn handsome. "He knew the public didn't give a damn if he had talent. They came to see his face."

Franchot was one hour late one morning, provoking Joan to give him a tongue-lashing that director Clarence Brown and the entire cast and crew applauded. The blowup was the beginning of the end of their marriage.

Barrymore and Beulah Bondi as his backwoods wife cunningly stole the show, and *The Gorgeous Hussy* cooled both Crawford's and Taylor's fans.

Bob in knee britches, however, caught the eye of Irving Thalberg.

The producer's latest prestige film was *The Good Earth*. As with *The Bitter Tea of General Yen*, it was out of the question to film the Pearl S. Buck saga with Chinese actors playing Chinese. Instead, Paul Muni and the Viennese actress Luise Rainer were made up as Chinese peasants. Louis B. considered *The Good Earth* dicey—it cost as much as any MGM film since the silent *Ben Hur*—and Thalberg had to be careful. His other recent big picture, *Romeo and Juliet*, starring his wife, Norma Shearer, and Leslie Howard, had been a box-office disappointment. With Garbo in the title role, *Camille* was a low-risk project.

Members of Thalberg's staff feared Bob Taylor was too unseasoned to match Garbo. The producer overruled their objections. Garbo's films demanded screen lovers who were young, clumsy, and irresistible so her disillusioned persona could treat men as love objects and never surrender her authority. In the spring of 1936, Thalberg and his director, George Cukor, decided Bob should play Garbo's young, inexperienced lover Armand Duval.

The immortal courtesan with a weakness for pleasure and camellias who drifts through the Parisian demimonde with scant regard for her own delicate health and in the end sacrifices herself for a penniless lover had been played on the stage by Sarah Bernhardt and Eleonora Duse. Clara Kimball Young, Pola Negri, Alla Nazimova, and Norma Talmadge had portrayed Marguerite Gauthier in silent screen versions and Yvonne Printemps in a French talkie. Thalberg and Cukor believed Garbo might give the Alexandre Dumas classic vitality if she could make audiences both understand that the story was of a period when a woman's reputation was everything and *forget* they were seeing a costume picture.

Cukor didn't particularly like Garbo. He found her too dour and lesbian and, in a letter to Hugh Walpole, said her noble suffering depressed him. Cukor's playwright friend Zoe Akins, the novelist James Hilton, and Metro's premier screenwriter Frances Marion came up with a script that turned on the delicate distinction between a "good" and a "bad" woman.

Lionel Barrymore was cast as Monsieur Duval, Armand's father, who, to save his son from the whore's clutches, makes Marguerite leave the boy she truly loves and return to her former life of dissipation. Henry Daniell, who had played coolly sadistic men of affluence before, was chosen for the Count de Varville, Marguerite's former lover who offers to relieve her debts if she will become his mistress again. Rex O'Malley was set to play the gay sidekick, Gaston. Mercedes De Acosta, Garbo's lover, was in on the production. In the executive screening room, Thalberg ran the dailies for De Acosta and had her read the French original. In a village in Normandy, Mercedes found a farmer's wife who was a descendant of Marguerite's sister.

If Garbo had Mercedes as an off-camera adviser, Robert Taylor had Barbara.

Although Thalberg and Cukor thought all Bob had to do was to be decorous and pretend undying love for Garbo, Bob had enough sense to realize Armand was his most demanding role. He confided in Barbara when the $1.5 million prestige production started. She told him she had made so many blunders that she was happy to help him not make the same mistakes. When he asked for specifics, she advised him not to approach Garbo between scenes. The suggestion was judicious. To maintain the tension she felt was needed between the doomed lovers, Garbo kept her distance from Taylor. She thought he was well brought up if a bit shy. "He used to have a gramophone with him that he would play because he knew I liked music," she would recall. "He told me that his best friend during his youth in Nebraska had been a Swede."

To be directed by Cukor was evidence of any actor's importance. Cukor sympathized with Bob's fear of being seen as "beautiful" Robert Taylor. "In those days you had to be very virile or they thought you were degenerate," the director would tell Gavin Lambert in 1972. "It can be hell for an actor to be good-looking." There were scenes in which Marguerite pulls Armand toward her, kisses him all over the face, on the mouth, and pushes him away. It was acting Bob had never tried before. Cukor's directions were demanding. Everybody put in ten-hour days on the set. Barbara told Bob to be patient with his director's demands for endless retakes.

After propositioning a boy in June 1936, MGM star William Haines, his boyfriend, Jimmy Shields, and a group of friends were chased from a beach by an angry mob. The story hit the Los Angeles front pages, and there was speculation that Cukor was one of the men in the group. Whitey Hendry and Howard Strickling worked fast. Within forty-eight hours, the charges were dropped.

Louis B. began to object to the public display of the Taylor–Stanwyck friendship. He hated having his crown prince of charm linked with a divorcée still in custody battles with her former husband over their adopted son. Helen Ferguson told Barbara to be cautious. It would be foolish to go against Mayer's wishes. Barbara only had to look at John Gilbert's ruin to see what happened to a star who defied the authoritarian boss of MGM. Whether ordered by Mayer or merely suggested by Howard Strickling, Taylor appeared at parties alone or with studio-supplied dates. Barbara didn't mind. She lived by the rules of the company town. Besides, she wasn't sure what she felt. She was free, successful, and in no hurry for serious involvement. Bob was a distraction. He was "nice," always understanding, and impressed by her independence. She sensed a fear of rejection and intimacy behind his well-behaved attention and assigned it to his inexperience. He hadn't had time to live. He had gone from college to stardom in eighteen months, and there were times when the four years between them felt like a generational chasm. So she told him he should enjoy his fame. At Helen's suggestion, she was seen with other escorts.

While Bob worked on *Camille*, Barbara returned to Fox to star with Joel McCrea in *Banjo on My Knee*, directed by John Cromwell. The film was based on a folk novel by Harry Hamilton and told the story of a newlywed Mississippi couple prevented from consummating their marriage when the groom runs into trouble with the law. The script was by Darryl Zanuck's favorite screenwriter and Hollywood wit, Nunnally Johnson, with additional screen dialogue by Hollywood's most famous writer-import, William Faulkner.

The author was better at developing atmosphere and plots than writing screen dialogue. One Faulknerian mouthful written for Barbara read like this:

> PEARL: Then he left me before we were even married. He fixed it so that his people could say the things about me they wanted to say. Then he left me, because when I left I wasn't running from him. I was running after him. If he had loved me he would have known that. If he had loved me he would not have left me. If he had loved me he would have followed me and overtaken me. He could have because no woman ever runs too fast for the man she loves to catch her, but he didn't. All he was after was to catch the man he thought had offered to give me what he had denied to give me. So that even this man would have to leave me just as he had left me.

None of Faulkner's scenes survived in Johnson's final script.

Stanwyck was happy to make a picture with John Cromwell. Seven years earlier the director had wanted her to repeat her *Burlesque* role opposite Hal Skelly in the *Dance for Life* film version, and since then Cromwell had made more than twenty movies at Paramount and RKO, including *Spitfire* with Katharine Hepburn, *Of Human Bondage*, and *Little Lord Fauntleroy*.

Even if the screen characters Barbara fleshed out were not intuitively natural for her, she knew how to make them look right. Her strength was cumulative, and compliments came from unsuspecting quarters. Crawford wondered aloud what, in the end, her twelve years with MGM had given her. She should have followed Stanwyck's example, she told friends. Filming *That Certain Woman*, Bette Davis told a news conference she was trying to emulate Ruth Chatterton's "nobility that Barbara Stanwyck seems to be inheriting." Loretta Young believed that if Barbara was gaining in self-assurance, it was because she molded her private self after the characters she played. "Barbara Stanwyck has always been strong, but she takes this strength from her pictures," said

Young. "She's drawn on every character; I know her well enough to say that."

Cromwell said it best. Presence, he believed, was what made an actor a real star. "Stanwyck had great star presence. Sometimes the word personality is interchangeable with presence although they aren't the same thing. But the principle applies."

Cromwell took his time with his actors. In *Banjo on My Knee* he got from Stanwyck a full-bodied performance. Walter Brennan's disarming Old Newt Holley came as close as any 1930s movie portrayal of Old Man River shanty boaters. As Old Newt's daughter-in-law, Stanwyck projected an earthiness, inner savagery, and loneliness that other directors would one day help lift to unsuspecting heights of intensity.

Barbara and Bob went to the races on Labor Day 1936. It was a long weekend, and everybody, it seemed, was out of town. With Harpo Marx, the directors Mervyn LeRoy and Sam Wood, and their wives, Irving and Norma Thalberg spent the weekend at the Del Monte Club in Monterey in Northern California. Thalberg caught a head cold playing bridge in the sea breeze. The cold turned into pneumonia when he returned to Los Angeles. On September 14, 1936, the thirty-seven-year-old wunderkind with a weak heart was dead.

Hollywood shut down for five minutes' mourning as his funeral began, and MGM suspended operations for the rest of the day. Bob attended the funeral at the Synagogue B'nai B'rith with the Barrymore brothers, the Marxes, Charlie Chaplin, Walt Disney, Howard Hughes, and MGM's top stars Spencer Tracy, Ramon Novarro, Garbo, Jeanette MacDonald, Crawford, Constance Bennett, Myrna Loy. In the face of speculation that Thalberg's death meant MGM would stop making classy pictures, Mayer immediately asserted his control. The well-organized Thalberg unit was dismantled. A new, confusing beginning was filmed for *Camille*.

Bob wanted a brief vacation, and Louis B. authorized a trip to Hawaii. Bob went alone, but the Matson Line's press agent made sure movie fans greeted him at the bottom of the gangplank in Honolulu. Screaming women pulled his hair and for souvenirs tore buttons off his clothes as he set foot in Hawaii. Police were unable to hold back the crowd, and in the melee Bob panicked. The next day, he caught the first boat back to California.

The January 22, 1937, Los Angeles premiere of *Camille* turned into a wake for Thalberg, with Garbo, a notorious no-show at celebrity events, attending. Taylor escorted Stanwyck to Grauman's Chinese Theatre on Hollywood Boulevard. *Camille* brought Garbo's career to a climax. For the first time, said the critics, she acted, giving a warm yet sardonic portrayal of Dumas's harlot. Barrymore was dismissed as too American for Monsieur Duval, but Taylor's romantic profile and his curiously touching portrayal of Armand were judged perfect. Unfortunately, the studio never trusted him with such subtleties again, and, perhaps more unfortunately, he never pressed for them.

Bob trusted Mayer. Where others told stories of L.B.'s real or feigned tantrums, fainting fits, and other histrionics when faced with demands for more money from his stars, the handsome young provincial had only nice things to say. L.B. was kind, understanding, and protective, even if he was not above resorting to sly fatherly blackmail when Bob asked for a raise. At his agent's urging, Bob once made a private appointment to see Mayer. Before Bob could ask anything, L.B. launched into a glowing description of how proud he was of his two daughters.

"God never saw fit to give me a son," the boss sighed. "He gave me daughters, two beautiful daughters, who have been a great joy to me. They're now married to fine, successful fellows, top producers, Dave Selznick and Billy Goetz. If He had blessed me with a son, I can think of nobody I'd rather have wanted than a son exactly like you."

After more of the same monologue, Bob left the office in a daze.

"Well," asked his agent, "did you get the raise?"

"No," the actor replied, "but I got a father."

In another version of Taylor's asking for a raise, Mayer imagined himself the father lucky enough to have a son like Bob. Misty-eyed, he said, "And if that son came to me and said, 'Dad, I am working for a wonderful company, Metro-Goldwyn-Mayer, and for a good man, the head of the company, who has my best interests at heart. But he's only paying me $75 a week, Dad. Do you think I should ask for a raise?'

"Do you know what I'd say to my son, Bob? I'd say, 'Son, it's a fine company. It is going to do great things for you—greater things than it has already done. It is going to make a great star of you. It is going to give you a wonderful career. You'll be famous! That's more important than a little money. Don't ask for a raise now, Son.'"

Barbara was in turn overpowering and dismissive with Bob. And not much better with Dion. Going on six, the boy was handsomely strawberry blond, but not living up to her expectations. Perhaps because her childhood had been miserable, she seemed at a loss as to how to make her own and Dion's life happy. All she could think of was to make sure he wouldn't grow up spoiled. She kept him at arm's length emotionally. Uncomfortable with physical displays, she never kissed or hugged him and justified her reserve by telling herself too much attention would ruin him. She despised weakness and didn't know how to handle a child's tears. To satisfy his need for attention, the boy veered between cloying sweetness and angry provocation, only strengthening her determination not to pamper or indulge him. Gifts had been few and far between in her own childhood so birthday and Christmas presents to Dion were limited to five, and any gift over that number was taken away from him and sent to orphanages. Only once did she take him to see her on the screen. The film was *Banjo on My Knee*. She was deeply offended when he said he'd liked Joel McCrea's fight. When she asked whether he had liked *her*, he said, "Well, your dress was pretty."

She accompanied Dion on his first day of kindergarten—Joan Blondell was bringing her son Norman to the same school, and together the mothers waited until the boys' first momentous day was over. Ordinarily, Barbara saw Dion only at breakfast and not at all if she went on location.

Work—and Bob's diffidence—kept their relationship on a relaxed, if mannered, dating basis. As a follow-up to *Camille*, MGM made him Jean Harlow's leading man in *Private Property* and RKO offered Barbara the female lead in an ambitious John Ford movie. Bob still shuddered thinking of how women had thrown themselves on him in Honolulu, but there were times when he had to go out. Howard Strickling not only kept a close watch on MGM's "most admired matinee idol since the late Rudolph Valentino," but demanded he be seen as a man about town.

Rather than take Barbara or a studio-mandated date dancing at Palomar's or the Cocoanut Grove, Bob liked to come out to Northridge on a Saturday night, go for a dip in the swimming pool, and throw steaks on the barbecue for everybody. To putter with the charcoal while the setting sun turned the Santa Susana Mountains cobalt blue and Barbara's "hands" led the thoroughbreds to the barns and a stable boy blew a tune on a harmonica was "real," like Nebraska.

There were people around, of course. Dion could stay up a little later on Saturdays, and Bob tried to throw him a ball. The child wasn't very coordinated—he squinted, maybe he needed glasses—but he was polite. Uncle Buck was there, always, in charge of the stable hands. Some people thought it odd that Barbara had her sister's onetime lover living with her. To Bob it made sense. He was sure Barbara could take care of herself, but, nevertheless, the ranch was somewhat isolated. A lady needed protection. Her former husband continued to make trouble. Frank was drunk, touchy, and abusive on the telephone. When Barbara refused to speak to him, he demanded to talk to his son, who beyond a timid "Hello, Dad" didn't know what to say.

Barbara turned thirty that summer. She had no regrets. She liked the life she was making for herself, the sprawling acres that were hers, the porch and the view of the valley below. Her pleasures were largely solitary: to slip into jeans and sneakers all day, to watch the brood mares or break a pair of yearlings to saddle, to pack a picnic for the beach, curl up with a book.

Serenity, however, was short-lived.

The summer of 1936 had provided a scandal so juicy, so loaded with names, so intimate, so far beyond anything journalists had ever turned up—and right out in court where the press was immune to libel—that Hitler's Berlin Olympics and the Spanish Civil War were knocked clear off the front pages. It also gave Frank Fay ideas.

George S. Kaufman and Mary Astor were the center of the uproar. Barbara knew them both, the playwright since *Burlesque*, Astor since their Warner Brothers days. Astor had literary aspirations and Barbara could easily have imagined Mary keeping a diary, perhaps even imagine her making notes of her intimate life. Barbara was shocked when, a year after the affair had ended with Kaufman returning to his wife, Bea, and Mary agreeing to a divorce, the actress contested the divorce. Astor had her lawyers sue to gain custody of her daughter from her husband, Dr. Franklyn Thorpe. To prove Astor an unworthy mother, Dr. Thorpe tried to have his former wife's diary entered as evidence. The scandal reached a fever pitch in August while Mary was filming *Dodsworth* for Samuel Goldwyn and Barbara's *His Brother's Wife* came out.

Without quoting directly from the diary, the August 17 issue of *Time* said Miss Astor's record of sexual events contained references to "thrilling ecstasy" and described Kaufman's powers as such that his amorous trysts reached twenty a day. Other papers published the actress's Top Ten list of lovers with Kaufman leading the list.

Barbara could only thank her lucky stars that Frank Fay's detectives had never unearthed anything on her.

When Kaufman failed to appear as a witness, Judge Goodwin J. Knight issued a bench warrant. What followed was out of a Marx Brothers script. When sheriff's deputies came looking for him at Moss Hart's rented house in Palm Springs, Kaufman fled through the bushes. MGM had him smuggled to Catalina island, the playground for tony film people. Judge Knight, who had been Frank Capra's classmate at Manual Arts High School, felt the movie industry was making a national fool of him, and sent deputies to Catalina. The chase continued on the high seas.

After another stay at Hart's house and another early-morning police visit that drove Kaufman to hysteria, friends managed to ship him out of California and, temporarily at least, out of the judge's reach. With the press jeering and cheering the "Public Lover No. 1," Kaufman reached New York. When reporters caught up with his wife, traveling in Europe with Edna Ferber, Bea said, "I'm not going to divorce Mr. Kaufman. Young actresses are an occupational hazard for any man working in the theater."

The end of the trial was a dud, with Judge Knight ruling in favor of joint custody.

Did Frank Fay think he could grab comparable headlines?

Barbara might be "seen" with Robert Taylor, but she was duly divorced. Even the one-year interlocutory of California divorce law, designed to give people pause before rushing into new marriages, had expired. Of course there was Dion.

Fay went to court in 1937, claiming Robert Taylor was his former wife's "consort" and that for the past sixteen months Barbara had denied Frank the right to see their adopted son "so that the child would become accustomed only to Robert Taylor." Fay claimed his former wife was in contempt of court for violating their 1935 divorce decree that allowed him to see their son. The contempt-of-court charge was filed as *A Star Is Born* started filming. To be sure the romantic melodrama starring Fredric March and Janet Gaynor was not caught up in the Fay–Stanwyck case, David Selznick took the extra precaution of having Ben Hecht rewrite the much rewritten story.

Fay believed the luck of the Irish was smiling down on him when the presiding justice was none other than Judge Goodwin J. Knight. Stanwyck's first day in court was inauspicious. It came on December 27, 1937, after a *Photoplay* article told how she was planning a special Christmas for her little boy, while the daily newspapers reported how she and Bob were seen at the Santa Anita racetrack on Christmas Day.

"Is it true you spent most of Christmas Day at the races instead of at home with your child?" asked Philip Klein, Fay's attorney.

She could only nod.

The cross-examination centered on Frank's charge that she was trying to alienate Dion's affection. "Wasn't it a fact that you were having Mr. Taylor to your house frequently so that the child could forget Mr. Fay?"

"Mr. Taylor was at the house frequently, but it was not so the boy would forget his father," she answered.

Judge Knight objected when Frank's lawyer brought up a $50 check that Bob apparently had made out to Dion and signed. "I don't care how many times Mr. Taylor came to her house," the judge ruled. "This is her personal life and has nothing to do with this proceeding."

Barbara's lawyer was Charles Cradick, who had defended her in her losing fight with Harry Cohn and in the Elizabeth Curtis "private nurse and companion" suit in 1934. On the stand, Fay testified that he had not seen his son in sixteen months, that since the divorce he had been permitted to see the boy only four times. Cradick asked the indignant father to specify the amount he contributed to the child's support. Fay answered that he did not contribute to Anthony Dion's support because Miss Stanwyck had never asked.

Cradick had Barbara tell the court that if she was keeping Dion away from his father she had her reasons.

"In the summer of 1935," she testified, "beside the pool of our Brentwood home, Mr. Fay was quite provoked because I had dinner the night before at the home of Mr. and Mrs. Marx and then we had gone to Minsky's *burlesque* in Hollywood. He struck me with his fist on the chin and I fell over a chair to the ground. It upset the baby. When my son was three years old, Mr. Fay was wandering about the house and his condition was not too good. I was in my room and the nurse was downstairs. I heard the nursery door bang. I went outside and saw Mr. Fay leaving the boy's room. He was drunk. I went into the nursery and found the carpet beneath my son's crib on fire from a smoldering cigarette stub." She accused Frank of neglecting the child and being opposed to his adoption, but asserted that when guests were at their home he would make a great show of his affection for the boy.

Cradick got Fay on the stand and asked, "Do you recall an incident at your home in Brentwood when you were gathered at the side of the swimming pool with the nurse and baby? Did you ask the nurse to place the baby in the water, but she protested that the child was scared of water and you picked the child up and tossed it into the pool?" Fay was not permitted to answer on a technicality, although Judge Knight ruled he would be required to relate the incident if recalled for direct examination.

In its December 30 edition, the *Los Angeles Examiner* splashed the story on page five: BARBARA STANWYCK HURLS SENSATIONAL CHARGES AT EX-MATE. TELLS OF FIRE BY CRIB; SAYS SON'S LIFE TWICE IMPERILED. A two-column photo showed Barbara on the stand, wearing a wide-brimmed, tucked-down man's hat and tweed suit. A four-paragraph story on the same page named Frank Fay as a target of an Internal Revenue Service lien for nonpayment of $9,573 in income taxes.

When the case resumed after New Year's, Barbara demanded a psychiatric evaluation of Frank Fay. Charging her former husband with being of "unsound mind" and submitting ten affidavits to support her allegation, she said Frank was someone who mingled prayers and profanities: "When he passed a church, Frank would remove his hands from the wheel of a car and pray, endangering the lives of others . . . He's an unfit guardian for the child. He drinks too much. He fell into Dion's crib once and fell asleep keeping the boy awake with his snoring. As far as I'm concerned he loves his new store teeth more than his son."

Judge Knight ruled in Frank's favor, giving him the right to visit his son twice a month on alternating Saturdays provided he was completely sober and always in the company of the child's nurse, who was required to report his conduct to Stanwyck.

Barbara told Cradick to appeal.

The headlines never matched the Astor-Kaufman screamers, but on January 18, 1938, Fay, his lawyers, and a horde of reporters drove in pouring rain to Barbara's ranch. With attorneys Philip Klein and Hy Schwartz waiting in a car, Frank marched past the KEEP OUT—PRIVATE sign to the gate telephone and announced he had come to see his son.*

"His face dropped," wrote the *Los Angeles Times* reporter. "Then he added, 'Whose orders are those?'"

Frank went back to the car and conferred with his attorneys. It was obvious, Klein explained to the press, that Stanwyck was continuing to refuse to let Frank see the boy.

Four men, described by the *Times* as "taciturn cowhands," and a Doberman pinscher peered out from behind the gate. Nobody, said the foreman, was getting through the locked gate. Under a picture of Fay, in trenchcoat and visored cap, at the gate, the next day's *Times* headline read: BARBARA STANWYCK'S GUARDS BLOCK FAY'S VISIT WITH SON.

---

*Schwartz sued Fay for nonpayment of legal fees a year later. The lawyer complained he had represented Fay in five lawsuits and was owed $19,600. In November 1939, Fay won a $611 reduction. In the end the court awarded Schwartz $3,750. It was par for the course. Earlier, Charles Cradick had sued Fay for nearly $50,000 in unpaid legal fees and settled for a fourth of that amount.

14

Stella

Even before Frank Fay filed contempt-of-court charges, Helen Ferguson thought Barbara needed to explain her marriage and ongoing custody battle on her terms. For the first time in her career Barbara Stanwyck would be available for an exclusive in-depth, Helen told *Photoplay*. The magazine was interested and assigned free-lance journalist Dixie Willson to do the piece. Thoroughly vetted by the Helen Ferguson Agency, Willson came to stay with Barbara at the ranch. It was indeed the first time Barbara—ever so cautiously—opened up to a writer, the first time she let someone explore her life. Perhaps she also wanted to distance herself from Bob because *Photoplay*'s subheadline of Willson's published piece read, "A fine searching story about the Stanwyck girl herself which doesn't ask her to bask in the shadow of Bob Taylor's—or anybody else's—glory."

The writer was sensitive to the situation of the movie star trying to make sense of her life. Courage was what mattered, Barbara said. She was going to bring up her son to learn to face hurts without crying. Tears never helped. "Perhaps I'm cruel to talk to him of things like that when he's so little, but I wish I had had someone to help me learn not to cry. I had to find that out by myself."

Willson divined a lot of hurt behind Stanwyck's brave front and, in the confessional celebrity-profile prose, said as much: "Of one thing you may be sure; her name is not spelled in letters of lights in exchange for merely looks or luck or imitation of drama as she imagines it, or life as she has read about it. It has taken tears more real than those of glycerine and camphor."

The writer got the facts about Barbara's early years, but nothing about the present circumstances or the whereabouts of Barbara's sisters and brother. To Willson's question of whether the teenaged Ruby Stevens had planned to study dancing, Barbara answered, "Oh no, we were really very poor. I knew that after fourteen I'd have to earn my own living. But I was willing to do that. I've always been a little sorry for pampered people . . . and of course, they're *very* sorry for me."

Willson saw Dion take riding lessons, and sketched the end of a day at the ranch, the "boys" bedding stalls for the night, the crack and smell of a log fire, and Barbara sitting on her porch:

> The distant mountains were turning from gray to cobalt blue. In dusty boots and grass-stained jodhpurs, knees locked in her arms, this girl of the husky, lazy voice sat on the flagstone floor, her eyes straying often from the paddock to the terrace where small Dion struggled with the balance of bright new stilts.
>
> "What do I like best . . . and least, about Hollywood?" Barbara Stanwyck said, repeating my question. "Best, that it gives me a place which is home. Least, the fanfare and ballyhoo that seems to be part of pictures. I really don't know why there should be fanfare for people who play in pictures are not incredible human beings. And I never quite know why the foremost impression of Hollywood should be glamour because glamour actually has nothing to do with pictures at all. Glamour is a separate thing altogether. Still, of course, there's my good friend Joan [Crawford] who just can't help being glamorous. But when I go with her into a restaurant or a shop and hear a little ripple of admiration and attention that follows her everywhere, I'm sure it isn't entirely Hollywood. I'm sure she is just the dynamic sort of person who would be glamorous anywhere.

Stanwyck was serene and successful, wrote Willson. Her existence was well ordered; she had few regrets: "Of course, I've always had a burning desire to be the best of all, and, though I know most things you dream of pass you by, I'll go on working with that same desire till the last role I play."

Photoplay ran the profile in its December 1937 issue with photos of Stanwyck under a huge straw hat, a head shot of Dion, and Barbara and Joan with their arms around each other.

For a while Fay took advantage of his visitation rights. Anything to get back at Barbara. Not that she was much better. Concerned with scoring points against a former husband she wanted completely out of her life, she proclaimed, through Helen Ferguson, both that she wanted her son to feel secure at home and, to make sure he didn't grow up a spoiled Hollywood child, that she intended in the near future to send him away to military school. Frank's court-ordered alternating Saturdays with Dion dwindled to once-every-other-month visits as he lost interest in the boy. By the time Dion was six, he was of little interest to either of his parents.

RKO was still counting the money from *The Informer*, when Jack Ford said he wanted to do *The Plough and the Stars*. Because of the play's ambivalence about the Irish cause, it had been greeted with such anger when it opened in Dublin in 1926 that Sean O'Casey moved to London. O'Casey's bar-room drama of the Irish character had language that was as fierce and inflexible as his social conscience. What was different—subversive to Dublin theatergoers a decade earlier—was Nora Clitheroe, who wants her man for herself, alive, and not out on the barricades fighting the Brits. In fact, O'Casey was not interested in glorifying the 1916 Easter uprising; he thought it tragic, foolhardy, and pitiful. Samuel J. Briskin, RKO's new production chief, wasn't sure a screen adaptation was what moviegoers wanted, but gave a reluctant go-ahead provided Ford agreed to star Barbara Stanwyck as Nora. Briskin, who had trained under Harry Cohn, believed in A pictures and strong box-office names. He signed Ann Sothern to a seven-year contract, Stanwyck to a two-picture deal, and added Barbara's *Woman in Red* costar Gene Raymond and her *Message to Garcia* vis-à-vis, John Boles, as "outstanding names for the studio roster."

The one-eyed Ford was Hollywood's "professional" Irishman, a director of a vast and diverse body of work that went back to the silent era. In *The Informer*, Liam

O'Flaherty's tale of a loser who, for steamship passage to America, betrays a comrade to the British, he had successfully mined the 1916 "troubles." To keep *The Informer* within its $340,000 budget, Ford had filmed it like a B picture. The inspired casting of Victor McLaglen as the "gutter Judas" helped vault the picture onto every critic's list of Best Pictures of 1935. At Oscar time, it won four awards: Best Director, Writer (Dudley Nichols), Actor (McLaglen), and Musical Score (composer Max Steiner).

Ford wanted an all-Irish cast for *The Plough and the Stars*. Briskin insisted on Stanwyck, then mellowed enough to let Ford import the Abbey Theatre's Barry Fitzgerald. Box-office exigencies demanded an American as Stanwyck's mate, and Preston Foster, with whom Stanwyck had already done *Ladies They Talk About* and *Annie Oakley*, was cast as her husband. Walter Plunkett, Katharine Hepburn's favorite designer, soon to be famous for his *Gone with the Wind* costumes, created a passably drab Dublin slum wardrobe for the film. Barbara's brogue was not unpleasant, but in Plunkett's 1916 dresses and head scarves she was, as one critic put it, "a grande dame in an Irish bog."

Ford imported half the Abbey Theatre's stock company to fill out the cast and took out his anger at having to submit to box-office requirements by misusing Barbara. She was too much a modern woman to submit to Irish machismo and squirmed at lines that had her plead with her man not to engage in the violence the audience expected.

Barbara sat with Briskin at the screening of the rough cut. "Halfway through, he said, 'Nobody's gonna understand those accents!'" she would remember. "So they called Preston and me back and we shot scene after scene of 'translations': 'Listen, Nora, you hear what they're sayin'? You know what it means. It means . . . ' Mr. Ford very wisely was unavailable on his yacht."

Indeed, Ford and his wife, Mary, sailed to Honolulu. While he was away, Briskin resigned and his second in command, Pandro S. Berman, took over as studio chief. In the time-honored tradition of Hollywood moguls denigrating their predecessors' work and canceling their deals, Berman took one look at the "translated" *Plough* and decided the film would be sexier if Stanwyck and Foster were lovers instead of married folk. Because Stanwyck and Preston Foster were already on other pictures, an assistant shot their scenes on Sundays. The new footage lacked consistency and sheen and jarred with Ford's footage.

When Ford returned, he pretended to be furious. "I've always felt that John should not have left the sinking ship," Barbara would recall. "God knows I had no power at that time, nor did Preston. Only John could have saved it and he should have." Instead of fighting for his cut, Ford moved to Fox to direct *Wee Willie Winkie*, the most expensive Shirley Temple vehicle to date.

Stanwyck went to work for the studio that might not match MGM in glamour, but was peerless in imagination and energy.

Paramount Pictures was the least regimented film factory, the one studio where directors, not supervisors or producers, shaped the films. Paramount favored chance over strategy and planning, and was reckless in the way it handled talent, but its output bore the stamp of cunning sensuality. It was there that Cecil B. DeMille, Ernst Lubitsch, Josef von Sternberg, and such lesser luminaries as Allan Dwan, Harry D'Arrast, and Mitchell Leisen held forth.

Barbara had eagerly sought the attention of Paramount's successive moguls, and getting the Paramount treatment was a pleasure even if *Internes Can't Take Money* was a programmer based on a Max Brand "Dr. Kildare" hospital novel. Max Brand was one of the many pseudonyms of Frederick Faust, an author of over a hundred fast-paced crime, spy, and western novels. *Internes Can't Take Money* was the first Kildare film, made a year before MGM took over the character for Lew Ayres. Paramount had bought the book at Joel McCrea's urging. Joel couldn't wait to play the young doctor who, under primitive conditions, operates on a gangster and helps a woman just released from prison find her missing daughter.

Before *Internes Can't Take Money* started, Barbara was told to make an appointment with John Engstead, the studio portrait photographer. His work appeared on the cover of every woman's magazine, and his subjects were the Paramount Who's Who, from Marlene Dietrich to Loretta Young, Cary Grant to Carole Lombard, Claudette Colbert to Mae West.

Barbara's showing up on time was Engstead's first surprise. He was used to Young's demands for retouching photographs, Nancy Carroll's bitchiness, and Colbert's tardiness. But there was Stanwyck walking into his gallery on the dot of two.

"My assistant Gene and I weren't ready, but there she was," he would recall. "She doesn't have the inspiration that Clara Bow had, or Lombard. But she was a good subject, and she was on time."

The *Internes* screen credits read costumes by Travis Banton, Paramount's alcoholic head designer catapulted to fame with the black feathers, veils, and chiffon ensembles he created for Marlene Dietrich. As a star with a one-picture deal, Stanwyck didn't rate the Banton treatment, however, and her white satin dress was designed by Banton's assistant, Edith Head. Both Banton and Head had been with Paramount since the mid-1920s, he coming from haute couture, she from teaching art in Los Angeles high schools.

"Barbara had been a little insulted that Travis didn't want to dress her," Head would remember, "but she and I hit it off immediately and it was the beginning of a long and important friendship." There were parallels to their lives. The designer was at the end of a marriage to an alcoholic. Friends couldn't understand why she stuck it out with Charles Head, a sales executive who in the face of his wife's success retreated to booze. Her Catholic upbringing kept her married, but the other man in her life, Barbara learned, was Wiard Boppo Ihnen, a set designer at Fox.

Barbara thought she and Bob should do another picture together.

So did Darryl Zanuck. Fan magazines reported gushingly on the Stanwyck-Taylor romance, and the Twentieth Century-Fox chief was sure moviegoers were eager to see the two of them together on the screen. Was Louis B. Mayer mellowing? MGM quickly agreed to loan Bob to Fox. Zanuck signed Barbara to a one-film deal, dusted off a G-man in costume setting script called *Private Enemy*, retitled it *This Is My Affair*, and got it into production.

The director was William A. Seiter, a former Keystone Kop who had directed Laurel and Hardy, Shirley Temple, and

Fred Astaire. Victor McLaglen and Brian Donlevy played the
villains. Frank Conroy incarnated President McKinley, and
Sidney Blackmer with a false set of teeth was President
Theodore Roosevelt. Bob was Lieutenant Richard L. Perry,
one of the victors of the 1889 Manila Bay encounter with the
Spanish fleet, who is secretly deputized by President
McKinley to break up a band of bank robbers whose astonishing knowledge of passkeys, vault combinations, and alarm systems has weakened public trust in the banking system.
Barbara is a dance-hall belle in the confidence of the gang's
leader. Taylor infiltrates the bank robbers, Stanwyck tests her
love for him, but then, of course, McKinley is assassinated.

The filming was a charm. Royer (Lewis Royer Hastings)
created an elegant period wardrobe for Stanwyck. To play on
the two stars' offscreen relationship, Harry Brand's press
releases trumpeted how intense their love scenes were, how
each remained on the set during the other's solo work, and
how flustered Barbara was when Bob sat in on the recording
of her one song in the film, "I Hum a Waltz."

If there was one part she lusted after—and pushed Zeppo to
get for her—it was the title role in *Stella Dallas*. Samuel
Goldwyn was preparing the picture with his usual panache,
trade-paper leaks, and planted announcements. William
Wyler, his premier in-house director and master of the high-
gloss filmmaking that Goldwyn unashamedly called "the
Goldwyn touch," was set to direct. "I would give up everything I own to make *Stella Dallas*," Barbara told Joel McCrea,
Goldwyn's fair-haired boy. Olive Higgins Prouty's bestselling
novel about a woman who marries an unhappy but socially
superior man and, when he drifts away, brings up their daughter alone, demanded an actress capable of playing on multiple
registers. There might have been faint parallels between
Barbara's life and Stella's had Rex Cherryman lived because,
like Ruby Stevens, the awkward young Stella has the wits to
impress the refined Stephen Dallas, an executive in the factory
where she works. Mother love was not the adult Barbara
Stanwyck's strong suit, whereas Stella's story is all about
maternal sacrifice and a mother trying to remake herself to
please her child. Playing Stella would be all *performance*, the
most demanding Barbara had ever tried. She would have to

be convincing both as a down-to-earth young woman alienating her upper-class husband and as a socially inept middle-aged mother who is a disgrace to their daughter. She would have to be brassy and touching, unselfish and embarrassing.

"Everybody was testing for it," Barbara would remember of *Stella Dallas*. "It was almost comparable to the search for a Scarlett O'Hara in *Gone with the Wind*, which was going on at the same time."

Stella Dallas had been Goldwyn's biggest success in 1925. The themes of upward mobility and of children ashamed of their elders echoed deep within the forty-two-year-old Polish-Jewish rags-to-riches mogul. Stella is an embarrassment to Laurel, the daughter she brings up alone. When Laurel's father marries a rich childhood acquaintance, she becomes immersed in their socialite world. She doesn't invite her mother to her high-society wedding, and Stella stands in the rain, behind an iron gate watching her daughter marry the attractive Richard Grosvenor.

In his own life, Goldwyn felt so humiliated by his mother that he never brought Hannah Gelbfisz to America. When he went to Europe in 1925, he made her journey from Warsaw to Berlin to see him. She had her suite next to his at the Adlon Hotel, but for the better part of a week she never left her room. Sam took all his dinners in his mother's suite. As for the daughter he had with long-since divorced Blanche Lasky, the relationship was little more than awkward vacations and letters demanded of Ruth by her father. He found her distant and resentful. When she was twelve and declined a trip with him to Europe, he threw her out of the Astor Hotel and resolved never to see or speak to her again.

When Prouty's novel was dramatized in 1924, Mrs. Leslie Carter, a legend past her prime, played Stella and a very young Edward G. Robinson was Grosvenor. *Stella Dallas* had been less than sensational on Broadway, but Goldwyn bought the rights both to the novel and to the stage version and hired Frances Marion to write the scenario. Marion was the writer of many of Mary Pickford's movies and a woman with a talent for picking people. She told Goldwyn he should cast Belle Bennett as Stella and matinee idol Ronald Colman as Stephen Dallas, the man she cannot live up to. To play the daughter, Sam himself discovered the fifteen-year-old Lois

Moran. Henry King directed Bennett as a genteel, aloof figure of pity. Warmth and compassion pervaded every scene, and the picture became Goldwyn's biggest silent moneymaker.

In 1937, however, the idea of redoing the old workhorse made Goldwyn's rivals hoot that Sam was losing his touch. The fact that every actress wanted to play Stella made him believe he'd have the last laugh.

Goldwyn ordered up a new screenplay and assigned the filming to William Wyler, his top director. When the writing duo of Victor Heerman and Sarah Y. Mason delivered their *Stella Dallas*, however, Wyler was on loanout to Warners directing Bette Davis in *Jezebel*.

Goldwyn hired King Vidor.

After *The Texas Rangers*, Vidor's second historical epic for Paramount, the studio had offered him *Sam Houston*. Vidor might be a Texan by birth, but, as he wrote production chief William LeBaron, "I've such a belly-full of Texas after the *Rangers* that I find myself not caring whether Sam Houston takes Texas from the Mexicans or lets them keep it." More to the point, Vidor was the president of the new Screen Directors Guild, and during the first critical year of the new union's life he had no intention of doing a location picture. Since *Stella Dallas* would shoot at the United Artists lot on Santa Monica Boulevard, he accepted Goldwyn's offer.

"See silent picture," Vidor noted to himself when he and Goldwyn came to terms on the remake.

There was little give-and-take with Goldwyn, a fact that made even reasonable arguments difficult. Goldwyn and Vidor immediately clashed on the title role. The producer wanted Ruth Chatterton or Gladys George and tested several actresses with less drawing power. Stanwyck was Vidor's first choice. Zeppo Marx was a poker partner of Goldwyn's, but thought it smarter to have Joel McCrea join Vidor in pulling for Barbara.

"She's just got no sex appeal," Goldwyn objected when McCrea made his pitch for his *Gambling Lady*, *Banjo on My Knee*, and *Internes Can't Take Money* costar.

John Boles was cast as Stephen Dallas, Stella Martin's ticket out of a drab, rigid home. Nineteen-year-old Anne Shirley got the part of their daughter, Laurel, whose birth widens the gap in class and manners between Stella and Stephen. Tim Holt, Marjorie Main, Alan Hale, Barbara O'Neil, Edward Norris, and Lillian Yarbo rounded out the cast.

When Zeppo took Barbara to see Goldwyn, the producer flatteringly objected that she was too young. It hurt when he said she had too little experience with children. When Goldwyn asked her if she had ever suffered over a child, she heard herself say, "But I can imagine how it would be."

Goldwyn agreed to let her test for Stella.

However much Barbara detested screen tests, she knuckled under. Stella was someone she had played before, the mockingly self-aware, self-sacrificing lower-class woman. With Anne Shirley, she rehearsed and played the script's birthday scene. Goldwyn said the part was hers.

Stanwyck found Vidor to be a director convinced of his own genius. Another John Ford, but without Ford's sometimes endearing crustiness, Vidor believed in motion. His camera setups were complicated—rapidly rising or dropping crane shots, often to pick out her character or to punctuate scenes that seemed to have their own climax. There was little creative rapport between Vidor and Stanwyck. Director and star did their jobs.

"I was spurred by memory of the magnificent performance of the late Belle Bennett in the first movie version," Barbara told the *Saturday Evening Post*. "Also, there was unusual stimulation in the dual nature of the part; it was like playing two different women simultaneously. Always Stella has to be shown both in her surface commonness and in her basic fineness." We see her wear outdated clothes and enjoying herself too noisily and, in the working-class and immigrant tradition, skimping and sacrificing to give a child upward mobility. As Stella peels potatoes, Laura prattles on about her father's new woman ("Well, she reminds me of a flower that grows in Maine, all pale and delicate, but strong too"). After overhearing she is the laughingstock of her daughter's new tennis-and-tea friends, Stella offers Laura to her husband's intended new wife ("Everybody would naturally think she was your little girl").

Boles played her husband with repressed gentility.

Stephen Dallas's millions were made by his father, who committed suicide, the woman he was in love with married another, and he has found anonymity in middle management at a Massachusetts mill. Stella wins his heart by polishing a glass in his office before a dissolve takes them to the movies, and as they leave the theater Stella wonders whether it is appropriate to take his arm. She says she envies the people they have just seen on the screen. Her ambition chills him. He says, "It isn't really well-bred to act the way you are." When they kiss, we know that it is a ploy for her, a polite condescension for him. Another dissolve, and they are married. She sees the birth of their daughter matter-of-factly; to him it is the miracle of life.

Stanwyck gave Stella's grating and seedy callousness the same intensity as the character's compassionate side, the clash of upward mobility. When Stephen unexpectedly calls on Stella, she quickly wipes off her lipstick and snips frills from her dress, trying once more to remake herself into the classy woman her former husband must want.

Anne Shirley remembered a scene in which Stella takes herself and her daughter to a fancy resort where Laurel meets eligible, collegiate Tim Holt. "Barbara Stanwyck was unforgettable," Shirley would say. "She stalks across the resort patio dressed outlandishly in a loud print dress, excessive, cheap jewelry and makeup." Rudolph Maté's moody camerawork underscored Stanwyck's acting, in which tragedy and comedy balance perfectly.

Vidor copied Henry King's silent finale. Alone and forgotten, Stella elbows her way through black umbrellas outside the town house where Laurel's marriage is being celebrated. She stands at the rail fence and watches through the three-panel windows, biting on a handkerchief until a street cop breaks up the crowd. However, where the silent movie cut between the society wedding inside and Stella watching outside in the rain, Vidor stayed on Stella. Before the fade-out the camera tracks backward in front of Stanwyck as she walks away.

Vidor's memories of the filming were bitter. Halfway through, Goldwyn stormed onto the set and berated Vidor and everybody else, calling the performances bad. He wanted to fire Vidor and Stanwyck and close down the picture. Late that night, he called Vidor at home, apologizing. He had seen the rushes again. They looked wonderful.

"It was painful," Vidor recalled. At the end of principal photography, he posted a note to himself above his desk: NO MORE GOLDWYN PICTURES! Barbara, however, remembered Goldwyn's directive that the flowers in the film be real. No actress of his would have to stick her face in a piece of wax.

Released in August 1937, *Stella Dallas* grossed more than $2 million. Calling the Prouty drama terribly dated for 1937 audiences, the *New York Times*'s Frank Nugent nevertheless found "Miss Stanwyck's portrayal is as courageous as it is fine. Ignoring the flattery of makeup and camera, she plays Stella as Mrs. Prouty drew her; coarse, cheap, common, given to sleazy dresses, to undulations in her walk, to fatty degeneration of the profile. And yet magnificent as a mother."

The film was nominated for an Oscar. The other Best Actress nominees for Best Performance in 1937 were Luise Rainer (*The Good Earth*), Irene Dunne (*The Awful Truth*), Greta Garbo (*Camille*), and Janet Gaynor (*A Star Is Born*). Perhaps a good omen for Stella, Anne Shirley was nominated in the Best Supporting Actress category.

With Bob as her escort, she attended the March 10, 1938, Academy Awards presentation. The klieg lights popped when Stanwyck and the costar of *Camille* entered the Los Angeles Biltmore Hotel. Early in the evening, Shirley lost to Alice Brady for *In Old Chicago*. When it came to the Best Actress award, the winner was Luise Rainer. Barbara was crushed. "My life's blood was in that picture," she said. "I should have won."

Her mistake was perhaps her own. She was someone who never pretended to be what she wasn't. She was too much a regular person, too much what studio and producers hoped regular people were like. Everybody accepted her work. No one questioned whether she was good. Incandescence is made by oversized presence, built-in glare, excess, inscrutability, and low cunning, not by being a hardworking pro and a good sport.

Ironically, she was the most natural American actress. Movies with irresistible foreign femmes fatales were becoming passé. Katharine Hepburn was slightly eccentric, Joan Crawford often outrageous. In Bette Davis, Warner Brothers created a homegrown *Evil Woman* who topped the fervid, hypnotic, and remote Garbo-Dietrich allure. With her startling eyes, disdainful mouth, clipped, almost British, speech, Davis was becoming the screen's ultimate bitch. In a series of reckless, unsympathetic but high-powered roles that no other star dared try, she interpreted connivance, neurosis, psychosis, and the vain Southern-belle heartbreaker in a series of box-office hits.

Stanwyck was the independent woman. Even if the roles she played weren't natural, she made them *look* that way. With her distinctive style and pulsating voice, she projected both toughness and warmth, cynicism and sensitivity. She had competition from Davis, Hepburn, and Crawford when it came to assertive women's parts, but as a free-lance she didn't have to ask for permission from Warner, Berman, or Mayer. Several prestige films eluded her, but her lack of pretensions and workmanlike professionalism made her a "director's actress" even when her relationship with Cohn, Warner, and Goldwyn remained prickly.

To 1970s feminists, Barbara's portrayal would be seen as Everywoman as victim. "Stanwyck brings us to admire something that exceeds in stupidity and beauty and daring the temperate limitation of her literary model and all the generalizations about the second sex," Molly Haskell would write. In a larger overview twenty years later, Elizabeth Kendall would see Stanwyck's ability to reveal grief and loneliness ever so movingly beneath a tough and efficient front as a side of her that made canny directors want to create parts explicitly for her: "Capra had been the first, but John Cromwell in *Banjo on My Knee* also dramatized Stanwyck's wild loneliness, and so, in another way, did King Vidor in *Stella Dallas*."

Although nominated three more times, she regretted most losing the *Stella Dallas* Oscar.

15

Offscreen

Barbara's quest for self-transformation worked splendidly on movie sets. Offscreen, she had never resolved her need to be in control and her wish to be taken care of. The conflict disappeared for a while in her relationship with Bob because she was so overwhelmingly in charge. Bob tried to please, tried to avoid arguments. He had a hard time expressing anger, felt guilty easily, was quick to assume blame, to continue to defer to his mother. However, both wished to continue their glasshouse professions unscathed. Bob would admit years later that they were not in love.

Barbara was all work and, for play, found sufficient distraction watching her horses run at the Santa Anita racetrack. Whereas her thoroughbreds were for racetrack winning and she had no real favorites, Bob raised quarter horses and gave them names. The respect of coworkers was enough for her, and most nights she was either reading scripts or learning lines. But her devotion to her work never inspired Bob to demand more of himself. She was protective of him. She called him "Junior"—behind her back he called her "The Queen." If anyone wondered about marriage, she said Bob was immature, that she didn't think he should be tied down.

People sometimes found them oddly stiff and, in the company of other stars, less than brilliant. Joan Crawford's know-it-all manner intimidated Barbara. Joan might put plastic covers on her furniture, but in her closets she had an index card with photograph and swatches attached to each dress to remind her when and where she had worn it. Before she went anywhere, she consulted her index cards so as to be able to tell her hostess, "So nice to see you. I haven't seen you since that premiere in New York." Barbara was too straightforward to be that brazen, but she enjoyed watching the effect of her friend's gall on people. When at Joan's, she hung back and observed.

In *Carnival Nights in Hollywood,* Elizabeth Wilson caught Stanwyck and Taylor at the beginning of a Crawford soiree:

> The guests are all assembled before Joan appears, pausing first at the top of the stairs. She has the best tan, Barbara Stanwyck the worst (busy working days on *Stella Dallas*). While long and lean Gary Cooper plays with the marble machine in the game room, challenging Una Merkel and Charles Boyer to a game, Cooper's lovely wife talks to Betty Furness and Pat Boyer. Luise Rainer and her husband, Clifford Odets, arrive, and Franchot Tone instantly goes into a huddle with Odets. The two know each other from New York. As Ginger Rogers eyes the food, Robert Taylor and his girlfriend, Barbara Stanwyck, who suffers the torture of the timid, play ping-pong while Joan Crawford looks on holding a little glass of sherry, which she never touches.

Barbara said she disparaged herself because she believed others were going to, and she wanted to beat them to it. She worried, mostly about things that didn't happen. She was intense about *everything,* "bitter about a lot of things and clinging to them (sometimes the chip on my shoulder wasn't exactly invisible either)."

One place she and Bob were relaxed was at Mary and Jack Benny's dinner parties. The Bennys loved to entertain in their grand Roxbury Drive home in Beverly Hills. Benny was the number-one radio comedian, the suave, vain, know-it-all braggart who seemed so on top of things even if his cast made a fool of him every week. His radio show paid him $25,000 a week, and he was also busy in movies. As a young man in vaudeville, he told Barbara, he had been influenced by Frank Fay.

Jack and Mary Livingstone (née Sadie Marks) had been married since 1927. Their adopted daughter, Joan, was Dion's age. Mary did everything for Jack. She made sure she was seen in the right restaurants, driving the right car, shopping in the right stores, and that everybody knew she was Mrs. Benny.

The Bennys' parties were celebrity events and ranged from intimate dinners for twelve to dining under a garden tent for sixty to a hundred. Mary always had the best food and the prettiest china, and she had her annual September barbecues catered by Chasen's. The guests were usually married couples, George and Gracie Burns, producer William Goetz and his wife, Edith, the Mervyn LeRoys, the Charles Vidors. Beatrice Kaufman, George S.'s formidable and much-cheated-on wife, would remember meeting Barbara and Bob with Sam and Frances Goldwyn at the Bennys'.

Besides being mothers of adopted children, Mary and Barbara had compatible temperaments. They were not late-night people. They tended to be reclusive, but knew how to make fun of their insecurities. The couples were comfortable together; Barbara, Bob, Jack, and Mary often went out as a foursome and were capable of sitting at a nightclub for almost an hour without saying a word to each other.

Bob never used his good looks to his advantage, said his friend Lloyd Nolan. If anything Bob considered his handsomeness something of an embarrassment that prevented him from being a regular guy. It was his impression that MGM wanted to maintain his bachelor image. When the reporters asked Barbara if she would marry him, she said no. When the press asked *him*, he said they were just good friends. Metro spent lavishly, and Howard Strickling worked assiduously, to make Robert Taylor a "man's man," giving him a series of rugged roles and honing his outdoorsy image. Bob's only insurrection was against his mother. As a movie star going on twenty-six, he felt it was time to create distance between himself and Ruth. She renewed her attacks on Stanwyck and blackmailed her son with teary forewarnings that he was killing her. What would happen if she had a heart attack? Bob got her twenty-four-hour nursing care. Promising he would look in on her every day, he bought a spread next to Stanwyck's ranch in Northridge.

Buying land in "the Valley" was the latest fashion among both irregular and married couples. Gary and Veronica "Rocky" Cooper lived on a ten-acre ranch in Van Nuys,

Spencer and Louise Tracy had bought a nearby hacienda-style house, and Hal and Louise Fazenda Wallis, a silent-film comedienne, had a sixty-acre spread on Woodman Avenue in Sherman Oaks. Carole Lombard and Clark Gable—he still married to Rhea Langham Gable—purchased a twenty-acre property in Encino. Surrounded by acres of citrus, fig, peach, and plum groves, fields of oats and alfalfa, a nine-stall stable, a barn, and a pigless sty, Bob's two-story white brick-and-frame house had nine rooms and spacious red-brick terraces. The second floor featured two adjoining master suites—a "his" decorated in brown and beige, a "hers" in blue and white.

It is impossible to say what their sexual relations were. Bob was known to be attracted to people of his own sex; Barbara lived the very private life of a successful independent woman. They could drive to the ocean on a date and sit silently watching the ocean. He was timid, she skittish, witty, full of fun, but had difficulties with intimacy. She had little tolerance for duplicity, but there was nothing she could do about his homosexual reputation.

Hollywood was not noted for its fondness for actresses over thirty. Paramount refused to renew Marlene Dietrich's contract in 1937, and for the next year the thirty-six-year-old Marlene, touted as the most glamorous, most alluring woman in the world, was out of work. The thirty-year-old Stanwyck nevertheless worked nonstop under the direction of the cream of filmmakers, made scads of money, and created for herself a well-controlled and increasingly private life. Whether Louis B. Mayer or some go-between warned her that Metro wanted Robert Taylor to stay single, she was smart enough to hang back. By *telling* Bob he shouldn't be tied down, she made him look to her with lofty consideration.

He knew he couldn't match her life experience. He told people he was in awe of the way she had practically brought herself up, that she was someone he could depend on. She had never emulated actresses who dressed too cute and too young and only managed to fool themselves, and with Bob she didn't pretend anything. She considered it a weakness to give in to moods. Yet as they saw more of each other, she began to like giving in to Bob's whims.

She liked who she was and how her life was going. The

booming film industry was a floating stock company. She had worked with some of the best and brightest in all sorts of combinations. Studios and directors paid attention to her. "If you say, 'I don't like this script, I don't like so-and-so,' most of them will listen to you," she would say in a career interview. "And if they think your ideas are valid, they will call in the writer and you discuss it as adults and professional people should."

Uncle Buck was a reassuring presence at the ranch, always there, always ready to help. He was her link to Mildred, who had brought her up. Byron was nearby, but Mabel's fate had been as tragic as their mother's. She had married, given birth to a son, and died before little Eugene Vaslett was two. Barbara felt her nephew was her responsibility, and over the next twenty years saw Eugene through college.

Barbara's friendship with Jack and Mary Benny deepened as their daughter and Dion became buddies. The Bennys loved the desert air and the golf and rented houses in Palm Spring before they bought a home next to Tyrone and Annabella Power. Barbara had finally learned to drive and on Sundays piled Dion into her Chevrolet and drove to Palm Springs. "My mother was not the easiest person to get along with but Stanwyck was constantly over at the house," Joan would recall. "I thought she was nice."

"Skip Stanwyck was my first boyfriend. We were five or six, and we were first on two-wheel bicycles. Skip used the surname Stanwyck. He was adorable with freckles and sandy blond hair. He sent me my first love letter—in almost indecipherable capital letters scrawled all over the place it said with classical simplicity, 'I love you.' Together we picked wild flowers in an enormous field behind the El Mirador, rode our bikes and explored the neighborhood. And possibly each other as well. To me he was Skip; later he became Tony. I remember us at my parents' home in Palm Springs, and pictures being taken of Skip and me with our bikes."

Joan Benny might find Dion adorable with his freckles and sandy hair. To Barbara, he was neither winsome nor stimulating. He was overweight and seemed to have little personality. Did it occur to her that her feelings confused him? There are no indications that she questioned herself.

Indifference and rejection are common reasons for overeating, but Barbara never associated Dion's overeating and unresponsiveness with her lack of interest in him. Barbara tried to teach Dion to be tough. As a child she had hated discipline. Responsibility was something that had been thrust on her, not something she had gone looking for. It had been the same for most of the other kids in Brooklyn. She recited a poem she had learned by heart. There was no down in eagles' nests. Eagles nests were built of scratchy sticks and little rocks.

> When comes the eaglet's time to fly
> No mother-softness robs him of his sky

If she wanted someone to look after her, she didn't permit anyone to do so. Nor should Dion. He had to learn to be responsible for himself. He sure couldn't count on Frank Fay. Besides, to be looked after meant being vulnerable, and, in example and words, she made it clear there was nothing more revolting that being weak. She made blunt demands on the boy and responded to his calls for reassurance with dismissal or pop psychology.

Bob might have thought he had successfully rebelled against his mother by buying a ranch in Northridge, but he visited or talked to her on the phone every day. Living next to Barbara with no strings attached was comfortable for Bob. She was no clinging vine. She came over for a swim or a barbecue and went home to study her lines. He liked to putter around. She kidded him about the cookbooks and dozens of watches he bought. On the weightier matter of remodeling and furnishing his ranch, it was Barbara who came up with ideas.

The press—and Ruth—deeply embarrassed Bob in February 1937. Newspapers revealed that his paternal grandfather was living on $16-a-month welfare. Reporters had a field day interviewing Ruth. She had told the Nebraska county assistant director that old Jacob A. Brugh's four children living in Nebraska should take care of him. At a time when laborers earned about $6 a week, the press was happy to point out that MGM was paying old Brugh's grandson $3,500 a week. Ruth made it worse by telling reporters Arly was too busy, that her son did give the eighty-two-year-old Brugh $20 the previous fall and actually paid several of his bills. Making sure the press couldn't get to Bob, Strickling professed the studio's dismay, hinted at a family feud, and said, "The old folks in Nebraska were trying to shove something over on Robert."

Louis B. Mayer abhorred disrespect of family and threatened to deduct enough money from Bob's pay to make the Nebraska story go away. An Associated Press story datelined Beatrice, Nebraska, February 24, reported Robert Taylor was taking his grandfather off the dole.

In the middle of the construction and redecorating of Bob's ranch, Metro sent Bob to England.

Alexander Korda had come a long way since the Stanwyck screen test. The British cinema owed him its renaissance. Yet despite his 1933 hit, *The Private Life of Henry VIII*, almost no British film other than a quickie could earn back its cost on the home market. The American market was therefore essential, but in spite of British producers' constant efforts the transatlantic target eluded them. Korda's remark that when the film business makes money it is in millions, "and so obviously, when we lose, it must be in millions" was typical of the industry's spendthrift delusions. While Korda cut salaries at his London Film Productions and a receiver was appointed at Twickenham Studios, debt-ridden Gaumont-British stopped making films altogether. To limit layoffs and studio closings, the government tightened its quota system limiting foreign films. MGM was the first American company to set up a British production division. Mayer hired Michael Balcon, with Korda the only real showbiz wizard in London, to head an ambitious program of Anglo-American films, each of which would justify its expense by being treated in the United States as a normal MGM release. Robert Taylor was assigned to star in the first MGM-British movie.

In the days before coast-to-coast and transatlantic air travel, it was quite a trip. The fastest travel from Los Angeles to London took at least ten days of continuous travel, via the Santa Fe's Super Chief to Chicago and the New York Central's no less famous 20th Century Limited to New York for a morning ocean liner, the Cunard's *Berengaria* or the French Line's swank new *Ile de France*.

Barbara had no intention of visiting Bob on his faraway location, and Helen Ferguson quoted her as telling Bob the six-month separation would test their feelings for each other. Bob's arrival in England to star in *A Yank at Oxford* with Maureen O'Sullivan and Lionel Barrymore caused a mob scene such as London had not seen since Charlie Chaplin's return to his native city in 1922.

Louis B. came to London with his son-in-law, William Goetz, and Howard Strickling. An elaborate press luncheon at the Savoy was arranged, and Strickling duly impressed on the English press the importance of having Mayer in their midst. Graham Greene was present and noted how Sir Hugh Walpole sat at the high table with O'Sullivan and Taylor. Mayer, Greene observed, spoke for forty minutes:

> The bright lights of Mr. Mayer's eloquence soar up: 'Thank God, I say to you, that it's the greatest year of net results and that's because I have men like Eddie Sankatz (can that have been the name?). It sounded like it after the Chablis Supérieur 1929, the Château Pontet Canet (Pouillac) 1933, G. H. Mumm Cordon Rouge 1928 and the Gautier Frères Fine Champagne.
>
> One can't help missing things, and when the mind comes back to the small dapper man under the massed banners, Mr. Mayer is talking about his family and God again . . . For forty minutes, we have listened to the voice of American capital itself: a touch of religion, a touch of family, the mixture goes down smoothly.

A Yank at Oxford told the story of a brash American college hero coping with English university life and two female students. Back in Hollywood, seven writers, including Scott Fitzgerald, had toiled on the script—the author of *Tender Is the Night* to add "collegiate gloss." Fitzgerald's participation was not substantial enough to earn him a screen credit, but when the film came out he wrote to his mother-in-law that "the sequence in which Taylor and Maureen O'Sullivan go out in the punt in the morning, while the choirboys are singing in Magdalene Tower, is mine, and one line very typically so—where Taylor says, 'Don't rub the sleep out of your eyes. It's beautiful sleep.' I thought that line had my trademark on it."

Fresh from directing a pair of Jean Harlow pictures, Jack Conway was shipped over to lend his brisk style to *A Yank at Oxford*. Korda loaned Vivien Leigh for the small but showy part of a bookseller's adulterous young wife who almost gets Taylor kicked out of Oxford. Leigh had her own notions of how an Englishwoman's character should be portrayed and, as Bob told Barbara on the transatlantic telephone, there was much tension on the set. Bob relayed all the gossip. Maureen and Vivien had gone to convent school together at Roehampton, and both owed their first movie roles to Korda. Vivien was living with Laurence Olivier, discreetly, since she was still married to Leigh Holman, Larry to Jill Osmond.* When MGM sent Bob to Stockholm for the Swedish premiere of *Camille*, Barbara told him to send flowers to Garbo's mother.

After working on nonexclusive contracts for RKO, MGM, and Fox, Barbara became a client of Morgan Maree, the business manager of Marion Davies, Cary Grant, David Selznick, and Mervyn LeRoy. What she liked about the stately Maree, who sat in a mammoth office in downtown L.A., was that he abhorred journalists and publicity. She also got a new agent.

Whether Barbara felt slighted by Zep's paying more attention to his brothers than to his other clients—he had just agented a record-breaking $250,000 contract for them for *Room Service*—or she believed Jules Stein was better for her, she left the Bren-Orsatti agency and signed up with Stein and the Music Corporation of America (MCA), an agency that was beginning to represent general talent in addition to musicians and had just landed Bette Davis as a client.

Unlike Zeppo, but very much like Barbara, the stubby,

*Only two other MGM British films were made before the outbreak of World War II caused Louis B. Mayer to suspend the program: King Vidor directed Robert Donat and Ralph Richardson in an adaption of the A. J. Cronin novel *The Citadel*, and Sam Wood directed Donat and newcomer Greer Garson in the world smash hit *Goodbye, Mr. Chips*.

wispy-voiced Stein was a workaholic. He had put himself
through medical school to become an ophthalmologist by
playing the violin and saxophone in Chicago and promoting
bands. After two years at Chicago's Cook County Hospital,
he realized he could make more money booking musicians
than as an eye doctor and in 1924 founded the Music
Corporation of America. Five years later he had a 10 percent
interest in half the major bands in the country. Bootleg
whiskey was usually part of the deal for booking bands in the
Prohibition 1920s, and Stein never shook his mob connection. When his boyhood chum James Caesar Petrillo became
the head of the American Federation of Musicians, the union
boss worked out a sweetheart deal that gave Stein a monopoly
over big bands that was only discovered in a Justice Department
investigation in 1945.

When Stanwyck joined MCA, Stein had just moved his
agency to Los Angeles. He was so obsessed with landing Bette
Davis as a client that he hired her husband Harmon Nelson's
friend Eddie Linsk (nicknamed "The Killer") at a high fee just
to convince her to sign with him. The feat was accomplished
in three weeks. Errol Flynn and John Garfield followed.

When the *Queen Mary* docked in New York in December
1937, Bob's masculinity became a national joke.
Women had mobbed Taylor in London, and Strickling had
him greet reporters in his cabin in pajamas with a day-old
stubble of beard. The P.R. strategy backfired when a reporter
asked Bob if he thought he was pretty.

"I'm a red-blooded American, and I resent people calling
me beautiful, and I've got hair on my chest," he snapped.

When he refused to unbutton his pajamas for photographers, the hair on his chest became a running joke. Damon
Runyon, the syndicated humorist, found the story irresistible:

> As we understand, Mr. Taylor's resentment of the sug-
> gestion that he is beautiful is offered as a sneer. Now
> this may not be altogether true. Some persons may truly
> think Mr. Taylor is indeed beautiful. We never have
> viewed the young man in the flesh, so we are unable to
> pass an opinion. However, if we were beautiful, we do
> not believe we would object to folks so stating. Apollo

was accounted beautiful, and there was no public record that he put up any squawk when there was public gossip about the matter.

Runyon reported that Ernest Hemingway was also hairless and that as a result of the brouhaha at least six engagements had been broken in suburban Westchester "because young men unwittingly admitted under crafty cross-examination by their beloveds that they lacked mustaches on their bosom."

But *did* Bob have hair on his chest? The question dogged him to Los Angeles. "Just what does a fellow have to do to be a regular guy?" he complained to the press. "Of course, I'm glad that I'm a popular actor, but I certainly don't get a kick out of a lot of girls who ought to know better pawing me and mauling me."

They still wanted to see his chest.

Instead of unbuttoning his shirt, he got to wear a low-slung bathing suit in *Three Comrades* that allowed him to show off a hairy chest.

16

Screwballs, Mr. C.B., and Golden Boy

Barbara decided she couldn't possibly do another emotional drama immediately after *Stella Dallas*. Reading the *Breakfast for Two* script RKO proposed for her and Herbert Marshall, she realized she had very little to do, that the comedy was practically Marshall's picture. Charles Kaufman was one of the writers of *Breakfast for Two*, and the comedy had some hilarious scenes as a headstrong Texas heiress turns a Manhattan playboy into a businessman and pursues him until he catches her. Alfred Santell was going to direct, and RKO promised a superb cast.

Stockholders were fighting over control of RKO-Radio, with studio boss Pandro S. Berman trying to get rid of Sam Briskin and three studio unions on strike, when *Breakfast for Two* went into production. Fred Astaire was filming *A Damsel in Distress* with Joan Fontaine (billed as RKO-Radio's "sensational new sweetheart"), John Boles, Jack Oakie, and Ida Lupino were in a little farce called *Fight for Your Lady*, and Burgess Meredith and Ann Sothern were shooting *There Goes the Groom*.

Santell did his best to give the "screwball" script spin, and Stanwyck and Marshall did their best in a boxing match in which she knocked him out with weighted gloves. She called *Breakfast for Two* a vacation, more play than work. She romped through the picture with her slow smile, he on his absent-minded charm. As Stanwyck and Marshall's maid and butler, Glenda Farrell and Eric Blore stole the show. Blore was a London lawyer-turned-actor who specialized in butlers—his discourse on crumpets and scones in *The Gay Divorcee* set a new high for a gentleman's gentleman hilarity.

In November 1937, RKO released *Breakfast for Two* on a double bill with *Don't Forget to Remember*, an amiable comedy starring Burgess Meredith and Ann Sothern. Berman spent the next two months looking for a story for Stanwyck. She hated his choices, and when one of her horses won at the Santa Anita racetrack, she quipped, "I'm glad someone in the family is working." She tried for Warner Brothers' *Jezebel*, to be directed by William Wyler. But Warners' own Bette Davis got the part of the impulsive, complex Southern belle who destroys her chances for happiness by perversely flouting convention.

By January 1938, Barbara's search for a role had become so desperate that columnists got wind of it. The *Hollywood Citizen-News* reported Stanwyck was being consulted about doing a picture for Paramount, but that neither RKO nor Paramount could come up with the right story. At Berman's suggestion she considered *The Son of Monte Cristo* with Douglas Fairbanks, Jr., for RKO. The film would be a sequel to the 1934 *Count of Monte Cristo* with Robert Donat and Elissa Landi.

Agreeing instead to do a part Katharine Hepburn refused gave Barbara a screwball hit. Hepburn's career at RKO was a succession of hits and misses. The studio's Broadway lookout, who had standing orders to "question every playwright and author in an attempt to find Hepburn material," signaled rehearsals were beginning on Edna Ferber and George S. Kaufman's *Stage Door*. Hepburn wanted it. Her decision meant she refused a Park Avenue screwball comedy in which the heroine inherits a haunted house—*The Mad Miss Manton*. Berman granted Hepburn her wish. But she found herself third in the *Stage Door* billings, behind Ginger Rogers and Adolphe Menjou. Stanwyck inherited *The Mad Miss Manton*.

With his lookalike twin brother Julius, Philip G. Epstein was fast becoming *the* screenwriter of "champagne comedies." The twins' fast, risqué, sophisticated dialogue gave them uncommon liberties and, in 1943, an Oscar for *Casablanca*. *The Mad Miss Manton* was a solo job for Philip.

For openers he had dizzy heiress Melsa Manton out walking

her dog at 3:00 A.M. after a costume ball and stumbling on a corpse. She immediately gets a bevy of scatterbrained Junior League girls in their best party dresses to play scavenger hunt at the crime scene, scampering all over to find clues. The corpse disappears before the police arrive, and everybody calls it another Melsa Manton hoax. The loudest hoax-crier is a newspaper editor. Miss Manton promptly sues for libel and enlists her bridge club in her detective work, leading to more bodies, absurd situations, and madcap romance.

Henry Fonda was cast as the sarcastic newspaper editor. He was on loan from Fox, hated his role, hated the script's sneering repartee with his leading lady, and tried his best to ignore everybody. For Leigh Jason, who directed with a light touch, he went through the motions. But he was smitten by Stanwyck. "Everyone who is close to me knows I've been in love with Barbara Stanwyck since I met her," Fonda would say forty years later. "She's a delicious woman. We've never had an affair. She's never encouraged me, but dammit, my wife will verify it, my daughter and son will confirm it, and now you all can testify to the truth. Stanwyck can act the hell out of any part, and she can turn a chore into a challenge."

Fonda was a challenge to work with for every-word-perfect Barbara. Hank had total recall, could read two pages of dialogue just once, put the script down, and recite the whole thing without making a single mistake. The summer was hot in Southern California. Wrapped in their furs, Manton and her debs were filmed at the Warner Brothers ranch in San Fernando Valley in hundred-degree weather. The Production Code objected to a scene that showed an elderly married couple in bed hearing strange noises. RKO printed the film so dark that the audience could not see the couple in bed, only hear their voices. *The Mad Miss Manton* lacked the zaniness of standard screwball comedies. Reviewers, however, called Fonda and Stanwyck refreshingly natural.

RKO publicity appreciated the irony of Barbara playing a Park Avenue debutante. Its press releases told of her being born "to the grimmest poverty at 246 Classon Avenue, Brooklyn."

Barbara's search for solid roles continued. Appalled by the paucity of good parts any studio had to offer, she renewed a campaign for *Dark Victory* she had begun a year earlier, when she heard David Selznick was adapting the George Emerson Brewer, Jr.–Bertram Block play. The part of a doomed-to-die woman who develops a brain tumor and learns to accept death with the help of a surgeon who is a friend and, finally, her husband was an actress's plum, and Stanwyck remained keenly interested in the project despite having been rebuffed in her earlier approaches to the always elusive Selznick. Now Selznick had put the picture on the shelf because no writer could lick the play, that is, find the middle ground between treating cancer as nature's scourge and romanticizing terminal illness. "That wasn't going to stop this girl," she would recall. "I'd done several Cecil B. DeMille 'Lux Radio Theatre' shows, so I pitched *Dark Victory* as a 'Lux' and I was set to do it on radio. It was a very successful show."

Her easily recognizable voice made her ideal for radio. With John Boles and Anne Shirley, she repeated *Stella Dallas* for "Lux Radio Theatre." DeMille used Barbara more than any other actress on his radio show. Besides *Dark Victory* and abridged radio adaptations of her movies, she did *Main Street*, *Morning Glory*, *Only Yesterday*, *Smilin' Through*, *This Above All*, and *Wuthering Heights*.

While she tried to goose Selznick into getting *Dark Victory* into development, she listened to Darryl Zanuck pitch *Always Goodbye*. She would play a woman faced with the choice of securing her little son's happiness or giving up the man she loved. The movie's Margot Weston gives up her illegitimate child to a couple and, after becoming a success, marries the now divorced adoptive father so as to become her own child's stepmother.

Barbara wanted to know who would play the man she marries.

Charles Boyer, said Zanuck.

Barbara signed on.

Boyer hated the Kathryn Scola–Edith Skouras script so much that Herbert Marshall was cast instead. Ian Hunter and Cesar Romero played two tiresome "other men" in Margot Weston's life. The child was a chubby little boy played by Johnnie Russell.

Variety called *Always Goodbye* "a fair summer attraction."

Stanwyck thought she had *Dark Victory* in the bag when

Variety reported Selznick was selling the rights to the play to Warner Brothers for $27,000. Never mind that Jack Warner bought it for Kay Francis, Barbara was ready. The word got around that Casey Robinson, WB's top writer, had licked the script.

"Then it was announced that Bette Davis would be doing it," Barbara would remember. "Well, I had the right idea, and so did Warners. The picture was nominated for Best Picture, Bette was nominated for Best Actress."

Barbara and Bob were among the first-nighters at the opening of Earl Carroll's theater-restaurant on Sunset and Vine. Photographers caught them with Clark Gable and Carole Lombard. Gable and Lombard were Hollywood's most brazen twosome. A 1938 poll of 20 million moviegoers declared Gable the "King of Hollywood" (the "Queen" was Myrna Loy).

DeMille gave Stanwyck a plum of a role in his new epic, *Union Pacific*. The director cast Joel McCrea as a kind of western G-man whose job it is to see that law and order are kept all down the line, Barbara as the engineer's daughter he marries, Brian Donlevy as the villain who tries to stop the progress of the iron horse, and newcomer Robert Preston as McCrea's rival for Barbara.

DeMille's last black-and-white film had the usual resplendent costumes and settings and feats of daring, climaxing in a spectacular train wreck. The picture was made with the cooperation of Union Pacific's president William M. Jeffers, who allowed DeMille's assistants to go through historical records stored in Omaha, Nebraska, where the railway started, loaned the film crews four 1860s locomotives and thirty-seven period cars and spectacular stretches of track. A replica of Cheyenne, Wyoming, was built in Utah, and a thousand Navajos were bused in for the location shooting.

The director staged a romantic interlude on a handcar hemmed in by grunting bison, a tender farewell in a caboose surrounded by hostile Indians, and a sentimental death beneath the smoking wreckage of a locomotive. There are Indian raids, shooting scrapes, brawls, fistfights, train robberies, fires, and chases.

The actors did their own stunts, Barbara leaping on and

off railroad cars, escaping from a herd of buffalo, and lying flat on her back in a boxcar while sulfur and molasses splashed over her.

Writing his autobiography twenty years later, DeMille would say he had never worked with an actress "more cooperative, less temperamental, and a better workman—to use my term of highest compliment—than Barbara Stanwyck. I have directed, and enjoyed working with many fine actresses, some of whom are also good workmen, but when I count over those of whom my memories are unmarred by anyway unpleasant recollection of friction on the set or unwillingness to do whatever the role required or squalls of temperament or temper, Barbara's name is the first that comes to mind, as one on whom a director can always count to do her work with all her heart."

Dispatches from Europe were outnumbered by *Gone with the Wind* bulletins during the summer and fall of 1938. Americans found more relevance in the latest scoop on who was going to play Scarlett O'Hara than in the mission to Munich of British Prime Minister Neville Chamberlain and French Premier Edouard Daladier's or Adolf Hitler's nonaggression pact with Benito Mussolini. War raged in China, civil war in Spain, and progressives in Hollywood gave money for the Republican, or Loyalist, forces battling Generalissimo Francisco Franco's rebel armies. Selznick's search for O'Hara, however, was a new national fantasy. After Samuel Goldwyn signed Stanwyck to star in *Golden Boy,* his publicity people pushed her for Scarlett. When Selznick did not test Barbara, a Goldwyn publicity release said he took a special note of her acting ability. In all, 1,400 Scarlett candidates were interviewed; ninety were given screen tests.

Not to be outdone, DeMille and Paramount staged a *Union Pacific* monster premiere in Omaha. On Easter Sunday 1939, the director, Stanwyck, McCrea, Preston, and a party of one hundred left Los Angeles in a special UP train, to be greeted at the Omaha station by two hundred thousand Nebraskans in period costume. Bands played, and the streets were jammed as the movie stars rode through in carriages, confetti filled the sky, and people hung from every window. The festivities were capped by a dinner for ten thousand.*

The Depression sharpened Americans' awareness of the deeper correlation of economic and other forces in society. Themes of the down-and-out flourished in theater and literature. Anxiety was universal on Broadway, but so was the creative ferment. Productions that in 1929–30 had reached nearly 250 were now under one hundred, and five thousand actors were out of work. As *New York Times* drama critic Brooks Atkinson would write in hindsight, "Perhaps the Depression had a ghastly dramatic undertone; perhaps it sharpened the minds, broadened the range of interests, and excited the notions of theater people. Perhaps it drew them closer. Whatever the reason it was one of Broadway's most stimulating times."

Golden Boy was a Depression play that focused on the tension between social ideals and people's obsessive desire for celebrity and money. Its author was Clifford Odets, an actor turned playwright identified with the New Deal's more aggressive social agenda.

The screen rights to the 1937 Odets play belonged to Rouben Mamoulian, the director of Garbo, Dietrich, Miriam Hopkins, and Irene Dunne. Frank Capra wanted to film the sentimental "we are the little people" morality play about a young Italian-American who wants to make it, abandons his musical talent, and turns to professional boxing. Like Odets, Capra felt the Depression raised questions about the validity of the country's political and economic system. Deep pessimism runs through Capra's movies and Odets's plays. The little guy may win in the end, not so much because evil is overpowered, but because the contrivance of the third act demands it. *Golden Boy* was the eternal American quandary: how to succeed in a society that trusts only one thing—success.

While Capra filmed *You Can't Take It with You*, he kept after Mamoulian. The Armenian-born Mamoulian considered himself a man of the theater. In 1935, he had directed the Alvin Theatre production of what Gershwin himself consid-

*In a historical perspective, aficionados of westerns would compare *Union Pacific* unfavorably with John Ford's silent *The Iron Horse*, which treated virtually the same empire-building theme.

ered his biggest achievement, *Porgy and Bess,* and he was revered in Hollywood for his broad stage experience, his technical abilities, and his high-strung independence. When Capra offered to buy the screen rights to *Golden Boy,* the monocled Mamoulian said no. He wanted to do it himself. Capra upped his price. Mamoulian refused offers that eventually reached a stratospheric $75,000. After much haggling and posturing, Cohn agreed to let Mamoulian do *Golden Boy* for Columbia. To Cohn's astonishment, Mamoulian accepted only what he had paid for the play, $1,500.

Mamoulian insisted Odets adapt his own work. Odets had burst onto Broadway with his effective and bitter *Waiting for Lefty* in 1935 and was acclaimed as the outstanding proletarian dramatist. Four of his plays had been produced in New York in 1935, propelling him to fame as Eugene O'Neill's successor—a playwright, as he mockingly said himself, "who receives fantastic offers from Hollywood, invitations to address ladies' clubs, one hundred and fifty phone calls a day and a lot of solemn consideration from guys who write pieces for the dramatic pages."

Odets arrived in Hollywood in December 1938, "hot as a pistol," as his agent put it, to visit his wife—Luise Rainer. Stanwyck's nemesis at the Academy Awards nine months earlier was terribly unhappy at MGM, and Odets was in no mood to do the *Golden Boy* screenplay for Cohn and Mamoulian. He was convinced a creative marriage between social drama and commerce was essentially unfeasible and that he would not work in Hollywood "unless I am broke." Hearing from Phil Berg, his agent, what kinds of money Cohn, Capra, and Mamoulian had tossed at each other over *Golden Boy,* he was determined to stay away from screenwriting and to rescue his wife from MGM.

Mamoulian went to New York to find writers with a feeling for Odets's Joe "*Golden Boy*" Bonaparte. Daniel Taradash, a scion of wealth and a graduate of Harvard Law School, and Lewis Meltzer, a wry, unpredictable playwright with one unfortunate play to his credit, were two twenty-five-year-old fringe members of the Group Theatre. For $200 a week, they agreed to come west to script *Golden Boy.*

To Mamoulian's annoyance, Cohn told the two young men to "make it sound like Capra." Mamoulian spirited

Taradash and Meltzer to the Mojave Desert so they could concoct a script far from Cohn's interference.

Mamoulian, Taradash, and Meltzer deleted a labor organizer and much philosophizing about Joe Bonaparte's forsaking a future as a sensitive, penniless violinist in favor of becoming a tough, brutalized but well-paid professional fighter. They coarsened Stanwyck's Lorna Moon character. Lorna is an orphaned "dame from Newark." She is the mistress of a fight manager who uses her to seduce Joe Bonaparte into real fighting. Instead of a sniveling, slightly tarnished girl, director and writers developed an embittered, wisecracking persona just right for Stanwyck.

The stage Lorna's third-act incantation after Napoleon has killed his opponent in a fight read:

LORNA: Somewhere there must be happy boys and girls who can teach us the way of life. We'll find a city where poverty's no shame, where there's no war in the street, where a man is glad to be himself; to live and make his woman herself.

Director and writers couldn't imagine Stanwyck spouting those lines and made the speech read:

LORNA: Be glad you're rid of him. You're free. Now you can go back to yourself, to your music.

The toughening process was helped by casting Adolphe Menjou as Joe's manager, Tom Moody, and Joseph Calleia, in a caricature of Bogart, as a gangster in pinstripe suit who wants to buy a piece of the new boxing hopeful. Menjou brought a touch of elegant despair to his love for Lorna.

Cohn sent a copy of the first-draft screenplay to the office of the Production Code Administration for preproduction clearance. Chief censor Joseph Breen replied that "the adulterous relationship between Moody, a married man, and your sympathetic female lead, Lorna . . . and a suggestion of a sexual affair between Lorna and Joe should be changed." Also, the following Stanwyck lines were unacceptable:

Page 1-2-25: "What the hell's so special in bed."
Page 1-3-31: "I don't like this seduction scene."
Page 1-3-37: "I'm a tramp from Newark, Tom, I know a
    dozen ways."
Page 2-1-11: "You expect me to sleep with that boy?"
Page 2-2-16: "He picked me up in Friskin's Hotel."
Page 2-3-29: "Because he's a queer."
Page 2-36: "This isn't a hotel bedroom."

The script went back for rewrites. It was submitted again, the Lorna-Moody relationship still found unacceptable and rewritten one more time.

Harry Cohn wanted Luther Adler, who had been a thrilling *Golden Boy* (to Frances Farmer's Lorna Moon) during the long run at the Belasco Theatre. Tyrone Power was the second choice, but Zanuck refused to lend him. "How about going for an unknown, Harry?" producer William Perlberg asked. "We could have a Search for *Golden Boy*, like Selznick did for Scarlett O'Hara."

Columbia publicity launched the campaign, and Alan Ladd was one young unknown who competed for the part with athletes and actors of all descriptions. Mamoulian was not amused. He preferred to watch screen tests to the *Golden Boy* search charade. Concentrating on finding someone to play Joe Bonaparte's sister, he saw six Paramount tests, including one of a young actress named Margaret Young. What made Mamoulian lean forward in the screening room, however, was the young Paramount actor reading lines to Young.

William Holden was sent for.

"Can you act?" Cohn growled when Mamoulian sent in the twenty-two-year-old newcomer with high praise.

"I'm not sure," Holden admitted.

"Can you box?"

"No."

"Can you play the violin?"

"No."

"Then why the hell are you here?"

"Because you sent for me."

Holden's forthright answer and Cohn's sense of a bargain

clinched the deal. Splitting Holden's salary with Paramount came to $25 a week.

William Franklin Beedle, Jr., was from South Pasadena. His appearance in a friend's play at Gilmor Brown's Playbox Theatre showcase in 1936 had led to a $35-a-week, seven-year Paramount contract. The studio had changed his name to Holden (after a *Los Angeles Times* associate editor) and used him as a member of a road gang in *Prison Farm*, starring Lloyd Nolan, and as a collegiate in *Million Dollar Legs*, a Jackie Coogan–Betty Grable musical. *Golden Boy* was his first loanout.

Before filming started on April 1, 1939, Holden boxed with an old-time fighter and studied the violin with a concert violinist and his lines with a dialogue coach, but the person who really helped was Stanwyck.

"Look, Bill, we all had to start in this business sometime," she told him on the first day of shooting. "You're going to be terrific, I know you are. Just hold on, and if there's any way I can help, for God's sake let me know."

The rest of the cast was less than charitable during the first three days. When he didn't show on the fourth day, but came back two days later complaining of "nerves," Mamoulian began to regret recommending the young actor. After one week, Cohn wanted to replace Holden.

Barbara went to Cohn and Perlberg and asked them to give the boy a chance. "My God, he's only had a week," she yelled at Cohn. "I don't know what you want. None of us can walk on water." Besides, Holden was sensitive and intelligent. He had the physique they wanted, his boxing was passable, and the story didn't make him a champion.

Her argument prevailed. She coached Bill and every night read the next day's lines with him in her dressing room. "I told him much of what Willard Mack had taught me," she would remember. Holden was still insecure, and the drinking that would eventually ruin his life started right there on the *Golden Boy* set. After a few nips of alcohol in his dressing room, he felt loosened up enough to face Mamoulian, Stanwyck, and crew.

Marriage

The January 1939 issue of *Photoplay*, with Hedy Lamarr on the cover, provoked a first-class scandal. The lead article in the influential and popular movie magazine was entitled "Hollywood's Unmarried Husbands and Wives." The byline read Kirtley Baskette, but within hours *le tout* Hollywood knew the writer was Sheilah Graham. Although the points were made entirely through innuendo, "Hollywood's Unmarried Husbands and Wives" was the most outspoken article about the stars' private lives ever published. It zeroed in on Gable and Lombard, Taylor and Stanwyck, Constance Bennett and Gilbert Roland, Charlie Chaplin and Paulette Goddard, and George Raft and Virginia Pine:

> Barbara Stanwyck is not Mrs. Robert Taylor. But she and Bob have built ranch homes next to each other. Regularly, once a week, they visit Bob's mother, Mrs. Brugh, for dinner. Regularly, once a week, too, Barbara freezes homemade ice cream for Bob from a recipe his mother gave her.
>
> Nowhere has domesticity, outside the marital state, reached such a full flower as in Hollywood. Nowhere are there so many famous unmarried husbands and wives . . . When Bob Taylor docked in New York from England and *A Yank at Oxford*, he waited around a couple of hours for a load of stuff he had brought over there to clear customs. Most of it was for—not Bob—but Barbara Stanwyck and her little son, Dion.
>
> They've been practically a family since Bob bought his ranch estate in Northridge and built a house there.

The story described their ranch life, their permanent seats together at the Hollywood Legion Stadium on fight nights, evenings together, how they were always invited together, "just like man and wife," and how they gave each other gifts—he a tennis court for her, she a two-horse auto trailer just like "old married folks" for him.

Louis B. Mayer was furious. Although more worried about Clark Gable's reputation in the middle of the *Gone with the Wind* shoot than Robert Taylor's, he called both male stars on the carpet. As popular as they were, he thundered, movie-goers might not pay to see anyone involved in scandal. Strickling took it from there.

Photoplay was informed of Louis B.'s wrath. If a retraction was not printed, MGM was not only going to cancel all advertising but choke off the magazine's access to its stars. *Photoplay* knuckled under and the following month published a full-page apology to the celebrities mentioned in "Hollywood's Unmarried Husbands and Wives," ostensibly because newspaper quotes from the piece had made "these friendships appear in a light far from our original intention."

Strickling took care of Gable next. Living apart from his older wife, Rhea, since 1936, Gable permitted the publicity department to tell the press he was going to ask for a divorce. The announcement was one too many insults for Rhea. He was robbing her of the one little triumph that had always been hers. She had understood that when the inevitable happened, *she* would do the announcing and the divorcing. A message from her lawyers notified Clark she would contest. The Gable divorce, one columnist informed her readers, "hit a snag."

Everybody knew Gable and Lombard had been together since 1936 and with her $40,000 had bought a ranch in Encino. At Carole's suggestion, a new lawyer was brought into Gable versus Gable. Clark could not pay Rhea's demands of $300,000 ($2.4 million in 1994 money), so Mayer agreed to an advance on Gable's new contract, which boosted his salary to $7,500 a week. After Rhea's settlement had been put in an escrow account in January 1939, she announced she was leaving for Las Vegas to seek a Nevada "quickie" divorce.

The Taylor–Stanwyck scrape was a breeze by compari-son. Bob had never been married, and it was exactly three years before that the Stanwyck–Fay divorce had been granted. Nevertheless, before the February *Photoplay* retraction appeared, Metro announced the formal engagement of Robert Taylor and Barbara Stanwyck. Louis B.'s ultimatum that Taylor marry Stanwyck had the force of law for Bob, of course. And Barbara was discerning enough to realize that if she wanted to sustain her star stature in the company town it behooved her not to offend MGM's formidable boss. Three months after their engagement, Strickling masterminded a wedding.

On Saturday, May 13, 1939, studio publicists whisked Bob and Barbara to San Diego for a wedding before Municipal Judge Phil Smith. To fool the press, their marriage license, taken out three days earlier, was in the names of R. Stevens and Spangler Arlington Brugh. To report back that everything was kosher, Louis B. made Ida Koverman, his secretary who had come up with Bob's stage name, join the party. Marion Marx was the matron of honor and Uncle Buck the best man. Strickling managed to squeeze an "item" out of the fact that the wedding party had a buffet supper and waited until after midnight so that Stanwyck and Taylor would not be married on the possibly ill-starred thirteenth. After midnight, Barbara, in blue silk dress and a hat borrowed from her hairdresser, pronounced her vows in a clear voice; Bob, in a brown business suit, mumbled his "I do."

At a press reception at the Beverly Hills Victor Hugo Café, they posed for photographers, arms entwined, smiling at each other. Joel McCrea phoned his congratulations, and a telegram from William Holden signed "The Golden Boy" read: GOSH, WHAT A BLOW! When photographers asked them to kiss, Bob refused, saying. "We'll just smile and look silly, I guess." Their raising horses led to a question of children. Again, Bob replied, "Well, we'll raise horses—definitely."

After the press reception, Barbara returned to the ranch while Bob went to see his hysterical mother. He gave Ruth a sedative. After a while they talked, but the word "wedding" was never mentioned. He assured her nothing would change. Didn't she know there were nights when he was too tired to drive out to Northridge? Why, he'd stay with her more often. She said she felt sick and asked him to stay and check her heartbeat every so often. He had learned to do that from his father and had done it many times before. How could he abandon her now? He spent the wedding night with his mother. The next morning, he reported to the set of *Lady of the Tropics*, filming a wedding scene with Hedy Lamarr.

Barbara went back to the set of *Golden Boy* and sometime during the next years became William Holden's lover. His alcoholism destroyed their relationship but not their friendship nor his affection for the woman who had helped him through his first movie. Every April 1, the starting date of *Golden Boy*, he sent Barbara two dozen roses and a white gardenia.

Frank Fay summed up his reaction to the marriage in one word. "Spite" was the reason Barbara had married again, Frank told actor Jay C. Flippen.

Louis B.'s diktat was propitious both for Barbara Stanwyck and for Robert Taylor. Fame was what effortlessly enveloped Bob, what Barbara hustled for. If being married was what it took, both were winners. Their celebrity was based on their ability to convincingly play love games with the opposite sex. Consummating the relationship was possibly easier for Barbara, who knew more about men than Bob knew about women. Crawford, who was "Aunt Joan" to Dion, would remember Bob telling her, "All I had to say about it was, 'I do.' I didn't know what happened." When he added that something good did come out of it, and Joan asked if he meant the marriage, he told her how the press had hounded him with the "pretty boy" epithet. "Overnight, I was a he-man but I still break out in sweat if anyone refers to me as pretty boy. MGM did all it could. Something came out of it though."

Did he mean marrying Barbara?

He hesitated. "Well, yes, but I was actually referring to the tough roles I'm assigned now ... boxers, cowboys, gangsters, that kind of thing."

At the wedding reception, he expressed the hope that marriage would mean the end of ordeal-by-fandom. No matter how much he loathed feminine hands groping him in public places, no matter his sexual preference, his ego demanded that, when challenged, he live up to the image a million women swooned over. Barbara had been married and perhaps thought she could limit any "slip" of Bob's that, if found out, could be catastrophic. Neither of them found exclusively homosexual circles attractive, although they were friends of Hollywood's newest lavender couple: Tyrone and Annabella Power. Bob might have been directed by George Cukor, but he was no more a habitué at Cukor's soirees than Barbara belonged to the so-called sewing circle, Hollywood's clandestine sisterhood of mostly rich, well-connected, and free lesbians who surrounded Greta Garbo.

Homosexuality was against the law in the 1930s, and it would be decades before anyone wrote that Stanwyck and Taylor were both drawn to same-sex love. In discussing Judy Garland's lifelong habit of having affairs with women and how commonplace so-called lavender marriages were in 1940s Hollywood, her biographer, David Shipman, would write that "the Stanwyck–Taylor marriage was obviously a precedent, since both were basically attracted to people of their own sex." In any event, Barbara and Bob lived their lives outside the gay subcultures. To themselves and each other, their busy lives allowed them, all too conveniently, to gloss over their differences.

For Barbara, marrying Metro's leading matinee idol meant radiance and gravity. For Bob, wedlock meant social acceptance, moorings, and confidence. Barbara gave little of herself to the marriage. Her seven years with Fay had taught her not to try to do anything for a man that he didn't want to do himself. For Bob, getting a wife sheltered him from marauding females and put a distance between him and his mother. Not that Ruth would ever stop intruding in her son's life.

MGM wanted to costar the newlyweds in a third movie together, but nothing came of it. At Mayer's insistence, however, Barbara and Bob sandwiched in a brief honeymoon before their next assignments. The honeymoon took them east to Bucks County, Pennsylvania, and the home of Moss Hart. Since the turn of the century, the hills above New Hope on the Delaware River had been a Bohemian retreat, first discovered by American impressionist painters. Buying Bucks County farmhouses was the rage with Broadway types in the 1930s, and the seventy-two-acre Hart estate in Holicong was just across from the fifty-nine-acre farm that Beatrice and

George S. Kaufman had bought to put some distance behind them after his tumultuous affair with Mary Astor. Moss and Kitty Hart had added wings and ells to the stone farmhouse, turned a toolshed into a library, built a swimming pool, and imported 3,500 pine trees for more shade, leading the acerbic Alexander Woollcott to comment, "It just goes to show what God could do if he had money." A 110-acre Pennsylvania Dutch farm in Pipersville belonged to Dorothy Parker and her husband Alan Campbell. The newlyweds considered buying an Italianate house with a view of the Delaware River a few miles north of New Hope.

Back in Los Angeles, the Taylors' engagement calendar quickly filled up. "They made you—*made you*—go out two or three nights a week," Barbara would say of MGM. Barbara and Bob were an attractive couple. And marriage was in style. Barbara's friends, from the Bennys to Crawford and Blondell, were married. Everybody was getting older, the hungry days were passé. The marriage put a still greater distance between Barbara and Dion. To a pair of role players like Barbara and Bob, the boy's presence no longer fit the play. To Barbara, he was a reminder of her failure with Frank. Joan Benny would come to believe Bob Taylor was the reason Barbara got rid of "Skip." "The boy was in the way when she married Robert Taylor," Benny would say, "so she put him in the closet, in a succession of boarding schools."

Dion was more forgiving. In 1959, he would say that Bob tried for a while to play his father. "At first he tried to teach me baseball and football, discussing the games and complaining when his favorite team lost. But I just didn't respond. These were things I had no knowledge of and the names and scores he talked about were completely foreign to me. After a while he gave up. I think he had a feeling I was Barbara's son, not his."

To the outside world, Barbara and Bob covered their differences with humor and jokes. They were seen to have struck an endearing balance between his quiet strength and her raw sense of humor, his level temper, her chip-on-the-shoulder quicksilver reaction. Their quirks were remarked upon. Where actresses habitually had their wedding rings taped over with flesh-colored adhesive, no-nonsense Barbara removed her wedding band when a role called for it. Bob refused to dance with his wife, insisting he was no good, she too terrific on a dance floor. In private he reacted to Barbara's authority as he had always responded to his mother's—by withdrawing. His wife, he discovered, was a lot like Garbo. Both were headstrong, stuck to their guns, and never gave in.

Few people glimpsed the Taylors' intimate lives or saw any reason to look askance at their separate bedrooms. Bob was the first to say he fell asleep the minute his head hit the pillow. Barbara made no bones about her chronic insomnia that had her read in bed until all hours.

Were the separate bedrooms a consequence of Bob's physical inadequacy? A story flying around the Los Angeles–Santa Monica Gun Club had Bob going on a hunting trip with fellow actors Andy Devine and Robert Stack. After much beer and a long haul over back roads, they could no longer refuse nature's call. As reported by skeet shooter and soon-to-be actor Robert Stack, the pair were irrigating the desert when Devine caught a glimpse of Taylor's penis. "That doesn't look like it belongs to the world's greatest lover," Devine said. Without missing a beat, Bob said, "I know, but don't tell my wife. She thinks they're all the same size." Bob would grow defensive over the years when it came to male intimacy and would refuse to hear out a fellow actor confiding his own homosexuality. Sal Mineo visited the set of the multinational flop *The Glass Sphinx* in Rome in 1967, and although Bob was not his type, he wanted to be seen with him. The twenty-seven-year-old Mineo's career had started at the top with *Rebel Without a Cause* but had gone nowhere since. When Mineo brought up his own homosexuality over cocktails, Bob said he didn't want to discuss politics.

After *Three Comrades*—a captivating adaptation of Erich Maria Remarque's wasted-youth romance that earned Margaret Sullavan an Oscar nomination for Best Actress—Bob played a prizefighter in *The Crowd Roars*, again showing his hairy chest. To build on the tough-guy Taylor image, Louis B. had him brawl with Wallace Beery in the action picture *Stand Up and Fight*. Myrna Loy, who made *Lucky Night* with Bob in 1939, thought him "a bit stuffy" and, she claimed, not above trying to play her off Barbara. "For some reason he tried to cook up a little triangle; he wanted her to think I was after him," Loy would recall. Barbara's maid talked to Myrna's maid, who could report back that there was nothing to it.

MGM renewed Bob's contract for another seven years—but Barbara insisted Morgan Maree become their joint business manager. Bob let MGM rule his life. As for Barbara, the fact that she had thirty-five movies behind her egged her on instead of slowing her down. Helen Ferguson and Mervyn LeRoy saw her battle with frequent back pain and insomnia. She made fun of their concern for her health, saying she was slowing to a gallop.

Work kept the Taylors apart for ten, twelve hours a day.

Barbara was scheduled to star with Fred MacMurray in a warm and witty Paramount picture called *Remember the Night*. After *Lady of the Tropics*, Bob went right into *Remember* with Greer Garson. On the *Motion Picture Herald*'s annual poll of ten thousand independent theater owners, he ranked number six in screen popularity. Stanwyck didn't make the 1939 Most Popular list, but she was nevertheless a star of such magnitude that to keep Henry Fonda under contract at Fox, Darryl Zanuck offered to have a part for her written into Fonda's next film. "Zanuck knew the propinquity of Stanwyck on a film set was a temptation Fonda would find irresistible," Leonard Mosley would write. Fonda had come to loathe the pictures Zanuck starred him in and turned down the offer.

The week Stanwyck and Holden were sent to New York for the *Golden Boy* launch war broke out in Europe. Barbara was more engrossed by the fact that Frank Fay was hitting the big time on Broadway again. His costars in *Frank Fay's Vaudeville* were ladies from his youth—Elsie Janis and the gay actress-writer-celebrity Eva Le Gallienne.

Barbara talked absentmindedly about the "trouble" in Europe. Nothing that happened an ocean away seemed very threatening. After overrunning Poland, Hitler and Mussolini seemed at a loss what to do next. There was no enthusiasm for the war in France and England, let alone in America, where opinion polls showed a majority against any involvement. French and German soldiers glowered at each other across the Rhine, and the conflict was quickly dubbed "the phony war." It was a beautiful fall in France. As Clare Boothe

Luce reported in *Time*, September and October had never been lovelier in Paris.

Barbara and Bob were dead set against seeing the United States tricked or stampeded into joining another war to bail out the English and the French. Let the Europeans fight their own wars. Neither of them was a Roosevelt Democrat. Archconservatism had run through her first marriage, and Bob was influenced by his mother's and Louis B.'s right-wing convictions.

The September 7, 1939, *Golden Boy* premiere at Radio City Music Hall was a disappointment. Not only did the outbreak of World War II four days earlier date the two-year-old Depression story, but its "Hollywoodization," including a long, brutish slugging match in the ring and a hokey happy ending, irritated critics. Odets's name was on the marquee, but the playwright stayed away.

Formal dinner parties remained the social distraction as Europe slid into the phony war. Barbara and Bob made their appearance when they had to. They were popular, she poised, stunning-looking, and attuned, he cordial, taking life as easily as it took him. If David Niven and Laurence Oliver felt obliged to return to defend England, the rest of the sizable English film colony concentrated on smart soirees and the occasional patriotic charity ball. Ouida and Basil Rathbone, Ronald Colman, Clive Brook, Herbert Marshall, Charlie Chaplin, Cary Grant, and MGM's distinguished C. Aubrey Smith set the tone. Ouida Rathbone was a superb hostess who requested formal attire—gowns for the women and white tie and tails for the men. "We dressed to the teeth for everything," said Barbara. "Never the same dress twice, a hairdresser would come to the house the day of the party, and for special events a makeup man would come from the studio to do my face." Barbara's clothes reflected her lifestyle perfectly. Her extensive wardrobe was smartly tailored. "She had dozens of suits, sports clothes and slacks, all made of men's material," *Hollywood Citizen-News* columnist Sidney Skolsky reported.

Edith Goetz and Irene Selznick were the movie colony's leading hostesses. No matter how famous, movie stars could be hired and fired. Louis B.'s two daughters were Hollywood princesses. An invitation to the Goetzes in the heart of fash-

ionable Bel Air or the Selznicks' Beverly Hills aerie implied
total acceptance. Barbara and Bob spent Christmas 1939 with
the Selznicks.

After *Gone with the Wind*, David wanted to celebrate, his
wife to catch her breath. He pretended annoyance when
Gone with the Wind was brought up, but was resentful if it
wasn't. He escorted Barbara to the dinner table and, to everybody's surprise, recited a hastily scrawled homage to her:

Barbara
A Quick Impression on a Drunken Christmas Night
by David O. Selznick

Without guile
O Henry style.
Evening prayers at home
Corned beef at the Court of Rome
Minsky learns emotion
Devotion
Grant Wood on 48th Street
Salome's Vine Street Beat
Guff
Helen Hayes gets tough
Situation found
Talent on a merry-go-round
Rhapsody in Blue
Spangles for Sunbonnet Sue
The Manhattan Nation
Appreciation.

Passions

The only real fighting in Europe in January 1940 was in the far north, where a Russian army tried to batter its way into Finland. Elsewhere the ominous calm of the *drôle de guerre* continued. The war made an impact on Hollywood's pocketbook as Germany and the Axis countries barred American films. The lull ended in April, when Hitler invaded Denmark and Norway to win bases for an impending assault on England and, with the northern flank secure, turned his armies against France and the Low Countries.

If Barbara scanned the newspapers every morning, Bob had little interest in world affairs. When filming, he was in bed by nine; she read half the night. Yes, she had her own bedroom, she told *Hollywood Citizen-News* columnist Sidney Skolsky, specifying that she slept on her right on the left side of her double bed. When she was working, she averaged three and a half hours sleep.

Jane Wyman and Ronald Reagan, Carole Lombard and Clark Gable were similar couples, the wives keeping up with current events, the husbands more interested in hunting trips and football.

Bob and "Dutch" Reagan were the same age. Reagan never tired of telling how, back in 1937, his agent, Bill Meiklejohn, had pitched him to WB's casting director Max Arnow: "Max, I have another Robert Taylor sitting in my office." To which Arnow said, "God made only one Robert Taylor" before agreeing to look at the radio announcer from Iowa.

Ron tried to please and at closer inspection was more

substantial than the characters Jack Warner had him play. Wyman believed in making her own breaks. She was articulate, cared about people, was loyal to friends, and active in the Screen Actors Guild. Barbara liked the fact that Ron and Jane drove to Warners together and managed to work together in *An Angel from Texas*, based on George S. Kaufman's play *The Butter and Egg Man*.

The Taylors were, of course, rungs above the Reagans and invited to glamour parties given by MGM executives. The stars were supposed to outshine each other, and the studio designers and workrooms busily dressed the screen goddesses for these soirees, where the same glittering people kept seeing the same glittering people. Bob and Barbara were never comfortable at these events—Barbara called them command performances. She liked to know the people she was to meet at the dinner party and disliked going to nightclubs. "I'll go to Ciro's or the Trocadero with Bob some evening," she would recall. "I'll be wearing a lovely gown, and my hair all doozied up. No sooner do I get there when I think, gee, I look awful. I see Claudette and she looks divine, or I see Dietrich looking something out of this world, and I imagine I look like some dowdy little shopgirl." Socializing at night spots meant being photographed—Jane Wyman with James Stewart, Reagan with Stanwyck and Claudette Colbert, Bob with Jane. These "on the town" impromptu sessions kept newspapers and magazines supplied with photos for weeks, sometimes months.

The Taylors were more comfortable with Mary and Jack Benny, Marion and Zeppo Marx, Lillian and Fred MacMurray. They became friends with Annabella and Tyrone Power, who had returned from Europe the day before war broke out. Bob didn't care much for the movies he made and hadn't even seen his most famous film until Barbara and he were dinner guests at the Louis B. Mayers one summer evening in 1940. *Waterloo Bridge* was MGM's summer hit, and Louis B. was proud of Bob.

"You were great in that one!" Mayer beamed over cocktails.

"Don't know," Bob responded. "I never saw it."

Mayer couldn't believe it. When the all-too-sincere Bob convinced him it was true, Louis B. phoned the studio and ordered a print to be dispatched to his home. After dinner, *Waterloo Bridge* was screened in the Mayer living room.

Fear of war ran through the national conscience. By mid-summer the defeat of Great Britain seemed entirely possible, and Americans were debating whether to rush material aid to Britain or stay out of the war. Henry L. Stimson, Roosevelt's appointee as Secretary of War, told the Senate Military Affairs Committee, "We may be next." Bob and Barbara were isolationists and against a third term for Franklin D. Roosevelt, as were Gable and Lombard, Reagan and Wyman, Mayer and Cohn. Capra spoke admiringly of Benito Mussolini. When William Wyler started *Mrs. Miniver* and wanted one fanatical Nazi youth in the film, Louis B. reminded him that the United States was not at war with anybody and that MGM had cinemas all over the world, including a couple in Berlin.

Senator Gerald Nye of North Dakota flayed Hollywood for trying "to rouse war fever in America and plunge the nation to her destruction." The Taylors agreed when Charles Lindbergh told a radio audience, "We are in danger of war today not because European people have attempted to interfere with the internal affairs of America but because we American people have attempted to interfere with the internal affairs of Europe." But screaming headlines of Germans smashing through Belgium and down into France made a lot of Americans nervous, and both the people who espoused open aid to the Allies and those who opposed it felt a need to rally around the flag. When Barbara was the guest of honor at the Athena National Sorority convention in Los Angeles she expressed the hope that the association was destined to become "one of America's foremost patriotic and humanitarian organizations."

Whether it was war, that traditional spur of population booms, or ticking biological clocks, Hollywood's birthrate soared in the spring of 1940. Douglas Fairbanks, Jr., Ray Milland, Anne Shirley, Janet Gaynor, Bill Henry, Geraldine Fitzgerald, John Garfield, Russell Hayden, Johnny Weissmuller, Madge Evans, Pat Ziegfeld, and several others were expecting "newcomers to their families," as the June issue of *Photoplay* put it. The year before Joan Crawford and her fourth husband

Phillip Terry had followed Barbara's example and adopted a baby they named Christina. Babies were a touchy subject. Glamour queens and screen heroes were supposed to lose all box-office appeal if they were known to be mothers or fathers.

Stanwyck and Taylor had no happy event to announce, but Barbara had followed Mary Benny's pregnancy that, by summer, resulted in a miscarriage. *Photoplay* asked Barbara to answer the question: Can Hollywood Mothers Be Good Mothers? In a sidebar to the June issue's cover story on Hollywood couples having babies, Barbara wrote effusively of bringing up Dion. No doubt ghostwritten by Helen Ferguson, the piece told of a day in the life of a movie star mother and her too busy son. She saw Dion for breakfast and had her chauffeur bring him to the studio at six P.M. so he could ride home with her. His bedtime was seven, she explained, seven-thirty when she was working.

"The Hollywood child is a desired child," she wrote. "Hollywood women want children so much they adopt them if necessary." Celebrity youngsters were not awed by actors or actresses. "Dion knows simply that Mr. Power and his wife, or Mr. Gable and *his* wife, are coming to dinner. He knows them as individuals, not as famous names."

When Bob and Barbara entertained on Saturday nights, Dion was taught to say the guests wore "evening gowns" and "dinner jackets," never "formal" or "tuxedo." The guests usually included the Bennys, Annabella and Tyrone Power, George Montgomery and his wife, Dinah Shore, Ray and Mal Milland, the Reagans, the MacMurrays. Divorces and remarriages might vary the pairings, but the dinner parties remained the same. Cocktails were followed by a catered sit-down dinner, which was followed by dancing to the strains of a professional band.

In the *Photoplay* piece, Barbara only mentioned Bob in connection with too many toys for Dion. She strongly condemned parents who, because of a deprived childhood, overcompensated by giving their youngsters too much. "I had to discipline myself to insure *his* future happiness. I'm not going to rob him of the excitement and triumph of a right perspective on possessions—and other Hollywood mothers discipline themselves on this matter as I do." The proof would be in how Hollywood children turned out as adults. Sounding like an echo of Nazi agitprop, she concluded: "In the face of wars and the rumors of general catastrophe, Hollywood women are taking time out to bear strong, beautiful children, or to adopt them. And whether the rearing of these children is good, bad or indifferent, at least they'll exist and they'll have healthy bodies, tans, straight teeth, and minds filled with the ideals of American democracy."

However wholesome her published view of her own motherhood, she was, in reality, appalled that Dion was not the beautiful and resilient child befitting her image, that he was not a clever, good-looking reflection of her. When he was six, she started sending him to a succession of boarding schools.

"She threw me away like so much garbage," Dion would remember when he was in his fifties. "When I was five or six, I got heavy. I was freckle-faced. I had to wear glasses, and I was awkward. And just by doing the normal things any active kid would do, like not picking up my clothes or playing in the dirt, I began to feel that I caused nothing but trouble for my mother. I can still see my mother standing over me, slim and beautiful but oh so threatening. She would say, 'What's the matter with you? Why do you do those horrible things? I'm disgusted with you.' Once I broke some toys and she screamed at me for what seemed like hours. 'You stupid child,' she yelled and began shaking me." Dion would not remember his mother ever touching him with affection or kissing him.

He called Taylor "Gentleman Bob" and saw him as a nice, ineffectual presence. Barbara never visited Dion at his boarding schools. Their living under one roof was limited to two weeks a year. During summer vacations, she sent him to camp on Catalina island.

Barbara's existence was entirely dedicated to her life before the cameras. Weekday mornings, her ritual consisted of drinking four glasses of water, followed by a hot and cold shower, and a copious breakfast. Assistant directors rarely had to call her because she checked her work schedule, drove herself to the studio, and never quibbled over early starting hours. On the set she was a quick study, knew her business, and demanded that her coworkers know theirs. She studied scripts at home, drank twenty cups of coffee, and chain-smoked all day, using a jeweled cigarette case given to her by Joan Crawford. She never allowed men to leap to their feet and light her cigarette or fix her chair. She ran the home on a budget, allocated her personal expenditures with the impassivity of an accountant, and admitted to no expensive tastes. Her favorite dinner was a thick steak and green vegetables.

Beatings by Frank Fay, falls from horses, and other work-related accidents had given her a bad back. To ease spinal pain a doctor once gave her five shots of a substance containing morphine, saying she would be out cold for at least twenty hours. After forty-five minutes she was awake. Bob insisted her case was written up in a medical journal.

Bob discovered a new passion—flying. *Flight Command*, a routine join-the-armed-forces flag-waver, was made with the cooperation of the naval air command, and for his navy ensign role Bob decided to take flying lessons. He found soaring into the air from Burbank airport liberating and exhilarating and soon began spending every spare moment at airstrips with instructors, flyers, and "hangar jocks," as general aviation enthusiasts were called. Bob's *Flight Command* was a Christmas 1940 release. With its exciting air sequences, the film was as fresh as the front-page news. The New York Post's review was music to Bob ears: "The story is pretty much what you would expect: flying thrills, tragedy, courage, misunderstanding, and eventually the heroism that proves to everyone that Robert Taylor has what it takes to be Clark Gable, even if he is less rugged."

Barbara was not only afraid of ocean travel, she was also terrified of "going up" in an airplane. *Flight Command* marked the end of any pretense of their ten-month marriage. Barbara tried to be patient. As much as she had disciplined Dion, she indulged her husband as if he were a wayward teenager. The pampering drove him further away from her. If he couldn't be up in the air, he enjoyed going to an airport and watching planes take off. Her response was to mock his enthusiasm. When he boasted about the number of flying hours he was racking up, she snapped, "Now you can do everything the birds can do except sit on a barbed wire fence."

*   *   *

To be one of the boys at the studio, Bob went on hunting trips with Victor Fleming, Clark Gable, and Spencer Tracy. Fleming, a former race car driver, was the open-air type who dressed for the part, sporting puttees and wielding riding crops. Gable owed much to him, and Bob's ardent wish was to be his friend. Once in 1943, Barbara went along. Bob was on one Sun Valley hill, Cooper on another, and Ernest Hemingway on a third, with a posse of guides beating the bush to drive the deer toward the hunters. "It wasn't hunting," she'd remember. "It was the damndest ambush I'd ever seen."

Hemingway loathed Bob, loved Barbara. In a letter to his editor, Maxwell Perkins, Hemingway called Taylor a miniature man who was neither very funny nor very impressive while Barbara struck him as being "very nice with a good tough Mick intelligence."

Bob wanted to be the man of the house. Barbara insisted he was, but didn't know how to make it a reality. She felt disappointed and looked for reasons to justify her unhappiness. Claiming she was tired of the long drives from Northridge to the studios, she suggested they move. He resisted her idea. She began looking for a house on the city side of the Santa Monica mountains. When she found a furnished home for lease in Bel Air—the house belonged to Colleen Moore's mother—she signed a one-year lease. Bob said he didn't want to live in somebody else's furniture. She told him she was tired of his hunting rifles, gun racks, and camping trips; he argued he had just installed the kitchen he liked. What would he do without his horses? She said they had so little time together. He said he considered Northridge his first real home.

Barbara got her way. She sold her interest in the thoroughbred stable to her partner Zep, the ranch to Jack Oakie, and found a house she liked at 423 North Faring Road in the Holmby Hills of West Los Angeles. There were four bedrooms, one each for Bob, her, and, downstairs, for Dion and Uncle Buck.

There was less to *do* for Uncle Buck on Faring Road, no thoroughbreds or stable hands to oversee, but he was someone Barbara couldn't be without. He had known her since she was twelve and lived with her even when she was married to

Frank Fay. Now in his fifties, he was the only stable influence Dion knew.

When asked what he meant to her, she said he was the one person she could always turn to for honest advice. In her world of flattering, self-serving agents and studio cronies, Uncle Buck told her the truth about her career moves and was the only one who could tell her that she was awful in a movie. He made himself indispensable not only as her level-headed critic but as front man and go-between when she wanted to remain anonymous. Charity was one such area. In a throwback to her hard-luck youth, she was easily moved to help little people struck by misfortunes, but too fearful of becoming a prey of cupidity and scams to let anyone know. If the morning newspapers told of Los Angeles victims of rotten luck, fire, or other calamities, she sent Buck with a cashier's check and orders not to reveal the donor's identity. During the depth of the Depression she tried to surround her money orders to a family that had been kind to young Ruby Stevens with the same discretion.

Eliminating their long studio commutes was supposed to give Barbara and Bob more time together. On his days off, however, Bob took to the air. She took out her frustration on the furniture and, as she had done in the waning days of the Fay marriage, became a compulsive redecorator. She laughed it off to the gossip columnists. "I have a passion for moving furniture from one place to another. Bob says he'd never sit down in any room in the dark because he'd be sure to land on the floor. I love to change colors in furniture, too. If I could afford it, I'd redecorate my house every month."

Rumors of a breakup began less than six months after Bob and Barbara were married. They dismissed the rumors as idle talk, saying they were just busy at different places, she going to work at Paramount, he taking flying lessons at Palm Spring's Odlum Ranch on days off. Bob's bosses nevertheless saw to it that he came under psychiatric care. Freudian analysis was fashionable and MGM wealthy enough to keep Eric Drimmer, a Swedish psychologist briefly married to Eva Gabor, as an in-house shrink. Besides Bob, Dr. Drimmer's patients included Clark Gable, Mickey Rooney, and Garbo (Judy Garland was seen by Ernest Simmel five days a week).

Barbara was not asked to be part of the therapy. She was careful not to come down too negatively on Bob's romance with flying even though she began to hate airplanes and the jocks Bob met around the general aviation hangars. She held her tongue because she sensed this was one area where he might become sarcastic and call her outdated. She tried golf but found herself uncoordinated on the green and after a few months gave it up. A smart movie offer from Paramount saved her from brooding.

*R*emember the Night was Stanwyck's third film for Paramount, her first with Fred MacMurray. With Cary Grant and Ray Milland, the former saxophone player belonged to the studio's new stable of dandies. The unflappable MacMurray was often teamed with "strong" women like Claudette Colbert and Rosalind Russell. He was married to Lillian Lamont, a dancer he had met playing in a band.

Their director was Mitchell Leisen, a gay former costume designer and art director sometimes dismissed as a poor man's George Cukor. However, every star under contract and the studio's best screenwriters wanted to work with the elegant Leisen, who fashioned Paramount's fizziest romances and smartest musicals. Edith Head was now Paramount's chief designer. Alcoholism had slowly killed Travis Banton's career, and for the last two years Edith was firmly in control of the wardrobe department. She was happy to work with Barbara. Her life was turning around, she told Barbara. Put off by one too many of her husband's binges, she had divorced Charles Head in 1938 and finally married her lover, Wiard Boppo Ihnen. The Taylors became frequent guests at parties at their rambling hacienda in Encino.

The clever *Remember the Night* script was by Preston Sturges.

Barbara saw a lot of the screenwriter. He was hard to miss. At the studio, Sturges held forth at lunch in the commissary, dominating the repartee at the writers' table. After hours, Sturges was a restaurateur. Howard Hughes, Orson Welles, and Humphrey Bogart helped make his Players restaurant-nightclub flourish. Barbara was a regular at the 8225 Sunset Boulevard hangout and was photographed in the Blue Room with Bogart and Welles.

Famed for his string of marriages and eccentric careers, Sturges wanted to direct the scripts he wrote, and Frank Orsatti, of Barbara's former Bren-Orsatti talent agency, was on the verge of getting him a directing job at Paramount by selling the studio a Sturges script for $1. All Barbara would remember of her first meeting with the thirty-nine-year-old Sturges was that she never got a word in. "As long as you didn't open your mouth, but let him do the talking, everything was fine."

The central conceit of *Remember the Night* is that love reforms Stanwyck and corrupts Fred MacMurray. The film opens in a New York department store during Christmas rush with a shot of a glittering jewel in a counter case and a hand reaching in to take it. As Lea Leander, Barbara is from the wrong side of the tracks, but a far cry from Frank Capra's early recession heroine stumbling onto good fortune. Lea is a shoplifter, quickly picked up with the jewel in her possession. Assistant district attorney MacMurray isn't going to let her off easy by bringing her before a tolerant, Christmas-besotted jury and instead has Lea's court appearance postponed until after New Year's. It is Christmas Eve, however, and he feels pangs of guilt when he realizes she will have to spend the holidays in prison. He arranges with a bondsman to obtain her temporary release. The bond agent mistakes the D.A.'s intentions and delivers Lea to MacMurray's apartment as he is preparing to leave for Indiana to spend Christmas with his mother (Beulah Bondi) and aunt (Elizabeth Patterson). Assuring Lea he has no ulterior motives, he takes her to dinner. The fun for the audience is to see MacMurray squirm at her total honesty as she tells him how she became a thief; the scene is highlighted when the deeply shocked judge enters the restaurant and sees D.A. and defendant at their table.

The film was Leisen's thirteenth, and during the shooting he endured jokes about surviving the jinx of thirteen. Since the story propelled Stanwyck and MacMurray from New York through Pennsylvania to Indiana and back again through Canada, and the remaining characters appeared only briefly, the director decided to typecast all other roles.

Leisen never really listened to dialogue during takes. He shot Sturges's script word for word and had a dialogue assistant who would nod to him before he would yell "Print!"

Leisen had a knack for becoming so engrossed in the filming that he would forget to call lunch breaks. The cast presented him with an alarm clock, set to ring at noon.

MacMurray was a disappointment to Sturges, who had imagined a livelier, more assertive D.A. "Preston was around a lot," Barbara would recall. "One day he said to me, 'Someday I'm going to write a real screwball comedy for you.' *Remember the Night* was a delightful light comedy, swell for me and Fred MacMurray, but hardly a screwball, and I replied that nobody would ever think of writing anything like that for me—a murderess, sure. But he said, 'You just wait.'"

An eye infection hospitalized Barbara in August 1940. Dr. Leo Bigelman performed an operation for what was attributed to makeup poisoning. The infection made her miss a scheduled picture opposite Joel McCrea, William Wellman's *Reaching for the Sun*. But Preston Sturges came to see her at the hospital. As soon as she was through recuperation, he would have the promised comedy ready.

The Lady Eve

Six people are leaning over the railing of the S.S. *Southern Queen*. The luxury liner is at anchor off a tropical island waiting for a motor launch to bring out a very important person. Colonel "Handsome Harry" Harrington and his daughter Jean, both in radiant tropical white, are there with somebody named GERALD. A woman in the group understands the VIP is *the* Pike. When somebody confirms the rumor, she tells her daughter to go put on her peek-a-boo.

THE CAMERA MOVES ON TO JEAN, whose real name is Eugenia. She is a smart-looking girl engaged at the moment in nibbling an apple. She looks down speculatively at the approaching motor launch.

> JEAN, COL. H.
> (together)
>
> Is he rich?

> GERALD
>
> He'd almost have to be to stop a boat. He's been up a river somewhere.

> JEAN
>
> Haven't we all.

> GERALD
>
> As the steward so picturesquely put it: he's dripping with dough.
>
> JEAN
>
> What does he own, Pike's Peak?

GERALD

No, no. Pike's Pale—the Ale that won for Yale.
JEAN holds the apple out over the side of the ship and
squints down as if aiming.

JEAN
(fervently)
I hope he's rich. I hope he thinks he's a wizard at cards . . .

COL H.

From your mouth to the ear of the Almighty.

JEAN

. . . and I hope he's got a big fat wife so I don't have to
dance in the moonlight with him. I don't know why it
is but a sucker always steps on your feet.

COL H.
(looking over rail)
And is a mug at everything.

JEAN

I don't see why I have to do all the dirty work. . . .
There must be plenty of rich old dames just waiting for
you to push them around.

COL H.

You find them and I'll push them.

JEAN
(grinning)
Boy, would I like to see you giving some old harpy the
three-in-one.

COL H.

Don't be vulgar, Jean. Let us be crooked but not common.

The first two pages of Preston Sturges's script set the tone
of his story about the elegant swindler and cardsharp, her
partner-in-crime father, and, coming toward them in the

motor launch, Charles "Hopsie" Pike, their millionaire prey, and his manservant-watchdog, Mugsy.

"He kept his word—and how," Barbara would remember of Sturges. "By that time I wasn't under contract to Paramount and he'd have to borrow me. Which would kill it, I figured. He also wanted to borrow Hank Fonda from Fox—another piece of intriguing casting. Hank had been Zanuck's Abraham Lincoln in so many things, whether his name was Tom Joad or Jesse James; how did Sturges know he was a sensational light comedian? Somehow *The Lady Eve* all came together."

The curly-haired Chicagoan had spent most of his childhood in Paris, where his mother was the founder of various perfume and cosmetics ventures. In *The Lady Eve*, Barbara plays a woman much like Sturges's mother, who changed her name six times by marriage and, with her precocious son, managed to catch a husband whenever they needed one. Mary Dempsey styled herself Mary d'Este. Her first salon in Paris was named after Leonardo da Vinci's model, Beatrice d'Este, a name Preston's mother arrived at through genealogical research. The Renaissance d'Este family, she declared, had spawned Irish offspring, and Dempsey was merely a corruption of d'Este. When the Italian family complained, she compromised by styling herself Mary Desti. Sturges was the inventor of a kissproof lipstick and of movable restaurant-booth tables, and his Players restaurant on Sunset Boulevard was hugely popular. He had started writing in 1927 after his first wife left him and he suffered a ruptured appendix. Immobilized for several weeks in a hospital bed, he wrote *Strictly Dishonorable*, a comedy hit that ran on Broadway for nearly two years and brought him $300,000 in royalties. Marrying eighteen-year-old Eleanor Hutton, the stepcousin of Barbara Hutton and equally rich, he came to Hollywood to look for a job. The Huttons regarded him as a dreamer, a dabbler, and a fortune hunter. Divorced after a few years, he was currently the lover of the wife of an older stockbroker. With a $350,000 budget and a three-week shooting schedule, he made his debut as a director with the uneven political satire *The Great McGinty* and followed up with the slapstick romance *Christmas in July*.

The Lady Eve started shooting during the last week of

October 1940, two months after Sturges finished *Christmas in July* with Dick Powell and Ellen Drew. Sturges chose a gleaming white ocean liner—and art director Hans Dreier's sleek shipboard dining room and staterooms—to show how impersonators can mock and fleece the rich. To play Jean Harrington's father, he picked Charles Coburn and introduced them at the cruise ship railing. A moment after the colonel utters the line, "Let us be crooked but not common," Jean drops her apple. It lands on the head of the embarking chump and makes him look up.

As promised by the title, the picture is a whimsical retelling of how Eve offered Adam the fruit of knowledge. Jean wastes little time finding out that the new shipboard mate is Charles "Hopsie" Pike of the brewing fortune. To complete the Old Testament metaphor, Sturges made Hopsie an amateur ophiologist, a student of snakes.

In the stateroom that evening, Jean has Hopsie under observation in her compact mirror. When he gets up and crosses toward the door, she sticks out a shapely leg that lands him on the floor.

Tripping Hopsie, however, breaks the heel of Jean's right shoe. She takes Hopsie down to her cabin to help her find a new pair of shoes. She sits, crosses her legs, and lets him kneel to try a pair on her feet.

Sturges's dialogue is sharp and suggestive. When Jean and Charles return to the salon, her father says: "It certainly took you a long time to come back in the same outfit." Replies Jean: "I'm lucky to have *this* on. Mr. Pike has been up the *Amazon* for a year!"

With that the Harringtons propose a card game. We *know* Charles is going to be fleeced when, joining the game, he shows the colonel how to palm a card.

Hopsie is the traditional befuddled rich-man foil, but Sturges's Jean Harrington has left behind the smart aleck, forgiving heroines that Stanwyck, Ginger Rogers, and Jean Arthur played with their eyes closed. More than one biographer would wonder whether much of this was not out of Sturges's youth. How many times did Mary Desti and Preston cheat in card games as a mother-and-son team on their numerous transatlantic crossings in pursuit of the good life?

Before the *Southern Queen* leaves the tropical waters,

Charles has proposed marriage, and Jean accepted. Things go wrong, of course. A news photo exposes the Harringtons *père et fille* as con artists.

"Are you an adventuress?" Hopsie asks bitterly coming up behind Jean.

"Of course I am. All women are."

Hopsie pretends he was aware of the father-daughter scheme all along. But she continues. "We have to be. If we waited around for men to propose to us, we'd die of old-maidenhood. That's why I let you try on my slippers, and put my cheek against yours, and made you put your arm around me . . . But then I fell in love with you. And that wasn't in the cards."

When they dock in New York everything is off. Hurt and humiliated, Jean vows revenge.

At a reception a few months later, Jean connives to snag her man by being accepted by his family as a member of the English nobility. Her lame excuse when Hopsie instantly recognizes her is that it was really her discredited sister he met aboard the *Southern Queen*. Love finally leads to marriage. Sturges condenses the nuptials into a silent montage, intercut with shots of a spiraling wedding cake, and concentrates instead on the wedding night. As a train carries the newlyweds on their honeymoon through tunnels and torrential rains, Jean concocts so many tales of love affairs that the disillusioned Hopsie jumps off. Jean opposes her father's pitch to try for a big-money settlement. When she discovers Hopsie and his ever faithful Muggsy leaving for South America aboard the *Southern Queen*, she gets passage on the ship. Her cabin is on a lower, cheaper deck than Hopsie's, but they meet, stumble into Jean's cabin, kiss, and explain their misunderstandings:

JEAN

Oh, you still don't understand.

CHARLIE

I don't want to understand. I don't want to know, whatever it is keep it to yourself. All I know is that I adore you, that I'll never leave you again, we'll work it out somehow . . . and that I have no right to be in your cabin.

JEAN

Why?

CHARLIE

Because I'm married.

JEAN
(softly)

But so am I, darling, so am I.
She pushes the door closed. After a few seconds it opens stealthily and MUGGSY flattens out through it. He closes the door very softly. He looks straight into the camera.

MUGGSY

Positively, the same dame.

Fade-out
The End

Sturges cast William Demarest as Muggsy, the ever suspicious valet whose curse it is always to be right but never to be taken seriously by his boss. Raspy-voiced Eugene Pallette plays Charles Pike's father, Eric Blore a phony earl engaged by Jean Harrington to pose as her uncle, and Vic Potel the purser who shows Charles photos incriminating the Harringtons. Jean was modeled on Sturges's mother Mary Desti, and several plot points came from the director's own life. The Hutton family's lawyers had been convinced that Sturges had married Eleanor Hutton only for her money, and when she wanted out of the marriage, he told the attorneys all he wanted was for her to ask him. In *The Lady Eve*, Jean telephones Charles's father to say she wants no alimony, just that Charles come and ask her for a divorce.

Barbara had a great time filming *The Lady Eve*. Whereas a Capra set was a "cathedral," she said, Preston's shoot was a "carnival." In Fonda, she met her match. He, too, always knew his lines and was affectionately called "One-Take Fonda." After *The Lady Eve*, he called Barbara his favorite leading lady. On her fourth birthday Jane Fonda—"Lady Jane" to everybody—came on the set to be feted by daddy and to be bounced on Barbara's knees. The set was so ebullient that instead of going to their trailers between setups, the players relaxed in canvas chairs with their sparkling director, listening to his fascinating stories or going over their lines with him. To get into the mood for Barbara's bedroom scene, Sturges wore a bathrobe.

The Lady Eve was one long series of pratfalls for Fonda. "I happen to love pratfalls, but as almost everything I like, other people dislike, and vice versa. My dearest friends and severest critics constantly urged me to cut the pratfalls down from five to three," Sturges would write. "But it was actually the enormous risks I took with my pictures, skating right up to the edge of nonacceptance, that paid off so handsomely. There are certain things that will convulse the audience, when it has been softened up by what has occurred previously, that seem very unfunny in cold print. Directing and acting have a lot to do with it, too. I had my fingers crossed when Henry Fonda went over the sofa. I held my left ear when he tore down the curtains, and I held everything when the roast beef hit him."

As for his leading lady, Sturges said, "Barbara Stanwyck had an instinct so sure that she needed almost no direction; she is a devastating Lady Eve." Barbara said she'd never had more fun. "He'd ask us how we liked the lines," she told a New York Times reporter. "If we didn't, we'd say so, and he'd say the scriptwriter was fifty kinds of an imbecile—and change them. But, you see, he wrote the thing himself."

"Eve was lucky for me another way," said Barbara. "My character is a very glamorous lady and for the first time, I got a really sensational wardrobe, designed by Edith Head."

The clothes were so gorgeous that Paramount gave her gowns the full publicity treatment. Edith Head, whose forte was expressions of simplicity and elegance, managed to outdo herself on The Lady Eve. Her twenty-five costume changes turned Stanwyck into an instant 1940s symbol and trendsetter. Barbara called Head's wardrobe the most beautiful she had ever worn and, for the first time, she felt like a clotheshorse.

"Lady Eve changed both our lives, it was Barbara's first high-fashion picture and her biggest transition in costuming," the designer would remember in 1979. "Barbara was quite trim and had a better shape than most of the other actresses around. She possessed what some designers considered to be a figure 'problem'—a long waist and a comparatively low rear end. By widening the waistbands in front of her gowns and narrowing them slightly in the back, I could still put her in straight skirts, something other designers were afraid to do, because they thought she might look too heavy in the seat. I just took advantage of her long waist to create the illusion that her derrière was just as perfectly placed as any other star's."

Stanwyck credited Head with changing her image and in gratitude hauled the designer off to her dentist to have her teeth fixed. "Edith always covered her mouth when she laughed and I didn't know why," Barbara said. "Finally she showed me her teeth and I understood. They were awful—not diseased, but some were missing and she felt self-conscious. She told me that she had been to dentists and they had said nothing could be done. I informed her that my dentist could fix anything. He had fixed my smile."

Head's pacifying manners with temperamental stars and directors and her quiet authority turned Barbara into an off-screen Edith Head fan. Since the early 1930s, stars had paid wardrobe departments to make their street clothes, and Edith designed a floor-length black dinner suit with a leaf motif on the back, shoulder, and front and a white crepe suit with flamboyant black mink tails for the personal Stanwyck wardrobe. Barbara's new fashion conscience reached the gossip columns when Hedda Hopper told of Dion secretly offering the designer $6 to make a nice dress for his mother for Christmas and Barbara adding a few hundred dollars.

The Lady Eve shoot wrapped in forty-one days, just two days behind schedule. To celebrate, Sturges closed his Sunset Boulevard restaurant to the public and invited cast, crew, and spouses for a party. The film was cut and scored with the routine speed of the golden-era assembly line. It opened Ash Wednesday, February 26, 1941, just over three and a half months after it started filming, and grossed $115,700 during its first three weeks.

In the larger overview of the American cinema, *The Lady Eve* is considered a screen classic. It represents the dizzy

high point in Sturges's short career—he would die in 1959—
as Hollywood's premier satirist of the American myths of success. The Jean Harrington role was also Stanwyck's most
sparkling comedy acting. Barbara never thought of herself as a
comedian. Slapstick yes, but not light comedy. Sturges's
inspired writing and directing brought out talents in her she
didn't know she possessed. "Like *Bringing Up Baby*," Pauline
Kael would write in 1982, *The Lady Eve* "is a mixture of visual
and verbal slapstick, and of high artifice and pratfalls. Barbara
Stanwyck keeps sticking out a sensational leg, and Henry
Fonda keeps tripping over it . . . neither performer has ever
been funnier."*

*The shipboard cardsharp had an afterlife. Mary Orr uses the name of
Stanwyck's title role in a 1946 *Cosmopolitan* magazine story, "The
Wisdom of Eve," and created the character Eve Harrington. Four years
later, Joseph Mankiewicz adapted "The Wisdom of Eve" to the screen,
called it *All About Eve*, and had Anne Baxter play Eve Harrington, the
young ingenue who dethrones the tempestuous aging star Margo
Channing.

20

The Sweater Girl

Barbara went straight from *The Lady Eve* to playing Capra's favorite character—a reporter who gets the hero into trouble and ends up saving him. They had both come a long way since *The Bitter Tea of General Yen*. After *Mr. Smith Goes to Washington*, Capra's options were unlimited. Before he even had a script, Gary Cooper, Edward Arnold, Walter Brennan, James Gleason, Spring Byington, and Barbara all accepted roles in his next picture.

After twelve years with Harry Cohn, Capra was leaving Columbia. Selznick wanted him, and there were offers from Samuel Goldwyn and Howard Hughes. The idea of total freedom and independence was so attractive, however, that he formed Frank Capra Productions, set up shop on Selznick International's Culver City lot, and made tentative plans to release his pictures through United Artists. Robert Riskin became a minority stockholder in FCP. In July 1940, five months before principal photography began, Capra and Riskin moved to Warner Brothers after Jack Warner agreed to advance $500,000 if the picture became a WB release.

Meet John Doe was supposed to be a statement on American fascism. Beyond the morality tales of ordinary folk standing up to the greed and corruption of the rich that Capra had perfected in *Mr. Deeds Goes to Town* and *Mr. Smith Goes to Washington*, the new picture was to be a comedy with a sting. Director and writer got excited about a story by Richard Connell and Robert Presnell in an old issue of *Century* magazine. They immediately decided they wanted Stanwyck as Ann Mitchell, a newspaperwoman who, after losing her job in a takeover of her paper, writes a fictitious letter about a man who claims he is so troubled by people's inhumanity that he will commit suicide on Christmas Eve.

The cooked-up story becomes a page-one favorite. Ann gets her job back, but the new owner's henchman (Gleason) is furious when he finds out there is no John Doe. Big boss D. B. Norton (Arnold) likes her idea of *fabricating* a John Doe, of bringing in some homeless nobody and using him to build circulation. In Long John Willoughby (Cooper), Ann finds a drifter and untalented minor-league baseball player lacking ideals who, despite warnings from his buddy the Colonel (Brennan), agrees to become Doe.

The story spins out of control.

The newspaper hires Doe and interviews him daily on the subject of Love Thy Neighbor. When his sermons touch local and national hearts, Doe makes a nationwide tour and becomes the subject of a *Time* magazine cover. Publisher Norton sees a chance to realize his political ambitions. He sets up a third political party and plans a rousing convention where Doe will nominate him for president. Doe discerns a would-be dictator in Norton and instead of nominating him at the podium starts denouncing the publisher. Norton manages to cut Doe's speech off and expose him as a fake.

The convention scene was filmed in Los Angeles's Wrigley Field. Fifteen hundred extras were paid $5.50 and a box lunch each night for several nights' work as delegates. The band plays "The Battle Hymn of the Republic," and the crowd cheers as John Doe makes his way to the platform. A chaplain asks for a silent moment to pray for "the John Does all over the country, many of whom are hungry and homeless." Scores of newsboys suddenly break the silence, shouting, "Extra! John Doe is a fake. John Doe movement is a swindle!" State troopers escort Arnold to the stand and hustle the astonished John Doe from the microphone. Norton grabs the mike and denounces Doe.

"It's a lie," Doe interrupts.

"It's not a lie," shouts the newspaper mogul. "Ask him who wrote his newspaper article. Ask him if he intended to jump off the building. Ask him. It's all in the paper. Go ahead and read it."

With this Norton leaves the stand. Doe tries to explain,

but the crowd is booing and throwing things (no bottles, please, suggested Capra). Brennan dashes up to protect his old friend, and with the help of "local police" Doe is led out of the angry mob.

Totally disillusioned, Doe decides to do what Ann's initial letter proclaimed—kill himself at midnight on Christmas Eve. Ann finds him on the roof of a tall building ready to jump. She convinces him to live and fight against the Nortons of the world. Stanwyck would remember a couple of different endings being written and filmed. Capra couldn't decide which one to use. The happy ending he did choose so distorted the meaning that Connell and Presnell, the original authors, sued.

Warners hyped *Meet John Doe* by calling the film "controversial" and keeping the screenplay a carefully guarded secret. Only Stanwyck, Cooper, Arnold, and Brennan received actual scripts; the rest of the cast were handed their lines scene by scene.

Barbara was perfect as the tough, wisecracking reporter, but the kudos went to Cooper's John Doe, whose naiveté and convictions end up melting her opportunism. *Time* gave Cooper its cover in January 1941, waxing lyrically about Gary and Veronica Coopers' social life, their tennis, bridge, and backgammon games with friends such as Tyrone Power and Annabella, the Fred MacMurrays, and the Robert Taylors. TWO DOWN AND ONE TO GO, the *New York Times* headlined a story on the busy Barbara Stanwyck. *Meet John Doe* was released on March 12, 1941, two weeks after *The Lady Eve*, and, reported the *Times*, Stanwyck had signed with Paramount to star in *Pioneer Woman*, her first Technicolor film.

Behind the polished front of Mr. and Mrs. Right, Bob reared up. Barbara loved their busy, regulated lives and, in public, was quick to say their careers were totally separate. Their smooth utterances occasionally got crossed. In a candid moment, Bob said his wife coached him for all his pictures while a Hunt Stromberg publicity profile quoted her as saying, "We have always agreed that our professional careers should be separately maintained at all times." Bob felt suffocated. Whenever they had time together, which wasn't too often, they argued, and he usually lost. He was the screen lover a million women swooned over, yet he was married to a cold, controlling woman. Despite Howard Strickling's denials that the Taylor marriage was in trouble, the relationship was strained. Bob was tired of Barbara's aloof perfection, her domineering ways, her calling him Junior, her objecting to his lifestyle, to his fondness for hunting and flying, to his wanting to be one of the boys. Shortly before their second anniversary he came home one night and told her he was having an affair with Lana Turner and wanted a divorce.

Lana was his costar in *Johnny Eager*. She was twenty and divorcing bandleader Artie Shaw after a three-month marriage. In the picture, Bob played a supposedly reformed gangster, Lana a society girl falling in love with him. Their director was Mervyn LeRoy. The love scenes were hot and heavy. Decades later, TV producer Norman Lear would say the sexiest woman he could think of was "Lana Turner, as she was held in the arms of Robert Taylor in the terrace scene in *Johnny Eager*."

Lana made a play for Bob. A female fan rushing toward him made him shudder in disgust, but a costar thrusting her thigh between his legs in the middle of a break demanded that he respond in kind.

"Bob had the kind of looks I could fall for, and we were attracted to each other from the beginning," Turner would write in her autobiography. She felt a pang of fear, however, when he told her how unhappy his marriage was, how all he felt for Barbara was respect. As she would put it, "I would never be responsible for breaking up a marriage, however unhappy it was. I wasn't in love with Bob, not really. Oh, we'd exchanged kisses, but we'd never been to bed together. Our eyes had, but not our bodies."

Lana had no intention of becoming a problem in the Taylors' relationship. "'I care for you,'" she would remember telling him, "'but don't make me the solution to your marital problems. Don't tell her.' But he did."

The Sweater Girl, provocatively sexy with a small-town winsomeness, had enough problems with men. Howard Hughes was after her, and she went out with Victor Mature and bandleader and legendary jazz drummer Gene Krupa. Before marrying Shaw, she had been the girlfriend of Gregson

Bautzer, a fashionable attorney taking care of her divorce. On his own—or at Strickling's urging—Bob joined the Lana Turner fan club, telling one reporter she was perfectly proportioned and not as "busty" as her pinup photos would make you believe. "I have never seen lips like hers and though I was never known to run after blondes, Lana could be the exception." Bob told friends he'd have to have Lana if only for one night.

Barbara lost her finely honed composure when Bob told her he wanted a divorce. She fled the house and for the next four days holed up in the home of Harriett Corey, her maid. Gossip columnists picked up the scent. Cornered, Barbara said it was not she but her husband who was away. Bob was tired, she explained. Since *Waterloo Bridge*, he had made five pictures in a row. "He wanted to take some extensive flying lessons and took his instructor to the Odlum Ranch in Palm Springs," she told a news conference.

Perhaps believing pregnancy might account for a moody overreaction or a marital tiff, a reporter asked if she were pregnant. A wistful smile creased her lips. "I'd shout it from the rooftop if I were." She suggested resentment might be behind the false rumors. "We are by no means separated and there are people, I suppose, who are jealous and would like to see me take a fall. Since my career has been successful lately, they attacked my marriage." Repeating almost verbatim her chin-up housewife defense she had used when the press questioned the Fay marriage, she said her husband and she were building a house in Beverly Hills. "Does that sound as if we're getting a divorce?"

Public appearances and busy schedules papered over the incident. What Bob later called his deep respect for Barbara made him rethink a divorce. Helen Ferguson would say he wanted neither to be alone nor to live with his mother. In a display of marital harmony, Stanwyck and Taylor made imprints of their hands in the forecourt of Sidney Grauman's Chinese Theatre and, with a stick, scrawled a thank-you note in the fresh cement to the celebrated showman. Others had planted their hand and/or footprints in the famous courtyard on Hollywood Boulevard, but Bob and Barbara were the only couple immortalized in fresh cement.

TAYLOR AND TURNER. THEY'RE HOTTER'N T-N-T,

screamed the MGM publicity when *Johnny Eager* was released.

Bob reported to George Cukor for *Her Cardboard Lover*. Norma Shearer was his leading lady in this French boulevard farce that Jeanne Eagels had played on Broadway just after Ruby Stevens was cast in *The Noose*. The script was witless, but Bob gave a wonderful performance as a gigolo hired by Shearer to impersonate her lover. *Her Cardboard Lover* proved to be Shearer's last film.

The Lady Eve was such a hit that Columbia quickly signed Stanwyck and Fonda to star in an imitation soufflé called *You Belong to Me*. Capra's *Meet John Doe* was also a success. *Variety* said, "Stanwyck has never had a better role," but most reviewers echoed the Baltimore Sun's affection for Cooper, "so right in every respect as this country's Everyman that it is hard to imagine anyone else in Hollywood filling the bill."* Before *You Belong to Me* went into production, however, Barbara was doing a woman-as-empire-builder saga.

William Wellman was the director of *The Great Man's Lady*, as Paramount renamed *Pioneer Woman*. An exception to 1940s westerns, the film had Stanwyck as a San Francisco matriarch who, in the early days, roughed it up and as a centenarian now rules as the dowager of Nob Hill society. "It's a kind of history, San Francisco history, and possibly sacred," she told reporters. The original story was by a husband-and-wife team who wrote under the wife's name, Viña Delmar. Eugene and Viña were the writers of the 1937 crazy divorce classic *The Awful Truth*. An oddity in golden age Hollywood, the couple worked at home, refused to go near any studio, appear on a set, or meet actors.

Barbara liked to meet her writers. "Whenever people ask me about the movies I've done," she'd say, "I always mention the writer first. I was very lucky, most of the time, in having good scripts. Good writers, directors. To me, the words come first. If it ain't on paper, it ain't ever gonna get up there on the screen."

Writers paid back her compliments, sometimes in spades.

*Cooper was the highest-paid man in the United States in 1939, earning $483,000 in period dollars.

Herman Mankiewicz, the prolific screenwriter and script doctor, said of her that she was the nicest woman he had ever met. "I could just dream of being married to her, having a little cottage out in the hills, roses round the door. I'd come home from the office, tired and weary, and I'd spy Barbara there through the door, walking in with an apple pie she'd just cooked herself. And no drawers."

Joel McCrea, Brian Donlevy, Katharine Stevens, Thurston Hall, and Lloyd Corrigan rounded out *The Great Man's Lady* cast. Wellman had Barbara dress in an unflattering raincoat and get drenched by a storm during a cattle drive. For the parlor stuff, Paramount publicity arranged for reporters to witness makeup artist Wally Westmore turn the thirty-four-year-old Stanwyck into a variety of ages. Stanwyck, Westmore, and an assistant director visited the Masonic Old Ladies Home in Santa Monica so Barbara could get a feel for how a centenarian walks and sits.

Wellman shot an exciting battle with Indians and the cavalry fighting in the middle of a shallow river. The complete battle sequence was so thrilling that Paramount sold the footage to Fox, which blew it up to CinemaScope and spliced it into two 1950s westerns, *Pony Soldier* and *Siege at Red River*.

The Great Man's Lady reinforced Barbara's iron-willed screen image. The film would remain one of her favorites because it cast a jaundiced eye on pioneer myths. Its deeper theme—the sense of loss that comes with uprooting—cut close to her personally. With Wellman she agreed it was the best picture they had made together.

"It broke my heart," Barbara said when *The Great Man's Lady* was not a success.

Stanwyck and Fonda's professionalism and Wesley Ruggles's brisk direction saved *You Belong to Me*, but the picture failed to repeat *The Lady Eve*'s success. Ruggles was the veteran of many Jean Arthur and Claudette Colbert comedies. Barbara played a doctor, Fonda her playboy husband who becomes jealous of a handsome patient of hers. Late in life she regretted *You Belong to Me* was her last film with Fonda. "He was delicious to work with," she would say in 1983. "I was sorry when each of the three pictures we did was over. I wish we had done more movies together. I loved Hank."

Bob moved from *Her Cardboard Lover* to *Stand by for*

Action, his first war movie, and Barbara to a romantic comedy when an odd event again thrust their marriage into the gossip columns.

Barbara was rushed to the Cedars of Lebanon Hospital on October 7, 1941, with severed arteries on her wrist and arm. Attempted suicide? No, Bob told the press, an unfortunate accident. His wife had tried to open a jammed window. Using the heel of her hand, she had broken the glass and cut herself.*

Barbara told Helen Ferguson to handle the press. The suicide angle was too tempting. To put a stop to further inquiries, Helen put an Irish proverb in Barbara's mouth. The press agent quoted Stanwyck as saying there was nothing more to add because "The more you kick something that's dead, the more it stinks."

It is hard to imagine Barbara deciding to end her life over a husband she saw as immature and called Junior, but the crumbling of her carefully constructed facade would have devastated her. She never tried to explain the slashed arteries. When asked much later, Bob also avoided a direct response. Clumsily, he said that what had troubled him, and apparently made him decide not to leave her, was realizing how much a divorce would hurt her, how deeply she loved him, implying that she might indeed have taken drastic measures.

Hollywood was full of divorces and recouplings. Behind Barbara's pride at being seen as one half of an ideal couple was little Ruby needing a home of her own. She had tried so hard to play house with Frank and little Dion. She had given herself a second chance, and it, too, wasn't working. She had known that from the start. She was thirty-four, running on a treadmill of success. She was a mother more than a wife to a man who had turned thirty in August and who, since their marriage, spent his working hours in celluloid romances with Hedy Lamarr, Vivien Leigh, Joan Crawford, Greer Garson, and saucy little Lana.

She never forgave "the other woman." More than forty years later, Lana Turner made an effort to see and talk to

---

*Lana Turner, ironically, tried a similar defense ten years later, after she separated form millionaire Bob Topping, her third husband. When her attempted sleeping pill and slashed wrist suicide failed, she would claim she had tried to take a shower while drunk, cutting her arm on the shower door.

Barbara, only to be intentionally and decisively snubbed. Helen put the blame for Bob's defection on Barbara herself. "She meant well telling him what to do and how to do it," Helen would say. "This was her way of helping. Bob wanted to be the man of the house, and Barbara didn't know how to accept that, despite the fact that she insisted he was."

Once more, Barbara immersed herself in an invented chorus girl and was rewarded with a smashing success. *Ball of Fire* was *The Lady Eve* with a twist—burlesque dancer collides with fuddy-duddy professor.

Gary Cooper was Samuel Goldwyn's hot property, used as much for trading purposes as for starring on his home lot. In exchange for the promise of his future service in Hemingway's *For Whom the Bell Tolls*, Goldwyn got a smash writing team from Paramount.

Billy Wilder and Charles Brackett were Paramount's top writing duo. In 1937, Paramount producer Arthur Hornblow had realized that Wilder's enthusiastic English revealed significant gaps in grammar and syntax and that the Writers Building also harbored Brackett, whose polished, elegant prose had adorned *The New Yorker* but who—like Wilder—was achieving little at the studio. Hornblow teamed the Viennese Jew and patrician New Yorker to write Ernst Lubitsch's *Bluebeard's Eighth Wife*. Since that picture, the pair had written *Ninotchka*, Paramount's comedy hit starring Garbo, and some of the best escapist entertainment—stories about millionaires, chambermaids, assassins, drunkards, smart-aleck cabdrivers, and nouveaux riches. The genre ceased to amuse with the outbreak of the war, and they charted its disappearance in two scripts for Mitchell Leisen—*Arise My Love*, set against a collapsing Europe, and *Hold Back the Dawn*, in which Charles Boyer is discovered trying to get into the United States by marrying an American schoolteacher.

After rejecting the projects Goldwyn had in development for Cooper, Wilder proposed a rewrite of a script he had written in Berlin eight years earlier. A variation on the *Pygmalion* theme, it was the story of seven professors who have labored nine years on a new encyclopedia. They have finally arrived at the letter 's', and one of them, the fuddy-duddy Bertram Potts, is given the word "slang." Professor

Potts's academic enquiry leads him to a gangster's moll. Sugarpuss O'Shea, as Wilder and Brackett named their heroine, is all jive and street talk. She disrupts the scholarly calm of Bertram and his colleagues and nearly gets him fired from the university. In the fade-out, the professor marries the burlesque queen. Twenty years later, Wilder would admit to the inherent creakiness of the plot, but in October 1941 everybody called the script superb. Goldwyn wanted the brassy Ginger Rogers to play the stripper and, to be on the safe side, sent the screenplay to Jean Arthur and Carole Lombard. As Rogers had just won an Academy Award for her performance in *Kitty Foyle*, she sent word that henceforth she would only play ladies. Columbia wouldn't lend Goldwyn Arthur, and Lombard wrote back that she didn't care for the Sugarpuss O'Shea character. Goldwyn convinced himself that as encyclopedist and showgirl Cooper and Stanwyck could repeat their *Meet John Doe* money-spinning.

The director was no studio toadie. Howard Hawks alternated between comedy and drama—he had just finished *Sergeant York* with Cooper. Goldwyn paid him $10,000 a week, which didn't prevent Hawks from walking off a picture when the ebullient producer got too "creative." Goldwyn thought Hawks had no character because he bet on horses and was involved in real estate schemes. On a studio set, however, Hawks's temper kept people on their toes—Barbara said his mind was as sharp as a rattler's fangs. Hawks was seen at nightclubs with the Taylors, but Barbara would remember their working together as less than cordial.

Goldwyn gave Dana Andrews his first break by letting him play the gangster Sugarpuss is supposed to marry, and in a life-imitates-art reversal, Virginia "Sugar" Hill, the mistress of mobster Bugsy Siegel, was cast as a showgirl.

Hawks's direction was clean and sharp. He gave boogie-woogie singer-stripper Barbara a zinger of a screen introduction. The first time we see her she slides onto a nightclub stage in a stripper's costume and, with Lana's former boyfriend Gene Krupa on the drums leading his orchestra, performs a rowdy rendition of "Drum Boogie." Her gown scintillates, her midriff is bare, her legs flash, and, after her vocal, Krupa switches from drumsticks to matchsticks that, at the end of his solo, burst into flames.

The cinematographer was the *Citizen Kane* cameraman

Gregg Toland. The master of ravishing studio camerawork photographed Stanwyck beautifully, experimenting with depth of focus that gave her face contour and relief. Hawks got Barbara to be sexy in the unlikeliest surroundings and made her stand on a stack of books to kiss Cooper. In a steal from *The Lady Eve*, Professor Potts gets to hold Sugarpuss O'Shea's bare foot. Cooper played Potts with a slightly bent neck throughout, as befitting a scholar who always has his nose in books. The previews were so promising that Goldwyn managed to book *Ball of Fire* into Radio City Music Hall for the first week of December 1941.

Like millions of Americans, Barbara and Bob stayed by the radio on Sunday afternoon, December 7. After the hourly headline news of the attack on Pearl Harbor, local bulletins demanded that all police and firemen report to duty and asked the public to use their telephones in emergencies only and stay off the streets. In Hawaii, bombing raids continued into the night; in L.A. a blackout was in force. All night the air sirens wailed. Southern California expected an invasion. A Japanese attack was believed to be imminent, and crude bomb shelters were thrown up at the studios. Monday morning Bob and Barbara heard President Roosevelt ask Congress for a Declaration of War.

Unlike the mood change that greeted *Golden Boy* in September 1939, the romantic collision of Sugarpuss O'Shea and Professor Potts lifted the spirits of a nation going to war. *Ball of Fire* was a hit. Daily *Variety* speculated that Barbara Stanwyck might win the 1941 Best Actress Oscar for *The Lady Eve*, *Meet John Doe*, or *Ball of Fire*. The competition was Crawford as an ugly crook who reforms after a facelift in *A Woman's Face*, Bette Davis's bravura performance in *The Little Foxes*, Olivia de Havilland in *Hold Back the Dawn*, and her twenty-four-year-old kid sister, Joan Fontaine, in the Alfred Hitchcock thriller *Suspicion*. When the nominations were announced, Stanwyck in *Ball of Fire* came up against Davis, the sisters de Havilland and Fontaine, and Greer Garson in *Blossoms in the Dust*. The nightly blackouts of Los Angeles killed the idea of a traditional glitter and pomp Oscar event, and on December 17 the Academy board announced there would be no banquet but that the awards would be given in a yet to be determined format.

Shortly after New Year's 1942, the Academy reinstated the February 26 Oscar event, calling it a dinner instead of a banquet and promising music but no dancing. "To boost civil morale," formal dress would be eschewed and women were to donate the money they would spend on orchids to the Red Cross.

On Oscar night, Barbara and Bob arrived late at the Biltmore Hotel ballroom, which was bedecked with American flags and the flags of the Allies. Ginger Rogers presented the Best Actress award. The winner, she announced, was Joan Fontaine.

Patriot Games

Two years of watching events in Europe had prepared Americans psychologically for war, but the country was desperately unprepared industrially. The prerequisite of planning a war was to finance it, and the sale of U.S. bonds became an immediate priority. The movie stars' value to the war effort was in making propaganda films, entertaining the troops, and selling war bonds. The Defense Department was keenly aware of Hollywood's promotional value.

World War II was fought with movies—obsessively. On the home fronts of both sides, audiences flocked to the only existing distraction. Movies were shown not only in cinemas, but in factories, schools, and union halls. Millions of men in uniform saw movies endlessly, aboard ships, in barracks and mess halls. In American boomtowns, movie houses remained open around the clock to accommodate swing and graveyard shifts. Attendance reached 80 million a week.

What were Americans fighting for? President Roosevelt and his chief of staff, General George C. Marshall, decided that the large armies—around 8 million men—the country was raising had to be told *why* and that movies were the best way. Because he was between assignments, Frank Capra was the first to fly to Washington. Quickly inducted and given the rank of major, Capra began organizing the Army Pictorial Service, which would soon make thousands of training films on every conceivable subject from venereal disease to spotting enemy aircraft and assembling M-1 rifles. Within months, freshly commissioned Colonels Darryl Zanuck, William Wyler, Anatole Litvak, and John Huston were in Washington working on a seven-hour "must see" *Why We Fight* series.

The *why* was to cast a long shadow. Buried deep in the question was the difficulty of what kind of a world an Allied victory would deliver. The Soviet Union was an ally, and large numbers of British and French soldiers were determined they and their comrades were not dying for the purpose of restoring the 1939 society of privilege and social strictures. A little over a year into the American participation in the war, Bob and Barbara were swept up in the left-right breach that was to fling them, and the country, into the postwar anti-Communist witch hunt.

The Taylors rang in 1942 at the Bennys' on Roxbury Drive. For Frederick De Cordova, the future producer-director who had just been hired as a dialogue director by Warners, the Bennys' New Year's Eve party was his first in Hollywood: "I was thrilled at the beauty of the home, the decorations, seeing all the big stars I had been reading about all my life. There was Clark Gable, Bob Hope, Bing Crosby and Stanwyck and Taylor and on and on. I thought it was the greatest night of my life, dancing with some of the girls who had been just a picture on a screen to me. I was standing at a bar in the garden having a drink when the lights went out at midnight, and I could see the shadows of all the famous couples kissing the New Year in."

The headlines remained ominous. During January and February, the military situation grew worse as the Japanese swarmed over the Philippines and captured Singapore and Burma. London was under the heaviest part of the German blitz. Californians were convinced the Japanese would launch a sneak attack on the Pacific Coast. The army rounded up Americans of Japanese descent and sent them to internment camps. British Prime Minister Winston Churchill flew to Washington to discuss joint military action.

The stars enlisted. Jimmy Stewart joined the air force as a private, eventually to become a bomber pilot and a colonel. Robert Montgomery enlisted in the navy; Tyrone Power abandoned both wife and male lover to join the marines; and Henry Fonda, who was thirty-seven and the father of two, volunteered as a sailor, only to be ordered back to Hollywood because Twentieth Century-Fox wanted him in a war movie. Clark Gable hesitated. MGM didn't approve of the idea of "The King" being drafted, and Louis B. was sure he could use his influence in Washington to have Gable go into the military as a commissioned officer. Carole Lombard was against "one of those phony commissions" for her husband.

Each celebrity's call to colors was an event in Howard Strickling's publicity department. He turned the first meeting of Gable's Victory Committee into a media event. Lombard came in a dark fur coat and black silk dress and told everyone she was disguised as a blackout. She beamed with pride when Clark addressed the assembled actors and urged everyone to volunteer. A subcommittee headed by Gable and including Myrna Loy, Claudette Colbert, Charles Boyer, Bob Hope, Ginger Rogers, and nine others was chosen to coordinate talent for war-bond rallies, camp shows, and hospital tours. As the wife of the chairman, Carole was the first to stand up and pledge her cooperation. Marlene Dietrich and Merle Oberon seconded. Barbara signed up for railway tours to help sell war bonds. The trains rolled into cities where defense plants were located, usually to be greeted by cheering Rosie the Riveters.

Bob couldn't wait to get into uniform, but Barbara discouraged his martial yearnings. She had had enough of his hunting trips, not to mention his new passion for flying. Wasn't all that dangerous enough? He should be thankful he didn't have to go, she told him. Behind her back, he volunteered for active duty. At thirty-one, he was overage, although the top brass hadn't considered the forty-four-year-old Capra too old to make him a major.

Hollywood was becoming an assembly line. A total of 488 features were made in 1942—a number never to be surpassed—and *somebody* had to star in all those movies. At Warners, Ronald Reagan and Erroll Flynn were playing RAF pilots shot down behind German lines in *Desperate Journey* when Reagan received his induction notice. Jack Warner personally wrote the army asking for, and, on January 1, 1942, receiving, a deferment.

Mayer was in no hurry to see the MGM stable drained of male stars either. Bob went with Barbara to the Reagans' send-off party when, in late April, Ron was told to report to Fort

Mason in San Francisco. Despite the birth of their daughter Maureen, gossip columnists speculated that the Reagan marriage was in trouble. In fact, the war brought them closer together. Bob was green with envy. Why couldn't Barbara and he be like "Dutch" and Jane Wyman, *the* tailor-made Hollywood "Mr. and Mrs. America Fighting the War"—wife as successful actress, actor-husband in the service?

Bob was further disconcerted when his wife got to do war duty. Actresses were turning out to be especially good at selling war bonds. Hedy Lamarr offered to kiss any man who bought $25,000 worth of bonds. Dorothy Lamour sold $30 million worth in four days. As the most famous native of Indiana, Lombard volunteered to "do" the Hoosier state. Barbara had no links to Canada, but she was "drafted" to do a Canadian railway tour.

Lombard's death in a plane crash on the last leg of her Indiana tour rocked Hollywood. Her devastated widower, Clark Gable, joined the Army Air Corps at forty-one—as a private—adding to Bob's discomfort. He was temporarily relieved when MGM cast him in a pair of war movies with all-male casts—*Stand by for Action* and *Bataan*.

While she commuted between Columbia, RKO, Paramount, and Warners, Barbara Stanwyck movies came out at three-month intervals—*You Belong to Me* and *Ball of Fire* before *The Great Man's Lady*. On days off she helped at the Beverly Hills Hotel USO canteen or appeared on radio broadcasts for servicemen. In collusion with Jack Warner, casting director (and soon-to-be Executive Assistant in Charge of Production) Steve Trilling forced Stanwyck, Davis, and Crawford to fight for the best roles. *The Little Foxes* was turning Bette into the screen's favorite man-eater, while Joan was in such a freefall that she was desperate about her career. To keep the stars on their toes, Trilling also developed a roster of new actresses, including Lauren Bacall, Joan Leslie, Susan Hayward, Ann Blyth, Brenda Marshall, Ann Sheridan, and Alexis Smith.

Davis didn't want to do *The Gay Sisters*. She found the story dull—three sisters become heiresses in 1915 when their father perishes aboard the sinking *Lusitania*. "I would be so grateful," she wrote Hal Wallis, "if you would give *The Gay Sisters* to someone else." Barbara had known Wallis since his publicist days. There was never a dull moment—or a free one—around Hal, and trading roles was his forte. Barbara wasted no time telling him she would love to do *The Gay Sisters*.

Reunited with George Brent in the intricate courtroom drama about inheritances, absent husbands, and unexplained children, Barbara played the bad apple in a respectable family. Adapted from a Chekovian novel by the recently returned Paris expatriate Stephen Longstreet, the story had Barbara marry engineer Brent to make herself eligible for a legacy. Vixenish Geraldine Fitzgerald and timid Nancy Coleman were her younger siblings.

Filmed in the spring of 1942, *The Gay Sisters* was Irving Rapper's third movie. The former London theater director decided newcomer Gig Young was the next Cary Grant and cast him in the picture as a dashing young artist the sisters fight over.

Gig Young was, like Bob, a graduate of the Pasadena Playhouse, and *The Gay Sisters* was his first chance. He was soon the object of Barbara's setside teaching. They had few scenes together, but she was there with advice. She gave him pointers on how to give his character a roguish charm that immediately came across on the screen. In Gig Young, Jack Warner thought the studio had another Errol Flynn—or at least a Ronald Reagan. *The Gay Sisters* was a typical wartime production. A week after wrapping the shoot, Rapper started *Now, Voyager* with Bette Davis.

Barbara joined Edward G. Robinson, Charles Boyer, Betty Field, Robert Cummings, Robert Benchley, and Thomas Mitchell in a stylish episode film at Warner Brothers. The Fall of France in June 1940 had brought a quartet of Parisian filmmakers to Hollywood—René Clair, Julien Duvivier, Max Ophuls, and Jean Renoir. Marlene Dietrich adopted them and a few actor stragglers who followed. During the First World War, the teenaged Marlene had handed flowers through barbed wire to French POWs; now she was closer to Hollywood's French emigrés than to the German and German-Jewish expatriate colony.

Marlene took in the uprooted Frenchmen—except for Renoir's companion there were no women among them—and enjoyed mothering these refugees from her triumphant fatherland. She was cook, counselor, and interpreter to them, and, when Jean Gabin arrived, his mistress. Gabin might be the star of Renoir's *La grande illusion*, Carné's *Quai des brumes*, and *Pépé le Moko*, Duvivier's answer to *Scarface*, but he was lost in Hollywood and clung to Dietrich and the little French colony.

With the help of Preston Sturges, Clair got his American career off on the right foot, directing Marlene in *The Flame of New Orleans* and Veronica Lake in the triumphant comedy fantasy *I Married a Witch*. Renoir found work directing *This Land Is Mine* with Charles Laughton as a French schoolteacher who finally revolts against the Gestapo occupier. Duvivier was hired by Universal.

Flesh and Fantasy was filmed during the late summer and fall of 1942. Robert Benchley, the humorist who wasn't above supplementing his writing income with acting stints and once ran an ad in *Variety* describing his specialty as "society drunks," plays a club bore who doesn't believe in the supernatural, but tells macabre stories by Ellis St. Joseph, Oscar Wilde, and Laslo Vadnay. Stanwyck and Charles Boyer were in the Vadnay story, the weakest of the half-hour vignettes, she as a refugee with unusual diamond earrings, he a trapeze performer who foresees his own death.

Although the decisive battles of the war were still to come, 1943 was a turning point. Out of reach of German or Japanese bombers, the "arsenal of democracy" was in full swing in the United States, and tanks, planes, and ships were coming off the assembly lines in ever-increasing numbers. Bob was sure the war would be over before he'd get into a uniform when he got word that because of his flying experience the navy wanted him.

Not so fast, said Louis B. *Song of Russia* must come first.

MGM's *Mrs. Miniver* had done more than a hundred speeches to help President Roosevelt overcome American isolationism and align the country with Britain. Directed by William Wyler and starring Greer Garson and Walter Pidgeon, *Mrs. Miniver* was the most popular film of 1942. A war film without battle scenes, it had happily grossed $6 mil-

Young Ruby
Stevens and big
brother Malcolm
Byron, Brooklyn.

David Porter Collection

Barbara Stanwyck,
1927.

*Courtesy of the Academy
of Motion Picture Arts
and Sciences*

Hal Skelly and Stanwyck in *Burlesque*, Barbara's first big stage hit, 1927.

New York Public Library

Frank and Barbara in Malibu, 1930.

Courtesy of the Academy of Motion Picture Arts and Sciences

Rising young star,
1931.

*Courtesy of the Academy
of Motion Picture Arts
and Sciences*

Barbara and Bob in *This Is My Affair*, Fox, 1937.

Remember the Night, with director Mitchell Leisen and Elizabeth Patterson, Paramount, 1940.

The Lady Eve
(Paramount, 1941):
Reeling Hopsie
(Henry Fonda) in.

*Copyright © by Universal
City Studios, Inc. Courtesy
of MCA Publishing Rights, a
Division of MCA Inc.*

Riding the director. *Lady
Eve* set-side antics: Barbara
on Preston Sturges.

*Courtesy of the Academy of
Motion Picture Arts and Sciences*

"Skip Stanwyck" and
Joan Benny in Palm
Springs, 1942.

Joan Benny Archives

Tourists in Paris, 1947.

National Archives

With Burt
Lancaster in
*Sorry, Wrong
Number,*
Paramount, 1948.

*Marc Wanamaker/Bison
Archives*

The Furies,
Barbara with
Walter Huston on
his last film,
Paramount, 1950.

Barbara and Bob,
reunited for *The
Night Walker,*
Universal, 1965.

Barbara Stanwyck

Larry Kleno Collection

lion for MGM and was now being showered with Academy Awards.

Mayer envisioned an encore. Joseph Stalin's Soviet Union was not Mayer's Russia—Louis B. didn't like to be reminded that he was born in Minsk, that his parents only emigrated to Canada when he was a youngster, but the land of his birth was an ally. Roosevelt and Churchill were set to meet Stalin at Teheran.

Song of Russia was Metro's contribution to the cause.

Bob threw a tantrum in Louis B.'s office. But Mayer put a call through to the Pentagon office of Secretary of the Navy Frank Knox. The secretary called back and said that of course the navy was happy to agree to give Robert Taylor time to make the film.

Whipped together in no time, *Song of Russia* was, like *Mrs. Miniver*, a war movie of the home front. Paul Jarrico and Richard Collins were responsible for the original story, and Leo Mittler, Victor Trivas, and Guy Endore wrote the screenplay. For authenticity, Russian-born Gregory Ratoff directed the big-budget story of an American symphony conductor on a Russian concert tour when Hitler's armies attack in June 1941. Bob was the conductor who, to the accompaniment of Tchaikovsky and Herbert Stothart's arrangements of other Russian composers, falls in love with the country, its people, and comely newcomer Susan Peters. Other members of the cast included John Hodiak and Robert Benchley. Wearing a sort of Russian garb out to lunch, Benchley explained his costume and appearance in *Song of Russia* by saying, "I'm a shill for Shostakovich."

"Grisha" Ratoff was a hammy actor with early experience in the Moscow Art Theatre, and he was a friend of Darryl Zanuck's. He had played the producer in *What Price Hollywood?* and directed Ingrid Bergman in *Intermezzo*. In *Song of Russia*, he tried to keep the inflections quasi-Russian. His cast, however, spoke in accents that derived from no known language. The *New York Times* hailed *Song of Russia* as "very close to being the best film on Russia yet made in the popular Hollywood idiom," but *Newsweek* called it MGM's "neatest trick . . . leaning over backward in Russia's favor without once swaying from right to left."

Bob hated *Song of Russia*.

* * *

A week before Spangler Arlington Brugh was sworn into the United States Navy, Barbara and Bob became founding members of the Motion Picture Alliance for the Preservation of American Ideals. The Alliance was both a backlash against the guilds that in the last ten years had unionized the industry and a reaction against the robust leftism of intellectuals and artists of the New Deal. The Alliance members included people Barbara and Bob had worked with—directors Sam Wood, Clarence Brown, and King Vidor, fellow actors Gable, Cooper, Adolphe Menjou, and Charles Coburn. Also signing up were Russian-born author Ayn Rand, columnist Hedda Hopper, and a pair of labor leaders—Roy Brewer and Hollywood Teamster boss Joe Tuohy. Stanwyck, Hopper, and Rand were the only women originally, although Irene Dunne and Ginger Rogers joined later. Wardell (Ward) Bond, a barrel-chested football player turned actor, would bring his friend John Wayne to meetings. According to the organization's Statement of Principles, the Alliance was created because "in our special field of motion pictures, we resent the growing impression that this industry is made up of, and dominated, by communists, radicals and crackpots."

Wood was the fire in the belly of the Alliance. A former assistant to Cecil B. DeMille, he was good with actors and astute in picking his assignments. As a free-lance director, his credits were a string of successes, from Reagan's only hit, *Kings Row*, to *For Whom the Bell Tolls*. Hemingway's tale of an American (Gary Cooper) joining the partisans fighting Generalissimo Francisco Franco's fascist army was too leftist for Wood. In various rewrites and during filming in southern Arizona *For Whom the Bell Tolls* became a Cooper–Ingrid Bergman love story set in an undefined political struggle. Behind the director's crusading single-mindedness was also his anger at losing the Best Director Oscar for *Goodbye Mr. Chips* to Victor Fleming for *Gone with the Wind*. Wood invited anti-Communist crusaders to speak at the American Legion hall on Highland Avenue. He carried a little black notebook in which he jotted down the names of liberal "subversives," beginning with his own *For Whom the Bell Tolls* screenwriter Dudley Nichols.

The Alliance had the steadfast support of press magnate

William Randolph Hearst and counted in its ranks a number of antilabor zealots. One was Walt Disney, who in 1941 had squashed a strike by cartoonists, saying he would "close down the studio and sell toys" rather than meet the cartoonists' union demands. Disney brought to the Alliance writers Kevin McGuiness, Rupert Hughes, and Howard Emmett Rogers, a trio who, with Disney, had tried to thwart the creation of the Screen Writers Guild.

Bob was a staunch Republican who loved to discuss politics. Barbara shared the Alliance members' fears of subversion. From FDR's New Deal to Broadway, Hollywood and brother-can-you-spare-a-dime populism, leftist sentiments had been the cutting edge in the arts. Whether it was Odets flaying the corrupting nature of free enterprise in *Golden Boy* or the *Song of Russia* quintet praising the Soviet Union, Barbara and her husband were easily convinced that writers, with their facility for manipulating ideas, had become too powerful.

Barbara's up-by-the-bootstraps gumption was making her the highest-paid woman in the land. Like so many self-made people of humble beginnings, she didn't believe she owed society anything in return. It was all her doing, not the consequence of a climate favorable to rapid social climbing. On studio sets she went out of her way to be chummy with electricians, camera assistants, and makeup and wardrobe personnel. But she abhorred their sons and daughters going to college to learn to question the social order as much as she hated the opportunities screenwriters gave themselves to write New Deal or far-left ideas of a reordered social order into scripts in which she was asked to star. The Alliance stood for the kind of robust self-reliance that had always been hers, and she quickly opened her purse and her door to her fellow members. She hosted its meetings in her living room after Bob flew off to basic training and a commission as lieutenant junior grade (the customary rank conferred on men over thirty with a civilian pilot's license).

To create a stir that would reverberate beyond the reporting of the Hollywood trade press, the Alliance members decided to go over the heads of the industry and alert sympathetic politicians in Washington. On March 7, 1944, they sent a letter to archconservative North Carolina Democrat

Robert R. Reynolds inviting a congressional investigation of communism in Hollywood. Reynolds read the letter into the Congressional Record. Wood followed up with letters to the House Un-American Activities Committee. HUAC owed its existence to Samuel Dickstein, a Jewish representative from Manhattan's East Side who, in 1938, had wanted a congressional investigation of "native fascists." Dickstein had been maneuvered out of power by Congressman Martin Dies of Texas. Under Dies, the committee had dropped the original purpose of exposing American Nazis. After Pearl Harbor, the Dies Committee concentrated on Communists, aliens, and Jehovah's Witnesses (who refused to salute the flag and whose church was considered a hotbed for conscientious objectors).

The move by the Alliance against its own industry—by its nature perhaps the most collaborative enterprise in the country—was to have incalculable consequences. The future would punish Odets, three of the *Song of Russia* authors, a half-dozen other writers and directors who worked on movies starring Barbara Stanwyck or Robert Taylor, and scores of others.

In helping to organize the Alliance, Barbara and Bob were ratcheting up their basic conservatism, which was largely in keeping with the general mood of the country at the time. Hindsight has accustomed us to seeing Hollywood's right-wingers as an excitable, often vicious, and ultimately discredited crowd and the witch hunt they instigated as a national embarrassment. But to judge the 1940s and '50s through end-of-the-century eyes is somewhat facile. All too soon, a majority of citizens in America—and in the Soviet Union—would believe a nuclear World War III was inevitable. By 1952, even the liberal voice of Adlai Stevenson would warn that the country's enemies "planned total conquest of the human mind."

Double Indemnity

T aylor was nervous the first time we went up together,"
Lieutenant Tom Purvis would remember. "He was concerned that I was thinking to myself, 'These handsome
Hollywood stars don't take anything seriously except their
box-office ratings.' We got up to five thousand feet in an
open plane and I said, 'Get ready for a right slow roll. It was
perfect, but when we came out of it Taylor looked like he was
going to throw up. I asked him what was wrong.

"'Hell, I just lost my cigarette lighter,' he cried. 'It's down
there in the Mississippi River!'"

Purvis laughed and said, "So what?"

"'So what!' Bob came back. "'That was a solid gold Zippo
with a raised gold replica of the naval station emblem.
Barbara gave it to me. She'll flip her lid! What the hell do I
tell her? A $300 lighter is at the bottom of the Mississippi?'"

Purvis thought Bob should just tell his wife. "If you ask
me, it's almost funny."

"'You don't know Barbara.'"

After the first adjustments, Bob liked going from celebrity
to dog-tag serial number. On his completion of basic training
at the naval air station in Dallas, the navy assigned him to its
Aviation Volunteer Transport Division. He quickly became
all navy, caring little about what was going on at home. He
was dashing in uniform and on one of his furloughs posed
with Barbara for news cameras on their front step. He looked
awfully young in his crew cut next to Barbara in a dressing
gown with her hair in a bun.

Bob requested active duty overseas. He was turned down

on the grounds that at thirty-one he was too old for combat.
When he made a second request, he was told he was needed
as an instructor. He was never satisfied with that line of reasoning and suspected he was being denied overseas assignments because of his movie stardom. Barbara came to New
Orleans once while he was stationed there. Fearing her wifely
concerns might hurt his warrior image, he vetoed any publicity
in connection with her visit.

William Wellman was the director of *Lady of Burlesque*,
which had Barbara as a nightclub dancer solving a
string of backstage murders. When Gypsy Rose Lee decided
she was too old to be taking her clothes off in front of
strangers, the famous stripper tried writing. To everyone's surprise, *The G-String Murders* was a bestseller. James Gunn's
screenplay was less than lively, but as Dixie Daisy, Barbara
sang the Sammy Cahn–Harry Akst "Take It Off the E-String,
Play It on the G-String" and did comedy skits with Michael
O'Shea. Barbara tried to get Hermes Pan to work with her,
but *Lady of Burlesque* was a United Artists production and
Pan was at Fox doing *My Gal Sal*. Even without the choreographer, however, Wellman and Barbara managed to stand a
cliché on its head by staging a striptease in which she never
takes off a thing.

Iris Adrian was a hoofer who joined the cast and became
a friend of Stanwyck's. Six years younger than Barbara, Iris
was a spunky, laugh-a-minute dancer who had sixteen pictures to her credit. A recent arrival from Broadway, she had
worked with Frank Fay on the stage and knew Bette Keane, a
woman whose two-movie career came to a halt after Frank
made her pregnant. Except for an occasional nightclub or
variety-show appearance, Fay was virtually retired, but still
plotting his return to Broadway. Barbara wasn't interested in
knowing what Frank was doing, but Iris told her anyway.
"Frank quit drinking when I worked with him in 1939," Iris
remembered. She was irreverent enough to speculate about
the fidelity of absent husbands, Lieutenant Taylor included.

"I used to kid around with Barbara," she would recall.
"She was always busy, so busy she'd never have time to cheat
on Bob. Ha! Frank used to tell me Bob and Barbara were living in sin since the Fay-Stanwyck marriage had been per-

formed by a Catholic priest. He never said anything about his own two previous marriages."

Iris could see how Stanwyck and Wild Bill Wellman were great friends, how the director thought Barbara was a wonderful actress. He had just finished *The Ox-Bow Incident*, a lynch law parable that was to loom large in the postwar ideological struggle, and had a hard time concentrating on directing the bump-and-grind numbers of *Lady of Burlesque*. People were embarrassed for Barbara, wondering what she was trying to prove doing cartwheels, splits, and high-heel dancing in scanty clothes. Perhaps *Lady of Burlesque* was revenge for the screen version of *Burlesque* Frank had prevented her from doing when she was twenty-one.

If former chorus girl Ruby Stevens needed confirmation that she had made it, the Treasury Department listed Barbara Stanwyck as the woman who earned the most in 1944—over $400,000, or $3.5 million in 1994 money. Bette Davis was second.

Hollywood was on a roll. MGM hit its highest net income since 1937 and the industry's record gross to date— $166 million in period dollars. Profits continued to increase, and even RKO was making money after seven years of short-earned dividends, with hits that ranged from Disney's *Bambi* to Howard Hughes's celebrated and much-censored Jane Russell western, *The Outlaw*.

Barbara became a pen pal to twelve assorted servicemen, two of whom requested a giant poster of her in her scanty *Ball of Fire* costume for their mess hall. Their letters all started out with "Dear Babs," or "Barb," or "Hiya Stanny."

During the winter of 1943–44, Barbara made her most famous picture.

Before Billy Wilder even started thinking about adapting *Double Indemnity*, Paramount submitted James M. Cain's novel to the Production Code office. Joseph Breen wrote back on March 13, 1943, telling Paramount not even to consider a movie about a pair of adulterers who kill the woman's husband to collect on his insurance. The story was a blueprint for murder.

Front-office deference was due Paramount's hottest writer-director. Wilder and his writing partner, Charles Brackett, didn't suffer fools lightly, whether Luigi Luraschi, the studio's legal department head who dealt with the Production Code office, or Breen himself. While other writers on the payroll acted like serfs, Wilder and Brackett were as uncompromising as their brilliant track record. Since *Ball of Fire*, Wilder had become a director because, he said, he was tired of seeing others ruin his scripts. His first two pictures were *The Major and the Minor*, a frothy wartime comedy starring Ginger Rogers, and the espionage thriller *Five Graves to Cairo*, with Erich von Stroheim as Field Marshall Erwin Rommel. Luraschi told Wilder to go ahead with a first-draft screenplay.

Wilder's writing partner on *Double Indemnity* was not Brackett but Raymond Chandler. During the summer of 1943, they turned Cain's novelette into a vastly revised screenplay that was carnal and criminal well beyond 1940s screen conventions. With *Mildred Pierce*, *Double Indemnity* was the best of the James Cain adaptations. The former reporter and screenwriter knew how to make violence vivid on the page. *The Postman Always Rings Twice* (categorically rejected by the Breen Office) and *Double Indemnity* both told stories of women plotting with their lovers to murder their husbands. In a clever concession to Breen, they told the story in flashback. Article 1 of the Production Code's "Particular Applications" read that "crime shall never be presented in such a way as to throw sympathy with the crime as against law and justice, or to inspire others with a desire for imitation." The first person seen on the screen is the wounded insurance salesman Walter Neff (Fred MacMurray) confessing the sordid story of murder into a Dictaphone. His accomplice, now dead, is Phyllis Dietrichson (Stanwyck), their victim her Los Angeles oilman husband (Tom Powers).

Wilder and Chandler told the rest straightforwardly, how Neff falls for Phyllis and sells her husband an accidental life insurance policy, how they kill him and place the body on a railway track so they can claim the *Double Indemnity* clause for accidental death (such as a fall from a moving train). Taking the crime to its lurid and logical resolution, the script had the deadly lovers shoot each other in a final embrace.

Phyllis was utterly without redeeming qualities. Wilder

knew that two things mattered: *how* he told the story and getting Stanwyck.

Chandler hated the seven weeks he spent writing with Wilder.

"Working with Billy Wilder on *Double Indemnity* was an agonizing experience and has probably shortened my life, but I learned from it about as much about screenwriting as I am capable of learning, which is not very much," Chandler would write to his English publisher, Hamish Hamilton. "Like every writer, or almost every writer who goes to Hollywood, I was convinced in the beginning that there must be some discoverable method of working in pictures, which would not be completely stultifying to whatever creative talent one might happen to possess. But like others before me, I discovered that this was a dream." The collaboration also left Wilder baffled. As a nondrinker, he had a hard time understanding how an intelligent man like Chandler could let alcohol ruin his talent.

By December, the Breen Office was down to nit-picking. "As we advised you before," the Production Office wrote, "this whole sequence in the death chamber seems very questionable in its present form. Specifically, the details of the execution seem unduly gruesome."

If Wilder and Chandler needed a boost, they got it from Cain. The original author loved what they had done to his novel. "It's the only picture I ever saw made from my books that had things in it I wish I had thought of," Cain said. "Wilder's ending was much better than my ending, and his device for letting the guy tell the story by taking out the office dictating machine—I would have done it if I had thought of it. There are situations in the movie that can make your hands get wet, you get so nervous—like the place where Eddie Robinson comes in to talk to Fred MacMurray. Robinson is working close to what the murder explanation is—connecting MacMurray and Stanwyck. And *she* comes and is about to rap on MacMurray's door when she hears something and pulls back; the door opens and Eddie Robinson comes out with MacMurray, and she's hiding behind the door. I tell you, there for a minute, it is just beautiful. I wish I had thought of something like that."

* * *

The *Double Indemnity* script left Barbara deeply troubled. She had never been asked to play an out-and-out killer. "I thought, 'This role is gonna finish me,'" she would remember forty years later. But it was also the best script she had ever been offered. "It's brilliant, of course, but what's amazing is that not one word was changed while we were shooting. Billy had it all there, and I mean *all*—everything you see on the screen was in the script. The moves, the business, the atmosphere, all written.

"When I mention 'atmosphere' in *Double Indemnity*— that gloomy, horrible house the Dietrichsons lived in, the slit of sunlight slicing through those heavy drapes—you could smell that death was in the air, you understood why she wanted to get out of there, away, no matter how. And for an actress, let me tell you the way those sets were lit, the house, Walter's apartment, those dark shadows, those slices of harsh light at strange angles—all that helped my performance. The way Billy staged it and John Seitz lit it, it was all one sensational mood."

The picture was filmed at Paramount during the winter of 1943–44. Wilder rehearsed a lot before rolling the camera and told his two stars to underplay the violence. He wanted Phyllis Dietrichson to look cheap and insisted on outfitting her with a blond wig. Watching the first dailies of her prompted Paramount chief Buddy De Silva to grin, "We hire Barbara Stanwyck and here we get George Washington."

Wilder was happy with Barbara's lurid blonde engineering her husband's murder. MacMurray played the insurance salesman with just the right touch of flabby dishonesty. Fred went to the rushes and reported back to Barbara that what he saw of her on the screen was not someone acting but someone enjoying herself. "I remember saying, 'Fred, really, how was it?' And very candidly he looked at me and said, 'I don't know about you, but I was wonderful!' And that's such a true remark. Actors only look at themselves." After she saw herself at the press preview, she had a nice quote for reporters: "I'm afraid to go home with her. She's such a bitch."

Audiences were riveted—and servicemen went wild— when Stanwyck appeared in the blond wig, form-fitting white sweater, and ankle bracelet. Males in the Los Angeles preview theater in Westwood whistled for five minutes, drowning out the dialogue. "There goes my picture," thought Wilder. "The season's nattiest, nastiest, most satisfying melodrama," said *Time* when the film was released September 16, 1944.

The year also marked the return of Frank Fay. Broadway friends who spoke of him in the past tense were stunned to see him burst from oblivion to national sensation in *Harvey*. His uncanny timing, soft voice, and faraway looks as the balmy tippler Elwood P. Dowd turned Mary Coyle Chase's play into the wackiest Broadway hit of 1944. The droll tale of Dowd and his outsized imaginary rabbit was made for Fay. "Elwood, who on stage could easily become incredible or dismaying, is played to perfection," *Time* cooed. Fay's "manner is almost prim, his delivery slow, his material largely pointless. For one drawled gag like 'Had a date with a newspaperwoman the other night—yes, she keeps a stand,' there are a dozen droll nothings that are triumphs of timing, and intonation."

Ironically, Chase had written the play for Tallulah Bankhead and a four-foot canary named Daisy. Bankhead, who met the playwright after she saw *Harvey*, called Fay's performance one of the greatest she had ever seen. Actress Maggie Root, whose art director husband, John, designed the *Harvey* set, said of Fay, "Nobody could touch him, not even Jimmy Stewart." In period dollars, *Harvey* grossed $12 million in five years, earning Frank almost $538,000 in two years on Broadway and two thousand road performances. Again, screen stardom eluded Frank. When *Harvey* was filmed in 1949, James Stewart played the whimsical Elwood.

The stage success brought a lawsuit by Frank's second wife, Gladys Lee Buchanan, alleging he was $56,500 behind in alimony payments. He had promised to pay her $75 a week when they divorced in 1925 (and Frank was then making $17,500 a week for his twice-a-day Palace show). Payments had been made "sporadically" for a few years, then stopped, she charged. Frank countered that he had paid until 1936, when he became too poor. They settled out of court.

Wilder wanted Stanwyck to play Ray Milland's girlfriend in *The Lost Weekend*, but Jane Wyman got the part. For Barbara, the last year of the war passed quickly as she made sure she was working all the time. By the late spring of

1945, she had four movies ready for release. "I don't like it, to take things this fast, but it couldn't be helped this year," she told a *Los Angeles Times* reporter. When asked if she wasn't exhausted, she laughed it off. "I guess I'm just stagestruck."

She was in *Hollywood Canteen*, Warners' all-star service musical, written and directed by Delmer Daves. Joan Leslie, Robert Hutton, Dana Clark, and Janis Paige were the stars and besides Stanwyck, the Andrew Sisters, Jack Benny, Joe E. Brown, Eddie Cantor, Bette Davis, John Garfield, Sydney Greenstreet, Paul Henreid, Peter Lorre, Ida Lupino, Dennis Morgan, Roy Rogers, Alexis Smith, and Jane Wyman saluted the many people in showbiz entertaining servicemen. Joan Crawford agreed to appear in the picture after she was told that Davis and Stanwyck were in it.

As Hitler staged a last-gasp but stunning counteroffensive in eastern Belgium and Allied troops fought to beat it back in the murderous Battle of the Bulge, the Defense Department sent Bob to New York on a war-bond drive and to promote the navy documentary *The Fighting Lady*, directed by William Wyler. Barbara joined him and made sure they were seen together in nightclubs. Less happily, the Taylors displayed—and quickly tried to cover—a fault line in their marriage. The witness was the *Daily News* columnist Earl Wilson.

Movie stars in uniform usually had no qualms about sitting still for celebrity interviews. Bob, however, found it unmanly to be interviewed by a gossip columnist as a member of the armed forces. To save the day for Wilson, Barbara agreed to see the columnist and to speak for both of them. But when Wilson arrived at the Taylors' hotel suite, he was met by Bob. Barbara would be joining them shortly, he explained. Barbara showed up late and after saying hello rushed to the bathroom muttering that she needed a shower.

The two men chatted awkwardly while they eyed the bathroom door. Bob banged on it a couple of times.

Wilson finally left. His column the following day was devoted to Lieutenant Taylor. When Barbara ran into Wilson in a nightclub several days later, she apologized. Her explanation for holing up in the bathroom was that she should never have agreed to the interview. Why? Because

Bob was on official Defense Department business. As a loyal citizen, it was her duty not to overshadow her husband.

Wilson didn't believe a word of it.

Barbara was nominated for Best Actress for *Double Indemnity*. So was Bette Davis, for the seventh time, for *Mr. Skeffington*, Greer Garson, for the fourth year in a row, for *Mrs. Parkington*, Ingrid Bergman for *Gaslight*, and Claudette Colbert for *Since You Went Away*. Oscar night, March 15, 1945, came in the middle of a strike by set designers, illustrators, and decorators. Bergman won for *Gaslight*. On the way out, good sport Barbara told the press she was a fan of Ingrid's.

In *Christmas in Connecticut*, magazine columnist Stanwyck writes about a Connecticut farm she doesn't own, a husband she doesn't have, and recipes she never cooks. The predictable but brisk comedy was fun to make. Reginald Gardiner is the fiancé with the thin mustache who does have a farm, Sydney Greenstreet the publisher who invites himself for Christmas and mustn't find out. Dennis Morgan is the young sailor Barbara is forced to entertain, and S. Z. Sakall the schmaltzy Hungarian who saves the day. The director was Peter Godfrey. After making a start in acting and directing in London, Godfrey had come to Hollywood in 1939. With fellow Englishman Greenstreet, Peter had cast and crew in stitches with impromptu spoofs.*

Warner Brothers offered Stanwyck *Mildred Pierce*. Barbara was eager to play another James M. Cain character. Cain was a lot more squalid than Olive Higgins Prouty—the attention on money and its effect was virulent and unrelenting—but it was another *Stella Dallas* tale of a sacrificing mother. Hard work allows the heroine of the title to climb from waitress to restaurant owner, but she has a despicable daughter who takes everything her mother can provide, including her second husband, himself a manipulative hanger-on.

The producer was Jerry Wald, a former writer with the irritating habit of announcing projects before the stars he wanted said yes. His infectious enthusiasm made him steal

---

*Nearly fifty years later, Arnold Schwarzenegger directed Dyan Cannon and Kris Kristofferson in a TV remake of *Christmas in Connectiticut*.

lines from Oscar Levant and smuggle plot points from books into the films he produced. A fast-talking manipulator of the press and all the channels of ballyhoo, Wald was the weasely original for Budd Schulberg's *What Makes Sammy Run?* The screen adaptation of *Mildred Pierce* was not by Wald, however, but by Catherine Turney. A year older than Stanwyck, Turney was Warners' top melodramatist. She would write three films starring Stanwyck.

Wald wanted to bury the taboo subject of daughter seducing her stepfather in a murder mystery. When Turney couldn't deliver a scene of police grilling Mildred, the producer turned to Albert Maltz, a specialist in action movies who had scripted *This Gun for Hire* and *Destination Tokyo*.

Barbara didn't like the Turney-Maltz script. Billy Wilder had spoiled her for Cain adaptations. The *Mildred Pierce* screenplay had nothing of the corrosive brilliance of *Double Indemnity*. The final script was little more than the story of a dowdy housewife who suffers the nasty, semi-incestuous goings-on of her cad of a husband and ungrateful daughter. Bette Davis, who had first refusal on all Class A scripts at Warners, didn't want to play the mother of a sixteen-year-old. Ann Sheridan, who was offered one of the early scripts, thought Mildred was too tough and the daughter an absolute horror. Rosalind Russell also passed on it. Because Michael Curtiz was the director, Stanwyck said yes.

But Wald kept tinkering with the script—and casting possibilities. In yet another rewrite, Louise Randall Pierson added a feminist polish to the script while William Faulkner gave it a Southern male perspective, including a scene in which a black maid holds the forlorn Mildred in her arms and sings the spiritual "Sing Away." Wald thought Crawford would be great in the title role. With Jack Warner's approval, he sent her a script with a note telling her the final draft would be written by Ranald MacDougall, noted for transferring the Hemingway mystique to the screen. Joan called the producer the same night beaming with enthusiasm.

After learning that Curtiz was hostile to her, Crawford humbled herself. She might have been in fifty-nine films, she told Wald, but she didn't mind testing for him. In October 1944, she auditioned for Curtiz, who swore at her in his inimitable Hungarian English. "After the test," Joan claimed, "he forgot all about Stanwyck."

Barbara was angry. "I desperately wanted the part. I went after it. I knew what a role for a woman it was, and I knew I could handle every facet of Mildred. I laid my cards on the table with Jerry Wald. After all, I'd done a dozen pictures at Warner's, including *So Big* and *Meet John Doe*. I'd paid my dues. I felt Mildred was me."

Within a week of filming, Curtiz wanted Crawford fired and Stanwyck reinstated. For her screen test, Joan had forsaken her star gloss for bare simplicity. For the film itself, she had no intention of appearing drab and dowdy. Joan, in turn, asked Wald to fire the director. Producer, director, and star settled into an uneasy truce after Jack Warner threatened to close down production. By the time the film was finished, everybody knew Warners had a winner.

Mildred Pierce brought Crawford an Oscar.

Two months after *Mildred Pierce* slipped from her grasp, Stanwyck accepted another Catherine Turney adaptation, consoling herself that *My Reputation* was much more important. It spoke to a predicament many of the war's homefront women were confronting.

Two women had written the pseudonymous novel about a young widow who, in all innocence, dates an army officer and in so doing almost loses the love of her teenage son. The story dealt with the war's dislocation of home-front certitudes and of a woman freeing herself from children, a sick husband, and a domineering mother. Barbara thought it had some of the power of *Mrs. Miniver*. Greer Garson had not wanted to play *Mrs. Miniver* because, at thirty-two, she was asked to portray a woman old enough to have a twenty-year-old son. Barbara had no such qualms.

My Reputation would remain one of Barbara's favorite films, perhaps more for its bold intentions than the final product. The picture was a screen adaptation of Clare Jaynes's 1942 novel *Instruct My Sorrows*, the story of Jessica Drummond's first year of widowhood. After her husband dies, Jessica is left with plenty of money, two young sons, and fear of loneliness. Considering the Production Code strictures, Turney's screenplay was adult both in treatment and concept.

Director Curtis Bernhardt, however, was no William Wyler.

Where Wyler gave emotional intensity to *Mrs. Miniver's* personal drama and knew how to suggest the larger canvas, the emigré Bernhardt had little sense of the tensions, anxieties, and expectations of men and women trying to cope with the conflict of wartime morality. As Kurt Bernhardt, he had embarked upon a promising career in his native Germany, directing Marlene Dietrich. As a refugee in France, he had made movies with Jean Gabin and Jules Berry. Since reaching Los Angeles in 1940, he had made six pictures, including the brilliant police thriller *Conflict* with Humphrey Bogart and Sydney Greenstreet.

My Reputation was quickly shot on familiar sets. Barbara is a widow in the Chicago suburb of Lake Forest, tattled about for dispensing too soon with her weeds. George Brent is a deskbound major who, during the nervous months after Pearl Harbor, courts her. She keeps saying no when she means yes until his intentions become honorable.

Bernhardt rubbed Americans the wrong way during the waning days of the war. As the German refugee painstakingly explained to Barbara, Brent, and Eve Arden, Americans were hopelessly, indeed laughably, naive.

Both Turney and Stanwyck found him hard to work with. James Wong Howe was the film's true asset. The cameraman, who shot his first movie at Paramount in 1923 and was still photographing Barbra Streisand in *Funny Lady* in 1974, gave *My Reputation* its mood. He used extreme high-angle shots of Barbara to emphasize her feeling of emotional loneliness, making her appear small and powerless. Turney and Stanwyck never quite connected. The writer found Barbara cold and felt she couldn't get close to her.

Warners released *My Reputation* for viewing by servicemen overseas before bringing it out Stateside. Barbara cringed at reviews that called it a sob story. She never gave up on *My Reputation* and years later would say it tried to come to grips with the quandary of the comparatively young widow "who does start to go out with eligible men, and then the gossip starts."

23

Rand and Warner

During the filming of *My Reputation*, Stanwyck discovered a new book that set her imagination soaring. She read hundreds of novels a year, but she had never come across a character she felt she had to flesh out on the screen. Racing through *The Fountainhead* in one night and one morning at the studio, Barbara saw herself not only in Dominique, the rich and beautiful woman torn between two men, but in the book's hero. She didn't have Howard Roark's enormous ego, but she, too, had made herself. Didn't her success justify her faith in herself? Wasn't she her own best creation?

The 754-page novel was by her fellow member of the Motion Picture Alliance for the Preservation of American Ideals, Ayn Rand. If an author stood for muscular capitalism and disdain for the common herd, it was this Russian-born philosopher-novelist. Her hero was an architect of unbounded ego who over two decades fights a society mired in tradition and mediocrity. A theme of antiauthoritarianism that appealed to Barbara ran through the pages. Here was the answer to the mushy left, the bleeding hearts, whiny social reformers, union bosses, and people in general who couldn't pull up their own socks. Rand said everybody should want to fulfill himself or herself, that to believe in yourself was paramount. The independent mind, she said, "is the fountainhead of all human progress." Barbara saw herself as Dominique, a woman of such private values that she is offended if others love the same books or music as she. "It's the things we admire and want that bring us into submission," says Dominique Francon, who marries the book's villain and loves the hero.

Barbara called Jack Warner's secretary and said she had

to see the boss. On the appointed hour she rushed into his office, threw *The Fountainhead* on his desk, and told him to buy the screen rights.

Next, she talked to the author.

Rand, née Alice Rosenbaum, lived on Marlene Dietrich's old ranch in Chatsworth, near the former Marwyck spread. Her strong Russian accent jarred with her streamlined, American prose. She had lived in the United States over twenty years and in the mid-1930s had been a reader at Paramount. Her husband, Frank O'Connor, was a former DeMille actor who managed the thirteen-acre ranch. Their friends included the lavender couple Janet Gaynor and MGM designer Adrian, whose theatrical clothes Ayn wore on dressy occasions. Rand was two years older than Stanwyck. Waving her long cigarette holder as she talked, she told Barbara she had written *The Fountainhead* heroine for Garbo.

"But Miss Garbo is not available," Barbara retorted. "I would just love to do it, because I understand this woman."

Jack Warner bought *The Fountainhead* and gave in to the headstrong author's demand that she adapt her book. Mervyn LeRoy agreed to direct with Humphrey Bogart as Roark, Stanwyck as Dominique.

Rand had done some screenwriting for Jerry Wald, but reducing her long novel to a 110-minute screen story was not easy. Nor was the character of Dominique, who leaves Roark because she can't bear seeing him destroyed and marries a newspaper tycoon in a deliberate act of self-destruction, only to join a triumphant Roark. Rand herself admitted Dominique was, if taken literally, "quite stupid" and suggested readers should see her "more as the projection of a certain attitude, taken to an extreme—an idealist paralyzed by disgust." She called Dominique "myself on a bad day."

While Stanwyck waited for the war to end, Bob dutifully telephoned every Sunday night. He was transferred to a naval base in Illinois, where, pending his discharge, he was still a flying instructor. One young student of his was twenty-year-old Roy Scherer Fitzgerald, who had been assigned to the Aviation Repair and Overhaul Unit and a tour of duty in the Philippines. When they met the next time, Roy was Rock Hudson.

More bored with her own boredom than anything else, Barbara fleshed out the last months of the European conflict filming *The Two Mrs. Carrolls* with Humphrey Bogart. Both were miscast in the adaptation of Martin Vale's play that had been a Broadway triumph for Victor Jory and Elisabeth Bergner.

Bogart is Geoff Carroll, an American in England with a small daughter (Ann Carter). He is a painter slowly going mad. He falls in love with Englishwoman Sally Morton (Stanwyck) and marries her. The couple settle in an English village, where Sally hears rumors that Geoff killed his first wife shortly after painting her in a portrait called *Angel of Death*. Sally discovers her husband has a similar portrait of her stashed away in the attic. Unfortunately, the screenplay by Thomas Job eliminated the first Mrs. Carroll and with her the play's big shocker—a scene in which the first Mrs. Carroll calls to warn Sally that Geoff is poisoning her nightly glass of milk. A very young and aggressive Alexis Smith plays a neighbor and would-be third Mrs. Carroll. The ending packs a wallop. Sally comes to realize what is going on when she invades her husband's locked studio and sees the distorted *Angel of Death* Dorian Gray–type portrait he has painted of her. Geoff crashes into her locked bedroom through a window, to be met by her brandishing a revolver. He subdues her and nearly strangles her with a curtain cord before her old beau (Pat O'Moore) and police burst in.

Offscreen, Bogart was plotting to divorce one wife so he could marry another. Mayo Methot was the actress who had set him on fire in 1930 and had become his third wife. Mayo's looks and figure had collapsed in alcoholism and in hideous scenes in which he goaded her until she started hurling bottles at him or, on one occasion, went after him with a carving knife. Now he wanted out so he could marry his nineteen-year-old leading lady in *To Have and Have Not*—Lauren Bacall.

Stanwyck and Bogart shared the same business manager, Morgan Maree. Bogart was the son of a painter. His mother was the fashionable New York portraitist and magazine illustrator Maud Humphrey, his father the noted physician Belmont De Forest Bogart. Between takes, Bogie told Barbara his mother had painted his portrait when he was one year old.

Behind the tough, hardened persona that Bogie perfected even offscreen, behind the sallow complexion and mocking smile, Barbara discovered a caustic, urbane, sophisticated man. There were emotional disturbances in the family, he told her. He had brought his mother to Los Angeles and was paying for her and his elder sister's institutionalized care. He was forty-six and in a ceremony squeezed in during *The Two Mrs. Carrolls* he married Lauren Bacall. Both bride and groom wept copiously during the ceremony.

The press was all over the newlyweds. Bogart was always good for a few punchy quotes, and Charlie Einfeld, Warners' publicity chief, took care of the Humphrey Bogart image. Barbara profited from the short hiatus Warners granted the Bogarts to visit Bob in Chicago. On her return she told reporters asking her if she had any plans, "How can anybody have plans until the war is over?" Bogie joked about Barbara being married to pretty Bob. "I'm not good looking," he admitted. "I used to be. Not like Robert Taylor. What I have is I've got character on my face. It takes an awful lot of late night drinking to put it there."

The Two Mrs. Carrolls was Stanwyck's second film with Godfrey. The English director, who gave himself a small part as a racetrack tout in the film, introduced Barbara to his wife Renee, a former Miss American Venus who had met Godfrey when she came west from a modeling career in New York. Barbara found Peter and Renée appealing. Going to dinner with them Friday nights soon became a routine.

As a director, Godfrey indulged his male lead, letting Bogart mug outrageously. But by constantly hinting at Geoff Carroll's insanity, Godfrey undercut the suspense. Warners held up the thriller's release for two years, and when it did come out it was laughed off the screen.*

Barbara worked nonstop while waiting for Bob's demobilization and in *The Bride Wore Boots* made a tolerably light comedy with Robert Cummings, Diana Lynn, and Robert Benchley. Cummings played Stanwyck's husband in this battle of the sexes that ends with hubby riding an old nag to victory, thereby winning back his wife. The director was Irving

---

*The film would be rediscovered by the French New Wave in the 1960s and, together with *Cry Wolf*, Godfrey's 1947 thriller with Stanwyck and Errol Flynn, earn praise as a superb *policier*.

Pichel, an escapee from Republic's low-budget pictures who had just scored with *Tomorrow Is Forever*, a conjugal drama starring Claudette Colbert, Orson Welles, George Brent, and eight-year-old Natasha Gurdin. Pichel changed Gurdin's name to Natalie Wood, after his director friend Sam Wood, and put her in *The Bride Wore Boots*. Barbara found Benchley the most entertaining member of the cast. He told her everybody becomes the type of person he or she hates most.

Ayn Rand finished her uncompromising *Fountainhead* script in six months. As sales of her book reached 400,000 in hardback, Jack Warner decided the film should be a major production. However, the story line requirement that Howard Roark blow up a housing development based on a castrated version of his architectural designs caused the War Production Board to cancel *The Fountainhead* on the ground that demolishing scarce housing stock amounted to despoiling strategic materials. Instead of fighting Washington, Warner decided to wait until wartime restrictions could be lifted. Director availability and the "major" picture status would bring King Vidor and Gary Cooper to the project in 1947. There was talk of a younger actress. Vidor didn't think Stanwyck was sexy enough to play Dominique. Ida Lupino, who often got the parts Bette Davis dismissed, was mentioned. In the end newcomer Patricia Neal was cast.

Barbara was furious. On June 21, 1948, she sent a telegram to Jack Warner:

DEAR JACK:

A COUPLE OF YEARS HAVE GONE BY SINCE I MADE A FILM FOR YOU AND SINCE THEN I AM SURE YOU WILL AGREE THAT THE SCRIPTS SUBMITTED TO ME HAVE NOT COMPARED WITH "THE FOUNTAINHEAD." I READ IN THE MORNING PAPERS TODAY YOUR OFFICIAL ANNOUNCEMENT THAT MRS. PATRICIA NEAL IS GOING TO PLAY THE ROLE OF "DOMINIQUE" IN "THE FOUNTAINHEAD." AFTER ALL, JACK, IT SEEMS ODD AFTER I FOUND THE PROPERTY, BROUGHT IT TO THE ATTENTION OF THE STUDIO, HAD THE STUDIO PURCHASE THE PROPERTY, AND DURING THE PREPARATION OF THE SCREENPLAY EVERYONE ASSUMED THAT I WOULD BE IN THE PICTURE, AND NOW I FIND

SOMEONE ELSE IS DEFINITELY PLAYING THE ROLE. NATU-
RALLY, JACK, I AM BITTERLY DISAPPOINTED.

HOWEVER, I CAN REALISTICALLY SEE YOUR PROBLEMS,
AND BASED ON ALL OF THE CIRCUMSTANCES IT WOULD
APPEAR TO BE TO OUR MUTUAL ADVANTAGE TO TERMI-
NATE OUR PERSONAL CONTRACTUAL RELATIONSHIP. I
WOULD APPRECIATE HEARING FROM YOU.

KINDEST PERSONAL REGARDS.

The moviegoers' romance with Hollywood was cooling.
By 1948, studios were negotiating early ends to star contracts,
and Warner obligingly thanked Barbara for firing herself.
"Naturally your interest in this property is well understood,
but our studio does not confine its operations to cases where
people bring in books and other stories and we buy them solely
on their suggestion," Warner wrote in his next day's reply.
"Since our actions have offended you and you desire to terminate your contract with us, it may be that, under the circumstances, this would be the best thing to do."

The Fountainhead "no-go" would remain a disappointment for Mervyn LeRoy as well. "For weeks we had gradually
whittled away at the book's 754 pages and had forged what I
think was an excellent screenplay," LeRoy would remember.
"Nothing came of it. That production would have to be
classed as a war casualty."

Barbara turned forty-one three weeks after backing out of
the Warner Brothers contract. *The Fountainhead* was her first
defeat to a younger actress.

24

Uneasy Peace

Bob's discharge came on November 5, 1945. Barbara was filming *The Strange Love of Martha Ivers* at Paramount when a telegram announced his homecoming. She rushed to Burbank airport, where her husband told reporters he wasn't sure how he'd feel about civilian life. "I met some great guys," he said. "It's rough splitting up as a group."

Bob looked as gorgeous as ever. Once Barbara and he were back behind closed doors, she played her most degrading scene—pleading with a man who didn't desire her to make love to her. He said he couldn't, that he had a prostate problem. She told him to see a doctor. Jane Ellen Wayne, Robert Taylor's biographer, quotes an unnamed psychologist telling Bob he was comparing Barbara to his mother, that no man was aroused by his mother in bed and the only way to restore his libidinous confidence was to have an affair with another woman. Viege Traub, a psychiatrist who treated a number of sexually dysfunctional actors, and knew Taylor and assumed he was gay, would find the two-mothers analogy atypical. A more likely cause would be the returning star's fear of somehow damaging his own success.

Behind her husband's professed prostate difficulty and his armed forces jargon, Barbara detected defiance against the responsibilities and improvisations of civilian life. He had never seen combat, but like so many returning soldiers, he was full of moralistic self-righteousness. Questions were never in doubt in the armed forces, issues were clear-cut and one-sided. In retrospect, life in uniform took on a rosy hue. Money hadn't mattered. The military was a tight-knit fraternity with precise and straightforward rules. "You know exactly who you are and what's expected of you," he said. Ronald Reagan was also shocked to come home and see the war effort had not reformed anyone. "I learned that a thousand bucks under the table was the formula for buying a new car," he would recall. "I learned that the real-estate squeeze was on for the serviceman. I discovered that the rich had got just a little richer and a lot of the poor had done a good job of grabbing a quick buck."

Bob resented men who had holed up at the studios (a "heart murmur" had excused Errol Flynn from serving). After a first luncheon at the MGM commissary, he came home saying there were too many new faces. It offended him that the war had made their old friend Zeppo Marx a millionaire. Zep had realized there was more money in the war effort than in actors' "ten percenting." After Frank Orsatti died, Zep left the talent agency in the hands of his brother, founded a company making coupling devices, and employed five hundred people. His company concentrated on U.S. Air Force procurement and clinched the contract for the clamping devices that carried the atomic bombs over Japan. He divorced Marion and was living in Palm Springs with a former Las Vegas showgirl twenty years his junior.

Bob returned to work, unhappy and confused. He hated more than ever the movies Louis B. Mayer had put him in before the war, the romantic parts that had made him a star. To him, the matinee idol roles the studio regarded as money in the bank were insults to his self-respect. He wanted to be a man's man on the screen, a guy like him, who rode, worked horses, hunted, fished, and loved big-sky country. As a welcome home gift, MGM presented him with a $7,500 twin-engine Beechcraft, and assigned his navy buddy Ralph Couser as his copilot. Bob and Ralph flew everywhere in the plane.

Barbara was jealous of her husband's all-male circle. When Couser phoned, she angrily yelled, "Hey, Bob, your wife wants to talk to you!"

Hollywood was turning its attention to peacetime opportunities. With a worldwide weekly audience of 235 million wanting new entertainment, MGM served up profits of $18 million, their highest ever, although gross income was slightly down. Paramount racked up a fantastic $39 million profit; Fox and Warners $22 million each. Many of the best creative minds wanted a new, freer, more relevant cinema. Returning Majors and Colonels Capra, Wyler, and George Stevens formed Liberty Films and started out on a happy foot with Capra's *It's a Wonderful Life*. "Gable's back and Garson's got him!" proclaimed the *Adventure* posters for Clark Gable's first postwar movie.

In response to audiences bored with maturing stars in formula entertainment, MGM was grooming a new crop of performers—Van Johnson, Cornel Wilde, Frank Sinatra, and Peter Lawford. Since 1916, the *Exhibitors Herald* had charted moviegoer comments across the United States and Canada. By March 1946, theater owners reported audiences spurning Spencer Tracy and Katharine Hepburn in *Without Love* and in their next effort, *The Sea of Grass*.

Bob was nevertheless happy when the studio assigned him to star with Hepburn in *Undercurrent*. Louis B. also wanted to test the chemistry of Bob and newcomer Robert Mitchum, whom William Wellman had catapulted to stardom as Lieutenant Walker in *The Story of G.I. Joe*, one of the most convincing films of the war. Mitchum was cast as Bob's good-guy brother and Hepburn's husband in the suspense thriller about a woman menaced by the mystery surrounding her brother-in-law. "I'm sure we'll get along," Hepburn told director Vincente Minnelli at the first read-through. Both Minnelli and Taylor thought the remark was as much a threat as an invitation to camaraderie.

Minnelli and Hepburn were at loggerheads throughout the shoot of what was new territory for both. Minnelli's specialty was musicals, and his forte was making films look beautiful and move gracefully. He had directed only one straight drama, *The Clock*, starring his soon-to-be wife, Judy Garland. *Undercurrent* was Hepburn's first thriller, and she had a hard time getting "the right horrified reactions." Compared with the assignments handed to MGM's other returning GIs, however, Bob still considered himself lucky. He had a strong script, a dazzling partner, and a chance to play a heavy. Gene Kelly was put in a new *Ziegfeld Follies* movie to dance with Fred Astaire. For Red Skelton, the studio trundled out *The Show-Off*, a Broadway staple already filmed three times. For Mickey Rooney it was back to playing Andy Hardy.

Stanwyck caught the updraft of the new genre moviegoers were beginning to enjoy—the film noir with its predilection for ambiguity, entrapment, sexual obsession, and vortex of crime. The studios liked the new class of action pictures as a replacement for the prewar B pictures because the films noirs could be shot on existing sets and easily promoted on the basis of sensational or violent story lines. *Double Indemnity* made Barbara an arresting choice when Hal Wallis and Paramount cast *The Strange Love of Martha Ivers*, in which the heroine is twice the hard-boiled, lustful Phyllis Dietrichson.

Like Zanuck before him, Wallis had become too successful for Jack Warner. After more than ten years heading up WB production, Wallis set himself up as an independent producer. Doing *The Strange Love of Martha Ivers* for him was, in Barbara's mind, a guarantee of taste and some daring. His choice of material ran toward adaptations of romantic novels and stories that didn't pigeonhole his productions in routine categories. *The Strange Love of Martha Ivers* was a twisted love triangle, an irresistible star vehicle about a murderous child who becomes a wealthy woman with a spineless husband. The drama begins when a former boyfriend returns to town. To make the movie, Wallis hired the writer and the director of the vivid war film *A Walk in the Sun*—Robert Rossen and Lewis Milestone.

Wallis and Milestone borrowed Van Heflin and Roman Bohnen from MGM and, at Lauren Bacall's recommendation, brought out a promising Broadway actor to make his screen debut—Kirk Douglas. "I knew I was taking a risk pitting a newcomer against that powerhouse, Stanwyck," Wallis would say of casting Kirk Douglas, "but she was extraordinarily considerate and played unselfishly with him in every scene."

Milestone knew how to grab an audience. He concentrated the action in night scenes, contrasting the opulent mansion of the corrupt rich with seedy third-rate motels, bars, blind alleys, and garages. As the wealthy neurotic of the title, Stanwyck gave a bravura performance. Toward the conclusion, she stands at the top of a long curving staircase, her arms slung over Van Heflin, urging him to finish off Kirk Douglas, who has collapsed in a drunken stupor below. Her face freezes into blank disbelief when Heflin fails to kill her husband. At the film's end, she embraces Douglas and tells him she will again love him. She smiles when he presses a gun into her stomach because she doesn't believe he has the guts to kill her.

Within weeks of the October 1945 filming start, *The Strange Love of Martha Ivers* was caught in a vicious labor dispute that set the stage for heightened ideological struggle and turned Stanwyck into a scab. During the war, the American Federation of Labor had pledged there would be no strikes before V-J Day. Japan's surrender in August brought a rising tide of strikes, shutdowns, and threats of strikes in oil, automobiles, coal, textiles, and many other industries. Enough of sacrifice was the word, time to concentrate on making money.

The film industry was 90 percent unionized in 1945, and on the surface the feud was an internecine David and Goliath dispute between a coalition of reformers and the sixteen-thousand-member labor umbrella organization, the International Alliance of Theatrical and Stage Employees (IATSE). Before the war, seventy-seven set decorators had formed their own union and in 1943 strengthened their little local by affiliating with the painters' union. IATSE wanted to represent the painters, but George Brown, the IATSE president, was in jail for racketeering, and the studios signed with the new combined decorators-painters union. Under its chief Herbert Sorrell ("I'm just a dumb painter"), the union was everything IATSE was not—leftist and honest. After winning a vicious fight with Walt Disney over the right to organize cartoonists, it quickly grew into the nine local Conference of Studio Unions.

Crossing the Conference picket lines was in total accord with Barbara's political convictions. While she, Douglas, Heflin, Milestone, and crew tried to concentrate on their scripted mayhem, nearly eight hundred members of the Conference marched outside Warner Brothers in Burbank and, to prevent IATSE workers from going to work, overturned three cars. People fought with knives, clubs, battery cables, and chains in the middle of Barham Boulevard while

Jack Warner and his executives on a stage roof watched Burbank police and Warner guards beat back the Conference picketers with clubs and spray them with fire hoses. The next day eighty people were injured in a pitched battle. The combined force of police, guards, and IATSE workers beat back the strikers. Roving groups of pickets arrived at Paramount.

"We continued to shoot, but it meant we were locked in at the studio—if we went out, we couldn't get back in," Douglas would remember. "Milestone favored the strikers, and went across the street to Oblath's restaurant, where a lot of strike supporters discussed it over coffee. For a while, the picture was directed by Byron Haskin. I felt guilty. What was I supposed to do? Stanwyck was working."

Milestone, Stanwyck, Douglas, *Martha Ivers*, and the rest of Hollywood were saved by Washington. At the end of October, the National Labor Relations Board ruled that the set decorators were entitled to join the painters. The studios and IATSE gave way. For Sorrell and his allies, however, it was a Pyrrhic victory. The cries of communist infiltration grew louder.

B ob and Barbara found readjusting to each other difficult. Whatever efforts to sustain a sexual relationship they had managed before were dropped. She possessed drive, energy, and ambition and was almost entirely self-directed. Bob successively surrendered the direction of his life to his mother, MGM, his wife, and the navy. *Double Indemnity* made her the quintessential actress of animal ambition—the tough, independent woman. The navy had shaped Bob in ways that made him rebel against his wife.

Few people were invited to their home, and those who did were appalled at what they saw and heard. It was painful to listen to her yell at Bob and to see him take it. She forbade conversation about guns, fishing rods, and airplanes. John Wayne would remember an evening at the Taylors when, after Barbara retired, the men drank downstairs and told tall yarns about fishing trips on which bears sniffed their sleeping bags. Suddenly, Barbara appeared in her nightgown on the top of the stairs and ordered Bob to bed. Recalled Wayne, "It was so humiliating for Bob that we all went home. He took it—in front of all those guys, my God."

Dion remained on the periphery. When he was twelve at summer camp and got a fishing spear through his leg, he was hospitalized for four or five days. "The doctors phoned my mother," he would recall. "I waited and waited for her to come, she never so much as called."

On the boy's level, neither Barbara nor Bob ran the household. Uncle Buck did. If anyone showed concern for Dion it was Millie Stevens's onetime lover. Barbara barely saw or spoke to Dion; nor did she talk about him. If reporters asked, Helen Ferguson came up with excuses, blaming the Taylors' marriage for Barbara's lack of interest in Dion. Bob claimed it was not his place to interfere. "Except for his bad grades, he was not a bad kid," Bob would recall. "It was hard to reach the kid because he saw nothing of his mother and father and had no personal affection, attention or direction."

Dion changed his name. After being Dion and Skippy, he was now Tony. His teenage years were difficult. With no love and little supervision from anyone except Uncle Buck, he was in scrapes that bordered on delinquency. In 1947, Barbara sent him half the continent away to the Culver Military Academy in Indiana. The military boarding school had a reputation for turning rebellious youngsters into little stalwarts in uniform and featured such traditions as hazings and older boys tormenting newcomers. The lifelong alienation of mother and son was cemented when she enrolled him in the academy. After a brief summer visit, Dion didn't see his mother for the next four years, as he never dared to come home without an invitation.

Barbara and Bob were in pictures that strangely echoed their subconscious sentiments. In *Cry Wolf* she can't be sure her husband is really her husband; in *The High Wall* he can't remember whether he murdered his wife.

Turning stars into producers was the studios' way of forgoing salary raises. New tax laws allowed producers to pay capital gains instead of income taxes on their earnings. To Jack Warner's considerable annoyance, Bette Davis took her producership seriously on *A Stolen Life*, scripted by Catherine Turney and directed by Curtis Bernhardt.

Errol Flynn didn't. He had top billing in *Cry Wolf*, but to Barbara's relief, he was totally indifferent to the functions of producer. Catherine Turney had adapted the Marjorie Carleton mystery bestseller. Barbara's friend Peter Godfrey directed, and Flynn sleepwalked through the film, his attention riveted on an upcoming expedition off Baja California that would include marine specialists from the Scripps Oceanographic Institute in San Diego and allow him to take a hefty tax write-off on his refurbished 118-foot yacht. A dark-house thriller with a hackneyed ending, *Cry Wolf* had Barbara claim her former husband Flynn's estate only to run into his mysterious uncle—and double—an uncommonly rigid Flynn. *Cry Wolf* was Stanwyck's most physical picture. Turney's script and Godfrey's direction had her batter down doors, run across tile roofs in spiked heels, and hoist herself up a dumbwaiter shaft.

Bob's *High Wall* was Metro's answer to Paramount's *Lost Weekend*. If Billy Wilder had persuaded Ray Milland to forgo his usual lightweight roles to impersonate an alcoholic on a binge that lands him in the psychiatric ward, why couldn't MGM's Robert Taylor play a guy going crazy in a rubber room? Bob tried his best as a war veteran in a mental ward after confessing he has killed his wife, but as Barbara had realized in *My Reputation*, director Curtis Bernhardt was no Wilder. Bob dutifully went berserk under the care of asylum doctor Audrey Totter, but the unconvincing whodunit eventually revealed he had been drugged when he confessed and that Herbert Marshall was the murderer.

The Bride Wore Boots was Barbara's first outright box-office bomb since the mid-1930s. Audiences were confused by *The Two Mrs. Carrolls*, released two years after it was made. At best, *Cry Wolf* was a thriller with a silly ending.

Stanwyck starred with Ray Milland in *California*, a rip-roaring, expensive adventure about California's 1848 bid for statehood with Barbara as a crooked politician's mistress. For her screen introduction, the frontier town's respectable ladies toss her, bags and baggage, out of a hotel and into a mud puddle. The director was John Farrow, and Barbara's forcing him to apologize to an actor made the rounds at the Screen Actors Guild. The Australian war veteran (and father of Mia) misused and humiliated the actor until Stanwyck walked off the set and refused to return until Farrow made amends before the entire crew.

To cap a busy year, Barbara got to play the doomed heroine

that had slipped from her grasp when David Selznick sold *Dark Victory* to Warner Brothers and Bette Davis's portrayal of the young woman dying of a brain tumor earned her a 1939 Academy Award nomination. *The Other Love* was based on Erich Maria Remarque's short novel *Beyond* and the similarities to the George Emerson Brewer, Jr.–Bertram Block play were striking. Where *Dark Victory*'s Judith Traherne had been a Long Island socialite, *The Other Love*'s Karen Duncan was a concert pianist. But both woman had doctors who fall in love with them, and both are tempted by last flings before redemption. Less daring than Judith Traherne's malignant brain tumor, Karen dies of consumption. David Niven played the doctor, who, for a last indulgence, takes her to the Riviera and an encounter with gambler Richard Conte. Niven and Conte looked uncomfortable with their parts and Barbara too serenely healthy for audiences to believe she was dying of consumption. Breathless publicity handouts told how Stanwyck practiced the piano three hours a day for a month so she could master the movements. On the day of the recording, however, the pianist Ania Dorfmann was hired. Her hands did not photograph like Stanwyck's. In close-ups, André Previn's youthful pianist hands were found to be a near-perfect match to Barbara's hands.

Stanwyck was the subject of intense glamour reporting. "She's that rarity of rarities—an actor's actor," wrote Dorothy Manners. "Ask the gang around the studios what they think of Barbara Stanwyck and you get the same answer from costar to prop boy: 'She's a swell guy.'" Manners reported that Barbara's favorite color was ruby red, her favorite perfume Tabu, that she brushed her hair one hundred strokes daily, ate a large breakfast, and then nothing until dinner. Louella Parsons was so struck by Stanwyck's finesse and polish that she had to remind herself of Barbara's humble beginnings. Hedda Hopper reported that the afternoon she dropped in on the Taylors, Bob had given Barbara a workout on the tennis court. "She was glowing with health," wrote Hopper, "her skin was tanned to a golden bronze. There's not a wrinkle in her face. She looks like a girl in her late twenties."

The Stanwyck-Taylor marriage ranked as one of Hollywood's strongest and healthiest. As promulgated by the Helen Ferguson Agency and echoed in the columns of

Hopper, Parsons, Manners, Sidney Skolsky, and the new Dorothy Kilgallen, Barbara and Bob were a fun couple who knew how to cover their differences with humor. They were portrayed as partners in a charming, congenial relationship, happy in their work, their home, devoted to their careers and each other. Tellingly perhaps, Dion disappeared from the fan press coverage. While a December 1946 Barbara Stanwyck feature by Manners referred to "young Tony" in the next-to-last paragraph, Parsons's May 1947 column called 1947 the "Barbara Stanwyck year," and Hopper's "Barbara and Bob" feature two months later no longer mentioned him.

25

Bearing Witness

Metro's answer to a shrinking box office was to buy and film bestselling novels. Even if the price was often inflationary and the time lag between literary success and release of the movie version a continuous peril, such source material was considered "presold." Linda Darnell starred in a much-bowdlerized version of Kathleen Winsor's sensational *Forever Amber*, Danny Kaye got the title role in the screen version of James Thurber's *The Secret Life of Walter Mitty*. William Lindsay Gresham's *Nightmare Alley* was filmed with Tyrone Power, Betty MacDonald's *The Egg and I* with Claudette Colbert. MGM brought John P. Marquand's *The Late George Apley* to the screen with Ronald Colman in the title role, and Alfred Hitchcock chose to adapt Robert Hichens's *The Paradine Case*.

Barbara signed to do Marquand's current bestseller, *B. F.'s Daughter*. It would be her first for MGM since working with Bob in *His Brother's Wife* ten years earlier. *B. F.'s Daughter* was number one on the bestseller list, and the title role was one of the top women's parts of the year. The picture was to start shooting in late October.

Bob was terribly frustrated when he wasn't cast in Sam Wood's *Command Decision*, the story of a general and his staff debating the aerial bombardment of Germany that featured many of his friends and rivals—Clark Gable, Walter Pidgeon, Van Johnson, Brian Donlevy, John Hodiak, Charles Bickford, Edward Arnold, Marshall Thompson, and Richard Quine. Bob felt so humiliated he refused to be seen at lunch at the studio commissary.

With no parts lined up for him, Louis B. allowed Taylor to make a short trip to Europe. The sight of Bob's tortured reaction to being passed over made Barbara want to indulge him. She was free until the start of *B. F.'s Daughter*. She had never been to Europe. And Helen kept telling her she needed a vacation.

They would go to Paris first, then travel through Holland and Belgium, perhaps get a glimpse of defeated Germany, before going to London, where they agreed to attend the British premiere of *The Other Love*. Gossip columns hinted the real reason for the trip was to shore up the marriage. Barbara, it was suggested, was desperately trying to find a way to keep her young husband.

Only once before had Barbara stood on the French Line pier in Manhattan. It was almost nineteen years ago that she had waved au revoir to Rex Cherryman and expected to follow him to Paris. Since then, she had married twice and become a star and a millionaire.

Bob and Barbara arrived at Le Havre on February 20, 1947.

Two years after the war's end, Paris and London were cities of diminished perspectives, shadows of their prewar glitter, and, for a pair of American movie stars, scrawny, drab, and dingy places of underheated hotels, temperamental telephones, and often surly, envious natives. Rationing was still in effect in Britain, and to American eyes even the meals served at the Savoy seemed tiny and uninviting.

The trip turned into a nightmare.

Their suite at Paris's George V was freezing. To Louella Parsons, Barbara would claim she had never suffered so much from the cold, and she took to spending her nights at the American Hospital in suburban Neuilly. The press sniffed a scandal and pressed Bob for an explanation. Lamely, he told reporters the most luxurious suite in Paris's luxury hotel was too cold for his wife. Enterprising reporters spoke to hospital nurses and shadowed Barbara. "Several times Miss Stanwyck has driven into Paris for dinner with Taylor but went right back to her hospital bed," a February 24 news wire dispatch reported.

Barbara was out of her depth and made a fool of herself wherever they went. After seeing the Folies-Bergère show, she told the press she was surprised to see "thousands of girls running around with just a piece of chiffon on." Charitably, no one reminded the former chorine that, in a famous Ziegfeld Shadowgraph tableau, she had once stood bare-chested on a New York stage. She offended the reviving couture industry by visiting several salons and buying nothing. "I think American designers did a terrific job during the war with inferior material," she sniffed, "and I think American women who go over buying French fashions are unfair."

From Paris, the Taylors went to Belgium. They liked Brussels more than Paris, and Barbara bought her husband a classic hunting rifle. They were disappointed that an invitation to fly to Germany came too late. Instead, a pair of MGM officials accompanied them to Holland, where Bob insisted on showing her Volendam, a town he had visited during the making of *A Yank in Oxford*. From Antwerp they crossed the English Channel for the only official function of their trip. United Artists publicized the Taylors' attendance at the April 2 London premiere of *The Other Love*.

Five hundred people surged through police lines as the stars' limousine approached the Empire Theatre. Three hundred feet from the floodlit, red-carpet entrance, fans mobbed the car. A woman grabbed Barbara's leg and wouldn't let go while a man grasped her hair. Bob had to be carried into the cinema by police.

The return voyage aboard the S.S. *America* was uneventful except for Stanwyck's seasickness and her heated reaction to European fellow travelers complaining too loudly about the shipboard service. In a tirade that the ocean liner's public relations officer telexed to the news services in New York, Stanwyck was quoted as snapping, "When American troops were going overseas not so long ago, we didn't hear any of you complaining about American service. You were pretty damn happy to see those GIs when they liberated Paris. You were pretty damn happy to get American food and supplies from the American Red Cross." On a ship-to-shore hookup, the Taylors were interviewed for the Louella Parsons radio program. Barbara and Bob sat up drinking black coffee with the captain until the 1:00 A.M. airtime. Barbara was so seasick she didn't think she would last through the broadcast. Bob had to hold her.

Getting off in New York didn't lighten her mood. *Harvey* was in its fourth year on Broadway, but when reporters asked her if she would see it, she snapped, "Not likely. I saw all the rabbits Frank Fay had to offer a long time ago."

Helen met them in New York. As their press agent, she insisted they be seen at least at one Broadway show. She arranged for tickets to Maurice Chevalier's sold-out evening of *Songs and Impressions*. Barbara knew Chevalier back in the 1930s when he and Yvonne Vallée lived in a small house perched above Beverly Hills and Franchot Tone and Joan Crawford had them to dinner. Chevalier had long since shed Yvonne, whose testy unpredictability had ruined Joan's dinner party. His Broadway show marked his postwar return to America, and Barbara, Bob, and Helen enjoyed the evening with an older but glittering audience eager to share in the nostalgia. The Taylors were that night's celebrity couple, and an usher asked them to join Chevalier backstage at the end of the show. They would have preferred a personal invitation, but, at Helen's urging, they went to Chevalier's dressing room. Other well-wishers were present, and when Chevalier finally came in he ignored the Taylors. Barbara turned purple. Bob grabbed her, and together they fled to the street and hailed a cab.

Bob hated the whole trip. He called Ralph Couser and asked the pilot to fly the Beechcraft halfway across the country to meet him in Chicago. In stony silence, Barbara, Bob, and Helen took the 20th Century Limited to the Windy City, where Bob said good-bye to wife and press agent. The two men flew to Los Angeles, while Barbara and Helen continued by rail. When they arrived home, Bob was on a fishing trip.

"Sure is good to be home," Barbara told the *Los Angeles Times*.

To have something to do until *B. F.'s Daughter*, she agreed to do a walk-on in Paramount's *Variety Girl*. Her *Message to Garcia* director George Marshall was in charge of this tribute to the Variety Clubs' philanthropy for underprivileged young people. Back in 1923, Paramount had been the first studio to feature stars playing themselves in James Cruze's *Hollywood*. William Holden was among the fifty featured players in the revue-format picture. Things were not going too well for him. He had served in the air force, married Ardis Ankerson, a divorcée who found parts in the movies under the name Brenda Marshall. It had taken Paramount eleven months to find a role for the returning airman, and his five postwar movies had done nothing to fulfill the promise of *Golden Boy*. Irv Glaser, the studio photographer who became a friend after Bill and Ardis separated in 1963, believed Holden and Stanwyck became lovers that summer. Whether the initiative was Bill's or Barbara's, they both needed a respite, he from a career going nowhere, she from a marriage that was all front. Barbara never admitted to an affair, but spoke affectionately of him. "Bill and I go way, way back," she would say thirty-five years later. "He's always been so grateful, simply because I helped him, in that I thought he would be a marvelous leading man."

Dion was allowed home for the summer. He was fifteen, and Barbara forced Bob to sit in on the family decision about the boy's future. "She gave me the lecture of my life," Dion would recall. Before she sent Dion back to the Culver Military Academy, he would claim that his mother saw to it that he was deflowered by a professional. On a sweaty Saturday night, Uncle Buck took him to Hollywood. "Uncle Buck explained that Mother had paid for the high-priced call girl to teach me the facts of life. Soon after this incident I got a call from Uncle Buck, and asked him if I could come home. He told me to forget it, to forget that Barbara Stanwyck was my mother. He said, 'She wants nothing to do with you.'"

Barbara's attitude toward her sisters and their families was somewhat more caring if no less aloof. She paid for college for Mabel's son, Eugene Vaslett, but made sure he didn't go to school too close by. Gene was sent to Indiana like Dion, to graduate from the University of Notre Dame. Maud and Mildred were still in New York. While Barbara helped her brother, Byron, after he married and made a career as a movie extra, she saw Millie only a couple of times during her infrequent East Coast visits.

Imperceptibly at first, the golden era was ending. Movie attendance was slipping—down to 62 million—from 80 million in 1946. MGM had no pictures for Bob. Barbara, however, was the most booked-up actress in Hollywood.

The studio against which all the other film factories measured themselves began a round of cost cutting. Twenty-five percent of MGM's workforce was furloughed. From the lofty New York headquarters of Metro's corporate parent, Loews Inc., came orders that Mayer better find another Irving Thalberg to ride herd on production. A year later, Louis B. persuaded Dore Schary—the studio boss at RKO until running afoul of Howard Hughes—to become Metro's production chief. Stanwyck was committed to do four pictures for Warners and four for Hal Wallis. She was also tentatively set to do four for Enterprise Pictures.*

Independent filmmaking was the wave of the future. Although theater owners complained as loudly as New York critics that the output was too bland, the studio bosses failed to see that the slipping movie attendance was a protest vote.

Barbara sensed that the screen fare the film factories put out reflected larger misgivings. The optimism of V-J Day was giving way to a vague defensiveness, to xenophobic and anti-communist hostility. When President Truman needed not only spiritual but tactical backing for the "devil" theory of communism, he sought the advice of Senator Arthur H. Vandenberg, the powerful chairman of the Foreign Relations Committee. Vandenberg's counsel was famous: "Scare the hell out of the country, Harry." The president set the course with the creation of his Temporary Commission on Employee Loyalty in November 1946. Under the new law 2.5 million federal employees were to be checked by loyalty review boards. As a guide, Attorney General Tom Clark prepared a list of organizations he considered "subversive." Truman was to regret the excesses four years later when the anticommunist hysteria came to a head with Joseph McCarthy and McCarthyism.

Communism had been a big issue in the 1946 congressional elections. In California, the Republican Committee of One Hundred asked soon-to-be-demobilized navy lieutenant

---

*Enterprise was a new company starting out with a splash. Its first picture was *Arch of Triumph*, Lewis Milestone's adaption of Erich Maria Remarque's current bestseller. Starring Ingrid Bergman and Charles Boyer, the $4 million film was a commercial disaster and proved to be not so much the promising beginning as the ignominious end. Enterprise had only one success, *Body and Soul*. After three years it folded.

commander Richard Nixon to run, all campaign costs paid, against Democratic incumbent Jerry Voorhis, who had been an effective member of Congress for many years and was the sponsor of the National School Lunch Act. Bob and Barbara were registered Republicans. Nixon had their endorsement as well as the backing of the Motion Picture Alliance for the Preservation of American Ideals. With never-proven charges that Voorhis was "the candidate of the Kremlin," Nixon won the election.

During the winter of 1946–47, the loyalty question was an irresistible grandstand for members of Congress. Not to be outdone by the president, the House Committee on Un-American Activities remembered Hollywood's prewar radical chic, its rallies for Spain, near-underground organizing of the Screen Writers Guild, the Federal Theatre and Federal Writers Project, which HUAC chairman Representative J. Parnell Thomas of New Jersey termed "sheer propaganda for communism or the New Deal."

Probing artists with a penchant for speaking up was nothing new. In 1938, when the House panel was called the Dies Committee after its chairman, Representative Martin Dies, its investigation of the Federal Theatre helped kill that New Deal project.

Bob and Barbara were swept up in the turmoil of political correctness that turned friends and coworkers against each other, Bob to become an informer, Barbara a superpatriot. Barbara denounced communists, and Bob hunted down subversives. Without saying *who* Stanwyck personally rebuked, Adela Rogers St. Johns wrote in the vernacular of the day that Barbara "blasted Hollywood Reds to their faces" and turned down a highly profitable proposition "entirely on grounds of patriotism."

Together with Ward Bond, Bob denounced suspect communists and fellow travelers. Hedda Hopper spent the summer of 1947 traveling across the country urging members of women's clubs to boycott films that featured "communist" actors.

Christian values were now seen as a cornerstone in America's ramparts against heathen Marxism. Ruby Stevens dreamed of being a missionary; Barbara Stanwyck never went to church. In her prewar custody battles with Frank Fay, she condemned her former husband's Catholic showboating, but at a Helen Ferguson party attended by Adela, Bob and Barbara, Dorothy Manners, and celebrity photographer Paul Hess, Barbara spoke passionately about the need for a vital, living Christianity and accused politicians of failing to guide people toward Christian enlightenment.

The Alliance met once a month at the American Legion auditorium on Highland Avenue, where its members listened to inspirational speeches from anticommunist crusaders like Louis Budenz, the former managing editor of the *Daily Worker* who had found God and sought to expiate his former sins. In radio speeches he denounced an all-powerful agent who, he claimed, traveled the country as the Kremlin's secret representative. Ayn Rand wrote in Alliance news releases that the purpose of Hollywood's communists was "to corrupt our moral premises by corrupting nonpolitical movies—in introducing small, casual bits of propaganda into innocent stories—thus making people absorb the basic principles of collectivism by indirection and implication."

Representative Thomas came to Los Angeles in May 1947 on an initial fishing expedition. With his assistant Robert E. Stripling, a former FBI agent, the congressman held a series of "interviews" in his hotel suite at the downtown Biltmore Hotel. The interviews were held in camera, but after each session Thomas and Stripling told reporters what they unearthed. One example, Thomas said, was the discovery that in 1943 the Roosevelt administration had "wielded the iron fist in order to get companies to put on certain communist propaganda." When asked for specifics, the U.S. representative said Robert Taylor had told him how government officials delayed his navy commission so he could complete *Song of Russia*.

The pressure, Bob had testified, had come right from the White House, from "Roosevelt aides." The charge was sensational.

Hedda Hopper, Bob and Barbara's fellow member of the Alliance, devoted a column to the Taylors and applauded Bob's testimony at the Biltmore hearings. "I admire Bob's courage in testifying in the investigation of communism in the film industry," she wrote. She quoted him as saying, "It's getting so that if a person is not a communist he's called a fascist."

Not everybody was ready to be branded communist or fascist. Dore Schary, the new production chief at MGM, called the Alliance members a bunch of "Yahoos." Hopper went after him and almost got herself fired for writing that the Schary appointment meant "the studio will be known as Metro-Goldwyn-Moscow." A threat of a lawsuit brought abject apologies from the columnist and, to smooth things out, a personal call on Schary by *Los Angeles Times* owner and publisher Norman Chandler.

Hysteria and guilt besieged the film industry. By midsummer, Bertolt Brecht and eighteen others were publicly accused of being agents of un-American propaganda. Larry Parks was an actor, and John Howard Lawson the first president of the Screen Writers Guild. Fellow writers were Alvah Bessie, Herbert Biberman, Lester Cole, Richard Collins, Gordon Kahn, Howard Koch, Ring Lardner, Jr., Albert Maltz, Samuel Ornitz, Waldo Salt, and Dalton Trumbo. Adrian Scott was a writer-producer, Robert Rossen a writer-director, and Edward Dmytryk, Lewis Milestone, and Irving Pichel directors. When only Bessie, Biberman, Cole, Dmytryk, Lardner, Lawson, Maltz, Ornitz, Scott, and Trumbo were subpoenaed to testify, along with Brecht, they became known as the Hollywood Ten.

In September, William Wyler and John Huston invited a few people to meet at Lucy's Restaurant on Melrose Avenue. Wyler, who was born in Mulhouse when Alsace was German and who, with the 1919 Versailles Treaty, had become a French citizen, was appalled that other foreign-borns— Samuel Goldwyn, Jack Warner, and even Frank Capra— wrapped themselves in the righteous mantle of superpatriots, Capra apparently at the advice of members of the Alliance. By the end of the evening, Wyler, Huston, screenwriter Philip Dunne, and actor Alexander Knox had formed the Committee for the First Amendment—an organization soon listed by the California Un-American Activities as a communist front. "We tried to defend not so much the Ten as a person's right to keep his political beliefs to himself, that no one would have to disclose whether he was a communist," Wyler would remember.

The committee gathered an imposing collection of supporters, from Bogart, Lauren Bacall, Katharine Hepburn, Billy Wilder, Groucho Marx, and Myrna Loy to literary heavyweights like George S. Kaufman and Archibald MacLeish, and a few producers, including Jerry Wald. Gene Kelly, Danny Kaye, Marsha Hunt, Ira Gershwin, Geraldine Brooks, Richard Conte, Paul Henreid, Robert Presnell, and others followed. Besides Bogart, Stanwyck had worked with many of them.

Bob received a subpoena dated September 25, 1947, demanding that he appear before the Un-American Activities Committee of the House of Representatives October 18. Barbara couldn't come with him to Washington since she was to start *B. F.'s Daughter* a week later. Bob traveled with Adolphe Menjou, Walt Disney, Gary Cooper, Screen Actors Guild president Ronald Reagan, and his two predecessors in that office, George Murphy and Robert Montgomery, and with Ginger Rogers's mother, Lela—all to be "friendly" witnesses.

Thomas brought his committee to order in the caucus room on the second floor of the Old House Office Building in Washington. The room was large enough to accommodate the press and give HUAC what it needed most—publicity. Nine newsreel cameras and broadcasting equipment lined the walls, and the press table held ninety-four reporters.

The first witnesses were Jack Warner, Walter Disney, Louis B. Mayer, and Sam Wood. "Ideological termites have burrowed into many American industries," Warner read from an opening statement. "Wherever they may be, I say let us dig them out and get rid of them. My brothers and I will be happy to contribute to a pest-removal fund. We are willing to establish such a fund to ship to Russia the people who don't like our American system of government and prefer the communist system to ours." He stressed his belief that screenwriters were "injecting communist stuff" into scripts. When asked how many employees this involved, he replied six, but named sixteen, including eight not identified before: Clifford Odets, Guy Endore, John Wexley, Julius and Philip Epstein, Sheridan Gibney, Emmet Lavery, and Irwin Shaw.

Of the "named," Barbara had worked with six. She had

starred in Odets's *Golden Boy*. Dalton Trumbo was the author of the *You Belong to Me* story, Philip Epstein was the writer of *The Bride Walks Out* and *The Mad Miss Manton*, Rossen of *The Strange Love of Martha Ivers*, directed by Milestone. Pichel directed her in *The Bride Wore Boots*, and Albert Maltz, who in a 1946 *New Masses* article said art was not so much the Marxist-Leninist weapon in the class struggle as a straitjacket, was the rewrite man on the *Mildred Pierce* script she had wanted to play.

Mayer's testimony amounted to damage control on the *Song of Russia* charge. The nattily dressed studio chief was anxious to "clear up a misunderstanding—how Robert Taylor had been 'forced'" into playing an American sympathetic to the Soviet Union in *Song of Russia*.

"I thought Robert Taylor ideal for the male role, but he did not like the story," Mayer testified. "At the time, Taylor mentioned his pending commission in the navy, so I telephoned the Secretary of the Navy, Frank Knox, and told him of the situation, recalled the good that had been accomplished with *Mrs. Miniver* and other pictures released during the war period. The Secretary called back and said he thought Taylor could be given time to make the film before being called to the service."

Ayn Rand tore into *Song of Russia*. Although she had last seen Moscow in 1926, she scornfully described MGM's Moscow as a city of "big, prosperous-looking, clean buildings, with something like swans or sailboats in the background." And Robert Taylor mingled with "happy peasants . . . children with operetta costumes . . . manicured starlets driving tractors and the happy women coming home from work singing."

John McDowell, a Pennsylvania Republican, wondered if nobody smiled in Russia anymore.

Rand was relentless. "Well, if you ask me literally, pretty much no."

"They don't smile?" McDowell came back.

"Not quite that way, no."

Wood denounced John Cromwell, one of Stanwyck's favorite directors, as an agent of a foreign power and testified that the film industry group to be watched most carefully was the writers. When Stripling asked if the director would care to name any he knew to be communists, he named Trumbo,

Stewart, and Lawson. Why them? Because when the *Hollywood Reporter* asked them, "Are you a communist?" they had refused to answer. When asked to give an example of how communist writers worked, he said they portrayed bankers and senators as "heavies."

Times and dates of the appearance of witnesses were classified. Crowds increased for the October 22 hearing when word leaked out this was the day Robert Taylor would testify.

Bob took his assigned seat at the witness table on schedule. Before investigator Stripling could ask any question, Bob started by backing down on the *Song of Russia* uproar. "In my own defense, lest I look a little silly by saying I was ever *forced* to do a picture," he began, "I was not forced because nobody can force you to make any picture." Elaborating on Mayer's "misunderstanding," he said the script had been written long before anyone in government could make suggestions.

So the story of the Roosevelt White House dictating to Hollywood was just that—a one-edition sensation.

Perhaps to make sure his testimony was not a total waste for the committee, Bob said he had been "looking for communists for a long time." He agreed with Stripling that it was primarily among screenwriters that "red" infiltration occurred. With newsreel cameras whirring, he named one writer, Lester Cole (but hastened to say he didn't know Cole personally), one character actor, Howard Da Silva, and the starlet Karen Morley.

He said he would refuse to work with any actor merely under suspicion of being a communist: "I'm afraid it would have to be him or me, because life is a little too short to be around people who annoy me as much as these fellow-travelers and communists do." Representative Richard Nixon congratulated Bob on his fearlessness in testifying. There was no mention of the fact that Cole was the screenwriter of *The High Wall*, the best script Bob had ever been offered.

When Bob was dismissed and headed for the door, spectators clustered around him for autographs and followed him out of the building to his car. The *New York Post*'s coverage of Bob's testimony was headlined: BOBBY SOXERS AND NATION CHEER ROBERT TAYLOR AS HE URGES BAN ON REDS, but the reaction of the establishment press was less approving. Responsible newspapers pointed out that attacking colleagues' reputations and livelihoods did not quite agree with American ideals.

26

Prejudice

Stanwyck had little taste for opinions that could be called "controversial." She was neither naive nor evasive. She was *practical*. Even if she, her husband, and their friends had no true understanding of the fierce ideological issues involved, the cold war favored right-wing sentiments. Americans were shocked when they heard the Soviet Union had detonated an atom bomb, Mao Zedong's communists were winning in China, and former State Department official Alger Hiss was accused of passing government documents to Whittaker Chambers. Threats of picketing and boycotts by such right-wing groups as the American Legion frightened Hollywood. The actor in Bob enjoyed his offscreen cold-warrior notoriety. When he was spotted in restaurants, Tom Purvis would remember, people sent drinks over and lifted their glasses in toast to the "Commie hunter."

Barbara was careful not to make any public pronouncements. As Bob went into strategy sessions with Louis B. and Hedda Hopper, she sensed a backlash in the making when the Committee for the First Amendment mobilized against the friendly witnesses. The committee organized two national broadcasts, chartered a plane so Humphrey Bogart could lead a star-studded delegation to Washington, and saw itself grow into a national Committee of One Thousand that included Albert Einstein. Bob had his boss in his corner, but among fellow actors, he was now regarded as being intolerant as Ward Bond, John Wayne, and Adolphe Menjou. Barbara and he became charter members of the new Hollywood Republican Committee, formed to encourage the industry to back Republicans in the 1948 elections. The committee favored California governor Earl Warren for president.

The "unfriendly" witnesses' defense was organized in Lewis Milestone's living room on Doheny Drive. Several top lawyers, including Robert Kenny, who had succeeded Earl Warren as California's attorney general, were present. A 1943 Supreme Court decision rejecting compulsory salutes to the flag held that the government could not make anyone profess his loyalty or punish him for refusing to do so. Disastrously, as it turned out, Kenny suggested that instead of politely invoking the Fifth Amendment against self-incrimination, the witnesses should evade and parry all questions and yet deny they were refusing to answer.

Brecht's German-English mumblings completely bewildered the committee, and he was quickly dismissed. The remaining Hollywood Ten all refused to discuss membership of any sort, whether in the Communist Party or the Screen Writers Guild, and cited the constitutional guarantees of free speech and assembly. Some of what they had to say never got a hearing, but Trumbo managed to yell into network microphones that this was the beginning of concentration camps in America.

Wyler told the congressmen that by their action they were poisoning the well to the point where he "wouldn't be allowed to make *The Best Years of Our Lives* today." Publisher Bennett Cerf testified that "if Hollywood can be bullied into producing only the kind of stories that fall in with this Committee's opinion and prejudice, it seems obvious to me that the publishers of books, magazines, and newspapers will most certainly be next on the agenda."

Da Silva, "named" by Bob, was out of work within days. Dmytryk, who had just directed *Crossfire*, about anti-Semitism in the U.S. Army, was dismissed by RKO. So was the movie's producer-writer Adrian Scott, the husband of Stanwyck's costar in *So Big* and *Stella Dallas*, Anne Shirley. MGM fired Cole and Trumbo, and Fox announced it would dispense with the services of Lardner. In November, the studio heads—Mayer, Goldwyn, Warner, Cohn, Schary, and Spyros Skouras and a slew of company lawyers—met at the Waldorf-Astoria in New York to settle on the industry's collective response. Goldwyn and Schary tried to resist calls for wholesale firings of suspected subversives. In an air of panic, they were overruled and a blacklist was established that eventually grew to about two hundred and fifty names.

On the basis of the testimony of the fourteen "friendly" witnesses, Thomas announced the committee's conclusion. The Roosevelt White House had pressured the studios to produce "flagrant communist propaganda," and communist writers were subtly writing Moscow's party line into scripts.

The Motion Picture Alliance for the Preservation of American Ideals cheered on the HUAC hearings and kept hunting leftists of every stripe. After working himself into a rage at the news that a liberal screenwriter was suing the Alliance for slander, Wood suffered a massive heart attack. On his deathbed he made a will saying his daughter was to receive most of his estate providing she didn't prove to be a communist.

The Alliance members chose John Wayne as their new president and IATSE chief Roy Brewer as principal enforcer and keeper of its growing Hollywood blacklist. The studio bosses maintained there was no such thing as a blacklist and counted on the talent guilds, the unions of directors, actors, writers, stagehands, and studio painters to somehow purge their own membership ranks. Under Reagan's leadership, the Screen Actors Guild drafted a loyalty oath and, in 1951, openly supported blacklisting. At the Directors Guild, Cecil B. DeMille and Frank Capra were the prime movers of loyalty oaths. Capra had first heard of the Alliance in 1946 when, during the casting of *It's a Wonderful Life*, he was told to clear Anne Revere with Wayne. Together with Reagan and Disney, Capra now became an informer for the FBI.

Da Silva, who had appeared in the original *Golden Boy* Broadway cast and since 1939 had been in twenty-two movies, changed talent agencies four times. Again and again, his agents reported back what film executives said: "We can't hire him, he's too hot." A backlash among actors began to hurt Gary Cooper and Bob Taylor. By cooperating too eagerly with the inquisitors, the two stars had betrayed the entire industry.

The charge, and the rancor Bob felt, made him paranoid. He became so afraid of being tricked into signing anything political that when fans pressed autograph books at him he looked for carbons under the proffered page before scrawling his signature.

Beyond the posing and posturing for "radical" causes that are acceptable as long as they are also chic, most actors crave acceptance. They want to be liked and often follow rather than lead. Decades later, when the House Un-American Activities Committee came to be seen as an hysterical aberration, Stanwyck would claim her husband had been betrayed by the studio. Yet Bob was the only *star* seen and heard on ten thousand screens in newsreels naming names.

Beneath Barbara's stance lurked profound hypocrisy. Not only had she worked with many of the Hollywood Ten, she continued to put her career ahead of beliefs. The hypocrisy was not that she had worked with Milestone and Pichel and had starred in pictures written by Odets, Trumbo, Epstein, and Rossen, but that she continued to do so, as did the industry. Her next picture was directed by Anatole Litvak, who chose to hide his leftist sympathies, and the one after that by blacklisted Michael Gordon. When MGM offered her *East Side, West Side*, she had no objections to acting in a screenplay by freshly blacklisted Isobel Lennart. Nor did she refuse to star in *Clash by Night*, an adaptation of an Odets play three years later. She was, of course, not alone. Jack Benny sailed through the witch hunt without one on-air barb or comment. Preston Sturges thought the HUAC hearings were a wonderful comedy.

As a whole, the Hollywood establishment managed to wink at the outcasts and to use their talents at bargain prices. The writers were hardest hit. Trumbo and the others struggled to make a living, writing under fictitious names at a fraction of what they had previously earned. Pichel and Milestone, on the other hand, barely skipped a beat as directors. A few months after the HUAC hearings, Pichel was at United Artists directing *Without Honor* and Milestone was back at Fox doing *Halls of Montezuma*.

If political conformity was vital to national security, sexual correctness was deemed no less essential. Homosexuals were a choice target of the witch hunt. Protestations of sexual conformity were insufficient since deviants, like communists, were known to lie about everything. To be accused was to be guilty. The popular press presented homosexuality as a chief cause of American ills.

"You can hardly separate homosexuals from subversives," Senator Kenneth Wherry told the *New York Post*. "Mind you, I don't say every homosexual is a subversive, and I don't say, every subversive is a homosexual, but [people] of low morality are a menace to the government." Alfred Kinsey was reviled because his statistics showed 37 percent of American men and 13 percent of American women had had homoerotic experiences at some point in their lives. The Senate decided homosexuals must be fired from government jobs because they lacked "emotional stability which is found in most sex perverts." Professional women had the most to fear when the FBI infiltrated the Daughters of Bilitis, a private organization of middle-class lesbians dedicated to improving the image of same-sex love. Most lesbians felt compelled to deny their sexual preferences, to live covertly, to marry gay men and make sure everybody addressed them as "Mrs." Many acceded to families' pleas to submit to psychoanalysis, which promised to cure lesbianism on the couch.

While the drama unfolded in Washington, Barbara started filming *B. F.'s Daughter* at MGM.

J. P. Marquand wrote about New England bluebloods, at once satirizing and indulging, but never offending, Boston Brahmins struggling to maintain aristocratic standards. His *Late George Apley* was a Proustian memoir of the flourishing of George and of his wife's fierce work on a committee to save Boston. *B. F.'s Daughter* was both a story of generational prejudices and attitudes and a canny character study of a wealthy industrialist's beautiful daughter. The story was in some ways Barbara's own. Polly Fulton is a doer married to a thinker whom she tries to mold in her own likeness. Van Heflin was cast as her poor but brainy husband, and, as in *The Lady Eve*, Charles Coburn was again her father. Robert Z. Leonard, who had scored with *The Great Ziegfeld*, was the director.

Barbara might have disdained Christian Dior in Paris, but the studio insisted on the Dior "New Look" for *B. F.'s Daughter*. The film was the first and only picture in which she was dressed by MGM's executive designer, Irene (née Irene Lenz-Gibbons), who, with her staff, never came onto the set without wearing immaculate white gloves and suitable hats. The wardrobe they created for Stanwyck spelled taste, position, and means and was memorable enough to earn Irene an Academy nomination.

Barbara cut her shoulder-length hair to play Polly Fulton. The haircut somehow underscored her gray streaks, which ran in her family—her brother's hair had turned white at twenty-six. MGM's ace cinematographer Joseph Ruttenberg, who had forty films behind him, wasn't alarmed—in black-and-white gray streaks appeared as blond highlights—but the publicity department routinely retouched outgoing photos. The front office ordered Leonard to tell Stanwyck to dye the gray out.

"Everybody said, 'Oh, my God, no actress can have white hair," she would remember. "No one wants to make love to a gray-haired lady. Everybody said, 'To be over forty isn't possible.'" Saying she had no intention of hiding the fact that she was forty-one, she refused to dye her hair. Publicity kept retouching the stills.

B. F.'s Daughter had lots of pithy dialogue, and Heflin figured he could use his stage tricks. For hours he practiced rolling a silver dollar from one finger to another as a piece of business. When Barbara asked him during rehearsal if he was going to roll his coin during their long, intricate scene together, he said no.

Leonard shouted "Action!" Barbara began her speech. Van played with his silver dollar. Halfway through the scene the camera focused on him. Delivering his lines, he heard the crew laughing.

Losing his concentration, he wheeled around and saw Barbara slowly lifting her dress.

"What are you doing?" he asked.

"Showing them a trick a helluva lot more interesting than yours."

She pulled another trick in a scene in which Heflin carries her, as his mink-coated bride, over the threshold. During the rehearsals he swept her off her feet and over the doorstep with such impudence she decided to teach him a lesson. When Leonard shouted "Action!" for the first take, Heflin pranced over, put his arms around her, and . . . nearly collapsed. With the help of the propman, Barbara was draped with eighty pounds of ship's chains wrapped in muslin under her mink.

Louis B. wanted safe entertainment, and the beginning

of the Hollywood witch hunt didn't favor criticism of economic, political and social values. Luther Davis's screenplay, the *Hollywood Reporter* noted when the film was released in February 1948, "never seems to get the social significance to jell and lapses comfortably into that old photoplay standard—the story of a poor but brilliant man who marries an heiress and is saved from the horrors of a life of luxury only through the understanding generated by a great love."

Despite its lack of action, *B. F.'s Daughter* was among MGM's best efforts in 1947.

Mayer shipped Bob to England in 1948 to play a communist traitor. When Hedda Hopper first heard about the casting, she called Barbara to say she thought it was a disgrace. The unconvincing plot of *Conspirator* had Bob as a British officer whose young wife discovers not only that he is a communist spy but that he is under orders to shoot her. In her first adult role, sixteen-year-old Elizabeth Taylor was Bob's wife.

MGM publicists concentrated on Bob giving Elizabeth her first screen kiss and enthusiastically reported how she closed her eyes and imagined herself in the arms of her twenty-three-year-old fiancé, army lieutenant Glenn Davis, stationed in Korea. They quoted Bob as saying all he had to teach her was to powder down her lips so her enthusiastic kissing wouldn't smear his makeup.

Conspirator ran into a diplomatic flap over its heavy-handed depiction of Russians. British censors threatened to ban the film, and after Guy Burgess and Donald MacDonald fled to the Soviet Union, the similarity to actual British traitors was too close for comfort. MGM feared libel suits from powerful British families. The release of the film billed as "Elizabeth Taylor's First Adult Love Story" was held up over a year.

The marriage of the Taylors' friends Ron and Jane Reagan was falling apart. Like Bob, Ron was stuck in neutral while Jane Wyman's career echoed Barbara's in a big way with *Johnny Belinda*. The Reagans separated in December 1947, after eight years of marriage—a month after he was elected to a full term as president of SAG. In her divorce suit, Jane said her husband's work with the guild had led to the breakup of their marriage.

Stanwyck spent the first three months of 1948 filming *Sorry, Wrong Number*, the first of her commitments to producer Hal Wallis. Both were happy to be out of the political limelight, and so was their Russian-born director Anatole Litvak.

After making movies in the nascent Soviet Union, France, England, and Germany, "Tola" Litvak had received the red-carpet treatment when he came to Hollywood in 1936 and somehow survived his background. A friend of Wyler's and Huston's, Tola and his wife, Sophie, had neglected to sign the Committee for the First Amendment manifesto. He now plunged happily into "all-American" themes, crime (*Sorry, Wrong Number*) and madness (*The Snake Pit*).

Sorry, Wrong Number was Lucille Fletcher's own adaptation of her twenty-two-minute radio play about a bedridden neurotic who happens to get crossed wires when she calls her husband at the office, hears a couple of men arranging a murder, and comes to realize she is to be the victim. Performed by Agnes Moorehead as a virtual monologue, the radio program was rebroadcast seven times between 1943 and 1948 and translated into fifteen languages.

Barbara demanded a copy of the script ten days before shooting and consulted physicians about manic-depressive behavior. She was told her new director was something of a martinet. After she met Litvak she decided a European who knew what he wanted wasn't automatically a Prussian. "When Litvak met me the first time, he was perfect. He asked me what I wanted. *Wrong Number* had several very difficult technical problems to solve, problems for everybody."

Litvak wanted to describe the self-imposed confinement of Leona Stevenson with a circling camera that moves from an array of useless medicines at her night table to the neurotic invalid herself. "Leona is in bed, with just the phone, for almost half the picture," Barbara would say. The production schedule or "board" allocated twelve working days for the bed scenes. "The first thing Litvak asked me—asked me—was: how did I want to do it? Break it up, a couple of days and then something else, or half a day for twenty-four days. Very considerate. No matter if it screwed up the board. I realized that Leona, after a very short time, starts to get worried, and then terrified, and finally disintegrates. Almost from the word go, she is way up there emotionally, and stays there day after day—twelve days. I decided I'd prefer to jump in, bam, go, stay there, up, try to sustain it all the way and shoot the works."

It all worked until Friday. "Five days I was handling it, starting the next day's work where I'd picked up, sustaining it all, and then I had two whole days to relax and not to worry about the character, and I tell you it was strange. It was really hard to pump myself up on Monday morning to try to feel that desperate tension."

Litvak poured on pyrotechnics. *Sorry, Wrong Number* had flashbacks within flashbacks, surrealistic and expressionistic devices to illuminate the murderer's shadow creeping up the stairs. Stanwyck scored with her bravura performance as the terrified and finally raving hysterical wife of Burt Lancaster. The film was not a success, however. The plot relied on too many obliging phone company snafus, and the virtuoso storytelling was ultimately too bewildering. Lancaster was miscast as the dull-witted, ineffectual husband, and, to stretch Fletcher's radio play to eighty-nine minutes, Litvak added too many subplots.

Both Barbara and Jane Wyman were nominated for Best Actress—Stanwyck for *Sorry, Wrong Number*, Jane for her deaf-mute rape victim in *Johnny Belinda*. Barbara didn't think her performance as a terrified and, finally, whimpering woman—or, for that matter, Olivia De Havilland's mentally deranged person in *The Snake Pit*—stood a chance against her friend Jane, Irene Dunne as the serenely beautiful mother image in *I Remember Mama*, or Ingrid Bergman as Joan of Arc herself. She was right. Wyman won the Academy Award and ran to the stage in a long-sleeved classic gown to make the shortest acceptance speech on record: "I accept this very gratefully for keeping my mouth shut. I think I will do it again."

At the Warners' celebration party (besides Wyman, Walter and John Huston, Jerry Wald and Claire Trevor won for Warners), four-time loser Stanwyck said, "If I get nominated next year, they'll have to give me the door prize, won't they? At least the bride should throw me the bouquet."

Radio was at its prime, and in late November Barbara came to the rescue of Jack Benny when Mary suddenly was unable to perform. The proximity of Christmas inspired the comedian to ask, "Do you believe in Santa, Barbara," a joke that California listeners might appreciate but mostly had Benny in stitches. Over the next years, Stanwyck filled in on several occasions. When "The Jack Benny Program" switched to television in 1950, she made her TV debut on his show.

The film industry was skidding. MGM managed to improve its profits a bit, but Universal and Disney went into the red for the second year in a row. A new crisis hit the industry in early 1948. The federal government's decade-old antitrust effort to break up the majors' control of both production and exhibition, a practice dating back to the nickelodeon days, finally wound its way through the courts. "Block booking," the practice that meant if a theater owner wanted the winners, he had to take B pictures, also-rans, and occasional turkeys, was the core of the fight. As early as 1933, the Department of Justice had looked into these monopolistic trade practices. Industry lawyers had obtained postponements and extensions through the 1930s and the war years, but the Truman administration reopened the entire case in 1948, winning a series of so-called consent decrees, which, in effect, forced the studios to sell their chains of cinemas.

The government's action was perfectly sound, but the Justice Department's victory over "wicked" Hollywood was disastrous for the industry. Fearing they could no longer unload four hundred movies a year on theaters they no longer controlled, the studios lost confidence in themselves. The immediate result was a slashing of scheduled productions and the cancellation of hundreds of long-term contracts with actors, directors, writers, and technicians.

With Clark Gable, Joan Crawford, Claudette Colbert, Spencer Tracy, James Cagney, and Robert Montgomery, Barbara Stanwyck was among the veterans still working, while Vivien Leigh, Merle Oberon, and Irene Dunne made no pictures in 1949. For Barbara, work was more important than billing and the perks that so often became ego traps.

She signed on with Universal for *The Lady Gambles*. The picture was a step down from *Sorry, Wrong Number*, but it meant a salary, and, if excuses were needed, a chance to work with old friends. Robert Preston played her patient husband, and Orry-Kelly did the wardrobe. For the first time she was in the hands of a director younger than she, the thirty-nine-year-old Michael Gordon.

Gordon was blacklisted, having been a member of the Group Theatre before the war and part of the stage production of *Waiting for Lefty* and *Golden Boy*. But Universal International was an agent's studio run by Jules Stein, and being an associate of producer Michel Kraike allowed Gordon to work despite the blacklist. Barbara closed her mind to politics for the duration of the shoot. She admitted she knew nothing about gambling to Gordon, who wanted to match Billy Wilder's startling exploration of alcoholic compulsion, *The Lost Weekend*. He made Barbara read Sigmund Freud on compulsive behavior. She got to like Gordon for the energy with which he worked to make *The Lady Gambles* an above-average psychological soap opera, although it did nothing for her career.

She had played them all, tough dames who wrecked homes, women sacrificing everything for no-good men, women neglecting their husbands, and rotten-to-the-heart wives. In 1948, she became the cheated-on wife in real life and, on celluloid, the deceived woman opposite Bob's lover.

Their marriage might be little more than a front, but Barbara had no intention of letting Bob out of her life. Keeping the career in forward was everything Barbara cared about. She insisted that Helen Ferguson get fresh news and magazine space to once more tout the marriage as close to ideal. Helen dutifully lined up interviews and planted stories that called the Taylors Hollywood's dream couple. Whether Bob was impotent with Barbara or impotence itself was a pretext, he no longer made any effort to have sex with her. When he wasn't with his male friends at the airport or on hunting trips, he was at the studio. He wanted to play tough guys, but knew his screen persona was against him. He wanted movies that showed him roaming the wilderness, flying airplanes, taming horses. He got to play opposite the premiere sex goddess of the day, Ava Gardner.

At twenty, the North Carolina hillbilly whose rich and provocative beauty was almost overwhelming had been transformed into an MGM startlet and had married Mickey Rooney. That was only the beginning. With her gritty earthiness, sloeshaped eyes, high cheekbones, chin and lush body, she had been promoted in Howard Strickling's press releases as "Hollywood's glamour girl of 1948." She was recently divorced from her latest husband, bandleader Artie Shaw, and at twenty-seven, was flitting from one liaison to another. Howard Duff forsook Yvonne De Carlo for her, and when her mercurial nature wore him down, he was followed by the bandleader at Ciro's on Sunset Strip, the impeccable Peter Lawford, and Howard Hughes, who was entranced with Gardner for the second time. Frank Sinatra was in hot pursuit of her. Merely to look at her, critic Kathleen Murphy would write, "suffices to make swine of men and advance the story."

The Bribe was Metro's bid to clone Warners' To Have and Have Not. But The Bribe had none of the sardonic patter or self-mockery that delighted audiences in Hawks's Bogart–Lauren Bacall starrer. Directed by Robert Z. Leonard, The Bribe was a pretentious, high-gloss melodrama that excused Gardner from her trademark slinky black dress and put her into Mexican huaraches and fetching native blouses. Taylor played a U.S. agent tracking down a gang smuggling surplus aircraft engines to South America and Charles Laughton a weakly aggressive, broken-down Graham Greeneish sot. The film was shot during August and September 1948 on MGM's all-purpose Mexican back lot. Despite a rousing chase sequence through a fiesta in the midst of exploding fireworks, both Bob and Ava thought it was the worst movie they had ever been in.

Gardner was a randy tease to her leading men, and for the duration of the shoot, she had her fun with Bob. "I was available," she would write in her memoirs. "And Bob Taylor surely fit the bill for me, and I did the same for Bob."

Their trysts were carried out, of all places, under his mother's roof. Ruth at first confronted her son. She relented after he asked if she would prefer him to go to a motel where he might be recognized. Ava would remember the liaison as a "magical little interlude [that] hurt no one because nobody knew." In her two-page description of the liaison in her 1990 autobiography, she found Bob to be warm, generous, and intelligent, forever typecast in parts that "demeaned his manhood" and in a marriage that had been on the rocks for a long time. She remembered him smoking fifty to seventy cigarettes a day before the cocktail hour and carrying around a big Thermos bottle of black coffee, even keeping it in his car. Cigarettes and black coffee kept him going all day long.

"I have never forgotten those few hidden months. I made two more films with Bob, *Ride Vaquero!* and *Knights of the Round Table*, where he played Sir Lancelot (of course!), but we never renewed our romance. And Bob, despite all his efforts, couldn't break the mold of the beautiful lover. The film world remembers him that way, and I have to say that I do, too," she wrote.

Stanwyck never indicated she knew of the affair. But the moment *The Bribe* was in the can, she insisted her husband come with her to New York in a demonstration of togetherness. She hated her own shrill stance, her need to be in control, to humble her husband. She longed for Bob to put demands on her, to insist on *something, anything*. As always when she put her foot down, he did as he was told.

Helen arranged for the *New York Daily News*'s Earl Wilson to lunch with Barbara. On cue, no doubt, the columnist brought up the rumors that the Taylor marriage was terminal. Barbara snappily answered if she ever sued for alienation of affection, the defendant would be Bob's airplane.

"Taylor lives in the airplane—*lives* in it," she said. "Oh, there are times when I go up with him with a tight grip and a tight lip to keep the family together. It's his life and none of my business and I wouldn't try to interfere."

"Ha, who am I kidding? If I did try to interfere, it wouldn't do any good. He had planes before he knew me."

She explained that on the half-dozen occasions when Bob managed to persuade her to take to the air with him, he never tried to let her fly the plane "because he knows I can barely operate a car."

"So I just stay home and worry about him while he's flying. I don't say anything because I'm modern and I know the airplane is here to stay—darn it!"

Wilson's September 26, 1948, column was illustrated with a photo of Taylor and Stanwyck kissing.

Six months later, Barbara played the cuckolded wife to Ava Gardner's homewrecker in a humorless, slightly awed look at Manhattan's gossip-column set. MGM's first choice for *East Side, West Side* was its own Greer Garson, but Mervyn LeRoy insisted on Stanwyck opposite James Mason as the deceitful husband.* Louis B. and Dore Schary invited Barbara to the gigantic studio luncheon that, in April 1949, marked MGM's twenty-fifth anniversary. In the afternoon fifty-eight of the eighty players in Metro's contract roster posed for the famous photo—Bob in the last row.

Stanwyck and Gardner had no scenes together, and managed to avoid each other throughout the eight-week shoot. The rest of the cast included Van Heflin as an ex-cop turned author whose sleuthing eventually clears Mason of murder, Cyd Charisse as a breathless young model, Gale Sondergaard, William Conrad, Raymond Greenleaf, and a newcomer named Nancy Davis.

Schary thought the aseptic Davis had a bright look. Besides, she was sponsored by Spencer Tracy and Clark Gable, who had both met and dated her in New York.

In her memoirs, *My Turn*, the future first lady would remember being nervous about working with Stanwyck: "She was known as a real pro who always knew her lines—and who expected you to know yours. We had a long scene together, in which I had all the lines, and got my part right on the first take, the crew broke into applause and Barbara congratulated me. That was probably my greatest moment in pictures—I felt I had really passed the test."

During the filming, Davis discovered her name was on the blacklist. She went to LeRoy and told the director she had been mistaken for another Nancy Davis in New York. LeRoy called Strickling. The publicity chief arranged for an item to appear in Louella Parsons's syndicated column pointing out that the Nancy Davis on the list of Communist sympathizers was not the Nancy Davis under contract to Metro.

When she was still unhappy, LeRoy suggested the Screen Actors Guild look into her case. SAG president Reagan reported back to LeRoy that there were at least three other

---

*Isobel Lennart's screenplay followed Marcia Davenport's 1947 bestseller. Making movies from novels was MGM's continued insurance policy, and *East Side, West Side* brought the total of novels filmed by MGM in 1949 to ten.

Nancy Davises in Hollywood. Next, Reagan called Nancy herself and invited her for dinner.

LeRoy had a gift for tearjerkers, and *East Side, West Side* offered him exemplary opportunities for moving his characters through a complicated plot that turns from a love triangle to an explosive whodunit when Gardner's femme fatale is found murdered. He cuts from sympathetic to hostile situations and punctures contrived situations with dramatic interludes that help overcome the stock characters of suffering wife, straying husband, and sultry siren. Barbara was never comfortable with Gardner in the cast and overacted so terribly as the wife who stops pretending her husband still loves her that critics made a note of it.

Clark Gable came on the set one day to ask Barbara if she would like to play a smart-ass newspaperwoman. *To Please a Lady* was the story of a professional race-car driver who is the menace of the Indianapolis 500 and a columnist and radio commentator who doesn't exactly fall for his style and says so. The dialogue was flip and fast. After playing *East Side, West Side*'s long-suffering wife, doing an energetic journalist in control of her emotions sounded so good she immediately said yes. Howard Strickling's news release quoted her as saying "Gable has the right to chose his leading lady. And I'm it."

27

Primal Women

Stanwyck's icy albino spider in *Double Indemnity* showed what a sensational dramatic actress she had learned to be. The rotten-to-the-heart femme fatale had not killed her career as she had feared when Billy Wilder offered her the part. Since *Double Indemnity*, she had starred in twelve movies. Audiences had come to admire her for the way she played self-assured women who, although ready to use feminine wiles, were smart and tough enough to survive without duplicity. Whatever the riches her screen characters were offered or inherited, whatever comforts and serenity they won or filched, none of them forgot the hard times. With an inflection of her voice or a glance, she knew how to impart an edge, a dignity, and an awareness of women's primal struggle, even when none was written into the part. She gave up analyzing every script offered her. What made her say yes or no to a role was whether it *worked* for her. "I couldn't take a part and tear it to pieces, analyzing it," she said when she was eighty. "See, I'd rather make a mistake than lose the vitality." She never hovered over her writers with suggestions. "I could never answer a question about a character until I was playing her so I was no help to writers."

Stanwyck knew she was no great beauty, but with grit, aches, and sex appeal she made versatility pay. "First I look for a good story. By that I mean one that says something. Does the public want to see and hear the story? Will the leading characters interest them? Then I read the character and ask myself, 'Can I do this part?' Do I know enough about this type of person?'" Douglas Sirk, who directed her in two 1950s films, said she was more expressive than any actress he had worked with. "She has depth as a person. There is this amazing stillness about her, and there is nothing the least bit phony."

She didn't think of herself as a comedienne, though she played comedy with great success. Comedy was in the writing, she said—Claude Binyon and Dalton Trumbo on *You Belong to Me*, Preston Sturges on *The Lady Eve*. "Both of those films I did with Henry Fonda, who is a wonderful comedian. If it's a situation comedy I'm all right, but just for me to be funny— I'm not a funny person."

Four Stanwyck pictures were in the can, in postproduction, or in release in the fall of 1949, and the romantic drama with Clark Gable was set to go. Offscreen Barbara's face adorned the pages of *Life, Time, Collier's,* and *The Saturday Evening Post* in Chesterfield cigarette advertising ("To my friends and fans I recommend Chesterfields. It's *my* cigarette"). She turned down a half-dozen films, but also talked herself into lending her name to movies that she should have been smart enough to reject. She justified her acceptance of less-than-promising scripts by saying an actress worth her salt could play *any* part.

The Motion Picture Alliance for the Preservation of American Ideals was at the height of its power. It had offices at 159 South Beverly Drive, two blocks from the Helen Ferguson Agency, where it compiled names of suspected communists for HUAC, issued press releases, and circulated anticommunist brochures. Alliance President John Wayne demanded "a delousing" of Hollywood and urged "all organizations within the film industry and all civic organizations in the community to press for a resolution to require registration of all communists."

Barbara applauded the Justice Department's prosecution of Charles Chaplin. The FBI had files on Chaplin stretching back to 1922, and J. Edgar Hoover's G-men were interviewing Hedda Hopper to bolster their never-proven allegation that the comedian had been a communist. Chaplin's gravest affront, in Barbara's eyes, was that he had never become a citizen. His second offense was mocking America's moral pomposity. She didn't speak out too loudly in public, however, perhaps because the writer of *The Strange Love of Martha Ivers,*

Robert Rossen, was now on the blacklist, and Lewis Milestone was part of the counteroffensive. After taking the Fifth Amendment, the ailing J. Edward Bromberg, Barbara's fellow actor from *Lady of Burlesque*, died of a heart attack, prompting Clifford Odets to say that at a time when citizens were "hounded out of home, honor, livelihood and painfully accredited career by the tricks and twists of shameless shabby politicians banded together into yapping packs," Bromberg's demise amounted to "death by political misadventure."

The Red hunt did nothing to improve the quality of American films. Finding it hard to adjust to new popular moods and aspirations, the industry dished out safe, light entertainment. The number of movies dealing with social and psychological affairs declined while production of intentionally anticommunist pictures rose. The sexual politics that pressured women to give up their jobs to returning servicemen influenced Capra's first postwar movie. Unlike the Barbara Stanwyck and Jean Arthur single-career women of his earlier films, *It's a Wonderful Life*'s Donna Reed is a housewife and a mother.

Television *was* proving a threat even though it remained an unmentionable in corporate Hollywood. While trade papers reported on the drop in movie attendance and the corresponding increase in TV viewing, television was a no-no subject among gainfully employed studio people. Episodic series were proliferating on the tiny black-and-white tube, almost all "kinescoped" in New York, although a pair of Helen Ferguson clients, Lucille Ball and her husband, Desi Arnez, were thinking of making a TV comedy series at the RKO studio on Gower Street. Barbara free-lanced for most of her career, but scores of her friends were set adrift without studio contracts. Many went to New York, assuming the capital of radio would also be the nerve center of TV production.

Bob felt he had gone beyond his patriotic duty playing a Commie in *Conspirator*. Echoing Ronald Reagan's crack that the parts Jack Warner gave him were so bad he could "telephone his lines in and it wouldn't make any difference," Bob said he wouldn't have to get out of bed to phone in his lines. Below his posturing lurked a new fear. He was afraid of the studio's fresh crop of leading men.

Rather than face his wife over the dinner table, Bob

went on hunting trips with his friends. When his navy buddy Tom Purvis came out from Chicago for a visit, he stayed at a hotel Bob paid for. "Barbara didn't like me, so I didn't like Barbara," Purvis would recall. "Understand we didn't know each other except for one or two brief encounters, but I was Bob's navy buddy and she was jealous. I felt kind of sorry for him because he put me up in a suite in the best hotel to make up for the lack of hospitality on Barbara's part—though he never put it to me that way. He knew that I knew." There was nothing to talk about even when Bob did bring a few friends home. In the company of Purvis, Bob called himself Dilly; Tom's nickname was Curly. Dilly and Curly talked hunting and fishing, and their conversation always excluded Barbara.

When Bob and Purvis flew off on their camping trips, Helen stayed with Barbara. Without neglecting Helen Ferguson Agency, she was adding movie-career counseling to her business and becoming a panelist on the television show "RSVP."

Before Metro could schedule the Gable drama *To Please a Lady*, Hal Wallis again went after Stanwyck. The producer asked Marty Holland, the author of *Fallen Angel* and its director, Otto Preminger, to come up with a thriller intriguing enough to lure Stanwyck. What Wallis wanted was a story that explored the neurotic fringes of passion and destructive triangles—a woman between two men as in Preminger's *Laura* and *Daisy Kenyon* or a man between two women as in *Fallen Angel*.

Holland delivered. She wrote a short story about a woman with a past who, to safeguard a criminal plan benefiting herself and another man, ensnares a district attorney only to fall in love with him. The Viennese Preminger with his trademark shaven head and Prussian manners was the hot film noir director. Preminger had Ketti Frings rewrite Holland's script. Working with Otto was supposed to be a form of shock treatment, but Barbara was ready to try. She quickly said yes to *Thelma Jordan*.

When Preminger ultimately proved unavailable, Barbara agreed to Wallis's choice of Robert Siodmak. The German-born director had followed the beaten track from Berlin to Paris to Los Angeles. His big break had come in 1944, when he met Joan Harrison, Alfred Hitchcock's English assistant. To make it on her own, Harrison bought the rights to *The Phantom Lady*, a mystery story by Cornell Woolrich, who wrote under a variety of pseudonyms. *The Phantom Lady* proved successful beyond all expectation. It kicked Siodmak's career into high gear and made him the master of moody, atmospheric thrillers.

Barbara was conscious of a change in public attitudes. Moviegoers seemed to want less sugarcoating when it came to depicting human nature. King Vidor was shooting *The Fountainhead* she had wanted so much. In *Pinky*, Elia Kazan was trying to come to grips with the taboo subject of interracial romance, and in *The Asphalt Jungle* John Huston was filming a caper from the criminals' point of view. *The File on Thelma Jordan*, said Wallis, was about the extremes to which people will go to get money. With her customary speed, Barbara read all of Woolrich's books, including those written under his pen name William Irish. Woolrich sold *I Married a Dead Man* to Paramount and a short story that Hitchcock turned into Rear Window.

The File on Thelma Jordan script spun the chilling logic of *Double Indemnity* in a new direction. Thelma Jordan tricks the innocent Cleve Marshall (Wendell Corey) into helping her with a crime that benefits her and another man, only to fall in love with Corey. Siodmak's thrillers delivered their punchy payoffs through expressionistic lighting and offbeat, sometimes loony characters—Franchot Tone in *The Phantom Lady*, Charles Laughton in *The Suspect*—and lustful women— Yvonne De Carlo in *Criss Cross*. In *Thelma Jordan*, he gave Barbara the screen's most erotic cigarette holder. He built action and suspense, but his best shock effects were missing. Paramount kept *Thelma Jordan* on the shelf for over a year. Before its halfhearted 1950 release, however, Barbara starred in another thriller by Woolrich.

I Married a Dead Man was the first and last of Woolrich's major crime novels that Mitchell Leisen, in league with Stanwyck, persuaded Paramount to buy as a Stanwyck vehicle. Bleaker than Woolrich's *The Bride Wore Black* and *Waltz into Darkness*, *I Married a Dead Man* told the story of Helen Georgesson, pregnant and fighting a sadistic lover, injured in a train collision and wrongly identified at the hospital as another pregnant woman found dead in the train wreckage. The joke around Paramount in the early summer of 1949 was that Leisen was spending more time shooting a train wreck than directing Barbara Stanwyck. In an inside-joke homage to Barbara's publicist friend, Catherine Turney rechristened the heroine of Woolrich's assumed-identity thriller Helen Ferguson.

Stanwyck is the haggard, sick, and very pregnant woman who embarks upon a transcontinental railway journey with five dollars to her name. The train is wrecked, and in the middle of the crash scene she goes into labor. The new mother assumes the identity of the dead woman next to her. When she meets the woman's family and sees its social position and inheritance, she is drawn into blackmail and near-murder.

As the male lead, John Lund was never better. The son of a Norwegian glassblower, Lund had reached stardom in 1946 opposite Olivia De Havilland in *To Each His Own*. Jane Cowl played the mother who assumes Helen is her daughter-in-law. Lund played Cowl's son and brother of the man whose death in the train wreck presumably has left the new mother a widow. Lyle Bettger was Barbara's blackmailing lover and father of her child and Phyllis Thaxter the woman killed in the accident.

Two stages over, Wilder was filming *Sunset Boulevard*, and besides concentrating on her Helen Ferguson role, Barbara had to soothe William Holden's frail ego and tell him a real actor can make love to an older woman. Montgomery Clift's agent had persuaded the sensational newcomer that teenage girls would never forgive him if he played a gigolo to Gloria Swanson's fading movie star. Bill, too, had been assailed by self-doubts once he agreed to play the screenwriter who can't hack it and lives off the wealthy and slightly dotty relic of the silent screen.

Leisen put as much gusto into filming hospital scenes as the train wreck. Helen is wheeled in to undergo surgery for her injuries, and her baby is delivered prematurely by cesarean section. The script cleverly teases the audience, revealing how Helen Ferguson is carried deeper into her own deception, how each time the new mother is on the verge of telling the truth, she is held back. Sooner than she thinks, however, Lund discovers the deceit, but she ingratiates herself in his and his family's favor. When evidence points to her as the murderer of her blackmailer, her new "family" staunchly defends her. For a happy ending, Bettger is revealed to have been killed by another woman altogether. Before its release, Paramount renamed the film *No Man of Her Own*, a title used in a 1932 Gable–Lombard comedy. Cue magazine suggested somebody should start a Society for the Prevention of Cruelty to Actresses and make Stanwyck a charter member: "For the punishment they're dishing out to her these days is murder. If she's not strangled to death (in *Sorry, Wrong Number*) she's being beaten to within an inch of her life (in *The Lady Gambles*), or shoved into suicide (*Thelma Jordan*) or left to die of tuberculosis (in *The Strange Love of Martha Ivers*)."

Barbara was thrilled when Hal Wallis invited her to match wits and acting tricks with Walter Huston. Ruby Stevens had watched Huston in *Desire Under the Elms* at the Greenwich Village Theatre in 1924. Now he would play her father, Wallis told her on the phone. "I'd carry a spear and hug the backdrop just to be in one scene with that one-in-a-million actor," she said.

The Furies was the first Freudian western, and Stanwyck's character a twin of her Polly Fulton part in *B. F.'s Daughter*. The McCarthy era explanation for a strong, aggressive woman was that her heart really belonged to Daddy. Whether he was an arrogant industrialist, a ruthless politician, or a hardened cattle baron, a father brought up his (usually only) daughter in his own image and swains had better beware: With her will and her money she would geld any suitor who tried to compete with her old man.

The Furies told the story of a cattle baron and his fights with the only person who dares oppose his iron will, his daughter. Huston played T. C. Jeffords, the tyrannical widow-father to Stanwyck's headstrong daughter. Their director was Anthony Mann, a former set designer who loved the big outdoors and made superb westerns. Inexplicably, Wallis vetoed Technicolor for this major production with its colorful cast and Arizona desert setting.

Wendell Corey was cast as a local gambler who dunks Barbara in a washbowl, bats her around, and then kisses her. Gilbert Roland played a squatter on the rangeland who becomes her lover, and Judith Anderson the "other woman," a scheming widow old T. C. Jeffords brings home as his new wife. When Jeffords hangs the squatter for horse stealing, his daughter sets out to ruin her father. It's an easy job since Jeffords has plastered the New Mexico countryside with "T.C.'s"—his own brand of currency redeemable in dollars he doesn't have. In the hate saga's most harrowing scene, Barbara forever alienates her father by disfiguring her stepmother with a well-aimed pair of scissors.

Niven Busch had adapted his own novel. Busch was an ex-rancher who came to Hollywood via sports reporting, and was an old hand at writing flamboyant westerns (*Duel in the Sun*). He was married to Teresa Wright, the star of his best screenplay, *Pursued*.

What he saw on *The Furies* set didn't impress him.

"I thought Stanwyck should have been better directed," he would remember. "And I thought the outdoor sequences should have been much better handled. They put Stanwyck on a miserable, fat-assed palomino that could hardly waddle. They were afraid she would get tossed off or something. They could have put her on a really good horse; she was a good horsewoman. I thought Gilbert Roland was good, but Wendell Corey was very insipid. They needed a very vital guy for that. That was a major weakness."

Barbara and Walter Huston, however, had a good time. They celebrated his sixty-fifth birthday on the set, and egged each other on. Doubles were ready to do a dangerous riding sequence one day, when Barbara decided she'd do her own riding. "I'm not going to let any broad show me," Huston shouted, hoisting himself into the saddle. Barbara said: "Thank God for the privilege of pitting all the skill I could beg, borrow or steal against Walter's greater skills in scenes we played together. I never won. But it was an honor to lose every scene to a guy like that."

After the shoot, John Huston invited Barbara to the birthday party he was arranging for his father at Romanoff's. Walter begged off that night, not feeling well. Twenty-four hours later he died of a heart attack.

Mann went from directing Barbara in *The Furies* to directing her husband in *The Devil's Doorway*, a pro-Indian western about a Shoshone who fights valiantly in the Civil

War but returns to Wyoming to find himself hated and threatened.

Barbara finally joined Clark Gable on *To Please a Lady*. Clarence Brown's set-side manners surprised her. Garbo's old no-nonsense director never raised his voice. In fact, he never told her and Gable what he wanted, but let them rehearse on their own. He spoke so softly they had to cross to the director's chair to hear his suggestions. Without explaining what engineering and directing had in common, Gable attributed Brown's skills as a director to his having started out as an engineer. *To Please a Lady* was Gable's and Brown's eighth film together.

After thirty years of studio filmmaking, Brown was discovering the fun of location shoots. He had just filmed William Faulkner's *Intruder in the Dust* in Faulkner's hometown of Oxford, Mississippi, with locals in bit parts and crowd scenes. To shoot authentic car racing, he took *To Please a Lady* to the Indianapolis 500 track.

Everything in Indiana was uneventful but for Barbara's brush with racial discrimination. She demanded a bedroom and bath for herself and the same for her longtime maid, Harriett Corey, with a sitting room between. Indianapolis's best hotel did not accommodate black persons. Barbara had MGM squirming when, as an alternative, she suggested the production make reservations for her and Harriet in the best "colored" hotel. When the company got to Indianapolis, Barbara and maid stayed in the city's best hotel.

Bob returned from *The Devil's Doorway* location in the deepest funk, not because of his director or location photography, which he said was exceptional, but because his career was going nowhere. It showed on the screen. His manner looked increasingly cantankerous.

He resented Metro's new stars—Van Johnson, Cornel Wilde, Frank Sinatra. Big was still big, of course—and with *Annie Get Your Gun*, *Father of the Bride*, and *The Asphalt Jungle* MGM-Loew made big money again. But movie attendance slumped to 60 million a week, the lowest since 1933. The falloff was sharpest in weak-to-medium attractions like *Ambush*, *Conspirator*, and The Devils' Doorway, precisely the pictures Bob starred in.

28

False Fronts

Darryl Zanuck told Joseph Mankiewicz to send copies of
his new script to Barbara Stanwyck, Claudette
Colbert, and Gertrude Lawrence. Barbara was shooting *To Please a Lady*, but read *All About Eve* in one evening.
There were in-jokes in this cruel and cynical backstage story
(the virago heroine's director-lover is preparing to leave
Broadway to direct a film in Hollywood for Zanuck) and
swipes at television ("That is all television is, dear—just auditions"). Barbara shuddered when she read a speech
Mankiewicz gave Margo Channing:

> Funny business, a woman's career. The things you drop
> on your way up the ladder—so you can move faster—
> you forget you'll need them when you go back to being
> a woman. That's one career all females have in com-
> mon whether we like it or not. Being a woman. Sooner
> or later, we've got to work at it, no matter what other
> careers we've had or wanted. And in the last analysis
> nothing is any good unless you can look up just before
> dinner—or turn in bed—and there he is. Without that
> you're not a woman. You're someone with a French
> provincial office—or a book full of clippings. But you're
> not a woman. Slow curtain. The end.

Mankiewicz knew more about women than any man
Barbara had ever met.

As Zanuck's fair-haired boy—and president of the
Directors Guild—Mankiewicz was another producer-writer

turned director to control his material. *All About Eve* explored the compulsion, camaraderie, cruelty, and self-indulgence of theater people, the skulduggery and bitchcraft of actresses, the neuroses, wit, fascination, and atmosphere of the backstage. When Zanuck phoned Barbara, she discovered Mankiewicz had already objected to having Marlene Dietrich as Margo, but the cast included Anne Baxter as Eve Harrington, George Sanders as the venomous and snobbish critic, and Fox contract player Gary Merrill as the director-lover. MCA's Lew Wasserman, Barbara's new agent, informed her the picture would start in San Francisco in mid-April 1950.

Getting Wasserman to represent her had been Jack Benny's idea. The dynamic, rail-thin Wasserman, who rose at five in the morning and spent his evenings screening features in his Beverly Hills mansion, was fast becoming the most powerful figure in the business. He rarely surfaced on the public record, opting instead for occasional appearances on the society pages. As president of MCA Artists, Ltd., he was gracious and soft-spoken, yet he was considered one of the most aggressive men in a business full of aggressive men. He had not only negotiated Benny's contract with the American Tobacco Company but advised Jack on his radio program. Barbara liked the fact that he had been married to the same woman for twenty years.

As Barbara pondered Margo, Bob flew in through the door to announce goddamn Louis B. was giving him the lead in goddamn MGM's biggest picture ever! Barbara hadn't seen her husband this excited since he went into the navy.

Bob had Louis B. Mayer down pat. "Yes, son, you are going to star in the biggest of them all. *Quo Vadis* will have everything in Technicolor, persecuted Christians, Rome in flames, a cast of thousands and you loving Deborah Kerr." The director would be their friend Mervyn LeRoy.

Barbara told her husband he'd better start taking fencing lessons.

Quo Vadis had been in the works for over a year. Henryk Sienkiewicz's 1896 worldwide bestseller had been filmed as a silent three times, and the script of this fourth edition was the object of a fierce battle between Mayer and his production chief, Dore Schary. Mayer wanted a Technicolor religious epic. Schary had hired John Huston, who, with a classics scholar, wrote a screenplay that stressed the parallel between Nero and modern dictators. Preproduction had started in Paris, and after seeing a screen test, everybody approved Peter Ustinov for Nero. Also okayed was the casting of Gregory Peck as the Roman aristocrat who eventually leads a revolt against Nero and Elizabeth Taylor as the Christian maiden he falls in love with.

Eager to show that *he*, not Schary, was still in charge, L.B. fired Huston and everybody else except Ustinov and gave the starring roles to Taylor and Kerr. The screenplay confected by John Lee Mahin, S. N. Behrman, and Sonya Levien was pure imitation Cecil B. De Mille.

MGM chose to film the colossal—the adjective was part of the billing—movie in Rome. Cinecittà's new studio offered bargain-price facilities and crowds of thousands. Five thousand extras would be used in the triumphal march to Nero's palace. Twenty lions would eat Christians, and two cheetahs would flank Patricia Laffan, who would play the jealous Empress Poppaea. Bob would be flying to Rome just a few weeks after Barbara started *All About Eve* in San Francisco.

Was it Bob's boyish enthusiasm that tipped the balance and made Barbara say no to Margo Channing? Or superstition, fear of playing the loser, the actress on the skids, the sharp-tongued star who realizes too late she hasn't learned to be a woman? Something in Mankiewicz's dazzling, corrosive story made Stanwyck wonder about her marriage and made her decide to stay closer to her husband. Telling Wasserman she had decided to say no to *All About Eve*, she asked her agent to look for a film she could do in Europe.

Wasserman came back with one possibility. *Another Man's Poison* would shoot in London. It was a thriller about a blackmailer who has proof that a woman murdered her husband. The author was the English writer-producer Val Guest.

Colbert got *All About Eve*. A back injury, however, forced her out. When Gertrude Lawrence insisted Margo's drunken scene be eliminated, Bette Davis read the script, thought it brilliant, and, ten days before shooting started, signed on. She wasn't Margo Channing, she said, but she understood her all too well. "I knew Margo felt every one of those years hitting her, and I felt down here in my gut every word she said when she told her lover, 'I hate men!' She hated them for staying attractive forever. From the day I was forty, I *screamed* every time I saw a mirror."

Bob left for the *Quo Vadis* location. The summer of 1950 proved to be one of the hottest on record for Rome, and the huge, complicated picture soon fell behind schedule. The feedback Barbara got from Cinecittà was positive. Bob didn't look silly in plumed helmet and short toga, and the fencing lessons had given him a kind of ease and grace he had never had before. Everybody was pleased with Bob as Marcus Vinicius and Kerr as the Christian maiden, even if Ustinov's Nero going mad ran away with the show. On the transatlantic telephone, Bob warned Barbara that principal photography was expected to stretch into October, perhaps even November.

But other rumors from Rome spoiled Barbara's preparations for her train-to-New-York-ocean-liner-to-Southampton-train-to-London voyage to start *Another Man's Poison*. Los Angeles newspapers published Rome-datelined wire service stories saying Robert Taylor was having an affair with a red-headed slave girl. Barbara ignored the gossip, but as the filming dragged on the slave got a name. She was Lia de Leo, a twenty-five-year-old Roman divorcée. Barbara began to panic when Howard Strickling swore he had nothing to do with it, that the rumors were certainly not publicity "plants." Los Angeles newspapers printed wire service stories from Rome quoting Lia as saying she was "Robert Taylor's big love."

Barbara felt exposed to pity and ridicule. Hedda Hopper and Louella Parsons phoned her at home for her reaction. When she refused to answer, the two columnists reported her embarrassed fumblings. To Hopper asking if it was true Bob wanted a divorce, Barbara snapped, "He didn't say anything about it at breakfast, but wait a minute, I'll ask him." In her column, Hopper reported how Stanwyck was back on the phone a few minutes later: "He says not today, Hedda. Sorry. Good-bye."

Maddeningly, the gossip columnists who predicted the collapse of the Taylors' marriage waxed heavenly on the Bette Davis romance with Gary Merrill on the set of *All About Eve*. The two wouldn't stop kissing when Mankiewicz shouted, "Cut!"

Barbara decided to take Helen with her to Europe. Again, despite Helen's advice on how to handle the press, Barbara said silly things that only added to the fire. She missed her husband, she told Parsons, but she was not going straight to Rome. She had made five pictures in eight months, she explained, so she would be taking a little vacation. It was so hot in Rome, Bob kept telling her. Besides he was busy with *Quo Vadis*.

Barbara hated the word "divorce." It had never been seriously used in connection with her and Bob. Despite occasional sniping and speculation, for twelve years they had been Hollywood's Happy Star Marriage. As Adela Rogers St. Johns put it when somebody criticized the Tinseltown divorce rate, "Someone else punched a button that lit up a neon sign saying Robert Taylor and Barbara Stanwyck—Their Happy Marriage."

Barbara burst her bubble of calculated serenity by flying to London. For someone as notoriously afraid of flying as she, getting on TWA's turboprop for the Los Angeles–Albuquerque–Kansas City–New York–Gander –Reykjavik–Shannon–London journey could only mean acute desperation.

Barbara and Helen's arrival in London was low-key, but the gossip from Rome wasn't letting up. The Robert Taylor dalliance followed on the heels of another Italian scandal— Ingrid Bergman's leaving America, husband, and daughter for Roberto Rossellini. Over thirty American reporters and photographers had stalked the pregnant Ingrid and laid siege to the clinic where her illegitimate child was born.

While reporters waited to cover the expected Bergman-Rossellini marriage, the *Quo Vadis* set was fair game. Celebrities passing through Rome got themselves invited to Cinecittà to see LeRoy lord it over his cast of thousands. Sam and Frances Goldwyn visited the *Quo Vadis* shoot, and, more embarrassing to Barbara, so did Mary and Jack Benny. To soothe Barbara and neutralize Lia's monopoly on press attention, Strickling ordered the *Quo Vadis* unit publicist to leak reports that Bob was seen "swimming, dining and dancing with numerous Italian beauties." The name of "starlet" Marina Berti was dropped.

Tom Purvis was staying with Bob in his rented Rome apartment. Enlisted by Bob, if not by Strickling, to try to restore a semblance of propriety, the old navy buddy told the press how, one night when they were relaxing in the apartment, an unnamed actress rang and said she was coming up. Bob told Tom to stay so the young woman wouldn't get any ideas. Said Purvis, "Seemed to me it was the usual crush-on-a-movie-star thing or maybe she thought he could get her into the movies."

In London, Guest and director Irving Rapper were doing a rewrite to calibrate the script to Stanwyck. Guest agreed to pay her fare to Rome, and, if *Quo Vadis* finished early enough, to her spending Christmas with Bob and starting *Another Man's Poison* after New Year's. While producer and director fine-tuned *Another Man's Poison*, Barbara decided to confront her husband, the *Quo Vadis* set, and the paparazzi. With Helen in tow, she flew to Rome.

Whether the crisis was the unforeseen slide toward a final parting or the last act of a twelve-year charade neither would ever say. Their private confrontation in Bob's rented apartment was brief and a total defeat for Barbara. With the intention of bringing Bob to his senses, she decided to frighten him by saying a divorce was in order. To her surprise, he agreed. She exploded in anger and told him that if he divorced her, she'd make him pay for it for the rest of his life.

They had never said an unkind word about each other in public. They were not about to. On orders from Strickling in Culver City, the unit publicists put a happy spin on the reunited man and wife. Press releases told how Bob greeted his wife with $8,000 worth of diamonds, how Barbara's gifts to her husband included cuff links bearing the likeness of him as Marcus Vinicius, and, when they got home, a Cadillac. Strickling tried to mastermind events with breathless handouts on how Bob was showing his wife the sights of the Eternal City. As the Taylors' personal press agent, Helen played along, filling in blissful details on how happy Barbara was to see her husband, how "tickled pink" he was seeing her.

Years later details of Barbara's desperation would come from Guest. The producer would remember her in tears on the telephone from Rome, calling to tell him she couldn't do *Another Man's Poison*. "I'm sorry. My whole life is in shreds after all these years we've been married," she told him. "I've got to go right back home and arrange a divorce."

Guest tried to salvage his picture by saying the best thing for her was probably to work, but she was adamant. She had to go back to California. As she had done in *All About Eve*, Bette Davis stepped into the breach. In July, she had made Merrill her fourth husband. A part was found for the groom in *Another Man's Poison*.

Bob refused all comments on his marriage, himself, and Lia when he returned from Rome, but newspapers announced the Taylors were divorcing. With his mother, Ralph Couser, and Ralph's wife, Bob moved into a rented house in Brentwood. In Rome, Lia fanned the flames by telling reporters Bob "is tired of her [Barbara] and told me so." When Louella Parsons got to Stanwyck, Barbara told her Bob and she would be going on a three-month vacation. Instead, Bob went to Palm Springs alone. Barbara refused to meet the press. On November 23, 1950, he was hospitalized for a double hernia operation. Barbara was forced to talk to reporters. She limited her comments to saying her husband's recovery was progressing "satisfactorily."

Adela Rogers St. Johns saw through the Taylors' front. When it was all over she wrote that Bob and Barbara "went around putting on false fronts, about as convincing as the masks children wear on Halloween. Behind them you could see Bob and Barbara, forlorn, lost, lonely, kidding nobody but themselves, maybe, and each other."

At a hastily called news conference a week before Christmas, Helen Ferguson read a joint statement:

> In the past few years, because of professional require-
> ments, we have been separated just too often and too
> long. Our sincere and continued efforts to maintain our
> marriage have failed. We are deeply disappointed that
> we could not solve our problems. We really tried. We
> unhappily and reluctantly admit that we have denied
> [it] to even our closest friends because we wanted to
> work things out together in as much privacy as possible.
> There will be a California divorce. Neither of us has
> any other romantic interest whatsoever.

Louella Parsons didn't buy that and in her column wrote the trouble that led to the Taylors' decision to part was buried much deeper than in "that Italian girl."

29

Herself

Looking chic in a cocoa-colored tailored suit and matching straw hat, Barbara appeared in Los Angeles Superior Court February 21, 1951. In a brief statement, she told Judge Thurmond Clarke her husband was tired of being married to her. "He said he had enjoyed his freedom during the months he was making a movie in Italy. He wanted to be able to live his life without restriction." To her attorney David Tannenbaum's question of what effect Taylor's request for a divorce had had on her, she said, "It shocked me greatly. I was ill for several weeks and under my physician's care."

Barbara did not charge mental cruelty—the popular charge by divorcing actresses. Her petition for a divorce decree was uncontested, and Bob chose not to be present. He was represented instead by his counsel, Lester Lappen. Helen Ferguson was Barbara's witness, testifying that she received a hysterical call from her friend to come right over to the Taylor house: "When I got there, I found Barbara in a tragic emotional state. She said to me, 'I want to make a statement. I am going to give Bob the divorce he wants.'" Helen said she stayed with Stanwyck until 5:00 A.M. and that it took "two hours for Barbara to calm down." During that time, Helen testified, "Mr. Taylor said hardly a word."

Judge Clarke interrupted. "That will be enough. Divorce granted!"

The proceedings were among the shortest in the records of movie divorces. A property settlement was approved by the court but not made public. Pressed by reporters, however, Bob's lawyer Lappen revealed that his client relinquished to

Stanwyck his interest in their Holmby Hills home, valued at $100,000, all furnishings, and 15 percent of his earnings until Barbara remarried or either party died. A judicial award for alimony was rarely made unless applied for, and her request for permanent alimony was exceptional by the standards of 1950s California divorce law. But as she had told Bob in Rome, she would make him pay for the rest of his life.

On the way out of the courtroom, Barbara spotted Harriett Corey. The two women embraced. Barbara cried softly. Reporters in the corridor wanted to know whether Bob had demanded the divorce so he could marry the Italian beauty. "You'd have to ask Mr. Taylor about that," she answered. Asked whether she had a boyfriend herself, she shuddered. "I've had enough. I don't want any more of that!"

The Los Angeles press reported the divorce as evidence that Robert Taylor had lost his heart to Lia de Leo in Rome. The next day's *Los Angeles Mirror* called Stanwyck a graying actress. The *Herald-Express* quoted her as saying she was tired of being "a long-distance telephone wife." News photographers hounded Taylor in L.A. and Lia in Rome. He blew up a couple of times. Once at a quiet cocktail party with Rex Harrison, he turned to the reporters and photographers and shouted. "I'm here, aren't I? Is Lia with me?" In Rome, Lia said it was no doubt for the best if she and Robert remained just friends.

Much later Bob would put it all rather simply. "Let's just say Barbara is a very strong personality. I respect her deeply and treasure her friendship . . . I always felt her talent was far greater than my own; it came easier to her, and she made the most of her gifts." Tom Purvis thought Bob and Barbara had simply tired of each other and of their way of life. "Maybe they should have adopted children," he said. "Bob loved kids, but Barbara had no time for them. Dion was a sad example. She and Bob had only one thing in common—the movie industry."

Standing in the entrance hall at North Faring Road the first night as a divorced woman, Barbara wasn't sure she would make it. As a little girl she had tried to kid away her sorrows by asking who had more fun—kids or cats? Now, she asked the empty house if anyone was home for a game of solitaire. The blow was not only to her pride. For the first time she felt existentially alone. Nothing had lasted in her quick-change life. Whatever their differences, she had wanted the marriage to Bob to last. In her late seventies, when Bob was long since dead, she would say it took her a long time to accept that he had wanted to be a married bachelor. "I remember telling him that every man who lived wants that, wants it both ways. I'm known as someone who takes care of herself, it's true, but I worked hard at the marriage because I wanted it."

At the suggestion of Clark Gable and Howard Strickling, Bob began seeing Gable's recent discard, Virginia Grey. The twenty-eight-year-old actress was a Metro contractee who never made it out of B pictures. Her romance with Gable had made headlines. Friends suspected Clark had found a successor to the late Carole Lombard and that he and Virginia would marry. Instead, it was the thrice-married Lady Sylvia Ashley who, after a whirlwind courtship, became the fourth Mrs. Gable.

Dating Taylor, Virginia would remember, was in many ways "very strange."

"At the end of the evening he would manage to disappear without saying goodnight. The first time it happened I spent hours looking for him, thinking something had happened to him. Nothing of the sort. Bob had simply gone home. He did not want to go through that sticky, phony 'I'll call you tomorrow or see you next week' business, so he left. Then he'd call and nothing was mentioned about his disappearance. He meant well. When he was on location making a film, he wrote to me regularly. Often Bob would say he was sorry I did not come along, but he never asked."

He insisted on keeping their dating secret. Virginia realized that if she wanted to see him again she shouldn't talk, and no rumors of Taylor's "new love interest" reached the gossip columns. Their "dating" ended when he was sent to Arizona to star in *Westward the Women*, a onetime Frank Capra project directed by William Wellman.

Barbara turned forty-four. Her private life was still the best-kept secret in Hollywood. Exhibiting grief and rancor was not her style, but friends and acquaintances found her moody, bitter, and "very tough." Did she mean herself or Bob when, in a commentary Helen ghosted for her for Edward R. Murrow's CBS Radio news show, she said that people who have been hurt lash out? She admitted she had a hard time learning to turn the other cheek. Was anyone to blame? She mentioned Bob's airplane, perhaps meaning Ralph Couser or Tom Purvis. She wondered whether she and Bob would find a way of reconciling. The self-imposed loneliness made her drink too much, and to get out of her funk she grasped at any chance to work.

Jack Benny said she had nerves of ice: "Maybe it's hammy, but that old line 'the show must go on'—that's Barbara." The trouper in her showed at the Screen Writers Guild's annual awards dinner. Since the divorce date practically coincided with the awards dinner, the guild organizers expected her to beg off, but she showed up exquisitely dressed and, facing the appraising stares of gossip columnists and fellow actors, launched into the planned skit, letter-perfect as always.

The divorce might have brought her closer to her son, but even if she had been so inclined, the twenty-year-old Dion had been drafted for a two-year tour of duty in the army that included a rotation to Germany.

Before Dion left for boot camp, Uncle Buck suggested that his mother at least see him. She agreed to a lunch. "When I met her, she just stuck out her gloved hand," Dion would recall. "She didn't kiss me, she didn't hug me. And after some small talk I learned the real reason for breaking the five-year silence—she began to lecture me on how to behave in the army."

That was the last time mother and son saw each other.

Claiming she could not bear to live in the house that had been her and Bob's home since 1940, Barbara auctioned the furniture, movie projectors, and a hundred other items. The auction hit the society pages as Lady Thelma Furness and her sister Consuelo Vanderbilt bought silverware and an unknown bidder carried away a series of ten studies of western pioneer women by Frederic Remington. Two days after the auction, the newly divorced were seen together at Ciro's on *Sunset Boulevard*. Letters, telegrams, and phone calls from fans pleaded for a reconciliation.

They continued to see each other. Bob was up for the fictionalized Frank Fay opposite Judy Garland as Barbara in Warner Brothers' musicalized remake of *A Star Is Born* (James Mason was the thirteenth and definitive choice). News-agency photos appeared showing Bob and Barbara together in a restaurant booth. Bob was "seen" with Sybil Merritt and Lane Trumbel, a pair of screen ingenues, but when reporters asked Barbara if there were a chance of reconciling, she said it was too early to say. For her July 16 birthday, Bob sent her a heart of diamonds. Always insecure and awkward at one-to-one interviews, he kept Helen as his press agent. As late as 1953, Bob was reported to be "dating" his former wife as well as Debra Paget and Darryl Zanuck's youngest daughter, Susan.

Barbara bought a smaller home at 273 South Beverly Glen Boulevard, on the fringe of Holmby Hills, and lived with Uncle Buck, Harriett Corey, a cook, and a twice-a-week gardener. Claudette Colbert and Irene Dunne were neighbors. Visitors found Barbara's new home at once feminine and austere. She sold the Renoir she and Bob had bought but kept a snowy Vlaminck landscape. To occupy herself during the few hours she allotted to leisure, she read ravenously—almost a book a day.

Uncle Buck was her only "family." Her brother, Byron, now a board member of the Screen Extras Guild, had married and lived in Los Angeles with his wife and son, but she rarely saw them. Maud was still in Brooklyn.

The day the Stanwyck-Taylor divorce became final in February 1952, Louella Parsons called Barbara. The columnist expected to hear the phrase she had heard so many times, that the new divorcée was glad it was finally all over. Instead, Barbara told her she and Bob had tried to reconcile. "My divorce from Bob was none of my doing," she said. "I think our unhappiness started from the time he bought an airplane. Then he went on fishing and hunting trips with other men and was always away from home. I finally asked him if I was making too many pictures and he insisted that I keep on." Parsons felt there was so much pent-up hurt behind those words that she suggested Barbara would marry again, that with her gray hair and young face she had never been more attractive.

Barbara would have none of it: "I hope I won't ever marry again. I'm a two-time loser."

A couple of cast-off wives became her friends. Joan Blondell kidded that Barbara shouldn't complain. Blondell had never abandoned her man, but crooner Dick Powell had left her for June Allyson, and Mike Todd had left her for Evelyn Keyes. Joan exuded a longing for home and domesticity. So did Nancy Sinatra, a thirty-two-year-old mother of three.

Nancy's marriage to Frank was ending in humiliation. Frank flaunted his tempestuous affair with Ava Gardner and tried to bully Nancy into granting him a divorce. Nancy hoped she could outlast Gardner and told the press, "Frank has left home, but he has done it before and I suppose he'll do it again." To save appearances, MGM shipped Ava to Spain to start work on *Pandora and the Flying Dutchman* and terminated Sinatra's contract one year early.

In August, the crooner forced the issue. With Ava he went on a press-hounded vacation to Acapulco. The news media assumed he would obtain a quick Mexican divorce and marry Ava. It was in Nevada, however, that the Sinatras finally divorced, he capitulating to every one of his wife's financial demands and Nancy walking out of the court a rich woman. In November, Frank married Ava in Philadelphia.

Barbara and Nancy were daughters of New York–area working-class parents—Nancy Barbato grew up in Hoboken, New Jersey. They had both married entertainers, and both tried to hang on to their husbands. Much separated them, too. The Sinatra marriage had been a traditional one, Frank as breadwinner, Nancy as homemaker. As a mother, Barbara had been a disaster; Nancy brought up her daughters, Nancy and Christina, and her son, Frank Jr., in the tradition of second-generation Italian-Americans. When Frank won an Oscar for *From Here to Eternity*, it was Nancy he phoned, not Ava. By 1954, Frank and Ava separated. Over the years, Stanwyck would become closer to the Sinatra children than she had ever been to Dion.

Oscar Levant would remember Barbara and Nancy arriving together at a party at the Ira Gershwins. "I hadn't seen Barbara in twenty years and out of what I think was a desperate loneliness, she came over and kissed me," he would write in his memoirs. "We had never kissed, good friends though we were. I was very touched. I had always pulled for her and had never forgotten her."

Stanwyck's circle of friends was small. It included fellow actors and their wives, Jack and Mary Benny, the MacMurrays, the McCreas, and William and Ardis (Brenda Marshall) Holden. Barbara remained close to Peter and Renée Godfrey, who had named their eldest daughter after her. Stanwyck lobbed gifts on the three-year-old girl and followed the development of her twin sisters, Jill and Tracy. Barbara described herself as serene. "I'm concentrating on work, and this is what it takes: serenity, beauty, quiet, friends when I want them, and the valuable state of being alone which a creative person must have in between," she told Hedda Hopper.

In fact, she was scared. She commanded top money—$150,000 per picture. Even if veteran stars were still working, how big was the demand for forty-four-year-old leading ladies? Stars younger than she had retired or were deemed passé. Rita Hayworth had left to marry Prince Aly Khan, and MGM had fired Judy Garland. Joan Fontaine's only film since 1948 had been the trashy *Born to Be Bad*, Katharine Hepburn had not worked since 1949, Ava Gardner's last picture had been *East Side, West Side*, and Jennifer Jones was used mostly in the vanity films her husband, David Selznick, produced.

With Bill and Ardis, Barbara attended a private studio screening of *Sunset Boulevard*. Previews in Evanston, Illinois, and Long Island, New York, had proved disastrous. Paramount postponed its release. As the Holdens and Stanwyck entered the screening for film luminaries, there were rumors the studio might shelve the film permanently.

Gloria Swanson was right behind them, making her entrance wearing a floor-length silver lamé dress. Once the lights dimmed, the audience saw Swanson play Norma Desmond ruthlessly, without regard for sympathy. The 111 minutes the film lasted went by in a hush, and after the shattering climax, silence greeted the end credits. When the lights went up, there was thunderous applause. Louis B. Mayer was in a rage. "You have disgraced the industry that made you and fed you," he yelled at director Billy Wilder as he stalked out. Barbara had tears streaming down her face as she pushed her way forward to congratulate Swanson.

The November premiere of *All About Eve* at Grauman's Chinese Theatre and the studio party at Ciro's turned Bette Davis into the actress of the year. Hedda Hopper called Bette Davis's performance the most thrilling comeback in 1950: "A succession of bad, yes, mediocre pictures had proved that not even the queen was immune to the skids . . . For my money, her performance in *All About Eve* tops anything she ever did." Two months later, *All About Eve* racked up a record fourteen Oscar nominations. *Sunset Boulevard* was listed eleven times.

Stanwyck and Claudette Colbert sat together at the Pantages Theatre on Hollywood Boulevard on March 29, 1951, watching Billy Wilder, Charles Brackett, and D. M. Marshman, Jr., pick up Oscars for the *Sunset Boulevard* screenplay and Franz Waxman the Music award. But it was Zanuck, Mankiewicz, and Sanders who stood grinning in their tuxedos with *All About Eve*'s Best Picture, Best Direction, and Best Supporting Actor Oscars. Judy Holliday scored as Best Actress in George Cukor's *Born Yesterday*.

At the post-Oscar party, Colbert told Mankiewicz a knife of jealousy was going through her heart. Barbara paid Davis a convoluted compliment that she might have meant for herself. Playing an older woman now, she said, meant Bette would never have to cross the age bridge again.

The ever-cynical Wilder embraced Barbara and, for hovering news-hounds, came up with an unprintable Barbara Stanwyck story. To prove she was earthy he told of a poolside risposte of hers. An aging actress complained to Barbara and Wilder how her young lover was spending $100,000 of her money on sports cars, jewelry, and clothes for himself. "Tell me, darling," Wilder quoted Barbara as telling the lady, "is the screwing you're getting worth the screwing you're getting?"

Barbara might have financed Frank Fay's Broadway comeback once, but no man could be said to have screwed her out of money. On the contrary, the divorce obliged Bob to pay part of his earnings to her as long as she lived or remarried. She felt cheated nevertheless, bought off, defrauded, not of a shared bed, but, as *Sunset Boulevard* and *All About*

Eve dramatized, of the respect without which a maturing woman cannot live.

Stanwyck embarked on a decade of film acting of little distinction. She was not alone. Davis might have had the guts to accept *All About Eve*, but in a fit of rage, she had fired herself after eighteen years with Warners. After clashing with King Vidor during the shooting of *Beyond the Forest* in 1949, she called Jack Warner to the set. "Jack, if you don't get another director, I want to be released from my contract," she screamed. "It's him or me!" Warner released her from her contract. Her departure left Joan Crawford as the reigning WB queen, but, like Barbara, she had to play domineering shrews in thrillers and westerns. In the fall of 1952, she was out of a contract. She announced her return to Broadway, backed out, and a year later was back at MGM for a two-picture deal with her old studio. *Torch Song* was a rip-off of *All About Eve* in which Crawford played an aging, neurotic musical comedy star. After undergoing slight surgical improvements to get the part, she told costume designer Helen Rose, "The face and the breasts are new, but my ass is the same, as flat as a twenty-year-old's." The second picture was never made.

Barbara and Joan remained friends. Shirley Eder called it a strange friendship, but Joan really liked Barbara. "It was always a kind of bond between them," writer Carl Johnes would recall. Every year on Joan's birthday, Barbara sent a big floral gift.

In March 1951, the House Un-American Activities Committee returned to Hollywood, where, four years earlier, it had struck gold. The cold war was at its chilliest. The Korean War was entering its second year, Americans were building fallout shelters in their backyards, Senator Joseph McCarthy warned of communists in every nook and cranny of the U.S. government, and the spy hunt nailed Julius and Ethel Rosenberg as the first civilians who would suffer the death penalty for espionage. Screen Actors Guild president Reagan announced the guild would not defend members who defied the committee. "It is every member's duty to cooperate fully," he proclaimed. Following the American Federation of

Musicians, the guild decided it would not take union action against any studio denying jobs to an actor whose "actions outside of union activities have so offended American public opinion that he has made himself unsalable at the box office." At the Directors Guild, a refusal by Joe Mankiewicz to insist on loyalty oaths for every member nearly cost him his career when Cecil B. DeMille led a move to unseat him.

Elia Kazan, Clifford Odets, *East Side, West Side* screenwriter Isobel Lennart, and twenty-seven others named three hundred of their colleagues as members or former members of the Communist Party. Ward Bond was nicknamed "The Hangman Ward" because he could smell a "commie-Jew a mile away." The Alliance's Roy Brewer said, "Communists created the blacklist themselves" and jeered individuals' desperate and often unsuccessful attempts to save their jobs. In July, Dashiell Hammett was arrested for refusing to reveal the names of contributors to a bail fund. When Edward G. Robinson sent a $2,500 check to help the destitute Trumbo, he was scolded by right-wing Hearst columnist Sidney Skolsky. The actor was not accused of anything, but his case turned Kafkaesque. Job offers declined until he begged the HUAC to hear him: "Call me as a witness," Robinson cried "Swear me in. I will testify under oath." On a visit from his Bucks County lair, humorist S. J. Perelman called Hollywood a terrible combination of boomtown gone bust and Nazi Germany in 1935.

The HUAC hearings continued until 1953, but the blacklist didn't begin to unravel until 1960, when Otto Preminger and Kirk Douglas admitted the screenwriter of *Exodus* and *Spartacus* was Dalton Trumbo.

William Wyler filmed *Carrie*, based on Theodore Dreiser's novel *Sister Carrie*, but Liberty Film partner Frank Capra refused to help cut the script because he considered its portrayal of a girl who chooses an illicit liaison with a wealthy man over working in a sweatshop to be a Marxist slur on the capitalist system. Very few of Barbara's director and producer friends dared to target political controversy. William Wellman showed a trapper marrying an Indian girl in *Across the Wide Missouri*, while Billy Wilder made media sensationalism the subject of *Ace in the Hole*. Barbara herself tiptoed around any subject that could be considered radioactive. Self-preservation made her turn down a parable on McCarthysm called *The Library*.

The Library was about book burning and guilt by association. It told the story of a New England librarian who resists pressures by vigilantes and elected officials to remove a controversial book, only to see *The Library* burned down. The original screenplay was by Daniel Taradash, imported from New York in 1938 to help rewrite *Golden Boy*. Taradash had won an Oscar in 1953 for his *From Here to Eternity* script and was such an outspoken opponent of the renewed witch hunt that Hedda Hopper wondered in print why anyone would even consider something as un-American as *The Library*.

Bette Davis felt the story had much to say about true un-Americanism and the need for a free and open society. She agreed to play the small-town librarian. Taradash directed, and after Harry Cohn blew hot and cold for three years, the film was made in 1955. Columbia renamed it *Storm Center* and nervously released it in 1956. More ominously, Davis did not work for three years afterward. It was rumored that Hopper and her conservative friends applied pressure to keep her from getting decent offers.

Stanwyck's first picture in 1951 was *The Man with a Cloak*. The limp period thriller was filmed on MGM's choicest sets with Joseph Cotton and the new French sensation Leslie Caron. *The Man with a Cloak* takes place in New York in 1848. A mysterious stranger who turns out to be Edgar Allan Poe enters two women's lives and helps Caron's character keep her inheritance. The director was Fletcher Markle, a Canadian TV writer-director who had graduated to the big screen directing Ronald Reagan's soon-to-be wife, Nancy Davis, in *Night into Morning*.

Barbara ran into Mae Clarke at the studio commissary. Her roommate from the days of the cold-water flat on Forty-sixth Street was under contract to MGM and up for a minor part in *Because of You*, a crime yarn starring Loretta Young. Barbara didn't have to fear running into her former husband during the filming because Metro sent Robert Taylor to England, this time to star in *Ivanhoe*. The big-budget adaptation of the Walter Scott novel was a pet project of Dore Schary's. Bob was *Ivanhoe*, Joan Fontaine the heroine, and

Elizabeth Taylor the woman who doesn't get him. Fontaine would remember Bob nursing his vanity over his divorce.

The success of *Quo Vadis*, released in November 1951, turned Bob into MGM's hottest male star. The film was Metro's all-time hit, generating the greatest cash flow since *Gone with the Wind*—$25 million worldwide. Bob and Deborah Kerr vaulted past Gregory Peck and Elizabeth Taylor as top stars. In his next film, *Above and Beyond*, Bob was in tune with the times and his aviator passion, playing Colonel Paul Tibbetts, the B-17 Enola Gay captain who dropped the first atomic bomb on Hiroshima.

Barbara rang in 1952 with Bill and Ardis Holden. Nancy and Ronald Reagan were there. So were Eleanor Parker and her husband, Paul Clemens, and Bill's lawyer, Robert Lerner, and his wife. At midnight, Bill put on a 78 rpm record of "Auld Lang Syne," and husbands and wives kissed. Since Barbara had no husband to kiss, Bill did the honors. New Year's Eve at the Holdens in Toluca Lake became a ritual after that.

Clash by Night, Stanwyck's first film in 1952 and her first for RKO since *Ball of Fire*, was touched by the witch hunt. The studio was now owned—and mismanaged—by Howard Hughes. The millionaire paid Warners $150,000 for the remaining months of producer Jerry Wald's contract so he could make Wald and former screenwriter Norman Krasna the day-to-day studio chiefs. Hughes was so gung-ho on the two "whiz kids" that besides weekly salaries of $2,500 each, he agreed to a profit-sharing contract with them. But the "wonder boys" couldn't get Hughes to okay *any* decisions.

In signing on for *Clash by Night*, Stanwyck again put aside her politics. The writing credits on *Clash by Night* were ticklish, and its director was on an unofficial blacklist. Fritz Lang, however, convinced Howard Hughes that calling him a communist was just too ridiculous and obviously the workings of personal malice. Questions about Lang's political correctness had popped up when he objected to an upbeat rewrite of Clifford Odets's 1930s defeatist ending.

The source material was Odets's panting play about jealousy, *The Lie*. A dozen writers worked on the script, including producer Harriett Parsons. Louella's daughter had been an in-house producer at RKO since 1943. The screen-writer of record was Alfred Hayes, favored by Darryl Zanuck for his clipped, realistic Hemingwayesque dialogue. He had spent several years in Italy writing novels and collaborating with Roberto Rossellini on *Paisan*. The first thing Parsons and Hayes cut out was the social dimension of 1930s unemployment in Odets's original drama. A "Commie" scene that supposedly belittled religion by showing a priest blessing a fishing fleet was excised when *Tiding*, the Los Angeles Archdiocese weekly, objected.

Lang's Hollywood career had never matched the experimental pyrotechnics of his Berlin years of Metropolis and Das *Testament des Dr. Mabuse*. He was obliged to labor in B pictures—he said he preferred lower-case "programmers" where he could create hostile nocturnal worlds full of ambiguity and incongruity. Movies, he told Barbara, must deal with people caught by fate, they must be about honest men or women driven to seek revenge in ways that turn them into criminals. Lynching was the theme in *Fury*, false accusations the focus of *You Only Live Once*. In *While the City Sleeps*, a newsman investigating homicides becomes a murder suspect himself. In *The Woman in the Window* and *Scarlet Street*, Edward G. Robinson becomes a murderer, and in *The Big Heat* Glenn Ford's wife is killed by a bomb meant for him. *Clash by Night* was Lang's second picture for Hughes. The first was the just-completed western made to order for Marlene Dietrich as an aging femme fatale operating a hideout for outlaws. Hughes recut the picture and changed the title from *Chuck-a-Luck* to *Rancho Notorious*, but the film remained an unappetizing western and a disaster for Dietrich.

Matching Lang with Odets's *The Lie* was a better fit. Stanwyck plays Mae Doyle, the hardened city girl and small-town adulteress Tallulah Bankhead had created onstage in 1941. Paul Douglas is her husband, Robert Ryan the wrong guy she can't help falling for. The characters' complexity helped the film overcome the eternal triangle. Stanwyck's Mae is both a woman with a dubious past and a liberated individual who comes to see her own flaws. Pain constantly flickers beneath a sardonic mien in Ryan's anguished performance. A caustic cynic, he tells Mae that in every decisive circumstance "somebody's throat has to be cut." But he also cries out to her, "Help me, Mae, I'm dying of loneliness."

Lang knew how to play on his stagy continental impertinence and suave authority. One morning when Barbara complained that the scene they were about to shoot was so badly written she couldn't play it, the director asked if he could talk frankly and openly to her. She said sure. "I think the scene reminds you of a rather recent event in your private life," he told her, "and that is why you can't play it." She looked at him for a second. "You sonofabitch," she snapped and went out to play the two-and-a-half-page scene so well Lang ordered no retakes.

On a loanout from Twentieth Century-Fox, Marilyn Monroe had a subplot part as Barbara's good-natured sister-in-law. By the time the movie reached neighborhood theaters Monroe was featured on the marquees. To promote the picture, RKO publicity chief Perry Lieber leaked the fact that Monroe had posed for a nude calendar in 1949. He supplied United Press International's Aline Mosby with a copy of the calendar. When Mosby's story became front-page news, Darryl Zanuck instructed Monroe to deny she was the honey-blond girl stretched out on a sheet of red velvet. Barbara encouraged Marilyn to face the music. She did and at a news conference told how the $50 she had been paid for the photo session paid her rent. Monroe's honesty paid off in supporting fan mail.

In the middle of the shooting, Hughes started a communist hunt at RKO that *Variety* suggested was an excuse to enable the millionaire to lay off people, cut production, and perhaps unload the studio. After Hughes removed Paul Jarrico's name as the screenwriter of *The Las Vegas Story*, a melodrama intended for Jane Russell and Victor Mature, the writer answered with a $350,000 damage suit. Incensed, Hughes challenged the Screen Writers Guild to call a strike against RKO, and, while he installed a "screening" system, placed some one hundred "loyal" studio employees on leaves of absence. "We are going to screen everyone in a creative or executive capacity," he said, "to make RKO one studio where the work of communist sympathizers will not be used." Jarrico was one of the writers of the now infamous *Song of Russia*. Hughes had him blacklisted.

Four months later, after RKO's 1952 losses reached $4

million, Hughes sold to a five-man syndicate. On October 16, the *Wall Street Journal* revealed that three of the new owners had been involved with "organized crime, fraudulent mail-order schemes and bigtime gambling."

To bolster Stanwyck's image as a star, Helen Ferguson talked Barbara into letting *Collier's* do a cover story on her. To write the profile, the magazine sent former *New York Times* film critic Frank Nugent, who in his time had disparaged many of her performances.

Nugent got to observe his subject at home and at work. Stanwyck refused to wear hats offscreen, he noticed. She hated jangling jewelry and had little interest in food. "Her dinner almost invariably is a small steak and a salad or a green vegetable," he wrote. "She can't stand hearing a telephone ring and invariably beats her maid to the phone. She likes a good story, but rarely tells one herself. She has a great laugh, right from the stomach."

She lived a cloistered life. A painting in her bedroom depicted a chorus girl in her dressing room, massaging her feet. "I know *her*," she said. "My feet have ached that way too!" Nugent interviewed Buck McCarthy. Uncle Buck told him Barbara could be impulsive, that her moods "come on her all of a sudden, and the only thing to do is to wait until she gets over them."

On the set, the former critic discovered that she was known to crew members as Queen Barbara, or, more affectionately, as Queen Babs. Watching her work, he likened her to the former boxing champion Joe Louis when he relaxed in his corner before the bell. "There is the same air of cool detachment, casual assurance," he wrote. "She sits on the doorstep of her dressing room—knitting occasionally, or reading a book, or sipping one of the 14 cups of coffee she consumes in the course of a studio day. She looks more like a housewife listening to the radio while shelling peas than an actress about to take off into the emotional stratosphere. Then the bell rings—and it's Killer Stanwyck in the ring, knocking the audience dead."

Lang called working with Stanwyck a pleasure. "She's fantastic, unbelievable, and I liked her tremendously. When Marilyn missed her lines—which she did constantly—Barbara never said a word."

Without identifying Marilyn Monroe, Nugent recounted how "an actress famed chiefly for her beauty and curvaceousness" was two hours late for her first scene with Stanwyck. To illustrate Barbara's grace and deadpan humor, Nugent reported how the actress blew her lines twenty-six times and how Barbara was as calm on the twenty-seventh take as on the first. Later when visitors to the set were milling around Marilyn, a crew member asked Barbara what she thought of Monroe. "With a figure like that," Barbara smiled, "you don't have to act."

It was Barbara, however, who caused a ten-day shutdown when she caught a cold that developed into pneumonia. They had been shooting the final scene at midnight. Barbara had been on the set since six that morning and the next day kept a scheduled appointment with Nugent. In the afternoon she was rushed to a hospital by ambulance.

It was not easy for Helen to convince her reticent friend to give interviews. Shirley Eder, the young columnist for the *Detroit Free Press*, had to agree to limit her questions to the present and the future and not ask about Stanwyck's past before she could have fifteen minutes with Barbara at the Helen Ferguson Agency. But the occasion of Eder's interview also revealed Helen's overprotectiveness of Barbara and her wish to control Barbara's every contact with the press. The interview was for NBC's "Monitor" radio show and while Eder was setting up her tape recorder and microphones, Helen was called to her private office to take a long-distance call. Stanwyck and Eder proceeded without the press agent. When Helen came back forty-five minutes later and said, "I'm sorry I was away so long; now you can begin," Barbara told her friend the interview was over and done. "Well," said Helen. "Shirley, you'll stay and play the tape for me, won't you?"

"No, Helen," Barbara cut in. "Shirley doesn't have to play the tape back to you. What's more, she has to leave, and so do I." With a wink to the journalist as if she had pulled one over on Helen, Barbara left the office. Helen called the columnist at her hotel a few hours later and asked for a copy of the tape. Shirley half promised to send it to her, but never got around to it.

30

B Pix

As a young actress, Barbara had told herself she would retire at forty. She was going on forty-six when she finally made an attempt to withdraw from the business that was her lifeblood. "I didn't work for one whole year," she would remember. "I went to Europe, but just how many cathedrals can you see? I simply didn't know what to do with myself, so I went back to work."

Work was a "panic thriller" about a woman who lets herself be ravished by an escaped killer so he will help save her husband from a rising tide and inevitable drowning. *Jeopardy* was directed by John Sturges, who was considered a master of the contemporary western. Barry Sullivan was the man trapped under his stalled car on a deserted beach and Ralph Meeker the escaped convict. Critics decided Sturges gave *Jeopardy* enough pace, Stanwyck and Meeker enough conviction to give the wildly improbable story enough spin to make its very short sixty-nine minutes seem like a cartoon or a documentary. MGM didn't expect much from the film, but *Jeopardy* turned out to a box-office winner.

The hit of 1953 was *Roman Holiday* and its scintillating newcomer, Audrey Hepburn. William Wyler's most romantic film was a fairy tale, where, for once, the prince doesn't marry the princess. It would be another twenty-five years before it leaked out that the script was by blacklisted Dalton Trumbo. During the summer of 1952, when Wyler shot the film in Rome, the screenwriter of record was John Dighton. Wyler loved the freedom of shooting in Rome. No sets, no back transparencies, nothing of the stage and back-lot Hollywood romances. Instead, twenty-three-year-old Hepburn and Gregory Peck rode through Roman streets and alleys on a motor scooter, danced on a Tiber river barge, hopscotched down the Spanish Steps, and kissed in front of the Barberini Palazzo. Darryl Zanuck had started the transatlantic migration in 1948 by sending Tyrone Power and Orson Welles to Italy to star in *Prince of Foxes*, a costume epic about the Renaissance Borgias. The power of the dollar and the tax implications of living and working abroad for part of the year soon became obvious to top-bracket showbiz people. Hollywood unions furiously opposed "runaway productions" and tried to stop the trend.

Stanwyck was no runaway. She was not alone. Edward G. Robinson was another maturing star who refused to uproot himself for London or Rome. What neither realized immediately was that staying at home meant a soft slide into B pictures. Under the pressure of television, the power structure was crumbling. Louis B. Mayer lost a fight with Dore Schary for control of MGM, resigned, and in 1957 tried a corporate finagle to seize control of Loew's, Inc. Two months after his coup failed, he died. The end of the contract system accelerated the decline of stars of Stanwyck's generation. Instead of being told to report to director so-and-so on Monday to start shooting such-and-such, they were suddenly in charge of themselves. Bette Davis, Joan Crawford, and Gary Cooper lacked the objectivity, judgment, or discipline to pick winners among the scripts agents and producers were pitching. Crawford did the ossified-star vehicle called *Torch Song*. Cooper was the fourth choice—after Marlon Brando, Montgomery Clift, and Charlton Heston—for *High Noon* and almost refused the role that saved his career because the script was written by blacklisted Carl Foreman.

As Barbara had done to prop up Frank Fay twenty years earlier, Judy Garland played scenes from her own movies on the stage of New York's Palace Theatre. Claudette Colbert returned to the Broadway of her youth. Marlene Dietrich and Noel Coward appeared in Las Vegas. Katharine Hepburn went to London to star in George Bernard Shaw's *Millionairess* and didn't make a movie until 1955. William Boyd had lost his big ranch and was flat broke when television asked him to play Hopalong Cassidy on the small screen. Bob Hope was getting $40,000 per each TV show, and David Niven and other "names" picked up grocery money by doing guest shots on the Hope and Jack Benny shows. Fear of offending the aging studio hierarchy, however, held back many stars. Charles Boyer and Dick Powell nevertheless formed a company to make films for television. Niven joined them and although Boyer, Powell, and Niven were unable to recruit a fourth star, they optimistically called their firm The Four-Star Playhouse. The idea was to have well-known actors appear once a month in an anthology series. During the 1953–54 season, Ronald Colman, Joan Fontaine, Merle Oberon, and Ida Lupino headlined Four-Star TV productions. Henry Fonda, who even had the guts to blow froth in beer commercials, became the show's host the following season. The fifth year they bought a series of Zane Grey western pulp novels and launched "Zane Grey Theater." Stanwyck appeared in Four-Star productions. She tried to be breezy with the press: "I'm an actress and an actress *acts*." In early 1956, she formed *her* independent production company, called it Barwyck, and looked for material suitable for television.

If Barbara was in B pictures, her former husband was hot again. Robert Taylor had never received an Academy Award, and MGM and his admirers thought he deserved an Oscar for his *Above and Beyond* portrayal of Colonel Paul Tibbetts, but only the picture's writer, Beirne Lay, Jr., and its composer, Hugo Friedhofer, were nominated. William Holden's cynical POW in *Stalag 17* won the 1953 Best Actor Oscar, but in playing Sir Lancelot to Ava Gardner's Guinevere in *Knights of the Round Table*, Bob gave his studio a blockbuster hit.

Barbara saw Bob now and then. Columnists reported he was going to marry a German divorcée with two children. Bob denied he planned to marry Ursula Thiess. When reporters asked for Barbara's reaction, she said she was tired of media speculation. "Bob and I didn't stay friends, we *became* friends again," she said. To put an end to speculation, she added, "Bob and I go to a nightclub or have dinner and talk. I know what I know, Bob knows what he knows. Other people don't."

The raven-haired Ursula was a former model brought to

Hollywood by Howard Hughes. After polishing her English with RKO's drama coach Florence Enright, the studio had sent her to India to star in *Monsoon*, paired her with Robert Stack in the costume drama *The Iron Glove*, and loaned her to Universal to costar in *Bengal Brigade* with Arlene Dahl and Rock Hudson. Bob's old friend from their Illinois naval base days was getting married by his studio. Universal was rumored to be paying off *Confidential* magazine not to publish an exposé on Rock Hudson's homosexuality. His bride was Phyllis Gates, his agent's secretary. Ursula's agent introduced her to Bob in April 1952. To bolster her up-and-coming status, they made the social scene.

While Bob was in Egypt playing an archeologist in *Valley of the Kings* and the Howard Strickling office hinted at an offscreen romance with his costar Eleanor Parker, Barbara kept herself busy playing a passenger on the S.S. *Titanic*.

She and Clifton Webb played a socially prominent couple on the brink of divorce in *Titanic*. Charles Brackett, Walter Reisch, and Richard Breen won Best Story and Screenplay Oscars for the reenactment of the 1912 maritime tragedy. Romanian-born Jean Negulesco directed the Twentieth Century-Fox production and managed to create suspense despite the all-too-well-known ending of the doomed ocean liner. Richard Basehart played a defrocked priest, Allyn Joslyn a meddlesome bore, Thelma Ritter a salty lady, and Brian Aherne the ship's captain. The cast also included twenty-three-year-old Robert Wagner.

Barbara took him under her wing, as she had done William Holden and Kirk Douglas. "She changed my whole approach to my work, made me want to learn the business completely," Wagner would remember. "She started me thinking. It means a lot when someone takes time with a newcomer."

Columnists hinted at a May-September liaison. As compared to dating someone Barbara's own age or older, a man in his early twenties possessed a blush, a kind of gauche innocence and capacity for bursting into flames that flattered her and reminded her of Bob when they first met. She called the rumors ridiculous. Press photographers caught them in a restaurant with Clifton Webb one night. In the published photo, Webb was cut out. Barbara tried humor when she was "seen" with Jean-Pierre Aumont. "I keep reading about these romances and it's embarrassing—to the other party," she told the *Los Angeles Daily News*. "A nice guy takes me out to dinner and then reads we're going to be married. To a sophisticated person I can say, 'Look, I don't want to get married,' but others might not understand. Another fellow might think I expect a proposal. He's not sure. So he doesn't call again. Paul Gregory, a producer, called to ask me if I would do a play for him. We had dinner, and the next day I read we're having a romance. He's a wonderful dinner companion but after those items, I don't know what he thinks."

She had little time for a love life, she added. "I only go out on Saturdays with the Jack Bennys and Nancy Sinatra."

Zanuck demanded a convincing sinking of the *Titanic*, and art directors Lyle Wheeler and Maurice Ransford created the fateful nighttime encounter of ship and iceberg in the studio's huge outdoor tank. Negulesco had Barbara swinging in a lifeboat high above forty extras in whirlpool-agitated waters. The realism of the scene made her think of the men and women drowning in the icy waters off Newfoundland forty years earlier. Did she think of Rex Cherryman dying in his ocean liner cabin twenty-five years earlier? "I burst into tears," she would remember. "I shook with great racking sobs and couldn't stop."

All I Desire put her in the middle of the deadliest 1950s combination of producer and director. Ross Hunter was a Harry Cohn graduate without the inspired crassness of the Columbia boss. Hunter had signed a long-term contract with Universal in 1951, and his first production there was *Take Me to Town*, a piece of stale schmaltz containing every known cliché stitched into a plot. The director of this Ann Sheridan–Sterling Hayden vehicle was Detlef Sierck, a Dane who spent his most creative years in Germany. Since his arrival in Hollywood, he styled himself Douglas Sirk. Hunter liked the cultivated director because Sirk could turn his hand to any genre, and he signed him for *All I Desire*. Sirk had attended Sergei Eisenstein's lectures in Hamburg, and, like the towering director of the Soviet cinema, his favorite dramatic prop was a set of stairs. The turn-of-the-century set of

All I Desire was built so that the action unavoidably was centered on a staircase.

Stanwyck's character, Naomi Murdoch, echoed Mae Doyle of *Clash by Night* and Stella of *Stella Dallas*. "I'm playing the type of part I've played many times—a bad woman trying to make up for past mistakes," Barbara told a press conference. "Namby-pambies have no interest for me. I'd rather not act at all than do a Pollyanna. I've got to play human beings. I think I understand the motives of the bad women I play." Her Naomi was superb. Her costars were Richard Carlson, a stage actor and friend of Bob Taylor's, Maureen O'Sullivan, Lyle Bettger, Richard Long, and Lori Nelson. Virginia Grey was also in the cast. Hunter considered her his good luck charm and put her in virtually every film he produced.

How Stanwyck knew Grey dated Bob Taylor remained a mystery to Virginia, but on the first day of shooting there was a confrontation Grey would never forget. Barbara resented any woman Bob dated, Virginia realized. "She let me have it with words I cannot repeat," Grey would recall. "There was no mention of Bob, but she had no other reason to dislike me so intensely. I had done the unpardonable. I had gone out with Robert Taylor."

Stanwyck's straight talk made her a choice interview. In March 1953, Helen and the Hollywood Foreign Press Association got her to sit still for a group press conference that revealed how tired she was of routine Hollywood fodder. Federico Fellini continued Italy's triumphant neorealism with *I Vitelloni*. In France, Henri-Georges Clouzot directed *Wages of Fear* and made Yves Montand a star. Japan made an impression with kenji Mizoguchi's *Ugetsu Monogatari*, and the whole world hummed the tune from Brazil's *O Cangaciero*. Barbara knew why these films received such praise and did so well commercially: "Because they recognized life for what it is and attempted to depict it that way on the screen. Their approach was adult, and the result was adult."

She thought *Clash by Night* came close to the grown-up nerve of the best foreign films. "I play a woman who for reasons which she feels are justified commits adultery," she said. "The audience may sympathize with me to an extent, for I am a woman who has a lot of good reasons for doing what is contrary to accepted social behavior."

"My entire role is written and acted, I hope, along the line of the European realistic approach to a situation which is not uncommon among people," she said. "It's offbeat, at least by Hollywood standards, and it is this, if anything, that sets it apart."

She returned to Warner Brothers for *The Moonlighter*. Jack Warner didn't think enough of the story of cattle rustlers and bank robbers to shoot it in Warnercolor, but it was filmed in 3-D. If CinemaScope and Cinerama were the winners of the lure-'em-into-the-tent studio gambles, 3-D was the big loser. The novelty of wearing tinted glasses to see a film faded quickly. The director was Roy Rowland, a jack-of-all-trades who had cut his teeth at MGM and made a reputation in westerns and thrillers. Barbara would make three movies with him. Fred MacMurray was her leading man, and the cast included Ward Bond, who later became famous in the TV series "Wagon Train." For Stanwyck and MacMurray, *The Moonlighter* was no reprise of *Double Indemnity*. The script gave them little to work with. Barbara enjoyed riding horses and doing stunts, including sliding down a waterfall, but called *The Moonlighter* a "dinky little western."

Still at Warners, she agreed to star in *Blowing Wild*, a movie Lauren Bacall had turned down. Barbara had known producer Milton Sperling since he was Darryl Zanuck's secretary in 1930. Sperling had Gary Cooper and Anthony Quinn lined up for *Blowing Wild* when he asked Barbara to play the wicked, scheming, power-crazy woman between the two men.

Blowing Wild was a lurid melodrama bursting with situations, scenes, and rewritten dialogue lifted from Cooper's current hit, *High Noon*, and *The Treasure of the Sierra Madre*. Cooper and Ward Bond are a pair of oil prospectors stranded in a Mexican town without a peso to their names. After being double-crossed by a white-suited, cigar-puffing Ian MacDonald, Cooper teams up with Mexican oil driller Quinn. Stanwyck is Quinn's no-good wife who wants to resume an affair with her husband's partner. When Cooper seems to be more interested in a stranded showgirl (Ruth Roman), Stanwyck shoves her husband to his death in some throbbing machinery, only to be blown to bits herself after screaming to Cooper, "I committed murder to get you!" The director was a friend of Cooper's, Hugo Fregonese, a wandering Argentine who made movies in half a dozen countries.

As usual, Barbara gave her all. She told Cooper not to fake it in a scene in which he chokes her. She wanted her eyes to pop and the veins of her neck to stick out. To make him sufficiently mad at her, she made snide remarks about his acting. Fregonese yelled action, and a livid Cooper grabbed her throat. "Her veins swelled, her mouth contorted," Cooper would remember. "The director yelled 'Cut' and she slumped. It was two days before Barbara could talk, and three days before I could stop worrying." Cast and crew were filming in Mexico when Barbara's two costars became Oscar winners—Cooper for *High Noon*, Quinn for his supporting role in *Viva Zapata!*

Jack Warner, Rowland, and Stanwyck convinced themselves that *Witness to Murder* could beat the thriller Alfred Hitchcock was shooting at Paramount. In the opening scene, Stanwyck looks across an apartment courtyard and sees George Sanders choke a young woman to death. Police lieutenant Gary Merrill doesn't believe her, but the murderer does. Alfred Hitchcock's *Rear Window*, in which wheelchair-bound James Stewart convinces himself he is seeing Raymond Burr murdering his wife across the courtyard, had a brilliant script by John Michael Hayes based on the short story by Cornell Woolrich. *Witness to Murder* had an attractive cast but floundered in producer-writer Chester Erskine's screenplay.

Barbara spent time with Merrill. He and Bette Davis were trying to build a new life in Connecticut. With few Hollywood offers, Bette tried a musical revue, but osteomyelitis of the jaw closed *Two's Company* early. It would be a year before she could work again. To solidify their marriage, they had adopted a newborn girl. Margot was found to be brain-damaged from birth.

When United Artists released *Witness to Murder* on April 15, 1954, the publicity promotion claimed it was "topping the thrills of *Double Indemnity* and *Sorry, Wrong Number*." *Rear Window* came out May 4, won the critics' applause, cleaned up at the box office, and gave Oscar nominations to Hitchcock, Hayes and cameraman Robert Burks.

On May 24, 1954, Bob married Ursula Thiess. The wedding took place aboard a cabin cruiser in the middle of

Wyoming's Jackson Lake, ten miles south of the Yellowstone National Park. Ralph Couser was the best man. Helen Ferguson was still Bob's publicist, but she got the news too late for the next morning's newspapers. Fearing Barbara would somehow interfere, Bob only phoned Helen hours after the wedding. When photographers showed up at Colter Bay, Bob at first refused to pose with his new bride, but relented and allowed one picture of the two of them in front of the mountain cabin. Two days later, he reported to the location of MGM's *Many Rivers to Cross*.

Barbara was in shock, but steeled herself to send a congratulatory telegram to the newlyweds. Why Ursula? Forgetting that her own much-papered-over studio-engineered marriage to Bob had begun to fall apart within months, forgetting Bob's eternal male hangers-on, his for-show affair with Lana Turner and for-real time with Ava Gardner, Barbara wondered why he had let himself be seduced by this thirty-year-old divorcée. It was the classic case. Ursula engineered a misunderstanding, refused to see Bob, and, while he was in Egypt on *Valley of the Kings*, made sure he heard she was dating other men until he begged for a minute of her time on a temperamental overseas telephone connection.

What Stanwyck didn't understand was that in marrying Ursula, Bob discovered a new way of relating and a manliness in himself that Barbara had never allowed him. For the first time he didn't disown his own strength, didn't have to feel a lot of guilt, hurt, and shame. Ursula was not consumed by ambition. She was ready to put Bob ahead of everything and everybody. If she continued to work it was only to make sure her children would not be a burden on Bob.

Like Barbara, Ursula came with a ready-made family. All comparisons with Dion and Barbara stopped there, however. Ursula's ten-year-old Emanuela—Mamela to everybody—and nine-year-old son, Michael, were with their mother. Their father was the Hamburg producer Georg Thiess. Younger than Bob, Ursula was more secure. The initiative in the relationship was totally his. "If I'm in love with a man, he doesn't have to know it," she told interviewers. "I can enjoy that feeling all by myself. My continental tolerance will keep my marriage from getting on the Hollywood divorce merry-go-round."

Ursula stayed in Los Angeles in 1955 when MGM sent Bob to England and France to shoot *Quentin Durward*. Sir Walter Scott's romantic tale set in Renaissance France was squeezed into the familiar screen mold. Absence made the heart grow fonder, and as Bob had done with Barbara during the shooting of *A Yank at Oxford*, he spent a good chunk of his per diem on transatlantic telephone calls. He wanted to be head of a household, with Ursula and the children included. He thought Ursula and he might have children of their own. When he came back from Europe, he bought a 113-acre ranch in West Los Angeles's Mandeville Canyon.

Ruth Brugh foundered in religion and spoke of the evils of Hollywood. Bob rented a small house for his mother on Selby Street in West Hollywood. She met her son's new family on birthdays and on Christmas. Slowly going senile, Ruth was an embarrassment to him. In a nursing home she outlived her son, although in such a vegetative state she never knew he died.

With an MGM contract that made him the longest-lasting contract player in Hollywood history—twenty-five years—Bob spent the next ten years trying to play his younger self.

Stanwyck might know how to endow her roles with a strength of purpose, but the politics she supported made scripts offering bold, fully realized women a rarity. There is a measure of irony in her slide into mediocrity during the Eisenhower years of guarded rectitude. She read Simone de Beauvoir's *The Second Sex*, which explained woman not as essence—mysterious or otherwise—but in terms of her situation, particularly her financial dependence or lack of economic emancipation. As a veteran star, Barbara was still big, and she was a millionaire, but the characters she was offered were one-dimensional, usually women with guns locked in deadly battles of the sexes. Flaunting her white hair and her small, shapely body, she lent her sneer and throaty laughter to wayward, evil women who, by the fade-out, were usually dead, unless they shared the reins with the one man who dared stand up.

Executive Suite was a happy exception. Her role as a corporate tycoon's neurotic daughter, major stockholder, and embittered mistress of the just-deceased top executive was not the largest part, but it was a strong one and a release from B-picture mediocrity. Moreover, the eight-week shoot in the fall of 1953 turned into two months of exhilarating work with energetic and ambitious behind-the-camera people and, in front, a team effort with talented players. The director was Robert Wise, the team players William Holden, June Allyson, Fredric March, Walter Pidgeon, Shelley Winters, Paul Douglas, Louis Calhern, Dean Jagger, Nina Foch, and Tim Considine. Most intriguingly, *Executive Suite* had a brilliant producer.

In Barbara's experience, producers were, for the most part, expendable. With the exception of Warners' stalwarts-turned-independents Hal Wallis and Jerry Wald, she repeated the old saw that a producer is an executive wearing a worried look on his assistant's face. In the emerging perspective of the director as the person whose emotions and viewpoint shape a film, David Selznick's craving for "creativity" appeared as little more than pathological interference. Even Irving Thalberg's uncanny gift for divining what audiences wanted appeared in retrospect as an eccentric example of middle-period baroque.

John Houseman was different.

The Romanian-born theatrical producer, director, and actor who with Orson Welles had founded the Mercury Theatre in 1937 lent his nervy intelligence and ability to inspire confidence to the project, his second for MGM, following the Vincente Minnelli-directed Hollywood "in" picture, *The Bad and the Beautiful*.

Houseman spent three quarters of the $1.25 million budget on actors, chosen for their ability rather than their box-office recognition, and saved on everything else. The picture had no music. Instead of giving in to designers suggesting new sets, he decided to rely on MGM's vast reserves of stock scenery. An existing interior needed only slight alterations to become the *Executive Suite* and boardroom of the title. The same was true of Holden's fashionable home and Stanwyck's sumptuous family mansion.

To direct the picture on Houseman's tight budget, Wise demanded exceptional rehearsal time for dialogue-heavy scenes. June Allyson, as Holden's wife, had a crucial scene with Stanwyck, who confides her unhappiness over never having been able to marry the deceased. Barbara jeered when Allyson walked in late not knowing her lines. Houseman received a phone call from Allyson's agent that night, saying the actress was in hysterics, that the cast hated and persecuted her. The next day, she was letter-perfect. The script included an explosive scene with Holden that forced her to unleash her pent-up emotions.

The theme of *Executive Suite* is ambition. Ernest Lehman's screen version of Cameron Hawley's novel made the power struggle for control of a company when the top man dies as tense as a thriller. The action takes place in a sparse twenty-four hours. Performance was paramount, as the eight characters do not appear together until they meet in a somber, imitation-Gothic boardroom, "nailed to their chairs," as Houseman would remember, "while the camera turned, twisted, and hovered around them in an endless series of master shots, two-shots, and closeups."

Nina Foch, who had just starred in a ho-hum MGM drama called *Fast Company*, played the "office wife" wedded to her husband's career. She thought Stanwyck and Holden might have been lovers once but not any longer. Working with the always letter-perfect Stanwyck was a pleasure. Watching her in a scene was a treat. "She was very sportsmanlike," Foch would remember, "and when I got an Oscar nomination for my part, she sent me a congratulatory telegram. I thought that was awfully nice." Foch lost the Best Supporting Actress Oscar to Eva Marie Saint in *On the Waterfront*.

*E*xecutive Suite was Barbara's seventieth movie. As her seventy-first she accepted the title role in a western to be filmed in Technicolor in Glacier National Park, Montana. The director of *Cattle Queen of Montana* was Allan Dwan, an old-timer she had long wanted to work with, her costar Ronald Reagan.

"Gives us a chance to play tourists on company time," said Reagan.

"Most of it on horseback," Barbara answered. She had read the script.

"Of course, in those days, Ronald Reagan wouldn't fly. Neither would [director of photography] John Alton," Dwan would remember. "So they came to location by train—took them three days to get up there from Los Angeles." Dwan made no mention of how airplane-shy Barbara reached Glacier National Park, but everybody marveled at the splendor of the northern Rockies.

Dwan was another Willard Mack, a Canadian-born jack-of-all-trades whose narrative flair could transform the most expendable genre material into something personal. Going on seventy, Dwan had been making movies since 1909, two-reelers in Arizona in the pioneer days, swashbucklers with Douglas Fairbanks, and high-society romps with Gloria Swanson in the high 1920s. Always the problem-solver producers hired to apply brains to idiotic projects, he had made fifty-three talkies since 1929, from Shirley Temple flicks and spy movies to war pictures (*Sands of Iwo Jima*). He had just finished a dazzling western, *Silver Lode*.

Dwan didn't share his two stars' right-wing sentiments. Like many artists working under oppressive regimes, he smuggled his protests into his films. His villain in *Silver Lode* is named McCarthy, a man who falsely accuses a character called Dan Ballard (John Payne) and dies of a bullet that ricochets off a liberty bell.

The blacklist was still a reality, but the Motion Picture Alliance for the Preservation of American Ideals was dying. The organization lost all credibility in 1955 after its members couldn't agree on whether to expel Screen Writers Guild members who took the Fifth Amendment when testifying before Congress. By three votes, the proposal failed.

Reagan's memories of the two months in Montana would be congenial. "Somehow working outdoors amid beautiful scenery and much of the time on horseback never has seemed like work to me," he would recall. The production rented horses from local ranchers and hired forty men as the *Cattle Queen* posse. On days when Reagan wasn't on call, he toured the scenic valley on horseback looking for real estate deals. There was money in land, he told Barbara.

Reagan's weather-beaten career was going nowhere. His agent wanted him to try Las Vegas. Since he could neither sing nor dance, he could only serve as master of ceremonies, telling a few jokes onstage before introducing the next act. Two months after they finished the Montana locations, he became the on-air host of "General Electric Theater," a CBS Sunday-night half-hour show. The $125,000-a-year "G.E. Theater" contract not only gave him the security he had never dreamed would be his, but brought him into a corporate world that would influence his political future. With *The Last Outpost*, *Cattle Queen* would remain the future president's favorite western.

Stanwyck was Edward G. Robinson's faithless wife and Glenn Ford a Civil War veteran looking for peace in The *Violent Men*, another sprawling Technicolor, CinemaScope western. The director was Rudolph Maté, her cinematographer on *A Message to Garcia* and *Stella Dallas*. Ford's cavalry officer has achieved peace on a western ranch and figures on going back east when he runs into Robinson, a crippled but ruthless cattle baron, full of old Colt slugs and greed, who drives small landowners from his valley. Brian Keith was Barbara's scum of a brother-in-law.

Robinson was the incarnation of iron stoicism: He had lost his son to suicide attempts, drugs, and mental disorders. More honest with himself than his costar, Robinson said *The Violent Men* was a B picture that clearly established him as a has-been.

For a reunion with Dwan, Barbara played an indomitable American in a trite jungle drama, in which, as she remarked, the animals were better than the picture. *Escape to Burma* was Dwan's first wide-screen film. Robert Ryan was the costar of hated plantation owner Stanwyck, playing a murder suspect who has a way with elephants. The eighty-eight-minute film mixes her and Ryan with elephants, tigers, and jungle bandits. "Even the title is a puzzle," wrote the *New York Times*. "It says 'Escape to Burma.' Yet everyone is in Burma, or a back lot decked out by industrious 'green men' to look like Burma, and how can you escape a place you're already at? Even the monkeys seem bewildered."

Stanwyck played the "other woman" opposite Fred MacMurray and Joan Bennett in a remake of a caustic, intelligent 1934 Universal picture. Ursula Parrott was the bestselling author of the original tale of emotions lying dormant in respectable, middle-class hearts. Without changing the title, Douglas Sirk filmed *There's Always Tomorrow* with

MacMurray playing a toy manufacturer with bratty kids, Bennett his self-absorbed wife whose life is given over to the teenage children, and Stanwyck the old flame who comes back into his life. Binnie Barnes, Frank Morgan, and Lois Wilson had played the trio in 1934 with Robert Taylor as the eldest teenager (William Reynolds played the son in the new version). "*There's Always Tomorrow* enlists Barbara Stanwyck in Hollywood's tearjerking division," wrote the *Los Angeles Mirror-News*'s Margaret Harford. "As an expert in womanly woe, she has few peers. The suffering is several cuts below her customary flashy style, but tears glisten often in Barbara's eyes and her admirers will find several opportunities to join her in a good cry."

How about a rip-roarin' western?

Barbara had her agent, Lew Wasserman, sign her on to play a lady rustler and owner of the Maverick Queen Saloon in South Pass, Wyoming. *The Maverick Queen* was a Republic picture, an adaptation of a novel by Barbara's favorite western author, Zane Grey, who had invented the immensely popular western story with its distinct codes of valor and toughness.

Republic was the small San Fernando Valley studio where Gene Autry and Roy Rogers were singing cowboys. The studio might be known as "Repulsive Productions" in the trade, but it was nevertheless the lot where John Ford directed Wayne and a brace of Abbey Theatre players in the superb *The Quiet Man* and Nicholas Ray made the cult western *Johnny Guitar*, which featured a butch Joan Crawford and an even more mannish Mercedes McCambridge.*

The Maverick Queen was Republic's first excursion into the wide-screen process. Naturama, as it called its proprietary anamorphic system, had a projection aspect of 2.35 to 1, which made it narrower than CinemaScope. Stanwyck plays Kit Banion, a lady who likes cowboys who can handle themselves in a poker game and a shoot-out. Republic stock actors Barry Sullivan, Scott Brady, Mary Murphy, Howard Petrie,

---

*Both Ray and Crawford had wanted Stanwyck for the McCambridge part, but Republic boss Herbert J. Yates said he couldn't afford *two* stars in one picture. Joan was so broke she owed two years' tuition for her adopted children. She was nipping vodka day and night, and her *Johnny Guitar* performance provoked new rumors of her lesbian tendencies.

and Wallace Ford fleshed out the rest of the cast. Joseph Kane was Republic's veteran action director who knew how to shoot fast—*The Maverick Queen* was his fourth in 1955.

Republic sent Joe Kane, cast, and crew to Silverton, Colorado, to shoot the exteriors. Thirteen years later Fox would send George Roy Hill, cast, and crew to the same location to shoot *Butch Cassidy and the Sundance Kid*. Both were variations on the same true story of the Pinkerton's National Detective agents hired by the Union Pacific Railroad in 1900 to go after the Hole in the Wall gang. In *The Maverick Queen*, Barry Sullivan is the Pinkerton agent Kit falls for, Howard Petrie is Butch, and Scott Brady is Sundance. Kit admits she is "part of the gang run by Butch Cassidy." Justice will out, and in the last-reel shoot-out she dies in the arms of the Pinkerton man.

As a favor to her friend Jack Benny, Barbara tested the waters of television with a parody of the Victorian suspense play. Their sketch was a takeoff on George Cukor's 1944 film *Gaslight*, with Jack in the Charles Boyer role and Barbara playing Ingrid Bergman. Since his radio days, Benny had satirized movies. The studios loved the publicity, and producers and executives constantly invited "The Jack Benny Show" to make fun of their latest release. In a satire of Charles Boyer driving Ingrid Bergman crazy and getting her committed so he can find the jewelry hidden in the attic, the skit opened with half-demented Barbara eating marinated salami while parts of the house collapse around her. To protect herself from falling plaster she cooly opens an umbrella and goes on munching. As the evil husband, Benny tries to drive her crazy by moving furniture, dimming lights, and turning pictures and things upside down. When he enters, she berates him for doing strange things. "Yesterday, Charles, you came back from the fox hunt, hung your riding habit in the stable and put the horse in the closet."

And on and on, until a Scotland Yard detective arrests Benny, ties him to a chair, and Barbara screams her husband has turned everything upside down, including an upside-down cake he turned right side up. The show was one of Benny's all-time favorites.

Before the skit could get on the air, however, CBS and

Benny were embroiled in a lawsuit with MGM. Metro insisted the network and the veteran comedian could not spoof *Gaslight* without its permission. Both sides saw the case as a matter of principle—CBS and Benny as a free-speech issue of the right to satirize, MGM as an infringement of copyright—and appealed all the way to the Supreme Court. MGM won and accepted a $1,000 payment, saying it didn't want to hurt Benny, just make the point. The skit was broadcast in 1959.

Television was booming. More than a hundred series were on the air or in production in 1956. Almost all were Hollywood products, and most were episodic series. The various family comedies copied "I Love Lucy," and crime action series followed the "Dragnet" formula. A genre that continued to surge—and impress network programmers—was the western. Since *Annie Oakley*, Barbara had acted in seven westerns, many of them second-rate. Echoing President Eisenhower's sentiment that everybody should know who Wild Bill Hickock was, she said the desperados, rustlers, and outlaws were America's nobility. "That's our royalty, our aristocracy. All the immigrants coming over on the covered wagons and atop the trains, the little Jewish peddler with his calico and ginghams on his back, the good men, the bad men, they all made this country."

Women, too, were part of the Old West. Maybe the way to propel her career forward was to play Calamity Jane, Belle Starr, or one of the other frontier legends on the little screen.

31

Sharp Reminders

Fiction, reality, and the past sharply and painfully crashed in on Barbara on June 18, 1955. She was on the set of MGM's *Somewhere I'll Find Him*, playing the head of an adoption agency fighting for all the good she had never given Dion, when a loudspeaker proclaimed the studio's very own Robert Taylor was the proud father of a baby boy. Robert and Ursula Taylor, the loudspeaker cooed, had decided to name their son Terry. Barbara rushed to her dressing room. Director Roy Rowland called a ten-minute break. Cast and crew stood around.

With Barbara, Bob had been impotent. Now, four years after their divorce, he had fathered a son. A decade earlier, Frank Fay had sired Bette Keane's child. It was there for all to see. If the men in her life could have children with other women, it must be her, not they, who was infertile. Against increasing odds, she had hoped that she and Bob could somehow reconcile, that he would see the error of his ways and come back to her. She chose to remember the best of their life together, their joshing camaraderie, the politics they shared, Bob with smoke in his eyes at the barbecue pit, the two of them at Santa Anita, the impression they made as a couple, the respect they earned from the community. How many second movie marriages lasted? Not her own to Bob, but his to Ursula. The woman might have given up her career for Bob. But Barbara imagined she had given up her son for Bob. Tiny Terry seemed to snuff out Barbara's last hopes.

Plunging into work to forget was unnerving for Barbara because *Somewhere I'll Find Him* was all about people's responsibility toward children, toward the kids they abandon and those they adopt. Her Ann Dempster character is the principled director of an adoption agency who opposes self-made millionaire James Cagney's attempts at tracking down the illegitimate son (Don Dubbins) he fathered and repudiated twenty years earlier. In the court fight to prevent Cagney from bursting into the life of the boy he once claimed couldn't be his, Frank Fenton's script gave her lines like these:

ANN

Even an animal feeds its young—and fights and dies for it.
(to the JUDGE)
I found homes for them, among human beings who didn't just exist for themselves, who gave them names and the love without which nobody grows into somebody with faith and decency.

If playing scenes like this affected Barbara, she didn't let anyone see it. On the set, Cagney and Stanwyck waxed nostalgically about their respective vaudeville days and, between setups, entertained cast and crew with dance improvisations. Like Barbara, Cagney was the child of a wayward Irish father who had died when he was sixteen. He told her he was going to play Lon Chaney next in *Man of a Thousand Faces*. In studying the private life of the silent screen star, he had discovered a story of abandonment. Lon's wife and the mother of Creighton Chaney—later Lon Chaney, Jr.—deserted them. Her name was unusual—Cleva. Trying to find his mother, the adult Creighton followed a lead to a desolate ranch. When he asked for Mrs. Cleva Fletcher, the woman who answered through the screen door said there was no one there by that name. A second later, a voice from inside the house asked the woman, "Who is it, Cleva?"

Children and parental responsibility were a subject Barbara rarely broached. She had given Dion little more than slapdash attention when it suited her. Unlike Ann Dempster, she had never given him her stage name. He might have been Skip Stanwyck to Joan Benny. Legally, he remained Dion Fay.

Robert Taylor had pretended indecision to Barbara, and she played on his guilt. Until his marriage to Ursula, he had tried to appease Barbara, to be disillusioned and world-weary, and to repeat after her that no more than she was he looking for a significant other. The birth of Terry Taylor altered that, although Bob still didn't have the courage or the heart to sever all ties. Whatever the Taylors' financial arrangements, it was not until Bob died that Ursula discovered he was paying alimony to his former wife. Not that Ursula would have objected. Viege Traub, the psychiatrist, found Ursula to be a shy woman. "She wouldn't do anything that Taylor didn't approve of," said Traub.

Barbara didn't need 15 percent of Bob's earnings, but she took the money, one last grip on him. Precisely because their marriage now seemed irrevocably lost, it took on an afterglow of regret that she would nourish with increasing solicitude.

The existence of Bob's baby made her feel lonelier than ever and in need of a stiff drink or two or three after work. On days off, she insisted that Uncle Buck mix her a very dry gin and tonic for lunch. Eleven days after learning of Terry Taylor's birth, she fell down a flight of stairs at home and cracked a vertebra. Whether the concoctions Uncle Buck mixed for her on Wednesday, June 29, 1955, were exceptionally potent or her irritation at having to flesh out her day with housework made her carelessly clumsy, she tripped over a clothes hanger while carrying an armload of clothing to the second-floor service stairs. The stumble sent her sprawling ten feet down the stairs. Her cries attracted Uncle Buck, who called an ambulance. Taken to St. John's Hospital in Santa Monica, she was X-rayed for fractures. Dr. George W. Ainlay's worst fears proved correct. She had suffered a cracked vertebra and torn ligaments in the fall. The hospitalization, which caused her to miss Dwan's next film, *Pearl of the South Pacific*, allowed the press to pierce her carefully veiled existence.

Uncle Buck was getting on in years, but, with Helen Ferguson, remained one constant in her bachelor existence. He stayed in contact with Dion. It was Buck who told her Dion got married in Las Vegas. His bride was Jan Porterfield, a showgirl. What former showgirl Barbara thought we do not know.

Fatherhood changed Bob. Airplanes and hunting trips with the boys were no longer the focus of his life. In 1959,

Ursula bore him a second child, a daughter they named Tessa. Bob became a strict disciplinarian. The children had to work for "wages" around the Mandeville Canyon ranch. Chinks, if not deep psychological scars, developed when Ursula's children, Mamela and Michael, reached their teens. The stepchildren had a harder time adapting than the Robert Taylor studio profiles and magazine write-ups would have it. In 1963, the eighteen-year-old Michael was sentenced in Munich for attempted murder—for trying to poison his father. Taking a leaf from Barbara's handling of Dion a decade earlier, Bob refused to let his stepchildren set foot on the ranch.

Dion worked for the Rand Corporation in Santa Monica for a while. In 1958, he and his wife had a son. Four years later Dion was arrested for selling pornography to teenagers. "Yes, I'm Barbara Stanwyck's adopted son, but we don't speak," he told the press. "The last time I talked to my mother was in 1952 when I left to go into the army. I haven't seen or heard from her since." Listed as an unemployed shipping clerk, he admitted he had sold the books to "tide me over until my unemployment compensation check arrived. I have never been in trouble before."

When people asked Barbara about her son, she brushed away all questions, usually with "Oh, he's long since gone." Only Uncle Buck kept in contact with Dion.

MGM held off releasing *Somewhere I'll Find Him* until the early fall of 1956. To boost its chances at the box office, the title was changed to *These Wilder Years*. Critics dismissed it as slushy, mawkish, and hackneyed, politely saying only the veteran cast saved a very modest drama.

Ambitious, nervy, and original projects were hard to find, and not just for Barbara Stanwyck. The directors of her triumphs were mostly laboring in the also-ran categories. While Rouben Mamoulian was satirizing Hollywood as much as Communism in *Silk Stockings*, a musical rewrite of *Ninotchka* via a Broadway show, and Billy Wilder was shooting a Marilyn Monroe comedy, *The Seven Year Itch*, Frank Capra was making *Riding High* and *Here Comes the Groom*, a pair of Bing Crosby vehicles, back to back. William Wellman was making movies for John Wayne's independent company, two aviation suspensers starring the Duke, an outdoor adventure with Robert

Mitchum, and, with Wayne again, a tacky escape-from-Red-China thriller. Howard Hawks reigned over ten thousand CinemaScoped extras, 1,600 camels, and 104 specially built barges in *Land of the Pharaohs*. Preston Sturges was an expatriate living in France shooting *Les Carnets du Major Thompson*, released in America as *The French They Are a Funny Race*. Paramount remade *The Lady Eve*, with Sidney Sheldon rewriting Sturges and Norman Taurog directing Mitzi Gaynor, David Niven, and George Gobel in the former Stanwyck-Fonda-Coburn roles. Barbara refused to see *The Birds and the Bees*, as the charmless reworking was called.

Producers with challenging scripts also passed on Bob. David Selznick called Taylor completely out of the question for the film version of F. Scott Fitzgerald's brilliant, flawed *Tender Is the Night*.

Money, again, obsessed the Hollywood mind. Mary Pickford followed Charlie Chaplin in selling her share of United Artists, which they had created with Douglas Fairbanks and D. W. Griffith in 1919. And although the studios kept blaming the small black-and-white tube for their troubles, Warner Brothers and Twentieth Century-Fox sold their pre-1948 films to television.

By the end of 1955, Dore Schary was given a $1 million golden handshake and fired. With his departure, MGM's efforts to sustain a centralized production system unraveled, and with it the contract system. Four years later, Bob Taylor was the last actor to be let go. By then, he no longer ate lunch at the studio commissary, he recalled, "because there are too many ghosts."

Corporate wisdom remained unchanged—only color, size, and casts of thousands could stop the alarming slump in cinema attendance. But the heirs to classic Hollywood were neither Selznick Jr., Louis B. Mayer II, nor the descendants of the stars, producers, and directors, but the agents and attorneys of the Beautiful People. As the studios decimated their stables of players, writers, and technical personnel, talent agents, who had to find work for their clients, seized the initiative. After acting as counselors-at-law, contract and tax experts, and general court jesters, the Beverly Hills "ten percenters" and lawyers were taking over the entertainment business. Jules Stein, Barbara's own agent since 1937, and Lew

Wasserman took the logical step of becoming the producers of the "packages" of scripts, directors, and talents they themselves put together. First they set up MCA's Revue film division and next bought Universal Pictures.

Columbia was still a one-man operation. Harry Cohn was the absolute ruler on Gower Street, although, he, too, was trying to trim his list of contract players, notably by making life miserable for Rita Hayworth. It was twenty-six years since Cohn had hired Barbara on a one-picture deal to play a bordertown temptress in *Mexicali Rose*. Now, she wanted him to give her the female lead in *Pal Joey*.

George Cukor was set to direct and Marlon Brando to star as the nightclub charmer-heel that Gene Kelly had played in the 1940 Broadway original with its gorgeous Richard Rodgers–Lorenz Hart tunes, "I Could Write a Book" and "Bewitched, Bothered and Bewildered." Barbara wanted to play Vera, the Chicago socialite who falls for Joey, the part Vivienne Segal had created on the stage. Dorothy Kingsley was doing the screenplay, and, from what Barbara heard, she was softening the story and changing the title role from hoofer to crooner to fit a new contender for the title role, Frank Sinatra. Kingsley was the writer of MGM's *Kiss Me, Kate*, the brisk, bright screen version of *The Taming of the Shrew*. George Sidney had been the director and, when Cukor couldn't come to an agreement with Cohn, Sidney won the *Pal Joey* assignment. Sidney brought along *Kiss Me, Kate*'s choreographer—Hermes Pan. That was Barbara's chance. Cohn didn't have to make accommodations to cast her. She could dance. Ask Hermes.

Choreographers don't cast million-dollar productions. Cohn hedged when Lew Wasserman pitched Stanwyck, saying he wanted Marlene Dietrich. He ended up using his in-house stars, Rita Hayworth and Kim Novak, opposite Sinatra. Hayworth's performance was painstaking, Novak's singing had to be dubbed, and the result was a smart but sugary replica of the profane hymn to racy nightlife.

Stanwyck knew what it took to make a great movie. "First of all comes the story," she said. "It's like building a house. That's your foundation, the basement, the cement. That's solid. That's the important thing. Then your interior decorator is the second thing—that's the director. *That* I want. The third thing is all your decorations. That's my actors. But without the story, good-bye. I think the little things will take care of themselves. If your story is good, and your direction is good, and the other actors, you have a chance." Unfortunately, these elements did not come together in a pair of low-budget, black-and-white programmers she made for United Artists.

Crime of Passion had all the ingredients for a superb thriller. The script was by Jo Eisinger, the writer of *Gilda*, the archetypal film noir, and of the disturbing thriller *The Sleeping City*. In *Crime of Passion*, Barbara is a San Francisco writer of a newspaper agony column who gets her big break when she convinces a murderess to give herself up. On her way to a better job in New York, she stops off in Los Angeles. A dinner with a LAPD detective leads to deeper involvement, marriage, and to her giving up her career. Realizing all too soon that life as a cop's wife in suburbia is a bore, she connives to socialize with her husband's boss as a way of increasing the prospects of promotion. Sterling Hayden is her husband, and Raymond Burr the inspector she almost has an affair with before she shoots him. It is left for her husband to discover the truth and arrest his wife.

Crime of Passion never lived up to Eisinger's ingenious premise: A writer who has only contempt for the pathetic letters from her lovelorn readers ends up in a sordid melodrama of her own making far more outlandish than anything she ever wrote about.

The cast included Royal Dano as a rival officer and, as his wife, Virginia Grey. It was five years since Virginia and Bob's odd dating, and Barbara apologized for her angry reaction during the *Clash by Night* shoot. Virginia, too, was an orphan. Virginia, too, was living alone on a ranch in Encino because she had never found a man who could or would take Clark Gable's place.

Filmed during the early summer of 1956, *Crime of Passion* was the third directing effort of longtime assistant director Gerd Oswald, whose direction was soft where the thriller format demanded relentless intensity. When *Los Angeles Times* reviewer Philip K. Scheuer called the film unworthy of her,

Barbara lashed out with a mixture of resignation and anger. Maybe she was through, she complained. "I can't stay up there forever. It's a man's world and it's getting worse. I don't know, they aren't writing beautiful adult stories anymore. In the past three years I haven't been sent any scripts, period. Oh, I know stars who say they can't find anything they want to do in films. But I couldn't lie like that. I just haven't had any offers."

Trooper Hook could have been a latter-day *Bitter Tea of General Yen*, miscegenation and racism on the range. Its director, Charles Marquis Warren, was the grand specialist of westerns, from the big-screen *Arrowhead* to television's "Gunsmoke" and "Rawhide." Besides directing *Trooper Hook*, Warren had a hand in writing the offbeat sagebrush drama that reunited Barbara with Joel McCrea, she as Cora, a white woman with a half-breed son, he as the cavalry officer who discovers her among the squaws. Rodolfo Acosta was the cruel Apache chief who fathered Cora's child. The cavalry sergeant takes Cora back to her husband (John Dehner) who rejects her half Apache child. When the Apache chief sets out to reclaim his son, both he and Cora's husband are killed, leaving her and the child to find comfort in the gallant cavalry officer's arms.

Between setups, Barbara discussed television with her director. She was interested in doing a TV series based on *Desperate Women*, James D. Horan's history of frontier women. Horan's title was silly. The frontier women weren't desperate. Some were good, some were bad, and they were all real. "In all the westerns these days the women are always left behind with the kids and the cows while the men do the fighting," she said.

Warren—and Lew Wasserman—were not encouraging. Television audiences weren't interested in Barbara Stanwyck on a horse. She insisted that was what she wanted to do. "People say it's not feminine. It isn't! Sure those women wore guns and britches. But don't kid yourself. They were all female."

She was back in the saddle in *Forty Guns*, playing a frontier tramp who, with the backing of forty gunslingers, makes her own law in corrupt Cochise County. *Forty Guns* was a

Fox film, and Barbara's initial satisfaction was that she aced out the studio's own Marilyn Monroe. Writer-director Samuel Fuller told Darryl Zanuck he had always had Stanwyck in mind. That was it. Barbara got the part.

Fuller was a character. Zanuck enjoyed this director of baroque B pictures, who pointed his long Havana cigar at people like a .45 caliber pistol. Zanuck saw Fuller as a soulmate, a fellow delinquent in a corporate Hollywood increasingly obsessed with tax angles and bottom lines. Trashy material never bothered either of them. Fuller made wildly physical and intense movies full of jagged inconsistencies and technical virtuosity, and no matter how far out he would go, Zanuck went along.

Fuller had a knack for dressing up the commonplace, for writing compressed dialogue, filming powerful close-ups, and setting up outrageous situations only to play them out quietly. His most famous western was *I Shot Jesse James*, his cruelest *Run of the Arrow*. He was a passionate right-winger, and *Pickup on South Street* was his heady mix of crime, violence, and anticommunism. He told Barbara that in *Forty Guns* she was Jessica Drummond, a composite portrait of two historical characters—Dora Hand, the most gracious sinner of the West, and Big Nose Kate Fisher, the girlfriend of the murderous dentist Doc Holliday. Her love interest was a peace officer who might have been Wyatt Earp. Barbara's *Maverick Queen* partner Barry Sullivan played the hard-ridin', square-dealin' sheriff, Gene Barry his brother who is eventually killed by Jessica's trigger-happy brother (John Ericson).

Forty Guns included the dizziest of Fuller's trademark crane shots. When *Cahiers du Cinéma*, the fiery French film magazine, crowned him, along with Howard Hawks, the essential American auteur, Fuller lovingly described his longest, most complicated take: "It opens in a bedroom with one of the brothers talking. He comes out of the bedroom, walks down the stairs and meets the other brother. They start to talk. They meet the sheriff. They walk four blocks. They go to the telegraph office, send a telegram. Barbara Stanwyck passes them with the forty horsemen, and then they walk past the camera. That's the longest dolly shot in Hollywood!"

As for Barbara, he would remember her as a trooper. "The stuntmen refused to do the scene where the Stanwyck character is dragged by horse. They thought it was too dangerous. So Stanwyck said she'd do it. We did it the first time and I said, 'I didn't like it. It was too far away from the camera truck. We're not getting what I want.' So we tried it again, and I didn't like it. She made no complaint. We tried it a third time, and it was just the way I wanted it. She was quite bruised."

For an encore Fuller wanted Barbara to play Evita Perón. But Juan Perón, Argentina's dethroned dictator, was very much alive in exile in Paraguay. From the Cannes Film Festival, Zanuck telegraphed his veto, and Fuller soon abandoned the idea.

Barbara turned fifty shortly after Fuller called it a wrap on *Forty Guns* and celebrated her birthday by turning down the female lead in Henry King's *This Earth Is Mine*. Unlike so many of her actress friends and rivals, she was rich. Crawford was one step ahead of the bankruptcy courts when she married the president of Pepsi Cola, Alfred Steele. Cameo roles were the death of stars, but Bette Davis was so crippled financially that she accepted $50,000 for two days' work in *John Paul Jones*. Gene Tierney, whose beauty had bewitched moviegoers a decade earlier, was found working in a dress shop in Topeka, Kansas. Paulette Goddard gave up on the movies in 1954 and became an expatriate in Gstaad, Switzerland, not far from her former husband, Charlie Chaplin. To be out of the reach of the IRS, Ava Gardner was living from hand to mouth in Spain.

Barbara was a millionaire. Her self-discipline and the years of Morgan Maree's management of her finances at one point made her the biggest stockholder in Atlantic & Pacific Tea Company.

Millionaire or not, the fear of facing her empty self, loneliness, and boredom made her consider ever more seriously the booming world of television. Fuller had been fun to work with, and westerns were a genre she loved. By 1958 thirty western series were in prime time, dominating all three networks. Even Ronald Reagan, who had not had much work since he finished "G. E. Theater," was the host of the half-hour "Death Valley Days." On a trail blazed by Hopalong Cassidy, Lash La Rue, Gene Autry, Roy Rogers, and Tex

Ritter came "The Californians," "Cheyenne," "The Cisco Kid," "Colt. 45," "Davy Crockett," "Frontier," "Gunsmoke," "Have Gun Will Travel," "Jim Bowie," "The Lone Ranger," "The Restless Gun," "Sugarfoot," "Tales of the Texas Rangers," "Tales of Wells Fargo," "Tombstone Territory," "Trackdown," President Eisenhower's favorite, "Wild Bill Hickok," "Wyatt Earp," and Zane Grey Theater.

Stanwyck considered herself the only unemployed cowboy in Hollywood. Although actresses appeared in single episodes of running shows, there were no women leads in TV westerns. Barbara went to "Zane Grey Theater" producer Dick Powell to suggest a series on frontier women. Powell forwarded the idea to CBS, which carried "Zane Grey Theater." The network agreed to let her star in a "Zane Grey" episode called "The Freighter" and to consider the result a pilot, perhaps for a "Barbara Stanwyck Theater" series. For source material, she wanted James D. Horan's documented stories of such colorful frontier women as Belle Starr and Pauline Cushman or Alice and Calamity Jane.

Belle was a bandit queen and the first woman tried in the courtroom of Isaac "Hanging Judge" Parker for being the leader of a band of horse thieves. After her husband was killed in a bar brawl, Belle took up with a handsome Cree Indian, only to die herself in an ambush. Pauline was an actress from New Orleans who served as a Union spy in the Civil War, married the wild and handsome Jere Fryer, and tried to hold on to him by substituting an infant born to a girl in a Casa Grande, Arizona, whorehouse as her own. The proud father stopped running after other women, but the sickly child died. The real mother exposed the plot, and a humiliated Pauline left her husband and Casa Grande to return to the stage, only to end up scrubbing floors in San Francisco theaters. Barbara was especially intrigued by the real Calamity Jane, who was so successful in playacting a man that she joined George Crook's 1876 expedition against the Sioux as a muleskinner. Louise Dresser had played a mannish Jane in *Caught* in 1931, and Doris Day played her as a tomboy in the 1953 *Calamity Jane*. Neither had caught the tragicomic figure Horan described: "There is no doubt Jane was tragically miscast by nature. Her figure was definitely not feminine. She was a good rider and could handle a mule team with ease. She lived to drink, and lived her short and merry life with a rowdy sort of happiness." In old age she joined the circus, like *Annie Oakley*, and sank into alcoholism. When she was dying, she asked to be buried next to Wild Bill Hickok.

Barbara adopted some of the frontier women's fearlessness. When the network failed to schedule "The Freighter," she persuaded Powell to take the telefilm directly to the advertising agencies in New York. When he came back empty-handed, she angrily went public. "Dick calls me a frustrated stuntwoman," she told the *Los Angeles Mirror-News*. "My one big frustration is that Duke Wayne never asked me to costar with him. Anyway, nobody would buy it for a series. The boys in the flannel suits said they didn't see how we could go for thirty-nine episodes. That's silly. I've got enough books on western lore at home for a hundred episodes."

Before "The Freighter" aired, she went back and did two more "Zane Grey" episodes and for Dick Powell's company a "Goodyear Theater" story of a vengeful woman. But she wasn't giving up on a western series: "I don't even want to have the big-cheese role in the series. I'd have guest stars like they do on 'Wagon Train.' In fact, that's the kind of series I wanted but nobody liked the idea. Then they turn around and do it with my friend Ward Bond."

Nolan Miller was a new friend. Miller was the strapping grandson of a Comanche and the son of a Louisiana oil rigger fresh out of Los Angeles's Chouinard Design School. He wanted to be another Travis Banton, Adrian, or Orry-Kelly, but the studios were not hiring. Television wardrobe departments were. It was while Miller was working for Dick Powell on "Zane Grey Theater" that he met "Missy," as he would always call Stanwyck. She introduced him to Aaron Spelling, a young writer on the show. "He's a terrific designer, you've got to use him," she told Spelling. The two men became friends, and Spelling vowed that when he became a producer, he would hire Miller.

Uncle Buck developed serious emphysema. When he could no longer care for himself, Barbara placed him in the Motion Picture Country House and Hospital, visiting him twice a week when she wasn't filming and on Sundays when she was working. He'd remember the old days when she was "a funny little girl with shining shoe-bottom eyes and brown pigtails." In September 1959, he died. She called a brother in Ohio, but the man was too sick to come to California. She arranged for Buck's burial.

Frank Fay died at St. John's Hospital in Santa Monica. The probate showed he had excluded Dion from his will and bequeathed everything to two Catholic institutions. Dion contested the will, and in 1962 a Superior Court ruled in his favor. However, half Frank Fay's $200,000 estate went to cover "debts, liens and other obligations."

"The Barbara Stanwyck Show"

For an actress who valued work more than leisure, the late fifties and early sixties were like crossing the desert. Barbara didn't get a picture for four years. When people asked why they hadn't seen her for so long, she was disarmingly candid. "Because nobody offered me a part." If the questions became more probing, she said there were no parts for women her age because America had become a country of youth.

Hollywood remained mired in the boring ethos of the fifties well past the end of the decade, but by 1965 even Tinseltown caught on to other times, moods, and assumptions. The readjustment was painful. The message of the chaotic 1960s was fractured spontaneity, emotional overloads, and the exaltation of the self. "New films" failed at the box office as often as the big, almost ritualistic, Hollywood productions that tried to have it every which way and relied on the time-honored values of bestseller source material and starry casts. The Aquarian Age demanded intense, visionary trading on an amplified "now" that was—cinematically and emotionally—the opposite of the perfection Barbara Stanwyck believed in. Intense new filmmakers made offhand movies full of distance and "cool" that nipped audiences in surprising ways. The charm of imperfection had creators preoccupied more with what they hinted at than with what they achieved. Youth openly displayed its strength, allure, and power. The forward thrust in the arts was measured in zap and complicity with the young.

Stanwyck hated it all.

She could be gracious and say she was going with the new trends or, as the divisive decade wore on with its political assassinations, Vietnam, Woodstock, and burning cities, lash out against "the great unwashed," as she called longhairs, hippies, draft dodgers, and young women in miniskirts. She loathed the drift in society, its permissiveness, lack of purpose, people's attitudes toward sex, women, business. The lodestar of her existence had been self-discipline. She saw the young take privileges and opportunities as their birthrights.

The distinction between cinema and television was increasingly a question of different mental landscapes. The big screen gave the decade form, style, and meaning. Television was the playback device, *the* mass media.

Barbara's idea of an anthology series on frontier women was not far off target. The August 1959 Nielsen ratings showed "Gunsmoke" and "Have Gun Will Travel" on CBS and ABC's "Rifleman" as the three most-watched shows. After "I've Got a Secret," "Peter Gunn," "You Bet Your Life," "Alfred Hitchcock Presents," and "The Joseph Cotton Show," "Wyatt Earp" and "Frontier Justice" rounded out the Top Ten.

Both the networks and her agents at MCA said she deserved something classier. Lew Wasserman suggested TV westerns were peaking. She countered that "from six [P.M.] on it sounds like the last frontier. On Monday it's 'Restless Gun' and 'Wells Fargo.' Tuesday it's 'Cheyenne,' 'Sugarfoot' and 'Wyatt Earp'—and so forth." She wanted to play a real frontier woman, "not one of those crinoline-covered things you see in most westerns. I'm with the boys. I want to go where the boys go."

CBS programming could not see thirty-nine episodes of frontier women. Negotiations continued over content and format. In the meantime, her former husband hit it big in "The Detectives." Bob told the press the reason he surrendered to television was money. Besides, he added, he had no idea how he looked on the small screen because he didn't *own* a TV set.

More important than appearing in Jack Benny's court-delayed *Gaslight* spoof, Dick Powell series, and Four-Star movies-for-TV, Barbara had substituted for Loretta Young twice in 1955 on "The Loretta Young Show." The half-hour NBC anthology series was popular and much copied. With her gown swirling, Young opened the show with a dramatic entrance. After she described the night's offering to her live audience, the drama of the week was presented, half the time starring Young herself. At the end she reappeared to say good-night. Barbara played hard to get when NBC and the Sam Jaffe talent agency offered her a series that would emulate Loretta Young's anthology show. "The Barbara Stanwyck Show" would not be all about frontier women, but several western-themed segments were a possibility. Fearing inferior scripts, she insisted she be given script approval or, failing that, completed teleplays before she committed to anything. On its own, the Sam Jaffe agency bought and developed half-hour teleplays. In January 1960, NBC announced the start of "The Barbara Stanwyck Show" Monday nights at ten for the 1960–61 season. The series would shoot at the Desilu (formerly RKO) studios.

The network gave her a news conference at which she was much too forthright for the insipid celebrity reporters and the *TV Guide* interviewer. Asked by the TV weekly why she was getting into television, she said because she was bored and wanted to work. "What else is there to do?" she asked. "I have no hobbies. I suppose that makes me an idiot, but there it is. You're supposed to paint or sculpt or something. I don't. I like to travel, but a woman can't travel alone. It's a bore. And it's a darned lonesome bore.

"People keep asking me what's the difference between doing pictures and TV, and I really can't see any difference. You're making film. The techniques are exactly the same. In television you work a little harder and a lot faster, that's all."

Her producer was Louis F. Edelman, a former WB and Fox executive active in both big-screen and TV production. To ensure a solid success for "The Barbara Stanwyck Show," producer and star offered top prices for scripts. "The foundation of any good show is the story, not the star," Barbara told reporters. "We have found several potential stories for our series, and I hope I don't louse them up."

Taking a swipe at the big screen, she said that although there were great roles for men in the movies, the film industry no longer seemed to make movies for female stars like Claudette Colbert, Joan Crawford, and Irene Dunne. "For my series, I hope to locate scripts with meaty roles for women, but that doesn't mean I intend to avoid stories centering on the male lead. If the story is good, I'll be happy to play an also-ran. I have no particular desire to be 98 percent of the script. In fact, I'd rather have a 50-50 situation, because then there would have to be an awfully good actor with me, and I need all the help I can get."

Veteran filmmaker Jacques Tourneur directed the initial presentation. In "The Mink Coat," Stanwyck played a lady on the skids. To cling to the high society she once belonged to, she uses her mink coat, her last vestige of wealth. Her make-believe world faces collapse when a baggage checkroom clerk loses the coat. The cast featured a young actor named Jack Nicholson.

The show made its debut September 19, 1960. Of the thirty-six episodes filmed for the black-and-white series, Stanwyck starred in thirty-two, usually opposite Lee Marvin or her friends and costars from the 1930s, Joan Blondell and Ralph Bellamy.

Four western scripts and three anticommunist stories were included. Albert Beich who had written *The Yellow Cab Man* for Red Skelton in 1950, came up with the script for "Dragon by the Tail," in which Stanwyck defended the United States against a communist agent. The segment was praised in Congress by Francis E. Walter, the chairman of the House Un-American Activities Committee. Communists were moving back into the entertainment industry, Walter said, praising such efforts as "Dragon by the Tail."

"The Barbara Stanwyck Show" was not a success. As herself, Barbara was stiff and awkward. Introducing segments and players at the opening of each half hour was torture for her. It was a sharp reminder of Willard Mack mocking her insecurity back in 1926. It was doing a Frank Fay, huckstering the audience. For nearly thirty-five years she had escaped into roles, into made-up characters, always letter-perfect not only with her own lines but her partners' dialogue as well.

Introductions to several segments were shot simultaneously. Since episodes were in various stages of readiness, Edelman didn't know in which order the segments would run, which meant Barbara could not learn her lines in advance. Already self-conscious saying, "I'm Barbara Stanwyck, your host tonight," she was even more uncomfortable reading off a teleprompter.

In May 1961, the Television Academy of Arts and Sciences gave her an Emmy award for Outstanding Performance by an Actress in a Series for "The Barbara Stanwyck Show." Two weeks later, NBC canceled the series.

"I never even got a free shampoo," she jeered at her hair-grooming sponsor Alberto-Culver. "Don't these guys send out samples?" She vented her spleen on her other sponsor, the American Gas Association, by saying, "I guess I should be happy the gas company was kind enough not to send me any samples, huh? I never even got a phone call. Whatever happened to manners?" Viewers sent her letters telling her how sorry and angry they were. When a coworker suggested the mail be redirected to NBC, she sneered, "What for? Nobody at NBC can read." The demise of her show inspired a round of second-guessing along broadcast row. When someone suggested a woman wasn't strong enough to hold down a prime-time slot, she threatened to Indian-wrestle any network vice president saying that to her face.

"As I understand it from my producer Lou Edelman, they want action shows and have a theory that women don't do action," she told Joe Hyams. "The fact is, I'm the best action actress in the world. I can do horse drags, jump off buildings, and I've got the scars to prove it." Only Donna Reed was left as a prime-time headliner, she said. Besides her own show, the networks dropped "The Loretta Young Show," "The June Allyson Show," "The Ann Sothern Show," and in 1963 "The Dinah Shore Show."

"I hated playing the role of hostess every week," she told columnist Kay Gardella. "I know Loretta Young loved it when she had her show on, but I couldn't stand it. I was lousy at it. I find I have to hide myself behind something. I can't just play myself."

Survivors of the fast-disappearing studio era returned to the stage, commuting between Los Angeles, New York, and summer-stock towns. Barbara, too, thought of returning to Broadway. At the end of 1961, she was reading Ira Wallach's *The Mistress of the Inn*, which had been given a tryout at the

Bucks County Playhouse in New Hope, Pennsylvania, in 1957. Since then, Wallach had scored on Broadway with his comedy *Drink to Me Only*.

It was not the first time she had thought of returning to the stage. While married to Bob she had hesitated because Broadway producers insisted on run-of-the-play agreements, not, as she wanted it, a six-month contract. "It would have been great to go back when I was young," she said in 1981. "I know that now. Hank Fonda went back again and again and he's as big a star as ever, and look at Katharine Hepburn! It's just one of those things that didn't work out for me."

Nothing came of *The Mistress of the Inn*.

Stanwyck happily accepted a role as the lesbian owner of a whorehouse on the big screen when, in April 1961, producer Charles Feldman offered her the fifth lead in *Walk on the Wild Side*. The screen adaptation of Nelson Algren's novel followed on the heels of William Wyler's remake of *The Children's Hour*. Lillian Hellman maintained her 1934 play was not so much about lesbianism as about slander, what a lie can do to people. Filmed with Shirley MacLaine and Audrey Hepburn as the maligned schoolteachers, the 1962 version of *The Children's Hour* was the first major Hollywood film about lesbianism, that is, the first movie with a major, visibly gay character. However, nothing is ever seen, the word "lesbian" is never pronounced, and, for a "moral" ending, MacLaine kills herself. A nervous Wyler nevertheless told a news conference they weren't trying to make "a dirty movie." MacLaine, who would say a few years later everybody is inherently bisexual, explained that she had researched her part by questioning psychiatrists.

Stanwyck's lesbianism in *Walk on the Wild Side* was thrown in for the effect. Feldman, who had produced the screen version of *A Streetcar Named Desire*, felt *Walk* could stretch the kind of material acceptable on the screen. "We're updating the story for 1960s audiences, who want more spice in stories about girls who go bad," he explained. By the time filming started, little was left of Algren's novel about the self-destruction of a young Depression-era Texan who finds the love of his childhood working in a New Orleans brothel. Louella Parsons was on the phone to Stanwyck when

Columbia announced Barbara had been cast as Jo Courtney, the bordello madam who lusts after one of her girls. "I hear you're going to play a madam and a lesbian," the columnist said. "I'm shocked." Barbara snapped, "What do you want them to do, get a real madam and a real lesbian?"

The picture was directed by Edward Dmytryk, a son of Ukrainian emigrants who had been one of the young hopefuls of the 1940s, directing Dick Powell in two brilliant thrillers, *Cornered* and the Raymond Chandler adaptation *Murder, My Sweet*. Accused of being a communist before the House Un-American Activities Committee, he was the only Directors Guild member to go to jail. Like Joseph Losey he found work in England, returned to Hollywood, and, after naming names at the 1951 HUAC hearings, was allowed to work at Columbia Pictures.

Walk on the Wild Side was a mess.

During the shooting, Feldman kept sending Dmytryk soft porn scenes that had no chance of passing the Production Code. Columbia's advertising and publicity staff breathed hot and heavy about the controversial nature of the film. To make *Walk on the Wild Side* both titillating and demure enough to pass the Breen Office, five writers worked on the script. Stanwyck's love for her best bordello worker, for example, was watered down to the point of unintended implications. Instead of insinuating that Stanwyck lusted after Capucine, their interaction came across as an employer's admiration for a productive employee. Ultimately, Capucine is killed accidentally during a shoot-out and vice queen Jo Courtney is hauled off by police.

The stars were a mess.

Laurence Harvey, who had helped Elizabeth Taylor win an Oscar in *Butterfield 8* and Simone Signoret in *Room at the Top*, fought with Dmytryk. Jane Fonda was in open rebellion against her father, her childhood, and her upbringing and came on the set every day with a Greek athlete she called her secretary. In danger of becoming a vapid sex symbol, she made everybody uneasy flaunting her newly acquired Actors Studio training. The twenty-eight-year-old Capucine (née Germaine Lefebvre) was Feldman's mistress and the producer's spy on the set. Anne Baxter, who played a man-hungry Mexican widow, was afraid her pregnancy would be discovered.

Feldman kept sending rewrites and added scenes that Dmytryk would show to the actors involved and, with their consent, throw out. Harvey, sullenly gay and fighting private demons, stalked off the set and made everybody wait until Barbara let him have it. "One day, he kept us waiting one hour and a half," Baxter would remember. "Highly professional Barbara was furious. So was I. But I had lied rather badly about my increasingly pregnant self and was keeping a rather low profile. Well, when he finally drifted back on the set, Barbara chewed him out with such icy grace that I wanted to cheer. He never did it again. Never."

Capucine, Fonda, and her Greek secretary formed their own cabal. "I didn't blame Capucine," Dmytryk would remember. "She was living with Charlie [Feldman] and had to go home every night to face his questions. There they were often joined by Jane and company, who added fuel to their fire." The inevitable blowup came one morning while they were filming Capucine's death scene and Dmytryk had to throw Fonda's secretary off the set. Fonda might not remember being bounced on Stanwyck's knees during The Lady Eve, but Barbara was so much of her father's generation that when it came to filming their confrontation Jane couldn't bring herself to spew her raw lines into Barbara's face. Dmytryk rearranged the setup so Fonda would not have to look at Stanwyck while delivering the offending dialogue.

The reviews were devastating. Playboy called it "a walk on the mild side, a soupy saga, and only a half-Nelson, adding that "Stanwyck, as a lesbian madam, seems made of chromium."

Barbara returned to television, where Sheila Kuel, the star of "The Zelda Gilroy Show," was dropped after she was found out to be a lesbian. The McCarthy era, during which thousands of lesbians were fired from jobs in libraries, schools, and the military, the FBI infiltrated the Daughters of Bilitis, and the postmaster general of Los Angeles confiscated lesbian magazines, left a legacy of suspicion. Barbara belonged to a generation that perfected the techniques of hiding innermost emotions and had no intention of leaving the twilight. In Walk on the Wild Side, she played the stereotypical lesbian villain, a woman whose acceptance of her sexual preference is what makes her the villain. Barbara was uncomfortable with anyone who so much as broached the subject of lesbianism.

When asked about her part, she was dismissive and said playing Jo Courtney "was a chance to get back into pictures and
see what would happen."

On the big screen, 1963 was the year of the first James
Bond film, of *Irma la Douce* and *The Great Escape*. For
Barbara, the year meant guest-starring in episodes of
"Rawhide" and "Wagon Train." Her costar in *Remember the
Night*, *Double Indemnity*, *The Moonlighter*, and *There's Always
Tomorrow* found a new career on television and told her how
to make it tolerable. As the widowed father in "My Three
Sons," Fred MacMurray worked only three months a year. All
his angles and close-ups were shot first, and the other actors
did the rest of the scenes later. In addition to his high salary,
he had a partnership. The series would run in prime time
until 1972 and many more years in syndication.

Barbara made two appearances on "The Untouchables."
Producer Quinn Martin wanted to spin off her guest-starring
role in the top-rated ABC show into a new series. "The
Seekers" would have her as the head of an FBI Missing
Persons Bureau. The network found the case histories too
grim, however, and passed on the idea. Another disappointment was the no-go former child star Jackie Cooper received
for a series called "Calhoun," based on Merle Miller's hilarious *Only You, Dick Darling: Or How to Write One Television
Script and Make $50 Million.*

Her brother died in 1964. Byron had suffered a first heart
attack in 1959. The fatal coronary thrombosis felled him
while he was filming a TV commercial at the El Caballo
Country Club. He was sixty and was survived by his wife,
Caryl, and his son, Brian. Three years later, Millie was gone,
leaving seventy-nine-year-old Maud Barbara's only living relative. Barbara hated to talk about any of this and claimed she
had said it all before.

She went out with people whose company she enjoyed
and kept up her own two annual dinners, at Christmas and
the Fourth of July. She never allowed journalists into her
house, although Renée Godfrey managed to have Shirley
Eder invited to 273 South Beverly Glen Boulevard one Friday
evening. "I can still hear Barbara saying, as I came through
the front door that night, 'I don't know what you're doing

here; I never let press come into my house,'" Eder would recall. "Apparently some sixth sense told her that once I came through the front door, nothing that I ever heard in her house would reach print without her express permission. For some reason she trusted me." Eder became a friend.

Helen Ferguson faded out of Barbara's life. Even before illness confined Helen to a wheelchair and forced her to relinquish her publicity agency, Barbara had tired of Helen's increasingly autocratic ways. Helen was still a confidante, but Barbara now called her "Mommy" Helen. Larry Kleno, a young man in the Helen Ferguson Agency, eventually took over the office. Helen went to live with a niece in Palm Springs.

Nancy Sinatra, Sr., remained Barbara's closest friend and, as such, perhaps the only person who could hurt Barbara if she sensed neglect in their friendship. Every July 16, Nancy gave Barbara a "surprise" birthday party. One year Barbara failed to show up. When Nancy called, an offended Barbara said she hadn't been invited. She never was, Nancy reminded her. Who ever heard of a birthday child being formally invited to her own party? Wasn't it always understood that she simply showed up?

Barbara's friend Peter Godfrey was diagnosed as suffering from Parkinson's disease. His wife, Renée, stood by him, got a job as a secretary, tried real estate, and went back to acting to help pay for a difficult operation. After she died a short time later, Stanwyck was appointed legal guardian of the Godfreys' seventeen-year-old daughter, Barbara, and the fourteen-year-old twins, Jill and Tracy. Friends like Shirley Eder had learned never to talk about Dion and, if the subject of children came up, only to talk about their own. As far as Shirley could tell, Barbara's devotion to the Godfrey daughters had less to do with affection for the girls than with a wish to right an injustice Barbara perceived in the parents' will. Although Stanwyck never told Eder what upset her after Renée's death, Shirley would remember Barbara not liking what she found in the personal papers.

Barbara kept up her self-deprecating humor, saying that for Academy Awards nights or other functions she felt obliged to attend, she relied on Cesar Romero. "I just call good ol' Butch Romero and he says rather reluctantly, 'Well if you *have* to go, I'll take you.' He does that for all of us old broads."

33

The Last Picture Show

Doris Day was the star of 1964, followed by four men—
Jack Lemmon, Rock Hudson, John Wayne, and Cary
Grant—followed by Shirley MacLaine. George
Cukor's *My Fair Lady* was the film of the year and Julie
Andrews the Oscar winner for *Mary Poppins*. Robert Aldrich,
a paunchy film noir director with a knack for money-spinning
"concepts," wanted to do an encore to *Whatever Happened to
Baby Jane?* His gamble that audiences would love to see Bette
Davis and Joan Crawford debase themselves as a pair of crazy
hags had paid off so wonderfully that dozens of copycat producers pitched imitation scripts to aging first ladies, demanding they look their worst.

Aldrich asked Henry Farrell, the author of *Whatever
Happened to Baby Jane?*, to come up with the sequel. The
Grand Guignol script about a pair of aging cousins Farrell
delivered six weeks later made Aldrich think of Stanwyck. He
had been assistant director on *The Strange Love of Martha Ivers*
and tried to get Barbara for *The Big Knife*.

Hal Wallis got her first, however. Calling her one afternoon, the producer of *The Strange Love of Martha Ivers*, *Sorry,
Wrong Number*, *Thelma Jordan*, and *The Furies* said he was
sending over a script he wanted her to read. She asked what it
was about. He said she'd love it. He'd have it delivered to her
house by messenger. She insisted. Before hanging up, he said
it was an Elvis Presley movie.

Barbara didn't know what to believe. "I thought, well, if
he's calling me, there must be something in it." She had
never seen an Elvis Presley movie.

She quickly found out that Mae West had turned down the part. Still, the idea of playing to a young audience flattered Barbara. She was Maggie Morgan, the never-say-die owner of a traveling carnival who hires wandering tough guy Elvis as a handyman. He makes assorted trouble for everybody, but, by singing in a honky-tonk on the midway, he saves Maggie's circus from bankruptcy. He falls in love with Maggie's daughter, coolly portrayed by Joan Freeman, and becomes the featured attraction. Playing Elvis's boss wasn't too bad. In *Flaming Star*, Dolores Del Rio had played his mother.

By the time *Roustabout* started, Wallis had had enough of Presley and Elvis enough of B pictures. Wallis was the first producer to put Presley under contract, and Elvis respectfully called Hal "sir." But John F. Kennedy's Camelot dated Elvis—the Beatles and the Rolling Stones were shooting up the charts, and the national hysteria that had surrounded Elvis Presley's meteoric rise in the late 1950s was evaporating. His record sales were down, and he was no longer trailed by squealing groupies. He blamed the "travelogue" movies he allowed himself to star in and his middle-of-the-road repertoire of songs. He was grinding out three movies a year, all cheap rock 'n' roll pictures that exploited him as much as his hard-core audience. *Viva Las Vegas*, his last one, was an exception, and the reason was Ann-Margret. For the first time, he had a talented, vivacious costar who nearly counterbalanced the cheap lewdness that was characteristic of most Presley formula movies like *Loving You*, *Jailhouse Rock*, *King Creole*, *G.I. Blues*, and *Blue Hawaii*.

In Roustabout, Presley sang eleven numbers and, said the critics, acted more convincingly than in any of his recent vehicles. Edith Head did the wardrobe. In a compliment that made Barbara blush, the designer told reporters Stanwyck was as well shaped as she had been on *The Lady Eve* in 1940. "Barbara looks terrific in a pair of blue denims, so I had no qualms about putting them on her," Head told the press. "She has so much presence that no matter what she wears, she owns the screen. Teaming her with Elvis was a stroke of genius. It gave him credence as an actor and it brought in some older audiences who would never have watched a Presley film otherwise."

Elvis hated *Roustabout*. He was in such a funk that his

handlers feared he might crack up if he didn't find something fresh to live for. On the set, there was no doubt who the star was, but Barbara pretended she enjoyed making the Hal Wallis Production, directed by TV graduate John Rich. Elvis was restless, and if a scene or a conversation didn't concern him he walked off. Barbara discovered she had one thing in common with him—they were both scared stiff of airplanes. Before the picture finished, a low-profile hippie spiritualist named Larry Geller became Elvis's swami.

To commemorate the wrap in April 1964, Elvis and his famous manager, Colonel Tom Parker, sent Barbara an enormous box of stuffed animals.

Aldrich and his screenwriters' follow-up to *Whatever Happened to Baby Jane?* was a piece of Southern Gothic they called *Whatever Happened to Cousin Charlotte?* Bette Davis hated the title, calling it cheap and revolting. Aldrich relented. The new picture in which Bette would star along with Joseph Cotton, Agnes Moorehead, Cecil Kellaway, and Victor Buono was renamed *Hush . . . Hush, Sweet Charlotte*.

With Bette as Charlotte, Cotton is the family doctor who was once the lover of both Charlotte and her cousin Miriam. A flashback opening establishes the cousins' tenuous relationship in their youth by showing the meat-cleaver murder of Charlotte's fiancé, a murder that unremittingly casts suspicions on her. Back in the present, we see the doctor and Miriam conspire to drive Charlotte insane so they can share her inheritance. When she overhears them below her balcony scheming to commit her, Charlotte pushes an enormous cement planter pot over the edge, crushing them. Vivien Leigh turned down the role, saying there was no way she could face Bette at seven o'clock on a movie set every morning. Aldrich signed Crawford to play Miriam.

A respiratory infection contracted during exterior filming in Louisiana landed Joan in the Cedars of Lebanon hospital in June 1964. Aldrich continued filming and shot all Bette's scenes in which Crawford didn't appear. When Joan didn't recover quickly, he sent copies of the script to Stanwyck, Olivia de Havilland, and Mary Astor. Treacherous cousin Miriam was drawn all black, but it was nevertheless a plum of a role. Barbara hesitated, as she had done when Joe Mankiewicz offered her Margo Channing.

Before she could decide, Joan improved enough to go back to work. Working three hours a day still proved to be too exhausting, however, and she was hospitalized again. The original $1.3 million budget escalated toward the $2 million mark, and the insurance company demanded Crawford be replaced. In the face of Stanwyck's vacillation and Astor's half-serious claim she was really retired, Aldrich closed down the production and flew to Switzerland, where de Havilland was vacationing. Olivia had played a murderess once before in *The Dark Mirror* and hated every moment of it. But Aldrich was desperate—and persuasive enough to make her agree to play Miriam. Stanwyck was offered the part of Jewel Mayhew—a little old lady sitting on her verandah waiting to die, but in her youth the meat-cleaver murderess who started all the trouble. Barbara said no.

When Astor grabbed the Jewel part, Barbara found herself in the uncustomary position of denying Aldrich had offered her the juicy Miriam role. "He did not offer me the part, and I didn't turn it down," she told a Hollywood Foreign Press luncheon. "But *had* he offered me the part, I certainly would have checked with Joan first, because Joan is a friend of mine, as to whether she was able to carry on or not."

Moviegoers loved Bette Davis's encore as a madwoman and de Havilland as the back-stabbing cousin. Producers were sure that what the public wanted was to see yesterday's screen goddesses exhibit themselves as demented, repulsive women. Tallulah Bankhead starred in *Fanatic*, a Columbia knockoff shooting in England and titled *Die, Die! My Darling!* in America. Geraldine Page and Ruth Gordon followed in *Whatever Happened to Aunt Alice?*

After hesitating on *Hush . . . Hush, Sweet Charlotte*, Barbara agreed to *The Night Walker*. She insisted this was a "shocker," not a horror film: "There's a difference. Horror is with the heads rolling and the blood and gore and all that sort of thing. This is a shocker-suspense film." The producer-director was William Castle, a cigar-chomping specialist in cheap horror flicks whose greatest triumph was three years in the future—producing Roman Polanski's *Rosemary's Baby*. Castle belonged to the carny type of moviemakers. For *The Tingler* he had vibrating seats installed in selected cinemas, for *Macabre* he insured his viewers at Lloyd's of London in case of sudden death. His latest was *Strait Jacket*, in which Joan Crawford played a deranged woman who, when she finds her husband and his mistress in bed, chops their heads off. The gimmick Castle had in mind for his newest chiller was to get Barbara Stanwyck and Robert Taylor together.

The Night Walker was about a woman trapped in a dream so starkly real that her days and nights blend into a nightmare. The script was by Robert Bloch, the author of Alfred Hitchcock's *Psycho* and Castle's *Strait Jacket*. When Stanwyck went to discuss it with Castle, he asked how she would feel if Taylor played her leading man. She tried to make her reply casual. "I think it would be a wonderful idea, but you'd better ask *him* and Mrs. Taylor." Castle had directed Ursula in the 1954 costume piece *The Iron Glove*. Bob wasn't keen on doing the picture, but Ursula convinced him it was a good idea.

Castle convinced Stanwyck and Taylor to invest in the picture, that is, to work for Screen Actors Guild minimum or "scale" in exchange for percentages of its future earnings. Without mentioning the money angle, he invited the entire Hollywood press corps to the first day's shooting. Louella Parsons wanted to know if the first Stanwyck-Taylor love scene wasn't a little bit embarrassing for Bob and Barbara. Castle answered for his stars. The scene was played across a table for two in a fashionable restaurant, he explained. As Taylor and Stanwyck took their seats, Bob said it all reminded him of a little place in Chicago. Barbara chimed in with "Do I remember! We ate ourselves out of shape there."

The jokes were window dressing. Bob looked terrible. His chain-smoking had given him lung cancer, and the counterculture he despised was claiming his stepchildren. Mamela was arrested for drunk driving and drug possession in California and in Germany.

The Night Walker started shooting during the late summer of 1964. Barbara played a somnambulist who keeps having a weird dream in which a stranger (Lloyd Bochner) tries to woo her away from her jealous, blind husband (Hayden Rorke). Bob played the family lawyer who helps her get to the bottom of her husband's disappearance in an explosion and fire. The stranger turns up again in a dream and takes her to an undertaker's chapel, where, in the presence of wax dummies and a model of her burn-scarred husband waiting to leap at her, the stranger insists she marry him. Barbara carried the picture.

Castle and Universal Pictures threw a premiere party at which photographers snapped pictures of Bob and Barbara standing together but never touching. She went on a promotional tour for *The Night Walker*, explaining that along with Bob and Castle she owned a piece of the film. "The whole thing would not be worth reporting," the *New York Times*'s Bosley Crowther said, "if it didn't have Barbara Stanwyck in the role of the somnambulist and Robert Taylor as her husband's lawyer who tries to help. Miss Stanwyck, silver-haired and seasoned, does lend an air of dignity to the otherwise unbelievable tale. And Mr. Taylor, lean and wrinkled, does at first make the lawyer seem something more than the spurious character he finally turns out to be." Because of the movie industry's Byzantine bookkeeping, most stars who "participate" in their movies' financial fortunes walk away feeling cheated. Barbara and Bob's investing in *The Night Walker* actually turned out to be a successful venture.

Castle got Crawford for his next suspense-thriller, *I Saw What You Did*. When Joan's character was killed off near the beginning of the film it was alleged the producer-director couldn't afford her. The rumor was deliberate, one of Castle's publicity stunts. Producers sent Barbara screenplays in the shocker-horror vein. She sent them right back, saying she was tired of scripts "about grandmothers who eat their children."

Barbara was in New York in the fall of 1965 for ten days of shopping, theatergoing and seeing old haunts. Shirley Eder and her husband, Ed, joined her. Shirley would recall the crowds waiting outside the Plaza Hotel to see Stanwyck and the audience at a *Golden Boy* revival with Sammy Davis, Jr., in the title role chanting, "Barbara Stanwyck!" as she stood up and acknowledged the applause. At the end of the stay, Shirley was with Barbara at her hotel suite one night when snow began to fall. Barbara sat at the picture window overlooking Central Park, her feet on the radiator, and began to reminisce about her youth.

"You know, Shirley, I can remember when I was poor—oh so poor and so cold because my coat was too thin to give warmth. But as cold as I was, I loved being outside when the first snow fell on New York City. It was a magic time for me then, and it's still magic, except now, with my feet on the radiator, I'm so nice and warm."

Matriarch

The television series on frontier women never got off the ground. Being her naked self on TV hadn't worked. *Playing* a western matriarch did. From 1965 to 1969, Stanwyck was the matriarch of a western clan on "The Big Valley" television series. "They don't write strong women's parts in movies or television," she told interviewers when the popular ABC series began its third season. "It just isn't like the great days when they had strong men stars and strong women stars—William Powell and Myrna Loy, Clark Gable and Joan Crawford, Gary Cooper and Greta Garbo. The wheel turns, so we'll probably get back to that. But meanwhile I like to work."

She could be even more emphatic. "I would go mad if I retired. I'm ready to work anytime. I'll take any part that comes along. I don't care about the money or the size of the role. All I care about is working."

Making a television series reminded her of touring vaudeville shows. There was never enough time. Before signing on with Levy-Garner-Laven Productions, she held out for a fully fleshed out character. What she wanted—and got— was rewrites that turned her matriarch character, Victoria Barkley, into a vital, frankly mature woman as active as her children. "I'm a tough old broad," she told the producers. "Don't try to make me into something I'm not. If you want someone to tiptoe down the Barkley staircase in crinoline and politely ask where the cattle went, get another girl. That's not me."

Hour-long segments were filmed in six days, averaging

twelve pages of screenplay a day. Three pages a day had been the average even for Warners: eighty-to-ninety-minute "working-girl" programmers. In movies, the hours were civilized compared to TV. Back in the studio days, everybody was home for dinner. On "The Big Valley," she was up at four and sometimes on the set till nine at night. "We do twenty-six shows in twenty-six weeks," she said, "twenty-six very fast movies, and no one bothers counting the hours. The script is here, the cameras are there, and you are here."

End-of-day aches had their own kick of adrenaline for her. "Late afternoons you feel you're so hot and tired—particularly on those hot locations—that you just can't do a thing. But somehow you always do. At night, you have a pot of soup and go to sleep. It's a brutal life."

She loved it.

During the nine months the series was in production each year nothing else existed for her. The three months when "The Big Valley" was in hiatus, she didn't know what to do with herself. When she was tired of reading, she went to the movies, sometimes staying all day. She joked that a script was much more dependable than a man.

As Victoria Barkley, she played the widowed matriarch of a powerful ranching clan in California's San Joaquin Valley in the 1870s. Barbara characterized Victoria Barkley as an old broad combining elegance with guts. Much of the series' drama centered on Victoria's fights with her sons. Richard Long played the eldest. Peter Breck and Charles Briles played the other two sons. Linda Evans was the only daughter and Lee Majors the bastard son of Victoria's late husband. Guest stars included Anne Baxter, Colleen Dewhurst, Katherine Ross, Carol Lynley, Leslie Nielsen, and Milton Berle.

Stanwyck found working with Evans and the other young TV players less than thrilling. "Most of these young people have no idea of what their obligations are; they don't know what an actress is supposed to do," she told writer-producer Robert Blees. As an example she said the actresses on the show ran to the makeup tables as soon as a scene was blocked. "That's the most important part of their performance—their hairdos. After that, their makeup, then wardrobe. Finally comes remembering their lines—A and B and C and D—and just that monotonous is how most of it comes out. Last on their list is the performance." When one of them asked why *she* was so blasé about her own makeup, Barbara answered that there were experts on the set who could do her in three minutes, that she had no interest in looking at herself in the mirror to pencil an eyebrow or a lower lip. What she was interested in was to start being the character. Evans cooed about their mother-daughter relationship. During the first season, however, Barbara scolded her young costar for being unprepared and late.

Linda Evans considered Stanwyck the greatest teacher. When Evans's character in a "Big Valley" scene needed more presence, Stanwyck told Evans she'd show her in the next take. "As the rehearsal went on," said Evans, "I waited for an explanation from Stanwyck about 'presence,' but she didn't say anything. I had to walk in this door and walk into the scene, but she didn't come over. Finally the director said, 'Action!' She came over behind me just as we were supposed to walk in the door. I thought, 'When is she going to tell me what to do?' Then, as I opened the door, she picked up her boot and kicked me in the butt! I went flying onto the set with my eyes wide open and she said, 'Now, *that*'s presence."

Frankly sixty and passably untroubled by playing the "blood and guts" matriarch, Barbara saw no point in trying to turn off the years. "There is no age in my life I want to be *again*! Certainly not thirty," she told *Pageant* magazine. "I have yet to understand the percentage, the advantage, the rhyme and reason, the necessity and/or compulsion to be never-older. Maybe I'm just too lazy—it seems much more practical to me to eat properly and to be too busy to be facialed, massaged, chin-strapped, and all the other time-consuming pampering age-fearing ladies submit to—not to mention hair dyes, face lifts, and the expense. At least the samples of the nice, youth-impelled, but I think, misguided ladies I've seen have made me think all the fretting, fussing, stewing, lying, and dyeing, all the tensions created by wanting to be forever young, age one faster. They look what they are—battle-scarred veterans of their lost war against time. I decided not to enlist in that war three years before I turned forty."

While the media were still largely deaf to the polite protests of homosexuals, a new lesbian movement emerged, made up of politically aware women. If these younger, assertive lesbians had a heroine it was "Big Valley's" Barbara Stanwyck and the sense of control she radiated. To many younger lesbians, her Victoria Barkley seemed genderless. Unlike Stanwyck's earlier roles in which the men always won or the situation got to her in the end, here she was a woman in full possession of her powers—no man needed. "You just *knew*," said Dana Henninger. "We weren't too impressed with her earlier career, *Stella Dallas*. She was a little too coy back then, but in her westerns, yes. And 'Big Valley!' There was no male testosterone in her Victoria Barkley. We were all just crazy about her." Anyone trying to tell her as much was met by a crushing brush-off. Boze Hadleigh, a committed homosexual journalist, was more or less thrown out of her house when he dared ask if she was gay.

Her elegant and gutsy aura was heightened by her affection for stunt work. Virgil Vogel, who directed her in forty-five "Big Valley" episodes, said no physical action ever frightened her. "She had great confidence. I would give her all the protection possible. I checked each stunt carefully, but in her extreme dedication to her work she always gave a little more than she was instructed to. If I asked her to jump eight feet, she would do ten." Over the "Big Valley's" four-year lifespan, Stanwyck appeared in all but seven of the 112 episodes.

Her white mane became a trademark and made her recognizable off the tube. During an L.A. visit of Ed and Shirley Eder and their young son and daughter, Barbara said she had never been to Disneyland. Once in the Anaheim theme park, Stanwyck was quickly identified. While she and the Eders queued up for the Matterhorn roller-coaster ride, public relations people swooped down to tell her they would move her and her party to the head of the line. To the Eder children's chagrin, Aunt Barbara snapped, "Not me, you don't." Later in the day, a group of Japanese businessmen spotted her. When their leader asked if they could snap a picture of her, she posed, movie star-style, for the shutterbugs and was rewarded with a bow and a respectful, "Thank you much, Miss Streisand." She never let on that she was not the thirty-five-year-younger La Streisand, and the Japanese went home convinced they had photographed the Funny Girl.

Barbara's aching back and emphysema gave her a no-nonsense respect for those who fought back illness and won. She attended the West Coast premiere of *The Subject Was Roses*, Patricia Neal's first film after recovering from a severe stroke. At the after-screening reception, everybody remarked on Neal's stunning comeback, on how her dramatic powers were not only intact but seemed intensified. Still, apprehension clouded her face as Stanwyck came up to her. *The Fountainhead* was long ago, but Jack Warner and King Vidor had given Neal the role Barbara had so much wanted.

Barbara betrayed no rancor. She smiled and said, "You're gorgeous."

"Oh," Neal laughed, "you finally saw *The Fountainhead?*"

Barbara had no use for jokes. She looked the younger actress squarely in the eye and said, "I admire you very much."

The Screen Actors Guild wanted to honor Stanwyck. Those who knew her on the SAG awards committee feared she would not show up if she was told she would be the recipient of an award. So they told her to come to the November 21, 1966, annual membership meeting to hand an award to newly elected California governor Ronald Reagan.

She was in the wings waiting for her cue when Reagan walked out onstage and began telling the audience the Screen Actors Guild award "is not presented just for longtime excellence on-screen. It should be called, perhaps, an above-and-beyond award, because it is given for outstanding achievement in fostering the finest ideals of the acting profession."

Barbara was totally confused as Reagan went on extolling the evening's recipient. "We have known her in this profession as truly a professional and an exponent of our art and craft of the best . . . "

At Reagan's ". . . Barbara Stanwyck," she covered her face. To the roar of a standing ovation, someone shooed her onstage and walked her to the microphone and an embrace by Reagan.

"It's the first time I've been kissed by a governor," she began. "I am very, very proud of this moment. I love our profession very much. I love our people in it. I always have and I always will. And whatever little contribution I can make to the profession, or to anything, for that matter, I am very proud to do so. It is a long road. There are a lot of bumps and rocks in it, but this kind of evens it all out, when an event like this happens in your life. From a very proud and grateful heart, I thank you very much."

Glittering occasions were few and far between. Nancy Sinatra hosted Stanwyck's sixtieth birthday July 16, 1967, and for the occasion invited Barbara's nephew and family. Gene Vaslett was a successful businessman in Oakland, California, and her grandnieces were artistically gifted, Victoria as a ballerina, Kathleen as a painter. Larry Kleno, who had taken over the Helen Ferguson Agency, became Stanwyck's press secretary, a position that would grow in influence over the next years.

Dion divorced and remarried. He was about to marry twenty-four-year-old Rose Bywalski in Las Vegas in 1968. Contacts between mother and son were nonexistent.

Stanwyck was proud of her independence, of living alone—she called herself a "bachelor woman"—but in 1968 she became in real life the besieged victim she had played to perfection in *Sorry, Wrong Number* and *Witness to Murder*.

It took her a while to realize there was someone outside her home, waiting for hours. One morning when she opened the front door, a man jumped forward, shouting, "I'm here, Barbara, baby, I love you!" She slammed the door, locked it quickly, and on the intercom told him that unless he left, she would call the police.

He left.

She waited ten minutes before she opened the door to retrieve her newspaper. From across the street, he came running toward her. She called the police.

When he came back again and again, she filed charges. Her tormentor was Henry Roy Belmert, a forty-five-year-old transient from Ohio. The judge ordered him to the Atascadero State Hospital for observation. The psychiatric evaluation was inconclusive.

California law required a jury trial before anyone could be committed as a "mentally disordered sex offender." The rules of evidence of the day prevented Stanwyck from testifying to the mental anguish she suffered because of Belmert's unwanted attention. At his Superior Court trial, however, she managed to say, "I don't know when I'm going to open the door and find him there. I don't know when he's going to jump out at me and grab me."

When neither Barbara nor Deputy District Attorney John Hoyt presented evidence of an actual sexual advance, the jury found Belmert not guilty. With terms of probation imposed, he was released.

The next thing police heard was Stanwyck's hysterical voice on the phone reporting that Belmert was cutting through her screen door. Again, he was arrested.

Barbara didn't wait for the wheels of justice to decide his or her fate. She sold the house on Beverly Glen Boulevard and found a small, one-story ranch house on Loma Vista Drive in Beverly Hills, part of the recently developed Trousdale Estates, where tight security was a priority.

In June 1969, Stanwyck and Governor Reagan met under unhappy circumstances, he to read the eulogy for Robert Taylor; she to make an embarrassing appearance at the funeral.

Not so long before, Bob had jokingly asked Nancy Reagan why the California Republican Party had chosen Ron, not him, to run for governor. Reagan's funeral speech was affectionate: "I know that some night on the late show, I am going to see Bob resplendent in white tie and tails at Delmonico's, and I'm sure I'll smile—smile because I'll remember how a fellow named Bob really preferred blue jeans and boots. And I'll see him squinting through the smoke of a barbecue as I have seen him a hundred times."

The words were too much for Barbara. She broke down in loud sighs and tears that interrupted Reagan. The stony silence of the other mourners amplified her sobs. Tom Purvis turned to stare Barbara down. Others thought she was heavily sedated or drunk.

Robert Taylor had spent his last years in the double-feature market, mostly in westerns. "The Detectives" series was canceled in 1962. Bob turned to television, taking over as host and star of "Death Valley Days" after Ronald Reagan left the show to run for governor. Bob refused to admit he had lung cancer. Ursula pleaded with him to undergo surgery. He pushed it off, saying there was no way he would be able to keep hospitalization from the producers of "Death Valley Days." In 1968, he and Charles Boyer had let themselves be talked into starring in a feeble espionage comedy with a telling title, *The Day the Hot Line Got Hot*. Shortly after the filming finished, Bob's lung cancer was diagnosed as inoperable. Doctors told the press he suffered from Rocky Mountain spotted fever.

Bob's last months were harrowing. He was in and out of St. John's Hospital in Santa Monica, insisting on going home, but after a few days yielding to Ursula and physicians' pleas for hospitalization and cobalt treatments.

Three weeks before the end, Ursula invited Barbara to come and see her former husband. Barbara had never visited the Taylors, but she came. The ravages of terminal cancer, three operations, and cobalt treatments left him an emaciated ghost of his former self. In May 1969, when Bob was home for the last time, Michael, his never mentally stable stepson, committed suicide. By early June, the news media reported that Robert Taylor was fighting for his life.

On the morning of June 8, he died.

The funeral of a Hollywood celebrity drew crowds to Forest Lawn, and Ursula offered the first Mrs. Taylor a seat with the family out of sight of the throngs. Barbara decided she would not attend, but on the morning of the funeral changed her mind.

She arrived—late. Steadied by two attendants, she entered the chapel in dark glasses, wearing a bright yellow dress that jarred with the mourners' black. The dress was later explained as fulfilling Bob's long-ago wish that she not wear black at his funeral.

Reagan managed to finish the eulogy despite Barbara's sobs. After the service Purvis and several other old buddies of Bob's shook their heads in silent protest when Ursula, escorted by her daughter, Mamela, crossed to Barbara and invited her to join a handful of others at the ranch "for a drink on Bob." Barbara was driven to Mandeville Canyon. When she was ready to leave, Purvis and the others saw Bob's two wives in a deep conversation in the middle of the driveway. All eyes were on them. No one dared walk up to them.

The two women talked, neither betraying any emotions. There was no comforting hand touching an arm, no brief hug, no handshake. Barbara got into her limousine. Slowly, the big car eased down onto Mandeville Canyon Road.

35

Golden Girl

Barbara soldiered on through her sixties and seventies. Cancer—and smoking—killed friend and foe. After Humphrey Bogart succumbed in 1957, Gary Cooper, John Wayne, Edward G. Robinson, William Powell, and Dalton Trumbo, whose screenwriting credit on *Exodus* marked the end of the blacklist, died of cancer. Massive coronaries felled Harry Cohn and David Selznick, and Sam Goldwyn spent five years bedridden, obese, partly paralyzed from a stroke before dying in his sleep. Barbara was a survivor. There were days when emphysema had her gasping for air, but she kept up her lifelong habit of smoking. "I'm not yesterday's woman, I'm tomorrow's woman," she said, tossing her white mane in a gesture of impatience and flicking cigarette ashes into an empty coffee cup.

She claimed she hated the past yet, when the golden era was brought up, talked longingly about it. She had never been under long-term contract to a single studio, but she marveled at the security that Bob, Joan, Clark, and Bette had enjoyed. She forgot the flip side, the ruthless meat-market breeding, the straitjacket contracts, and the punishing suspensions of the star system. "Two or three pictures a year written for them by the top writers. It was like a baby being bathed and all wrapped in a blanket. Today, it's catch as catch can. Today someone buys a book or a play and asks, 'Who can we go to a bank with?' not 'Who's right for it?' It was a good system for a while but Hollywood today is like a series of Mobil or Standard Oil stations leased to a distributor."

Work rescued her in 1970. Aaron Spelling, the "Zane

Grey Theater" writer she had introduced to Nolan Miller, was on his way to becoming television's most successful producer. Spelling offered her two ABC Movie of the Week assignments. In *The House That Wouldn't Die*, she inherits an old house in which strange things begin to happen the moment she arrives. Barbara Michael's novel, *Ammie, Come Home*, was adapted by *Whatever Happened to Baby Jane?* and *Hush . . . Hush, Sweet Charlotte* writer Henry Farrell. Next she was cast in *A Taste of Evil* opposite Barbara Parkins and Roddy McDowell. Looking every inch the regal matriarch in a Nolan Miller creation, she terrorized her daughter, ranting and raving in a supercharged ending.

Miller was very much part of Spelling's upward mobility. "Dynasty," "The Love Boat," "Fantasy Island," and a half-dozen other glamour shows were still in both men's future, but Spelling realized that the way to lure film stars to television was to promise designer wardrobes. "We dangled Nolan," Spelling would recall. "Instead of offering more money, we said Nolan will do your clothes."

"Stanwyck taught me not to worry about shoes," Miller would say twenty years later. "'If they are looking at the shoes,' she said, 'everything else is a mistake.' She thought the top of the dress was the most important, especially in TV where it's all close-ups. She called them 'table-top' dresses."

The couturier and his wife, Sandra, became Barbara's friends. Sandra was the daughter of New Orleans socialite Matilda Streams, one of Nolan's earliest private clients. Miller did Sandra's sweet-sixteen party dress, her debutante gowns, and her first wedding dress. "That marriage lasted ten minutes," he said. "Ten years later I married her. It sounds like a miniseries." The Millers called Barbara "Missy" and realized her idea of a good time was a quiet dinner with them, Jane Wyman, and Nancy Sinatra, Sr. "Missy thought she ran my life for me," Nolan would recall. "She'd call and ask what I had for breakfast. She wanted to be sure I *had* breakfast."

Of the old stars, Crawford remained Barbara's closest friend. Visitors to Crawford's New York apartment commented that the only photos displayed in the living were one of President John F. Kennedy and one of Stanwyck. In New York, the ladies did lunch at the "21" Club, always at the same corner table at the front of the room so Joan could see and be seen by everyone who entered. "She looks like a million bucks when she goes out," said Barbara of her friend. "She's a star, and don't you forget it."

With her take-charge style, Joan usually ordered the menu. Nolan sometimes joined them and would remember Crawford and Stanwyck reminiscing about how wonderful it had been when the studios, however brutally, built careers. Stars were stars back then, one of them would say, disparaging modern-day actors who after one television series thought of themselves as stars.

If the dinner was at the Beverly Wilshire Hotel's Don the Beachcomber restaurant, Jack Oakie usually came by to offer a drink and thank Stanwyck for selling him her ranch back in 1940. "Made me a rich man," he winked. Southern California's postwar sprawl had swallowed Northridge and made it L.A.'s newest lily-white suburbia of palm-treed, rectilinear streets laced with cookie-cutter ranch homes, swimming pools, malls, freeways, and smog.

Crawford eventually stopped coming to California. "All of my friends are out of work, it's so sad," she said.

In November 1971, Stanwyck began a pilot for a TV series about a woman lawyer and her young partner, played by James Stacy. She was especially happy to have Lee J. Cobb in the cast. It had been over thirty years since they had worked together on *Golden Boy*.

On the second day of shooting, she felt a sharp sting in her left side. Her lifelong smoking had aggravated her bronchitis, but she decided to tough it out. She wasn't going to hold up production. At the end of the day, she returned home feverish and exhausted. The pain grew worse. In the middle of the night she called Nancy Sinatra, Sr., and asked her friend to take her to the hospital. Diagnosed as suffering from a ruptured kidney wall, she was rushed into surgery at St. John's Hospital in Santa Monica, where both Frank Fay and Bob had died. When she woke up in recovery thirty hours later, she was told the kidney had been removed. "Plenty of people survive with one kidney, you know," she whispered. "I'll be fine."

St. John's Hospital kept her for two weeks. She apologized to the producers of "Fitzgerald & Pride" and especially regretted not being able to work with Cobb. Susan Hayward took her place, and the filming was rescheduled. Hayward sent Barbara twelve dozen roses.

Nolan presented the two actresses to each other. "When I introduced Missy and Susan, they were very formal about it. 'Hello, how are you,' in very elegant tones of voice," he would recall. "At the end of the afternoon, they were both hugging and kissing, with tears and the whole thing."

For the convalescing Stanwyck, Hayward was a mirror image of her younger self. Susan told of being born Edythe Marrener on Church Avenue, Brooklyn, in 1918, attending the Girls' Commercial High on Classon Avenue, and dreaming of becoming an actress like her idol, Barbara Stanwyck. Whenever a Stanwyck film played the Glenwood Theatre or the RKO-Kenmore, Edyth persuaded her father to give her a dime so she could go and see it. "I studied the way you walked and talked and dressed," she told Barbara. "I was forced to wear middy blouses and skirts at Girls' Commercial, but I vowed that once I got out of school, I'd wear the same smart suits Barbara Stanwyck always wore in movie magazine photos." She was a pretty, dignified, and scared-stiff twenty-year-old when the David Selznick sweep for Scarlett O'Hara brought her to California, to be screen-tested by George Cukor. An agent got permission to show her failed *Gone with the Wind* test at Warner Brothers, where she was renamed Susan Hayward. She, too, had married twice, her first husband the failed actor Jess Barker, her second the late FBI agent Floyd Eaton Chalkley.

In January 1973, Barbara was well enough to work in *The Letters*, a third ABC Movie of the Week. She could grin and bear it during the day, but the kidney forced her to spend most evenings in bed. It was in bed that she watched Mae Clarke, her roommate from Forty-sixth Street, greet James Cagney on stage at the televised American Film Institute's Lifetime Achievement Award dinner in his honor.

Susan Hayward was diagnosed with brain tumors. Nolan did a forest-green sequined gown for Hayward to wear as a presenter at the 1974 Academy Awards. She was terminally ill and died a few weeks later. In March 1977, Helen Ferguson died. Two months later Crawford was dead.

"There's a lot of gold being given out tonight, but Hollywood will never run out of it as long as we have treasures like the next two stars," Bob Hope told the audience at the fiftieth presentation of the Academy Awards. "He made his sensational screen debut in *Golden Boy*, and we'll never forget his leading lady whose performances were never less than twenty-four karat. The *Golden Boy* and The Golden Girl are together again tonight. William Holden and Barbara Stanwyck!"

Looking stunning in Nolan Miller's rhinestone-studded black gown, Barbara walked down a flight of glittering stairs with Holden at the April 3, 1978, Oscar event. In close-up at the podium, the tuxedoed Holden looked older than his co-presenter as he launched into an impromptu speech:

Before Barbara and I present this next award, I'd like to say something. Thirty-nine years ago this month, we were working in a film together called *Golden Boy*. It wasn't going well because I was going to be replaced. But due to this lovely human being and her interest and understanding and her professional integrity and her encouragement and above all, her generosity, I'm here tonight.

A roar of applause rang through the Dorothy Chandler Pavilion.

When it died down, she cried, "Oh, Bill."

After a deep breath, they alternated reading the nominees for Best Achievement in Sound. Barbara turned to Holden, handed him the traditional envelope, and said, "And here, my *Golden Boy*, you read it."*

Celebrity journalism sold movie tickets, theater tickets, books, and records of the famous and the glamorous. Barbara shrugged when magazines called her a near-recluse, but reacted sharply when the *New York Times* reported fan letters forwarded to her from studios asked where she was buried.

On Golden Pond ran for 128 performances on Broadway with Tom Aldreidge and Frances Sternhagen as the couple who have been married fifty years and come once again to

---

*The winners were Don MacDougall, Ray West, Bob Mindler, and Derek Ball for *Star Wars*.

their summer cottage in Maine. Stanwyck fought to do the 1981 film version with her old friend Henry Fonda, and so did Greer Garson. Producer Jane Fonda held out for Katharine Hepburn. Barbara accepted a guest appearance on "Charlie's Angels"—to prove she wasn't dead. The producers floated the idea of a spin-off to be called "Tony's Boys," with Barbara as Tony, a female version of Charlie, and three good-looking boys, but the series was ultimately shelved.

Two months after her "pardner" from *Cattle Queen of Montana* was inaugurated as President of the United States in 1981, Ronald Reagan sent a personal message to New York's Lincoln Center, where Frank Capra, Henry Fonda, and a glittering audience paid tribute to Barbara Stanwyck. "You are a woman whose strength of character, vitality and energy permeate every word you play," read the White House telegram. "Long before it was fashionable, you were a paradigm of independence and self-direction for women all over the world."

Walter Matthau summed her up: "She has played five gun molls, two burlesque queens, half a dozen adulteresses and twice as many murderers. When she was good, she was very, very good. And when she was bad, she was terrific."

Escorted by Holden, she stood on the stage, a vision in white, from her white hair, to her silver-sequined white gown wrapped in a white mink stole, to her white shoes. When the ovation died down, she thanked the Lincoln Center Film Society:

> When the Film Society first notified me about this event, I thought they made a mistake. I thought they meant Barbra Streisand. Well, we got that straightened out. And then I thought that I had to tell them I had never won an Academy Award. So, we got that straightened out. They said it didn't make any difference to them.

Back in Los Angeles, Nancy Sinatra, Sr., threw a dinner party for her. Holden came in from Palm Springs and was joined by producer Ray Stark and director Richard Quine. Holden drove Barbara home. Did she know he was losing his long battle with alcoholism? Although he had spent a great deal of the last years in Europe and Africa with Stephanie Powers, they had always stayed in touch.

When he bid her good night on her doorstep, she said, "Good night, *Golden Boy*. Take care of yourself." Three weeks later Holden was found dead in his Santa Monica apartment. A friend called Barbara. "N-n-no, it can't be. Are you sure it's Bill?"

The Reagan administration pledged to wage war on crime. On March 30, 1981, the president, his press secretary, James Brady, and two police officers were wounded in a fusillade of bullets. Twenty-five-year-old John W. Hinckley, Jr., was arrested. He seemed to have acted from a desire to impress Jodie Foster, the teenage movie star he had never met. Seven months later, Barbara was terrorized by a pistol-packing burglar.

It was 1:00 A.M., October 27, when she was awakened by someone standing in her bedroom door and shining a flashlight in her face. Before she could turn on the light, a man's muffled voice asked where her jewelry and purse were.

She switched on the light and saw a man in a ski mask pointing a gun at her. He ordered her not to look at him and to turn out her bedside lamp.

"I want your jewelry or I'll kill you," he said.

She decided jewelry was not worth her life and told him her valuables were in the top drawer in her dressing room. Beverly Hills police lieutenant Russ Olson would later report the robber was confused as to the location of the jewelry, that when she turned her light on again, she was hit with a blunt object.

"I told you not to look," the burglar shouted. "I'll kill you."

After taking diamond rings, a diamond necklace, earrings, and the cigarette box Robert Taylor had given her, he grabbed her and threw her into a bedroom closet, and slammed the sliding door shut. He did not lock it, but shouted, "If you come out, I'm going to kill you!"

For what seemed an eternity, the seventy-four-year-old actress lay bleeding in the closet. Blood trickled down her forehead and into her eyes. She told herself to stay calm, and when everything was silent, she stumbled out and called police. An ambulance took her to the Cedars-Sinai Medical Center, where she was treated and released.

The psychological repercussion was worse than the night's ordeal or the loss of jewelry, estimated by police at $5,000. The thief had cut the glass on the living-room window, noiselessly and professionally. BARBARA STANWYCK SURVIVES NIGHTMARE ATTACK, read one headline. Another said, ACTRESS RELIVES ROLE IN BURGLARY.

She was too distraught to attend Edith Head's funeral two days later. Larry Kleno told reporters how calm and cool she had been, how after being released from the hospital she had joked about the disinfectant "painted over my hair." No one was arrested. Did that mean a repeat of the Belmert ordeal? From neighbors police pieced together a description of the street that night suggesting the burglar had an accomplice. Barbara wondered if Henry Belmert had discovered her new address, whether *he* was the accomplice. Now two men who had threatened her were on the loose.

Stanwyck spent $10,000 on an elaborate security system. Racoons, squirrels, and chipmunks always rattled the swank hillsides of the Trousdale Estates by setting off alarms. Now, the slightest nighttime noise had her freeze in fright. Invitations from friends went unanswered. When they called, they found her changed. In November, Nancy Sinatra managed to convince her to come to dinner one night. Barbara had to be picked up and delivered back to Loma Vista Drive by trusted friends.

She was torn when the Academy of Motion Picture Arts and Sciences decided to give her an honorary Oscar. Her impulse was to stay holed up at home, but Hollywood had been good to her. How could she refuse?

The March 29, 1982, presentation was a night of upsets. *Chariots of Fire* was the unexpected winner as Best Picture, but Katharine Hepburn and Henry Fonda were the evening's sentimental favorites, winners of the Best Acting awards for *On Golden Pond*. Neither was present, Hepburn performing in Washington, Fonda too ill to attend.

"Four years ago, William Holden and Barbara Stanwyck came on this stage to present an award," John Travolta began.

"When they did, Mr. Holden departed from the script to speak from the heart. He said that his career derived from the lady standing next to him, that all he was came from her generosity, her support, her abiding belief in him. Barbara was completely surprised by this. She listened, her public face letting her private face show . . . but only for a second."

Introducing scenes from her career, Travolta mentioned she had been nominated four times—for *Stella Dallas*, *Ball of Fire*, *Double Indemnity*, and *Sorry, Wrong Number*—and, to a standing ovation, brought her onstage.

For a moment she seemed to fight back tears. Then she took a deep breath and said, "A few years ago I stood on this stage with William Holden as a presenter. I loved him very much and I miss him. He always wished that I would get an Oscar. And so tonight, my *Golden Boy*, you got your wish."

Backstage, the honorary Oscar winner told the press, "Of course I was disappointed those times I was nominated before and lost. Anyone who says they're not is lying. I'd like to do more as an actress, and better. It might be in a wheelchair but what the hell."

Depending on her mood, her answers to adulation tended toward the wry or the blasé. "Look, believe it or not, I don't walk on water," she liked to caution. She lived in the present, and her complaints were about now. "Some actors and actresses in my position say they can't find the right role, but I can't fool myself that easily. Why lie about it? I just don't get many offers. There is a whole new team at the studios, and I'm just another aging woman to them. They are more interested in new faces. And let's face it—mine isn't new."

A month later, her face filled the TV screen in *The Thorn Birds*.

She created an imperious portrait of a wealthy and spiteful matriarch in the miniseries. Colleen McCullough's sprawling saga, with its hammer blows of fate, was Australia's *Gone with the Wind*, and in scope, passion, and tribulations the bestseller matched Margaret Mitchell's Civil War novel. Barbara had read *The Thorn Birds* without casting herself as Mary Carson. Yet she knew she had no competition for the role when Herbert Ross was hired to direct it as a feature.

A year after Michael Cimino's *Heaven's Gate* had essentially bankrupted United Artists, however, the $21 million price tag producers David Wolper and Stan Margulies came up with for a big-screen *Thorn Birds* was too steep. Scaled back and, ironically, blown up to a ten-hour miniseries for a worldwide TV audience, the project looked financially realistic.

Stanwyck's portrayal dominated the first three hours of Carmen Culver's screenplay. "I do four takes—that's all," she told director Daryl Duke. Richard Chamberlain, who was cast as Father Ralph de Bricassart, the handsome parish priest, was sure no more would be needed. Drogheda, a prosperous Aussie sheep station, was re-created on a spread in the Simi Valley not too far from the Northridge of Stanwyck's rancher days. The cast included Rachel Ward as Mary Carson's granddaughter and Father Bricassart's earthly love, Jean Simmons as Fee Cleary, Richard Kiley as Paddy Cleary, Christopher Plummer as the archbishop, and Mare Winningham as Barbara's great-granddaughter. Duke filmed the interiors at Burbank Studio—as the merged Warner and Columbia studios were now called.

The Thorn Birds gave Barbara a chance to play a woman of seventy-five assailed by sexual urges. Widowed and embittered, Mary Carson wants only one thing—the passionate embrace of the young priest. Her yearning is played out in a verandah scene in which she comes upon the priest getting out of wet clothes after a storm.

Duke told Barbara to stroke Chamberlain's bare chest, and for once she flubbed her line.

"Cut!" shouted Duke.

"What the hell," she grinned. "It's the first time in twenty years I've had a naked man in my arms."

Like a trouper she finished a house-burning scene on the Simi Valley set. Film technicians added special-effects smoke to the controlled fire. She was not the only one to gag on the thick, black smoke that Duke and cinematographer Bill Butler said would give the picture a special beauty, but she took several lungfuls. She stayed on the assigned spot in the wooden inferno until Duke yelled Cut!" Gasping for air, she was rushed to St. Joseph's Hospital.

Her lifelong smoking habit added to the gravity of the smoke inhalation. She had seen what emphysema had done to Uncle Buck, but refused to believe the disease, brought on by her heavy smoking, could turn her into an invalid. The hospital kept her for three weeks of breathing exercises, twice-daily deep-breath therapy. When she returned to work, cast and crew gave her a champagne welcome and, as a gag, a bottle of special-effects smoke.

Nine months later she was still suffering bronchial after-effects. She watched *The Thorn Birds* in bed. Broadcast over four nights in March 1983, the ABC miniseries proved so popular it ranked as the runner-up to the highest-rated-ever miniseries "Roots."

The Television Academy gave her an Emmy for her Mary Carson portrayal. Although she had never won an Oscar for any of her big-screen performances, the *Thorn Birds* Emmy was her third, following her "Barbara Stanwyck Show" and "Big Valley" awards. She walked briskly onstage to accept the Emmy, but in the wings two minutes later she had trouble catching her breath. Four times she was rushed to the hospital, gasping for life. Doctors told her a cold could kill her. A virtual prisoner of emergency equipment at home, she lived in fear of smog, chills, and dampness developing into crippling pneumonia. She was forced to say no to offers for appearances in her friend Richard Quine's remake of *Hotel* for TV and "The Love Boat."

36

Closing Number

Queen Babs was, in her late seventies, one of the best-loved stars. For over fifty years she had played the women that a new assertive feminist agenda took as models—women who lit their own cigarettes, opened their own doors, and ran their own lives. Cable TV and home electronics gave a second life to many of her films and inspired new appreciation. Her screen persona was a woman who knew how to survive without feminine wiles but was not above using them. Her dancer's figure and sassy demeanor illuminated her Depression-era dames, and poise and independence entered the mix with her 1940s screwball comedies and film noir cynicism. In the long view, her emotional range and lack of pretension gave her life on the screen honesty and sarcasm, toughness and warmth. Film historian Stephen Harvey thought her acting technique so deceptively simple and elusive that he called her the least mannered and pretentious of the major stars of her period. Pauline Kael, the doyenne of American film critics, called *The Lady Eve* "a frivolous masterpiece." Richard Schickel unearthed *The Miracle Woman* and praised Stanwyck for never being "ditsy, cuddly or passive—modes that the reigning conventions of romance of the period encouraged" in *The Mad Miss Manton, The Lady Eve*, "and maybe best of all, *Ball of Fire*." Not all reassessments were that flattering. Gavin Lambert, whose *Inside Daisy Clover* was becoming a cult film for its subliminal homosexuality, told a UCLA cinema class that Stanwyck in *Double Indemnity* "comes across like a drag queen," that "there is something simply 'too much' about her." New hotshot director Lawrence

Kasdan came out with an imitation of *Double Indemnity*, *Body Heat*, with Kathleen Turner in the Stanwyck role and William Hurt as the Florida lawyer with whom she plots to murder her husband. For Christmas–New Year's 1984–85 holidays the independent Los Angeles station, KTLA-5, put on a Barbara Stanwyck Week, with a like celebration periodically scheduled on other stations.

Dion surfaced in print to tell his side of the story of a lifetime of hurt and rejection. Prodded by a tabloid and a would-be biographer digging into the marrow of Stanwyck's life, the fifty-one-year-old Dion remembered the mother who was never there, the father who beat her up in raging arguments. He remembered turning freckled-faced and heavy when he was five or six, his bad grades, and being shipped to a military academy. He remembered how she never phoned, never sent for him on weekends.

"She never touched, kissed or held me—except when cameras flashed," he told the *National Enquirer*, pouring out a litany of blame as he detailed his unhappy childhood and adolescence. "I want to see my mother again—even for just half an hour—and experience just once more what it feels like to be a son," he told the tabloid. "Mother, perhaps if we meet once more, we can both live the rest of our lives in peace."

Had she agreed to see him earlier, had she given him an explanation that might salve thirty years of misunderstanding, perhaps Anthony Dion Fay might not have taken the *Enquirer*'s money to spill his story. However exploitative the *Enquirer*'s editing, the interview was all the more pathetic as it was addressed to someone who had spent her own childhood in foster homes, rejected and kicked around.

Was Dion after her money? He admitted his life had not been exemplary, that he had brushes with the law, that he had passed bad checks when hurting for money, but that was decades after she had cut him out of her life. People who knew Barbara admitted she had always treated her adopted son with indifference bordering on contempt, that it was all very tragic.

She refused to see him.

Reporters trying to get her side of the story were rebuffed.

Mommie Dearest, Christina Crawford's harrowing memoir of her mother, was a bestseller, and now Dion was dragging *his* mother through the tabloid press, telling of abandonment and lifelong antagonism. Larry Kleno said there was nothing to explain, that Stanwyck considered Dion "an unfortunate situation." Asked to elaborate, the press secretary said Dion had never learned from his mistakes. Stanwyck had gotten him out of so many scrapes when he was young that she had just given up on him. She was deeply hurt, but Dion was a closed issue.

"She wouldn't talk about him," her friend Shirley Eder would recall. "She kept a picture of him in a closet. She had a way of shutting off things, to close the door behind her."

To Barbara's mental aches was added the physical indignity of growing blindness.

Four months after the *Enquirer* article, she was losing her sight. In May 1984, she was diagnosed as suffering from cataracts on both eyes, with the left eye by far the worst. In early December, she was hospitalized for surgery. After removing the cataracts in both eyes, doctors inserted a plastic lens inside the left eye. She was pronounced legally blind, but doctors said her vision would improve. The recovery was slow. By the summer of 1985, however, her right eye healed sufficiently for her to see well enough to read.

She shunned formal affairs, and her favorite evenings were spent at the house parties given by Nancy Sinatra, Sr. Aside from her few women friends, Barbara kept to herself, easing her pain and loneliness with drink. "Life is a pretty difficult thing to get through," she said. "But I'm not an unhappy person." When she turned eighty and was asked if she liked what she had made of herself, she said, "Let's say I did what I was supposed to do. Okay?"

Her private existence was one of the best-kept Hollywood secrets, and publishers wanted the Stanwyck story. Over breakfast at the Beverly Hills Hotel, the William Morris Agency's Norman Brokaw broached the subject of an "as told to" Stanwyck autobiography to Shirley Eder. He was sure he could get a huge sum for a book written with Stanwyck's collaboration.

When Eder mentioned Brokaw's idea, Barbara said that

the complete honesty and openness with which she would have to approach such a project would be too wrenching. "I had a scrapbook as a kid, but I never wrote down the bad things that happened," she told her friend. "Since I'm not about to let it all hang out—which could be dull reading even if I did—I'm *not* going to do it." As an afterthought that spoke volumes, she added, "Besides, it would be too damn painful for me to go back through so many personal experiences." She declined to help others write her story. Without her collaboration, Al DiOrio, the biographer of Judy Garland and Bobby Darin, published a slim Stanwyck biography.

By early spring 1985, her eyesight and bronchitis were on the mend. Aaron Spelling had a TV movie for her he hoped to spin off into a series. To play her husband in *Dark Mansions*, Spelling was trying for Sterling Hayden, her lover in *Crime of Passion*. Going on seventy-six, Stanwyck made Spelling agree that if *Dark Mansions* should go to a series, her scenes would be filmed so she would only work two days a week.

By April, *Dark Mansions* was out and "The Colbys" was in.

"Dynasty" was at the height of its popularity. In the United States alone, over 50 million people watched each episode, and Spelling decided to match the success of "Dallas" with a new series that in its early weeks was formally titled "Dynasty II: The Colbys." Set in Los Angeles, its central characters were the members of the family of one of "Dynasty's" main characters, Jeff Colby, played by John James. Charlton Heston was the corporate magnate Jason Colby, Jeff's father, and Emma Samms was Fallon Carrington, Jeff's wife. Stanwyck would be Constance Colby Patterson, Jason's elder sister. The character was a spunky woman with a brain for business, a mixture of Barbara's *Executive Suite* heiress and her "Big Valley" matriarch.

Besides her two-days-a-week work rule, Barbara made Spelling and producer-writer Esther Shapiro agree she would never have to work past 6:00 P.M., never the week before Christmas, and never do interviews.

The step outline had Constance Colby Patterson controlling half the family fortune and determined that neither Jason nor anyone else in the family would trample on her.

Charlton Heston claimed the reason he agreed to be in the series was Stanwyck's presence.

Spelling and his team of writers planned interaction between the casts of "Dynasty" and "The Colbys." However, Joan Collins (one of "Dynasty's" major stars) hated the rival series, and, according to *TV Guide*, she urged her fellow actors on "Dynasty" to have nothing to do with the spin-off.

A month before filming started, Barbara's home was gutted in a blaze. She was inside Saturday morning, June 22, 1985, when the fire started in the attic of her Loma Vista Drive home. She heard the smoke alarms go off and went outside to see the roof on fire. Seven fire engines responded as did neighbors, including Ross Hunter, her producer on *All I Desire*. "Anyone else would have been hysterical but Barbara was magnificent, seeing her beautiful paintings covered with ashes," Hunter said. Nancy Sinatra managed to get through police barricades and chase away news crews pestering Barbara for interviews.

Stanwyck tried to be brave but looked like someone whose life is crumbling around her, despite Hunter's statement. News photographers caught her in the street in an old cardigan, watching with Hunter, touching her lips in disbelief, distraught at losing so many personal belongings.

Press reports told of her trying to dash into the burning house to save Robert Taylor's letters to her. The tabloids played it to the hilt. "Even after their divorce and after Taylor's death, Barbara still loved him, was still obsessed by his memory—and his memory was tied up in those letters, certain mementos from him and personal photos of him," reported the tabloid. "She started to rush back into the house to save these precious mementos but a fireman held her back. Barbara said, 'Please . . . ' but then her voice broke and tears welled up."

Damages were estimated between $1.5 and $1.8 million. After spending a week with Nancy Sinatra, she moved into a rented house. Her home was rebuilt.

Joan Collins was so noticeably absent for the July taping of the first "Dynasty" and "Dynasty II" scenes that Spelling had to admit to the press he hadn't spoken to her and, in any case, would never speak to her fiancé-manager, Peter Holm. Stanwyck and Heston were so perfect they shot their first scene—a three-pager—in one take, but the two of them didn't get along. Barbara nicknamed him "Moses" for his *Ten Commandments* role. "He has a bad memory," she said. "He still thinks he's parting the Red Sea."

They nevertheless thought of themselves as examples for the younger cast members. The sentiment was far from mutual. "Both Barbara and Heston are not exactly unsusceptible to their egos," said newcomer Michael Praed. Tracy Scoggins, who played Barbara's niece, said, "She's rough on the younger players." Heston admitted she was "no little Mary Sunshine on the set."

When Barbara had to wait while Scoggins and Stephanie Beacham had their hair fixed, she called Spelling and had him issue an order: When Stanwyck is ready, *everybody* else in her scene must be ready!

Stanwyck looked frail and jittery, clutching the arm of Nolan Miller as she entered the Beverly Wilshire Hotel ballroom for the publicity bash that ABC and Spelling threw for the season debut of "Dynasty and Dynasty II: The Colbys." Stanwyck and Linda Evans, now the costar in "Dynasty," wore stunning Nolan creations, Barbara a black chiffon dress that set off her trademark white hair. The average costume budget per episode of the new show was $25,000, and at $10,000 a week, Nolan was the highest-paid costume designer in the business. When a magazine reporter approached, Nolan said to her, "Barbara dear, say hello. This gentleman would like to do a story."

"With or without my help I'm sure," she snapped.

As the taping progressed, character developments promised in the series' step outline were not in the scripts. Constance Colby Patterson never moved into the Colbys' boardroom, and her love interest, played by Joseph Campanella, was eliminated. Barbara saw her part dwindle to the point where she was little more than a well-dressed mouthpiece for the good guys in the family. Although Spelling and Shapiro respected her two-days-a-week shooting schedule, constant rewrites made it a six-day job to learn her lines and attend story meetings and rehearsals. When she complained that she was playing the same scene she had done the week before, she was told, "Don't worry. It'll work."

"I say the same line every week," she told Shapiro, "the only thing different is my dress." Rock Hudson, who created a sensation flying to Paris seeking experimental treatment for AIDS and died of the disease in October 1985, was cheap fodder for her anger: "Even if Rock Hudson had been healthy when he did 'Dynasty,' the scripts would have done him in," she spat.

One day in March 1986, when Shapiro came on the set, Barbara faced her down and said, "This is the biggest pile of garbage I ever did—it's lucky I signed only for thirteen episodes. I'll be surprised if it lasts half that long."

By April, Stanwyck's revolt was out in the open. Tabloids had a field day. *The Star* quoted her as telling Shapiro, "It's one thing to know you're making a lot of money off vulgarity, but when you don't *know* it's vulgar—it's plain stupid." She called the show "a turkey."

She went to Spelling and told him she had never walked out on a contract before, but, reluctantly, she was going to leave the show. "I've played the same damn scene twenty-four times," she told him. He asked her to reconsider.

To write her out of the series, a last episode had her on the phone arranging an around-the-world cruise for herself and her absent boyfriend. "The Colbys" didn't outlive her prophecy by much. It wrapped its second, and final, season on ABC with a cliffhanger improbable even for television standards—Fallon's kidnapping by a UFO—although she surfaced on "Dynasty" the following season.

The Screen Actors Guild had resorted to subterfuge to give Stanwyck its award. The American Film Institute tried to be up front with her in 1986 when it wanted to make her the fifteenth recipient of its Lifetime Achievement Award at a televised tribute dinner. "I can't go through with that evening," she told AFI's president George Stevens, Jr. "I'm not that kind of person." Stevens, whose father had directed her in *Annie Oakley*, turned to AFI board member Heston to persuade her. "My TV brother Moses called me and said, 'I'll take care of everything,'" she told *Variety*. "'I'll not hear any more from you. You will be there!' And he hung up."

She almost didn't make the April 9 black-tie ceremony. A week earlier she had sprained her back, and she checked out of St. John's Hospital only hours before the Beverly Hills Hotel award dinner. During the long evening Stanwyck stayed in a wheelchair in the wings for all but ten minutes. The organizers showed clips from many of her movies and her kiss with Ronald Reagan frame frozen on the screen. The long evening of tributes was emceed by Jane Fonda. In keeping with the actress being honored, the evening was short on sentimentality and long on clear-eyed fun.

"I only made one movie with Barbara Stanwyck," Fonda announced, shook her head, and walked offstage. She came back, did her intro again, and said her condition for appearing was that no clip from *Walk on the Wild Side* be run. "My father was in love with her all his life," she told the glittering audience. "He openly admitted it to all his wives."

The testimonials were delivered from the audience as assorted well-wishers simply stood at their tables and spoke. Walter Matthau called himself an admirer of Stanwyck because she knew how to wrap both a good girl and a bad girl into one performance. Fred MacMurray called Stanwyck "the most wonderful girl to work with." He summed up their four films together. "Once I sent her to jail, once I shot her, once I left her for another woman and once I sent her over a waterfall." Richard Chamberlain called Stanwyck's raw voice "a million dollar case of laryngitis."

With a supreme effort, she got out of the wheelchair and, to the accompaniment of a standing ovation, walked onstage. Unable to mask her pain, she leaned on the glass podium and responded to the applause with "Honest to God, I can't walk on water." Matter-of-factly, she said she was there because of what others had taught her. She singled out Frank Capra, who let her in on all the secrets of filmmaking, and Billy Wilder, "who taught me to kill—and thank God for him!" She thanked the crews—"I refer to them as my boys"—the writers—"Oh, God, how important they are"—and other actors.

With that, she picked up her award, made it to the wheelchair and an oxygen tank, and returned to the hospital.

She had nothing planned for her eightieth birthday, but on July 16, 1987, friends and *Variety* columnist Army

Archerd showered her with attention. Her illnesses kept her confined to her home, thin and weak, but clinging to hopes of doing one more movie or a TV series. Ironically, the back problems that almost made her miss the AFI tribute were aggravated by treadmill exercises to strengthen her lungs against the combination of chronic emphysema and pulmonary obstruction that weakened her. Her eye condition remained painful, but she was able to read and watch television.

The limitations and humiliations of invalidism were especially grating to the fiercely independent Stanwyck. It was certainly not how she had imagined her later years would be. She had accepted *The Thorn Birds* and "The Colbys" not only to work but also hoping to recapture her fame. She had wanted to go out in a blaze of glory.

Stanwyck let her mind drift to the past. Her sickroom became a dimly lit shrine to Bob Taylor and herself. Photos of them together were everywhere. On the night table stood her honorary Oscar. It was almost twenty years since Bob had died, but she talked of her late husband as if he were there yesterday, and she came to believe she could communicate with him through the Oscar. If anyone asked why she was clutching the statue in bed, she said, "It brings Bob to me."

"When I hold this Oscar and I'm very quiet, I feel young and beautiful again. I discovered some time ago that Bob is still with me and that our love for each other will continue on the other side. Bob comes to me in the early hours of each morning. I wasn't frightened when he first appeared—just pleased and grateful. That was a year ago and I was tossing and turning in my sleep. I turned on the light and saw the Oscar gleaming on the table. Something told me to pick it up. As I touched it there was a little electric shock and then my beloved Bob was standing by me. A look of incredible tenderness was on his face. We were together again and I knew he was there to help me to the other side."

What she feared most happened in June 1988. Pneumonia put her in St. John's Hospital with few chances of survival. Dr. Robert J. Kositchek could do little to ease her gasping pains because of her allergy to many painkillers and because doctors found ten broken vertebrae in her brittle back. Isolated in an oxygen tent in a room where the lights were dimmed to protect her eyes, she could barely wave to

Larry Kleno, Nancy Sinatra, Sr., and her old friends Loretta Young and Jane Wyman. From the White House, President Reagan phoned, but she was too weak to take the call.

Once more she rallied. Three weeks later she was back home, cared for by round-the-clock nurses. When she wasn't on oxygen, she was able to sit up in bed and make household decisions. She liked to have her hair combed out and groomed herself for the day in case an unexpected visitor dropped by. The variety and dosages of painkillers made it difficult to say when she'd be awake, however, and visitors inevitably became scarcer. With the exception of Nancy Sinatra, she was surrounded by paid staff, Kleno, and medical technicians.

She felt utterly forgotten and even on good days sank into despair. Nolan Miller came by to show her a videotape of his newest couture collection. A more concerted effort to cheer her up was devised by Kleno with the consent of Morgan Maree, her longtime business manager. Kleno talked to the tabloids. Stories appeared on "The Forgotten Barbara Stanwyck," with Maree's address at the bottom for readers who might want to send a cheerful postcard. "She doesn't know what day it is or if she's eaten breakfast yet or why she needs a nurse," wrote The Globe. "She can't leave her bedroom at all. That's where she'll probably die. She knows there's not much time left and what would give her the most peace would be to know she's not forgotten." Dion was variously reported as never calling or reconciled with his mother.

Staff members read the postcards that did come in. They gave her a scrapbook to leaf through, but found her sitting staring out the window. There were days when she seemed to give up hope. A bladder infection added to her distress.

She was readmitted to St. John's Hospital in May. Hospital workers reported that she had instructed nurses not to admit Dion to her bedside, no matter how close to death she might be. Again, she was sent home.

Months went by in a monotonous haze. She told Kleno she wanted to be cremated and have her ashes strewn over Lone Pine, the stretch of California desert on the eastern slope of the Sequoia and Kings Canyon national parks, where she had made several westerns.

She was too ill to react to Bette Davis's death from cancer and to the ultimate indignity that befell Bob's memory. MGM was only a shred of its former self, and the huge, mostly idle film factory in Culver City was now named Lorimar Studios. Reacting to the neoconservatism of President George Bush and to Senator Jesse Helms's art bashing, fifty Lorimar screenwriters petitioned to have the building they were working in stripped of the name the Robert Taylor Building.

A taint of anti-Semitism had trailed the actor for years, but, said director Judy Chaikin, it was the days of the blacklisting that gave Taylor a special place of infamy. "Taylor is the only one on film actually naming names," she said. "When people see it, it takes their breath away; the star who named names." Ursula, who had remarried, came to the defense of her second husband. Bob, she said, had been betrayed by the studio he promoted. But the speed with which Lorimar stripped Taylor's name from the Writers Building and renamed it the George Cukor Building astonished even the petitioners.

Barbara was back at St. John's Hospital January 9, 1990, for treatment of her chronic lung condition. Medication made her refuse food.

Eleven days after admittance she went into a coma. Nancy Sinatra and Kleno were at her side with her nephew Gene Vaslett, his wife, and two daughters. In the late afternoon of January 20, 1990, her heart gave out, and she died in her sleep.

There was no funeral. According to her wishes, her body was cremated. Kleno rented a helicopter and scattered her ashes over Lone Pine.

"It Worked—Didn't It?"

Barbara Stanwyck knew that what counts is to be in the last act. "Put me in the last fifteen minutes of a picture," she said. "I don't care what happens before. I don't even care if I was in the rest of the damned thing—I'll take it in those last fifteen minutes." Between the memorable and the forgettable, between *The Lady Eve* and *Always Goodbye*, *Double Indemnity*, and *Escape to Burma*, she is part of Hollywood's preferred vision of itself.

Stanwyck felt restless and empty without a movie role to slip into, and her insistence on the importance of being in a film's final quarter hour reminds us that life, like the movies, unspools in the present tense. She never found out what it was that gifted directors saw in her, what millions responded to up there on the screen.

If we flash back to 1917, little is expected, less is calculated or planned for ten-year-old Ruby Stevens. All she can think of a few years later is getting enough money to buy a nice coat. At the dawn of the talkies, she is someone who learns to defy the special gravity of the screen. Still later, she realizes style and reticence make for the larger-than-life images that allow audiences to lose themselves in screen fantasy. Classical Hollywood never cast actresses for their acting abilities, and moviegoers accepted the bigger-than-life fantasy, the tension, and the glamour. Like her threadbare Depression audiences, she learned to let the flair, distinction, and strength of the people she played rub off on her. She became the Barbara Stanwyck who was said to be not fully dressed until she screwed a sneer on her lips. She knew that drama and laughter originate in character as much as in circumstance.

She knew the world didn't owe her a living, and her compulsive dedication to work was lifelong. Since her childhood taught her she wasn't important to anyone, she decided early on to take herself seriously. She learned to control situations and people in her life and was unable to surrender, even if it meant unsatisfying intimate relationships in her personal life. She felt guilty and responsible for her husbands and never quite trusted anyone—other than herself.

Psychiatrists tell us the orphan's greatest quandary is whom to trust, that people without a consistent identity are prone to role playing, to making up identities. They also tell us that the result is often a lifelong conflict between a need to be in charge and a wish to be taken care of. She never resolved this inner tension. Had she done so, had she been all in control or all clinging vine, she would have been a much less intriguing performer. Acting may be indefinable, but what moviegoers react to is the appeal of the oversized presence on the screen. The trick is not to defeat expectations but to surpass them.

Unlike many who climb from nothing, she managed to hang on to a basic emotional honesty. She was straightforward and as far as she could recall never said anything she didn't mean. She hated the trappings of celebrity and found the public's assumed familiarity somewhat presumptuous. As a matter of principle rather than vanity, no one ever saw her in cold cream or curlers. Prematurely gray, she was not afraid to say how old she was. Yet the humiliations of old age frightened her. More than a decade after turning down *All About Eve*, she refused the ravings of *Hush . . . Hush, Sweet Charlotte*.

Screen acting is not progressive. Movie actors do not go from strength to strength toward ever more demanding parts, but slide sideways at best, typecast and shackled by past successes. To be asked to repeat oneself is in itself a drift toward mediocrity. Stanwyck realized early on that the mechanics of moviemaking never really favored performers. The industry might be star-oriented—graven images of mystery and allure sell tickets—but the prime initiative does not belong to actors. People who are not performers decide what gets made and with whom. With the movies' built-in glare, massive inadvertencies, and trendy obsessions, hanging on to a career is in itself an art. The climb is unpredictable, the room at the top tenuous. Stanwyck played her hand superbly.

She *looked* as if she could handle herself in any situation. Whether she was called upon to endure happiness or doom, she tempered her projected competence with irony, which is why she aged better than more mannered performers.

She created a body of characters as complex as any of her peers' performances, but was careless in the myth-creating business. The orphan, chorus girl, and Gower Gulch beginnings were the stuff of stardust, but she didn't throw tantrums like Crawford, didn't walk off pictures like Davis. Except for a pair of Clifford Odets adaptations that were overlooked, she missed the cinematized versions of the classic and classy Broadway theater. She incarnated ladies named Sugarpuss O'Shea, Dixie Daisy, and Sierra Nevada Jones while others embodied Mrs. Miniver, Tracy Lord, Regina Giddens, and Margo Channing. It is hard to imagine Hepburn playing second fiddle and taking second billing to Elvis Presley, Colbert in her sixties getting back in the saddle, Davis or Crawford suffering Aaron Spelling and Linda Evans for more than one script read-through. To Stanwyck, however, the point of working was to keep busy, not to pole-vault herself onto some pedestal. Invariably, when Hollywood handed out its annual awards, she was passed over. She had little faith in acting theories. She had mocked Marilyn Monroe, who came to the set of *Clash by Night* trailing Actors Studio's Paula Strasberg, and Jane Fonda, who couldn't do a scene in *Walk on the Wild Side* without Strasberg. "I marvel at people who have theories about acting," Barbara said disdainfully in 1987. "I never had an acting lesson."

Preston Sturges felt her instinct was so sure that she needed almost no direction. In her own opinion, she worked best with directors who allowed her to compose her own portraits. "To me the essence of a good director is not to say, 'Walk to the table, then turn around and face left.' The good director will walk you through gently and give you some air." Capra gave her the feeling she was directing herself. "He allowed you to express yourself. Then, and only then, if you were wrong, he would tactfully suggest something else. He was never didactic. Billy Wilder works the same way, and I think I've done some of my best work for them."

She didn't like directors who brought their writers on the set and changed dialogue on the run. Capra had Robert Riskin around and every morning brought scene changes on color-coded pages. "It used to drive me crazy," Barbara acknowledged. "Sometimes he would change two or three pages of nothing but talk, talk, talk. Some of them were bastards to learn on the spot. But I never said anything about it; he was the boss." She considered the writer paramount—perhaps that was what made her turn with such vehemence during the McCarthy era on writers she felt had betrayed her country's ideals.

Barbara's professional memories were positive. Her fondest recollection was Sturges, who after *Remember the Night* told her he was going to write her a marvelous comedy. She was funny, he said, adding, "I'm going to the front office and insist they let me direct it." That was in 1941. Forty years later, she smiled and said, "A lot of people said that sort of thing, and fifteen minutes later it was forgotten. But two months later, Sturges handed me *The Lady Eve*. He was marvelous. He loved actors. Some directors get along with actors, but they don't really like them."

Stanwyck didn't pretend she knew more about camera angles than the cameraman, more about makeup than the head of makeup. If a setup called for her to wear a hat, she let wardrobe put the hat on her head and walked onto the set without looking at herself in the mirror. Her no-nonsense professionalism made her the Queen to her crews over the years. Although working crews rarely take up collections to "gift the star," at the end of a Stanwyck shoot someone always stepped forward to present her with a token of respect—a silver locket, a coffee maker, record player, or upholstered director's chair. The inscriptions read "To the Queen" or "To the Queen from her Drones."

"She was just the most wonderful actress in the whole business, and I've worked with a lot of them," said Fred MacMurray. "She was one of a kind." Her peers nominated her for Best Actress Academy Awards four times, for the tough-talking guileless mother in *Stella Dallas*, the slang-slinging chorus girl in *Ball of Fire*, the murderous blonde in *Double Indemnity*, and the bedridden neurotic in *Sorry, Wrong Number*. But the only Academy Award she won was an honorary Oscar. Television was more generous, giving her Emmys for "The Barbara Stanwyck Show," "The Big Valley," and "The Thorn Birds."

She became an "actor's actor," often more enthusiastic about other performers' work than her own. When the *Hollywood Reporter* asked her to write a guest column for its vacationing Rambling Reporter Mike Connelly in 1954, she wrote effusively about seeing Jeanne Eagels in *Rain* and in *Her Cardboard Lover* on the stage, of Henry Fonda on the stage in *Mr. Roberts* and on the screen in *The Ox-bow Incident*. She remembered Spencer Tracy in *Captains Courageous*, Katharine Hepburn in *The Philadelphia Story*.

"I wrote a fan letter to Olivia de Havilland for *The Snake Pit*, to Bette Davis for *Jezebel* and *Dark Victory*. I'll never forget Victor Mature's scene at the foot of the cross in *The Robe*, nor the breathtaking, heartbreaking farewell scenes of Jack Gilbert and Renée Adorée in *The Big Parade*. I don't want to forget Orson Welles in *The Third Man*, which, so far, I've only seen six times. I saw Victor McLaglen in *The Informer* ten times—what an actor and wonderful guy. I cherish the memory of Jackie Cooper as *Skippy*—just writing it brings a lump to my throat and a sting in my eyes. I'll buy Claire Trevor, period. And what about that Ida Lupino . . . I lack the words to express the last but not the least of my memories—no words are worthy of the unforgettable, the incomparable—Hell, I need only one word anyway. Here it is—GARBO."

Stanwyck had developed an aversion to the screen tests early on, for herself and others. Instead of having an actor walk on a cold stage, she was convinced that producers should give a new talent a small role in a real film, and if he or she showed talent, successively more important parts. "A role of any sort provides a challenge," she said in 1953. "Newcomers instinctively feel this and prepare themselves to meet it. The result is a more accurate indication of their ability than a screen test could provide."

Maureen O'Sullivan was a rare dissenting voice in fellow

performers' praise of Stanwyck. O'Sullivan ranked fifth below Stanwyck on the *All I Desire* credits and felt it. "I found her a cold person," O'Sullivan would recall. "She was the only actress in my working experience who ever went home leaving me to do my closeups with the scriptgirl, which I thought was most unprofessional."

Unlike Robert Taylor, whose middle years were tough and humbling, Barbara never surrendered the direction of her life to anybody. She knew how to bring an edge of reality to roles that were often absurd—sentimental, spunky bad girls who both mirrored and modeled four decades of the movies. To breathe life into screenwriters' paper women, to make them work, was an intoxicating surrogate for love.

Her fatal attraction to Frank Fay might have played out differently today when "two-track" careers are both cliché and truism and marriages are more egalitarian. Barbara and Frank were of an age when a woman's drive and ambitions were accomplished through the man she chose. But she and Frank fought for the same turf, each in turn using success to hurt the other. He slipped all too easily into delusion and bitterness. As their marriage careened into jealousy and alcoholic brawls, her willingness to deny herself to stay with him must also count against her. She never made the mistake again, of course.

Was sexuality just another role, as arbitrary as any part she played? Once past Fay, the little intimacy she craved she got from faithful women friends. The inventions of the soundstages fulfilled her deepest wants. Life offscreen was something of a bore, to be filled with reading books and scripts, adopting a child, watching one's horse at the racetrack, getting ready for tomorrow's shoot. With Robert Taylor she had it all figured out except that, like a plot twist in a Stanwyck movie, he would leave her. Returning to the big empty house on North Faring Road after the divorce, she said, was the lowest point of her life.

She was a social drinker by day and evening and a solitary boozer during sleepless nights. Stepping out of a wet raincoat and into a dry martini was more than a line of dialogue in 1940s Hollywood. Movie stars of her generation drank and smoked themselves to death, and so did Bob and Barbara.

The cause of her death was congestive heart failure complicated by emphysema.

Ava Gardner, the woman Stanwyck never forgave for inciting her husband's passions as she never had, died in London five days after Barbara. After Ava and Bob's love affair during the summer of '48, the two actresses played the roles life had assigned them—seductress and cuckolded wife—in the glossy *East Side, West Side*. Ava went on to marry Frank Sinatra, and after Bob and Barbara divorced, long-suffering Nancy Sinatra became Barbara's best friend. Stanwyck was eighty-two when she died, Gardner sixty-eight.

For a film star living sixty years in the Hollywood klieg lights, Barbara's existence was surprisingly private. She disapproved of scrutiny, and even after her death, friends felt that talking about her violated her will. There are phases of her existence we will never know. Then again, what *do* we know of the celebrities that our unoriginal times worship? Indeed, how many of us will acknowledge witnesses to our innermost thoughts and acts? The question of whether she loved women and tolerated men is less a matter of evidence than of attitude and affinity. She balked at introspection, loathed analytical meanderings and meditations on happiness. Gay women like her for her scrappy, brainy, and winning self-reliance, for the way she could imply moral outrage at the lousy hand society can deal a woman. Los Angeles lesbian get-togethers appreciate the two or three women who dress up and madly vamp the crowd as Barbara Stanwyck in "The Big Valley." Dangerous females are also part of male sexual fantasies. Lily "Baby Face" Powers, Lorna Moon, Phyllis Dietrichson, and Thelma Jordan belong to a long line of femme fatales that stretch from *Manon* to *La Femme Nikita* and *Menace*.

When she was seventy, she said she wouldn't like to be young again. "I would hate to do it all over again. Life is a pretty difficult thing." She could never forget the let-down secondhand dresses Ruby Stevens was forced to wear. As a star she asked Nolan Miller to give her sumptuous gowns with four-inch hems because a tiny hem said "poor."

After the seven years with Fay, she started out on her own with a son she didn't like. People tend to treat their offspring as they were treated. The parallels between Stanwyck and Crawford are striking. Both married ineffectual men, both were distracted, overworked actresses who, among other roles, wanted to play motherhood. They blamed their children when the kids didn't fit the images their celebrity moms cultivated, when they weren't enough of an extension of their mother's movie-star identities. Dion felt guilty because he was not the child Barbara wanted. Perhaps he was luckier than Christina Crawford; he was merely discarded. On the other hand, Crawford's four adopted children had each other.

We do not know why Barbara could never bring herself to fully embrace Dion. His offense may have been just to exist, to being there and getting in the way of an insecure adoptive mother's wish to concentrate on a younger, sexually indifferent husband. Later, Dion may have been a reminder of her shortcomings, her twin failed marriages, proof of the danger of emotional surrender. Her friends say Taylor never liked Dion. Bob's relationship with the two children Ursula Thiess brought into their marriage was equally tenuous. Whether or not Bob had a part in the discarding of the young Dion, Barbara's rejection of the boy gives us a glimpse of a flinty inner self that probably masked deep psychic scars.

There were things she'd like to forget and nothing she would change, she often said. She was not good at giving of herself, whether it was names to her horses, affection to a son, or intimacy to a lover. She had a hard time sharing emotions. As a young woman, she gave advice too freely, and, in old age, she remembered with alarm her intolerable certainty in counseling others. Giving professional advice was different. She was generous with her talent, and the young actors she helped stretch from Robert Taylor on his first brush with egos bigger than his on *Camille*, through William Holden, Robert Wagner, and Linda Evans in their early years. She also championed the "little people," for whom she stood up to bullying directors and front offices. But she could only give of her heart if no one knew. In her heyday she sent Uncle Buck with cashier's checks and the strictest orders not to reveal the donor to Los Angeles victims of bad luck, fire, and other calamities reported in the morning's newspaper. Her need to rely on herself was buried as deep in her earliest years as her self-awareness.

"Many people will hurt you, and you can't change that," she told Dion when he was six. "And you can't run away from it because at the end of every day you wind up with yourself, after all."

The admonition sounds like bitter experience seared into her own consciousness. She reached out twice, devoted herself to Fay and Taylor, only to learn that *wishing* they would change didn't make them change. She walked out on Fay and felt humiliated when Bob did it to her. She declared she had no talent for the games of love.

In the end, she gave the best of herself to make-believe, to an image of a self she never really understood. But, as she said, "What the hell, it worked—didn't it?"

Notes On Sources

Interviews with those who knew Barbara Stanwyck, including Iris Adrian, Joan Benny, Frank Capra, Shirley Eder, Maggy Maskel Ferguson, Larry Kleno, Frank McCarthy, Nolan Miller, Viege Traub, Gertrude Walker, Billy Wilder, and many other professional colleagues of hers are the sources of this book, as are the credits and documentation of her films and earlier books on Stanwyck. The author has read most of the celebrity journalism, gossip columnists, and fan magazines about Barbara Stanwyck (BS) and has used such sources as *zeitgeist* and examples of her image. Several individuals, archives, and libraries helped in the research. Details of BS's films and period news clippings of BS's films were gleaned from production files at the Center for Motion Picture Study, Academy of Motion Picture Arts and Sciences, Los Angeles, and her theatrical beginnings at the New York City Library for the Performing Arts at Lincoln Center. Source citations are given in the bibliography. Documentation supporting certain portions of the narrative are cited below:

1. *"I hope she lives."* BS, "I just wanted to survive": to author, 1985. BS, "All right, let's just say": *Los Angeles Times*, May 5, 1987. BS, "Some of my most interesting roles have been completely unsympathetic": *Saturday Evening Post*, October 5, 1946. BS, "Maybe we're just more used": BS to author, 1985. BS, "Then the makeup man fixes it," and "Don't teach me": *Los Angeles Times*, May 5, 1987. BS, "I think living in the past": *Pageant*, May 1967. BS, "I see things": *Pageant*, May 1967. BS, "It's gone and done": *Los Angeles Times*, May 5, 1987.

2. *Brooklyn.* Details of BS's birth and early childhood are based on the author's research in New York and, selectively, on BS's remarks to several interviewers and studio biographies. Ernest Hemingway wrote on BS's "Mick intelligence" in November 15, 1941, letter to Max Perkins. BS, "I'll always be an orphan," "Nobody Knows Stanwyck as I Do," Ruby Stevens as told to Margaret Lee Runbeck *Good Housekeeping*, July 1954. BS, "Cats and dogs": *TV Picture Life*, November 1967. BS, "At least nobody beat me": *TV Picture Life*, November 1967. BS on her father, "squaring" his shoulders against circumstances: *Photoplay*, December 1937. BS, "Growing up in one foster home": undated 1938 RKO studio biography. BS scrawling name on sidewalks "to show everybody": *Photoplay*, December 1937. BS, "I didn't relish the disciplines": *Pageant*, May 1967. BS called herself the "stupidest" student in several interviews. *Film-Comment* March-April, 1981 reproduced Rev. Carter's book inscription as part of 13-page Stanwyck "Midsection" assessment. BS attending Erasmus Hall High School noted in *Burlesque* playbill, 1927. BS, "The plain wrapping, not the fancy": *Collier's*, July 12, 1952. BS, "I knew that after fourteen": *Good Housekeeping*, July 1954. BS, "Once in a while my sister Millie": *Hollywood Reporter*, April 23, 1954. BS, "I'll always love Earl Lindsay": Helen Ferguson publicity release, January 1951. BS, "Then pretty soon": *Photoplay*, December 1937. BS, "I gave up trying to follow the 'sensible' advice": *Pageant*, May 1967. BS's employment at Jerome H. Remick Music Company detailed in Jerry Vermilye, *Barbara Stanwyck*, p. 14.

3. *"Stark naked, I swear."* BS, "I might, just might, be tempted" and "I was in the 16th row": *Pageant*, May 1967. Details of Ziegfeld, the Follies, and mid-1920s Broadway life are described in Gerald Bordman, *The American Musical Theatre.* The description of the Follies as representing "the businessman's ideal" is from Brooks Atkinson, *Broadway*, p. 114. BS, "We lived over a laundry": BS to author, 1985. BS, "stark naked" and "Ask Mae Clarke" quoted in "The Lady Stanwyck," interview with *New York Times*, March 21, 1943. Jim Kepner to author on Sheldon Dewey's memories of BS in Jimmy Guinan's gay speakeasy, 1993. BS, "Even in the early 1920s": *New York Times*, March 21, 1943. Louise Brook's quote "Eligible bachelors" is from unpublished book, allegedly

destroyed by Brooks in 1954, after she gave copies of most of the manuscript to James Card, quoted in Barry Paris, *Louise Brooks*, p. 68. Levant on BS from Oscar Levant, *Memoirs of an Amnesiac*, p. 82. BS told the LaHiff story in numerous interviews, including *Collier's*, July 12, 1952. BS remembering introduction to Mack in "Nobody Knows Stanwyck as I Do," by Ruby Stevens as told to Margaret Lee Runbeck; *Good Housekeeping*, July 1954.

4. *Rex*. BS, "I was a dancer": Helen Ferguson publicity release, January 1951. BS on Loew's WHN radio detailed in Dana Andrews, *Hollywood East*, p. 140. BS, "I was temperamental": Jane Ellen Wayne, *Stanwyck*, p. 15. Pittsburgh rehearsals of *The Noose* detailed in Al DiOrio, *Barbara Stanwyck*, p. 30. *The Noose* tryout was review in the *Pittsburgh Gazette*, October 10, 1926, and *Pittsburgh Press* October 12, 1926. BS, "It's got to be the chorus girl": Helen Ferguson publicity release. BS, "Bill Mack was going": *Good Housekeeping*, July 1954. Belasco, "Yes, I've been watching you": *New York Times*, February 23, 1941. A Hunt Stromberg Production BS biography dated October 15, 1942, relates the story of the newly named Stanwyck inviting her sister to *The Noose*. Elisha Cook, Jr., "She had a scene": quoted in Jordan R. Young, *Reel Characters*, p. 15. BS, "It was my first chance at dramatic acting" and "Bill Mack was going": BS to author, 1985. BS, "Rex was handsome": Jane Ellen Wayne, *Stanwyck*, p. 17. BS biography from details of *Broadway Nights* and most of BS's films are culled from individual production files at the Center for Motion Picture Study. BS, "I sat down and waited": BS to author, 1985. Levant, "If we were invited": Oscar Levant, *Memoirs of an Amnesiac*, p. 82. Cherryman's obituary: *New York Times*, August 11, 1928.

5. *Faysie*. Levant touched upon Frank Fay's anti-Semitism in *Memoirs of an Amnesiac*, p. 80, as did Harry Golden in *The Right Time*, p. 175. Levant described his European trip with Fay and Fay's attitudes toward religion and Helen Hayes in *Memoirs of an Amnesiac*, pp. 80–83. Levant, "Barbara fell madly in love with him": Oscar Levant, *Memoirs of an Amnesiac*, p. 83. "It was 'Hi there, Frankie'": *Photoplay*, October 1931. Fay's personality and early years are detailed in *Photoplay*, January 1933, and *New York Times* obituary, September 27, 1961. Milton Berle, "Fay's friends" and Fay's

court appearance on a business matter: Milton Berle with Haskel Frankel, *Milton Berle*, pp. 100–101. Stanwyck-Fay wedding detailed in Al DiOrio, *Barbara Stanwyck*, p. 41. "Pretty little Barbara Stanwyck": *New York Times*, February 28, 1929. Schenck, "If you ever want to do a movie part": "Nobody Knows Stanwyck as I Do," by Ruby Stevens as told to Margaret Lee Runbeck, *Good Housekeeping*, July 1954. Descriptions of Hollywood, Joseph Schenck, United Artists, and industry switch to talkies in 1929–30 are author's own, based on Axel Madsen, *Gloria and Joe*, pp. 6, 8, and 232ff. Schenck, "Three weeks is a short time": *Photoplay*, January 1933.

6. *Hollywood*. George Fitzmaurice background: *Dictionnaire du Cinéma*, ed. Jean Tulard, pp. 273–74. BS, "He kept arranging all kinds of drapery" and "I staggered through it": *Film Comment*, March-April 1981. "They never should've unlocked": DiOrio, *Barbara Stanwyck*, p. 45. *Show of Shows* summary: *Leslie Halliwell's Film Guide*, 7th edition, p. 915. The author interviewed Harry Cohn and Frank Capra in 1964. Their early relationship is detailed in Joseph McBride, *Frank Capra*, pp. 197ff. BS, "You memorize the script": *New York Times* interview, February 23, 1941. BS, "I made a frightful thing": *New York Times*, June 21, 1931. Gloria Swanson told author of Alexander Korda's screen test of BS. Wallis, "This was before the days": Hal Wallis and Charles Higham, *Starmaker*, p. 10. Author interviewed Adela Rogers St. Johns in 1969.

7. *Capra*. Jo Swerling's early years and quotes of story meetings detailed in "Failure to Be 'Yes Man' Started Swerling's Career," *New York Herald Tribune*, April 29, 1934. *Ladies of Leisure* dialogue from screenplay at Center for Motion Picture Study, Beverly Hills. Harry Cohn, "Capra is going to do": Bob Thomas, *King Cohn*, p. 111. BS, "No thanks, I've had my experience with tests": Thomas, *King Cohn*, p. 111. BS, "Oh hell," and Capra, "Harry, forget Stanwyck": DiOrio, *Barbara Stanwyck*, p. 50. Capra told author of working with Howell and Swerling in interview in 1966. Capra's work method with BS detailed in Frank Capra, *The Name Above the Title*, pp. 116ff. Capra, "Naive, unsophisticated, caring nothing about makeup": Capra, *The Name Above the Title*, p. 116. Bernds, "My God, we were all on our

toes": quoted in Joseph McBride, *Frank Capra*, p. 213. Capra, "I wish I could tell you more": Joseph McBride, *Frank Capra*, p. 216. BS, "It isn't what you do": *Los Angeles Times*, June 21, 1931. BS, "Frank Capra taught me" and "You never really look at yourself," *Los Angeles Times*, April 5, 1987. BS, "If the part calls for": *American Film*, July–August 1989.

8. *Low-budget Life*. Joan Blondell, "This town": quoted in John Kobal, *People Will Talk*, p. 185. Cagney, "They were squeezing": James Cagney, *Cagney by Cagney*, p. 65. The author interviewed William Wellman in 1966. Wellman mentioned his friendship with Hal Skelly in Wellman, *A Short Time for Insanity*, p. 184. BS, "Directors are very vain": BS to author, 1985. BS, "Does this sound like": *Los Angeles Times*, July 25, 1931. BS, "Our dandy little opus": BS to author, 1985. Los Angeles newspapers reported Zanuck firing Fay, June 5, 1931. BS, "I'm a star now": *Los Angeles Times*, June 21, 1931. BS, "He's old-fashioned": *Los Angeles Examiner*, June 21, 1931. Capra, "I weaseled. I insisted on a 'heavy'": Frank Capra, *The Name Above the Title*, p. 131. *The Los Angeles Times* and *New York Times* covered Columbia's court request for an injunction against BS September 5 and September 11, 1931. BS, "You didn't argue": Joseph McBride, *Frank Capra*, p. 239. Bellamy, "I can remember vividly": McBride, *Frank Capra*, p. 231. "It hurt," quoted in McBride, *Frank Capra*, p. 240. *Photoplay* on BS not liking Hollywood, *Photoplay*, April 1932. Frank Fay at Palace review, *Photoplay*, May 1932. *Hollywood Herald*, "tawdry and cheap": quoted in Mason Wiley and Damien Bona, *Inside Oscar*, p. 38. BS, "She had the kind of creative ruthlessness": Lawrence Quirk, *Fasten Your Seat Belts*, p. 53.

9. *What Price Hollywood?* The author interviewed David Selznick in 1963. "It was a story based on things": Wellman to author, 1966. York, "Suddenly Broadway's favorite son": *Photoplay*, October 1932. Harrison Carroll column, *Los Angeles Times*, July 25, 1931. Foch, "She did one odd thing": Foch to author, 1993. The Fays' Brentwood house and architect James E. Dolena details: *Architectural Digest*, April 1990. Ruth Biery's feature on the Fays appeared in *Photoplay*, Jan 1933. BS, "I chose that picture" and "You may take a trip to Palm Springs": *Photoplay*, January 1933. Nude photos of Crawford with woman published in Kenneth Anger's,

Hollywood Babylon II, pp. 117–18. Crawford, "I knew of my mother's lesbian proclivities": Christina Crawford, *Mommie Dearest*, p. 157. Livingstone, "Why do you always bring that maid": quoted by Shirley Eder to author 1993. Helen Ferguson, "We certainly present": Academy of Motion Picture files, 1992. Author interviewed Iris Adrian and Shirley Eder on BS's relationship with Helen Ferguson in 1993. Homosexuality in Hollywood is detailed in Patrick McGilligan, *George Cukor*; Denis Brian, *Tallulah, Darling*; David King Dunaway, *Huxley in Hollywood*; Kenneth Anger, *Hollywood Babylon II*; and Rebecca Bell-Metereau, *Hollywood Androgyny*. Elizabeth M. Curtis's suit against BS and Cradick's response reported in *Los Angeles Times*, March 10 and 30, 1934. Barbara climbed over the wall and "Their fights were dreadful": Jane Ellen Wayne, *Crawford's Men*, p. 6. Brice, "Who the hell?": quoted in Herbert Goldman, *Fanny Brice*, p. 144. BS, "I love you just as much": Jane Ellen Wayne, *Stanwyck*, p. 48.

10. *Depression Blues*. Thomas Reddy's column in *Los Angeles Times*, February 26, 1933. Court records date John Charles Greene's birth as February 5, 1932, and his adoption by the Fays December 6, 1932. BS, "Too much attention": *Los Angeles Examiner*, December 28, 1932. *The Nation* reviewed Grace Zaring Stone, *The Bitter Tea of General Yen*, January 7, 1931, *The New Republic*, October 29, 1930. Capra, "The missionary was a well-bred": Frank Capra, *The Name Above the Title*, p. 143. Garbo, "Don't kiss": quoted in Charles Higham, *Merchant of Dreams*, p. 145. BS, "Any revulsion": Joseph McBride, *Frank Capra*, p. 280. The *Bitter Tea* opening at Radio City Music Hall: *New York Times*, January 12, 1933. BS, "The story was far ahead": *American Cinematographer*, August 1973. Howard Smith's November 1932 story conference notes are quoted in Leonard J. Leff and Jerold L. Simmons, *The Dame in the Kimono*, pp. 28–29. Joseph Schenck, "You and I will start": Mel Gussow, *Don't Say Yes Until I Finish Talking*, p. 59. Marx, "It was the prettiest house": Hector Arce, *Groucho*, p. 198.

11. *Single*. BS, "Frank Fay was causing": *Film Comment* March-April 1981. Graham Greene review of *Red Salute*, Greene, *Graham Greene on Film*, pp. 36–37. BS asks for divorce, reported in *New York Times*, November 10, 1935.

Comedians' barbs against Fay quoted in Milton Berle, *B.S. I Love You*, p. 55. Golden, "He would go on binges": Harry Golden, *The Right Time*, p. 175. Levant, "She loathed him": Oscar Levant, *Memoirs of an Amnesiac*, p. 83.

12. *Arly.* Adela Rogers St. Johns on Robert Taylor: *Liberty*, October 24, 1936. Hay, "Every year Gilmor Brown": Hay to author, 1993. Author interviewed agent Paul Kohner on Taylor, publicist Don Prince on Strickling, and MGM police lieutenant John Hollywood on 1930s studio security. Strickling, "We told stars what they could say": *Los Angeles Times*, July 16, 1982. Horne, "MGM created a certain name": quoted in Ava Gardner, *Ava*, pp. 147–48. Ingersoll, "Taylor was careless": Ingersoll to author, 1968. Gilbert, "I have been on the screen": *Movie Classics*, June 1934. McCrea, "I took Arlington out to MGM": quoted in John Korbal, *People Will Talk*, p. 292.

13. *Private Lives.* Crawford, "He knew the public": Jane Ellen Wayne, *Crawford's Men*, p. ix. Garbo, "He used to have a gramophone": Sven Broman, *Conversations with Greta Garbo*, p. 148. Cukor, "It can be hell": Gavin Lambert, *On Cukor*, p. 115. William Faulkner's deleted dialogue from *Banjo on My Knee* detailed in Tom Dardis, *Some Time in the Sun*, p. 97. Bette Davis on BS inheriting Ruth Chatterton's screen nobility: Bette Davis, *The Lonely Life*, p. 213. Young, "Barbara Stanwyck has always been strong": Lyn Tornabene, *Long Live the King*, p. 193. Cromwell, "Stanwyck had great star presence": Larry Swindell, *Charles Boyer*, p. 115. Mayer, "God never saw fit to give me a son": Bosley Crowther, *Hollywood Rajah*, pp. 6–7. Fay, "Well, your dress": *Photoplay*, June 1940. Author interviewed Wyler, who directed Mary Astor during Astor-Kaufman scandal, 1972. BS and Frank Fay testimony quoted in *Los Angeles Examiner* court coverage, December 29–30, 1937. *The Los Angeles Times* reported Fay's attempt at visiting Dion, January 19, 1938.

14. *Stella.* Dixie Willson, "Barbara For Her Own Sake" feature appeared in *Photoplay* in December 1937. BS, "I've always felt that John": *Film Comment*, March-April 1981. The author interviewed John Ford in 1966, William Wyler in 1972. John Engstead on BS quoted in John Kobal, *People Will Talk*, p. 520. Head, "Barbara had been a little insulted": Edith Head and Paddy Calistro, *Edith Head's Hollywood*, p. 33. BS,

"Everybody was testing for it": *Film Comment*, March-April 1981. Vidor to LeBaron, "I've such a belly-full": Raymond Durgnat and Scott Simmon, *King Vidor*, p. 173. Vidor, "See silent picture": Durgnat and Simmon, *King Vidor*, p. 200. Goldwyn, "She's just got no sex appeal": A. Scott Berg, *Goldwyn*, p. 294. BS, "But I can imagine": Wayne, *Barbara Stanwyck*, p. 67. BS, "I was spurred by memory": *Saturday Evening Post*, October 5, 1946. BS, "My life's blood": BS to author, 1985. Haskell, "Stanwyck brings us to admire": Molly Haskell, *From Reverence to Rape*, p. 6. Kendall, "Capra had been the first": Elizabeth Kendall, *The Runaway Bride*, p. 246.

15. *Offscreen*. Wilson's description of Crawford dinner is quoted in Shaun Considine, *Bette and Joan*, p. 74. BS, "bitter about a lot of things": *Pageant*, May 1967. BS, "If you say": John Kobal, *People Will Talk*, p. 508. Shirley Eder and Lloyd Nolan detailed to author BS's relations to nephew Eugene Vaslett, 1983. Joan Benny, "Skip Stanwyck was my first boyfriend": Benny interview with author, 1993. United Press carried story of Taylor's grandfather on welfare, dateline, Beatrice, Nebraska, February 4, 1937. Graham Greene on Louis B. Mayer, *Night and Day* magazine, November 4, 1937. F. Scott Fitzgerald, "the sequence in which": Matthew J. Bruccoli, *Some Sort of Epic Grandeur*, p. 506. Taylor's New York arrival and hairless chest brouhaha covered by *Los Angeles Examiner*, December 14 and 17, 1937. Damon Runyon column was a King Features Syndicate release August 22, 1937.

16. *Screwballs, Mr. C.B., and* Golden Boy. BS, "I'm glad someone": *Daily Variety*, December 20, 1937. Fonda, "Everyone who is close to me": Howard Teichmann, *Fonda: My Life*, p. 125. BS, "Then it was announced": *American Cinematographer*, August 1937. DeMille, "more cooperative": Cecil B. DeMille, *Autobiography*, p. 364. Comparisons of *Union Pacific* and *The Iron Horse* in George N. Fenin and William Everson, *The Western*, p. 237. Atkinson, "Perhaps the depression": Brooks Atkinson, *Broadway*, p. 285. Author interviewed Rouben Mamoulian in 1966. Clifford Odets on money for *Golden Boy*: Margaret Gibson, *Clifford Odets*, p. 524. BS, "Look, Bill, I know": Bob Thomas, *Golden Boy*, p. 29. BS, "My God, he's only had a week": Al DiOrio, *Barbara Stanwyck*, p. 102. BS, "I told him much of what Willard

Mack": Stanwyck as "Rambling Reporter" guest columnist, *Hollywood Reporter*, April 23, 1954.

17. *Marriage*. Kirtley Baskette, "Hollywood Unmarried Husbands and Wives," *Photoplay*, January 1939. National press covered the May 14, 1939, BS-Taylor marriage and press reception. Taylor, "We'll just smile": *Los Angeles Herald*, May 15, 1939. Holden as BS's lover, Billy Wilder to author, 1969. Taylor to Crawford, "All I had to say about it": Jane Ellen Wayne, *Crawford's Men*, p. 154. Shipman, "the Stanwyck-Taylor marriage": David Shipman, *Judy Garland*, p. 139. BS, "They made you": *Los Angeles Times*, April 5, 1987. Benny, "The boy was in the way": Joan Benny to author, 1993. Fay, "At first he": *National Enquirer*, January 3, 1984. Andy Devine on Taylor's penis: Robert Stack, *Straight Shooting*, p. 43. Sal Mineo going out with RT and confessing his own homosexuality in 1967: quoted in Boz Hadleigh, *Confessions with My Elders*, pp. 26–27. Loy on Taylor: James Kotsilibas-Davis and Myrna Loy, *Myrna Loy*, p. 156. Mosley, "Zanuck knew the propinquity of Stanwyck": Leonard Mosley, *The Rise and Fall of Hollywood's Last Tycoon*, p. 185. BS, "We dressed to the teeth": BS to author, 1985. Bob Thomas excerpted David Selznick's homage to BS in *Selznick*, p. 183.

18. *Passions*. BS, "I'll go to Ciro's or the Trocadero": Al DiOrio, *Barbara Stanwyck*, p. 116. BS, Can Hollywood Mothers be Good Mothers? *Photoplay*, June 1940. Fay, "She threw me away": *National Enquirer*, January 3, 1984. BS, "Now you can do everything": DiOrio, *Barbara Stanwyck*, p. 148. BS, "It wasn't hunting": *Collier's*, July 12, 1952. Hemingway on BS's "Mick intelligence" in November 15, 1941, letter to Max Perkins. BS, "I have a passion": *Hollywood Citizen-News*, August 17, 1944. MGM hiring Eric Drimmer is detailed in Sven Broman, *Conversations with Greta Garbo*. Preston Sturges's youth and early screenwriting are detailed in Diane Jacobs, *Christmas in July: The Life and Art of Preston Sturges*. BS, "Preston was around a lot": *Film Comment*, March-April 1981.

19. *The Lady Eve*. Dialogue and stage directions of opening pages of *The Lady Eve* taken from unrevised November 6, 1940, shooting script. BS, "He kept his word": *American Cinematographer*, August 1973. Sturges, "I happen to love pratfalls": quoted in Jacobs, *Christmas in July: The Life and Art*

of *Preston Sturges*, p. 294. BS, "He'd ask us how we liked the lines": *New York Times*, February 23, 1941. BS, "*Eve* was lucky" and "*Lady Eve* changed": Edith Head and Paddy Calistro, *Edith Head's Hollywood*, p. 45. Kael, "Like *Bringing Up Baby*": Pauline Kael, *5001 Nights at the Movies*, p. 313.

20. *The Sweater Girl.* Sidney Skolsky's column on BS, *Hollywood Citizen-News*, July 2, 1940. Filming of *John Doe* crowd scene at Wrigley Field detailed in *Los Angeles Downtown Shipping News*, September 11, 1940. BS, "We have always agreed": October 15, 1942, Hunt Stromberg Production press profile. Turner, "Bob had the kind of looks": Lana Turner, *Lana*, p. 74. Taylor, "I have never seen lips": Jane Ellen Wayne, *Stanwyck*, p. 93. BS, "It's a kind of history": *Movie Digest*, September 1972. Mankiewicz, "I could just dream of being married": Leonard Mosley, *The Rise and Fall of Hollywood's Last Tycoon*, p. 219. BS, "It broke my heart": BS to author, 1985. BS, "He was delicious": *U.S.* magazine, March 28, 1983. Ferguson, "She meant well": Wayne, *Stanwyck*, p. 96. Wilder on his screenwriting career detailed to author, 1969. Howard Hawks on *Ball of Fire* detailed to author, 1974.

21. *Patriot Games.* The Jack Bennys' 1942 New Year's party detailed in Irving A. Fein, *Jack Benny*, p. 83. Ronald Reagan's deferment is detailed in Anne Edwards, *Early Reagan*, pp. 258–61. BS in Canada: documented in National Archives wartime photo service. Davis, "I would be so grateful": Charles Higham, *Bette*, p. 149. Rapper on Young: George Eells, *Final Gig*, p. 59. *Mrs. Miniver*, Louis B. Mayer, and *Song of Russia*: Wyler to author, 1972. Creation of Motion Picture Alliance for the Preservation of American Ideals detailed in Otto Friedrich, *City of Nets*, p. 168, Joseph McBride, *Frank Capra*, pp. 515*ff*, and Donald Shepherd and Robert Slatzer, *Duke*, p. 236. Alliance statement of principals published in full-page ad in the *Hollywood Reporter*, February 20, 1944.

22. *Double Indemnity.* Purvis, "Taylor was nervous": Jane Ellen Wayne, *Robert Taylor*, pp. 114–15. Irish Adrian, "Frank quit drinking": Adrian to author, 1993. BS's GI pen pals, *Hollywood Citizen-News*, August 17, 1944. Author interviewed Wilder on *Double Indemnity* in 1968. Chandler, "Working with Billy Wilder": Raymond Chandler, *Raymond*

Chandler Speaking, p. 237. Cain, "It's the only picture": Pat McGilligan, *Backstory*, p. 125. BS, "I thought, 'This role'": *Los Angeles Times*, April 5, 1987. Buddy De Sylva, "We hire Barbara Stanwyck": Billy Wilder quoted to author, 1968. BS, "I remember saying, 'Fred, really'": Wilder to author, 1968. BS, "I'm afraid to go home": *Variety*, July 8, 1944. *Time* review of Frank Fay in *Harvey*, November 13, 1944. Root, "Nobody could touch him": Maggie Root to author, 1993. BS, "I don't like it, to take things this fast": *Los Angeles Times*, July 22, 1945. Jane Ellen Wayne quoted Earl Wilson's column in *Stanwyck*, p. 103. Details of *Mildred Pierce* casting and BS quote, "I desperately wanted the part": author's interview with Wald, 1973.

23. *Rand and Warner*. BS on wanting to do *The Fountainhead* and meeting Ayn Rand are detailed in John Kobal, *People Will Talk*, p. 507. Bogart, "I'm not good looking": Ezra Goodman, *Bogey*, p. 51. Coe on *The Two Mrs. Carrolls*: Jonathan Coe, *Humphrey Bogart*, p. 117. BS telegram to Jack Warner is from Warner Bros. Archives at University of Southern California. LeRoy, "For weeks we had gradually whittled": Mervyn LeRoy, *Take One*, p. 255.

24. *Uneasy Peace*. Taylor's army release and airport news conference reported in *Los Angeles Examiner*, November 6, 1945. Reagan, "I learned that a thousand": quoted in Anne Edwards, *Early Reagan*, pp. 299–300. BS, "Hey, Bob, your wife": Jane Ellen Wayne, *Stanwyck*, p. 121. Wallis, "I knew I was taking a risk": Hal Wallis and Charles Higham, *Starmaker*, p. 116. BS, "You know they could get fired": *Los Angeles Daily News*, March 28, 1983. Douglas, "We continued to shoot": Kirk Douglas, *The Ragman's Son*, p. 136. Wayne, "It was so humiliating": Wayne, *Stanwyck*, p. 117. Fay, "The doctors": *National Enquirer*, January 3, 1984. Taylor, "Except for his bad grades": Wayne, *Stanwyck*, p. 118. Dorothy Manners's syndicated column was published December 8, 1946, Louella Parsons's "Barbara Stanwyck year" feature May 18, 1947, and Hedda Hopper's "Barbara and Bob" July 6, 1947.

25. *Bearing Witness*. BS, "I think American designers": Louella Parsons in *Los Angeles Examiner*, May 18, 1947. Louella Parsons detailed BS and Taylor ship-to-shore broadcast in *Los Angeles Examiner*, May 18, 1947. BS, "Bill and I go

way, way back": *Hollywood Studio Magazine*, March 1982. Fay, "She gave me the lecture of my life" and "Uncle Buck explained": *National Enquirer*, January 3, 1984. The HUAC hearings are covered in Larry Ceplar and Steven Englund, *The Inquisition in Hollywood*, p. 439, and Lester Cole, *Hollywood Red*, pp. 265ff. Adela Rogers St. Johns discussed BS's anticommunism in *Los Angeles Examiner*, June 3, 1951. Hopper, "I admire Bob's courage": *Chicago Tribune* syndicate, July 6, 1947. Wyler, "We tried to defend": Wyler to author, 1972. Ayn Rand's HUAC testimony is detailed in Otto Friedrich, *City of Nets*, pp. 317–18. Taylor's verbatim testimony is published in *Thirty Years of Treason*, ed. Eric Bentley.

26. *Prejudice*. William Wyler and Bennett Cerf HUAC testimony is covered in Larry Ceplar and Steven Englund, *The Inquisition in Hollywood*. Joseph McBride details Capra's informing for the FBI and State Department in *Frank Capra*, p. 609. Senator Wherry, "You can hardly separate": *New York Post*, July 11, 1950. BS, "Everybody said, 'Oh, my God'": *Pageant*, May 1967. BS's refusal to color her graying hair during *B.F.'s Daughter* is detailed in Jane Ellen Wayne, *Stanwyck*, p. 112. Nancy Reagan details her irritation with suspected communist namesakes in *My Turn*, pp. 80–91. BS, "The first thing Litvak": *People*, November 25, 1985. BS on Jack Benny's Show is detailed in Milt Josefsberg, *The Jack Benny Show*, pp. 475–76. Kathleen Murphy on Gardner, "Farewell My Lovelies," *Film Comment*, July-August 1990. Gardner, "I was available": Ava Gardner, *Ava: My Story*, p. 119. Earl Wilson column quoting BS on Taylor and airplanes appeared in *New York Daily News*, September 26, 1949. Reagan, "She was known as a real pro": Nancy Reagan, *My Turn*, p. 91.

27. *Primal Women*. BS, "I couldn't take a part": *Los Angeles Times*, April 5, 1987. BS, "First I look for a good story": *Hollywood Citizen-News*, March 28, 1952. Sirk, "She has depth": Sirk to author, 1964. Capra, "She can give out that burst of emotion": *Variety*, January 24, 1990. BS, "I wrote a fan letter": *Hollywood Reporter*, April 23, 1954. Stephen Harvey, "The Strange Fate of Barbara Stanwyck," *Film Comment*, March-April 1981. BS, "I burst into tears": quoted by unit publicist Don Prince to author, 1968. Purvis, "Barbara didn't like me": Jane Ellen Wayne, *Stanwyck*, p. 117. Walter Huston, "I'm not going": *Film Comment*, March-April 1981.

BS, "I'd carry a spear": Stanwyck guest column, *Hollywood Reporter*, April 23, 1954. Busch, "I thought Stanwyck should have been better directed": Pat McGilligan, *Backstory*, p. 107.

28. *False Fronts.* Davis, "I knew Margo": Charles Higham, *The Life of Bette Davis*, p. xiv. Guest on BS's reaction to pending divorce detailed in Charles Higham, *Bette: The Life of Bette Davis*, p. 223. Taylor moving into rented house: *Los Angeles Herald-Express*, February 22, 1951. St. Johns, "What Shattered the Taylor-Stanwyck Perfect Movie Marriage": *American Weekly*, May 1951.

29. *Herself.* The *Los Angeles Daily News* carried the divorce proceedings, including Helen Ferguson's testimony, February 22, 1951. Taylor, "I'm here": Jane Ellen Wayne, *Stanwyck*, p. 134. "Let's just say"; Lawrence J. Quirk, *The Films of Robert Taylor*, p. 11. Purvis, "Maybe they should have adopted children": Jane Ellen Wayne, *Stanwyck*, p. 136. BS, "I remember telling him": *Los Angeles Times*, April 5, 1987. Virginia Grey career: Patrick Agan, *Whatever Happened to . . . ?*, pp. 82–83. Grey, "At the end of the evening": Jane Ellen Wayne, *Stanwyck*, p. 137. Jack Benny on BS's nerves of ice quoted *Collier's*, July 12, 1952. BS, "I hope I won't": quoted by Louella Parsons, *Los Angeles Examiner*, April 6, 1952. Dion, "When I met her": *National Enquirer*, January 3, 1984. BS, "My divorce from Bob": quoted by Louella Parsons, *Los Angeles Examiner*, April 6, 1952. Nancy Sinatra, "Frank has left home before": Jane Ellen Wayne, *Ava's Men*, p. 116. Levant, "I hadn't seen Barbara in twenty years": Oscar Levant, *Memoirs of an Amnesiac*, p. 83. BS, "I'm concentrating": quoted by Hedda Hopper, *Chicago Tribune* syndicate, March 11, 1951. Mayer, "You have disgraced": quoted by Billy Wilder to author, 1968. Hopper, "A succession of bad": *Los Angeles Times*, December 24, 1950. Crawford, "The face and the breasts are new": Shaun Considine, *Bette and Joan*, p. 259. Johnes, "It was always a kind of bond": Considine, *Bette and Joan*, p. 374. Ronald Reagan's directives as Actors Guild president are detailed in Cogley, *Report on Blacklisting*, p. 163, and Larry Ceplair and Steven Englund, *The Inquisition in Hollywood*, p. 367. Ward Bond nicknamed "The Hangman Ward": Carl Foreman in *Punch*, August 14, 1974. Brewer, "Communists created": from minutes of Brewer meeting with producers released years later by Congressman Carroll Kearns

in congressional investigation of labor. Robinson, "Call me as a witness": Otto Friedrich, *City of Nets*, p. 380. Fritz Lang detailed *Clash by Night* shoot, repartee with BS, and her relationship with Marilyn Monroe to author, 1968. Dorothy Parker on Hollywood fear: Marion Meade, *Dorothy Parker*, p. 345. *Daily Variety*, June 3, 1952 reported scenes cut from *Clash by Night* after Catholic archdiocese objections. Nugent's cover story, "Stanwyck," appeared in *Collier's*, July 12, 1952. Howard Hughes, "We are going to screen": *Daily Variety*, October 2, 1952.

30. *B Pix*. BS, "I didn't work for one whole year": *Family Weekly*, August 4, 1968. The Writers Guild of America decision to credit Dalton Trumbo with *Roman Holiday* screenplay was reported in *Daily Variety*, October 22, 1991. BS, "Bob and I didn't stay": *Photoplay*, August 1954. Wagner, "She changed my whole approach": Jane Ellen Wayne, *Stanwyck*, p. 140. BS, "I keep reading about these romances": *Los Angeles Daily News*, December 12, 1952. BS, "I'm playing the type": Jane Ellen Wayne, *Stanwyck*, p. 141. Grey, "She let me have it with words": Jane Ellen Wayne, *Stanwyck*, p. 137. BS, "Because they recognized life for what it is": *Hollywood Citizen-News*, March 31, 1953. BS, "My entire role is written": *Hollywood Citizen-News*, March 31, 1952. Cooper, "Her veins swelled": Swindell, *The Last Hero: Gary Cooper*, p. 295. Houseman on *Executive Suite* filming: John Houseman, *Front and Center*, p. 420. Foch, "She was very sportsmanlike": Foch to author, 1993. Dwan, "Of course in those days": Peter Bogdanovich, *Allan Dwan*, p. 157. Jack Benny described the *Gaslight* parody in Joan and Jack Benny, *Sunday Nights at Seven*, pp. 241–42. Reagan, "Somehow working outdoors": Ronald Reagan, *An American Life*, p. 221. Harry Hay told author of Joan Crawford pursuing Mercedes McCambridge during *Johnny Guitar* filming, 1993. BS, "That's our royalty": *Film Comment*, March-April 1981.

31. *Sharp Reminders*. Vierge Traub on Ursula Thiess to author, 1993. *The Los Angeles Mirror News* detailed arrest on pornography charges of Dion Fay April 8, 1960. Taylor, "because there are too many ghosts": to screenwriter Andrew Fenady in 1968. BS, "First of all": BS to author, 1985. BS, "In all the westerns": *Los Angeles Mirror News*, May 29, 1961. Fuller, "It opens in a bedroom": quoted in Jean-Pierre

Coursodon and Pierre Sauvage, *American Directors*, pp. 150–51. Fuller, "The stuntmen refused": Eric Sherman and Martin Rubin, *The Director's Event*, pp. 149–50. BS, "I don't think he wanted": *Los Angeles Mirror News*, June 25, 1958. Horan, "There is no doubt": James D. Horan and Paul Sann, *Pictorial History of the Wild West*, p. 127. BS, "Dick calls me": *Los Angeles Mirror News*, June 25, 1958. BS, "He's a terrific designer": *New York Times*, October 18, 1992.

32. *"The Barbara Stanwyck Show."* BS, "From six on it sounds like": *American Film*, September 1968. BS, "What else": *TV Guide*, January 22, 1961. BS, "The foundation of any good show": Al DiOrio, *Barbara Stanwyck*, p. 170. BS, "I never even got a free shampoo": *Los Angeles Mirror News*, May 29, 1961. BS, "As I understand it": *Hollywood Reporter*, April 17, 1961. BS, "I hated playing the role": Kay Gardella interview, quoted in Jerry Vermilye, *Barbara Stanwyck*, p. 129. BS and *The Mistress of the Inn*, *Los Angeles Times*, December 27, 1961. BS, "It would have been great to go back": *Film Comment*, March-April 1981. Charles Feldman, "We're updating": at January 12, 1962, news conference. BS described Louella Parsons's reaction to BS's casting in *Walk on the Wild Side* in *Film Comment*, March-April 1981, interview. Baxter, "One day he kept us waiting": DiOrio, *Barbara Stanwyck*, p. 178. Dmytryk, "I didn't blame Capucine": Edward Dmytryk, *It's a Hell of a Life But Not a Bad Living*, pp. 246–48. Byron Steven's obituary: *Hollywood Citizen News*, December 15, 1964. Eder, "I can still hear Barbara": Eder, *Not This Time, Cary Grant*, p. 115.

33. *The Last Picture Show.* BS, "I thought, well, if he's calling me": Earl Greenwood and Kathleen Tracy, *The Boy Who Would Be King*, p. 288. Head, "Barbara looks terrific": Edith Head and Paddy Calistro, *Edith Head's Hollywood*, p. 140. Author interviewed Aldrich in 1972. BS, "He did not offer": Whitney Stine, *Mother Goddam*, p. 308. BS insisted *The Night Walker* was a shocker, not a horror movie: John Kobal, *People Will Talk*, p. 511. BS, "I think it would be": Kobal, *People Will Talk*, p. 511. William Castle quoted BS on first day's shooting to author, 1966. Bosley Crowther, "The whole thing": *New York Times*, January 24, 1965. BS, "It was a chance": Jerry Vermilye, *Barbara Stanwyck*, p. 132. BS, "You know, Shirley": Shirley Eder, *Not This Time Cary Grant*, p. 119.

34. *Matriarch.* BS, "They don't write": *Miami Herald,* April 9, 1967. BS, "I'm a tough old broad": *Family Weekly,* August 4, 1968. BS, "We do twenty-six": *Miami Herald,* April 9, 1967. BS, "Most of these young people": *Movie,* January 1973. Evans, "As the rehearsal went on": *People,* February 5, 1990. BS, "There is no age in my life I want to be *again!*": *Pageant,* May 1967. Vogel, "She had great confidence": Vogel to author, 1985. Neal on *The Fountainhead:* Neal, *Patricia Neal: As I Am,* p. 306. BS, "It's the first time": Al DiOrio, *Barbara Stanwyck,* p. 189. BS, "A role of any sort provides a challenge," *Hollywood Citizen-News,* March 31, 1953. The Henry Roy Belmert case was extensively covered by Los Angeles media in 1971. Taylor's death on June 8, 1969, and his funeral was covered by the *Los Angeles Times,* June 9, 1969; also *The Star,* November 26, 1985.

35. *Golden Girl.* BS, "I'm not yesterday's woman": *New York Times,* March 22, 1981. Spelling, "We dangled Nolan": *New York Times,* October 18, 1992. Miller, "Stanwyck taught me": Miller to author, 1993. BS, "She looks like a million": quoted by Shirley Eder to author, 1993. Oakie, "Made me a rich man": Eder to author, 1993. Crawford, "All of my friends": Shaun Considine, *Bette and Joan,* p. 402. BS, "Plenty of people survive": *Photoplay,* November 1971. Nolan, "When I introduced Missy": Nolan to author, 1993. Holden, "Before Barbara": Associated Press news transcript, April 3, 1978. Matthau, "She has played": *Daily Variety,* April 15, 1981. BS, "N-n-no, it can't be": Bob Thomas, *Golden Boy,* p. 5. The burglary and terrorizing of BS, March 30, 1981, covered by Los Angeles media, including *Los Angeles Times* and *Herald-Examiner,* October 29, 1981, and *People,* November 25, 1985. Travolta, "Four years ago": Thomas, *Golden Boy,* p. 265. BS, "Look, believe it or not": Singer syndication, May 18, 1982. *Thorn Birds* casting of BS announced: *Daily Variety,* April 1, 1982. Details of Wolper-Margulies production setup: *Daily Variety,* March 15, 1983. BS's hospitalization for smoke inhalation: *Hollywood Reporter,* August 3 and 20, 1983.

36. *Closing Number.* Stephen Harvey's BS career assessment published in *Film Comment,* March-April 1981. Kael on *The Lady Eve:* Pauline Kael, *5001 Nights at the Movies,* p. 313. Richard Schickel surveyed Stanwyck's and Taylor's careers in *Architectural Digest,* April 1990, and BS's career in April 15,

1992, TNT TV special "Barbara Stanwyck: Fire and Desire." Gavin Lambert quote: *Ten Percent* magazine, UCLA, summer 1993. *National Enquirer* interview with Dion Fay, January 3, 1984. Kleno on Dion Fay and BS's "unfortunate situation": Kleno to author, 1993. Eder, "She wouldn't talk about him": Eder to author, 1993. BS, "Life's a pretty difficult thing": BS to author, 1985. BS, "I had a scrapbook": quoted by Eder to author, 1993. Fire at BS's Loma Vista home reported by Los Angeles media, including *Daily Variety*, June 24, 1985, *Hollywood Reporter*, June 25, 1985, and *The Globe*, July 16, 1985. Praed, "Both Barbara and Heston": *People*, November 25, 1985. Miller, "Barbara dear": *People*, November 25, 1985. BS, "I say the same line": *The Star*, July 15, 1986. BS, "Even if Rock Hudson": *The Star*, July 15, 1986. BS, "This is the biggest pile": *The Star*, September 3, 1985. BS, "It's one thing to know": *The Star*, July 15, 1986. American Film Institute award: *USA Today*, April 10, 1987, and *New York Times*, April 11, 1987. BS, "Honest to God, I can't walk on water": *New York Times*, May 29, 1987. BS, "When I hold this Oscar": *National Enquirer*, February 6, 1990. The campaign soliciting fan mail: *The Globe*, October 18, 1988. Renaming of MGM's Robert Taylor Building: *Los Angeles Times*, January 1, 1990. BS's hospitalization, last days, and death are detailed in *Los Angeles Times*, January 21, 1990, *Daily Variety*, January 22, 1990, *Los Angeles Daily News*, January 23, 1990.

37. *"It worked—didn't it?"* BS, "Put me in the last": BS to author, 1985. BS, "I marvel at people": *Los Angeles Times*, April 5, 1987. BS, "It used to drive me crazy": Joseph McBride, *Frank Capra*, p. 297. BS told author of Preston Sturges' desire to write a comedy for her, 1985. BS on Sturges, *New York Times*, March 22, 1981. MacMurray, "She was just the most wonderful": *Hollywood Reporter*, January 22, 1990. O'Sullivan, "I found her a cold person": David Shipman, *Movie Talk*, p. 193. BS, "I would hate": *Pageant*, May 1967. BS, "Many people will hurt you": *Photoplay*, December 1937.

Bibliography

Alpert, Hollis. *The Barrymores*. New York: Dial Press, 1964.

Altman, Dana. *Hollywood East, Louis B. Mayer and the Origins of the Studio System*. New York: Carol Publishing, 1992.

Andersen, Christopher. *Citizen Jane: The Turbulent Life of Jane Fonda*. New York: Henry Holt, 1990.

Anger, Kenneth. *Hollywood Babylon II*. New York: New American Library, 1984.

Arce, Hector. *Groucho*. New York: G.P. Putnam, 1979.

Arce, Hector. *The Secret Life of Tyrone Power*. New York: William Morrow, 1979.

Atkinson, Brooks. *Broadway*. New York: Macmillan, 1970.

Bell-Metereau, Rebecca. *Hollywood Androgyny*. New York: Columbia University Press, 1985.

Benny, Jack, and Benny, Joan. *Sunday Nights at Seven: The Jack Benny Story*. New York: Warner Books, 1990.

Bentley, Eric, ed. *Thirty Years of Treason: Excerpts from Hearings before the House Committee on Un-American Activities, 1938–1968*. New York: Viking, 1971.

Berg, A. Scott. *Goldwyn: A Biography*. New York: Alfred A. Knopf, 1989.

Berle, Milton, with Haskel Frankel. *Milton Berle: An Autobiography*. New York: Delacorte, 1974.

Blum, Daniel. *A Pictorial History of the American Theatre: A Chronicle 1860–1970*. New York: Crown 1969.

Bogdanovich, Peter. *The Last Pioneer: Allan Dwan*. New York: Praeger, 1971.

Bookspan, Martin, and Yockey, Ross. *André Previn: A Biography*. Garden City, NY: Doubleday, 1981.

Bordman, Gerald. *American Musical Theatre: A Chronicle*. New York: Oxford University Press, 1978.

Branden, Nathaniel. *Judgment Day: My Years with Ayn Rand*. Boston: Houghton Mifflin, 1989.

Brian, Denis. *Tallulah, Darling: A Biography of Tallulah Bankhead*. New York: Macmillan, 1972.

Broman, Sven. *Conversations with Greta Garbo*. New York: Viking, 1992.

Bruccoli, Matthew J. *Some Sort of Grandeur: The Life of F. Scott Fitzgerald*. New York: Carol & Graf, 1981.

Cagney, James. *Cagney by Cagney*. Garden City, NY: Doubleday, 1976.

Capra, Frank. *The Name Above the Title*. New York: Macmillan, 1971.

Ceplar, Larry, and Englund, Steven. *The Inquisition in Hollywood: Politics in the Film Community*. Garden City, NY: Anchor Press/Doubleday, 1980.

Chandler, Raymond. *Raymond Chandler Speaking*. Boston: Houghton Mifflin, 1962.

———. *Selected Letters*, ed. Frank MacShane. New York: Columbia University Press, 1981.

Coe, Jonathan. *Humphrey Bogart: Take It & Like It*. New York: Grove Weidenfeld, 1991.

Cogley, John. *Report on Blacklisting*, 2 vols. New York: Fund for the Republic, 1956.

Cole, Lester. *Hollywood Red*. Palo Alto: Ramparts Press, 1981.

Collins, Joan. *Past Imperfect*. New York: Simon and Schuster, 1984.

Considine, Shaun. *Bette and Joan: The Divine Feud*. New York: E.P. Dutton, 1989.

Coursodon, Jean-Pierre, and Sauvage, Pierre. *American Directors*. New York: McGraw-Hill, 1983.

Crawford, Christina. *Mommie Dearest*. New York: William Morrow, 1978.

Crowther, Bosley. *Hollywood Rajah: The Life and Times of Louis B. Mayer*. New York: Henry Holt, 1960.

———. *Vintage Films*. New York: G.P. Putnam, 1977.

Da, Lottie, and Alexander, Jan. *Bad Girls of the Silver Screen*. New York: Carroll & Graf, 1989.

Dardis, Tom. *Some Time in the Sun: The Hollywood Years of Fitzgerald, Faulker, Nathaniel West, Aldous Huxley and James Agee*. New York: Scribner, 1976.

Daum, Raymond, and Muse, Vance. *Walking with Garbo*. New York: HarperCollins Publishers, 1991.

Davis, Bette. *The Lonely Life: An Autobiography*. New York: G.P. Putnam's Sons, 1962.

De Acosta, Mercedes. *Here Lies the Heart*. New York: Reynal, 1960.

DeMille, Cecil B. *Autobiography*. Englewood Cliffs, NJ: Prentice-Hall, 1959.

DiOrio, Al. *Barbara Stanwyck: A Biography*. New York: Coward-McCann, 1983.

Dmytryk, Edward. *It's a Hell of a Life but Not a Bad Living: A Hollywood Memoir*. New York: Times Books, 1978.

Douglas, Kirk. *The Ragman's Son: An Autobiography*. New York: Simon and Schuster, 1988.

Dunaway, David King. *Huxley in Hollywood*. New York: Harper & Row, 1989.

Durgnat, Raymond, and Simmon, Scott. *King Vidor: American*. Berkeley: University of California Press, 1988.

Eames, John Douglas. *The MGM Story*. New York: Crown, 1975.

Easton, Carol. *The Search for Sam Goldwyn*. New York: William Morrow, 1975.

Eder, Shirley. *Not This Time, Cary Grant*. Garden City, NY: Doubleday, 1973.

Edwards, Anne. *Early Reagan: The Rise to Power*. New York: William Morrow, 1987.

————. *Vivien Leigh*. New York: Simon and Schuster, 1977.

Eells, George. *Final Gig*. San Diego: Harcourt Brace, 1991.

Ewen, David. *The Life and Death of Tin Pan Alley*. New York: Funk and Wagnalls, 1964.

Faderman, Lillian. *Odd Girls and Twilight Lovers: A History of Lesbian Life in Twentieth-Century America*. New York: Penguin, 1991.

Fairbanks, Jr., Douglas. *The Salad Days*. Garden City, NY: Doubleday, 1988.

Fein, Irving A. *Jack Benny: An Intimate Biography*. New York: G.P. Putnam, 1976.

Fenin, George N., and Everson, William. *The Western*. New York: Bonanza Books, 1976.

Fireman, Judith, ed. *TV Book: The Ultimate Television Book*. New York: Workman, 1977.

Fonda, Henry, as told to Howard Teichman. *My Life*. New York: New American Library, 1981.

Fontaine, Joan. *No Bed of Roses: An Autobiography*. New York: William Morrow, 1978.

Friedrich, Otto. *City of Nets*. New York: Harper & Row, 1986.

Gardner, Ava. *Ava: My Story*. New York: Bantam, 1990.

Gibson, Margaret Brenman. *Clifford Odets*. New York: Atheneum, 1981.

Golden, Harry. *The Right Time*. New York: G.P. Putnam, 1986.

Goldman, Herbert G. *Fanny Brice: The Original Funny Girl*. New York: Oxford University Press, 1992.

Goldstein, Malcolm. *George S. Kaufman: The Life, His Theater*. New York: Oxford University Press, 1979.

Goodman, Ezra. *Bogie: The Good-Bad Guy*. New York: Lyle Stuart, 1965.

Greene, Graham. *Graham Greene on Film*. New York: Simon and Schuster, 1972.

Greenwood, Earl, and Tracy, Kathleen. *The Boy Who Would Be King: Elvis Presley*. New York: E.P. Dutton, 1990.

Guiles, Fred Lawrence. *Jane Fonda*. Garden City, NY: Doubleday, 1982.

Gussow, Mel. *Don't Say Yes Until I Finish Talking: A Biography of Daryl F. Zanuck*. Garden City, NY: Doubleday, 1971.

Hadleigh, Boze. *Conversations with My Elders*. New York: St. Martin's Press, 1986.

Halliwell, Leslie, ed. *Halliwell's Film Guide*, 7th ed. New York: Harper & Row, 1989.

Hart, Moss. *Act One: An Autobiography*. New York: Random House, 1959.

Haskell, Molly, *From Reverence to Rape: The Treatment of Women in the Movies*. New York: Holt, Rinehart and Winston, 1974.

Haver, Ronald. *David O. Selznick's Hollywood*. New York: Alfred A. Knopf, 1980.

Head, Edith, and Calistro, Paddy. *Edith Head's Hollywood*. New York: E.P. Dutton, 1983.

Higham, Charles. *Bette: The Life of Bette Davis*. New York: Macmillan, 1981.

————. *Merchant of Dreams: Louis B. Mayer, MGM and the Secret Hollywood*. New York: Donald I. Fine, 1993.

————. *Warner Brothers*. New York: Scribner, 1975.

Horan, James D., and Sann, Paul. *Pictorial History of the Wild West*. New York: Crown, 1954.

Houseman, John. *Front and Center*. New York: Simon and Schuster, 1979.

Hudson, Rock, and Davidson, Sara. *Rock Hudson: His Story*. New York: William Morrow, 1986.

Jacobs, Diane. *Christmas in July: The Life and Art of Preston Sturges*. Berkeley: University of California Press, 1992.

Josefsberg, Milt. *The Jack Benny Show*. New Rochelle, NY: Arlington House, 1977.

Kael, Pauline. *5001 Nights at the Movies*. New York: Holt, Rinehart and Winston, 1982.

Kahn, Gordon. *Hollywood on Trial: The Story of the 10 Who Were Indicted*. New York: Boni & Gaer, 1948.

Kaminsky, Stuart. *Coop: The Life and Legend of Gary Cooper*. New York: St. Martin's Press, 1980.

Kelley, Kitty. *Elizabeth Taylor: The Last Star*. New York: Simon and Schuster, 1981.

————. *His Way: The Unauthorized Biography of Frank Sinatra*. New York: Bantam, 1986.

Kendall, Elizabeth. *The Runaway Bride: Hollywood Romantic Comedy of the 1930s*. New York: Alfred A. Knopf, 1990.

Keyes, Evelyn. *Scarlett O'Hara's Younger Sister: My Lively Life In and Out of Hollywood*. Secaucus, NJ: Lyle Stuart, 1977.

Klauber, Bruce H. *World of Gene Krupa*. Ventura, CA: Pathfinder Publishing, 1990.

Kobal, John. *People Will Talk*. New York: Alfred A. Knopf, 1985.

Korda, Michael. *Charmed Lives: A Family Romance*. New York: Random House, 1979.

Kotsilibas-Davis, James, and Loy, Myrna. *Myrna Loy*. New York: Alfred A. Knopf, 1987.

Kurth, Peter. *American Cassandra: The Life of Dorothy Thompson*. Boston: Little, Brown, 1990.

Lambert, Gavin. *On Cukor*. New York: G.P. Putnam, 1972.

LaVine, W. Robert. *In a Glamorous Fashion: The Fabulous Years of Hollywood Costume Design*. New York: Scribner, 1980.

Lee, Hermione. *Willa Cather: Double Lives*. New York: Pantheon, 1989.

Leff, Leonard J., and Simmons, Jerold L. *The Dame in the Kimono*. New York: Grove Weidenfeld, 1990.

LeRoy, Mervyn, as told to Dick Kleiner. *Take One*. New York: Hawthorne, 1974.

Levant, Oscar. *The Memoirs of an Amnesiac*. New York: G.P. Putnam's Sons, 1965.

McBride, Joseph. *Frank Capra: The Catastrophe of Success*. New York: Simon and Schuster, 1992.

McGilligan, Patrick. *George Cukor: A Biography of a Gentleman Director*. New York: St. Martin's Press, 1991.

———. *Backstory: Interviews with Screenwriters of Hollywood's Golden Age*. Berkeley: University of California Press, 1986.

Madsen, Axel. *Gloria and Joe: The Star-Crossed Love Affair of Gloria Swanson and Joe Kennedy*. New York: William Morrow, 1988.

———. *William Wyler: The Authorized Biography*. New York: Crowell, 1973.

Marx, Arthur. *Goldwyn*. New York: Norton, 1976.

Meade, Marion. *Dorothy Parker: Who's Fresh Hell Is This?* New York: Villard Books, 1988.

Mellow, James R. *Hemingway: A Life Without Consequence*. Boston: Houghton Mifflin, 1992.

Meredith, Scott. *George S. Kaufman and His Friends*. Garden City, NY: Doubleday, 1974.

Milne, Tom. *Mamoulian*. Bloomington: Indiana University Press, 1969.

Morella, Joe, and Epstein, Edward Z. *Jane Wyman*. New York: Delacorte Press, 1985.

Mosley, Leonard. *Zanuck: The Rise and Fall of Hollywood's Last Tycoon*. Boston: Little, Brown, 1984.

Neal, Patricia, with Richard DeNeut. *Patricia Neal: As I Am*. New York: Simon and Schuster, 1987.

Paris, Barry. *Louise Brooks*. New York: Alfred A. Knopf, 1989.

Preminger, Erik Lee. *Gypsy and Me: At Home and On the Road with Gypsy Rose Lee*. Boston: Little, Brown, 1984.

Previn, André. *No Minor Chords: My Days in Hollywood*. New York: Doubleday, 1991.

Quirk, Lawrence J. *Fasten Your Seat Belts: The Passionate Life of Bette Davis*. New York: William Morrow, 1990.

———. *The Films of Robert Taylor*. Secaucus, NJ: Citadel Press, 1975.

Reagan, Nancy. *My Turn*. New York: Random House, 1989.

Reagan, Ronald. *An American Life: The Autobiography*. New York: Simon and Schuster, 1990.

Robinson, Edward G., and Spigelgass, Leonard. *All My Yesterdays*. New York: Hawthorn, 1973.

Rosen, Marjorie. *Popcorn Venus: Women, Movies and the American Dream*. New York: Coward, McCann & Geoghegan, 1973.

Russo, Vito. *The Celluloid Closet: Homosexuality in the Movies*. New York: Harper & Row, 1987.

Schatz, Thomas. *The Genius of the System: Hollywood Filmmaking in the Studio Era*. New York: Pantheon, 1988.

Schumach, Murray. *The Face On The Cutting Room Floor*. New York: William Morrow, 1964.

Shepherd, Donald, and Slatzer, Robert. *Duke: The Life and Times of John Wayne*. Garden City, NY: Doubleday, 1985.

Sherman, Eric, and Rubin, Martin. *The Director's Event*. New York: Atheneum, 1970.

Shipman, David. *Judy Garland*. New York: Hyperion, 1993.

————. *Movie Talk: Who Said What About Whom in the Movies*. New York: St. Martin's Press, 1988.

Silver, Alain, and Ward, Elizabeth. *Film Noir: An Encyclopedic Reference to the American Style*. Woodstock, NY: Overlook Press, 1979.

Sinclair, Andrew. *John Ford*. New York: Dial Press, 1979.

Smith, Ella. *Starring Miss Barbara Stanwyck*. New York: Crown, 1974.

Sperber, A. M. *Edward R. Murrow*. New York: Freundlich Books, 1986.

Spoto, Donald. *The Dark Side of Genius: The Life of Alfred Hitchcock*. Boston: Little, Brown, 1983.

Stack, Robert, with Mark Evans. *Straight Shooting*. New York: Macmillan, 1980.

Stine, Whitney. *Mother Goddam: The Story of the Career of Bette Davis*. New York: Hawthorn, 1974.

Sturges, Preston. *Preston Sturges: His Life in His Words*. New York: Simon and Schuster, 1990.

Suskin, Steven. *Opening Night on Broadway: A Critical Quotebook of the Golden Era of the Musical Theater*. New York: Schirmer Books, 1990.

Swindell, Larry. *Body and Soul: The Story of John Garfield*. New York: William Morrow, 1975.

————. *The Last Hero: Gary Cooper*. Garden City, NY: Doubleday, 1980.

————. *Charles Boyer: The Reluctant Lover*. Garden City, NY: Doubleday, 1983.

Teichmann, Howard. *Smart Alec: The Wit, World and Life of Alexander Woolcott*. New York: Morrow, 1976.

Thomas, Bob. *Golden Boy: The Untold Story of William Holden*. New York: St. Martin's Press, 1983.

————. *Selznick*. Garden City, NY: Doubleday, 1970.

————. *King Cohn: The Life and Times of Harry Cohn*. New York: G.P. Putnam, 1967.

Thomas, Tony. *The Films of Ronald Reagan*. Secaucus, NJ: Citadel Press, 1980.

Tornabene, Lyn. *Long Live the King: A Biography of Clark Gable*. New York: G.P. Putnam, 1976.

Tulard, Jean, ed. *Dictionnaire du Cinéma*. Paris: Laffont, 1985.

Turner, Lana. *Lana: The Lady, The Legend, The Truth*. New York: E.P. Dutton, 1982.

Tyler, Parker. *Screening the Sexes: Homosexuality in the Movies*. New York: Holt, Rinehart, 1972.

Vermilye, Jerry. *Barbara Stanwyck*. New York: Pyramid, 1975.

Wallis, Hal, and Higham, Charles. *Starmaker: The Autobiography of Hal Wallis*. New York: Macmillan, 1980.

Walker, Alexander. *Elizabeth: The Life of Elizabeth Taylor*. New York: Grove Weidenfeld, 1990.

Wayne, Jane Ellen. *Ava's Men*. New York: St. Martin's Press, 1990.

————. *Gable's Women*. New York: Prentice Hall, 1987.

————. *Robert Taylor*. New York: St. Martin's Press, 1977.

————. *Stanwyck*. New York: Arbor House, 1985.

Wellman, William A. *A Short Time for Insanity: An Autobiography*. New York: Hawthorn, 1974.

Wiley, Mason, and Bona, Damien. *Inside Oscar: The Unofficial History of the Academy Awards*. New York: Ballantine, 1986.

Young, Jordan R. *Reel Characters*. Beverly Hills: Moonstar Press, 1975.

Filmography

BARBARA STANWYCK

(1907-1990)

Broadway Nights. Director: Joseph C. Boyle. Screenplay: Forrest Halsey, from a story by Norman Houston. Camera: Ernest Haller. Cast: Lois Wilson, Sam Hardy, Louis John Bartels, Philip Strange, Barbara Stanwyck (dancer), Bunny Weldon, Sylvia Sidney. Music: Fritz Kreisler. First National, 1927.

Stanwyck's only silent (with music and sound effects) film has her as a friend of heroine Wilson (star of *Covered Wagon*). Without mentioning Stanwyck, the *New York Times*'s Mordaunt Hall called it a story well told with clever camerawork.

The Locked Door. Director: George Fitzmaurice. Screenplay: C. Gardner Sullivan, from the play *The Sign on the Door* by Channing Pollock. Dialogue: George Scarborough. Camera: Ray June. Editor: Hal Kern. Cast: Rod La Rocque, William Boyd, Barbara Stanwyck (Ann Carter), Betty Bronson, Harry Stubbs, Harry Mestayer, Mack Swain, Zasu Pitts. United Artists (UA), 1929.

La Rocque plays the heavy, and Stanwyck is William Boyd's bride in this remake of the silent story of husband and wife trying to save each other by assuming guilt for a murder.

Mexicali Rose. Director: Erle C. Kenton. Screenplay: Gladys Lehman (Dorothy Howell). Continuity: Norman Houston. Camera: Ted Tetzlaff. Editor: Leon Barsha. Cast: Barbara Stanwyck (Mexicali Rose), Sam Hardy, William

Janney, Louis Natheaux, Arthur Rankin, Harry Vejar. Columbia, 1929.

Stanwyck hated this Harry Cohn cheapie about a border-town belle done in by her husband. To get revenge, the wanton Rose marries his younger brother (Janney), but she is ultimately murdered by the village half-wit (Rankin).

Ladies of Leisure. Director: Frank Capra. Screenplay: Jo Swerling, from the play *Ladies of the Evening* by Milton Herbert Gropper. Camera: Joseph Walker. Editor: Maurice Wright. Cast: Barbara Stanwyck (Kay Arnold), Lowell Sherman, Ralph Graves, Marie Prevost, Nance O'Neil, George Fawcett. Columbia, 1930.

Stanwyck's breakthrough picture. She is a "party girl" in this early Depression comedy who falls in love with upper-class gent. The *New York Times* headlined its review MISS STANWYCK TRIUMPH. Posterity tends to see *Ladies of Leisure* as only fitfully interesting despite its refreshing toughness and sardonic edge. The film is usually cited as a museum piece of the early-talkie gold-digger weepie genre or as an example of a breezier Capra before his bighearted river of sentiments of *It's a Wonderful Life*, *Mr. Smith Goes to Washington*, and *Meet John Doe*.

Ten Cents a Dance. Director: Lionel Barrymore. Screenplay: Jo Swerling. Continuity: Dorothy Howell. Camera: Ernest Haller, Gil Warrenton. Song: Richard Rodgers, Lorenz Hart. Editor: Arthur Huffsmith. Cast: Barbara Stanwyck (Barbara O'Neill), Ricardo Cortez, Monroe Owsley, Sally Blane, Blanche Frederici, Martha Sleeper. Columbia, 1931.

Barbara's dance-hall hostess is lusted after by her husband's employer who won't prosecute her embezzling mate if she surrenders her lovely self. The *New York Times* called the denouement interesting, but said *Ten Cents a Dance* "goes no more deeply into the story of the girls who dance for a living than does the popular song from which the new film at the Strand is derived."

Illicit. Director: Archie Mayo. Screenplay: Harvey Thew, from the play by Robert Riskin and Edith Fitzgerald. Camera:

Robert Kurrle. Costumes: Earl Luick. Editor: William Holmes. Cast: Barbara Stanwyck (Anne Vincent), James Rennie, Ricardo Cortez, Joan Blondell, Natalie Moorhead, Charles Butterworth, Claude Gillingwater. Warners, 1931.

For Stanwyck, a good follow-up to *Ladies of Leisure*, but one of producer Darryl Zanuck's "working-girl" programmers of little distinction despite screenplay by Robert (*It Happened One Night*) Riskin. A year later, Warners remade *Illicit* with Bette Davis and Gene Raymond. Davis resented being handed a Stanwyck hand-me-down. Renamed *Ex-Lady*, the new version was tawdrier than *Illicit*. Davis spent most of her screen time in dishabille, and the publicity campaign pictured her half-naked under the headline WE DON'T DARE TELL YOU HOW DARING IT IS.

Night Nurse. Director: William Wellman. Screenplay: Oliver H. P. Garrett, from the novel by Dora Macy. Additional dialogue: Charles Kenyon. Camera: Barney McGill. Costumes: Earl Luick. Editor: Edward M. McDermott. Cast: Barbara Stanwyck (Lora Hart), Ben Lyons, Joan Blondell, Clark Gable, Blanche Frederici, Charlotte Merriam. Warners, 1931.

Gable goes around socking everybody. His bullying of Stanwyck is ghastly. *Hollywood Reporter*: "A conglomeration of exaggerations, often bordering on serial dramatics."

The Miracle Woman. Director: Frank Capra. Screenplay: Jo Swerling, from the play *Bless You, Sister* by John Meehan and Robert Riskin. Camera: Joseph Walker. Editor: Maurice Wright. Cast: Barbara Stanwyck (Florence Fallon), David Manners, Sam Hardy, Beryl Mercer, Russell Hopton, Charles Middleton. Columbia, 1931.

A thinly disguised retelling of the life of Aimee Semple McPherson with Stanwyck giving peerless performance as the young evangelist who is taken over by a carny promoter and becomes a big-time preacher. "There is no doubt that after reviewing this release, picture and theatermen will agree that Capra can do more with Barbara Stanwyck than any other director she has worked with," *Variety* said.

Forbidden. Director: Frank Capra. Screenplay: Jo Swerling, from a story by Frank Capra. Camera: Joseph

Walker. Editor: Maurice Wright. Cast: Barbara Stanwyck (Lulu Smith), Adolphe Menjou, Ralph Bellamy, Dorothy Peterson, Charlotte Henry. Columbia, 1931.

Barbara as a loving adulteress who murders her husband so her lover can continue his upward mobility. Movies with women sacrificing everything for their married lovers or their illegitimate babies were big in the 1930s. *Forbidden* would rank low in the careers of Capra and Stanwyck. *Variety* called *Forbidden* "a cry picture for the girls." It was Columbia's 1932 top moneymaker.

Shopworn. Director: Nick Grinde. Screenplay: Jo Swerling and Robert Riskin, from a story by Sarah Y. Mason and Frances Marion. Camera: Joseph Walker. Editor: Gene Havlick. Cast: Barbara Stanwyck (Kitty Lane), Regis Toomey, Zasu Pitts, Lucien Littlefield, Clara Blandick, Robert Alden. Columbia, 1932.

Barbara as a waitress who becomes a stage star, marries a socialite whose mother railroads her daughter-in-law on a morals charge. The *New York Times*'s Mordaunt Hall: "Vacillating characters with ludicrously poor memories trip on and off the screen and harangue each other during the tedious proceedings in *Shopworn*. It is beyond the powers of such players as Barbara Stanwyck, Regis Toomey, Clara Blandick and Zasu Pitts to make their actions in this film convincing or even mildly interesting."

So Big. Director: William Wellman. Screenplay: J. Grubb, Alexander and Robert Lord, from the novel by Edna Ferber. Camera: Sid Hickox. Costumes: Orry-Kelly. Editor: William Holmes. Cast: Barbara Stanwyck (Selina Peake), George Brent, Dawn O'Day (Anne Shirley), Hardie Albright, Dickie Moore, Guy Kibble, Bette Davis, Mae Madison. Warners, 1932.

The first talkie remake of Edna Ferber's 1924 novel of a widowed teacher and her mother in rough rural community, and Stanwyck's first A picture. *New York World-Telegram*: "No matter what one thinks about the picture, the final conviction of anyone who sees Miss Stanwyck's Selina Peake will be that she herself contributes a fine and stirring performance."

The Purchase Price. Director: William Wellman. Screenplay: Robert Lord, from the story "The Mud Lark" by Arthur Stringer. Camera: Sid Hickox. Editor: William Holmes. Cast: Barbara Stanwyck (Joan Gordon), George Brent, Hardie Albright, Lyle Talbot, David Landau. Warners, 1932.

To escape a gangster, torch singer Barbara impersonates a hotel maid and becomes a mail-order bride.

The Bitter Tea of General Yen. Director: Frank Capra. Screenplay: Edward Paramore, from the novel by Grace Zaring Stone. Camera: Joseph Walker. Costumes: Edward Stevenson. Music: Frank Harling. Editor: Edward Curtis. Cast: Barbara Stanwyck (Megan Davis), Nils Asther, Toshia Mori, Gavin Gordon, Walter Connelly. Columbia, 1933.

Interracial romance that 1933 audiences couldn't stomach. Barbara is a straitlaced New England girl sexually drawn to Chinese warlord. Capra entwines Barbara in the most sensuous camera movements.

Ladies They Talk About. Directors William Keighley and Howard Brethertton. Screenplay: Sidney Sutherland and Brown Holmes, from the play *Women in Prison* by Dorothy Mackaye and Carlton Miles. Camera: John Seitz. Costumes: Orry-Kelly. Editor: Basil Wrangel. Cast: Barbara Stanwyck (Nan Taylor), Preston Foster, Lyle Talbot, Dorothy Burgess, Lillian Roth, Maude Eburne. Warners, 1933.

Gun moll Stanwyck believes evangelist Foster is responsible for her imprisonment, hunts him down, and shoots him before realizing she really loves him.

Baby Face. Director: Alfred E. Green. Screenplay: Gene Markey and Kathryn Scola, from a story by Mark Canfield (Darryl Zanuck). Camera: James Van Trees. Costumes: Orry-Kelly. Editor: Howard Bretherton. Cast: Barbara Stanwyck (Lily Powers), George Brent, Donald Cook, Alphonse Ethier, Henry Kolker, Margaret Lindsay, John Wayne, Theresa Harris. Warners, 1933.

Gold digger Barbara moves from bank teller to executive penthouse in raunchy, fast-paced melodrama. *New York Times:* "Evidently there is not a decent man in this bank—not one who scorns to have an affair with this tarnished Lily."

Ever in My Heart. Director: Archie Mayo. Screenplay: Bertram Millhauser, from a story by Milhauser and Beulah Marie Dix. Camera: Arthur Todd. Costumes: Earl Luick. Editor: Owen Marks. Cast: Barbara Stanwyck (Mary Archer), Otto Kruger, Ralph Bellamy, Ruth Donnelly. Warners, 1933.

World War I drama with Kruger as deported German, Stanwyck as his American wife who discovers he's a spy. *Variety*: "A clean picture more for the nabes than the first runs."

A Lost Lady. Director: Alfred E. Green. Screenplay by Gene Markey and Kathryn Scola from the novel by Willa Cather. Camera: Sid Hickox. Costumes: Orry-Kelly. Editor: Owen Marks. Cast: Barbara Stanwyck (Marian Ormsby), Frank Morgan, Ricardo Cortez, Lyle Talbot, Phillip Reed. First National, 1934.

A lightweight remake of 1923 Willa Cather novel with Stanwyck as a fashion model in love with an older man.

Gambling Lady. Director: Archie Mayo. Screenplay by Bertram Ralph Block and Doris Malloy, from a story by Malloy. Camera: George Barnes. Costumes: Orry-Kelly. Editor: Harold McLernon. Cast: Barbara Stanwyck (Lady Lee), Joel McCrea, Pat O'Brien, C. Aubrey Smith, Claire Dodd, Arthur Treacher. Warners, 1934.

The daughter of a professional gambler who committed suicide follows in her father's footsteps and becomes involved in murder.

The Secret Bride. Director: William Dieterie. Screenplay: Tom Buckingham, F. Hugh Herbert, and Mary McCall, Jr., from the play by Leonard Ide. Camera: Ernest Haller. Costumes: Orry-Kelly. Editor: Owen Marks. Cast: Barbara Stanwyck (Ruth Vincent), Warren William, Glenda Farrell, Grant Mitchell, Arthur Byron. Warners, 1935.

Attorney General William is secretly married to the daughter (Stanwyck) of the governor he's trying to impeach.

The Woman in Red. Director: Robert Florey.Screenplay: Mary McCall, Jr., and Peter Milne, from the novel *North Shore* by Wallace Irwin. Camera: Sol Polito. Costumes: Orry-Kelly.

Editor: Terry Morse. Cast: Barbara Stanwyck (Shelby Barret), Gene Raymond, Genevieve Tobin, John Eldredge, Philip Reed, Dorothy Tree, Arthur Treacher. First National, 1935.

Rich horsewoman Stanwyck marries poor polo player Raymond and is vindicated of suspicion of adultery.

Red Salute (*Runaway Daughter*, in Britain *Arms and the Girl*). Director: Sidney Lanfield. Screenplay: Humphrey Pearson and Manuel Seff, from a story by Pearson. Camera: Robert Planck. Editor: Grant Whytock. Cast: Barbara Stanwyck (Drue Van Allen), Robert Young, Cliff Edwards, Hardie Albright, Ruth Donnelly, Purnell Pratt, Gordon Jones. UA, 1935.

Stanwyck's first comedy is modeled after *It Happened One Night*. Early road picture with Barbara dabbling in campus Communism and taking a cross-border hike with soldier Young. Stanwyck and Young are funny jostling and bickering, and some of her lines are biting.

Annie Oakley. Director: George Stevens. Screenplay: Joel Sayre and John Twist from a story by Joseph A. Fields and Ewart Adamson. Camera: J. Roy Hunt. Music: Alberto Columbo. Editor: Jack Hively. Cast: Stanwyck (Annie Oakley), Melvyn Douglas, Preston Foster, Moroni Olsen, Pert Kelton, Chief Thunderbird. RKO, 1935.

Stanwyck in the title role of the Ohio backwoods sharpshooter who became famous when they made *Annie Get Your Gun*.

A Message to Garcia. Director: George Marshall. Screenplay: W. P. Lipscomb and Gene Fowler, suggested by Elbert Hubbard's essay and Lieutenant Andrew S. Rowan's book. Camera: Rudolph Maté. Music: Louis Silvers. Editor: Herbert Levy. Cast: Wallace Beery, Barbara Stanwyck (Rafaelita Maderos), John Boles, Mona Barrie, Alan Hale, Herbert Mundin, Enrique Acosta. Fox, 1936.

A ridiculous screenplay spins a piece of historical claptrap out of an 1898 incident from the Spanish-American War. Señorita Stanwyck is a Cuban nobleman's daughter helping an American agent get through to rebel general Calixto Garcia. The *New York Evening Post*: "It bothers us that Barbara, cast as the Cuban señorita, should talk perfect Brooklyn."

The Bride Walks Out. Director: Leigh Jason. Screenplay: P. J. Wolfson and Philip G. Epstein, from a story by Howard Emmett Rogers. Camera: J. Roy Hunt. Costumes: Bernard Newman. Music: Roy Webb. Editor: Arthur Roberts. Cast: Barbara Stanwyck (Carolyn Martin), Gene Raymond, Robert Young, Ned Sparks, Helen Broderick, Hattie McDaniel. RKO, 1936.

Barbara as the spendthrift bride more interested in shopping than in budgeting her husband's $35 a week. Affable marital comedy with no surprises.

His Brother's Wife. Director: W.S. Van Dyke. Screenplay: Leon Gordon and John Meehan, from a story by George Auerbach. Camera: Oliver T. Marsh. Costumes: Dolly Tree. Music: Franz Waxman. Editor: Conrad A. Nervig. Cast: Barbara Stanwyck (Rita Wilson), Robert Taylor, Jean Hersholt, Joseph Calleia, John Eldredge. MGM, 1936.

Barbara's first film with Taylor. The shoddy script has him snub her for jungle research, and she, to get even, marry his brother (Eldredge).

Banjo on My Knee. Director: John Cromwell. Screenplay: Nunnally Johnson, from the novel by Harry Hamilton. Additional dialogue William Faulkner. Camera: Ernest Palmer. Costumes: Gwen Wakeling. Music: Arthur Lange. Songs: Jimmy McHugh. Editor: Hansen Fritch. Cast: Barbara Stanwyck (Pearl Holley), Joel McCrea, Walter Brennan, Buddy Ebsen, Walter Catlett, Helen Westley, Katherine De Mille, Anthony (Tony) Martin. Fox, 1936.

Barbara becomes a waterfront entertainer and has a hair-pulling match with DeMille. *Banjo on My Knee* was a Christmas 1936 release. Twentieth Century-Fox publicity said the film "combines the setting of *Tobacco Road* with the mood of *Steamboat 'Round the Bend*," to which the *New York Times*'s Frank Nugent took vigorous exception: "Only Mr. Brennan's Newt, the sporadic hoofing of Buddy Ebsen, the Hall Johnson choir's collaboration with an anonymous soloist on 'The St. Louis Blues,' Anthony Martin's singing of

'There's Something in the Air,' and a sound comedy performance by Walter Catlett as an abused photographer emerge as definite entertainment factors."

The Plough and the Stars. Director: John Ford. Screenplay: Dudley Nichols, from the play by Sean O'Casey. Camera: Joseph August. Costumes: Walter Plunkett. Music: Roy Webb. Cast: Barbara Stanwyck (Nora Clitheroe), Preston Foster, Barry Fitzgerald, Denis O'Dea, Eileen Crowe, Arthur Shields. RKO, 1936.

Elementary film version of Sean O'Casey's play of the months leading up to the 1916 Dublin uprising. Inherent in the source material, too much screen time is devoted to the Stanwyck-Foster story and not enough to dramatizing the Easter uprising. In postproduction, Ford failed to defend his film against front-office "improvements" and failed to match his success of the year before: *The Informer*.

Internes Can't Take Money. Director: Alfred Santell. Screenplay: Rian James and Theodore Reeves, from a story by Max Brand. Camera: Theodor Sparkuhl. Costumes: Travis Banton. Editor: Doane Harriuson. Music: Gregory Stone. Cast: Joel McCrea, Barbara Stanwyck (Janet Haley), Lloyd Nolan, Stanley Ridges, Lee Bowman, Barry Macollum. Paramount, 1937.

Barbara is a patient with a dead bank-robber husband, Lloyd Nolan a gangster, and McCrea is young Doc Kildare patching up Nolan with a bottle of whiskey as an antiseptic, two lime squeezers for retractors, and a violin string for sutures. The *New York Times* singled out director Alfred Santell for a "blend of Hitchcock suspense and American verve" and Stanwyck for being pleasantly subdued "in contrast to the stormy time she had in her last picture."

This Is My Affair. Director: William A. Seiter. Screenplay: Allen Revkin and Lamar Trotti. Camera: Robert Planck. Costumes: Royer. Music: Arthur Lange. Editor: Allen McNeil. Cast: Robert Taylor, Barbara Stanwyck (Lil Duryea), Victor McLaglen, Brian Donlevy, Sidney Blackmer, John Carradine, Frank Conroy, Richard L. Perry. Fox, 1937.

Taylor as undercover agent who has a hard time proving his identity; Barbara as dance-hall belle with mob connections.

Stella Dallas. Director: King Vidor. Screenplay: Sarah Y. Mason, Victor Heerman, Frances Marion (and Elizabeth Hill, uncredited), from the novel by Olive Higgins Prouty and the play by Harry Wagstaff Gribble and Gertrude Purcell. Camera: Rudolph Maté. Editor: Sherman Todd. Costumes: Omar Kiam. Music: Alfred Newman. Cast: Barbara Stanwyck (Stella Dallas), John Boles, Anne Shirley, Barbara O'Neil, Alan Hale, Tim Holt, Lillian Yarbo. UA, 1937.

Celebrated tearjerker about the girl from the wrong side of the tracks.

Breakfast for Two. Director: Alfred Santell. Screenplay: Charles Kaufman, Paul Yawitz, and Viola Brothers Shore, from a story by David Garth. Camera: J. Roy Hunt. Costumes: Edward Stevenson. Cast: Barbara Stanwyck (Valentine Ransom), Herbert Marshall, Glenda Farrell, Eric Blore. RKO, 1937.

Barbara as headstrong Texas heiress who chases Marshall until he catches her.

The Mad Miss Manton. Director: Leigh Jason. Screenplay: Philip G. Epstein, from a story by Wilson Collison. Camera: Nicholas Musuraca. Costumes: Edward Stevenson. Music: Roy Webb. Editor: George Hively. Cast: Barbara Stanwyck (Melsa Manton), Henry Fonda, Sam Levene, Frances Mercer, Stanley Ridges, Whitney Bourne, Hattie McDaniel. RKO, 1938.

Variety: "Stanwyck brilliantly enacts the title role of the madcap heiress. Henry Fonda is excellent as the newspaper editor in love with the deb but, when a scoop looms, tosses aside romantic inclinations."

Always Goodbye. Director: Sidney Lanfield. Screenplay: Kathryn Scola and Edith Skouras, from a story by Gilbert Emery and Douglas Doty. Camera: Robert Planck. Costumes: Royer. Editor: Robert Simpson. Cast: Barbara Stanwyck (Margot Weston), Herbert Marshall, Ian Hunter, Cesar Romero, Binnie Barnes, Johnnie Russell. Fox, 1938.

Fashion designer Stanwyck gives up an illegitimate son and, after becoming a success, becomes the child's stepmother. A remake of a tearjerker Darryl Zanuck had produced with

Ann Harding in 1933 as *Gallant Lady*. The *New York Times*'s Frank Nugent summed up the plot in one sentence: "The script lets her [Stanwyck] have Mr. Romero to keep her amused, Herbert Marshall's shoulder to cry on, Ian Hunter's comforting arm to surround her at the last."

Union Pacific. Director: Cecil B. DeMille. Screenplay: Walter DeLeon, C. Gardner Sullivan, and Jesse Lasky, Jr., from an adaptation by Jack Cunningham of a story by Ernest Haycox. Camera: Victor Milner, Dewey Wrigley. Costume: Natalie Visart. Music: Sigmund Krumgold, John Leopold. Editor: Anne Bauchens. Cast: Barbara Stanwyck (Mollie Monahan), Joel McCrea, Akim Tamiroff, Lynne Overman, Robert Preston, Brian Donlevy, Anthony Quinn, Evelyn Keyes, Stanley Ridges, Regis Toomey. Paramount, 1939.

Stanwyck as postmistress of a rugged railroad camp in big-scale western climaxing in spectacular train wreck.

Golden Boy. Director: Rouben Mamoulian. Screenplay: Lewis Meltzer, Daniel Taradash, Sarah Y. Mason (Frances Marion) and Victor Heerman, from the play by Clifford Odets. Camera: Nicholas Musuraca, Karl Freund. Costumes: Kalloch. Music: Victor Young. Editor: Otto Meyer. Cast: Barbara Stanwyck (Lorna Moon), Adolphe Menjou, William Holden, Lee J. Cobb, Joseph Calleia, Sam Levene. Columbia, 1939.

Hokey film version of Clifford Odets's 1937 play. The role of Lorna Moon is built up to fit Stanwyck's star status and the story rearranged to provide a happy ending.

Remember the Night. Director: Mitchell Leisen. Screenplay: Preston Sturges. Camera: Ted Tetzlaff. Art director: Hans Dreier. Costumes: Edith Head. Music: Frederick Hollander. Editor: Doane Harrison. Cast: Barbara Stanwyck (Lea Leander) Fred MacMurray, Beulah Bondi, Elizabeth Patterson, Sterling Holloway. Paramount, 1940.

Urbane comedy-romance specialist Leisen directs Stanwyck in one of her best performances in Preston Sturges's last screenplay before he became a director and writer. Love reforms convicted thief Stanwyck and corrupts D.A. MacMurray even if the brew is sweetened in the end. *New York World-Telegram*: "glowing and heart-warming."

The Lady Eve. Director: Preston Sturges. Screenplay: Sturges from the story "Two Bad Hats" by Moncton Hoffe. Camera: Victor Milner. Art directors: Hans Dreier, Ernst Fegté. Costumes: Edith Head, Vic Potel. Music: Leo Shuken. Editor: Stuart Gilmore. Cast: Barbara Stanwyck (Jean Harrington), Henry Fonda, Charles Coburn, Eugene Pallette, William Demarest, Eric Blore. Paramount, 1941.

Sturges's best romantic comedy. Sleek and saucy satire about a dopey and sweet young millionaire (Fonda) and a lady cardsharp. The film includes one of Hollywood's great drunk scenes. *Variety* set the critics' tone, calling it "smart, light, frothy, romantic and invigorating tonic for the [1941] spring box office." A screen classic.

Meet John Doe. Director: Frank Capra. Screenplay: Robert Riskin, from a story by Richard Connell and Robert Presnell. Camera: George Barnes. Costumes: Natalie Visart. Music: Dmitri Tiomkin. Editor: Daniel Mandell. Cast: Gary Cooper, Barbara Stanwyck (Ann Mitchell), Edward Arnold, Walter Brennan, Spring Byington, James Gleason, Gene Lockhart, Rod La Rocque, Regis Toomey. Warners, 1941.

Odd social conscience-raising picture with Stanwyck as ruthless reporter exploiting washed-up ballplayer Cooper until she realizes she loves him. *New York World-Telegram:* "Stanwyck is supremely good as the columnist, lovely and talented; they don't come better than this one."

You Belong to Me. Director: Wesley Ruggles. Screenplay: Claude Binyon, from a story by Dalton Trumbo. Camera: Joseph Walker. Costumes: Edith Head. Music: Frederick Hollander. Editor: Viola Lawrence. Cast: Barbara Stanwyck (Helen Hunt), Henry Fonda, Edgar Buchanan, Roger Clark, Ruth Donnelly. Columbia, 1941.

Dr. Stanwyck neglects her husband (Fonda) for a handsome patient who feigns illness.

Ball of Fire. Director: Howard Hawks. Screenplay: Charles Brackett and Billy Wilder from the story "From A to Z" by Wilder and Thomas Monroe. Camera: Gregg Toland. Costumes: Edith Head. Music: Alfred Newman. Editor: Daniel Mandell. Cast: Gary Cooper, Barbara Stanwyck

(Sugarpuss O'Shea), Oscar Homolka, Henry Tavers, Dana Andrews, Tully Marshall, Leonid Kinskey, Richard Haydn, Aubrey Mather, Kathleen Howard, Virginia Hill. RKO, 1941.

The way slangy Stanwyck manhandles the English language fascinates linguistics professor Cooper. He got the kudos in *Meet John Doe,* she ran away with the *Ball of Fire* reviews. Cooper's absent-minded professor was a nice piece of light acting, but Barbara as Sugarpuss O'Shea was sensational.

The Great Man's Lady. Director: William Wellman. Screenplay: W. L. River from the story by Adela Rogers St. Johns and Seena Owen, based on the story by Viña Delmar. Camera: William C. Mellor. Costumes: Edith Head. Music: Victor Young. Editor: Thomas Scott. Cast: Barbara Stanwyck (Hannah Sempler), Joel McCrea, Brian Donlevy, Katharine Stevens, Thurston Hall, Lloyd Corrigan. Paramount, 1942.

Stanwyck as a young pioneer bride who ages from fifteen to over one hundred. A personal favorite of Stanwyck's.

The Gay Sisters. Director: Irving Rapper. Screenplay: Lenore Coffee, from the novel by Stephen Longstreet. Camera: Sol Polito. Costumes: Edith Head. Music: Max Steiner. Editor: Warren Low. Cast: Barbara Stanwyck (Fiona Gaylord), George Brent, Geraldine Fitzgerald, Donald Crisp, Gig Young, Nancy Coleman, Gene Lockhart, Larry Simms. Warners, 1942.

Stanwyck marries engineer Brent to make herself eligible for another legacy. While awaiting a court decision on their father's will, impoverished society girls refuse to sell their New York mansion.

Lady of Burlesque (in Britain *Striptease Lady*). Director: William Wellman. Screenplay: James Gunn, from the novel *The G String Murders* by Gypsy Rose Lee. Camera: Robert De Grasse. Costumes: Edith Head. Music: Arthur Lange. Editor: James E. Newcome. Cast: Barbara Stanwyck (Dixie Daisy), Michael O'Shea, J. Edward Bromberg, Iris Adrian, Pinky Lee, Gloria Dickson, Charles Dingle. UA, 1943.

Wellman's saucy comedy has stripper Stanwyck sing, dance, do comedy skits, and solve three murders.

Flesh and Fantasy. Director: Julien Duvivier. Screenplay: Ernest Pascal, Samuel Hoffstein and Ellis St. Joseph from the stories by St. Joseph, Oscar Wilde, and Laslo Vadnay. Camera: Paul Ivano, Stanley Cortez. Costumes: Edith Head. Music: Alexandre Tansman. Editor: Arthur Hilton. Cast: Charles Boyer, Edward G. Robinson, Barbara Stanwyck (Joan Stanley), Betty Field, Robert Cummings, Thomas Mitchell, Robert Bentley, C. Aubrey Smith, Edgar Barrier, David Hoffman. Universal, 1944.

Stanwyck plays a fugitive who foretells aerialist Boyer's fall from a high wire in the weakest of three strange stories.

Double Indemnity. Director: Billy Wilder. Screenplay by Wilder and Raymond Chandler, from the short story by James M. Cain. Camera: John F. Seitz. Costumes: Edith Head. Music: Miklós Rózsa. Editor: Doane Harrison. Cast: Fred MacMurray, Barbara Stanwyck (Phyllis Dietrichson), Edward G. Robinson, Porter Hall, Jean Heather, Tom Powers, Byron Barr, Richard Gaines. Paramount, 1944.

Stanwyck's most famous movie has her as the rotten-to-the-heart femme fatale who helps insurance man MacMurray bump off her husband. *Time* called the movie "the season's nattiest, nastiest, most satisfying melodrama" when it was released September 16, 1944.

Hollywood Canteen. Director: Delmer Daves. Screenplay: Delmer Daves. Camera: Bert Glennon. Music: Ray Heindorf. Editor: Christian Nyby. Cast: Joan Leslie, Robert Hutton, Dane Clark, Janis Paige, and guest appearances by Barbara Stanwyck, the Andrews Sisters, Jack Benny, Joe E. Brown, Eddie Cantor, Joan Crawford, Bette Davis, John Garfield, Sidney Greenstreet, Paul Henreid, Peter Lorre, Ida Lupino, Dennis Morgan, Roy Rogers, Alexis Smith, Jane Wyman. Warners. 1944.

Salute to the many people in showbiz entertaining World War II servicemen.

Christmas in Connecticut (in Britain *Indiscretion*). Director: Peter Godfrey. Screenplay: Lionel Houser and Adela Commandini from a story by Aileen Hamilton. Camera: Carl Guthrie. Costumes: Edith Head. Music: Frederick Hollander. Editor: Frank Magee. Cast: Barbara

Stanwyck (Elizabeth Lane), Dennis Morgan, Sydney Greenstreet, Reginald Gardiner, S. Z. Sakall. Warners, 1945.

Magazine columnist Stanwyck writes about Connecticut farm she doesn't own, husband she doesn't have, and recipes she never cooks. Morgan is the sailor who wants to sample her cooking. Predictable but funny.

My Reputation. Director: Curtis Bernhardt. Screenplay: Catherine Turney, from the novel *Instruct My Sorrows* by "Clare Jaynes." Camera: James Wong Howe. Costumes: Edith Head. Music: Max Steiner. Editor: David Weisbart. Cast: Barbara Stanwyck (Jessica Drummond), George Brent, Eve Arden, Warner Anderson, Lucille Watson, John Ridgely, Jerome Cowan, Esther Dale, Scotty Beckett. Warners, 1946.

Wartime soap opera about a young widow who dates an army officer and is the victim of gossip and almost loses her sons' love. The *New York Herald-Tribune:* "A domestic sob story put together out of stock situations and old scraps of dialogue." *The New Yorker* chided "Hollywood's fierce preoccupation with the small woes of the wealthy." One of Stanwyck's own favorites.

The Bride Wore Boots. Director: Irving Pichel. Screenplay: Dwight Mitchell Wiley, from a story by Wiley and a play by Harry Segall. Camera: Stuart Thompson. Costumes: Edith Head. Music: Frederick Hollander. Editor: Ellsworth Hoagland. Cast: Barbara Stanwyck (Sally Warren), Robert Cummings, Diana Lynn, Patrick Knowles, Peggy Wood, Robert Benchley, Willie Best, Natalie Wood. Paramount, 1946.

Horsewoman Barbara heckles author-husband Cummings and shows preference for her stallion.

The Strange Love of Martha Ivers. Director: Lewis Milestone. Screenplay: Robert Rossen, from a story by Jack Patrick. Camera: Victor Milner. Costumes: Edith Head. Music: Miklós Rózsa. Editor: Archie Marshek. Cast: Barbara Stanwyck (Martha Ivers), Van Heflin, Lizabeth Scott, Kirk Douglas, Judith Anderson, Roman Bohnen. Paramount, 1946.

Stanwyck is the ruthless and fabulously wealthy Martha Ivers with one murder on her hands and a second in her heart. Heflin plays a childhood friend who in Martha rekindles old passions and long-forgotten guilt feelings. Douglas is the alcoholic district attorney who uses his office to execute an innocent man for a crime Martha committed as a young woman. In fact, he witnessed the killing of Martha's cruel aunt and helped Martha lie her way out of the accidental tragedy. His father guessed what happened, however, and, to help his son to the Ivers's wealth and social position, coldly engineered the hateful marriage. Something of a perennial. Cinephiles call this melodrama of a woman haunted by memories of a murder one of Milestone's best (together with *All Quiet on the Western Front* and *The Front Page*).

California. Director: John Farrow. Screenplay: Frank Butler and Theodore Strauss, from a story by Boris Ingster. Camera: Ray Rennahan. Costumes: Edith Head. Music: Victor Young. Editor: Eda Warren. Cast: Ray Milland, Barbara Stanwyck (Lily Bishop), Barry Fitzgerald, George Coulouris, Albert Dekker, Anthony Quinn. Paramount, 1946.

Stanwyck's first color film is an expensively cast western about California's 1848 bid for statehood. The picture, said *Newsweek,* "quickly loses its stirrups and ends up caught by the chaps in a bed of cactus."

The Other Love (No Other Love or *Man Killer)*. Director: André De Toth. Screenplay: Harry Brown and Ladislas Fodor from the short story "Beyond" by Erich Maria Remarque. Camera: Victor Milner. Costumes: Edith Head. Music: Miklós Rózsa. Editor: Walter Thompson. Cast: Barbara Stanwyck (Karen Duncan), David Niven, Richard Conte, Gilbert Roland, Natalie Schafer, Joan Lorring, UA, 1947.

Erich Maria Remarque novelette about concert pianist Stanwyck leaving a Swiss sanatorium and Dr. Niven for a last fling on the Riviera with gambler Conte. Barbara is too radiantly healthful to be believable as dying of tuberculosis.

The Two Mrs. Carrolls. Director: Peter Godfrey. Screenplay: Thomas Job, from the play by Martin Vale. Camera: Peverell Marley. Costumes: Edith Head. Music: Franz Waxman. Editor: Frederick Richards. Cast: Humphrey

Bogart, Barbara Stanwyck (Sally Morton Carroll), Alexis Smith, Nigel Bruce, Isobel Elsom, Pat O'Moore, Ann Carter. Warners, 1947.

Stanwyck looks great as the wife who realizes she is her mad husband's next victim. Bogie gave one of his worst performances as artist who paints his wives as Angels of Death before bumping them off. Together with *Cry Wolf*, Godfrey's 1946 thriller with Stanwyck and Errol Flynn, this stilted adaptation of Martin Vale's warhorse of a play was rediscovered by the French New Wave and declared a superb *policier*.

Cry Wolf. Director: Peter Godfrey. Screenplay Catherine Turney, from the novel by Marjorie Carleton. Camera: Carl Guthrie. Costumes: Edith Head. Music: Franz Waxman. Editor: Folmar Blangsted. Cast: Erroll Flynn, Barbara Stanwyck (Sandra Demarest), Geraldine Brooks, Richard Basehart, Jerome Cowan, John Ridgely. Warners, 1947.

To collect her rightful inheritance, Stanwyck goes to the brooding mansion of her brother-in-law (Flynn). Dark house thriller with a hackneyed solution.

Variety Girl. Director: George Marshall. Screenplay: Edmund Hartmann, Frank Tashlin, Robert Welch, Monte Brice. Camera: Lionel Lindon, Stuart Thompson. Costumes: Edith Head. Editor: LeRoy Stone. Cast: Mary Hatcher, Olga San Juan, De Forest Kelley, Bing Crosby, Bob Hope, Gary Cooper, Ray Milland, Alan Ladd, Barbara Stanwyck, Paulette Goddard, Dorothy Lamour. Paramount, 1947. A tribute to the Variety Clubs' good work on behalf of underprivileged youngsters.

Of all the young hopefuls in Hollywood, one girl becomes a star, and Paramount has all the stars under contract doing bits. Stanwyck explains how Variety Clubs started. Crosby and Hope have the best lines.

B. F.'s Daughter. Director: Robert Z. Leonard. Screenplay: Luther Davis, from the novel by John P. Marquand. Camera: Joseph Ruttenberg. Women's costumes by Irene. Music: Bronislau Kaper. Editor: George White. Cast: Barbara Stanwyck (Polly Fulton), Van Heflin, Charles Coburn, Richard Hart, Keenan Wynn, Margaret Lindsay, Spring Byington. MGM, 1948.

Elaborate treatment of John P. Marquand novel of the wife of a penniless lecturer who secures his rise to fame without his knowing she is a millionaire's daughter. Stanwyck is miscast as an industrialist's daughter.

Sorry, Wrong Number. Director: Anatole Litvak. Screenplay: Lucille Fletcher from her radio play. Camera: Sol Polito. Costumes: Edith Head. Editor: Warren Low. Cast: Barbara Stanwyck (Leona Stevenson), Burt Lancaster, Ann Richards, Wendell Corey, Ed Begley, Harold Vermilyea, Leif Erickson, William Conrad. Paramount, 1948.

Anatole Litvak is no Alfred Hitchcock, and Lucille Fletcher's gimmicky one-woman radio play is turned into gimmicky movie redeemed only by Stanwyck's performance as the bedridden neurotic trying to summon help before an unknown killer can murder her. The film's ghoulish ending still packs a punch.

The Lady Gambles. Director: Michael Gordon. Screenplay: Roy Huggins, from an adaptation by Halsted Welles of a story by Lewis Meltzer and Oscar Saul. Camera: Russell Metty. Costumes: Orry-Kelly. Editor: Milton Carruth. Music: Frank Skinner. Cast: Barbara Stanwyck (Joan Boothe), Robert Preston, Stephen McNally, Edith Barrett, John Hoyt. Universal, 1949.

Stanwyck in the title role of a relentless gambler who can't quit and Preston as her patient husband.

East Side, West Side. Director: Mervyn LeRoy. Screenplay: Isobel Lennart, from the novel by Marcia Davenport. Camera: Charles Rosher. Women's costumes: Helen Rose. Editor: Harold F. Kress. Music: Miklós Rózsa. Cast: James Mason, Barbara Stanwyck (Jessie Bourne), Ava Gardner, Gale Sondergaard, Van Heflin, Cyd Charisse, Nancy Davis, William Conrad. MGM, 1949.

Society matron Stanwyck tolerates husband James Mason's mercurial temper but suspects he killed a Manhattan playgirl. Reviewers called the film everything from a triangle that equals zero to a slick article that can't decide whether it is a polished love story or a thriller and objected to Lennert's every-line-is-a-gem dialogue. London newspapers had fun with British-born Mason for trying a new mid-Atlantic accent.

Thelma Jordan (The File on Thelma Jordan). Director: Robert Siodmak. Screenplay: Ketti Frings, from a story by Marty Holland. Camera: George Barnes. Costumes: Edith Head. Editor: Warren Low. Music: Victor Young. Cast: Barbara Stanwyck (Thelma Jordan), Wendell Corey, Paul Kelly, Joan Tetzel, Stanley Ridges, Richard Rober, Barry Kelley. Paramount, 1949.

A district attorney falls for murder suspect Stanwyck and has her acquitted by losing the case. Could have been *Double Indemnity* redux. Murky script but superior star vehicle although lacking Siodmak's usual shock effects.

No Man of Her Own. Director: Mitchell Leisen. Screenplay: Sally Benson and Catherine Turney from the novel *I Married a Dead Man* by William Irish. Camera: Daniel L. Fapp. Costumes: Edith Head. Editor: Alma Macrorie. Music: Hugo Friedhofer. Editor: Alma Macrorie. Cast: Barbara Stanwyck (Helen Ferguson, Patrice Harkness), John Lund, Jane Cowl, Phyllis Thaxter, Lyle Bettger, Henry O'Neill, Richard Denning. Paramount, 1949.

Much-recommended Leisen classic about down-and-out woman who changes identities with wealthy war widow when the latter is killed in a train wreck.

The Furies. Director: Anthony Mann. Screenplay: Charles Schnee, from the novel by Niven Busch. Camera: Victor Milner. Costumes: Edith Head. Editor: Archie Marshek. Cast: Barbara Stanwyck (Vance Jeffords), Wendell Corey, Walter Huston, Wendell Corey, Judith Anderson, Gilbert Roland. Paramount, 1950.

Walter Huston's last screen appearance as a tyrannical cattle baron. Stanwyck is his headstrong daughter. This slice of an Old West that never was has aged well and is constantly revived. Critics weren't overwhelmed in 1950. "As a film it is no fitting swan song for one of the screen's best actors," said *Newsweek* at the time after Huston died. "And it does little for the reputation of Barbara Stanwyck whose ability to suffer and die photogenically has led her into such recent cinematic debacles as *No Man of Her Own*."

To Please a Lady. Director: Clarence Brown. Screenplay: Barre Lyndon and Marge Decker. Camera: Harold Rosson. Costumes: Helen Rose. Editor: Robert J. Kern. Cast: Clark Gable, Barbara Stanwyck (Regina Forbes), Adolphe Menjou, Will Geer, Roland Winters, Emory Parnell. MGM, 1950.

Gable as race-car enthusiast and Stanwyck as his newspaperwoman friend who objects to his risking his neck.

The Man with a Cloak. Director: Fletcher Markle. Screenplay: Frank Fenton, from a story by John Dickson Carr. Camera: George Folsey. Women's costumes: Walter Plunkett. Music: David Raskin. Editor: Newell P. Kimlin. Cast: Joseph Cotten, Barbara Stanwyck (Lorna Bounty), Louis Calhern, Leslie Caron, Joe DeSantis, Jim Backus. MGM, 1951.

In nineteenth-century New York, a mysterious stranger who turns out to be Edgar Allan Poe enters two women's lives. Cotton is Poe, Stanwyck is Cal-hern's sinister housekeeper who tries to grab his fortune, and pretty Caron the rightful recipient. Playful literary allusions enliven the eighty-one minutes, but Markle's direction lacks sparkle.

Clash by Night. Director: Fritz Lang. Screenplay: Alfred Hayes, from the play *The Lie* by Clifford Odets. Camera: Nicholas Musuraca. Costumes: Michael Wolfe. Music: Roy Webb. Editor: George J. Amy. Cast: Barbara Stanwyck (Mae Doyle), Robert Ryan, Marilyn Monroe, J. Carrol Naish, Paul Douglas. RKO, 1952.

Heavy, slow-moving adaptation of Clifford Odets's 1941 drama of fishing boat skipper who marries a hometown stray and discovers she loves his best friend. Monroe plays Barbara's sister-in-law. Always mentioned in film noir anthologies. *The New Yorker*: "Miss Stanwyck is one of the most sedulous flatteners of 'a's in modern times and in this film her range of emotions goes from a dull 'Nah' to a dreary 'Keep yuh hands offa me.' Even so, she comes out of the ideal well ahead of Mr. Douglas, who seems desperately ill at ease among the fish and the oratory."

Jeopardy. Director: John Sturges. Screenplay: Mel Dinelli, from a story by Maurice Zimm. Camera: Victor Milner. Music: Dimitri Tiomkin. Costumes: Helen Rose.

Editor: Newell P. Kimlin. Cast: Barbara Stanwyck (Helen Stilwin), Barry Sullivan, Ralph Meeker, Lee Aaker. MGM, 1952.

Contrived but efficient suspenser about a woman who lets herself be ravished by an escaped killer so he will help save her husband from a rising tide and inevitable drowning.

Titanic. Director: Jean Negulesco. Screenplay: Charles Brackett, Walter Reisch, and Richard Breen. Camera: Joe MacDonald. Costumes: Dorothy Jeakins. Music: Sol Kaplan. Editor: Louis Loeffler. Cast: Clifton Webb, Barbara Stanwyck (Julia Sturges), Robert Wagner, Audrey Dalton, Thelma Ritter, Brian Aherne, Richard Basehart. Fox, 1953.

Best story and screenplay Oscar for flat reenactment of famous 1912 maritime tragedy.

All I Desire. Director: Douglas Sirk. Screenplay: James Gunn and Robert Blees, from an adaptation by Gina Kaus of the novel *Stopover* by Carol Brink. Camera: Carl Guthrie. Costumes: Rosemary Odell. Music: Joseph Gershenson. Editor: Milton Carruth. Cast: Barbara Stanwyck (Naomi Murdoch), Richard Carlson, Lyle Bettger, Marcia Henderson, Maureen O'Sullivan, Lori Nelson, Richard Long. Universal, 1953.

Sirk loved Greek drama where everything happened *en famille* and in one place. *All I Desire* obeyed the Aristotelian unities of action, time, and place. The theme of Carol Brink's original novel, *Stopover*, was responsibility, the triumph of order over confusion. Ten years before the story begins Naomi Murdoch walked out on her schoolteacher husband and their three young children. Now, in 1910, she returns to the Minnesota town to see her younger daughter graduate from high school. She is determined to return to the big city. The story details the five days of her visit.

The Moonlighter. Director: Roy Rowland. Screenplay: Niven Busch. Camera: Bert Glennon. Costumes: Joe King, Ann Peck. Music: Heinz Roemheld. Editor: Terry Morse. Cast: Barbara Stanwyck (Rela), Fred MacMurray, William Ching, Jack Elam, Ward Bond. Warners, 1953.

A 3-D western that was a complete fiasco.

Blowing Wild. Director: Hugo Fregonese. Screenplay: Philip Yordan. Camera: Sidney Hickox. Music: Dimitri Tiomkin. Editor: Alan Crosland, Jr. Cast: Gary Cooper, Barbara Stanwyck (Marina), Ruth Roman, Anthony Quinn, Ward Bond, Ian MacDonald. Warners, 1953.

Wicked, power-crazy Stanwyck wants control of Mexican oil fields. She is married to one wildcatter (Quinn) and in love with another (Cooper).

Executive Suite. Director: Robert Wise. Screenplay: Ernest Lehman, from the novel by Cameron Hawley. Camera: George Folsey. Women's costumes: Helen Rose. Editor: Ralph E. Winters. Cast: William Holden, June Allyson, Barbara Stanwyck (Julia Tredway), Fredric March, Walter Pidgeon, Shelley Winters, Paul Douglas, Louis Calhern, Dean Jagger, Nina Foch, Tim Considine. MGM, 1954.

MGM returns to the all-star formula that worked so well in *Grand Hotel* and *Dinner at Eight*. First and best of the 1950s boardroom films with Stanwyck as the stockholder whose vote can swing the election of chief executive officer to Holden.

Witness to Murder. Director: Roy Rowland. Screenplay: Chester Erskine. Camera: John Alton. Costumes: Jack Masters, Irene Caine. Music: Herschel Burke Gilbert. Editor: Robert Swink. Cast: Barbara Stanwyck (Cheryl Draper), George Sanders, Gary Merrill, Jesse White, Harry Shanon, Claire Carleton. UA, 1954.

Stanwyck is a Beverly Hills fashion designer who witnesses the murder that Sanders commits and Merrill investigates. Predictable but well-acted minor suspenser.

Cattle Queen of Montana. Director: Allan Dwan. Screenplay: Howard Estabrook and Robert Blees, from the story by Thomas Blackburn. Camera: John Alton. Costumes: Gwen Wakeling. Editor: Carl Lodato. Cast: Barbara Stanwyck (Sierra Nevada Jones), Ronald Reagan, Gene Evans, Lance Fuller, Anthony Caruso, Jack Elam, Yvette Dufay, Chubby Johnson, Rod Redwing. RKO, 1954.

Slow, not very believable, but, with *The Last Outpost*, Reagan's favorite western. *Los Angeles Examiner*: "Barbara Stanwyck, that ever lovin' darling of the box office, steps out in a brand new kind of starring role—on horseback yet, and some cowgirl she is, too. *Cattle Queen* is a lush, expensive looking production in Technicolor with the bright fresh scenery of Montana—untouched heretofore by Hollywood cameras—and the story has enough action to satisfy the most frenetic western fan. Indians, whisky, guns, cattle stampedes, killin' and romance—what more could you ask for?"

The Violent Men. Director: Rudolph Maté. Screenplay: Harry Kleiner, from the novel by David Hamilton. Camera: Burnett Guffey, W. Howard Greene. Music: Max Steiner. Costumes: Jean-Louis. Editor: Jerome Thomas. Cast: Barbara Stanwyck (Martha Wilkinson), Glenn Ford, Edward G. Robinson, Dianne Foster, Brian Keith. Columbia, 1955.

Sprawling western in color. Stanwyck is married to crippled rancher Robinson, has an affair with foreman Keith. Critics praised Stanwyck and Robinson, but complained they were snarling so much at each other that audiences might be forgiven for thinking they were watching a gangster flick.

Escape to Burma. Director: Allan Dwan. Screenplay: Talbot Jennings and Hobart Donavan, from the story, "Bow Tamely to Me" by Kenneth Perkins. Camera: John Alton. Costumes: Gwen Wakeling. Music: Louis Forbes. Editor: James Leicester. Cast: Barbara Stanwyck (Gwen Moore), Robert Ryan, David Farrar, Murvyn Vye. RKO, 1955.

The depth of B pictures. Hated Burma plantation owner Stanwyck has a way with elephants. She eventually helps adventurer and murder suspect Ryan.

There's Always Tomorrow. Director: Douglas Sirk. Screenplay: Bernard C. Schoenfeld, from a story by Ursula Parrott. Camera: Russell Metty. Costumes: Jay Morley, Jr. Music: Herman Stein, Heinz Roemheld. Editor: William M. Morgan. Cast: Barbara Stanwyck (Norma Miller), Fred MacMurray, Joan Bennett, Pat Crowley, William Reynolds, Jane Darwell. Universal, 1956.

A remake of 1934 Frank Morgan–Binnie Barnes starrer. MacMurray is married to Bennett but wonders what it would be like with old flame Stanwyck.

The Maverick Queen. Director: Joseph Kane. Screenplay: Kenneth Gamet and DeVallon Scott, from the novel by Zane Grey. Camera: Jack Marta. Costumes: Adele Palmer. Editor: Richard L. Van Enger. Cast: Barbara Stanwyck (Kit Banion), Barry Sullivan, Scott Brady, Mary Murphy, Wallace Ford, Howard Petrie. Republic, 1955.

Fast-paced Zane Grey western by Republic Studio's prolific western director has bandit woman Stanwyck fall for Pinkerton detective sent out to arrest her. Remade as *Butch Cassidy and the Sundance Kid* fourteen years later.

These Wilder Years. Director: Roy Rowland. Screenplay: Frank Fenton, from a story by Ralph Wheelwright. Camera: George Folsey. Music: Jeff Alexander. Costumes: Helen Rose. Editor: Ben Lewis. Cast: James Cagney, Barbara Stanwyck (Ann Dempster), Walter Pidgeon, Betty Lou Keim, Don Dubbins, Edward Andrews, Basil Ruysdael, Grandon Rhodes. MGM, 1956.

Stanwyck as principled director of an adoption agency who opposes self-made millionaire James Cagney's attempt at tracking down the illegitimate son he fathered and repudiated twenty years earlier. Reviewers said only veteran cast saved modest drama.

Crime of Passion. Director: Gerd Oswald. Screenplay: Jo Eisinger. Camera: Joseph La Shelle. Costumes: Grace Houston. Music: Paul Dunlap. Cast: Barbara Stanwyck (Kathy), Sterling Hayden, Raymond Burr, Fay Wray, Royal Dano, Virginia Grey, Dennis Cross, Robert Griffin, Jay Adler. UA, 1957.

Executive wife Stanwyck's ambition for her husband leads to murder. *Los Angeles Times*'s Philip Scheuer: "Stanwyck's characterization is one for the book—and the police blotter: the woman's character is so completely amoral—as is the tone of the whole picture—that I never found it quite convincing. And this despite an attempt to explain her 'drive' in terms of psychological instability. Also, as I say, this is our Barbara. She really shouldn't do this to us."

Trooper Hook. Director: Charles Marquis Warren. Screenplay: Warren, David Victor, and Herbert Little, Jr., from a story by Jack Schaefer. Camera: Ellsworth Fredericks.

Women's costumes: Voulee Giokaris..Music: Gerald Fried. Editor: Fred Berger. Cast: Joel McCrea, Barbara Stanwyck (Cora), Earl Holliman, Edward Andrews, Susan Kohner, Royal Dano, John Dehner, Susan Kohner, Terry Lawrence, Celia Lovsky, Rudolfo Acosta. UA, 1957.

Slow, downbeat western in which the U.S. cavalry razes an Apache village and discovers Barbara among the squaws only to see her become an outcast when returned to her own.

Forty Guns. Director: Samuel Fuller. Screenplay: Samuel Fuller. Camera: Joseph Biroc. Costumes: Charles LeMaire, Leah Rhodes. Music: Harry Sukman. Editor: Gene Fowler, Jr. Cast: Barbara Stanwyck (Jessica Drummond), Barry Sullivan, Dean Jagger, John Ericson, Gene Barry, Robert Dix, Paul Dubow, Gerald Milton, Ziva Rodann, Hank Worden, Eve Brent. Fox, 1957.

Fuller classic. Powerful ranchwoman and corrupt boss of corrupt Tombstone, Arizona, Stanwyck protects her hoodlum brother.

Walk on the Wild Side. Director: Edward Dmytryk. Screenplay: John Fante and Edmund Morris from the novel by Nelson Algren. Camera: Joe MacDonald. Costumes: Charles LeMaire. Music: Elmer Bernstein. Editor: Harry Gerstad. Cast: Laurence Harvey, Capucine, Jane Fonda, Anne Baxter, Barbara Stanwyck (Jo Courtney), Joanna Moore, John Anderson, Ken Lynch, Todd Armstrong, Lillian Bronson, Adrienne Marden, Sherry O'neil, John Bryant, Kathryn Card. Columbia, 1962.

Talkative, self-conscious adaptation of the 1956 Nelson Algren novel. In the 1930s, a penniless farmer finds his childhood love working in Stanwyck's New Orleans brothel. *Newsweek*: "The latest nightmare out of Hollywood is *Walk on the Wild Side*, wrenched from Nelson Algren's novel." *New York Times*'s Bosley Crowther: "It is incredible that anything as foolish would be made in this day and age." Not to miss: Bernstein's jazz score and Saul Bass's title sequence of the alley tomcat on the prowl.

Roustabout. Director: John Rich. Screenplay: Allan Weiss, Anthony Lawrence, from a story by Weiss. Camera:

Lucien Ballard. Music: Joseph J. Lilly. Editor: Warren Low. Cast: Elvis Presley, Barbara Stanwyck (Maggie Morgan), Sue Ann Langdon, Pat Buutram, Joan Staley, Dabbs Greer, Steve Brodie, Joan Freeman, Leif Erickson. Paramount, 1964.

An Elvis picture. Barbara runs a carnival, and Presley is a vagabond youth who joins the show.

The Night Walker. Director: William Castle. Screenplay: Robert Bloch. Camera: Harold Stine. Music: Vic Mizzy. Editor: Edwin H. Bryant. Cast: Robert Taylor, Barbara Stanwyck (Irene Trent), Judith Meredith, Lloyd Bochner, Rochelle Hudson, Judi Meredith, Hayden Rorke, Jess Barker, Tetsu Kumal, Ted Durant, Lloyd Bochner. Universal, 1965.

Stiff suspense drama with Stanwyck terrorized by nightmares, which seem instigated by her husband, who supposedly was killed in a fire. *Time* called it a lukewarm bloodbath that "does afford Veteran Horrorist Barbara Stanwyck a chance to unleash her hysteria of yore."

The House That Wouldn't Die. ABC Movie of the Week. Director: John Llewellyn Moxey. Teleplay: Henry Farrell from the novel *Ammie, Come Home*, by Barbara Michaels. Stanwyck costumes: Nolan Miller. Editor: Art Seid. Cast: Stanwyck (Ruth Bennett), Richard Egan, Michael Anderson Jr., Katherine Winn, Doreen Lang, Mabel Albertson. Aaron Spelling Productions, 1970.

A Taste of Evil. ABC Movie of the Week. Director: John Llewellyn Moxey. Teleplay: Jimmy Sangster. Stanwyck costumes: Nolan Miller. Editor: Art Seid. Cast: Stanwyck (Miriam Jennings), Barbara Parkins, Roddy McDowall, William Windom, Arthur O'Connell, Ring Russell, Dawn Frame. Aaron Spelling Productions, 1971.

The Letters. ABC Movie of the Week. Director of Stanwyck segment: Gene Nelson. Teleplay: Ellis Marcus, Hal Sitowitz, from a story by Marcus. Stanwyck costumes: Nolan Miller. Editor: Carroll Sax. Cast: Story 1: John Forsythe, Jane Powell, Lesley Ann Warren; Story 2: Stanwyck (Geraldine Parkington), Leslie Nielsen, Dina Merrill; Story 3: Ida Lupino, Ben Murphy, Pamela Franklin. Aaron Spelling Productions, 1973.

The Thorn Birds. ABC. Director: Daryl Duke. Teleplay: Carmen Fulver, from the novel by Colleen McCullough. Costumes: Travilla. Editor: Robert F. Shugrue. Cast: Richard Chamberlain, Rachel Ward, Jean Simmons, Ken Howard, Mare Winningham, Piper Laurie, Richard Kiley, Earl Holliman, Bryan Brown, Philip Anglim, Christopher Plummer, Allyn Ann McLerie, Barbara Stanwyck (Mary Carson). David L. Wolper Production, 1982.

Index

HarperPaperbacks *By Mail*

CELEBRITY FARE

Dolly
My Life and Other Unfinished Business
by Dolly Parton

Dolly Parton is a one-of-a-kind sensation, who, after releasing sixty-two albums that have sold more than fifty million copies worldwide, still considers herself a simple country girl. (32 pages of photographs.)

Diva: The Totally Unauthorized Biography of Whitney Houston by Jeffrey Bowman

Whitney Houston has been a magnet for rumors and scandal sheets worldwide. Now, her fans will see what life is really like for the queen of pop.

Out of the Madness:
The Strictly Unauthorized Biography of Janet Jackson by Bart Andrews

Janet Jackson has rebuilt herself through hard work and discipline. Now for the first time, her fans can learn the truth of how she fought her way out of the madness.